THE POLITICS OF LITERATURE

Poland 1945–1989

The Politics of Literature

Poland 1945–1989

Carl Tighe

UNIVERSITY OF WALES PRESS
CARDIFF
1999

British Library Cataloguing-in-Publication Data.
A catalogue record for this book is available from the British Library.

ISBN 0–7083–1524–0

Typeset at University of Wales Press
Printed in Great Britain by Dinefwr Press, Llandybïe

CONTENTS

Preface   vii

Acknowledgements   x

1 Cultural Pathology: The Roots of Polish Literary Opposition
  to Communism   3

2 The Writing Profession   65

3 Jerzy Andrzejewski   100

4 Jan Kott   134

5 Stanisław Lem   158

6 Kazimierz Brandys   177

7 Ryszard Kapuściński   203

8 Tadeusz Konwicki   224

9 Adam Michnik   244

10 Writers, Language and Party   278

11 Socialist 'Unreality' to Capitalist 'Reality'   305

Notes   339

Biographies   362

Index   404

PREFACE

This study explores the relationship between literature and politics. It asks what literature can tell us about politics, and it does so by exploring Polish literary-political culture in the years 1945–89. During these years the Communist Party, for all its opposite intent, preserved the power of the word and the moral and political position of writers at a time when in western Europe and America writers were no longer taken very seriously as political commentators. This was a period when writers in Poland occupied a position of great moral authority. Many believed that, in spite of Soviet power, an independent Polish socialism was a possibility, and that even if they were not able to shake off the power of Moscow they might still be able to turn communism into a force for good. For many writers the post-war years started with a brief honeymoon period, followed by increasing disenchantment with the authoritarianism and boorishness of the Party, then open opposition to the one-party state: if they remained in Poland (and many did not) writers became successively fellow travellers, Party members, revisionists, dissidents, oppositionists, underground organizers, Solidarność (Solidarity) advisers, political prisoners, and, finally, democratic politicians.

My subject is the interface between literature and politics in post-war Poland, but more particularly the Polish literary *lewa laicka* (lay left). Though it is difficult to define left and right with any precision in post-war Poland, this label, however inadequate, serves to identify writers who were largely ex-Party, non-communist and non-Catholic, but who are broadly in sympathy with the underlying humanitarian aims of liberal Marxism and who made their contribution to post-war Polish history from outside the Catholic Church. Many, whether they knew it or not, harked back to the long-suppressed aims and ideology of the liberal element of the old PPS (Polish Socialist Party). At various points in the post-war period these writers might equally have been referred to as fellow travellers, independent Marxists, revisionists, dissident Marxists, the generation of 1968, or just simply ex-Party.

After the final dissolution of the various resistance groups in the civil war up to 1947, the destruction of the opposition parties in 1949, and the breaking of the revisionists in the anti-Semitic purge of 1968, there was no satisfactory connection between the scattered groupings opposed to communism. However, in 1976 Adam Michnik, anxious to unite dissidents, independent trade unionists, Catholic leaders, disaffected intellectuals, and the frustrated professions, showed that in many ways revisionists (ex-Party or non-Party socialists), the more humanist and liberal-leaning elements of the right-wing nationalist opposition, the liberal sections of the émigré community, neo-positivist Catholic writers and editors, liberal Catholics in the Church hierarchy, Catholic deputies in the Sejm, and even one or two members of Pax, were all very close in their strategies and concerns (though not in their ambitions). He dubbed them all New Evolutionists.

The driving force behind New Evolutionism was the democratic socialism of Adam Michnik, the creative humanism of the writing community and the moral authority of the Church. New Evolutionism was a broad series of social, political and artistic movements (the Party had made it so) seeking resolution and unity in opposition to the Party and, for most but not all, in a vision of a democratic Poland. It encompassed, sometimes uneasily, fund-amentalist free-marketeers, nationalists of all kinds, gung-ho supporters of Reagan and Thatcher, conservative authoritarians, Catholic anti-Semites, members of the Catholic hierarchy, lay Catholic organizations and libertarian-socialist idealists, revisionist and dissident ex-communists. I have chosen to look at the literary-political career trajectories of particular writers on the *lewa laicka* of the New Evolution movement.

Unlike many émigré and Catholic writers, these are writers whose relation-ship to the Party was problematic and constantly developing. Andrzejewski, Kott, Brandys, Lem, Kapuściński, Konwicki, Michnik are all examples of literary *lewa laicka* evolution: their starting-points are diverse but over the years their outlooks converge. Although these writers do not easily form a political group or a literary movement, their common themes, the similarity of their careers, their shared experience, their general sympathy for the ideas of democracy and 'socialism with a human face', all make it possible to treat their careers as a synchronic meta-narrative within the larger political and historical framework.

All these writers have substantial international reputations and consider-able prestige in Poland. Between them they represent most of the options (apart from silence) available to writers over the post-war years. These people, many of them ex-Party members, gave the lie to Stalinist and Catholic Church claims that what existed in post-war Poland was socialism. They were clear that what they had was not socialism as they understood it, but a decayed and decaying Stalinist communism. Even in 1996 Michnik, Kott and Kapuściński did not find the idea of liberal social democracy, 'socialism with a human face', utterly ludicrous, nor were they persuaded that the fall of Soviet power presaged the end of history – though they agreed it meant the end of Utopian dreams.

Although I have labelled these oppositionist writers *lewa laicka*, I doubt this would have made them all happy. Ex-Stalinist Jacek Trznadel believed that, in spite of his impeccable social-democratic credentials, Adam Michnik was a communist plant within the opposition. Andrzejewski was unhappy about being connected to social-activists like Michnik and Kuroń, both of whom were very up-front about their socialism. But it was Michnik who pointed out that the first task of the various factions of the opposition movement was not to fight each other but to find common ground, combine, and link up with the Polish working class. Michnik felt that the only way to do this was outside the structures of the Party, which could be relied on only to destroy their efforts. He also felt it necessary to operate outside the structures of the Church, which, though its moral values were often inspiring, could not be trusted to follow through reforms from which it did not benefit or which it did not control.

The opposition movement that grew up in the late 1970s was led largely by the intellectuals of KOR (Workers' Defence Committee), which specialized in fronting legal cases for accused workers and had a large number of writers among its membership, including J. J. Lipski, Andrzejewski and the poet Stanisław Barańczak.[1] As Michnik has repeatedly pointed out, there can be no doubt that in the formation of independent public opinion, literature played a decisive role. It has been difficult for the right wing and for the Catholic Church to accept that the most creative and persistent oppositionists facing the Party, did not come from within the Catholic Church, as western observers might have expected, but from the highly exposed ex-Party writers of the *lewa laicka*. Michnik has claimed a wide-ranging list of contemporary writers for the liberal and humanist elements of the social-democratic Polish left. As far as he is concerned, without a close reading of the life and works of these particular writers it is simply 'impossible to understand the moral and intellectual dilemmas of Polish oppositionist thought'.[2]

ACKNOWLEDGEMENTS

My thanks for their hospitality and good fellowship during the period of research and writing to: Madeleine and Luke Rose, Linda and Brian Wasileski, Mick and Pat O'Rourke, Cathie and Tony Gard, Ela Jarosz, Janina Stupnicka, Richard Boulez, Darek Oleksiak, Chris and Danusia Scott-Barrett, Mariola Żychowska, David, Anne and Grace Downes, Avshalom Douek and Ravid Admon, Frankie Hudson and David Emmerson, Harry Turner, Desmond Smith and Corine Deliot, Mike Kenny, Alan Sennett, Daryl Glaser, Joanna Wróblewska, Maryla Rosółkowska, Karen Hall, Maria Nedeva; Sharon Wood, Niamh Dowling, Jacqui David, Morag Patrick, Shirley Bor, Nicci Loader, Shinobu Yasumuro, Yvonne Lyon, Corine Ferry and Tina Wade. I would also like to thank: Marcus Wheeler, Eamon Wright, the late Walter Jeffrey of the Writers Guild of Great Britain, English PEN, John Osmond and Nigel Jenkins of the Welsh Union of Writers; Andrzej Tarnowski, Christopher Bobiński, Jane Curry, Solidarność Press Secretaries Mateusz and Joanna Wyrwich, Dr Zdisław Jagodziński of POSK, Andrzej Zgorzelski of Gdańsk University, Joanna Zach of the Polish Philology Department at the Jagiellonian University, Pani Szwajcer of DK-SWS Book Distribution Services Warsaw, Agencja Autorska in Warsaw, Anna Iwaszkiewicz, Tomasz Stawecki, the Lancaster Polish Club, the staff of the Poster Museum at Wilanów, Chis Binns, Professor Norman Davies, Professor Mike Waller, Professor Paul Lewis, Professor Robin Okey, Ned Thomas, Czesław Miłosz, Jerzy Jarzębski, Ryszard Kapuściński, Juliusz Żuławski, Artur Międzyrzecki, Eva Hoffman, Kasia Mroczkowska-Brand, Bill Brand, Piotr Rypsen, Ignacy Krasicki, Bozena Koszińska, Teresa Halikowska, and Krystyna Kęplicz of the Polska Fundacja Upowszechniania Nauki; Andrzej Wajda, who, in the hectic closing months of 1980, was kind enough to spare time to talk about his film of the Gdańsk strike negotiations; and Tadeusz Różewicz who in 1975 ignored the advice of his doctor (and the wrath of his wife) to spend a while in conversation. I also wish to express a debt of gratitude to Mary Niesłuchowska.

Parts of this book have appeared in *Contemporary European History*, *The Journal of European Studies*, *The Modern Language Review*, *Science Fiction*, *Social Change and War* (MUP), *Our History*, *Monthly Review* and *The Works*. I would like to thank the editors of these journals.

Whether by instinct or meditation, writers have always been aware of their special position in communist ideology. They have taken communism seriously because *it* has taken them seriously. Thus a history of the relations between communism and modern literature is, in certain vital respects, a history of both.

George Steiner, *Language and Silence*

Literature is our Parliament too. Printing, which comes necessarily out of Writing, I say often, is equivalent to Democracy; invent Writing, Democracy is inevitable . . . Whoever can speak, speaking now to the whole nation, becomes a power, a branch of government, with inalienable weight in law-making, in all acts of authority . . . the nation is governed by all that was tongue in the nation: Democracy is virtually *there*.

Thomas Carlyle, *On Heroes, Hero-Worship and the Heroic in History*

CULTURAL PATHOLOGY
The Roots of Polish Literary Opposition to Communism

Let me start with my family. It is by no means unimportant. I come from a noble family which, for some four hundred years, owned estates in Lithuania, not far from Wilno and Kovno. On account of the property it possessed, the offices it held and the marriages it contracted, my family was slightly above the average run of Polish nobility, though it never formed part of the aristocracy. Although I was not a count, a certain number of my aunts were countesses, but even these countesses were not of the first water – they were just so-so.
Witold Gombrowicz, A Kind of Testament (1973)

And my malice from that time, that terrible obstinate malice, came from a sort of intellectual hoodlumism. From a feeling that though the outward forms had been preserved, inside everything had been eroded, removed, cleaned out. It turned out that this was more than I could bear. I closed my eyes to it. I locked up all my ideas, everything. I threw the key into the abyss, the sea, the Vistula, and I threw myself into the only faith that existed then. There was only one alternative, only one global answer to negation. The entire illness stemmed from the need, that hunger for something all-embracing. In fact communism arose to satisfy certain hungers. The phenomenon was inevitable in so far as powerful hungers had arisen in modern societies, even in those of the nineteenth century. One of those hungers was for a catechism, a simple catechism. That sort of hunger burns in refined intellectuals much more than it does in the man on the street . . .
Aleksander Wat, My Century: The Odyssey of a Polish Intellectual (1977)

Identifying the roots of Polish literary opposition to communism is a kind of cultural pathology. Those roots often lie in cataclysmic events (partition, the Second World War), in ideas (Revisionism, neo-Positivism, New Evolutionism), in institutions (the Catholic Church), and in individuals (writers and intellectuals). But they also lie in smaller independent organizations (the Writers' Union, International PEN, pre-war political parties), in traditions (officer corps, military leadership, resistance), and in intellectual and artistic movements (Romanticism and Positivism). And they may be traced in ambitions (Polish Independence), national mythology (Sarmatianism), lingering gentry social style, and in the experience of the *inteligencja* (intelligentsia).

Throughout the forty-five years of communist rule in Poland, literary opposition, drawing upon established historical models, was a far more complex and nuanced phenomenon than is often supposed. The exact point at which the various historical roots intersect in the post-war period is crucial to the nature and formation of literary opposition, and as a result the map has some surprising contours. Inevitably, opposition to communism in Poland also had its roots in a shifting sense of purpose, a particular combination of circumstances, and a fleeting, even fugitive, sense of identity. Whatever version of Polish identity writers chose – Polish Catholic, Polish Jew, inheritor of noble traditions, exiled Pole, even Polish anti-Stalinist socialist – it was far from easy for post-war intellectuals to situate themselves in any corner of the map of opposition. Given the problems of catching such a difficult subject, it has been essential to adopt a wide-ranging approach, using historical, philosophical, cultural, political, and literary materials.

Literature and Partition

In Poland literature has often been political life conducted by other means. And there are good reasons for this. Between 1772 and 1795 Poland was swallowed up in partition by the Russian, Prussian and Austrian monarchies. Long before Poland disappeared the Prussian Emperor Frederick the Great had aimed to eliminate the 'lazy Catholic Poles' on his territory and turn them into 'good Prussians'. After partition the Russians and Prussians attempted to stamp out Polish national aspirations. Prussia in particular hoped to absorb Poles into a German-speaking identity by eliminating Polish culture, history and language, and by reducing the area of political, economic and civil life in which Poles could operate as Poles. It is primarily because of the experience of the partitions that language, literature and writers came to occupy an unusually important position in Polish society. They were seen as indispensable to the survival of the nation. As Paweł Hertz wrote: 'Things which elsewhere were arranged in Parliament, here, because of the lack of Polish national institutions and the great weight of the partitioning authorities, were arranged in journals and pushed their way into literature – particularly into poetry.'[1]

During the partition years Poland's poorly developed (and mainly noble) civil society came to reside increasingly in the institution of the family, in the Catholic Church and in the literary life of the nation's language. The intellectuals, along with the Catholic Church, became the political, moral and ideological life of Poland, but they did so at several removes from the centres of power. As political action foundered in intrigue and competition, and military failure brought about increased suffering, the Polish language and its literature came to be of vital importance in resisting pressures on Polish identity. Writers, philosophers – indeed anyone who managed to obtain an education and who still remained Polish – acquired a didactic national purpose and substituted for the absent stratum in the absent political state in what was seen by some as a leading national role, and by others as a tribal tyranny. As Zdzisław Najder said:

Talking about Polish literature and culture in general, one has constantly to repeat that it is almost devoid of the so called *bourgeois* element. It is traditionally a gentry culture. The origins of this phenomenon are very, very complex . . . When you talk about culture and cultural values in Poland, these values are always connected with the typical gentry code of behaviour: a code of honour, in which the most important notions are those of duty, of honour, of loyalty to your nation, loyalty to your group. Much less important, sometimes virtually non-existent, are the notions of maintaining an economic standard, of preserving life for the sake of preserving life itself.[2]

The experience of partition produced the bulk of Poland's most influential and lasting literature and exercised a profound influence on national thought. The works of Adam Mickiewicz (1795–1855), Juliusz Słowacki (1809–49) and Zygmunt Krasiński (1812–59) reached the height of their influence between the insurrections of November 1830 and January 1863. It is precisely at this period that the Polish word *wieszcz* (possibly derived from the Latin *vates*) came to mean not only a person inspired, a seer into the future, a genius of some kind, but also, particularly in the works of the great Romantic poet Mickiewicz, came to assume the meaning of national poet. That is, a poet whose prime responsibility was to write for the nation, a poet who lived as he wrote, for the spiritual life of the nation. The works of these poets are still considered vital to the health of the nation, so much so that the banning of part III of Mickiewicz's play *Dziady* was the cause of student riots in 1968.[3]

Throughout the nineteenth century the Polish *inteligencja* concentrated its energies on 'serious national literature' simply because there had been few other outlets for its energies. Norman Davies has spelled out the centrality of literature to Polish political life:

Polish politics, driven from the public arena by an army of police and censors, took refuge in the metaphors of the poets and the allegories of the novelists. It developed its own vivid literary code, a corpus of symbols and conventions which assumed a life of their own. For this reason, nineteenth-century Polish literature, which in quantity, variety, and artistic accomplishment, was comparable to all the great literatures of Europe, has proved markedly unsuitable for export, and largely untranslateable. But in Poland its role was paramount. It quickly became a great fortress, a cultural Fort Knox, impregnable because its invisible walls could not be breached by guns and search warrants . . . it began to assume the role of a political surrogate, a substitute for 'normal' political discussions and activities. In Poland, Literature did not merely reflect Politics as it did elsewhere; it threatened to replace it. For long stretches of Poland's 'Babylonian captivity', in the long watches of Poland's political night, the 'word' was at least the equal of the 'deed'.[4]

This model of poetic-national endeavour was to survive, changed and challenged, with only a brief alteration during the inter-war years, into the post-war communist period.

Poles paid dearly for allowing Romantic literature to rule over their heads and cool military calculation. The physical effort of trying to shake off the partitioning powers in the various uprisings, culminating in the failure of the January uprising of 1863, radically altered Polish literature and broke the will to win by force. This defeat set many Poles on the road to Positivism. Polish Romanticism had elevated literature to a 'national level' by confirming the life of the nation as the only fit subject for the writer, but in doing so it almost put an end to disinterested metaphysical literary speculation. Up to the January uprising it had been possible for an individual to justify the most abominable behaviour on the grounds that it was a patriotic duty to be antisocial, even criminal, if the powers defining what was acceptable were not Polish. Polish literature had fostered anti-authority attitudes that fitted perfectly into an atmosphere of partition. Indeed, Adam Mickiewicz produced a historical narrative poem called *Konrad Wallenrod* (published in St Petersburg, 1828), in which a young Pole joins the Teutonic Knights, appears to collaborate, rises through the ranks to become Grand Master of the Order only to lead them into total disaster, and which thus seemed to sanction and justify a whole range of activities and attitudes that in other circumstances would be socially and politically unacceptable. Some writers began to see this national function as a strait-jacket. Mickiewicz's contemporaries, Juliusz Słowacki and Zygmunt Krasiński, helped inspire the notion of a 'national bard', but later came to question the notion. Cyprian Norwid (1821–83) in particular, rejected Mickiewicz's Polish messianism, but Norwid's poetry remained unpublished until fifty years after his death.

The reaction against Romanticism was increasingly clear. In 1882 Henryk Sienkiewicz (1846–1916) wrote the short story 'Latarnik' (Lighthouse Keeper) in which Skawiński, an exiled and wandering Polish insurrectionary of 1830, works as a lighthouse keeper at Aspinwall. The old man takes delivery of a parcel of books in Polish, one of which is a copy of Adam Mickiewicz's magnificent epic poem *Pan Tadeusz*, a portrait and history of Lithuanian-Polish gentry society in 1811–12, the years just before Napoleon's invasion of Russia.[5] Lost in his reading and his emotions, recalling the battles of his youth and the cause of his exile, Skawiński forgets to light the lamp and causes a shipwreck. He loses his job and his lighthouse home, but 'in his breast he carried into the new roads of his life his book, which from time to time his hand grasped as though fearful lest that too should be taken from him'. On one level with this story Sienkiewicz, though an heir to Polish Romanticism, had written its epitaph by recognizing the limitations of military and national action inspired by literary and poetic dreams.

Though Sienkiewicz was later to lose interest in Positivism and move on to write a series of massively popular historical novels in a more traditional and Romantic vein, his work was to to have a profound impact on Władysław Reymont (1867–1925), Eliza Orzeszkowa (1841–1910), Stefan Żeromski

(1864–1925) and Bolesław Prus (1844–1912). These writers were to form the backbone of the Polish Positivist movement. As a student Prus had taken part in the 1863 uprising and had been badly wounded and imprisoned by the tsarist authorities. His novels *Faraon* (Pharaoh, 1896) and *Lalka* (Doll), which appeared in serial form in the years 1890–6, though rooted in Romanticism, constituted a decisive break with the Romantic idea of the poet as insurrectionary national leader. Instead of lamenting the fate of the nation or urging revolt, Prus studied Polish society and ancient Egypt in an effort to understand the nature and workings of 'the social organism', civic, social and national responsibility, the roots of political power, and the process of nation-building.[6]

During the nineteenth century Polish literature and political experience had diverged hugely and significantly from almost the whole of western Europe. After this time however, the Positivist movement, in literature as in politics, increasingly gained ground. Positivism stressed a realistic and pragmatic appreciation of the political situation. It recommended an end to Polish resistance, acceptance of 'geo-political realities', 'grass roots' activities, self-help, social and welfare work. Positivism saw 'organic work' as a necessary evil within the existing political set-up. For the Positivists it was clear that work, education, and quiet organization were the only ways of preparing for the possibility of restoring Polish independence. Positivism became increasingly popular, but the old insurrectionary traditions died hard and it was still possible to characterize Positivism as collaboration with a foreign army of occupation. Wacław Berent (1873–1940) was to satirize Positivism in his novel *The Expert* (1895), and the 'Young Poland' movement of the 1890s was to seek further connection with the 'norms' of west European literature, moving even further along the path of romantic counter-revolution, but the Romantic traditions lingered. The poet Jan Lechoń (1899–1956), one of the founders of the Skamander group, confronted Poland's literary and political past in *Karmazynowy Poemat* (Crimson Poem, 1920) and in the collection *Srebrne i czarne* (Silver and Black, 1924), and pleaded: 'In Spring let me see only Spring. Not Poland.'

The clash between Romantic rebellion and realist acceptance of the world 'as it is' can be seen in the family background of Joseph Conrad (Józef Teodor Konrad Nałęcz Korżeniowski, 1857–1924). In 1900 Tadeusz Bobrowski, Joseph Conrad's maternal uncle, wrote a description of Conrad's father, the distinguished and revered poet, translator and revolutionary Apollo Korżeniowski (1820–69). In doing so he left a description of the peculiar mentality that had become the *szlachta* (nobility) scheme of things. According to Bobrowski, Apollo Korżeniowski had an exceedingly tender and soft heart – hence 'his great sympathy for the poor and oppressed':

> . . . and this was why he and others thought he was a democrat. But these were only impulses of the heart and mind inherent in a member of a good family of the

gentry; they were not truly democratic convictions. I could never establish the real composition of his political and social ideas, apart from a hazy inclination towards a republican form of state incorporating some equally hazy agglomeration of human rights as set out by the constitution of 3 May – which for our times was not far-reaching enough.[7]

Bobrowski had opposed the 1863 uprising and regarded his own family as a model of good sense and balance, but he thought the Korżeniowskis inclined to frivolous Romantic gesture and debt. He may have been right. In 1861 Apollo Korżeniowski had conspired with the 'Mierosławski Reds' and founded the underground Warsaw City Committee: he had been denounced by an informer, arrested and, with his wife and four-year-old Joseph Conrad, exiled to Vologda. In the 1863 uprising Apollo's father Teodor had died on his way to join the partisans, his brother Robert was killed in the fighting and his brother Hilary was exiled to Tomsk. However, the difference between Conrad's maternal and paternal lines was not as clear as Bobrowski wished. Bobrowski's brothers held attitudes and opinions almost identical to those of Korżeniowski: Kazimierz had been arrested and imprisoned at the start of the 1863 uprising; Stefan, leader of the leftists and head of the underground national government, a key figure in preparations for the uprising, had been murdered by a political opponent in a rigged duel.

This 'hazy agglomeration' of national and political feelings, powerful though it was in opposition to authority, was no more than that. The fact of occupation and partition by foreign powers was to rob Poland of any developing sense of a hierarchy of values. While the *Sarmata* vein encompassed the Catholicism and cosmopolitan toleration of the old Polish Republicans like Apollo Korżeniowski, it also encompassed intolerance, obscurantism, messianism, and extreme boorish nationalism. The anarchic self-interest of the small landowner changed very easily into contempt for political authority and into intellectual contempt for middle-class materialism and middle-class values. The culture of the *szlachta* as a whole tended towards the trivial and the formless simply because it lacked direction and reason in national politics. The *szlachta* sense of honour mutated easily into the speculator's greed, his cosmopolitanism into xenophobia, his sense of democracy into provincial boorishness and his sense of pride at being a Pole sometimes became anti-Semitism. Towards the end of the partitions the *inteligencja* showed very clear signs of high-spirited isolationism that after 1918 developed into a mentality of selfish opportunism and permanent cynical opposition. In some this isolationism became the cultured attitude of the élitist *szlachcic*; in others the anarchic self-interest of the bourgeois black-marketeer; in some the pietistic religiosity of the Catholic devotee; in a few the responsibility of being an artist on whom the future of the country's cultural life depended; in others it became the need to get on by the clearest route of social advancement, that is in the growing administration and bureaucracy; in others it manifested itself as a burning need for political action, often in the idea of revolution and membership of the tiny and powerless parties of the left.

At the age of five Joseph Conrad had described himself as 'Pole, Catholic, nobleman', and was throughout his life conscious of his descent from the noble Nałęcz *ród* (Nałęcz clan). He was very well aware of the suffering on both sides of his family at the hands of the Russians during the 1863 uprising: it left an indelible mark on his personality and on his writing. Conrad never shook off his Polish Romantic literary heritage, but was also deeply affected by the Positivist work ethic as a way of numbing Romantic aspirations and cooling dreams which could not be realized:

> I don't like work – no man does – but I like what is in work – the chance to find yourself. Your own reality – for yourself, not for others – what no other man can know. They can only see the mere show, and can never tell what it really means.[8]

In assessing the inward-looking literary patrimony of the partition years, Kazimierz Brandys (b.1916) was to complain that as long as the figure of the hero was automatically assumed to stand for Poland, it was, even in late twentieth-century Polish literature, impossible to present human suffering without readers assuming that this was a metaphor for Poland's suffering, and impossible to present human passion in anything like its full complexity. For Brandys the question of what Polish literature 'knew' by 1918 hinged upon whether it was, or ever could be, universal and available to outsiders, or whether it would remain purely local. For Brandys, while the literature of France, Spain and Britain reflected the experience of empire-building, colonization, class conflict, political awareness and ambition, industrial and urban growth, and the steady advance of material prosperity, Polish literature reflected the overwhelming experience of continual loss, deprivation, defeat and calamity. Poland was in danger of disappearing for ever and Polish literature was increasingly that of a linguistic ghetto, a literature that knew everything there was to know about conspiracy, patriotism and dying for Poland, but which understood less and less the responsible exercise of political power. For Brandys, Polish literature could scarcely conceive that it might one day hold such power.

Brandys attempted something unusual in Polish literature in that he tried to reveal the ways in which Polish national consciousness manifested itself – a kind of literary national pathology. For Brandys, though he could hardly expect it of any literature in any massive or thorough way, it was important that by 1918 Polish literature knew little or nothing of the inner workings of power, parties, ideologies and political struggle, banking and economics, but knew much more of resistance, military struggle and sacrifice in the name of the nation. Brandys said bluntly that Poles were the children of the nation rather than the products of civilization. Their lack of freedom through the partitions had meant that their knowledge of the world was gained through catastrophic uprisings, military defeat, exile, oppression and conspiracy. He described the experience of living within the 'national myth' as the very opposite of the 'individual's relation to civilisation':

> There is no chance to reveal the social, biological, and metaphysical components of life if they cannot be developed to the full in the life of the hero, if one must stop before the final consequences. One mustn't sink into madness, mustn't betray, mustn't kill, mustn't bring dishonour on oneself by one's weakness – how can one under such conditions avoid some feeble compromise, even if purely literary? . . . The result: society has ceased to know itself . . . Poland has suffered from a provincial complex made up of bitterness, pride and a somewhat perverse élitism . . . in these admonitions and allusions, this muttering which is incomprehensible to the uninitiated, there is a note of truth. Truth which is no less true for not being understood by strangers – in general, one does not grasp the truths that one has not been able to experience. And once again doubts arise: are these local truths or universal?[9]

Sarmatianism

Sarmatianism is important to any consideration of the connection between literature and politics in Poland. *Sarmata* may mean 'a person of the old Polish type', a 'character of the old school', 'a noble type', 'a figure from a previous era'. The Sarmatians were an Iranian people noticed by classical writers in the second century BC. They invaded eastern Europe and settled in southern Poland around AD 200–500, conquering the local population. It is from a supposed Sarmatian warrior caste that the Polish *szlachta* claim descent: by AD 1200 Sarmatian property signs known as *tamgas* had begun to appear in *szlachta* heraldic symbols. The complex of dogmas that supposed the nobility to be under special protection from God, that they had somehow only to dispense law and maintain their own golden freedoms, may be termed Sarmatianism. The *szlachta* saw their function as the ownership of the 'grain basket of Europe' from which they mainly derived their livelihood, while the peasantry remained in ignorance and poverty. Sarmatianism disliked foreigners and alien influence and sought to protect Polish territory from all change, with the result that from the sixteenth century onwards, when the Sarmatian myth first emerged, Poland fell further and further behind the developing economies of western Europe.[10]

Sarmatian personal style is still everywhere apparent in Poland, particularly in a hankering after a strong, preferably martial, ruler. Lech Wałęsa, though no writer and no *szlachcic*, along with thousands of other Solidarność members sported a drooping walrus moustache – the inseparable adornment of every Polish nobleman's face – that was unmistakably Sarmatian and whose line of descent can be traced back through Józef Piłsudski (ruled 1926–35) to Jan Sobieski (ruled 1674–96) and thence to Władysław Jagiełło (ruled 1386–1434). Tadeusz Konwicki pondered the meaning of the survival of this phenomenon:

> The Poles are a wonderful, charming, intelligent nation, but a nation that is infantile, adolescent, arrested at an early stage of development. The splendid Poles, so proud of their Polishness, are childlike . . . That is why they have an acute father complex. What the Poles dream of is a normal, mature, responsible man who will assume responsibility for their childish ways. Poles long for a father, a great big man with a moustache, blunt but decisive.[11]

While in western Europe the Enlightenment was an aristocratic and international affair, in Poland it was an affair of the progressive and increasingly nationalist gentry alienated from political power and forced to make connections with a peasantry it despised. They saw the Enlightenment as a national and increasingly nationalist affair: Sarmatianism fed into the Polish uprisings. After the failure of these uprisings the ethos of Sarmatianism was absorbed into the very idea of 'Polishness', into a whole range of attitudes and social postures, and came to inform Polish social activities. 'Polishness' was defined increasingly in terms of opposition to authority – the partitioning powers initially, but later all state power. Sarmatianism emerged in the failure of Polish democracy and in the military government of the inter-war years, in the political and social attitudes of some AK (Home Army) leaders, and in the attitude of many Poles towards the Soviet Union and communism in the post-war period.[12] The post-war 'socialist' government saw literature as a particular stronghold of Sarmatianism and sought to dilute and eventually to eradicate this spirit from Polish culture.

Sarmatianism is still massively embedded in Polish culture. General Jaruzelski may have subconsciously counted on this aspect of Polish political culture – admiration for the powerful Sarmatian soldier/father figure of Piłsudski – to pull him through the declaration of Martial Law in December 1981. Jaruzelski came from a *szlachta* family in the Lublin area and his grandfather had taken part in the 1863 uprising. Jaruzelski had joined the PPR (Polish Workers' Party) in 1947, and his route into politics was not so very different from that of many other displaced younger members of the Polish nobility who, like Piłsudski, moved from military service into political activism. The Jaruzelski family's heraldic symbol was the *ślepowron* (blind crow): WRON (*wrona*, crow) was the acronym of the Council of National Salvation, the military government set up by Jaruzelski after Martial Law. However, though massively decorated for his heroism in the Second World

War, Jaruzelski was a resolutely uncharismatic leader who consistently miscalculated Polish feeling. He was not what Poles, with memories of Piłsudski, expected of a military leader: he wore dark glasses (a blind crow), was clean-shaven (no Sarmatian moustache), and steadfastly refused to promote himself to *marszał*. On the other hand his opponent was the massively charismatic Lech Wałęsa, an open admirer of Piłsudski (a bust of the *marszał* stands on Wałęsa's desk), who had the necessary drooping moustache. It is no accident that Solidarność adopted the sixteenth-century *szlachta* motto of *Nic o nas bez nas* (Nothing about us without us) as one of its slogans.

Polish Independence

Since the first of the partitions the restoration and maintenance of Polish independence had been an overriding national concern. Poland's restoration in 1918 was unexpected, and the task of government proved to be very difficult. In addition to the military struggle to re-establish secure borders and expel foreign troops, there was enormous social disruption and war damage to contend with. After more than a hundred years of invisibility Poland had no agreed mechanisms for social and political decision-making; nor was there an established public consensus as to what kind of place the new Poland should be. This, coupled with a long-established tradition of haughty Sarmatian individualism and hostility to authority almost guaranteed problems. Gabriel Narutowicz, the first president of Poland, was elected in 1922 with the backing of socialists, liberals and national minorities, but was immediately assassinated by a nationalist. As Poland drifted further into confusion many looked to the military to provide a strong and simple solution. In May 1926, more by accident than design, Józef Piłsudski returned from retirement, put an end to Poland's flirtation with democracy, led a military *putsch* and established a regime that was to last until September 1939. The military and the Church, in combination with the tiny surviving class of landowners, ruled in exclusive and repressive partnership. After Piłsudski's death in 1935 the military regime of the 'Colonels' became increasingly repressive, anti-Semitic and, though suspicious of Nazi Germany, sympathetic towards the ideals of Fascism.

Poland's economic achievements in the inter-war period are not clear-cut. According to the Polish census of 1921 the *inteligencja* numbered around 1.4 million, that is, about 5 per cent of the Polish population. Landowners had been reduced to about 1 per cent, but the industrial proletariat still amounted to only 17 per cent, and industrial entrepreneurs about 2 per cent. In contrast to this peasants and agricultural labourers constituted around 74 per cent of Polish society. Because of partition the Polish middle classes had been slow to emerge from the soup of feudalism. As a result, throughout the inter-war years, Polish civil society was underdeveloped compared with neighbouring Germany. Civil society could develop no faster than the growth of Polish cities, the absorption of a rural peasantry into an urban labour force, and the consequent upward mobility of second- and third-generation town-dwellers into the tiny middle class.

In the inter-war period, radio, film, architecture, journalism and the universities all went through a brisk expansion. Illiteracy, running at 33.3 per cent, but as high as 76 per cent in some parts of Galicia, was reduced by the introduction of compulsory primary education. There was also a huge growth in independent out-of-school educational facilities organized by the farmers and peasants, and a massive increase in the circulation of newspapers in Polish, German, Czech, Ukrainian, Yiddish, Russian and Byelorussian. Museums, public libraries and the universities (there were over 50,000 Polish students by the 1930s) went through a massive expansion in this period, but it seems that the institutes of learning produced more members of the *inteligencja* than society and the economy could usefully absorb. The *inteligencja* seems to have increased from about 3.5 per cent (488,000, but 1,134,000 with dependants) of the population in 1921, to about 4.7 per cent in 1931, and 5.2 per cent in 1939. Successful centrally planned industrial projects in Warsaw, Łódź, and Dąbrawa Basin were mere pockets, existing amid a vast agricultural hinterland which lacked finance but which supported much more than 50 per cent of the population. In spite of the beginning of centralized economic planning and industrialization, the economy was still dominated by the massive rural population, a vast peasantry, and by agriculture. Although by 1918 the independent professions were growing rapidly, the *inteligencja* still found little place in public and political life. Poland's National Income was about the same as Romania's, but better than that of the Balkan states. The real earnings of skilled workers were better than in almost all other European countries except Germany, yet throughout the inter-war period 30 per cent were unemployed.[13]

Inevitably Polish independence and the development of the inter-war military regime had an impact on the arts. The end of the First World War, the upheaval of the Russian revolution, the chaos of self-government, and the sudden freedom from the crushing weight of national responsibility (or the reaction against it), meant that while some writers felt themselves disorientated and cut adrift from traditional Polish cultural landmarks, they were also free for the first time to explore new territory in Polish literature. For example, homosexuality made an appearance in Polish literature in operatic collaborations between Jarosław Iwaszkiewicz (1894–1980) and the composer Karol Szymanowski (1882–1937). This was a period when all the arts went through a massive experimental expansion in Poland, with the avant-garde reaching out to modernism and to the folk culture of east central Europe.

One of the consequences of the release from the confines of national responsibility was that literature was in the open market, and as such was 'normalized' along west European lines. By some, writers were now seen as slightly disloyal political irritants who made difficult times worse, and by others as an increasingly expensive luxury. A few writers, particularly Maria Dąbrowska (1889–1965), were still taken seriously, but in general between the wars writers were a small and socially isolated section of society.[14] Writers, lacking any sense of national focus for their political thinking, felt themselves blocked. They had little or no influence on the country's political life. They had no opportunity to make an input on such vital political issues as the alliance of Catholic Church and Polish state, the interests of the remaining noble landowners on their massive provincial estates, the growth of anti-Semitism, the impact of foreign finance capital from France and Italy, the investment plans of central government or the entrepreneurial plans of the growing middle class.

With Polish independence, those who might normally have become frustrated provincial poets sheltering within the 'national myth' could turn to the new and rapidly expanding bureaucracy. The growing administrative class was influenced by a lively, nationalist and rather opportunistic intake, and began to display signs of what Norman Davies has called a 'mongrel Sarmatianism', a new middle-class populist boorishness, in its encounters with the art and literature of the new Poland. The arts between the wars were still largely unfunded and unsupported by the state, and inevitably there developed an artistic community that regarded the state, and was regarded by the state, with considerable suspicion. Nor were the arts a powerful force for social change when it came to Poland's undeveloped and backward rural districts. The 'market' for all kinds of art works, including literature, seems to have shrunk considerably and any artist working in a non-representational or avant-garde style was likely to be marginalized. Between the wars modern Europe and the Third World existed side by side in Poland. It is a relationship, a nexus of history, culture and politics, that is preserved in the Polish language, where the word *mieszczaństwo* means townspeople, bourgeois and also philistine.[15]

Between the wars the *inteligencja* were still denied a place in national politics and government. Instead, as they had done in the partitions, they devoted themselves to languages, literature, philosophy and revolutionary politics:

> Completely hemmed in as they were, how could the intellectuals, who thought themselves more intelligent and more honest than the counts and ministers, have helped thinking that the whole system had to be overthrown? Land reform, universal suffrage, a democratic constitution, autonomy for national minorities, democratic social policies were all needed. The bourgeois revolution was ripe, but there was no one to make it . . . In eastern Europe there was no bourgeois-democratic alternative to early rational redistribution, so the political impact of

bourgeois radicalism was slight. The members of the second reform generation came to form an elite opposition which offered a real alternative to the conservative-bureaucratic intelligentsia in the sphere of culture, but politically they represented a utopian alternative.[16]

Polish literature, bereft of the national function built up during the partitions, cut off from its messianic role, was now simply irrelevant to politics. Yet the Positivist strand of literature, which insisted on social improvement, was also out of step with the ultra-conservative military regime. As utilitarian attitudes prevailed, inter-war writers had a particularly difficult and confusing time. It was possible to move to the right. Juliusz Kaden-Bandrowski (1885–1944) became a senior spokesman for the military government and a fanatical Piłsudski supporter. This earned him the hatred of many of his contemporaries. However, his close relationship with the authorities did him little good, and in his novel *Czarne skrzydła* (Black Wings, 1925–9), set in the Dąbrawa coal basin, he flayed French capitalists investing in Polish mines, toadying Polish civil servants and businessmen, sycophantic Socialists, self-serving union leaders and the system that allowed these people to flourish: virtually the only positive portrait in the novel is that of a young communist. Konstanty Ildefons Gałczyński (1905–53) also turned to right-wing politics, anti-Semitism and nationalism in his search for certainty and a place in the Polish scheme of things: but his poem 'Bal u Salomona' (Ball at Solomon's) presented Poland as gloomy, oppressive and sinister.

Though there was little joy to be had, it was possible to occupy a kind of neutral centre. For the most part Julian Tuwim (1894–1953) took refuge in translation, fake etymology and catastrophist pessimism, but in 1936 he produced a long poem called *Bal w operze* (Opera Ball) in which his frustrations with the regime overflowed: there he satirized the Fascist dictator Pantokrator and the prostitutes, bankers, generals and secret policemen who attend a palace ball. Antoni Słonimski (1895–1976) wrote exuberant lyrical verse as part of the Skamander group; in despair at the rise of Nazism in Germany, he visited the USSR in 1932, only to be disappointed by what he saw. As a Wellsian rationalist and pacifist Słonimski criticized Polish anti-Semitism and nationalist chauvinism.

It was also possible to move to the left, but this almost certainly meant conflict with the Polish authorities. Aleksander Wat (1900–67), a Marxist but never a Party member, was jailed for several months in 1932. The poet Władysław Broniewski (1897–1962) had fought and been decorated for bravery in the Polish–Soviet war of 1920, but later went on to become a supporter of the Russian revolution and helped write a communist manifesto in verse in 1925. In spite of this he never engaged in direct political activities and never joined the Party, but was protected from the Polish police by his former army officers in the military regime – presumably out of loyalty for his bravery in 1920. For other writers a move to the left brought them within Stalin's murderous orbit.

The outbreak of the Second World War affected the whole range of 'normal' literary activity in independent Poland; poetry was perhaps less affected than other literary forms, but the developing strands of anti-realistic fiction and experimental theatre were brought to an abrupt halt. It would be many years before Poland could begin to re-establish an interest in this work. Bruno Schulz (1892–1942) was an art teacher who translated Kafka's *The Trial* into Polish. Through the magical and brilliantly effective prose of his two short novels *Sklepy Cynamonowe* (Cinnamon Shops, 1934) and *Sanatorium pod Klepsydrą* (Sanatorium under the Sign of the Hourglass, 1937) he had explored his own sexual sado-masochism and relations with his father, relating these to the changing pattern of familial and religious orthodoxy in the face of the new industrial society growing up in the oilfields around the rural and mainly Jewish town of Drohobycz. And these in turn he related to the mythical aspects of national and personal identity seen from the poverty of a complex Polish-Jewish identity and Poland's eastern provinces:

> To what genre does *Cinnamon Shops* belong? How should it be classified? I think of it as an autobiographical narrative. Not only because it is written in the first person and because certain events and experiences from the author's childhood can be discerned in it. The work is an autobiography, or rather spiritual gene-alogy, a genealogy par excellence in that it follows the spiritual family tree down to those depths where it merges into mythology, to be lost in the mutterings of mythological delirium. I have always felt that the roots of the individual spirit, traced far enough down, would be lost in the matrix of myth. This is the ultimate depth; it is impossible to reach farther down.[17]

Schulz managed to survive the initial months of the Nazi occupation, but was found outside the Drohobycz Jewish ghetto and shot by an SS officer in 1942.

Witold Gombrowicz (1904–69) had been born in Małoszyce. He studied law, philosophy and economics, and made his début as a writer with a volume of short stories published in 1937. His writing was experimental, lacking in conventional plot, illogical, distorted. Gombrowicz's method was that of constant provocation, relentlessly satirizing the very notion of 'Polishness'. He attacked cultural reliance on the mentality of the manor and the old nobility, portraying them as examples of 'the degeneration of forms'. He satirized the 'infantilism' and snobbery of the decayed Polish nobility and the boorishness and mental poverty of the new middle class, exposing meticul-ously the childishness that lurked in *inteligencja* attitudes and postures. For Gombrowicz Poland was fatally obsessed by noble myths about itself. For him Poland was the place where Europe drew to an end, where the cultural and political forms of the east and west met and softened each other, where

Form and Degradation had made a great compromise to create Polish culture, where the harsh contours of western European politics, art and social order began to blur and dissolve into the 'chaos' of the east, a place in desperate need of the sharpest realism, but which because of its history was dominated instead by the Romantic tradition. Gombrowicz took it as his personal task to break free from this historico-cultural complex, to cease being a Pole in his writing. He wanted to prise the Poles free of Poland and 'local' Polish obsessions so that they would become, as he put it, 'simply human beings':

> Everything was effaced, disintegrated . . . Poland, deprived of those great cities (and their bourgeoisie) where life can be concentrated and complicated, where it can arise and flourish, had a rural, peasant culture, yes, a culture represented by squires and priests. The nobleman sitting in his farmstead made the peasant do the work, and the village priest was the oracle. This feeling of formlessness tortured the Poles, but at the same time it gave them a strange sense of liberty. It was one of the basic causes of their admiration for their 'Polishness' . . . Of course there was a Polish form – a fairly obvious one, Sarmatian style! But it was not very substantial, it already contained a destructive fragility.[18]

Ferdydurke (1938), Gombrowicz's summation of these themes, caused a massive scandal when it was first issued, but its impact and its insights were overtaken by the outbreak of war. Gombrowicz was on a trip to Argentina when the war started: he never returned to Poland and did not return to Europe until 1963. Gombrowicz was to become a frequent contributor to *Kultura* (Paris). He was frequently denounced by Catholic conservatives and championed by radical intellectuals. He died in Vence, France.[19]

Stanisław Ignacy Witkiewicz (Witkacy, 1885–1939) introduced a feverish eroticism into his analysis of the sometimes Fascistic impulses and inner life of the *inteligencja*. It was he who stated most clearly and explored most fervently the problems of the independent Polish literary community. He was born in Warsaw, brought up in Zakopane and studied painting at the Kraków Academy of Fine Arts. He was a close friend of the anthropologist Bronisław Malinowski and travelled with him to India, Ceylon, Australia and New Guinea. In 1914, as a Russian citizen, he had been compelled to return to Europe. He had enlisted in an officers' training school, took up a commission in an élite Russian regiment and was decorated with the Order of St Anne for bravery. Instead of shooting him in 1917 his troops elected him commissar. In spite of this Witkiewicz remained opposed to Marxism (along with most contemporary philosophy), and preferred to develop his experimental theatre of Pure Form, his interest in hallucinogenic drugs, and his Catastrophist perception that humanity in the twentieth century was heading for unmitigated disaster with 'happiness for all'.

Those who had read Witkiewicz's massive novel *Nienasycenie* (Insatiability, 1930) knew that he was acutely aware of the problems of Poland's geographical and political position, of the precise nature of the Polish *inteligencja*, and of what lay in store for Poland under the rule of the Nazis and the cultural commissars from the east. In this novel Witkiewicz satirized the *inteligencja*, the philosophy of Marxism, and the provincial boorishness he predicted the communists would find and manipulate in Polish society. He showed a nation ruled over by a clever dictator called Dirty Face, an effete, bored and decayed gentry at the head of a primitive country that had fallen prey to a mysterious eastern philosophy and to the devastating effects of a pill of well-being called Murti-Bing. The Chinese Army, having subdued the Russians, approaches the Polish border. Dirty Face, famed for his ability to maintain neutrality, instead of fighting agrees to let the enemy behead him with full ritual honours. Poland is allowed to continue as it was, except that now social life is determined by the pill of Murti-Bing and by the Ministry for the Mechanization of Culture. For the artistic community Witkiewicz's suicide on the evening of 17 September 1939, upon hearing news of the Russian invasion of Poland, marked very clearly the end of literary experiment and the life of the independent nation.

For these three writers literature marched to its own drum, not that of the nation. In many ways the trio – Witkiewicz the visionary iconoclastic drug-taker, Schulz the masochist Jewish provincial art teacher, and Gombrowicz the sometime homosexual satirist – represented the most experimental forms of art, the most hard-headed attitudes to national identity and myth, the most outrageous life-styles available to challenge the conservative Polish *inteligencja*, and a serious alternative to the basic assumptions of the military-clerical inter-war Polish leadership. War, Nazi occupation, resistance, civil war and communism were all to force Polish literature back into its older 'national' mode.[20]

The Second World War

While material destruction in Poland was almost beyond belief, the country could nevertheless be restored. However, the massive loss of life and the damage to Polish culture and cultural patterns was to have far-reaching and unpredictable consequences. The Soviets had been waging war on the Polish *inteligencja* for some time before 1939. The Polish military had been a focus for traditional patriotic and national values, and many of the nation's professional intellectuals were officers either in the standing army or in the reserve. Thus when the Soviet secret police (NKVD) massacred 15,000 Polish prisoners of war at Katyń and two other camps in April 1940 it was a direct strike at the Polish *inteligencja*. The bodies exhumed by the Nazis at Katyń in 1943 included three generals, a rear-admiral, 100 colonels, 300 majors, 1,000 captains, 3,500 lieutenants, 500 cadet officers, 200 naval and air force officers; reservists included twenty-one university professors and lecturers, 300 surgeons and physicians, 200 lawyers, judges, prosecutors, solicitors and court officials, 300 engineers, and hundreds of teachers, journalists, writers, industrialists and businessmen. In June 1990 the USSR 'found' the bodies of 13,000 Poles, buried at various locations mainly in the Ukraine. Gorbachev ordered a full-scale investigation in November 1990, but it was blocked by the KGB. Only in October 1991, with the arrest of powerful KGB officials after the failed coup, did the Soviets admit that orders for the execution of the Poles came directly from Stalin.[21]

The Soviet experience of the poet Aleksander Wat was not so very unusual. What was unusual was that he survived. Born Aleksander Chwat, of a Warsaw Jewish *inteligencja* family, he had studied philosophy and psychology at Warsaw University, became a Dadaist poet and a founder of the Polish Futurist movement. He had published a book of experimental verse, *Me from One Side and Me from the Other Side of My Pug Iron Fire* (1919), and in the years 1921–5 edited *New Art* and *Almanac of New Art*. In 1927 he published a story collection, *Lucifer Unemployed*, and from 1929 edited the communist magazine *Miesęcznik Literacki* until it was closed down and he was imprisoned by the Polish authorities in 1932. He was a Marxist whose conversion coincided with a long literary silence: though never a member of the Party, he was an important fellow traveller on the intellectual left. In 1939 he escaped to the Russian zone of occupied Poland and in 1940 was arrested by the NKVD as a Trotskyite and Zionist agent of the Vatican. He was imprisoned in the Lubyanka and then deported to Kazakhstan in Soviet Asia where he lived under conditions of great hardship. After his release as part of the 1941–2 amnesty for Poles, he travelled to Alma-Ata in an attempt to find his wife and child. After a long search he eventually found them on a kolkhoz (collective farm) tending oxen, but shortly afterwards, as they would not accept Soviet citizenship, they were all exiled to Ili and released to return to Poland only in April 1946.[22]

Other Polish writers told of similar brutal experiences in the USSR. Of 230,000 Polish troops taken prisoner by the Soviets in September 1939, only 82,000 were found in time to join Anders's army. Approximately 112,000 other Poles eventually left the Soviet Union with General Anders's army, but many were left behind because the Soviet authorities delayed processing their cases, and others did not hear about the 'amnesty' for Poles until it was too late. Many more had difficulties in finding the Polish collection centres. Of the 1.8 million Polish civilians deported to Siberia in the years 1939–41 over 688,000 perished. Some 600,000 Poles were not allowed to return to Poland until after the war; 30,000 did not return until 1959; unknown numbers were forced to accept Soviet passports, and there are still thought to be 1.5–2 million Poles in the territory of the former USSR.[23]

One of the consequences of the war was that the *inteligencja*'s conspiratorial tendencies, learned during the long years of partition, had been massively confirmed by the occupation. Through the war years over 70,000 students graduated in secret from the universities in Warsaw, Wilno and Lwów. Theatre, publishing, libraries, art and graphic design all went underground. In 1940 there were about thirty underground journals in circulation: by 1945 there were over 600. Of these no less than fifteen spanned the whole wartime period. Inevitably the Polish *inteligencja* also suffered hideously under the Nazis. In the Warsaw uprising alone some 550,000 Poles were sent to the camps, 150,000 sent on forced labour, 245,000 died. Among the 6,000,000 Polish war dead (only 11 per cent of whom died as a result of military action) were 50 per cent of doctors, 57 per cent of lawyers, 18 per cent of clergy, 40 per cent of university teachers, 25 per cent of archaeologists, 21.5 per cent of the legal professions, 35 per cent of all graduates, 30 per cent of scientists, 20 per cent of of school teachers, 20 per cent of artists; almost the entire Jewish community of 3.4 million had been killed. More than 4,000 writers, journalists, broadcasters and virtually an entire generation of poets perished at the hands of the Nazis. The lyric poet Józef Czechowicz (1903–39) died in a bombing raid on his home village near Lublin; Tadeusz 'Boy' Żeleński (1874–1941) was shot by the Nazis when they occupied Lwów; Andrzej Trzebiński (1922–43) died in a Nazi street round-up. The poets Stanisław Stroiński (1921–44), Tadeusz Gajcy (1922–44), Karol Irzykowski (1873–1944), Krzysztof Kamil Baczyński (1921–44) and Juliusz Kaden-Bandrowski (1885–1944) all died in the Warsaw uprising.[24]

By 1945 the pre-war Polish *inteligencja* and the professions had almost ceased to exist. The intellectual centres of Warsaw and Poznań were smashed, their populations killed, dispersed, exiled, imprisoned. The Polish state had been moved 100 miles westwards, losing the important cultural centres of Wilno and Lwów, which had become Lithuanian Vilnius and Ukrainian Lviv (Russian Lvov), both under Soviet control. The new People's Republic of Poland sat on the ruined German cities of Danzig (Gdańsk), Stettin (Szczecin), Oppeln (Opole) and Breslau (Wrocław), all so badly damaged that it would be the mid-1960s before reconstruction would make any significant impact on their lunar landscapes. As Czesław Miłosz was to write:

> To understand the course of events in eastern and central Europe during the first post-war years it must be realized that pre-war social conditions called for extensive reforms. It must further be understood that the Nazi rule had occasioned a profound disintegration of the existing order of things. In these circumstances, the only hope was to set up a social order which would be new, but would not be a copy of the Russian regime. So what was planned in Moscow as a stage on the road to servitude, was willingly accepted in the countries concerned as though it were true progress. Men will clutch at illusions when they have nothing else to hold to.[25]

The deaths of so many intellectuals, professionals, writers and other artists effectively closed a period of Polish literature and drew a line under the social, political and cultural experiment that had been independent Poland. Even without the arrival of Soviet communism, cultural life in Poland could never be the same again.[26]

Polish Socialism

The history of Polish socialism begins with the Proletariat Party, Poland's first socialist party, founded by Ludwik Waryński in 1882. Even at this period the Russians treated the Polish Left with particular savagery. Waryński was arrested in 1884: he served sixteen years' hard labour; four other leaders were hanged and dozens more were exiled or imprisoned. Stanisław Mendelson and Bolesław Limanowski drew the remainder together and from the wreckage in 1892 founded the PPS (Polish Socialist Party) in Paris. Apart from its gradualist Fabian principles, its prime intention was to unite all elements of Polish labour within the cause of national liberation.

The PPS saw no great need for a world revolution, and refused to open a class war, saying that a mere massacre of tyrants would solve nothing. It emphasized the needs of the masses, predicting an end to economic systems powered only by the profit motive. To this end it launched the London-based journal *Przedświt* (Dawn), which it smuggled into Poland, and after January 1893 recruited Józef Piłsudski as a regular contributor. With around 12,500 members it was the largest left-wing party in Poland with its power base in the textile industry of Łódź, Żyrardów and Białystock, the glass industry of Piotrków, the foundries and mines of the Dąbrawa basin, and the growing urban proletariat of Warsaw. The PPS represented mainstream Polish socialist opinion. From the start it was committed to Polish cultural values, to democracy and a wide range of political rights and freedoms, and it consistently looked to the west European left for support in its policies and in regaining Polish independence.

The years after 1863 had seen intense debate on the future of a possible Polish state. From its foundation the PPS was increasingly concerned to unite the peasants, middle class, intellectuals and gentry under the banner of Positivism and nationalism. The leaders hardly mentioned the idea of socialism, or political ideology at all, but emphasized Polish national aspirations and campaigned for the restoration of the 1772 Polish borders. These policies had little appeal for Jews, Ukrainians and Lithuanians, whose feelings and aspirations they largely ignored. At the turn of the century the PPS seriously considered notions that it should help form overseas legions of Poles to fight for Poland's independence, and that the PPS should prepare itself to become a national government. Rupture within the left seemed inevitable. The 1905 revolution divided opinion within the PPS and it began to split into rival factions. The PPS issued a manifesto and called for an immediate general strike. Though the writer Bolesław Prus opposed the idea, other members felt this was not enough and formed a fighting section to join the Warsaw street battles. PPS-Lewica (Left), the largest of the rival factions, wanted a more traditional trade union- and labour-orientated policy, and believed the struggle for national independence was harmful to the class struggle. PPS-Lewica saw no advantage for Polish workers in siding with Polish patriotic gestures towards restoring an independence that would simultaneously re-install the power and privilege of the gentry, the Church and the landed few. Predictably, in 1918 PPS-Lewica split from the PPS and amalgamated with the revolutionary SDKPiL (Social Democracy of the Kingdom of Poland and Lithuania) to form the KPRP (Communist Worker's Party of Poland).

After the failure of the 1905 revolution Piłsudski broke with the timid main body of the PPS to form PPS-Rewolucja (Revolution). This was a conspiratorial faction led by Piłsudski, which formed military volunteer units in the Austrian provinces and organized for military action to restore Polish independence at the earliest opportunity. Under Piłsudski's leadership this faction moved towards a far more nationalist outlook, in which the recovery of national independence was their prime aim. This was to be the strand of politics which informed Piłsudski's legions, and which, after the collapse of the partitioning powers in 1918, took a leading role in restoring Polish independence. Neither the rival communists nor the Jewish Bund had supported the pursuit of Polish independence, so after 1918, as the new Polish government turned its attention from the struggle against the partitioning powers to the internal issues facing the infant Polish state, the PPS had little choice but to move steadily rightward to encompass nationalist opinion. By 1926 the PPS was one of the the largest parliamentary parties in Poland. But the left never managed to present its case or its achievements as clearly and coherently as the right-wing nationalist Endecja (ND: National Democracy), led by Roman Dmowski. It was perhaps inevitable that with independence Polish politics would lurch towards nationalism and the right, but the Polish–Soviet war of 1919–20 gave Poland another push in this direction.

For the most part Polish political thought during the nineteenth century (on both right and left) had focused on speculation about the prospect of Polish independence, a vehicle for Romantic dreams rather than the project of politics. The basic question throughout the partitions was whether an independent Poland could be revived. For those on the left the question was whether Poland would be restored by a socialist revolution, or whether socialism would become possible only with the revival of Poland. But for many on the left, Poland's independence and Polish nationalism were in themselves barriers to revolution. For those under the influence of Róża Luksemburg the question was: would socialism lead to an independent Poland or away from it?

Although Krzywicki, Brzozowski, Kostrzewa, Kelles-Krauz, Daszyński and Luksemburg had all written original works of socialist theory, compared with the strength of nationalist feeling that allowed the right-wing military regime to stay in power between the wars, the left as a whole exerted only intermittent influence on political and cultural developments. Only the PPS, which functioned in the Sejm (Parliament) as a powerless liberal intellectual opposition to the military Sanacja (literally, purging) regime and to the right-wing nationalist Endecja, had any real left-wing influence in Poland between the wars.

In the 1930s the PPS moved towards an anti-communist pose, and (unlike Endecja), co-operated with the Jewish Bund. There was a significant difference in the way the PPS and Endecja related to the 3.5-million-strong Jewish minority. Endecja portrayed Jewish and communist failure to support Poland's struggles for independence in the years up to 1918 as evidence that they were anti-Polish and instruments of Russianization. The PPS condemned anti-Semitism, but refused to recognize Jews as a distinct national group with a separate agenda and ambitions. PPS wanted Jewish workers to be recognized as part of the Polish proletariat, but also thought it best they should be thoroughly integrated into Polish society.

By the late 1930s the Polish left resembled the left of western Europe in that it was anti-Fascist, campaigned for land reform, agreed with the notion of a planned economy and saw the need for a separation of Church and state. The PPS, however, was a radical socialist party committed to parliamentary methods: it espoused national independence, a tolerant attitude to ethnic and religious minorities, a policy of social equality, the ambition to achieve socialism by democratic means and legitimation of trade union activity. During the Second World War most of the membership of the PPS went underground or formed part of the coalition government in London. Socialists who stayed in Poland were hounded by the Nazis, and untold thousands ended their lives like Norbert Barlicki (1880–1941), a leading leftist member of the PPS, murdered in Oswięcim. In 1945 the party split again. PPS-WRN (Freedom Equality Independence), the party's resistance movement throughout the war, decided to be 'true' to the London government, and even though the AK (Armia Krajowa, Home Army, London-backed resistance of which PPS-WRN was a part) had been dissolved at the end of the war, PPS-WRN stayed underground, resisting the communists by force of arms until 1947. The leftist faction of the PPS, however, came out of hiding and appropriated the name PPS. The two wings of the party were never reunited.

In 1948 the communists forcibly merged the leftist rump of the PPS with the PPR (Polish Workers' Party) to form PZPR (Polish United Workers' Party). The official line was that the PPS supported the government installed by the Red Army and the 'new reality'; post-war communist ideologues often asserted that this merger enhanced the 'ideals of the left', which were common to both the PZPR and the PPS, but one of their first acts was to set about purging the less malleable sections of PPS membership. The older 'independent leftist' activists of the PPS were hunted down by the SB (Security Service).

Many left-wing thinkers refused to acquiesce in Stalinist lies and tyranny and it is necessary to keep this in mind when considering the politics of the post-war intellectual opposition. While some PPS members favoured collaboration with the communists, the majority of the pre-war PPS social-democratic leadership opposed the 'new reality'. Several prominent intellectuals of the left, Maria Dąbrowska, Jan Nepomucen Miller, Zygmunt Żuławski, and Maria and Stanisław Ossowski, made their opposition clear. The journal *Kuźnica* (Forge) emphasized the PZPR's 'progressive' programme of social reforms, but the social democrats and the old PPS membership stressed, where they were able, the totalitarian and obscurantist history and methods of the PZPR. For many ex-PPS members it was not possible to equate the ruling 'Progressive System' of the PZPR with the political programmes of the entire left. Although there was considerable intellectual interest in the history and traditions of pre-war PPS, this interest was not grounded in any daily practice or existing organization and consequently had very little impact on the Polish working class. Also, the fact was that 'geopolitical realities' made it unlikely there would be any revival of PPS fortunes. The PZPR, having absorbed or marginalized the old PPS membership, was unlikely to look with favour on any resurgence. With the creation of the PZPR there was no left-wing *inteligencja* tradition outside the control of the Party.

In spite of the physical disappearance of the PPS, and the difficulties intellectuals had in reaching the Polish working class with 'radical socialist ideas', the pre-war PPS was a persistent undercurrent in the left-liberal intellectual humanist politics of the revisionists and later of KOR (Committee Defending Workers). Indeed, of the fourteen founder members of KOR no less than five had been active members of the inter-war PPS. In the sixth issue (1980) of the underground journal *Krytyka*, edited by Michnik, it is possible to find an extended history of the PPS. There Kuroń and Starczewski distanced themselves from the post-war merger with the communists, claimed Christian ideals as the highest values of European culture, made it perfectly clear that the membership of the editorial board had a long-standing interest in the history and ideals of the PPS, but also that the inter-war PPS anti-Catholic stance was only warranted when it opposed intolerance, chauvinism and xenophobia in clerical garb.[27]

The PPS was revived illegally in November 1987 specifically to oppose communism and to reclaim socialist ideology from the reconstituted PZPR. At that time the PPS declared that, even though it was drawing on right-wing and nationalist sympathies and was dissatisfied with the work of KOR, it would 'shape the socialist option in Poland' through its alliance of workers and young *inteligencja*. After the collapse of communism in 1989 there were no fewer than three parties calling themselves PPS, all claiming direct descent from the pre-war PPS. The PPS parties, whose membership consisted mainly of members of the pre-war PPS and ex-members of KOR, were briefly united with the London-based survivors of the pre-war PPS under the leadership of writer and ex-KOR leader J. J. Lipski. However, they had only a small electoral following and almost at once the revived PPS was riven by dissent over its attitude to Marxism and to the Catholic Church. The Provisional National Committee of the PPS split from the main party over attitudes to the Catholic Church. The crypto-Trotskyite faction PPS-RD (Revolutionary Democratic) opposed the move to a market economy and proposed policies for socialist self-management. The remaining PPS in the Sejm were led by Piotr Ikonowicz into co-operation with the Democratic Left Alliance. While it may be an irrational fear, for many the PPS is still too close to the communists in many of its social policies. However, the fact that the PPS exists at all, and has enjoyed some electoral success in opposing the transition to a totally unfettered free market economy has puzzled right-wingers, anti-communists, Catholics, émigrés and western observers alike.[28]

It is important to emphasize just how much of a black hole surrounded the history of independent pre-war Polish socialism. When, in the mid-1960s, Fiszman questioned twenty Polish *lyceum* graduates he found that only two had any knowledge about pre-1939 Poland – one because his family were connected to the pre-war military regime and later to the AK (Home Army: London backed resistance movement), the other because he had recently visited his exiled family in the west. The group were ignorant of the history of the Polish labour movement, the PPS, and the names and fates of pre-war Polish communist and socialist leaders.[29]

The PPS represented a strand of socialist thought that was independent of Moscow, and which, until 1945, was far more visible and important to Polish domestic politics than communism. In many ways the post-war writers and oppositionists of the *lewica laicka* (lay left) were in the direct line of spiritual descent from most liberal humanist sections of the pre-war PPS, though this influence was transmitted through the life-style, moral values and activities of the members of Polish PEN (international literary club) and ZLP (Polish Writers' Union), disseminated in their books and through public readings. Often quite consciously the writers maintained an orientation towards pre-war liberal politics and the *inteligencja* style of the pre-war PPS. Although Moscow's communism failed them and revisionism did likewise, although there was no recognizable literary or political movement to contain them and foster them, the post-war writers of the *lewica laicka* held out quietly and stubbornly for the social-democratic ideals of the old PPS. Writers saw multi-voiced debate in literature as a project for democracy and as an important part of the reconstruction of civil society: the post-war Communist Party, on the other hand, saw anything which was not unanimously approved and led by the Party as a threat to its power and a recipe for chaos.

Polish Communism

Communism in post-war Poland may have been imposed by a foreign power, but it was not without domestic roots: it was not simply a kind of anti-Polish virus parachuted into Poland from Moscow in 1942. Communism represented one strand of Polish left-wing thought, albeit eventually massacred and threatened into passivity by Stalin. Uncertain, half-hearted, shifty and ambiguous, reluctantly informed of its failings by the activities of independent socialists, the post-war Polish Communist Party cannot be passed off as a kind of foreign 'occupation'. It is one of the most fruitful sources of its own opposition.[30]

The history of the Polish Communist Party begins with the SDKP (Social Democracy of the Kingdom of Poland), founded by Julian Marchlewski and Róża Luksemburg in 1893. However, having rejected nationalism the SDKP soon found itself in difficulties. In 1898–1900 it merged with the SDL (Social Democracy of Lithuania) to become the SDKPiL (Social Democracy of the Kingdom of Poland and Lithuania), and its fortunes revived a little. It was dominated by Marchlewski, Luksemburg, and Feliks Dzierżyński (later known as 'Bloody Feliks', founder of the Cheka), who opposed the revival of Poland, claiming that nationalism would inevitably arise in a new Polish state and would play into the hands of the newly emerging national bourgeoisie. Communist theory dictated the liberation of subject peoples – and many Polish revolutionaries felt themselves to be, if not members of the ethnic minorities, then at least 'outsiders' to Polish society in one sense or another.

Luksemburg and the SDKPiL opposed Polish independence on several grounds. Firstly Luksemburg believed that Lenin used the idea of self-determination too loosely. She claimed that it should only be used to mean the self-determination of the proletariat, something which at that time Poland hardly possessed. She also believed that an increased number of nation-states would make the revolutionary task impossible since it would mean further fragmentation of the working class and would require a countless series of revolutions in small states. In the mistaken belief that revolution in Germany was imminent the SDKPiL repeatedly resisted attempts to restore the revival of Poland to the communist agenda, much to the annoyance of Luksemburg's Russian comrades. The SDKPiL believed that independence under capitalism was an impossible sham, but that independence under socialism would be unnecessary. Luksemburg blackened her name for ever in the eyes of most Poles by fighting against the restoration of the Polish state in a capitalist formation, and by agreeing to work in an uneasy alliance with the German Social Democratic Party in East Prussia, an area where they were Germanizing the Poles out of existence.

The strange, persistent, subterranean fact was that by 1918 the peoples of the emerging east-central European states saw their national survival bound up in the growth of states that would contain and protect specific cultures and peoples. The state of Poland could hardly have been expected to wither away when the national people it contained had taken such pains, over very long periods, to preserve some form of underground cultural, linguistic, literary and religious existence. In 1918 Poland was re-formed out of a national identity created in opposition to Russian and German efforts to deny, suppress and absorb the Poles. The SDKPiL failed to take into account the strength of the Polish will to re-create a state, and consistently underestimated the element of Russian nationalism contained within Bolshevik revolutionary aspirations. After the Russian revolution and the re-emergence of Poland the SDKPiL even campaigned, against Lenin's wishes, for Poland to become an 'organic part' of the Soviet Union, a Soviet republic. The SDKPiL appeared to many not as Polish socialists, but as traitors. It had always seen itself as an intellectual elite (which in many ways it was) but it had little or no mass appeal.

To complicate things further, the bulk of the SDKPiL membership were seen as marginal to Polish national identity. Only a tiny proportion were workers; the bulk of the membership – about two-thirds – were Lithuanians, Ukrainians and Byelorussians and it was in the *kresy* (eastern borderlands) that they enjoyed their highest level of support and membership between the wars. Also, many of the SDKPiL leadership were Jewish, and though they were less prominent in the 1920s when there was an influx of Byelorussian and Ukrainian peasants, they made up about 26 per cent of the party by 1933, though they made up only about 10 per cent of the Polish population as a whole. Since Jewish members had often received a better than average education they quickly rose to positions of power within the party. Predominantly Jewish leadership on the left made it much easier for the right-wing parties, the Catholic Church and the inter-war government to foment anti-Semitism. In spite of these problems in 1905 the SDKPiL planted bombs in Warsaw and organized demonstrations in Kraków. Probably because of these activities they attracted the support of a large number of the *inteligencja* with revolutionary tendencies, including Wacław Nałkowski (1851–1911), Andrzej Strug (1871–1937), Stefan Żeromski (1864–1925) and Stefania Sempołowska (1870–1944). In the first half of 1906 membership is thought to have been about 35,000.

Róża Luksemburg had pointed out repeatedly that Poland's history was unusual. She believed that Lenin's stress on the formation of bourgeois-led independence and nationalist movements had not taken into account circumstances in Poland. She stressed that the development of the nation-state was a phenomenon linked with the growth of an industrialized proletariat and substantially with the growth of a unified national bourgeoisie. Poland, then a series of colonial possessions, was still largely pre-capitalist and there was almost no major influence on nationalism from the Polish bourgeoisie. In

Poland neither a substantial bourgeoisie nor a substantial proletariat existed at the start of the partitions. They only barely existed by 1918, and even then contributed very little to Poland's history or developing national feeling. Nor were they a powerful political or economic force in opposition. In Lenin's terms the way things happened in Poland did not make sense: the bourgeoisie were not the 'builders of the nation'.[31]

In 1918 the SDKPiL and PPS-Lewica (PPS-Left) amalgamated to form the KPRP (Communist Worker's Party of Poland). The KPRP line on Polish independence was the same as that of the SDKPiL: they had no intention of struggling to free a bourgeois Polish republic, and thought Poland should be 'organically integrated' into the Soviet Union. It was this, more than anything else, which prevented them from achieving any mass appeal for Polish workers and peasants, and which left the party unprepared for Polish independence and the popular success of Piłsudski's PPS. The SDKPiL had a very small membership and was hampered by having almost no working-class following outside Czerwona Dąbrowa, Zamość and the poorer working-class districts of Warsaw. Nevertheless the newly formed KPRP represented the largest organized left-wing structure in Poland: for the first time there was one left-wing party with a consistent policy. The KPRP refused to accept Poland's independence, boycotted elections to the Sejm, and was made illegal by the Polish authorities in 1919. At the same time the government arrested trade union leaders, suppressed the main trade unions, banned the Jewish Bund and dismissed thousands of Jewish workers suspected of communist sympathies. The KPRP, aware, as a result of the Polish-Soviet war, that its ambition for Poland to become a part of the Soviet Union was unpopular and unfeasible, was in any case betrayed by the signature of the Treaty of Riga in which the Soviet Union recognized the Polish Republic. The KPRP emerged again in 1923, changed its name to KPP (Communist Party of Poland), agreed to take part in the forthcoming elections and formally accepted and supported the idea of the Polish state. The Party seemed to be the natural leader in the struggle for minority rights in Poland but soon made a powerful enemy in Moscow.

The eventual fate of Polish socialism under Soviet direction was there for those with eyes to see it in the Polish-Soviet war. As Soviet military units entered Polish territory, poor support for the Party among the Polish peasantry, and mistrust of Polish communists among Red Army commissars meant that Moscow kept a firm check on all attempts by the Polish communists to assume control of their own organization. In 1920 the Polish communists in Mińsk were disconcerted to see their All-Russian Conference of Communist Poles Commissariat of Polish Affairs forcibly merged with the Bolshevik Party's own Bureau of Polish Affairs. Soviet commissars assumed that Russian and Yiddish were to be the languages of administration in the new socialist Poland instead of Polish. They proved insensitive to Polish national feeling and, under the ruthless guidance of Dzierżyński, provoked a Polish nationalist reaction by making liberation seem more like occupation, imposing popular and desirable reforms at bayonet point. Reforms like the eight-hour working day (which under normal circumstances would have been attractive to Polish workers) appeared anti-Polish.

In Soviet eyes the KPP did itself no favours. On the 'agricultural question' the Polrewkom (Polish Revolutionary Committee) failed to follow Lenin's orders to redistribute land and destroy the *kulaks* (peasant landowners), claiming that this would later hinder collectivization. Lenin was to dub this independence from Moscow, and incessant concern for the details of how communism could be applied in Poland, as a peculiarly Polish infantile disorder, 'leftism'. The KPP, it seemed, were more communist than Bolshevik. But in fact this was part of the Polish party's dilemma. It was a party seen to be imported by the Russian enemy, expected to operate where it had little hope of finding sympathy or support, and even less chance of repairing the damage or allaying the fears caused by the Red Army. As a result of Soviet policies and attitudes the newly created Polish Red Army failed to recruit enough volunteers to field even one company of soldiers, and the project was abandoned. The Soviets proved incapable of understanding Luksemburg's earlier warnings about the depth of Polish national feeling. Their behaviour damaged the image of communism in Poland and demolished for nearly a decade any chance of electoral success the tiny KPP might have stood. The war, however, forced all other parties to the right in order to ride the tide of nationalist feeling, and boosted the image of the right-wing nationalist *Endecja* movement.[32]

As a result of mass agitation, deep unease at Poland's poor pace of modernization and a nagging belief that perhaps cousins in the Soviet Union were faring better than the national minorities in Poland, communists and socialists did very well in the Polish eastern borderlands in the relatively free elections of 1928. Of a possible 444 seats in the Sejm the PPS won sixty-four and the communist bloc, with 7 per cent of all the votes cast, won fifteen. However, their success in this area of very mixed population and language meant that the Soviet Union's suspicion of the KPP's cosmopolitanism was deepened further. Also the various factions within the Polish left were split over the question of national minorities and 'national deviationism'. Inter-war Poland had a large Czech, German, Ukrainian, Ruthenian, Lithuanian, Byelorussian and Jewish population totalling 10,000,000 people from a total population of around 29,000,000. The political questions of identity and loyalty could hardly be avoided in a context of such mixed language and settlement, especially when the area was undergoing a slow, but nevertheless unsettling, economic transformation.

While the KPP supported Piłsudski's May 1926 coup in order to prevent a right-wing take-over, in the years that followed they found themselves reviled by Moscow for what became known as the 'May error'. Piłsudski had started out as a socialist, but claiming that there could be no socialism without independence (the opposite of Polish socialist orthodoxy which assumed that there could be no independence without socialism), he had used the idea of socialism to assist independence and thereafter blended his own unorthodox variety of vaguely socialist paternal nationalism in a country that was massively Catholic and agricultural, in his rule through a combination of military, Church, landowners and the rising power of industrial capital. Piłsudski failed to implement any far-reaching and thorough land reform to alleviate economic tensions, and his political police and anti-Soviet nationalism quickly gained the upper hand until, far from being the springboard of revolution in its leap into the Danube region, the Polish east by the mid-1930s became increasingly nationalist and staunchly anti-Soviet.

Throughout the 1930s the KPP pursued an ultra-leftist line that post-war First Secretary Władysław Gomułka was later to label 'abstract revolutionism'. Although nominally the KPP had agreed to take part in an anti-Fascist front, in practice they still thought collaboration with the bourgeois parties would weaken their resolve and they worked for a Polish revolution along classical Bolshevik lines: they attempted to undermine the parliamentary parties, prepared for armed insurrection to seize power, supported militant occupation strikes, terrorist attacks on the authorities, and backed the ethnic minorities (including the large, vociferous and increasingly Nazified German minority) in their struggle against Polish chauvinism. Many of the KPP leadership resided abroad through the 1930s, and those who remained in Poland spent time in prison. By 1938 over 7,000 KPP members were in Polish prisons. The KPP membership, increasingly seen as traitors to Poland, lost their Sejm deputies and failed to make common cause with the PPS against the Sanacja regime.

Throughout the 1930s the KPP had become associated in Soviet eyes with independent 'leftist Piłsudski-ist Trotskyite Fascist' opinion. Although the KPP realized it had miscalculated in supporting the 'socialist' Piłsudski and recanted its 'error', Stalin nevertheless considered their independent streak to be a threat: at bottom he suspected that their cosmopolitanism was just a complicated form of Polish patriotism. The party was unable to operate effectively in Poland, and Stalin lost patience not only with the Polish communists in particular, but with Poles in general. Stalin was more than willing to get rid of Polish communist intellectuals whenever he could. Several Polish communist writers, anxious to avoid the prisons of the Polish military regime, took refuge in the USSR: Tadeusz Żarski (1896–1934), Witold Wandurski (1891–1934/38), Jan Hempel (1877–1937), and the 'proletarian poet' Ryszard Sztande (1897–1938?) were all killed by the NKVD.

In 1937–8 Stalin invited the KPP leadership, who were being hounded mercilessly by the Polish authorities, to take refuge in Moscow. At the time, in the wake of the Bukharin trial, the NKVD were actively engaged in killing 50,000 Polish refugees, exiles and émigrés (most of whom were not communist). On the pretext that KPP had fallen prey to the influence of Trotsky, that the party was riddled with Polish secret police informers and that the Poles were planning to co-operate with the Nazis against the Soviet Union, Stalin had the KPP leaders, Bronkowski, Krajewski-Stein, Unszlicht, Walecki (Horwitz), Bobiński, Ryng (Heryng), Ciszewski, and Henrykowski arrested, tried and executed. Another victim of the NKVD was Warszawski (Adolf Warski, 1868–1937). He had been a close associate of Róża Luksemburg and one of the leadership of the SDKPiL; he had been a communist deputy at the Warsaw Diet, and a leading member of the Political Bureau of the Central Committee of the KPP. Wera Kostrzewa (Maria Koszutska, 1876–1939), a leader of the PPS-Lewica, later an important member of the KPP and their representative to the Comintern, an expert on the workers' movement in Poland and on all matters relating to the peasantry, perhaps the party's most important surviving intellectual on the left, was also killed. The Soviets even killed their ally, Leński (Julian Leszczyński, 1877–1939). He had been a leading KPP theorist, a member of the Party's Political Bureau and Party General Secretary from 1929. He had been the chief Polish opponent of anti-Stalinism; in 1932 he had expelled the young Isaac Deutscher from the party for his anti-Stalinist opinions. Another victim was the writer Bruno Jasieński (1901–38?). He had written Marxist journalism and Futurist poetry in Paris before being expelled by the French authorities; unwilling to return to Poland, where he feared arrest, he took up residence and worked as an editor in Moscow: in 1938 he was arrested, sentenced to fifteen years hard labour and died of typhus in transit to a camp at Kolyma, nobody knows exactly when or where; his wife was sentenced to ten years' hard labour.

Perhaps 5,000 KPP members (practically the entire active membership) were purged, imprisoned, sent to the camps or executed. Virtually all these people were veterans of the left and had joined the KPP either from the SDKPiL or PPS-Lewica. Eventually all the Polish members of the Soviet Communist Party Executive Committee and all the Polish members of the Control Commission of the Comintern had been killed. Only one member of the KPP Central Committee, Władysław Gomułka, survived. Stalin had the KPP disbanded and its name struck from the Comintern register.

The Soviets, when it was convenient, allowed a revival of the KPP in late 1941. Terrified of its association with the KPP, the new party's first act was to rename itself as the PPR (Polish Workers' Party). The intention was that the Party should, at least in Stalin's mind, distance itself from the old KPP and its mistakes on the 'Polish question'. The new party had a Soviet-imposed leadership, at least two of whom had not been members of the party before the war. Located mainly on Russian-controlled territory, with membership hovering around 4,000, the PPR was subject to Moscow's potentially lethal guidance and to enormous internal rivalry. In 1942 the party leader Nowotko was murdered by his own executive officer, who was later condemned to death by a Party court. In 1943 Finder, who had parachuted into Poland, was arrested by the Gestapo under mysterious circumstances and killed. Władysław Gomułka, who had survived the 1938 purge because he was under arrest by the Polish authorities for agitation among chemical workers, emerged to become first secretary.

Gomułka set out to make independence, communism, nationalism and a military alliance with Moscow the four cornerstones of Party power. Nevertheless, the PPR inherited most of the surviving KPP membership and with them seems to have inherited a number of the KPP's old habits: its factionalism, its dislike of liberal reformism and an inability to make alliances with left-leaning bourgeois parties. The KPP, however, had seen itself as an embattled party of revolutionary opposition and was pleased that it had maintained its intellectual and ideological purity. This was not the case with the new Party. The imposition of communism in Poland after 1945 lacked any legitimacy in national politics, a fact which the PZPR found great difficulty in recognizing, but which both shaped and limited its efforts to remodel Polish society. There was very little to distinguish the post-war communist regime from the pre-war military Sanacja regime apart from the notion (rather than the fact) of ideology. The Party could dictate from a narrow élite just as well as the old regime, manipulate the various institutions in its own favour, develop a Jesuitical line on 'truth' when necessary, uphold a hierarchy of its own, appear radical and anticlerical when it needed to, and, in making populist gestures to the 'proletariat', appeal to a narrow and intolerant version of Polish national identity, preferably dignified by the idea of 'national unity', just as Endecja and Piłsudski had done before it. To a very great extent it was this similarity that helped enable the patriot of old to emerge from the war as the modern comrade.

Right from the start the PZPR lacked legitimacy and was seen to have been installed by Soviet bayonets. Nevertheless, by the mid-1950s the PZPR had effected a remarkable change in Polish politics. By threat of violence it had silenced the surviving pre-war parties and created a useful 'tame opposition'; in absorbing the PPS it abolished criticism of its claim to be socialist. By hijacking the language of socialism the PZPR made any alternative to its own version of socialism difficult to conceive and all but impossible to articulate. For many who came into contact with it, it discredited the left as a whole. And yet the PZPR was to prove the creator of many of communism's most dedicated critics and opponents. The idealistic writers and intellectuals who joined the Party after 1945, discovered in 1949, 1956, 1968, 1970, 1976 and 1980–1 that if they had any self respect they could not continue their membership. Writers like Andrzejewski, Kołakowski, Barańczak, Brandys, Konwicki, Kapuściński, Michnik, Kuroń and many more, repeatedly found their ideals warped, their dreams of social improvement betrayed, their protests stifled, their creative initiatives spoiled, and their moral support perverted by the Party.

Polish communism was a remarkably ambivalent creature, but Poles were surprisingly willing to give it a chance. Joining the Party meant that a structured and ever-ascendant career was virtually guaranteed, no matter what the calibre of the applicant. Poles knew the Party lacked legitimacy, but it was the only recognizable avenue of social and economic advancement. It is one of the ironies of Polish social life (and testimony to the Party's demoralizing effect) that, contrary to popular mythology, Party membership rose steadily throughout the post-war period (particularly in the 1970s), and in times of economic distress tended to rise rather than fall. The Party grew from 34,000 members in January 1945 to 300,000 members by April 1945 – a substantial figure, even if many were merely opportunists. Membership of the PZPR reached its zenith, 3,150,000 members, in July 1980 just a few days before shipyard strikes broke out in Gdańsk.[33]

The PZPR was the creature of Moscow, but never fully so. It was a half-hearted Polish variant of Stalinism, caught between Polish national aspirations and a version of socialism that was not its own. After years of increasingly poor leadership the Party was suspended by the Martial Law authorities in 1981. Although it was later restored, the Party never achieved any real authority, collapsed and nearly disappeared in the 'almost democratic' elections of 1989, reformed itself, and then split into two social-democratic parties in 1989–90. The successor parties of the Democratic Left Alliance made a remarkable recovery and came second out of eighteen major groupings with 11.7 per cent of the vote in the 1991 general election. At the 1993 elections, together with the Peasants' Party, their old allies from the communist years, they were the largest bloc in the Sejm and formed the coalition government.

Many western observers, particularly those on the right, assumed that with the events of 1989 all varieties of the left had been decisively dismissed. But, as if somebody had forgotten to tell the Poles about the end of history, left and right have once more emerged from the stew. Arguments between left and right have resumed. The shock has been that arguments were picked up not from November 1989, but from September 1939, when independent Polish political life, with all its faults and problems, was interrupted by the Nazi-Soviet partition. As Poles have come to understand that socialism is no longer subject to Moscow and that perhaps the western pursuit of an untrammelled free market is not necessarily for them either, there has been a steady swing away from the free market, privatization, the unpredictable autocracy of Wałęsa and the retrograde ambitions of the Church, followed by disillusionment with the speed of democratic progress. There has been a steady polarization of left and right, a clear disappointment with the very notion of participatory politics on the part of the bulk of the population, and a slow but clear revival of interest in both dictatorial politics and in the social-democratic principles of the old PPS. Poland, it is clear, is rediscovering left and right, and at the same time is recovering an independent liberal-socialist intellectual heritage largely buried by Moscow.

The Inteligencja

The Party, through its failure to allow any development of self-awareness from within its own structures or through criticism of its actions from outside, developed a language that was increasingly meaningless and irrelevant to Polish daily life, while the writers and independent intellectuals struggled to restore meaning to a language devastated by the Party. The clash between the writers and the Party was for the most part low-key and unspectacular, but there could be no mistaking the fact that the efforts of the Party were in direct contradiction to the work of the writers, in direct opposition to virtually the whole range of modern professional economic activities and hampered social, political and personal self-awareness.

Contrary to expectations, the Party did not destroy the *inteligencja* – instead it encouraged it to grow and made laws designed to protect it. Yet it is clear that many of the problems the post-war communist government faced were the direct result of its failure to manage or satisfy the Polish *inteligencja*. The precise definition of the Polish *inteligencja* is problematic as it has varied considerably through history. In the years 1918–39 the Polish *inteligencja* comprised 14 per cent of those employed outside agriculture. It included those who could command fees of over 1,200 złoties per month right down to those who perhaps earned only 260 złoties per month. In pre-war and post-war Poland the term *inteligencja* referred to a wide range of people whose political opinions often stressed their spiritual independence from the government along nationalist, democratic, revolutionary, ethnic or religious lines.

All groups and classes within Polish society faced massive change in the post-war period. But none, it seems, have faced the challenge of change more than the *inteligencja*. Leszek Kołakowski, following Soviet practice, claimed that the post-war *inteligencja* signified a class-group of educated people who earned their living by their knowledge and skills. Sociological research has traced some of the transformations that have affected (and afflicted) this social group. The '*inteligencja* stratum' is now divided into 'intelligentsia proper' (with academic degrees) and 'white collar' (office clerks and similar workers). Thus the post-war Polish *inteligencja* is a very large and varied entity comprising all those with higher education, further education, and those who only have their secondary school diploma: this included all professional intellectuals, all white-collar workers and those with secondary education, a very large proportion of those engaged in non-manual independent and semi-independent occupations: physicians, lawyers, highly qualified engineers, intellectuals, dentists, surgeons, lawyers, judges, university and secondary school teachers, writers and artists, architects, administrators, technicians, heads of state economic enterprises, civil servants, the religious hierarchy, engineers, journalists, junior technicians, clerical workers, some shop assistants and humble provincial primary school teachers. Thus by the mid-1970s the *inteligencja* comprised over 35 per cent of Polish society. Topolski has said that while many could be said to have joined the stratum because of their education or work experience, their backgrounds differed widely: 35 per cent came from worker backgrounds, 20 per cent from peasant backgrounds, 40 per cent from the old *inteligencja*, and 5 per cent from the old bourgeoisie and *szlachta*.[34]

However, while the Party nurtured the new *czerwona burżuazja* (Red Bourgeoisie), at the same time it tried to ensure that the *inteligencja* remained politically powerless. As Hirszowicz put it:

The geography and sociology of culture eliminated the figure of the old *inteligent*. He has been replaced by the professional, who for better or worse operates within a strictly designed division of labour. The Polish intelligentsia ceased to exist with the Second World War . . . Today in Poland the intelligentsia exists on a verbal level, partly in customs, in the style of life, in bric-à-brac, in the home atmosphere. That is all. It does not exist in the social structure or in the social life at large.[35]

The Polish middle class, technocracy and industrial proletariat are predominantly the product of the post-1945 communist rulers of Poland. Predictably, the *czerwona burżuazja* is a mass of contradictions: these people may have been saved from rural idiocy by the Party and by industrialization, their opportunism and ambition may have been made possible by a communist education and their future employment may have resided in the state *biurokracja*. However, their value system was still largely derived from, or heavily influenced by, the Catholic Church; their political thought and national view were massively influenced by the displaced *szlachta* ethos. The *czerwona burżuazja* was as nationalist and, in its own way, as obsessed by the idea of a Polish state as the pre-war *inteligencja* had ever been. By creating a red bourgeoisie and by playing the national card repeatedly, the Party fostered a class and a strand of thinking that in the short term helped it create a state. In the long term, however, it made the withering away of the state much less likely, and made the idea of internationalism simply a nationalist variation on the theme of plots against Poland. The PZPR could not avoid the trap. Though Moscow-trained, they were, after all, Poles – products of a particular history and culture.

Kołakowski said that in a country which was still predominantly agricultural it would be very hard to withstand the overwhelming pressure of the petit-bourgeois culture and customs imposed by the Party. He also said that only the Polish creative *inteligencja* had the 'skill to educate and influence culturally' and could help the Polish working class to free itself from the stifling peasant tastes and habits of the lower middle classes, the Party and *biurokracja* (bureaucracy). Kołakowski claimed that the Party needed independent creative intellectuals precisely because they were able to help it reach wise decisions. They could do this because they were free in their thought and 'superfluous as opportunists'. But Kołakowski had few illusions about how they were regarded by the authorities:

> Those in power in all social orders strive to maintain the closest possible cooperation with the intellectuals. Failing this, they must rely exclusively on the support of the police and the army – apparently the most efficient method, yet experience has shown it to be deceptive if it is the sole means of ruling. The participation of the pedagogic intelligentsia (scientists, teachers, artists, journalists, propagandists) in the system of government is, other things being equal, in inverse proportion to the degree of repression; for the less one is capable of ruling by intellectual means, the more one must resort to the instruments of force. That is why intellectuals so often attract the instinctive animosity of the police and the army.[36]

Kołakowski has located both the attractiveness and the weakness of socialism for a society where class struggle has largely been absent from national history, and where civil society still aspires to capitalism, bourgeois society and bourgeois democracy:

> Communism, in its promise of abolishing classes and class struggle, thereby cutting out the roots of social conflict, makes the bourgeois 'negative freedom' and human rights – rights of individuals isolated from, and hostile to, one another – useless. The division between civil society and the state, indeed the very distinction between the two, is done away with: 'real life' and spontaneous community, having absorbed the state, law, and other instruments of government that kept bourgeois society, with its privileges, exploitation, and oppressiveness intact and served to perpetuate it, has no need of such supports. Communism ends the clash between the individual and society; each person naturally and spontaneously identifies himself with the values and aspirations of the 'whole', and the perfect unity of the social body is recreated . . . by a movement upward on an 'ascending spiral' that restores human meaning to technological progress. Human rights, in other words, are simply the facade of the capitalist system; in the new unified society they become utterly irrelevant.[37]

Throughout the 1970s creative intellectuals – a tiny group within the *inteligencja* – were the main focus of opposition to the Party, in direct rivalry with the Party for the allegiance and opinion of the bulk of the *inteligencja*.

The writers hinted to their readership that they knew what they were doing, that they understood the latest nuances of Party policy and that they were against it. Readers became adept at reading between the lines. In the early 1970s there were still interesting books to read, but as that decade ended and the censorship became increasingly entrenched, writers became less interested in 'saying something' and grew more and more obsessed with the act and process of writing, of speaking only and at length about the difficulties of writing under this social and political set-up. Another aspect of this development could be seen in the 'defeat' of literature by the censor and restrictive publishing policies and in the epidemic growth of underground publishing in the late 1970s. Not all underground literature was of high quality or of any great political significance, but to a readership starved of public debate, much – possibly too much – was read with a wink and a nudge. The struggle with the censor and strategies to defeat or subvert censorship, rather than any other content, became major literary preoccupations. In the universities too, pure literary theory came to assume an awesome and stultifying stature: at almost every level there was a move away from the study of creative literature, away from literary history. Doubtless these were symptoms and reflections of the defeat of ideological thought within the Party itself.

It was not that the post-war *inteligencja* felt the pursuit of material wealth was a soulless activity, or that writers believed Mickiewicz was better than a Mercedes (owning even a Trabant was beyond the ambition of most Poles). It was simply that in reaction to the living standards and 'achievements' of the Party (which were profoundly un-Polish, lacking in spiritual value, and embedded in a hideously inefficient economy) the creative *inteligencja* insisted that it should be they rather than the Party who set standards of moral and social behaviour. Increasingly it was to the creative *inteligencja* that journalists and politicians turned as the dangerously demoralized working class of Poland emerged from the heady broth of rapid industrialization and showed that it could be boorish, unsophisticated, undisciplined, ill-mannered, ruffianly and determined – traits which contributed to Poland's poor economic performance. This did not necessarily mean that the *creative* inteligencja were models of intellectual clarity or honesty, nor did it mean that they had any programme to offer beyond the concept of national identity and national survival.

Polish writers, in opposition or in the Party, were but two representatives of the east-central European *inteligencja* as an aspect of the emerging middle class on the road to class power. The *inteligencja* began to re-emerge as a problem in the mid-1970s precisely because Gierek's technical revolution contradicted the Party efforts to retain power by controlling the flow of information. However, the problems of the *inteligencja* emerged primarily as moral and normative – that is as a cultural phenomenon of political significance. The futurology of classical Marxism-Leninism had not predicted the rise of technological society. Nor had it foreseen the professional problems, economic demands and spiritual discontents such a society would voice. It failed utterly and repeatedly to accommodate or even appreciate the stress these developments would place on the vertical command structures of the Party.

The Catholic Church

The Catholic Church had evolved a very strong role in expressing Polish national opposition to partition and occupation (particularly in the Russian-controlled area) throughout the nineteenth century. In the inter-war years this role became intertwined with Piłsudski's nationalism as the dominant ideology, so that in the post-war years, under 'Soviet occupation', the Church resumed its role as the guardian of Polishness and Polish nationhood, even though in practical terms its continued existence as an independent institution necessitated compromise with the secular authorities.

Catholic social doctrine in Pope Leo XIII's encyclical *Rerum novarum* (1891) and Pius XI's encyclical *Quadragesimo anno* (1931) (two documents directed against socialism and trade unionism which hampered understanding between socialists and Catholics for decades) was included in the Polish Constitution of 1935. This allowed the legal implementation of an alliance between Church and state. The inter-war Polish government gratefully accepted the Church's anti-communist stance and did so to the social and economic advantage of the Church. As the Church owned over 1,000,000 acres of land and massive holdings in buildings, it functioned as a large magnate. The inter-war government treated it as a trusted partner and in return for its support the Polish state disbursed to the Church some 20,000,000 złoties per year: in 1935–6 the state paid out 17,465,499 złoties in salaries to priests, cardinals and bishops. The state also paid out 2,867 stipends to seminary students, but offered only 2,584 other studentships. The ultra-conservative Church resisted every progressive movement in the inter-war years – everything from socialism to trade unions and independent peasant organizations.[38]

Pre-war Poland had been about 64 per cent Catholic. Post-war Poland, mainly because of the expulsion of the Germans and the extermination of the Jews, Mariavites, Jehovah's Witnesses and most other religious minorities, and the boundary shift which excluded most Uniate and Orthodox Ukrainians, was more than 90 per cent Catholic. After 1945 the Church and the Party took a long time to adjust to each other. The new government assisted the Church in reopening the Catholic University in Lublin and gave the Church huge sums of money from a very depleted budget to reconstruct damaged buildings: 100 million złoties in 1944, 590 million złoties in 1945, 89 million złoties in 1946, 188 million złoties in 1947.[39] Indeed it looked for a while as if they might find a way of working together: Catholic funeral rites were observed when communist General Karol Świerczewski (the International Brigade's General 'Walter' in the Spanish Civil War) was buried; in addition, Polish radio broadcast Sunday mass until 1947, and Bierut's presidential oath in 1947 ended with the words 'so help me God'. This changed with the completion of the communist take-over in 1949.

It took the Party some time to learn that the more they tried to combat the Church the more Poles would run to its aid: they found it very difficult to reconcile the idea of an orthodox socialist Poland and a prominent Catholic Church. With the defeat of the political opposition in 1947–9 the position of the Church changed dramatically. Under First Secretary Bolesław Bierut the 1950 Church-state accord failed. The Church had been dispossessed of much of its inherited property with the land reform of 1944, and while it lost land in the old Polish east, it failed to secure the property of the German Church in the new western territories. This left a lingering resentment. After 1948 many of the clergy were accused, among other things, of assisting or hiding AK members and about 900 priests were imprisoned. Cardinal Wyszyński himself was put under house arrest. For a while, like Jacob and the Angel, the two organizations appeared locked in mortal combat. But this was not to last.

In 1954 a slow dissolution of the Stalinist bonds began. Against a background of intellectual unrest and increasing industrial dissatisfaction the government sought and obtained the support of the hierarchy in reasserting its authority. In October 1956 Cardinal Wyszyński addressed Poles to call for 'calm, caution and prayers'. In return for this support the government agreed to give the Church certain privileges and concluded a new agreement in December 1956 which reinstated the Church's jurisdiction over its own affairs, confirmed the right to select its own hierarchy and mark its own administrative areas. The Party allowed the revival of the Catholic journal *Tygodnik Powszechny* (Universal Weekly), which had been given to Pax when it failed to produce a slavish obituary for Stalin, and the journal *Znak* (Sign); it also allowed five Catholic deputies to be elected to the Sejm, and monks and nuns to return to their monasteries. As Bogdan Szajkowski commented, from that point on the relationship between the Catholic hierarchy and the PZPR changed from that of dangerous enemies fighting an everlasting battle for the control of Polish souls, to that of indispensable allies. Although in the following years both sides indulged in wasteful squabbling, neither would overstep the unwritten rules of the game.[40]

The deeply ambiguous role of the Catholic Church under communism has yet to be examined in any great detail, but it is clear that after an initial period of difficulty, both the Party and the Church realized that pragmatic co-operation rather than confrontation would be more fruitful: apart from their disagreement about the Polish episcopate's letter to German Catholics in 1965, the Church and the Party had very few open clashes. After 1956 it seems that the Church made valuable 'trade offs' with the Party: the Party and the Church were not the deadly enemies many supposed. In almost every sphere the Catholic Church grew under communism. In exchange for co-operation in maintaining social calm and good order, the Church again received material benefits. In the years 1945–77 the Church built or gained planning permission for 1,900 new churches. This was a rate of construction unequalled in the 1,000 years of Polish Church history. In 1977, when Poland had regained its pre-war population of about 35,000,000, a Church census revealed that the Church was actually bigger under the communists than it had been before the war: in addition to the two cardinals, seventy-five bishops, forty-five seminaries, 18,000 catechism centres, 15,792 catechism teachers and twenty-nine episcopal commissions, there were 19,000 priests (only 13,934 in 1937), 36,261 monks and nuns (only 23,696 in 1937), 14,152 Church-owned buildings (only 7,257 in 1937); there were also twenty vocational and secondary schools, a Catholic university in Lublin with over 2,000 full time students, a theological seminary and eight major religious festivals. The Polish Church had 20,000,000 regular communicants. The post-war Church was never the hunted, furtive, underground creature of western imagining.

The Catholic University of Lublin (KUL), which had first produced matriculations in December 1918 and which remains the main centre of Catholic learning, had been re-established after the war with four faculties – theology, canon law, moral teaching, law and the social sciences. KUL was the first university to resume operations after the war and its inauguration ceremony was attended by Soviet Foreign Minister Nikolai Bulganin. In the post-war period KUL expanded considerably. In 1937–8 it had 1,400 students; by 1979 it had 2,140 full time students. During the sixty years of its existence over 30,000, including more than two-thirds of the episcopate, graduated from KUL or undertook post-graduate study there. Karol Wojtyła (later to become Pope John Paul II) was a professor there for several years, and KUL published his *Selected Problems of Christian Culture*, along with a wide range of books. In addition there was also the Academy of Catholic Theology (ATK), a state-operated and -funded establishment founded in 1954 as a continuation of the theological faculties at Warsaw University and the Jagiellonian University. ATK was closely linked with KUL. The lecturers (who specialized in theology, Christian philosophy, canon law and a full range of other courses including Christian archaeology, sacred art, patrology, mission study, apologetics, dogmatic theology), many of whom also taught at KUL, had state appointments and a canonical mission from the Polish primate, who is also grand chancellor of ATK. In 1978–9 ATK had 1,655 students.

It is also important to realize the size of the Church's publishing effort (which avoided state censorship by operating its own system of self-censorship), and its importance as an outlet for intellectuals throughout the post-war period: the Catholic Church has probably always had more freedom to publish than mythology supposes. In the years 1945–78 the Church published over 8,000 book titles and a very wide range of its own journals. In total, by 1979, there were forty-eight Church publishing ventures, including KIK (Clubs of the Catholic Intelligentsia), bringing out a total of ninety-two periodicals. The Catholic University at Lublin and the Catholic Theological Academy both produced several dozen titles per year. ATK published a wide range of theological and religious titles.

The Znak group of Catholic deputies to the Sejm (1957–76) were closely associated with the journals *Znak*, *Więź* (Link) and *Tygodnik Powszechny* (Universal Weekly). In addition there are a number of publishing houses specializing in particular aspects of Catholic life and interest. The most important concerns are: Apostolstwo Modlitwy (New Testament, Acts of the Apostles, Gospels); Pallotinum, publishing religious literature, including detailed accounts of the Second Vatican Council, Vatican documents, moral theology and a history of the Polish Church; Znak published a wide range of Catholic writing; Księgarnia św.Jacka, Katowice, prayer books and devotional literature, catechisms, theology, Gospels, Acts of the Apostles and material intended to preserve the Catholic-Polish character of Silesia; Księgarnia św.Wojciecha, Poznań, publishes the New Testament translated from Greek (eighteen editions by 1979), the Lives of the Saints, Bibles, Catechisms, prayer books and Catholic *belles-lettres*, totalling about twenty new titles per year. In addition, the Episcopal Commission, the Polish Secretariat for the Apostolate for the Sick, each archdiocese, twenty five of the diocesan chapters, twelve diocesan centres, the Sisters of Our Lady of Loretto, the Reformed Carmelite Nuns, the Franciscan Friars, the Dominican Friars and the Divine Word Missionaries, and eight small Catholic organizations all had their own presses.[41]

In spite of its social and diplomatic achievements in the post-war period the Polish Church had enormous difficulties in shaking off its pre-war past. It was bound by the pre-war expectations of the hierarchy and by the old papal encyclicals. The Polish Catholic hierarchy was at home with the certainties of Pius XI and Pius XII. It was distinctly uncomfortable with the uncharted territory opened up by John XXIII's eastern policy and his encyclical *Pacem in terris*, and by Paul VI's commitment to conciliation, *détente* and the improvement of the position of the Church in eastern Europe. The traditionalist Wyszyński was more concerned with defending the past and the Church as an institution, with preserving the role of the Polish Church as a repository of morality independent of the Party, than he was with finding a way for Church and Party to co-operate further. He was a man of remarkable determination, but little flexibility; he accepted *Rerum novarum* in toto, and saw no reason to move far from this. He argued that the Party never gave away anything of substance – and he was right: for him the Church was not free to act as a political force and therefore it was not free at all. That the Church was able to conduct its own business, publish his sermons, build churches and generally go about its business for most of the post-war period mattered little to him, compared with this basic limitation of its freedom. Thus, while Wyszyński's powerful sermons were relayed from the pulpit and the Church was a refuge for those who ran to it, and while it moderated the excesses and insensitivity of the Party, it was hardly a powerhouse of active opposition. Until the constitutional reforms of 1975–6 and the events at Ursus and Radom in 1976, the Church was modestly complacent about its social achievements and satisfied with its growth under the communists.

The Church and Dissidents

Adam Michnik attempted to put the best face on the possibility of links between atheist and socialist intellectual dissidents and the Church in his book *Kościół, lewica – dialog* (Paris, 1977). He emphasized the moral role of the Church, and gave the Church hierarchy a very clear indication that even a dissident Marxist might have expectations of it which were not being fulfilled. Michnik believed that the fundamental weakness of the Polish opposition had arisen from the division between the Church and the anticlerical Marxists who were fighting for democratic socialism in the 1950s and 1960s. This division went back into the peculiarities of Polish history, to the partitions, to the fact that Poland had never experienced for itself the disestablishment of the Church, the separation of temporal and spiritual authority, and to the fact that in a country where there was no large middle class to criticize and moderate the Church, all criticism would come from the left. The repression and anti-Semitic campaign of 1968, which the Church had failed to oppose or criticize, had effectively destroyed the power of the anticlerical Marxists outside the Party. But for Michnik, while this may have been to the temporary strategic advantage of the Church, it did not mean that the common moral and spiritual interests of the Catholic Church, Marxist intellectuals, and workers could be ignored. Michnik argued that it was in the interest of the whole of Polish society to oppose any system that placed restrictions on the liberty of the individual, since this was one of the fundamental tenets of the Christian value system, and, in Michnik's view, was also one of the prime objectives of 'socialism with a human face'. His message, doubtless tailored to Wyszyński's tastes, was a shrewd tactical manœuvre, allowing the *lewica laicka* to put the Church on the spot.

The Church also found it difficult to make an alliance with independent Marxist thinkers like Michnik, Kuroń, Geremek and Modzelewski, not only because they were ex-Party independent socialists, but because many of the dissidents were of Jewish origin and the Church could not shake out from the hierarchy a residue of pre-war anti-Semitism. In February 1936 Cardinal Hlond had circulated a pastoral letter in which he made it clear that in his opinion Jews fought against the Catholic Church, that Jewish freethinkers constituted the vanguard of atheism, that they represented revolution and the Bolshevik movement and as such were deeply anti-Polish. Bishop Kaczmarek and Cardinal Hlond later said publicly that the Jews had only themselves to blame for the 1946 massacre in Kielce, since they occupied too many leading prominent positions in an imposed alien communist government.

In view of persistent opinions like this it is important to look at educational standards and social origins within the priesthood. Even as late as the 1970s more than 60 per cent of priests came from southern Polish villages, while 8 per cent came from towns and cities; 82 per cent of priests came from families with four to ten children; more than 65 per cent of priests came from families where parents had only a primary or incomplete primary education; 15 per cent came from families where the parents had only a secondary education; a mere 10 per cent came from families with parents who had some kind of academic education.[42]

Most distant from the dissident Marxists of KOR (Committee Defending Workers) were the conservative elements of the Catholic hierarchy, conservative Catholic oppositionists and the right-wing émigrés. By the late 1970s the Church hierarchy was busy developing links with ROPCiO (movement for the defence of human and civil rights), Młoda Polska, Catholic intellectuals like Leszek Moczulski (who saw KOR members as little more than communists in disguise), and the Catholic writers of KIK like Kisielewski, Mazowiecki and Cywiński (who refused any such simple schema). The Catholic hierarchy was always uneasy about the sheer activism of the revisionist Marxists, and the wide range of discontented, state-educated, atheist and secular youngsters associated with KOR. They, it seemed, proposed to challenge the power of the state, but not in the name of God or the Church. While KOR supported the episcopate, the episcopate did not necessarily reciprocate. Both organizations supported each other's social achievements, but the Church, while it entertained political ambitions, did not want to be seen as engaging in politics.

The failures of both the Party and the Church gave rise to the growth of independent social movements in Poland after 1976. Quite suddenly an amorphous third force sprouted between Church and Party. This was indicated by the birth of ROPCiO and KOR in the years 1975–6, but was made clear to all by the appearance of Solidarność in 1980. This growth put the Church in an awkward position. For Wyszyński and key members of his hierarchy, their fear was that if the Catholic workers and the *inteligencja* were infiltrated by the atheists of KOR, the Church would lose its leadership and moral authority. Any move whereby the Church was seen to offer more than mere toleration of these dissidents would lose the Church the confidence of the Party; any move which denied support to the hard-working champions of working-class struggle would compromise the hierarchy in the eyes of the faithful. The murder of Stanisław Pyjas in 1977 brought the Church and KOR into even closer connection. After a sharp rebuke to the authorities by Cardinal Wojtyła, in May 1977 St Martin's Church in Warsaw became the scene of a KOR-led hunger strike.

First Secretary Gierek, like Wyszyński, was alarmed at the prospect of dissident intellectuals and the Church converging, but unlike Wyszyński, Gierek was constrained by the flow of international finance, and in theory by the Helsinki Accords on Human Rights. In May 1980 the Party granted the Church substantial concessions, including a Polish edition of the official Vatican newspaper, the end of military service for some 200 seminarians and extended state pension rights for a wide range of Church employees. The Church, at the 173rd conference of the episcopate later in May 1980, maintained its ethical and political stance and made it clear to the Party that these concessions did not answer their problems, that the improvement of the economy and social conditions and an end to reprisals against people who held different opinions from those of the Party (a clear reference to the arrest of TKN and KOR members) were still necessary. By the end of 1981 Solidarność had wrung substantial concessions from the Party in the area of religious affairs. The Party, under pressure, feared that it had given away too much, that the dissidents were gaining confidence.

It was the strength and entrenched character of this role that prevented the post-war authorities from carrying out any Soviet-style assault on the Church, even in the Bierut years. The Church remained a powerful independent institution to an extent that is unique in east central Europe. By the great shipyard strike of August 1980, more than one in ten of the Polish population were either Party members or held *nomenklatura* (Part-nominated) appointments. However, the communists had failed to collectivize the peasantry or control the *inteligencja*, and this meant that while opportunists swelled Party ranks, communist ideological penetration of Polish society was very weak. The combination of independent farmers, independent intellectuals, an independent Church with a Polish Pope at its head, coupled with a mightily discontented industrial work-force and extensive connections with Polish communities abroad, including Pope John Paul II, Nobel prizewinner Czesław Miłosz, well-placed Senator Muskie, and White House advisor Zbigniew Brzeziński, made Solidarność possible. The support of the Church for Solidarność (however cautious) was reciprocated by the union's demands for the extension of religious rights and activities.

The election of a Polish pope had had an electrifying effect on Poland. It was as if their nationhood was recognized, acknowledged and guaranteed from outside. The pope's first visit to Poland was an astonishing spectacle in which the secular authorities were shown to be irrelevant by their virtual absence from every public event. The pope's visit to Poland gave Poles a sense that they could be responsible for themselves, and that the power of the Party could be challenged. The election of a Polish pope was a powerful input to the developing independent trade union movement and to the independence of dissident intellectuals. Just by the virtue of its existence outside Party control, the Church was a powerful beacon, a contradiction of everything the communists were trying to achieve. However, it must be said that for most of the post-war period the Church saw its role as offering passive resistance to communism rather than in actively challenging the secular authorities.

By 1980–1 it was possible to see that the Church hierarchy was not, as many Catholic Poles had imagined it to be, the sole focus of opposition to the Party, nor was it the fundamental adversary of the state that many had assumed. Also, at a grass roots level throughout the late 1970s, parish priests in contact with industrial workers soon became steadily politicized. Many were not averse to assisting KOR, TKN, ROPCiO and the Free Trade Unions of the Coast in whatever way they could. In the 1980s several parish priests were to work very closely with Solidarność parishioners and had become politicized to the point of going against the instruction of their bishop. On several occasions in 1980–1 the Church disappointed the faithful by failing to take a lead, by underwriting the deals offered by the Party (which the Party subsequently and consistently reneged on) and by constantly appealing for peace and harmony when, even though this was most ardently desired by striking workers, the ORMO and ZOMO riot police and the various provocateurs would not have it so.

The new primate, Cardinal Glemp, though he disappointed many, was dominated by a pope who understood in detail the requirements of Poland and who had no intention of squandering the material and social achievements of the post-war years; while the USSR was still a power, he had no intention of provoking intervention by the Red Army; and while the Party was still there to be reckoned with he had no desire to admit KOR to the Church's monopoly on the role as spiritual guide, or its growing share in the confidence of the Party. After martial law the Church defined its role, much to the confusion of the congregation and many priests who had become politicized after working with Solidarność, but much to the relief of the authorities, as a social rather than a political campaigner. The Church had a difficult role to fulfil in trying to ensure calm and tranquillity, trying to reassure the military, assist the populace, succour the needy, sustain intellectual protest and still, somehow, to make it clear that it was not aiding the reinstatement of communist power directly or indirectly by offering support to left-leaning dissident intellectuals.

With the collapse of communism in 1989 the Church, proving Cywiński's point about it's 'Julianic' ambition and orientation, tried to resume its inter-war role and began to campaign for changes in the abortion laws, for the reinstatement of religious education in schools and for the enshrinement of

Catholicism as the legally recognized state religion with its position recognized in a new constitution. The Catholic writer Cywiński warned that the moral authority of the Polish Church was inverse to its participation in political power. Deprived of that power by communism, the Catholic Church could do no more than survive the difficult times and wait for the moment of its return. Although written in 1971, his words were to predict quite accurately not only the line the Church would take on KOR and TKN in the late 1970s and early 1980s, and even on Solidarność, but also the line they would take after the fall of communism:

> Deprived of its political strength, the Catholic Church fights to preserve its spiritual leadership over the nation. It refuses to accept that there is any way other than the Church to bring about the spiritual or ideological integration of society, and it refuses to acknowledge the existence of any form of opposition other than those that it promotes and controls. If the existence of another form of opposition becomes quite obvious – one that offers some kind of ideological alternative, allowing it to come together apart from the Church – then the Julianic Church condemns this opposition, or at least tries to disavow and devalue it in the eyes of public opinion. Never will the Julianic Church be anxious to engage in any form of collaboration against the state with any independent centre of oppositionist thought.[43]

These changes provoked an upheaval within the Church itself: it no longer occupied a monopoly position and was not the only institution offering spiritual shelter. It had been worth supporting the Church in the post-war years, even when it had disappointed, because it had nevertheless sustained the spirit simply by existing outside the orbit of the Party. However, after the collapse of communism Poles discovered that in a free and open society they need support neither the Church ambition to control the private lives of Polish citizens, nor its bid to share state power. In the 1993 elections to the Sejm, as much as a result of protest at the pace of economic reform and changes in the abortion laws as at the Church's bid for a share of political power, the parties of the right and those backed by the Church lost heavily to the reformed PZPR, which was now a social-democratic party, and to the PZPR's old ally, the Peasant Party.

In Poland, where no sizeable middle class had developed to confront the Church with substantial opposition and criticism during the eighteenth and nineteenth centuries, the only possible source of dissent lay in the radical left, in the literati and, after the war, in the Party. This is something the Church, almost always in the position of moral monopolist and sole independent repository of 'Polish values', has found difficult to accept. It is clear that the malaise of post-war Polish literary culture was rooted in its relationship to a regime that lacked moral legitimacy and political authority but which aspired to be both a moral authority and a major and dynamic social force, the result being that it was nothing more than a failed and failing authoritarian regime. The Party ran the country on the basis of primitive political and personal assessments rather than ideological considerations. However, it was also clear that throughout the post-war period the Party and the dissidents learned a great deal from the Church, and had gradually learned to take into account the life of the individual and the life of the spirit. Also under the influence of Marxism and contact with the dissidents, and through the politicization of its priests in the early 1980s, the Church learned a greater understanding of the problems of its own flock.

The confluence of a party that had learned about the inner life, spirituality, morality and conscience, and the possibility of a Church that had an impact on public life by responding fully and openly to the political ambitions of trade unions and the congregation, that was not afraid to comment on political life but which saw beyond its own institutional survival, these were all much to be desired in Poland (and elsewhere). The tragedy was that these lessons had to be learned again and again, on a personal and on an institutional level, by both Church and state. Every lesson learned was under severe domestic economic pressure, pressure from Moscow and the Warsaw Pact allies, and was likely to evaporate at each and every change of circumstances. To a very great extent the limitations, intransigence, intelligence, inabilities, talent and determination of both the Party and the Church mirrored each other. By the 1970s they were each other's products. And for this reason progress could not lie with either, but lay instead in the hands of the individuals and small independent groupings that lay between the Church and Party, groups and individuals that were suspected by both Party and Church and which were supported by neither. The rise of the independent social, artistic and political movements (particularly KOR) and the sudden growth of Solidarność threatened not only the power of the Party, but also the authority of the Church.

Catholic Writers

Those who claimed to be 'Catholic writers' paid a price for this allegiance. But it was not levied by the Party. The issues these writers faced and chose to write about were of necessity very different from those of writers who chose to publish abroad or underground. Doubtless many Catholic writers felt they had occupied the moral high ground in declaring their allegiance. Almost all of them published in *Znak*, *Więź* and *Tygodnik Powszechny*. However, by publishing in these journals they approached a neo-Positivist point of view in that they indicated acceptance of the power of the Party and allowed their work to be subject to the censor. Dissident writers who published abroad or underground rather than in these journals often regarded Catholic writers as 'safe'. Miłosz has written:

> The task of defining who is a Catholic writer is a hard one. Is he a man who belongs to a given denomination or one whose ideas, expressed in a literary form, are in agreement with Church dogma? Instead of losing ourselves in subtleties, we may apply a purely external criterion and call Catholic those writers who cooperate with Catholic magazines and publishing houses. Those writers have shown an obvious predilection for the historical novel, perhaps explainable by their longing for larger perspectives on human time.[44]

Miłosz has specifically listed only Hanna Malewska, Antoni Gołubiew, Teodor Parnicki and the public figure of Jerzy Zawieyski as Catholic literary figures. But there were others: Zofia Kossak, Jan Dobraczyński, Karol Bunsch, Roman Brandsteatter, Władysław Grabski, Kazimiera Iłłakowicz-ówna, Jerzy Piechowski, Ewa Szelburg-Zarembina, Jerzy Krzysztoń, Andrzej Piotrowski, Zdzisław Umiński, Maria Starzyńska, Marek Skwarnicki, Stanisław Stomma, Jerzy Turowicz. However, as Miłosz warns, even where they were popular and translated into other languages, Catholic writers were generally 'behind' in their literary techniques and were often dependent upon French Catholic literature of a conservative or rightist slant for their literary models and political opinions.[45] In general when they were writing prose rather than poetry, Catholic writers often found their rationality inhibited by their Church stance: it was difficult to write inventively, out of a free-wheeling imagination and personal conviction (no matter how deeply held), when the institution of the Church had to be both represented and protected, and when its moral schema and political position were 'givens'. Before 1956 it was a rare writer who dared portray the clash between two kinds of 'good', between Catholic sanctity and Party loyalty, between the desire to enter heaven and the attempt to create a workers' paradise, between divine justice and social justice. After 1956 these were no longer fit subjects since the argument, if not won by the Church and the Catholic writers, had certainly been lost by the Party.

Michnik, a sensitive non-Catholic supporter of the best that the Church can do, has written that to try to divide Polish literary culture into Catholic and non-Catholic is both pointless and unnecessarily divisive:

> As religion, Roman Catholicism may inspire, and has inspired, cultural diversity. But culture is one. There is no Catholic culture, Protestant culture, or non-believer's culture; there is only Polish culture. And it is precisely this culture – pluralistic, yet understood as a unity – that we must defend. We on the secular Left must defend this culture regardless of what the Church does. Let us say loud and clear: the confiscation of any book, even a religious book, we must treat as a confiscation of

our own book. We must treat every act of police repression as repression aimed at us. We must defend every persecuted person as if he or she were our closest comrade. Only then will we be faithful to our ideals. All the rest is sham.[46]

For Michnik and most other Marxist revisionists and members of the secular left, the ideals of the Church were not a problem, even if the Church itself was. Michnik repeatedly stressed that contemporary Christian thought had a huge impact on Polish intellectual life (even on non-Catholic writers) and that it would be difficult to overestimate the role of Stefan Kisielewski, Hanna Malewska, Jerzy Turowicz, Jerzy Zawieyski, Stanisław Stomma, Antoni Gołubiew and Jacek Woźniakowski, not because they were Catholic, but simply because they contributed to a culture that was broadly based and independent of official forms and norms.

Jewish Writers

It is important to remember that although Polish national identity is often seen, and is certainly presented by the Church as being, indissolubly linked with Catholicism, the culture of Poland would be massively impoverished without its non-Catholic contributions. Adolf Rudnicki, Bolesław Leśmian, Julian Tuwim, Antoni Słonimski, Mieczysław Jastruń, Paweł Hertz, Roman Brandstaetter, Julian Stryjkowski and Artur Sandauer were all major non-Catholic literary figures in the pre-war years. By 1939 the Jews constituted perhaps 10 per cent of the total population but probably as much as 22 per cent of the professional class: 56 per cent of doctors, 34 per cent of lawyers, 2 per cent of the civil service. Although many Polish Jews became culturally assimilated, they rarely converted to Catholicism.

By 1945 the Polish Jewish community had been almost totally destroyed in the Nazi camps. Those few surviving Jewish communists emerged from the war with a very peculiar world view – shaped by conspiratorial pre-war politics, by Hitler's death camps and by Stalin's prisons. Virtually the only thing left to them was their political faith in the creation of a communist Poland – though the circumstances in which this might grow and prosper were severely curtailed, even in their imagination.[47] That so many surviving Jews were or became communists after the war complicated political life enormously. It raised in many Polish minds the prospect of a *Żydokomuna* (International Jewish Conspiracy) determined to destroy Poland. One way or another the connection put almost all Polish Jews at risk. After the war survivors were subject to a pogrom in Kielce, a purge in 1959 and an even more determined purge and expulsions in 1968.

In spite of the fact that Poland's practising post-war Jewish population never numbered more than about 40,000 and was to drop to less than 15,000 in the 1980s, there were nevertheless significant Jewish contributors to literary life in the People's Republic of Poland. Both before and after the war Catholic writers tended to prefer the historical novel, while Jewish writers tended towards poetry and the essay. Though they largely avoided specifically Jewish themes, they were nevertheless attacked by the right-wing for 'judaizing' the Polish language.

Linking Jewish humanist traditions with Polish politics and literature, Miłosz has said:

> The truth is that in pre-war Poland the leftists were mainly Jews. There's no racial mystery in any of that. They simply had an international outlook, whereas since the nineteenth century the Poles had a very strong tradition of fighting for independence. The Poland that had reappeared on the map of Europe seemed so precious to them that the very idea of any end to this unique arrangement that allowed Poland to exist was unthinkable. A whole series of imponderables prohibited any sympathy for the Communist Party . . . the Communist Party in pre-war Poland would be like a party in Mexico that called for incorporation in the United States.[48]

Although they had intended communism to give them entrance to a more egalitarian Polish society, Jewish membership of the Communist Party actually worked to the contrary. Jan Błoński has said Jewish involvement in socialist politics and literature in the post-war years sprang from the same roots as Jewish involvement in Zionism and revolutionary politics in the 1930s and 1940s, namely the ongoing crisis of Jewish identity in its relationship to the ghetto and 'the need to belong to a community'. For many Polish writers with a Jewish background – Jan Kott, Adam Michnik, Kazimierz Brandys, Zygmunt Bauman, to name but a few – left-wing politics and Polish literature (as opposed to Zionism and Yiddish literature), were a way into a wider world and appeared to offer an 'eschatology of brotherhood'.[49]

Exile and Emigration

Throughout Poland's history the frustration of intellectuals and peasants alike found expression in emigration. Accordingly, exile and emigration both have an important part to play in the history of Polish literature: for various reasons Kochanowski, Potocki, Mickiewicz, Norwid, Krasiński, Sienkiewicz, Dąbrowska, and many other Polish writers all spent long periods of time in western Europe. Any attempt to draw a map of post-war Polish thinking must register the persistent fact of exile (voluntary or enforced) and the influence of Poles resident abroad on Poland and Polish opinion.

In the years 1870–1939 4.2 million Poles (15 per cent of the inter-war population) emigrated to the USA, France, Canada, Scandinavia and Brazil. A staggering 2,000,000 of these left Galicia in the years 1890–1914. A further

2,000,000 Poles per year went abroad as seasonal workers. In the nineteenth century Paris had been the great centre for Polish émigré activity, but by 1939 the states of Illinois, Pennsylvania, Connecticut and New York (with Polish populations accounting for more than 6 per cent of the total), were serious rivals. With those who emigrated for purely financial reasons went a large number of political refugees and even larger numbers of well-educated, talented Poles who could find no place, either in partition society or in independent Poland – a movement that has lasted right up to the present day. In the latter half of the nineteenth century the scope for action, for bourgeois radicalism, for the grounding of 'organic intellectuals' in political work of any kind was reduced almost to zero. The middle class was so small that no matter how ripe the rest of the social and economic structure was for change, the class that might have made that change was almost entirely absent.[50]

After 1945, London, Paris, New York and Chicago were to play an important part in Polish literary-political culture. In addition to the massive waves of Poles who had gone abroad before the Second World War, there were soldiers of the Polish Army who had fought in the west and did not wish or were unable to return to post-war Poland, thousands of displaced persons, people who had left Poland with Mikołajczyk after the 1947 rigged elections and Poles of Jewish origin forced out in 1959 and 1968. There was also the powerless and outmanœuvred remnant of the London-based Polish government-in-exile, who provided a focus for a dwindling generation of ageing Poles who invested it with lingering legitimacy. These groups were supplemented from time to time by individual Polish intellectuals who, in a linguistically ugly but vivid example of Polish humour, found themselves 'emigrated' because of their political opinions.

Boorish and unimaginative though they were, the Polish Communist Party preferred to exile opponents rather than kill them. As a consequence some of the finest minds, though lost to Polish communism, continued to work abroad including Czesław Miłosz, Leszek Kołakowski, Zygmunt Bauman, Jan Kott, Aleksander Wat, Tadeusz Nowakowski, Konstanty Jeleński, Jerzy Peterkiewicz, Jerzy Stempowski, Józef Mackiewicz, Julian Tuwim, Witold Gombrowicz, Gustaw Herling-Grudziński, Kazimierz Wierzyński, Marek Hłasko, Jan Lechoń, Witold Wirpsza, Stanisław Barańczak, and Eva Hoffman.

Among the various post-war émigré cultural organizations pride of place doubtless goes to *Kultura*, a literary-political monthly published by the Institut Literacki in Paris under the editorship of Jerzy Giedroyć. Among its frequent contributors were: Czesław Miłosz, Gustaw Herling-Grudziński, Witold Gombrowicz, Leszek Kołakowski. This journal and these writers provided a focus for talent, dissent, opinion and information outside Party control. *Kultura* was read particularly among Warsaw and Kraków university lecturers. Although the fact of the journal was very important for Polish literary and political culture, the journal was not sufficiently widely available to be influential except at third and fourth hand, and writers like Parnicki had to wait until Polish state publishers (who also read *Kultura*) were allowed to print them before they reached a popular audience.

While the importance of the Polish exile and émigré community cannot be denied, Lipski has made the point that the anti-socialism of some of the émigré community was sometimes ill-advised and misinformed, and in short it was a dangerous and unpredictable ally. For example, in July 1976 one hundred copies of a letter reached Poland from the extreme right-wing Catholic writer Jędrzej Giertych in London. Giertych claimed that all dissident activities in Poland were sponsored jointly as part of a plot between the intelligence services of the USA, West Germany, Israel and China as revenge for Soviet success in Angola and Cuba. While Lipski and others in KOR assumed this letter was a fake it turned out to be an 'authentic expression of the political thought of Jędrzej Giertych'.[51] Lipski has suggested that whether he knew it or not Giertych's attempt to smear the political and literary opposition was assisted by the Polish security services.

After the war the older generation of exiles and émigrés were petrified in their political attitudes and in their literary tastes. They saw Poland as they remembered it or as they imagined it under communism. They did not necessarily see it as it was or have any experience of the place after they had left it – most could not return even for visits. Unlike right-wing groups in the rest of east central Europe where the old order and the nobility had often been compromised by a readiness to 'do business' with the Nazis, in Poland there had been almost no collaboration with the Nazis. Even the extremist parties of the right had fought against the Nazis and all could lay legitimate claim to unimpeachable patriotic credentials. In Poland the pre-war right was anti-Nazi, anti-Soviet and often anti-Semitic, so that by the end of the war there was no need to rethink the fundamental national and political values that underpinned Polish identity. Unlike the rest of Europe, where the traditional right wing felt a distant but compromising kinship with Fascism and Nazism, in Poland there was no crisis on the right. This confidence was backed up by the record of the Polish armed services (the fourth largest of the allied armies) in the fight against Nazism: fiercely nationalist, the Polish military acquitted itself magnificently in the campaign of September 1939, the Battle of Britain, Narvik, Tobruk, Monte Cassino, Falaise and Arnhem.

Few of the older émigré community could understand how the younger left-leaning post-war writers and intellectuals could lend their support to the communists in the early post-war years. For them this was simply unpatriotic and anti-Polish. Their attitudes often provoked hostility. Young Poles, products of the People's Republic whether they liked it or not, were often informed upon arriving in the west, not only that they were somehow not quite 'real' Poles, but that they were also communists. However, there is now a younger generation of diaspora Poles, bilingual children of exiles and émigrés who have been educated abroad. They had no contact with pre-war Poland except through their parents' memories. Unlike their parents, they are not simply anti-communist and they see contemporary Poland through a complex prism of influences.

Neo-Positivism

Catholic Sejm deputy Stanisław Stomma is generally credited with coining the term neo-Positivist to describe those who aimed to create a political movement based on a tradition that went back to the failure of the 1863 uprising. It was a tradition that recognized 'geopolitical realities', forsook direct military confrontation and worked for improvement in status within whichever regime held power at the time. However, Stomma, like Piłsudski before him, remained poised for the moment when he and his party could act decisively in regaining Poland's independence, and when he and his followers could become the leadership of the nation. For Piłsudski the moment came in 1918. The moment the neo-Positivists awaited was the disintegration of the USSR.

The neo-Positivists included all those members of the Catholic Church who found they could co-operate with the state through licensed but independent Catholic organizations like Znak, KIK (Clubs of the Catholic Intelligentsia), and the Catholic journals, and those who wrote for and edited the Catholic journals which had accepted self-censorship. The most important of these Catholic periodicals was *Tygodnik Powszechny* (Universal Weekly), an independent Catholic journal run by KIK and Znak, with a variable print run of around 40,000, depending on relations with the Party. *Więź* (Link), established in 1958 by ex-Pax members, was financed by KIK as an independent Catholic monthly, edited by Tadeusz Mazowiecki, with a print run of 7,000 copies. There was also *Znak* (Sign), an independent Catholic monthly financed by KIK and Znak, with a print run of 7,450 copies, subject to censorship.

Neo-Positivists took for granted Poland's enforced loyalty to the powerful USSR (they had no option, especially since the USSR was the sole guarantor of Poland's post-war western border), but at the same time they rejected Marxism and socialist ideology. Znak adherents (unlike the revisionists) stressed their ideological and financial independence from the Party but they nevertheless expected rights to be granted from above rather than organized from below: they were hampered by their acceptance of the *status quo* and by their acceptance of the Church as the main moral and spiritual opposition leader. The Catholic Church, working through Znak, had tried to establish that there was a useful distinction to be made between the State and the Party, that it was possible to co-operate with the one without succumbing to the atheist ideology of the other. This was always a delicate balancing act and open to criticism by hard-line Catholics and communists alike. The behaviour of the Znak deputies to the Sejm, in taking an active part in the Party's ersatz political pluralism, even in dignifying the Sejm with their presence, opens questions about the 'collaborationist' line chosen by the neo-Positivists and the hierarchy itself.

In the late 1960s and early 1970s a succession of personnel changes among the Znak deputies led to an increasing conformity of the Znak line with the Party's requirements: Tadeusz Mazowiecki, who protested to the premier about the behaviour of the security forces in 1968, was replaced by Wacław Aulaytner; Stanisław Stomma walked out of the Sejm chamber rather than cast his vote in favour of the 1975–6 constitutional reforms and was replaced at the next session. Control of Znak finances was handed over to a new group called Neo-Znak. The Neo-Znak deputies were connected to ODiSS (Centre for Documentation and Social Studies). Set up in 1969 by ex-Pax writer Janusz Zabłocki, this organization published several journals, research on Polish Catholicism, and books by Zabłocki and Andrzej Micewski. The views of ODiSS, like those of Pax, were consistent with official perspectives. In the summer of 1976 the ODiSS-Znak deputies voted for price increases when the government wanted them to, and then for the restoration of the old prices when the government backed down. They remained silent in the aftermath of the Ursus and Radom demonstrations. By the end of 1976 Znak had disowned the Neo-Znak Sejm deputies. This was effectively the end of the Znak group in the Sejm. In spite of their failure it was the Znak deputies of the 1960s and early 1970s that Pope John Paul II entertained at the primate's residence on his visit in 1979. Members of KOR, who were far more active and much more effective in their opposition by this time, were not invited.[52]

Revisionism

Isaac Deutscher wrote that in the propaganda skirmishes against the USSR and communism, the ex-communist was the most active sharpshooter.[53] There is a bitter and undeniable truth in this, a truth which would be recognized by leftist writers like Arthur Koestler and George Orwell, ex-members of the British communist party, historians and writers like Basil Davidson, E. P. Thompson, Eric Hobsbawm, Christopher Hill, Gwyn Alf Williams, Raymond Williams, 'sympathetic Marxists', followers of the independent Italian socialist thinker and writer Antonio Gramsci, and a host of east European ex-party members like Kołakowski and Kott. Certainly the battle joined in Poland was not so much a simple confrontation between the moral authority of the Catholic Church and the police power of the state, as a subtle and only occasionally bloody war of manœuvre between the Party and the dissident revisionists, members of KOR, their allies in the neo-Positivist reaches of the

Church, politically active priests, Catholic writers and editors in *Tygodnik Powszechny*, the Znak deputies, and the liberal, socialist and ex-Party exiles. It must also be said that one of the prime allies of all the wide range of oppositionists was the Party itself. Party members found themselves persistently undermined by the moral authority of the Church, outmanœuvred by oppositionist ex-members, out-organized by the underground publishing industry and KOR, outraged at the persistent provocations of the *milicja* and security services, lacking respect and self-respect, frustrated by the power and ambition of Moscow, alienated, misinformed and abused. Deprived of basic information about the activities of their government, their country and the world around them, Party members read whatever they could get their hands on, knowing that if it was written by 'the opposition' (émigrés, Catholic hierarchy, dissidents, revisionists) it was far more likely to be truthful and accurate than the Party's own 'organs'.

Everyone active in public, literary or political life after the war was a part of the moral and political dilemma of Poland. Many chose active participation in public affairs, saving what could be saved of Poland for Poland. Others chose internal immigration or exile; a few chose permanent opposition, but in the early years those that showed their dissent did not avoid prison for very long. Many intellectuals worked with the new authorities grudgingly, but in the spirit of 'wait and see': Tadeusz Kotarbiński, Kazimierz Ajdukiewicz, Tadeusz Manteuffel, Kazimierz Wyka, Maria Ossowska and Stanisław Ossowski, Maria Dąbrowska, Leon Schiller, Antoni Słonimski, Jerzy Zawieyski. There were also those who became Party members or who lent their support in the early years: Leszek Kołakowski, Oskar Lange, Maria Hirszowicz, Włodzimierz Brus, Krzysztof Pomian, Bronisław Baczko, Witold Kula, Kazimierz Brandys, Adam Ważyk, Władysław Bieńkowski, Jerzy Andrzejewski, Edward Lipiński, Julian Przyboś, Wiktor Woroszylski, Jacek Bocheński, Bronisław Geremek, Jerzy Jedlicki, Adam Kersten and Stefan Amsterdamski. All these people believed that something other than Soviet communism could be developed in Poland. They wanted to develop what Michnik called an 'enlightened socialist despotism'.

The revisionists opposed passivity and internal exile, and they stressed activism and participation in public life. They had great faith in their ability to influence events, and believed that the Party could be reformed. Their main idea was that enlightened and progressive people of ideas and culture should take over the Party. Surprisingly, when it became possible to make critical comments on the government's literary policies, during the debates of 1954–5, and later in the years up to 1968, it was not the Catholic writers like Zawieyski and Gołubiew who led the way, but the socialists and dissidents, the revisionists like Julian Pzyboś. The majority of oppositionist initiatives during the years 1956–68 originated with the revisionists rather than the steadfast oppositionists and anti-socialists of the Church or with the neo-Positivists around *Znak*, *Tygodnik Powszechny* and *Więź*, who had, after all, accepted censorship. From the late 1960s onwards the secular left struggled to make a connection with the powerful industrial working class and to develop a new method of approach. By this time many intellectuals in this circle had gone beyond revising Marxism and had distanced themselves from the Party.

After 1976 the majority of initiatives to combat the Party and the bureaucracy came not from the Church and its neo-Positivist allies, but from the revisionist-descended KOR and the secular left. As ex-Party members moved further away from the Party and state publishing ventures, they began to publish underground in *Zapis* and made connection with writers like Jerzy Ficowski and the writers around *Znak*: Adam Stanowski, Władysław Bartoszewski, Bohdan Cywiński and Tadeusz Mazowiecki. Many of these, revisionists, ex-Party and Catholic neo-Positivists alike, made alliance, not in the Church but in TKN, KOR and the underground journals of the late 1970s. They originated and disseminated dissenting points of view among the *inteligencja*. They took on the power of the courts, the police and the educational system. Among workers and the *inteligencja*, as well as among the Party membership, they laboured to restore and revive independent civil life in Poland.

There were many similarities and points of contact between the neo-Positivists and the revisionists. As Michnik put it:

> To use a metaphoric comparison, if one considers the state organisation of the Soviet Union as the Church and Marxist ideological doctrine as the Bible, then revisionism was faithful to the Bible while developing its own interpretations, whereas neo-positivism adhered to the Church but with the hope that the Church would sooner or later disappear.[54]

The particularities and peculiarities of Polish history could not but make this a very ambiguous 'movement'.

Revisionism and neo-Positivism were fragile entities, and the more social conflict became apparent in the 1960s the less tenable these movements appeared. Unlike the other political groupings the revisionists had an enormous influence on Polish learning, education, philosophy and literary culture, and they promoted political activism in a way that the Party and the Church did not. However, like the Catholic neo-Positivists, the revisionists expected rights granted from above in response to sensible intellectual exchange. They were hampered by this and by the fact that they accepted and used, and were therefore limited by, the language of the Party, and by the party's acceptance of the USSR and, at least in the early years, by a sense of loyalty to the idea of Party discipline. The revisionists enjoyed a brief 'springtime' in 1956, but were broken and scattered by the anti-Semitic, anti-intellectual purges and expulsions of 1968 – events which severed the links between the Party and the revisionists and creative *inteligencja*.[55]

New Evolutionism

In October 1976 Adam Michnik wrote a short essay entitled 'The New Evolutionism', in which he harked back to the traditions of the suppressed PPS (Polish Socialist Party) and said that since October 1956 there had been a profound hope that somehow socialism could evolve out of the failure of Stalinism. He identified revisionism and neo-Positivism as two avenues of evolution which had already failed.

Michnik noted that the revisionists had believed that Soviet power could be humanized and democratized and that official Marxist doctrine was capable of assimilating contemporary arts and social sciences without imposing *socrealizm* (socialist realism) as the only correct artistic form. He faced up to the fact that the revisionists were profoundly wrong, and that they had lost their battle to 'transform from within the doctrine and the Party in the direction of democratic reform and common sense'. However, he also made the point that it was the revisionists who encouraged enlightened people with progressive ideas to lead the Party, and it was the surviving revisionists and their evolutionist descendants of the next generation who in the 1970s forged links with the more progressive Catholics and social activists, put the established relationship between Church and Party under pressure and obliged the hierarchy to rethink their attitude to independent social movements. In spite of the intellectual muscle wielded by the revisionists and their neo-Positivist allies, it gradually emerged that they had made fundamental tactical errors in assessing their position in society and in dealing with the Party. Michnik wrote:

> Revisionism had been tainted at its very source by the belief that the strivings and goals of the 'liberal' wing in the party apparatus were identical to the demands of the revisionist intelligentsia. I think that the revisionists' greatest sin lay not in their defeat in the intra-party struggle for power (where they could not win) but in the character of that defeat. It was the defeat of individuals being eliminated from positions of power and influence, not a set-back for a broadly based leftist and democratic political platform. The revisionists never created such a platform.[56]

By the mid-1970s the term 'revisionism' was no longer applicable to the opposition: not only was the group broken by imprisonment, exile and expulsion from the Party, but the revisionists had come to realize that they could not revise or reform the Party from within, could not make it aware of the need for reform while the power of the USSR remained unshaken, and could not communicate anything from outside the Party using the language of the Party. In 1968 the hopes of the revisionists were dashed; by the time of the constitutional changes of 1975–6 the hopes of the neo-Positivists in Znak had likewise been shown to be illusory. Both groups found themselves faced with a stark choice: they could co-operate with the Party or they could refuse. They realized that open and consistent criticism of the Party would earn them nothing more than absorption of their energies and eventually consistency of viewpoint with the authorities. To challenge the intra-party strategy of the revisionists and the muted criticism of the neo-Positivists, it was necessary to create social solidarity outside the Party through the struggle for the reform of the law and legal practice, through the expansion of civil liberties and human rights, and by steady and persistent pressure on the government to withdraw its stranglehold on education, the media and the state-run society.

It was left to the surviving revisionists and neo-Positivists, the writing fraternity, the furtive independent trade unionists, students and independent Catholic intellectuals to make the point that if the Party would not engage in dialogue with oppositionists, then society had no alternative but to go 'independent' of state sources of finance and build outside established Party and state structures. Revisionism and neo-Positivism may have been finished as political movements, but their impulse (the reforming, humane, subtle, creative aspects of secular-left thought) was a powerful undercurrent through-out the 1970s and 1980s, informed the guiding principles of organizations like KOR, TKN, many of the dissident journals, and could be felt in the principles of the post-communist Democratic Union Party. The moral and political principles of the revisionists, coming via KOR, had a powerful impact on the Catholic Church in the late 1970s.

The New Evolutionists of the 1970s and 1980s did not address themselves to the authorities but to an independent public; they did not instruct the authorities on how to reform themselves but showed the public how to behave in the face of an unlicensed authority. Michnik did not trust the Party. He pointed out that the Party could always produce another revisionist move-ment from within its ranks whenever it was convenient or when the going got rough, and that the aim of the New Evolutionists was gradual change towards democratic socialism. Michnik wrote:

New Evolutionism is based on faith in the power of the working class, which, with a steady and un-yielding stand, has on several occasions forced the government to make spectacular concessions. It is difficult to foresee developments in the working class, but there is no question that the power élite fears this social group most. Pressure from the working classes is a necessary condition for the evolution of public life toward a democracy . . . The intelligentsia's duty is to formulate alternative programs and defend the basic principles. More precisely, I refer to those small groups of intellectuals who believe in continuing the traditions of the 'insubordinate' intelligentsia of the early 1900s – the tradition of writers such as Stanisław Brzozowski, Stanisław Wyspiański, Stefan Żeromski and Zofia Nałkowska. I feel solidarity with those traditions and those people, although I am the last person to overestimate the importance of their actions. But those voices, albeit weak and sporadic, are nevertheless authentic: they form an independent public opinion, with nonconformist attitudes and oppositional thought. This course is being followed by people from various traditions and social strata: former revisionists (including the author of this article), former neo-positivists, and those who became ideologically aware after the events of 1968.[57]

There can be little doubt that the opposition movement which grew up in the late 1970s was led largely by the left-leaning intellectuals of KOR (Workers' Defence Committee), which specialized in fronting legal cases for accused workers and had a large number of writers among its membership, including J. J. Lipski, Andrzejewski and the poet Stanisław Barańczak. As Michnik has repeatedly pointed out, there can be no doubt that in the formation of independent public opinion, literature played a decisive role. However, it is difficult for the right and for the Catholic Church to accept that the most creative and active, the most wily and persistent oppositionists facing the Party, did not come from within the Catholic Church, as western observers might have expected, but from the *lewica laicka* (the lay left). And significantly the *lewica laicka* often consisted of highly exposed ex-Party writers.

Michnik has claimed for the liberal and humanist element of the Polish left specific works and a wide-ranging list of contemporary and past writers: Zofia Nałkowska, Maria Dąbrowska, Zbigniew Herbert, Czesław Miłosz, Antoni Słonimski, Adam Ważyk, Stanisław Ossowski, J. J. Szczepański, Kazimierz Brandys, Gustaw Herling-Grudziński, Tadeusz Borowski, Wiktor Woroszylski, Jacek Bocheński, Tadeusz Konwicki, Oskar Lange, Edward Lipiński, Leszek Kołakowski, Włodzimierz Brus, Krzysztof Pomian, Bronisław Baczko, Władysław Bieńkowski, Witold Kula, Maria Hirszowicz, Stanisław Barańczak, Ryszard Krynicki, Adam Zagajewski, Bohdan Cywiński, Kazimierz Wierzyński, Juliusz Mieroszewski, Marek Hłasko, Witold Gombrowicz, Jerzy Turowicz, Tadeusz Mazowiecki, Stanisław Stomma, Jerzy Zawieyski, Stefan Kisielewski, Jacek Woźniakowski, Anna Morawska, Hanna Malewska and Antoni Gołubiew. Whether they liked each other or not (and sometimes they did not), Michnik saw these people as his natural allies; for him, without a close reading of these particular writers, it was simply not likely that any observer would ever get to grips with the problems and dilemmas of Polish oppositionist thought.

Without doubt these were some of the best minds of their generation(s). The inability of the Party to win or retain the sympathy of intellectuals who were generally sympathetic to the cause of socialism, and who as independent intellectuals, knew they stood to lose in any capitalist 'open market', is a measure of the Party's failure. That the Party could not make use of their goodwill, talent and loyalty, could not absorb or respond to their record of life in the People's Republic of Poland is an indication of the total lack of originality and intellectual dynamism within a Party crippled and made tame by the stifling hand of Stalin and the Stalinists. The revisionists may not have created a broadly based leftist, democratic political platform, but it was precisely to overcome this error and promote a new civil society that KOR and TKN were founded, and, in order to make an even closer connection with the Polish industrial working class, that the intellectuals of these organizations, many of whom were writers, ex-revisionists and ex-Party members, became advisers to Solidarność in 1980–1.

Left and Right

The American writer William Woods visited Poland in 1967. He tried to define the range of political opinions he found. For him ODiSS (founded in October 1957 by secessionists from Pax) occupied the centre; Pax, the tame 'Catholic' front organization, stood to the left. He characterized the Catholic Znak group and its associated newspapers as organizations of the far right; Cardinal Wyszyński he characterized as to the right of both the Vatican Council and Znak.[58]

Things have changed a great deal since 1967. With hindsight it is possible to see that the range of opinion in post-war Poland was much wider, more convoluted, and much less clear-cut than Woods had been able to discern. Clearly there was a problem with the notions of left and right (also: progressive, liberal, conservative, reactionary) when applied to post-war Poland. But the problem of what exactly constituted the 'right' and the 'left' became particularly complex in the late 1970s and early 1980s. The visible array of Party-approved organizations gave little hint of the complexity that underlay the official picture, and the wide variety of unofficial organizations that sprang up in the late 1970s gave little indication of the complexity that underlay both the official and the unofficial positions. The intersections, conjunctions and alliances possible within Polish opinion were confusing, but in any case largely hidden to outside observers. Now, from the vantage point of post-1989, it is also possible to see not only that the Party, the Church and the opposition all imposed their own orthodoxies, but that political, social, religious and artistic opinions were interwoven to a remarkable degree. Artistic, religious and political developments reflected this.

In Poland the supposed certainties of the Cold War and the revealed contradictions pile up with frightening speed. After the war Polish society became atomized and ill-informed about itself to a remarkable degree. By the 1980s, however, its structures and social and political layers were by no means as solid or impermeable as outside observers often supposed. Indeed, the biographies of individual writers show that it was possible for an individual to move from one grouping and milieu to another. Even though many see Polish post-war society as polarized into the main blocs of Party and Catholic Church, in fact the Polish literary-political scene was much more divergent, covered a far wider spectrum, and, even within Party and Church circles, was infinitely more divided against itself and wary of making alliances than any simple formula of government and opposition, communists and Catholics, could portray. The supposed monoliths of Church and Party stand neither in such stark contrast, nor in such clearly defined opposition to each other, as was once supposed.

Opposition, the style of opposition, opposition alliances, were not written in stone. Throughout the communist period opposition was far more various, and more subtly nuanced, than many western observers could ever credit. A writer and intellectual like Tadeusz Mazowiecki could start off in Pax, move into editing the Catholic journal *Więź* (left-liberal-leaning and therefore from the hierarchy point of view unreliable), become an adviser to Solidarność, and then become prime minister in the first post-communist government, only to be smeared and sacked by Wałęsa after a few months in office, accused (with Geremek, Michnik, Kuroń and others who had helped Solidarność through difficult times) of being a Jew and a crypto-communist. Bohdan Cywiński could edit the Catholic journal *Znak*, lecture for TKN (Flying University) and still be a member of the left-orientated KOR.

Czesław Miłosz on the other hand could accept a diplomatic post with the communists, break with the regime, write a devastating critique of the crippling effect communism had on Polish literary intellectuals, and find himself banned from publication in Poland for many years, only to be welcomed back by the Party and awarded (in spite of his communist past) an honorary degree by the Catholic University of Lublin after achieving international repute as a Nobel prizewinner. Pax and the partisan organization ZBoWiD (Union of Fighters for Freedom and Democracy) could link up in an anti-Semitic campaign, and their opinions, along with those of the Party-sponsored Grunwald Patriotic Union, could find damaging resonance within the Church hierarchy. In 1980 one-third of the membership of the Solidarność MKS (Inter-Factory Strike Committees) were also members of the Party.[59] Clearly even these few examples contradict any simple dichotomy.

Post-war Polish writers often came to understand the politics of literature and their highly ambiguous relationship to government, Party and society not through *socrealizm*, the literature of politics (boy meets tractor, odes to the six-year plan, hymns to Stalin, poems about storming the productivity norms, songs in praise of our state security bureaus) but rather through the politics of literature. Their struggle was to observe and write as they saw fit, to be judged on their merit by artistic and social standards, on the accuracy of their perceptions rather than according to Party needs. Their opinions and attitudes changed constantly. For many it was a matter of initial enthusiasm and then gradually refusing consent. For them aesthetics was an important part of politics. Zbigniew Herbert, who refused to have anything to do with the communists right from the outset, wrote:

It didn't require great character at all
our refusal disagreement and resistance
we had a shred of necessary courage
but fundamentally it was a matter of taste
Yes taste.[60]

Literature

Literature is a complex and rich human creative act: books aid awareness, particularly in the individual's relationship to society. As such, literature is of profound interest not only to free and independent readers, but also to any government attempting to monitor and change the life and thought patterns of its citizens. The existence of any work of literature has inherent moral, social and political implications: complex, layered and fused. To any regime, but particularly an authoritarian one, literature is an important gauge of popularity and civil ambition, a record of success, a target for correction and suppression. If we ever want to remind ourselves of the power of literature, we have only to think of how aware of literature and writers reactionary governments can be (USSR, China, Iran, Nigeria). It is not merely the content of literature that they fear, the explicit doctrine, but the energy and independence implied by the aesthetic qualities a book may have. Intensity, irony and ambiguity are in themselves a threat to the impassive power of the state. They constitute a *secret* other, inner life, over which the state has little or no control. For many writers in Poland, literature itself was a project for democracy, a 'return to Europe', for deliverance from the barbarous yoke of Tatar-communism.

For most of its recent history, writers and literature have been very important to Poland: they have also played an important role in the history of the Polish left. Writers played a key role in developing national thought during the partitions and in developing socialist thought between the wars; they were instrumental in installing the communists after 1945; they played a key role in undermining and opposing the Party after 1949. In 1989 they helped negotiate a post-communist democratic, free-market Poland into existence. Often, in order to 'enter' a particular moment in Polish politics or literature, it is essential to trace the biographies of those involved, and to examine their literary products.

The exploration of the literary-political interface in Poland raises a number of issues. It questions the idea of People's Poland as a 'totalitarian' society – how did the writers survive if it was totalitarian? It brings into question the role of the Catholic Church. It holds up for scrutiny the limitations of the dissident community ranged against the Party, showing that the dissidents were not as unanimous about the form a 'free' Poland might take as many in the west assumed. It raises the possibility that the west did not understand what many of the the opposition movement wanted, and consistently played down the extent of their socialism. These questions all have implications for our understanding of the kind of place Poland is likely to become in the twenty-first century.

Since the collapse of communism life in Poland has become infinitely more complex: truth is far more elusive, lies and half truths so much more difficult to pin down in the free press. When truth was simply the opposite of whatever the government said, it was a much simpler matter to know what you thought. But in the half-truths of the free market, readers have lost their leaders, they can no longer rely on writers to guide them in knowing what to oppose, or what to support. Among many other confusing developments, ex-communist social democrats were elected to government, the anti-Stalinists who had opposed the Party in the name of democratic socialism failed to achieve power, the Church failed to find the populist support it expected for its political aims, privatization plans for industry stalled, and ex-communist Kwaśniewski ousted Wałęsa from the presidency. In the long, hard haul to 'normality' Polish readers lost their writers and gained politicians. Nothing is certain now except that in east central Europe literature and politics, writers and politicians, are still closely intertwined. In Poland literature remains a major site for the generation and clash of ideas. Literature is the place where ideas and words are tested.

Much to the consternation of Russia, Poland (along with Hungary and the Czech Republic) is moving towards membership of NATO and the increasingly powerful and self-conscious European Union. If the membership of this strategically important east central European state is to succeed it is vital that the west attempts to understand the new Polish leadership – and an integral part of that is the complex connection between the left, literary culture and political history. As a new political class emerges from the wreckage of communism and its opposition, it is clear that writers remain important and influential in east central Europe in a way that they do not in western Europe. Yet it is clear that the literary *lewica laicka*, along with the whole of the Polish *inteligencja*, must adapt themselves to greatly altered and altering conditions. While the increasingly autocratic solutions favoured by ex-President Wałęsa found favour with many, the democratic ideals of Michnik, Kuroń and the rest of the *lewica laicka* are still but weakly anchored in Polish politics. Indeed, part of the legacy they have to contend with is not only that the Party effectively smeared all opinions of the left with its own Stalinist dirt, but that the opinions of the left are widely perceived to have failed. For many, the failure of communist economic theories means that all socialist thought is mistaken. This is not something that Polish socialists can dismiss out of hand. Indeed, while it was possible for writers under communism to exist on a language of hints and guesses, this is no longer the case.

The speed of the communist collapse, the political naivety and unpreparedness of the writers for the realities of political power, exposed writers, socialists and a large slice of the *inteligencja* as unfit for power. On the other hand, in spite of propaganda from free-marketeers, it is clear that the emerging political class (of which *lewica laicka* and the old *nomenklatura* are a part), does not view capitalism as a necessary evil, nor does it assume that socialism is necessarily evil.

The collapse of communism allowed Poland to break away from the Soviet empire, to break with what it saw as 'Asia'. It allowed Poles to 'return to Europe' and gave them the opportunity to reaffirm their connection to west European culture and style, and it freed Polish literature from the fetters of the national conscience. Michnik, the most politically articulate member of the *lewica laicka*, is keen that intellectuals on the left should disinter the traditions of the old PPS from the clutches of communism, even though this is bound to be an uphill struggle in a country where the working class has no living experience of the PPS. Michnik is also keen that the *lewica laicka* and slowly re-emerging Polish socialism are seen as allied to western liberal and social-democratic traditions rather than Stalinism. Michnik says that ROAD, the post-communist broad left alliance, is not so much left of centre as west of centre. Needless to say, the idea of 'west of centre' contradicts much of the historical experience of Polish literature, social experience and political tradition. In Poland, as the writer Witold Gombrowicz often remarked, the west melts into the east, western ambition clashes with eastern history. It is a collision which west European historians and political scientists cannot chart with any ease: it is best read, as Polish writers and their readers claim, through contemporary Polish literature, through the politics of literature and through the twisted and twisting lives of Polish writers:

> What does the political scientist know?
> The political scientist knows the latest trends
> The current state of affairs
> The history of doctrines

> What does the political scientist not know?
> The political scientist does not know about desperation
> He doesn't know the game that consists
> Of renouncing the game
> It doesn't occur to him
> That no-one knows when
> The changes may appear
> Like an ice-floe's sudden cracks

> And that natural resources
> Include knowledge of venerated laws
> Ability to wonder
> And a sense of humour.[61]

2

THE WRITING PROFESSION

Citizens of the Polish People's Republic have a right to enjoy cultural achievements and to participate creatively in the development of their national culture . . . The Polish People's Republic is concerned for the all-round development of scholarship, literature, and the arts, and surrounds with particular care the creative intelligentsia and those engaged in scientific, educational, literary and artistic work.

The Constitution of the Polish People's Republic, 1952.

It is tempting to see Poland's post-war communist regimes as uniformly grey and undifferentiated. However, it is important to distinguish differences in the style and content of communism in these years. Two distinct 'periods' are discernible. The period from July 1944 to December 1948 was a time of civil war when a very large proportion of the population resisted the imposition of an illegitimate Moscow-backed government. The institutions of communism at this time were still underdeveloped, largely nascent and lacking in confidence. Communism had not fully penetrated all the institutions of the Polish state. However, this was not the case in the period from December 1948 to October 1956, when Poland was effectively a Stalinist state. Then, under the leadership of First Secretary Bolesław Bierut, with armed resistance to communism broken, the PPS (Polish Socialist Party) forcibly 'unified' with the PPR (Polish Workers Party) to form the PZPR (Polish United Workers Party), the legitimacy of the regime confirmed by rigged elections and referenda, against a background of growing Cold War and West German claims to Polish territory, the Stalinist ethos spread through the institutions of the state. Industry was dominated by shock brigades, norms, quotas and Heroes of Labour. Priests were arrested in their hundreds. Church lands were confiscated. Statues of Stalin were erected. The town of Katowice was renamed Stalinogród. Informers and denunciations were commonplace and any kind of foreign contact was suspicious. But, Polish Stalinism was not as frenzied as that of its neighbours: the Church was harried but not suppressed; collectivization proceeded (if at all) very slowly; peasants were not deported; intellectuals were censored but not liquidated; there were very few show trials.

Soviet treatment of Polish writers had been unpredictable in the years 1939–44, but, putting Soviet experience to one side, the Polish communists made a good start. In the manifesto of the Polish Committee of National Liberation (provisional Moscow-backed government) published in Lublin on

22 July 1944, it declared that the new Polish government intended to democratize culture and offer the *inteligencja* 'special protection'. This vague
announcement was designed to attract the support of a wide range of leftist
and left-sympathetic Poles. Many writers believed they would now be
recruited to build the new Poland and, being necessary to a new social order,
they would reap all the benefits of 'rational redistribution'. There can be little
doubt that simple selfishness also played a part. The communists offered an
enormously enhanced financial and social position to writers of all kinds. For
many writers this was their first (and possibly only) chance to create a stable
and secure home life and to build an artistic and professional reputation. A
significant number of writers sensed the opportunities the new regime offered
and genuinely wanted to take part in building the new Poland.

Socialism seemed to offer a way out of the pointlessness and confusion that
afflicted the world in general, and Poland in particular. An alliance with
Moscow was seen by some as the only way to preserve the Polish state. The
development of Polish society out of its long semi-feudal history, out of the
horrors of the war, towards a new, modern industrial future was bound to be
complex and was bound to offend traditional *inteligencja* moral values, and in
this it probably made little difference whether that development was towards
communism or towards capitalism. That it was undertaken by communists
backed by Moscow was certainly offensive. Even so, many of the *inteligencja*
were inclined to take malicious delight in the communist persecution of the
materialist and unimaginative bourgeoisie and the exclusion of the old
nobility from public life. They saw no allies in the peasantry who resisted
modernization, saw no great friend either in the Church, that property-
owning ally of the inter-war military, nor in the radio propaganda broadcasts
of the western 'allies' who had abandoned them at Yalta. For many, the
communists were state- and nation-builders, determined to create a strong
unified Poland without national and ethnic minorities, within strong borders
and with strong alliances. A very large number of people accepted communism in 1945 simply because they were exhausted by years of bloodshed and
privation and had no clear idea of any other alternative. By 1945 many Poles
had run the gamut of twentieth-century human and political possibilities in a
very short space of time.

In what had become eastern Europe after 1945, the writer faced a complex
situation in which cultural sensibilities and political loyalties were stretched in
several directions. In Poland the literary culture was rooted in the values of
the *szlachta* (gentry) and in the nationalist resistance movements, the secret
codes and language of the partitions and occupation years. The reorientation
involved, now that all work, commissions, publication, trade union membership, domestic accommodation and pensions came through state patronage,
was massive. Although Poles were not happy with censorship and the omni-
present UB (Department of Security), many felt that in order to establish the

new and secure Polish borders these things were necessary evils which would in time (as the theory had it) wither away. Writers were surprisingly willing to give communism a chance. However, after an initial honeymoon period, as Bierut's Stalinist Poland developed after December 1948, writers, particularly those who had joined the Party, found it increasingly difficult to reconcile their liberal and libertarian vision of socialism with the repressive, illiberal, paranoid and sometimes lethal reality of life in the Soviet satellite state. However, they also found it difficult to abandon their hopes. As Andrzej Szczypiorski wrote:

> Artists are people inclined to fideism. Artists have to believe in something, otherwise they cannot be artists. Having, not without reason, lost their faith in democratic principles and in humanist civilisation that had effectively failed to oppose Hitler's tyranny, the intellectuals began feverishly to search for a new faith. They found it in the doctrine of collective living, scientific forecasting of the future, in the Hegelian spirit of history that comes from the East. The decline of the world of values that had bred Hitlerism was undeniable. The spiritual vacuum in the Polish graveyard could not last indefinitely. Stalinism filled that vacuum.[1]

Among the creative intellectual community it was not unusual to find writers of the younger generation, particularly those who had spent the war in Poland, who joined the Party with considerable enthusiasm in the immediate post-war years: Tadeusz Borowski, Julian Przyboś, Paweł Hertz, Adolf Rudnicki, Julian Stryjkowski, Jerzy Andrzejewski, Kazimierz Brandys, Tadeusz Konwicki, Leszek Kołakowski. Other writers, such as Tuwim, Iwaszkiewicz, Gałczynski and Słonimski (who had visited the USSR, only to be disappointed by what he saw), made it clear that although they would not join, they were prepared to work with the Party. A number of writers who were sympathetic to communism were even given official appointments: Czesław Miłosz worked as cultural attaché in the USA and France between 1946 and 1951, Przyboś spent the years 1947–51 as a diplomat in Switzerland, Pruszyński spent 1948 to 1950 as a diplomat in Holland, and Putrament worked as a diplomat in France from 1945 to 1950. Tadeusz Borowski joined the Party and in 1949 was sent to Germany as Press Attaché to the Polish military mission. Mieczysław Jastrun, Aleksander Wat, Stefan Żółkiewski and Adam Ważyk had all been KPP members before the war; Leon Kruczkowski, Jan Kott and Jerzy Putrament had joined the Party during the war. Władysław Broniewski had been a loyal fellow traveller before the war, but after his arrest and imprisonment by the NKVD, had raged: 'Why should a revolutionary poet rot to death in this Soviet hole?'[2]

There must have been a very strong suspicion that there would be no Soviet liberation of Poland, merely 'liberation'. But there was no way to ignore the new Poland and it was not possible to refuse to take part: this was as good as they were going to get. Refusal to co-operate could make things worse; co-operation stood a slim chance of actually improving things. Whatever their motives, and however ambiguous their alliance, supporters of the new régime were a very small group within the Polish *inteligencja*, and a minute group within Polish society as a whole. They regarded themselves as representatives of the future and hoped by the power of their example to persuade others to give their support to the new regime. They took up the challenge to revolutionize Polish literary culture and enjoyed the ambiguous national, social, artistic and economic benefits of belonging to a profession that was wooed by the communists, but which had always been oppositionist and conspiratorial, spiritually and morally powerful, if politically weak. Among all these writers there was a realistic appreciation that what happened in Poland depended on what was happening in the USSR, and there was also a clear understanding that whatever Polish communists might say for public consumption, they and their literary supporters were Poles first and communists second. As Polish PEN chairman Juliusz Żuławski said:

> It was complicated. I believe that many Polish communists were afraid of Russia and some acted in a double way: they wanted it to be seen that they were very good communists, but at the same time they were also Poles, and they also tried to preserve what they could of the Polish identity. Many Polish communists acted this way. Double thinking, double acting. Of course they mouthed communist propaganda, but behind that they tried not to spoil everything. In Poland this was especially the case, much more so than in other communist countries.[3]

In contrast, right from the very start, Zbigniew Herbert and Mieczysław Jastrun had no difficulty in seeing Sovietization for the thing it was. They both suffered horribly at the very idea of a communist take-over and for many years they published little, infrequently and reluctantly.

The implementation of central planning after 1945 was not the work of writers and artists dreaming of transplanting western-style bourgeois democracy to east central Europe, but the work of a tiny previously marginalized party who had accidentally survived the murderous intent of the NKVD. While aware of the specific nature of Soviet communism and the supposed cultural and political break this represented, there were many in the *inteligencja* who felt that communism was the end towards which societies of all kinds, but particularly those of east central Europe, were destined to travel. They did not see co-operation with the Party or entry into the *biurokracja* as 'selling out'. A significant number of the *inteligencja* (including a number of prominent writers) were inclined to see communism as offering a way out of Poland's long history of culturally and socially entrenched poverty and lack of investment, a way to avoid a repetition of the semi-Fascist inter-war military government, a guarantee of Poland's new borders. The war itself was seen as a way of breaking apart the old values: in its scale and disruption of the old order the war had been as effective as revolution, show trials, five-year plans, collectivization and purges. In this way communism was an idea that appealed to dissatisfied and frustrated intellectuals, and it depended upon them for its impetus and its legitimation, its moral, visionary and cultural input. Acceptance of post-war Polish communism was also pragmatic. These people lived in that place at that time. They had to find some way of accommodating themselves to the totality of the new situation. It could not have been a more ambiguous transition.

Because of the extent of the social, human and material damage caused by the Nazis, a high degree of centralization was necessary in reconstruction. The post-war publishing industry in particular was influenced and shaped by the experience of wartime publishing in the USSR for the PPR (Polish Workers' Party) and the AL (People's Army). The initial 'Implements of the Dissemination of Culture' were set up in the late 1940s and expanded from central institutions into regional centres in the 1950s with campaigns like: 'Building a New Culture for the Happiness of the Fatherland, for the Consolidation of World Peace: Days of Enlightenment, Books and the Press – May 1951'. The 1960s and 1970s saw the expansion of the entire cultural apparatus, not only through institutions and organizations, but also through a series of national campaigns: 'Review of the Cultural Activities of the Working People – Man – Work – Creation'; '1974 – The Alliance of the Working People with Culture and Art'; '1976 – The Year of Libraries and Reading'; 'The Programme of Developing Libraries for the 1980s'. From the start the communists stressed that the media should be aware of the continuing external threat to Poland's existence, and should foster a spirit of national unity, and that pluralism, even in journals run by the Church and by Catholic societies, should always be in harmony with Marxist-Leninist ideology.

The Polish authorities organized the whole of the publishing industry through the Ministry of Culture's Department of Books. All matters relating to publication were overseen by the Central Committee Department of Culture and the Central Committee Department of the Press who worked through the Ministry of Culture and Art and through that Ministry's Panel on Arts and Publishing. They took control of the distribution and retail systems, took over typesetting, printing, binding, packaging and paper-making facilities and enabled the state postal service to monitor the circulation of all printed and manuscript matter and, in conjunction with the security services, to monitor the private dissemination of printed materials. They also established the BMWW (International Bureau for the Exchange of Publications), a monopoly import-export concern to control the purchase of printed materials from abroad. The government also started a bureau for the protection of intellectual property, which was not so much the copyright protection agency it claimed to be but simply a clearing house for information about publishing projects. The government soon subsidized almost all legal publishing, printing, distribution and retailing; it taxed and rewarded authors, controlled the revenues of publishing houses and to a very great extent determined each publisher's annual list. None of this vast state publishing industry was subject to cost-accounting, or to marketing or distribution costing. Publishers published what they were allowed to publish, distributors distributed what came their way, bookshops sold what they were given.

The first method of controlling the artistic and creative world was financial. It is difficult to establish the exact size and value of the Polish arts budget. Nevertheless, while it was small compared with the budgets for almost every other aspect of the Polish economy, and minute compared with the amounts spent on maintaining a huge military apparatus, compared with the arts budgets wielded by most west European governments the Polish state arts budget was enormous. According to official statistics for the period 1971–80 approximately 14,300,000,000 złoties was spent annually by the Ministry for Arts and Culture (0.3 per cent of the national budget, compared with 0.7 per cent for science and technology, and 0.5 per cent for forestry). In the same period the ministry invested the sum of 3,800,000,000 złoties (a cumulative figure representing 0.5 per cent of the national budget) and needed a further 4,400,000,000 złoties (0.3 per cent of the national budget) in order to complete its various planned cultural projects.[4]

A second method of control was by direct appointment to important posts. It has been estimated that of the 1,200,000 'management and responsibility' posts in the Polish economy, something like 200,000 were *nomenklatura* posts for Party members, and perhaps a further 900,000 were *nomenklatura*-controlled appointments for Party members and others who were deemed suitable by the Party. It is thought that, when families were taken into account, over two million Poles (perhaps 10 per cent of the population) owed their jobs, their incomes or their place in society to *nomenklatura* appointments or protection. Chief appointments in publishing were made or approved by the Central Committee. These posts included: the chief and deputy editors of the influential Party journals *Trybuna Ludu*, *Nowe Drogi*, *Życie Parti* and *Chłopska Droga*; the senior editors of *Ideologia i Polityka* and *Zagadnienia i Materiały*; the chief, deputy editors and directors of the Polish Press Agency, Interpress, the Central Photographic Agency, the Society for Artistic and Graphic Publications, the Society for Documentary Film Production, and Kronika (Polish Film News); the senior editors of all national circulation daily, weekly and monthly newspapers; the directors and senior editors of all scientific and literary publishing houses; the directors of all specialized national institutes of scientific research; at the Polish Academy of Sciences they appointed the president, vice-presidents, administrative secretary and assistants, the directors of all foreign-language publishing and broadcasting services, as well as the departmental secretaries and assistant secretaries and directors; the chairman, vice-chairmen and directors of the RSW publishing conglomerate; the director of the important Książka i Wiedza publishing cooperative; the chairman, deputies and directors-general of the radio and television boards; the president and secretary-general of the Society of Polish Journalists; the president and secretary-general of the Writers' Union.[5]

The Regional Party Committees had power to control further appointments: the presidents and full-time leaders of artistic, social, cultural, sporting and paramilitary associations, also of professional bodies such as the Higher Technical Organization and the Association of Polish Jurists; the chief and deputy directors of local Polish radio and television broadcasting stations and centres; the chief and deputy editors of the main local daily newspapers and cultural and social magazines; the chief and deputy editors of regional press and book-publishing houses; the rectors and vice-rectors of higher educational establishments; the directors of regional museums. In addition to the Party-nominated posts there were also the ordinary Party members in less crucial positions. Although most editors and journalists were encouraged to become Party members they were rarely if ever forced to do so. It has been estimated that in 1970–7 Party membership in the giant print combine RSW (Workers' Co-operative Publisher) ran at about 51 per cent. In the Polish Press Agency it was thought to be about 56 per cent. In the Polish Radio and Television Committee membership was about 44 per cent. On the publishing editorial boards membership was much higher: about 80 per cent of RSW editors were Party members; in radio and television, among editors and controllers membership was thought to be about 70 per cent.[6]

By 1976 there were 2,409 papers and journals published in Poland: 56 daily, 136 weekly, 86 bi-weekly, 571 monthly, 200 bi-monthly, 465 quarterly, 214 annual, fifty-six bi-annual and 625 others. By 1986 a total of 3,083 magazines, newspapers and periodicals appeared, and of these 2,986 were regular periodicals – 170 official gazettes, 500 for general consumption, the remainder designated 'specialist interest' journals; no less than fifty-eight publications (totalling 2,255,800 copies) paid attention in varying degrees to literary matters. The important state literary journals were: *Twórczość, Miesięcznik Literacki, Kultura, Nowa Kultura, Literatura, Poezja, Dialog, Przegląd Kulturalny, Życie Literackie, Literatura na Świecie, Nowe Książki, Rocznik Literacki, Pamiętnik Literacki, Ruch Literacki, Nowy Wyraz, Poglądy, Odra, Kamiena, Pismo, Magazyn Kulturalny, Kuźnica, Polityka, Forum, Trybuna Ludu, Odrodzenie, Perspektywy, Panorama, Tydzień, Głos Pracy, Polska.* There were also twenty-one Pax (Stowarzyszenie Pax, Pax Association) journals including *Słowo Powszechne* (daily 100,000–180,000 copies), and *Kierunki* (20,000 copies weekly); ODiSS, Caritas and the other official religious publishers produced journals totalling over 70,000 copies per week.

Of the fifty state publishing houses, all co-ordinated through the Central Publishing Board of the Ministry of Arts and Culture, twenty produced fiction. The most important state literary publishing houses were: Spółdzielnia Wydawnicza Książki i Wiedza; Państwowy Instytut Wydawniczy; Biblioteka Narodowa; Biuro Wystaw Artystycznych; Wydawnictwo Arkady; Wydawnictwa Artystyczne i Filmowe; Polskie Wydawnictwo Muzyczne; Ludowa Spółdzielnia Wydawnicza; Wydawnictwa Literackie; Wydawnictwo Ministerstwa Obrony Narodowej; Spółdzielnia Wydawnicza Czytelnik; Wydawnictwo Zrzeszenie Księgarzy. In addition there were also eight major regional and 'youth' publishing houses which occasionally produced literature. Pax was also a massively diverse publishing enterprise with a hand in a great many journals. It offered the annual Włodzimierz Pietrzak Prize for the best achievement in the literary field. *Belles-lettres* accounted for 18 per cent of Pax publications. The favourite foreign writers for Pax publication were François Mauriac, G.K.Chesterton and Graham Greene. The Polish authors most favoured by Pax were Zofia Kossak and Jan Dobraczyński.[7]

By far the largest and most important state publishing house was RSW. It had been established in 1947 and was run by the Party Press Department to publish 'the central organs of the Party', such as *Trybuna Ludu* and twenty Party regional and local papers. All profits from this enterprise went directly to the Party. For most of its existence RSW supervised and controlled the production of 160 journals, including *Trybuna Ludu, Trybuna Robotnicza, Życie Warszawy, Dziennik Polski, Echo Krakowa, Przyjaciółka, Kobieta i Życie, Przekrój, Perspektywy, Panorama, Tydzień, Polityka, Kultura, Literatura, Życie Literackie, Tworczość, Poezja, Dialog, Literatura na Świecie, Magazyn Kulturalny, Poglądy, Polska.* Many of these had a substantial interest in literature. RSW produced forty-six daily newspapers comprising 80 per cent of all daily Polish newspapers. It also controlled three press agencies, twenty-five printing houses, and 30,000 'Ruch' street kiosks where the newspapers were sold. By the mid-1970s RSW employed 85,000 people in its own immediate concerns and a total of 500,000 people in related enterprises. RSW was not only a tame print monopoly, it was also the largest press conglomerate in Europe – bigger even than the giant West German Springer Press. While it was titled a 'workers' co-operative', RSW had little to do with workers or with co-operatives. Very few of those who worked for RSW were members of the 'co-operative management committee'; rather, they were simply employees. The notion of co-operative was contradicted at almost every turn by RSW. Not only was RSW the creation of the Party rather than an independent entity, but its publications (supervised by the censor) were entirely for the Party. RSW was a direct extension of the Party machine: the chairman and vice-chairman of RSW, along with the editors of all the various journals and publications produced by RSW, were Party-approved *nomenklatura* appointments. RSW was in every sense an official publishing house: it was not possible to say where RSW began and the Party ended.

Poland's print distribution system was a nightmare. Printers, publishers and the distributors were tied to the latest five-year plan, and in the absence of marketing skills and cost-accounting had to 'plan blind' two or three years ahead. Every publisher sent new books to the state monopoly distribution service DSK (Repository Book Store), which had eleven large warehouses. They in their turn would send books out to eighteen regional organizations known as DK (Book Store), which would then place books in particular bookshops. Bookshop managers had almost no say in the process and could exert very little influence over what appeared on their shelves. DSK would often order books at a fixed price and a fixed number of copies – this was the only 'business calculation' that might possibly affect the size of the print run and the cost levels for the publisher. Inflation and shortages were not taken into account; the standard contracts between DSK and publishing houses were never amended to take note of altered circumstances or demand. Storing books is always extremely expensive, and without cost-accounting and adequate records it was neither easy to store books nor to find stocks of stored books when they were required. By 1989 DSK warehouses were packed with unsold books and it owed the publishers PAN and Ossolineum several billion złoties.

The Polish publishing industry was gigantic but clumsy. Subsidy meant that only books the government thought inoffensive or desirable were likely to appear, but it also meant that a great number of serious and scholarly books (which would not necessarily have found a publisher in a market economy) were published, distributed and sold cheaply. The enormous print and publishing industry was as efficient as the rest of the economy. It was massively over-staffed (probably by around 50 per cent) and hugely subsidized, publishing books that were cheap but took an enormous amount of time to produce. It was easier for the publishing houses to handle large print runs than short ones, which always proved to be more expensive. It is not unusual to hear writers' tales of manuscripts, accepted for publication and approved by the censor, languishing in the publishing houses for five to ten years before appearing in the shops. In part this was due to the inefficiency and low productivity of the publishing houses and to censorship, but it was also due to the massive print and paper shortages that plagued Polish publishing throughout the post-war period.

There was considerable tension over the fact that classics of modern literature and important translations took second place to political publications supported and promoted by the Party and the Ministry of Culture. In the years 1944–87 translations of foreign literature accounted for a total of 16,877 titles (due to a quirk in the way publishing is classified, 760 of these were translations from Polish into other languages): 4,862 from Russian,

3,734 from English, 1,976 from French, 1,574 from German. In 1978 over 54 million copies of modern literature were published: that is one and a half books of fiction for everyone in Poland. Of this, 12 million copies were translations. Translations may have taken second place to Party publications, but they took up a huge, perhaps disproportionate amount of time and money, and this meant less attention for living Polish writers. As in the west, foreign writers, preferably dead, were cheaper and safer to publish than living writers. Publication of works in translation was conducted through particular state publishing houses: PiW; the Nike series by Czytelnik; Spanish and South American literature by Kraków Wydawnictwo Literackie; Scandinavian literature by the Poznań Publishing House. This was supplemented by the monthly journal *Literatura na Świecie* (World Literature). Over the years fluctuations in the number of Polish foreign-language publications and translations into Polish reflected not only the growing economic crisis – though Poland rarely paid for foreign rights to books and was not part of the international copyright conventions – but also the political difficulties of allowing potentially 'dangerous' foreign material on to the domestic market. Translations of foreign literature into Polish peaked at 2,370 editions in 1960, rose again to 2,101 in 1975 and then slumped to 400 by 1986.[8]

Books by Polish writers usually appeared in editions of about 10,000 copies (the average print run of a new book of fiction in the UK is 1,600 copies). The office of the censor used the weapon of a very short print run (as small as 300) and the system of subscription-only purchase, to limit the power and influence of books which were deemed necessary but dangerous and whose circulation, therefore, was limited to professional readers and the inner Party. The Party could also rule that while a book might appear it was not to be reviewed or not to be reviewed favourably. In this way authors could not complain that they had not been published, but the effect of the book was minimal.

The Ministry of Arts and Culture had in its gift a series of *wynogrodzenie dodatkowe* (special awards) available upon the demonstration of artistic, ideological or pedagogical worth. There were also about a hundred very large annual awards. The most prestigious of these was the state literary prize, given in alternate years: Lem, Kott, Andrzejewski and Brandys were all recipients. Publishers, various ministries including the Ministry of National Defence, Polish radio and television, various large industrial enterprises and other 'social organizations' all offered their own awards to writers and several of them even commissioned new works, often referred to as 'social commissions'. There was also a special annual prize offered by the Central Trade Union Council. There were a large number of competitions and festivals, all funded by the Ministry for Art and Culture, with a budget running into unspecified thousands of millions of złoties. The Ministry of Art and Culture also had in its gift trips abroad, either for research or literary tours to Polish communities in the USA, Canada, Brazil, France and England, appointments to the foreign embassies, work on delegations and international committees. The Polish publishing community found outlets at the MTK (International Book Fair). This festival, held annually in May, started in Poznań in 1956, but moved to Warsaw in 1958. In general it had about 300 stands representing 700 publishers from as many as twenty countries. This, with the Annual Warsaw Poetry Festival, was one of the main showcases for domestic publishing.

The Party believed fervently in mass literacy and in further and higher education. As well as a programme to eliminate the secondary illiteracy that resulted from Germanization policies and Nazi educational restrictions, a programme which had been particularly effective in the new western border districts, the early post-war government set out to 'popularize and socialize the means of cultural production in all fields' – the task of an entire generation of cultural workers. Throughout the post-war period the Ministry of Art and Culture paid particular attention to the creation of public libraries. In 1956 Poland had 42,000 libraries, averaging 8,164 readers each, a total of 116,200,000 borrowings per year and a library book stock of 89,300,000 volumes: by 1970 that had risen to 52,400 libraries, a book stock of 214,700,000 volumes, an average of 17,387 borrowers per library, and 276,700,000 borrowings per year; by 1978 there were 37,600 libraries, 276,400,000 volumes in stock, an average of 18,239 borrowers per library, and 271,100,000 borrowings per year. At peak effectiveness in 1969 there were 50,000 libraries: approximately one local library for every 10,000 people. However, the bulk of these were poorly stocked, and it seems that by 1971 they spent an average of only thirteen złoties per registered reader per year. The Party was in fact storing up trouble for itself with its libraries and mass literacy campaigns. By fostering literacy the Party contradicted its efforts to control the formation of opinion and thought and the free flow of information. The only way that mass literacy policies could help the Party was in combination with the Party's strict and exclusive control of the print and publishing industry and its use of censorship.[9] As the famous aphorism from Stanisław Jerzy Lec had it: 'Illiterates must dictate'.[10]

In considering the relationship of writers to the Party it is essential to remember just how unreliable the Party was, not only politically, but culturally. As a result of Stalin's murderous policies, the Party inherited a mentally impoverished membership, made worse by the generally poor educational levels of the Party leadership through the 1940s. The Polish communists who formed the new PPR after 1941 were almost all released from the camps. They were by no means the pick of the bunch: they were not the best-known, most active, most imaginative, best-experienced, most knowledgeable, most original or the most sensitive – as Władysław Gomułka, sole surviving member of the KPP Central Committee after the 1938 purge, was to prove. They were merely those who had survived. By 1961, 26.1 per cent of Party membership had less than a primary school education, 49.1 per cent had a primary school education, 19.5 per cent had a secondary education, and 5.3

per cent had a university education. Of its three million members in 1984, only 369,000 qualified as *inteligencja* – that is, had some form of higher education, or had successfully completed their secondary schooling. National data, on the other hand, showed that in the general population, one in three had completed some form of education above the primary and vocational levels. This said, it is perhaps easy to see why the Party was more interested in writers than in literature. In contrast to the Party, by the mid-1960s, 28 per cent of writers were graduates; 40 per cent possessed Master's, Doctorate or *Habilitacja* degrees; the highest qualifications were to be found among critics and essayists, the lowest among poets; 18 per cent studied foreign languages, 17 per cent Polish philology, 16 per cent the humanities, 14 per cent law, and 8 per cent fine arts, theatre and music, 8 per cent economic and political sciences, and 4 per cent history. Of those who had completed professional training before becoming writers, by far the largest groups were teachers (11 per cent), and journalists (10 per cent).[11]

Education of ZLP membership (% of membership)

	1929	1964
domestic	5	1
lower than secondary	1	1
secondary school	11	18
incomplete tertiary	28	10
tertiary – graduate	7	28
tertiary – masters	30	31
tertiary – doctorate	18	9
tertiary – *habilitacja*	—	1
no information	—	1

Source: A.Siciński, *Literaci polscy: przemiany zawodu na tle przemian kultury współczesnej* (Wrocław-Warsaw: 1971), table 34.

The period 1944–9 was one in which writers were left pretty much to their own devices, to work out their own style, content, methods and relationship to the state and the reading public: by and large a continuation of pre-war arrangements. The newly 'elected' government of 1947 had allocated, along with the ministries of forests, post and telegraph, agriculture and agricultural reform, the post of minister of culture to the SL (Peasant Party); and while the appearance of liberal opinion was maintained by these allocations, in fact the post of minister was less important than the Party-approved post of deputy minister or secretary of state. The Party, in cultural matters, was anxious to appear as a benevolent dictatorship engaged in a *łagodna rewolucja* (gentle revolution), though in every other sphere of activity it was busy criminalizing and repressing all opposition. In 1945 the Party set the agenda for the Kraków conference of the ZZLP (Union of Professional Polish Writers), where the major subject of discussion was the question: 'Was the Second World War an ideological watershed?'. Chairman Julian Przyboś, a fanatical avant-gardist who, while reluctant to support official cultural policies, was desperate to modernize Poland, directed writers not to look back to already established Polish literary forms, but to look to the USSR, which, he said, had the most progressive avant-garde poetry in the world.

Catholic writers and the older writers were certain to resist any form of coercion, so the Party did not push too hard. In any case the Party wished to enlist influential Catholics to its side without necessarily enrolling them in the Party. In an effort to subvert the authority of the Church Jakub Berman set up Pax in 1945, a 'Catholic' front organization for discussion and publication, under the ex-Falangist Bolesław Piasecki. Pax was prepared to 'co-operate' with the new order. The younger, newer writers were more easily influenced in favour of the Party, and soon both these groupings had become isolated from the bulk of the ZZLP membership, who were neither Party members nor active Catholics. In spite of the violence that marked some aspects of the communist take-over, in the early years there was a great deal of give-and-take within the literary-political fraternity. In Kraków, where conservative Catholicism, enlightened liberalism and informed socialism rubbed shoulders, and where literary reputations were not established simply by hitching one's talents to Communist Party power, it is said that:

> The onset of social realism did not take the usual course of self-critiques and conversions to the new communist faith . . . Only in Kraków, in the house administered by the Polish Literary Union (ulica Krupnicza 22) . . . could representatives of all attitudes towards the new system live side by side. Creators of revolutionary rhetoric, literary henchmen of the new power and editors of *Tygodnik Powszechny* (published under the auspices of the Church and opposed to the new government) borrowed salt and vodka from each other.[12]

Meetings and discussions between opposing political factions within the writing community in Kraków seem to have passed off without rancour or violence, and the Party attempted to swing this generosity of spirit and interest in resolving the issues suspended by the war around to its own ends by focusing writers' attention on the meaning of the war rather than on the experience of war. The censor only intervened on clearly defined issues and on specifically forbidden topics. In general writers wrote about the war years rather than about new issues – they had a great deal of experience to catch up on both culturally and individually.

In 1945 the Party had created the literary magazine *Kuźnica* in an attempt to forge a link between the Polish Enlightenment and the socialist 'camp of reform'. The magazine was deemed the communist-Positivist flagship, devoted to fighting reactionary clericism, misplaced *szlachta* idealism and outdated, outmoded Polish patriotism. Although it pushed the party line on *socrealizm*, it did not do so exclusively or dogmatically, but in a broad and questioning attempt to restore some of the best humanist and socialist elements of nineteenth-century literature. In July 1948 the Party held its first Congress and Jakub Berman was appointed a member of the Politburo, the Secretariat of the Central Committee and the Central Committee's Organizational Bureau. Although nominally his most powerful office was only that of under-secretary in the Council of Ministers, in effect Berman oversaw ideology, education, foreign affairs, security, culture and propaganda. Jerzy Boresza, working under Berman, was director of several major state publishing concerns and secretary-general of the 1948 Wrocław Congress of Intellectuals, which invited foreign intellectuals to Poland to see the changes being wrought.

This was the situation up to the end of 1947, when the Party went over to the attack in cultural matters. The policies of the Party, up to this point directed at obtaining support for their programme from the *inteligencja*, began to develop into a contradictory combination of mistrust of the writers' individualism and independence, disgust at writers' ingratitude, rewards to those who went along with the Party line and efforts to coerce or silence those who proved unreliable or less tractable. First Secretary Bolesław Bierut, opening a Wrocław radio station on 16 November 1947, during the ZZLP Wrocław Writers' Congress, signalled that a direct attempt to control writers was on the way. He complained that artists of all kinds, rather than lagging behind the 'mighty current' of important political and economic developments, should reflect the great changes the country was experiencing. He looked to artists to 'popularize and socialize cultural production in all its fields and manifestations', 'to shape the culture of the entire nation for a new period in its history'. He made it clear that work to a plan was necessary along the 'entire cultural front', and called for an 'artistic offensive' to create the 'culture of a people's democracy'. The project of controlling writers fell largely to Jakub Berman, who said he had decided to use 'every conceivable means' to influence Polish writers because 'It was especially important to us to enlist the cultural circles on our side.'[13]

The most important fixed point in the life of Polish writers was their union. The pre-war ZZLP (Professional Union of Polish Writers), an organization whose good works and reputation still linger warmly in the memory of older Polish writers, was devoted to the practical work of the writer, to improving pay and conditions and protecting the rights of authors. In the particularly Polish interface of literary ideas and political morals the union followed the line that writers had to be free to express their own judgements and thoughts, and regarded itself as an organization whose function was to protect the ability of writers to remain free to say and write just what they chose. Inevitably this led to the union's intervention in a number of cases, conflict with the authorities and charges that it was politically motivated. The union, however, maintained throughout its existence that it was above party politics and that its criteria were always primarily aesthetic and professional. In the inter-war years the union had been a primary focus of liberal ideals and tolerance of difference. In its lifetime ZZLP had protested against the assassination of Polish President Gabriel Narutowicz in 1922, against anti-Semitism, against the notorious internment camp set up by Piłsudski at Bereza Kartuska, against the imprisonment of extreme right-wingers such as Ferdynand Goetl, and left-wing members of KPP such as Leon Pasternak. Its membership included Catholics, Jews and atheists, nationalists, socialists, communists and supporters of the ruling military *Sanacja* regime. In a period of rising extremism and dramatic social conflict ZZLP stood out as a bastion of tolerance, humanism, pluralism and the acceptance of human difference.

When Polish writers took refuge in the USSR in September 1939 they tried to reinstate their union, but after an initial period of reasonable relations, found that the Soviets had reorganized the union for them as a subsection of the Union of Soviet Ukrainian Writers. The Poles had little control of their own funds, no control over union policies, and could publish only in approved Soviet magazines. The German attack on the USSR prevented the full development of Soviet policies towards the Polish writers. Approximately 25 per cent of the membership survived the war, but post-war membership was probably never more than about 1,200: possibly as many as 20 per cent of the post-war union were Party members. Union membership was spread through seventeen regional branches, the largest and most vociferous of which was always the Warsaw branch. The next-largest centre of union membership and activity was Kraków. The chairmanship of the union varied in quality, particularly in the early post-war years, reflecting not only the particular political climate, but also the personality and the experience of each chairman. But in general Przyboś, Czachowski and Iwaszkiewicz, the first three post-war chairmen of ZZLP, worked hard to return Polish literary life to 'normality'. Although the Party did not at first interfere directly with the union, the Party believed, with Stalin, that once it had control over the writers it would have control of the 'engineers of human souls'. Writers would be of enormous use in ideological legitimation, rather than in purely literary tasks. The Party desperately needed writers and intellectuals. It had no capacity to 'buy' the nation, but there was a possibility that it could buy some writers and coerce others.

Membership of ZLP, 1945–1967

1945	358
1946	563
1947	654
1961	862
1962	918
1963	937
1964	949
1965	997
1966	994
1967	1,025

Source: Siciński, *Literaci polscy*, table 1.

At the fourth congress of the ZZLP (20–3 January 1949) in Szczecin the Party characterized contemporary Polish literature as the bourgeois reactionary art of 'the philosophy of catastrophism, helplessness, mysticism and irrationalism' (*Trybuna Ludu*, 20 January 1949). The Party, under Berman's direction, rewrote the statutes of the Writers' Union to make it conform to those of the other eastern-bloc writers' unions, and assist it in mobilizing the membership to support the new authorities. Berman had spent the war in the USSR and was one of the authors of the Party's ideological programme which included the decision to collectivize agriculture. Backed by Party members of the union, Leon Kruczkowski, the new union chairman, formally acknowledged the leading role of the Party and accepted Berman's decree on the tenets of *socrealizm*, now judged the only worthwhile form of literature. Berman instructed Kruczkowski to prepare a 'production plan' by which literature would become part of the Six-Year Plan. Also the union changed its name: instead of ZZLP it became ZLP (Union of Polish Writers). The change of name signified a 'democratization' of the membership which enabled Party and bureaucracy *grafomani* (graphomaniacs) to secure membership. The party chose to see the influx of new members as rejuvenation, but for the surviving pre-war membership the result of the change was a demoralizing levelling-down, and a serious drop in the standing and prestige of their professional organization. Many were unhappy about the changes and felt that, in spite of its liberal appearance, the new union would not have sufficient independence from the Party to maintain either its own professional competence or the prestige of its members.

The situation of *socrealizm* changed considerably after the 1949 conference. *Socrealizm* was formally introduced by the minister for the arts, Włodzimierz Sokorski, at the writers' conference in 1949, and it was formally adopted and ratified with solemnity at each annual writers' congress, but abandoned with the thaw of 1956. Under the guidance of Jakub Berman, it became Party policy to foster and publish *socrealizm* in a Polish variant. The new ZLP was (in theory at least) tied to the Six-Year Plan for literature imposed by Berman and to the *pion* (plumb line) of social organization, the downward transmission of ideas and directives from the Party. While in theory the ZLP remained non-political, in practice the Party hoped that the union could now do no other than interpret the directives of the Central Committee's Department of Culture, as they were transmitted by the Ministry of Arts and Culture.

Almost at once the changes in ZLP's structure and function became apparent. Overseen by Włodzimierz Sokorski the Party cadre within the ZLP began to organize educational and organizational meetings, conferences, congresses and factory visits for writers. There now appeared a hierarchy of political preference for publication, stipends and prizes. The main administrative divisions within the ZLP were Executive Committee (twenty members elected at the annual congress, plus the chairmen of the regional branches), the Qualifications Commission (controlling membership admissions), Court of Colleagues (arbitrating within the union) and the Accounts and Auditing Commission. The ZLP were also instructed to develop *sekcje twórcze* (creative genre sections), which met regularly to discuss the ideological content of work in progress and to consider the implications of the latest edicts from the Party. The creation of these sections was an attempt to fragment and control decision-making processes within the union, but also to control the creativity of individual writers. As if to confirm the new line, the final Kraków issue of *Twórczość* in December 1949 carried an eighteen-page poem in praise of Stalin. That same week the collected works of Joseph Stalin were published in Polish, and the journal *Nowa Kultura* began a series of articles on Marxist theory and the arts. There followed a series of meetings in 1950 between the union and the officials of the Ministry of Arts and Culture about the fulfilment of literary instructions concerning *socrealizm* and the problems created when the Party decided to place the production of certain books and publications in the hands of inexperienced military and youth organizations whose literary aims were quite different from those of professional writers: Lem's novels *Śledztwo* (1959), *Solaris* (1961), and *Niezwyciężony* (1964) were produced by the publishing section of the Ministry of National Defence.[14] The union was in great danger of being bureaucratized into dull conformity.

ZLP membership by region, 1964 (% of membership)

Bydgoszcz	1.7
Gdańsk	2.5
Katowice	2.7
Kraków	12.7

Lubelsk	1.6
Łódź	4.8
Olsztyn	1.8
Opole	1.8
Poznań	4.1
Szczecin	2.1
Wrocław	3.5
Zielona Góra	1.2
Warsaw	59.5

Source: Siciński, *Literaci polscy*, table 14.

From the late 1940s the ZLP offered a range of incentives to membership: insurance and pension schemes for writers and their families, *wczasowiski* (holiday centres in the countryside), financial encouragement to young writers, grants, loans and scholarships for researching particular projects, or to travel abroad, access to well-placed editors and intercession with the censor. ZLP also provided in its Warsaw branch and through co-operation with other larger unions a club with a good, cheap subsidized restaurant and coffee shop where writers could meet and mingle with workers and officials from the Ministry of Culture and the Association of Tourists and Sightseers, who also shared the facilities. The writers' club, though famed for its uncomfortable chairs and its heating failures during the winter, was also well known for its good coffee and excellent *befsztyk* (beefsteak). Wednesday evenings were often given over to readings by particular writers, and the club frequently hosted exhibitions of contemporary art. Entry was restricted to members of the club, which did not necessarily include all members of the union.

The union's provincial branches, sometimes in co-operation with MPiK, the Club of International Press and Books (a unique organization in the Soviet bloc), each provided a reading room where a wide range of foreign journals and newspapers and some items of food were available. ZLP also had good relations and shared certain facilities with the Association of Polish Architects, the Union of Authors and Composers for the Stage, and the Association of Polish Artists of Theatre and Film, the actors' and performers' club. In co-operation with these and other arts organizations branches often supplied take-out sales of canned goods, sausage, vodka, paper, typewriter ribbons and writing materials, and access to foreign books not generally available. Members of ZLP also had access to the 'Czytelnik' coffee shop – established in 1956 by the Czytelnik publishing house on Wiejska Street, where notices and announcements from ZLP usually appeared on the wall near the cloakroom. This was a favourite haunt not only of the editors from Czytelnik but of the editors of the magazines *Twórczość*, *Pryzjaciółka*, *Nowa*

Wieś and *Współczesność*, employees and officials of the nearby Ministry of Foreign Trade and members of the Polish Press Agency and the Central Committee, all of which were located nearby. This was the coffee house favoured by ZLP chairmen Iwaszkiewicz and Putrament.

Membership of the writers' union indicated a certain practical degree of *dyspozycyność* – willingness to co-operate. But in general throughout the post-war years, the ZLP protected writers and quietly fostered intellectual opposition by acting as a fall-back for disaffected creative Party members – something not envisaged by Berman. Although it was technically possible to be a writer without being a member of ZLP, in practice it was unlikely that, apart from new writers, anyone outside the union would ever get much written, let alone published by the state. Even so ZLP facilities were far from grand. Its premises were located in a reconstructed house once owned by the novelist Władysław Reymont (1867–1925), near Warsaw Castle, and were certainly not as lavish as those of the Soviet writers' union. Brandys has described the ZLP canteen:

Two small rooms in a cellar, separated by an arcade and three small steps. The tables are crowded; seven people are waiting in line by the wall. Stuffy, airless. Tin forks and spoons, no tablecloths or napkins; when a chair becomes available, you have to sit with the remains of someone else's food. Prize-winning writers and poor poets come here for lunch, famous actors and older women living off translating and their memoirs, as well as a few popular lawyers. And quite a few striking, fashionably dressed girls . . . Well-known film-makers, owners of foreign cars and villas on the [Gdańsk] Bay, rubbing shoulders with blacklisted writers and a mob of skinny critics, mixed in with a few literary informers. All together, eating their cabbage soup with tin spoons.[15]

Nor was the writers' 'home' very grand. Formerly a private estate consisting of a noble palace and park at Obory, near the picturesque town of Konstancin just south of Warsaw, writers shared the place with the Main School of Farming. Konwicki fondly recalled:

Obory, poor Polish literature's phalanstery. Hideous allotments of garden plots at an ancient bend in the Vistula, in the midst of an ancient landscape with age-old trees and an old-fashioned road paved with fieldstone. Neglected gardens, crooked paths lined with chestnut trees, and a park in terrible condition . . . I've remembered everything. Thirty years of this place, part prison, part hospice, part bordello for Warsaw's writers. I've spent so many months there. I've drunk so much vodka there. Been through so much there. The only problem I had was the writing.[16]

In co-operation with Klub MPiK (Club of International Press and Books), the ZLP helped provide more than 10,000 meetings per year at the 1,900 literary appreciation circles where writers gave lucrative public readings. In the years 1962–72 MPiK served a total of thirty million 'customers'. However, while many regarded MPiK with great affection, the facilities offered were friendly but basic:

> There is a club in my neighbourhood which I have been visiting for years and where I am treated like an old customer . . . We all know each other although we seldom exchange greetings. We gather in this small smoke-filled room to sit in silence together, sipping black coffee and occasionally reading something. Some have their favourite journals. There is a respectable looking lady who does the crossword puzzles . . . a number of young women who study the fashion magazines. A young man devotes two hours each day to the sports papers. There are loyal readers of *The New York Times, Pravda, Frankfurter Allgemeine,* and *Le Monde.*[17]

In 1950 Jakub Berman moved the magazine *Twórczość* from Kraków to Warsaw, presumably to control it better, and 'amalgamated' the literary journals *Kuźnica* and *Odrodzenie* to form *Nowa Kultura*: 'one journal, with a line that was better adapted to the times'.[18] Berman's idea was that Polish writers should take over established Soviet models, but the effect was to strangle much Polish writing by forcing publishing houses and editors to refuse almost everything that did not conform to the precepts of *socrealizm*. The Party effectively reduced writing to a dull, grey, conformist imitation of dull, grey, conformist Soviet models. Given that Poland's literary culture was that of the *szlachta*, the Party felt it could not trust its writers not to stab it in the back. Also given the long tradition of Polish resistance in literature, the language of hints and guesses, of smuggled messages, it was inevitable that the Party should also take a great interest in controlling the products of its writers, of scrutinizing their work for disloyalty and treachery. For the writers of the immediate post-war period the Party was prepared to provide far greater material comfort and ensure far greater success than they would have been able to enjoy in free-market circumstances. But in return this meant that they repeatedly had to indicate a willingness to follow Party guidelines. Provided they did not fall foul of the censor or the police, writers in Poland enjoyed an incredibly privileged position within communist society. Even though communism had brought about a great levelling of Polish society, the literati occupied by tradition a place of unusual influence and moral significance, and occupations linked to the creative and semi-independent *inteligencja*, rather than to industry, finance, politics or the *biurokracja*, were still ranked first in social prestige. In the late 1960s the three most highly regarded professions were professor, doctor and teacher; ministers and nurses were ranked eighth, priests seventh, the *milicja* fourteenth. In fact, writers occupied the position that the Party would have liked to hold – and in this writers and the Party may be seen as rivals.[19]

The Party offered writers a far higher level of financial reward than they would have enjoyed under capitalism. Though still substantially behind anything that western Europe could manage, the Party offered financial stability and a standard of living substantially better than the average Polish factory worker, university teacher or engineer. The carrot offered to writers in return for co-operation was enhanced in 1949 when the Party announced a revised taxation system. As part of a programme of capital accumulation and investment in heavy industry, income from capital and sales of property was now subject to 92.5 per cent taxation: tax for tradesmen, those in handicraft enterprises and the independent professions (doctors, engineers, dentists, accountants, solicitors and legal counsel) rose to 80 per cent of gross income. However, the taxation of writers, artists and publishers was minimal, the lowest of all possible categories.[20] It was clear that in terms of its tax structure the Party valued the support of writers and artists far more than it valued the support of other independent professionals, or at least that it considered that writers needed more positive 'encouragement' if they were to be won over. By the late 1960s, for example, a book of 250 pages might appear in a print run of 10,000 copies, but the writer would receive a royalty on the book that was the equivalent of about five months' salary. A reprint of the book would earn the author a further royalty of 80 per cent on the original royalty payment, and subsequent reprinting would earn another 60 per cent royalty. This was further supplemented by the Ministry of Art and Culture Authors' Fund, sometimes by as much as 250 per cent on the original royalty sum.

Writers could also be rewarded by further editions of their book in a cheap version at a low and popular price. A writer deemed to be in favour could earn in total from a modest edition of a book four to eight times as much as the average monthly Polish wage. A prolific writer looked upon with favour by the regime could become very wealthy within a short space of time. On average, writers aged up to thirty-five earned 4,000 złoties per month; aged thirty-five to fifty earned 5,700 złoties; aged fifty to sixty earned 3,950 złoties; and those over sixty earned 3,100 złoties. Once they began to earn more than 2,500 złoties per month almost all agreed that their material situation was good/improving, but even top earners complained that it was difficult to live from creative work alone and, like ordinary Polish workers, many had another income – from teaching, radio, film, TV, journalism, editing. The only exceptions were the 300 or so ZLP members engaged regularly in full-time work for radio, film or TV. Official special treatment for writers was well established by 1968. At that time, when the average Polish salary was about 2,200 złoties per month, some forty-five writers and artists earned over 10,000 złoties per month (the same as the salary of the deputy prime minister), while some writers were thought to have earned over 40,000 złoties per month.[21] William Woods is surely mistaken in saying 'a Polish novelist, while unlikely to make a living from novels alone, will probably earn about as much in purchasing power as will his western equivalent'. Certainly the Polish writing profession was much better off than it had been in the inter-war period, but for all the writer's enhanced earnings and social standing, finding something in the shops to spend their money on was a real problem.

Average monthly earnings of ZLP membership, 1959 (% of membership)

up to 500 zł	2
500–1,000 zł	4
1,000–1,500 zł	5
1,500–2,000 zł	8
2,000–2,500 zł	7
2,500–3,000 zł	11
3,000–4,000 zł	17
4,000–5,000 zł	10
5,000–7,000 zł	15
7,000–10,000 zł	9
10,000+ zł	6
no information	6

Source: Siciński, *Literaci polscy,* table 47.

The Ministry of Arts and Culture made one further radical change in publishing practice: from the late 1940s onwards payment to the author was dependent on the size of the print run rather than on actual sales. Thus a book deemed favourable by the censor might prove unpopular, even unsaleable, but the author would nevertheless receive payment. The increasingly centralized production of books rose from 10,454,000 copies of 1,107 titles in 1945 to 118,000,000 copies of 4,611 titles by 1950 – more than four books per year for every man, woman and child living in Poland.[22] As late as 1 January 1974 the Party was still trying to woo writers and improve the material conditions of those who offered it support or who did not cause trouble, and the Sejm passed a special Pensions Act which enhanced the standing of writers, and raised writers' pensions by 20 per cent over the normal state pension. The act made more than modest provision for family, disability and funeral allowances, medical treatment and accommodation for any writer who had been 'in the creative arts' for fifteen years or more.

The effect of such blandishments was undoubtedly to make some of the more successful of the older generation of writers both demoralized and cynical about their work, and as a result there was a temptation to become engaged in the defence of their personal privilege rather than the practice of writing. Some saw the manipulation of the publishing and print industry through the ZLP and the Ministry of Art and Culture as little more than the management of ignorant political bosses. The majority of writers seemed sincere about their work, though, and believed wholeheartedly in the usefulness of their writing. Even so it was impossible to escape the fact that writers had become institutionalized and that their union had become bureaucratized to a remarkable degree. They were more like civil servants who happened to receive a slice of the enormous state arts budget, and, as such, even the most honest of these writers found it increasingly difficult to see criticism of the political system as anything more than an unjust and irresponsible personal attack on them and their work. According to Siciński, between 1929 and 1964 the number of full-time professional writers in Poland rose from 700 to 900, increasing from 358 to 1,025 between 1945 and 1967. However, the number of professional writers remained small. In June 1979 the ZLP mustered only 1,220 members.[23]

So much for the carrot. The stick was equally well developed. The powers of the censor were particularly useful. The GUKPPiW (Main Office for the Control of Press, Theatre and Exhibitions, the censor) was initiated on 5 July 1946, with its head office on Mysia Street in Warsaw. It dealt mainly with the control of press references to state secrets. This function was expanded to include a wider range of 'sensitive' materials in 1949, when the GUKPPiW grew rapidly and expanded its operations into the provinces. It could recommend that a book should be withdrawn from circulation, or that its author could be blacklisted: this might mean that a writer was banned from writing for the newspapers or making radio and TV broadcasts, that the writer was not allowed to publish, that the writer was confined to working on translations of foreign literature, no longer mentioned in the press or media, or perhaps with only negative references allowed. A ban might be for a particular period or it might be indefinite. In the case of a ban, the withdrawal of state subsidy, readings, prizes, awards and reprintings were all shown to be of particular importance not only in maintaining a writer's life-style, but in some cases for simply earning enough to live on. A ban coupled with the withdrawal of state finance usually signalled that the Party no longer wished the writer to continue working and that perhaps it was time to emigrate. After the Szczecin conference it became very difficult for a writer to get challenging new work to a readership through the increasingly effective net of censorship: first the writer had to get past comment and criticism from the *sekcje twórcze* (creative genre sections), then the editorial boards of the various reviews and journals dealing with creative literature, then past the editorial board of the state publishing houses, and finally past the censor. A writer who refused to follow the Party line or who offended the Party in some way could be entirely ignored by the critics so that a book did not sell. The writer could also be threatened with expulsion from the union or denied reprints of books already issued or denied additional awards and prizes.

The advent of communism brought about a massive transformation in Polish society. In the years 1931–60 the percentage of the population involved in agriculture shrank from 60 per cent to 38.2 per cent while the number of those employed in industry rose from 12.7 per cent to 25 per cent; in the post-war period the *inteligencja* went through a rapid expansion. Officially the major divisions within post-war Polish society were: workers, peasantry, *inteligencja* and self-employed artisans. It is generally agreed that the war and the impact of communism did away with the old-style *inteligencja*. But a new communist *inteligencja* has nevertheless emerged. Some question whether communist *inteligencja* is not a contradiction in terms. The distinguished poet Artur Międzyrzecki said:

> The fact is that always in Poland the *inteligencja* has practically not existed. It is a very, very tiny percentage of all Poles. A very small and politically powerless section of Polish society. Influential, maybe, but powerful, no. Also, for all practical purposes they practically ceased to exist after the war. Now we have a very different kind of intellectual, more a technical person. These people, the writers, the creative *inteligencja*, they now have the same training as the bureaucrats and the technocrats, and for that reason we can hardly say any more that we have a true *inteligencja*. The real difference lies in their family background – what their parents and grandparents were, and because of that in their education and their moral attitude. We don't any longer necessarily think of officials or bureaucrats as *inteligencja*. They have given all that up when they entered the Party or the machinery of state. They tend towards technical competence, *eksperci* – experts. No, we tend now to think of those who remain independent, the oppositionists, as real intellectuals.[24]

The conditions prevailing under communism gave the emerging *inteligencja* the opportunity to enhance their social standing. This was reflected in education where, given Poland's social and political structure, the *inteligencja* was over-represented at every voluntary or higher level to an incredible degree. In 1964–5 children of the *inteligencja* (43.1 per cent) constituted the largest group of students at the Lyceum Ogólny (pre-university high school): children of the working class made up 26.3 per cent, those of the peasantry 18.3 per cent. At university (1965–6) the *inteligencja* made up 53.3 per cent of students, workers 26.1 per cent, the peasantry 14.1 per cent. At teacher-training colleges proportions were less extreme but similar: the *inteligencja* made up 38.3 per cent, workers 35.6 per cent, peasantry 20.9 per cent. At university children of the *inteligencja* made up 65.5 per cent of the Arts Faculties, 55.9 per cent of Medicine, 51 per cent of Technical Faculties, 50.9 per cent of Physical Education departments, 43.2 per cent of Economics, 40.3 per cent of Agriculture Faculties. Only in Theology were the 20.1 per cent of *inteligencja* dominated by 45.6 per cent of peasant and 27.8 per cent worker students.[25]

It is hard to be precise about the social background of contemporary Polish writers because very little research has been done on the subject. Only one sociological survey of writers has been undertaken in the post-war years, that by Siciński published in 1971. Siciński's materials are based on the results of a survey of ZLP members conducted by J.Szczepański of the PAN Instytut Filozofii i Socjologii in July 1959 and on a survey conducted by ZLP under President Iwaszkiewicz, initiated and organized by the ZLP Documentation Commission, led by Centkiewicz, Łopalewski and Kozikowski in January 1964, but also drawing on pre-war statistics. His study provides a unique portrait of the writers in years 1963–4. While membership of the union may have increased between 1929 and 1967, alone among the post-war social and class groupings, there seems to have been little change in the social structure and origins of this group. According to Siciński the social composition (by origin) of the literary intellectuals at the turn of the century was: *szlachta* (nobility) 57.1 per cent, *inteligencja* 23 per cent, *burżuazja* 15.4 per cent, peasantry 4.1 per cent. It seems that by 1964, in spite of a huge effort by the Party, fewer than half of Polish writers derived from a working-class or peasant background. Indeed, it has been estimated by Gömöri that at least 50 per cent of post-war Polish writers were descended from the pre-war, land-owning, professional class.[26]

Social origins of ZLP membership, 1929–1964 (% of membership)

	1929	1964
agricultural	33	4
commercial, industrial, banking	5	6
intellectual, independent trades	56	64
factory worker, artisan	4	15
peasant	2	9
unknown	—	2

Source: Siciński, *Literaci polscy*, table 9.

Siciński produced figures showing that in general writers were married (75 per cent), male (3:1), prose writers (4:1), were between forty-one and sixty years old, came from 'managerial' and 'independent trade' backgrounds (64 per cent), lived in Warsaw (60 per cent) or Kraków (13 per cent), made their début in the years 1930–8 (28 per cent) or 1940–8 (30 per cent), completed their university course or obtained a master's degree (usually in Polish philology, foreign languages, the humanities or law) trained to be teachers or journalists, published between five and seven books, supplemented their income as writers from another related source of work, frequently wrote essays and literary sketches for magazines, gave one to five public readings per year, possessed a radio (86 per cent) rather than a TV (31 per cent), owned a typewriter and a telephone, sometimes a fridge (43 per cent) and rarely a car (11 per cent). Fifteen per cent of writers owned more than 200 books, 26 per cent owned over 500 books, 19 per cent owned over 1,000 books, 15 per cent owned more than 2,000 books, 4 per cent owned more than 4,000 books, and 2 per cent owned around 6,000 books. Polish writers are a predominantly urban phenomenon: 5.4 per cent lived in towns or villages of up to 20,000 inhabitants, but 92 per cent lived in towns of over 20,000 inhabitants.[27]

The majority of post-war writers did not think their earnings from writing were satisfactory; their leisure activities were radio and television, theatre, hobbies, hunting, water sports, walking and sitting in coffee shops or meeting with other writers; their reading was predominantly creative literature; they thought of their profession as politically and ideologically influential, and as socially responsible, but they did not see themselves as a social élite, and were not necessarily on the side of the authorities; 46 per cent of writers had a positive opinion of the ZLP and its work on their behalf and did not think of Party members in the union as a separate group. They regarded the most pressing problems facing literature as the social standing of writers, lack of opportunities in society and the economy and the difficult material conditions of life in Poland.

By the late 1940s Polish writers occupied a rather shabby velvet prison located somewhere in the first circle of Hell. Their privilege, though it was not the stuff of a pact with Mephistopheles, could not be denied. Pre-war ideology and values persisted, particularly among the writing profession, but were connected with a union which, if it was not exactly tame, was certainly severely hampered by the Party. There was considerable pressure on writers to become absorbed either into the approved mode of production or into the Party ethos, and to revise their historical role within Polish society. The Party insisted there was no social conflict in People's Poland: the official line propounded in the Party press was that the 'socialist transformations' under way in the People's Republic of Poland had abolished the 'basic exploiting classes' so that there were now two entirely non-antagonistic classes, the workers and the peasants, led by their vanguard, the Party, all in total harmony.[28]

Clearly not all writers in Poland were opposed to the government. Many were members of the Party and some bureaucrats and Party officials 'dabbled' in the arts or 'became writers' because they had managed to get a poem, a story or an article published in an obscure departmental magazine or an internal Party journal. Many of these enjoyed protection from the Party and when necessary would turn out *en masse* to block union decision-making. After 1949 the literary magazines published a steady stream of translations from Soviet *socrealizm* alongside Polish *socrealizm*, much of it from these people: poems about the victorious Red Army, Polish-Soviet friendship, the

Polish People's Army, hymns to the security services, to the joys of the new People's Constitution, to the sons of labour, to individual Stakhanovite workers in the new industrial centres, hymns in praise of the new communist industrial city of Nowa Huta, poems urging the realization of the latest Five-Year Plan, or the 1950 Six-Year Plan, odes praising Stalin. And of course there were poems denouncing Truman, Churchill and Tito. And professional writers sometimes made fools of themselves. In 1949, for example, Broniewski, his suffering at the hands of the NKVD forgotten, wrote his ode 'Word about Stalin': 'Glory to the name of Stalin, bringer of peace to the world, peace'. In spite of the tension that existed between the ZLP and the PZPR there was very little hostility to the Party cadre within the ZLP. In 1964 Siciński asked ZLP members how they regarded writer members of the PZPR. The replies were as follows: as a separate group within the ZLP, forming its own circle, 5 per cent; not as a separate group within the ZLP, 39 per cent; as a non-artistic group, sharing ideology, world-view and politics, 6 per cent; non-artistic group, formed on another basis, e.g comradeship, 11 per cent; as a group founded on other principles or another basis, 10 per cent; don't know or did not reply, 29 per cent (table 62). Considering the antics of people like Putrament and Ważyk this shows remarkable restraint on the part of the ZLP membership.

Zbigniew Herbert said, 'Society resisted until 1948.' After that the writers, or their silence, were bought:

> The financial situation of the majority of the Writers' Union in those days was fantastic. Their careers were brilliant and fast. Italian, English, German and French writers are miserably poor. The great essayist Cioran, for example, is said to dine in some students' canteen and to be supported by Ionescu. His books bring him no money. An average writer in the West cannot support himself from his writing. He has to work at a university – if he has a suitable education – or in a bank, like Eliot. Whoever chooses to become a writer takes an immense risk, whereas here they lived in the lap of luxury, above the average of other professionals. The only risk was political. One had to know which way the wind blew. The material and social position of a writer is very important. I keep harping on about this inelegant subject like some kitchen maid. But here we come to the question of talent. If one was a member of the Writers' Union it was obvious that one's books would be published. I do not know of a single case where a book was turned down because it was badly written.[29]

Very few writers resigned from the ZLP, and only a few were ever expelled; the science fiction writer Stanisław Lem was one of them. His union membership was withdrawn in 1951 on the grounds that he had failed to produce enough. Herbert, who was particularly resistant to the blandishments of the new regime, was one of the few writers to resign from the ZLP. He described his reasons:

Because of a lie. Socialist realism had sounded. I had no chance to publish what I was writing then, and by my withdrawal I think I anticipated a dismissal from the union. It was like this: I was taken to observe an action to destroy *kulaks*. Armed bands of 'workers', who were not workers at all, would come and loot the property of the foes of the proletariat. They took away everything. Grain was loaded on horse carts; and the carts would stand outdoors in the rain and snow, the grain going to waste. It was the economic price of an historical experiment. I was a writer and could join a band to see for myself, in practice, not in the papers. I wanted to find out who was right, the spirit of the day or common sense. And conscience. They took grain away from a woman, Malcowa, who worked for a *kulak*. She went wild with despair. What could one do? Give the woman a hundredweight of grain lest she and her son should die of starvation in the coming winter. I went to see the organiser of the action so that I could write a report and get them to give her a sack of grain. They explained that I did not understand the dialectic of history. Some time later I learned that Malcowa had hanged herself. I unstuck my photo. I sent my membership card back to the union. I went down to the bottom.[30]

Although many writers had been inclined to shrug helplessly at the extraordinary spectacle of a communist take-over in Poland, a significant number had been prepared to go along with the new regime – particularly the ardent Stalinists like Putrament and enthusiastic young Polish intellectuals with no experience of the USSR, but also writers who had taken refuge in the USSR in 1939 and had seen at first hand just how ruthless the Soviet system was with its opponents. However, the drive to impose conformist *socrealizm* as part of the latest economic plan simply alienated writers. Juliusz Żuławski said:

The worst period for me was the period 1950–4. In this period, rather than risk new creative work of my own, I decided to translate English and American poetry. In 1951 for example, I ran to Byron (for political reasons); he was very much against British imperialism and against the Congress of Vienna. And so for many years I was a translator, and this was the case with a number of my friends. The classics were always considered safe: they were not dangerous; the authors were dead; they didn't write about Poland, about our situation. And it was possible to make a living out of the classics.[31]

For many writers the year 1949 was a professional and ideological crossroads at which they chose either to collaborate or to preserve their individual stance and remain aloof in increasing danger of poverty and harassment. Some, the lucky few like Tuwim, managed to preserve their independence simply because the Party made no effort to win them over.

Tadeusz Borowski (1922–51), who was to be the model for Beta in Miłosz's *The Captive Mind*, who was perhaps one of the most determined supporters of *socrealizm*, was among the first to see the severe limitations of the approved style in both literature and political life. Born in the Ukrainian town of Zhitomir, USSR, Borowski's parents had been imprisoned in Stalin's camps in 1926 – his father, a bookkeeper, was transported to Karelia to dig the White Sea Canal as a result of belonging to a Polish military organization during the First World War. Borowski lived with his aunt for several years and the family was reunited in Poland in 1932, when Soviet communists were exchanged for Poles by the Red Cross. After being educated by Franciscan monks he graduated from an underground high school in 1940, worked as a night-watchman and played the black market, publishing his poetry in underground magazines. A cycle of his poems was published by the underground in 1942. He had an active role in the wartime resistance but was arrested by mistake in 1943 and sent to Auschwitz, where he worked as a hospital orderly. He was later evacuated to Dachau and was liberated by the Americans on 1 May 1945. He lived in Munich and Murnau for a while, working for the Red Cross, returning to Poland in 1946 or 1947, where he joined the PPS.

His first book *Farewell to Maria* (1948) depicted the cruel, amoral street life of occupied Warsaw and the camps. The stories that seemed to finish him were those of his second volume, *World of Stone* (1948). This was a stunning, closely observed set of stories about his experiences in the Nazi concentration camps, steeped in despair and horror, depicting without flinching the choice to be made if a prisoner were to survive the camps. They displayed a brutal nihilism, and bitter realism. Although on the surface his writing was a graphic and detailed depiction of the camps, the amorality of his observation was at odds with the view of the world the Party wanted to present. Criticism of this collection led to a mental crisis and soon, in an effort to find a new and satisfying direction and a reason for persevering with his life he became a frantically active journalist and cultural worker and a convinced *socrealist*, and for his efforts he received a state literary prize. If the strain of trying to record the unspeakable had begun the process of driving him mad, the strain of trying to live the 'new life' of communist culture finished the job. Borowski had joined the Communist Party in 1948 and become an enthusiastic and highly active supporter of the new regime. But he came to understand that his view of the senselessness and catastrophic quality of his wartime experience, the failure of the Party to provide any deep-seated answer to his probing of the darkest side of human nature, and his failure to see any real solution in communism, had only one possible conclusion. He had embraced communism as a rigid moral form in an effort to give shape to what he saw as an immoral and pointless world.

In 1949 Borowski went back to Germany as a press officer attached to the Polish military mission. He was still unable to reconcile himself to the post-Holocaust world, unable to find anything but emptiness within himself, unable to realize the huge hopes of personal fulfilment he had placed in the Party, unwilling to accept the reality of life under communism or to believe that it was for Stalinism the world had waited and fought. The effort of continued political activism at the height of the Cold War, the arrest of one of his best friends by the Polish Security Service, and Borowski's own involvement in an espionage mission of some sort all proved too much and he gassed himself in Warsaw on 1 July 1951.[32]

The warm breeze of reform had been blowing very gently through Poland even before Stalin's death and it is clear that change was coming to Poland, whether the Party liked it or not. This point was made by the Catholic journal *Tygodnik Powszechny*. The paper had started publication in Kraków several weeks before the end of the Second World War, published by the Polish Catholic primate's office (Metropolitan Curia) and supported by a number of Catholic intellectuals. For a long while it was the only genuine Catholic independent weekly newspaper, and while it was initially non-political, in 1946 it sharply criticized the Marxist ideas of the new authorities from a very Catholic moral standpoint. In 1953 all Polish newspapers were instructed to print laudatory comment on the recently deceased Stalin. The editor of *Tygodnik Powszechny*, Jerzy Turowicz, failed to comply. In March 1953 police occupied the journal's premises, arrested Turowicz and prevented publication. The journal was taken away from the Metropolitan Curia and handed over to Pax, who moved in their own staff and resumed publication under new editorial guidelines. The new editorial board included Professor Tadeusz Lehr-Spławiński, Professor Andrzej Mycielski, Jan Dobraczyński, Anna Morawska and Jan Prokop. In their hands the paper languished for several years before it was handed back to the original editorial team. After the March 1954 Party congress, the police were given additional resources, and provisions were made to tighten the censorship laws again. The Party had made it clear they were prepared to tolerate licensed criticism, but nobody could yet act with impunity. Even so, the Polish Stalinists had clearly hesitated: the Catholic editors of *Tygodnik Powszechny* were not shot, did not disappear. It was possible to challenge the Party and live.

Khrushchev's disclosures about Stalin's crimes at the Twentieth Congress of the Soviet Communist Party in February 1956 unveiled an ongoing crisis among Polish communists by opening up the dubious nature of their alliance with Moscow, by showing the political realities behind the 'inevitable march of history' and by revealing the very low level of ideological thought within the Party – a factor most writers and intellectuals were already well aware of. But by the time of Khrushchev's revelations, the Polish writers, particularly the revisionists within the Party, had been steadily working towards change for nearly two years. Writers and intellectuals on the left who had gone along with the idea of building communism as part of rebuilding Poland, knew that things had gone badly adrift. Ważyk, Miłosz, Brandys, Kott, Słonimski,

Tuwim, Jastrun, Gałczyński, Andrzejewski and Konwicki saw that the prospects for independent Polish literature and culture under Soviet-style communism were increasingly bleak. Some, like Przyboś and Herbert, continued to write, but refused to publish, waiting for better times. They all agreed that the war on illiteracy, opening up the educational system to the entire population, mass publication of the classics and cheap large-scale publication of new works by living writers were progressive policies. However, the literature of *partyjność* (Party-mindedness), no matter how imperfectly adopted, did not interest the *inteligencja* readership, bored the relatively undiscriminating new mass readership, satisfied writers not at all and, ironically, was hardly a thing of delight even to the Party. For these writers the actuality of communism came nowhere near their idea of socialism, and their dreams of an independent Poland were not satisfied by the peculiar satellite life of the People's Republic of Poland.

Almost immediately after Stalin's death in 1953, and in spite of its bungling of the *Tygodnik Powszechny* affair, the Party relaxed its policy on *socrealizm*. At the Eleventh Session of the Council of Culture and Art in February 1954, Minister of Culture Władysław Sokorski, who had been described by Stefan Staszewski as 'foaming at the mouth' over opposition to the introduction of *socrealizm* at the 1949 writers' conference, now revealed his distaste for attempts to direct literature or intervene in cultural and creative processes.[33] He admitted that *socrealizm* (which he had introduced at the Fourth ZLP Congress in 1949) had been a mistake and that the basis for such literature did not yet exist in Poland. He criticized prevailing Party orthodoxy on *socrealizm*, saying that there could never be any such 'definite artistic school or style or recipe' for creative literature. While the idea of *socrealizm* was still valid it had been clumsily implemented and had stifled the individual 'free development' necessary to underpin objective truth. He also admitted that the Party's insistence on content over form had been misguided, and promised that the system of Party directives to writers would now cease. Sokorski's comments (*Przegląd Kulturalny*, 22–9 April 1954), along with supporting arguments from Hertz, Kott and Przyboś (*Życie Literackie*, 2 May 1954) opened up serious and unusually public debate. The discussion attracted critical comment from the loyal Stalinists Grzegorz Lasota, Kruczkowski (*Twórczość*, July 1954, and *Życie Literackie*, 13 June 1954) and Putrament (*Życie Literackie*, 19 June 1955). They saw Party cultural policy in a far more favourable light and claimed rather weakly that only the system of 'incentives' to writers was misguided. Within the ZLP the debate dominated the annual conference in June 1954. A tense period of watching and waiting followed as the argument rumbled on into the following year: it was clear from Sokorski's speech that the Party was uncertain of itself, but that change was possible.

The real question was: who had the nerve to set about making changes? Many writers sensed a growing opportunity. For those writers who had been in the Party, or who were still members, the frustration of inactivity was intolerable. They felt the Party should have taken the lead, but when it did not they realized they would have to summon the will to organize and force the pace. In January 1955 Leszek Kołakowski, then a young lecturer at Warsaw University, wrote in *Nowa Kultura* to protest at the primitive nonsense that masqueraded as ideological thinking, at the crudity of Party language in reducing Marxist literature and thinking to tired phrases, second-hand slogans and meaningless jargon. He also protested at the primitive categories of thought and dogmatism that limited perception, understanding and cognition, talents needed not just to solve existing problems, but to uncover and identify new problems for solution. Kołakowski complained that most writers were paralysed by fear of the censor. As far as Kołakowski was concerned, the more the Party acknowledged different views and shared power with the *technokracja* the more stable Poland's economy would become: as it was, the *technokracja* felt frustrated, abused, constricted socially and politically, their professional work made difficult if not impossible by inefficient central planning.[34]

The ideological vacuum and the flurry of activity by revisionist writers led to a rejuvenation of the ZLP (which had largely fallen silent after 1949) at their spring 1955 congress. Lively public debate from the writing community was something the authorities claimed they desired, but which they soon realized they could not control. The difference between the vague ideological recommendations and exhortations of the Third ZZLP Congress of 1947 and the hard-headed assault of the Fourth ZLP Congress in 1949 had been noted in Roman Szydłowski's article 'Nowe drogi polskiej literatury' (The New Ways of Polish Literature, *Trybuna Ludu* (29 January 1949)), but critical comment on the changes to ZLP and the adoption of *socrealizm* could not emerge in print until the thaw was under way. A great number of writers now made their feelings on Party interference clear: Artur Sandauer in *Nowa Kultura* (March 1956), Julian Przyboś in *Nowa Kultura* (April 1956), Adam Ważyk in *Nowa Kultura* (October 1956), J.Stanisławski in *Po Prostu* (25 March 1956).

In March 1955 *Przegląd Kulturalny* published new poems by Słucki, one of which was provocatively entitled 'Rehabilitation'; *Twórczość* published new poems by Jastrun and Hertz in which anti-Stalin allusions were clearly intended; *Po Prostu* ran a number of sympathetic articles about the AK. In April and May 1955 the young critic Jan Błoński assessed the literary achievements of the post-war years and the Party's drive for *socrealizm*. He argued, in a series of articles published in *Życie Literacki*, that between 1949 and 1955, under the '*socrealist* Five-Year-Plan for Literature' Polish publishing houses had flooded the poetry market with appalling pseudo-verse, but had nevertheless actually managed to reduce the amount of verse appearing in print. He also pointed out that, as the result of imposed Party schematism, no new poets had made their début with a first volume of verse in the years 1950 to 1954.[35]

On 21 August 1955 Adam Ważyk published his 'Poem for Grown-Ups' in *Nowa Kultura*, a journal which had already published full accounts of the ZLP's spring congress. Ważyk's poem was a bombshell, and the magazine, much to the Party's embarrassment, sold out at once. Ważyk had been sent to the new industrial city of Nowa Huta to research an article about the life of industrial shock workers. It was this visit, the images, phrases and conversations with workers, that forced him to break with the 'paper myth' of the successful creation of a communist city to house the New Man, and which formed the material of his poem. Ważyk's visit to Nowa Huta (literally, New Factory) was meant to be a pilgrimage to a special place in the iconography of Polish communism. The Party had decided to build this first-ever communist city, centred on the massive steelworks, as a way of watering down neighbouring Kraków's bourgeois-conservative character. There was no sound economic rationale for the venture: coal had to come from Silesia, iron ore had to be hauled over 1,000 miles from the USSR. The decision to build Nowa Huta was taken in February 1949, the foundations of the steelworks were laid in April 1950, by which time there were already sixty work brigades on site: an uncharacteristic dynamism which was to mark the growth of the city as a whole.

By 1955 the city had swallowed up several nearby villages and there were over 70,000 inhabitants and 30,000 construction workers living on estates of up to 20,000 residents. Nowa Huta was designed as a visual hymn to Labour. The main streets are the road to Kraków, a street of housing estates and blocks of flats, and the massive boulevard Aleja Lenina leading to the Lenin steel mill. The town boasted Europe's largest statue of Lenin. In line with the idea that there would be only one class under communism, there was no shopping centre, no proletarian suburb and no middle-class suburb. As the new life would be collective it was initially planned that each flat would have a loudspeaker in it, that each district would have its own day-care centres and nurseries, a large canteen and a central kitchen. There was also a theatre, a hospital, an art gallery and a Klub MPiK. No car parks were provided because it was believed that cycle paths would be of more use to the new workers. The assimilation of large numbers of poorly educated agricultural workers into city life and to industrial demands was always problematic, and the city's large-scale brawls, alcoholism, prostitution, theft and gang warfare were (and still are) legendary.

The design of the Huta Lenina Steel works had been made available to Poland by the USSR in an agreement dated 1948: it was one of the largest steel mills in Europe and became operational in July 1954. By the mid-1960s the mill was producing over six million tons of steel per year – one third of Poland's total steel output. What no one knew at the time was that the design of the mill had been purchased by the Russians from the USA at the turn of the century. It was outdated even then. It could produce only low-grade steel and spewed a lethal fume of toxins and acid rain on to the surrounding countryside, causing massive health problems in nearby Kraków. By 1990 bronchial complaints in the Kraków-Nowa Huta area were 30 per cent higher, and sick leave 40 per cent higher than in the rest of Poland.[36]

Ważyk (1905–82) had been born in Warsaw of a middle-class Jewish family and had worked as a translator from Latin, French and Russian. An avant-gardist of the pre-war poetry circle and an enthusiastic Cubist poet, he had made his début in 1924. He switched to fiction in the 1930s but returned to poetry with the rise of Hitler. With the German invasion his poetry had become increasingly communist and documentary. He had spent the war in the USSR where he co-edited *Nowe Widnokręgi*. He returned to Poland as an officer of the Soviet-backed AL and a devotee of *socrealizm*, claiming that his poetry was purified of the language and concerns of the inter-war period. He co-founded *Kuźnica* (where his function was that of ideological watch-dog) and edited *Twórczość* 1950–4. Throughout the Stalinist period his credit was high. In 1952 he was awarded the state literary prize and the PEN prize in 1953. He viewed himself as a severe and intellectually aggressive theoretician, a Marxist propagandist and advocate of *socrealizm*. Although he had written very little of his Cubist poetry after the war (and that was judged poor), he had instead produced a great deal of prose about the role of artists under communism, and about how Polish writers needed to overcome their 'pre-war Sarmatian sensibility'; he was a classic example of the effect that *socrealizm* could have on a creative imagination and had once described Stalin's mind as a 'river of wisdom'. He was an opponent of all 'rotten bourgeois liberalism' and one of the most intensely disliked of the Party writers.

Ważyk, who had returned from the USSR at the end of the war in military uniform and with an enormous pistol strapped to his thigh, a style of dress he persisted with for some time, had up to this point been a staunch Party member. Now he denounced the simplistic brutality of Stalinist thought, referred to Poland's communist literature as a 'five-year-old youngster which should be educated and which should educate', derided the 'achievements' of Polish Stalinism, emphasized the material, intellectual and spiritual poverty of the industrialization programme, depicted the peasant workers of Nowa Huta as inert and cultureless and raged against the hopelessness and helplessness of what he called the 'un-human Poland, howling with boredom on December nights':

> All this is not new.
> Old is the Cerberus of socialist morality.
> Fourier, the dreamer, charmingly foretold
> that lemonade would flow in seas.

Does it not flow?
They drink salt-water,
crying:
'lemonade!'
returning home secretly
to vomit.[37]

In spite of his poem, Ważyk remained a Party member, still saw himself as 'with the Party' and wished to channel progress and reform through the Party. The Party could not understand how such a slavish Stalinist could have become an 'anti-socialist element'. Ważyk refused to admit that publication of the poem was a mistake, so the Party sacked Paweł Hoffman, the magazine's editor, and most of the editorial board. Jakub Berman failed to get Ważyk expelled from the Party, however, and had to settle for getting him reprimanded. The Party criticized Ważyk's 'petit-bourgeois gesture' and labelled the poem an 'anti-Party composition, a harmful and distorted picture of our reality, an insult to the working class'. However, the Party was disconcerted to find that workers and Party members from all over Poland refused to sign spontaneous petitions condemning the poem, and instead endorsed Ważyk's observations, saying that faults should not be hushed up and that the facts of life in Nowa Huta were well known. Thousands of illicit copies of the poem circulated from hand to hand and made Ważyk a popular figure, and fed into the increasingly bold stream of revisionist criticism directed at the Party. Before the end of 1955 censorship had virtually collapsed, and demoralized and confused censors were debating whether to dissolve their office voluntarily.[38]

On 12 March 1956 Bolesław Bierut, Polish leader since 1948, died of natural causes in Moscow (many said he died of a stroke on being told the full extent of Stalin's crimes). On 20 March the PZPR (Polish United Workers' Party) elected its new first secretary, Edward Ochab. He was a communist of long standing, approved by Khrushchev and generally thought to be Moscow's man. However, caught between Soviet fear of democratization and nationalism in Poland and the increasingly vociferous demands of the Polish people, Ochab began a cautious process of liberalization, including the rehabilitation of numerous political prisoners. Ochab hoped he had done enough to calm the public and the writers, but what was to become the 'thaw' of 1956 was well under way. By the end of 1956 it was clear that the communist bid for totalitarian control had more or less failed, though for the next thirty-three years the Party consistently failed to replace this strategy with any other.

3

JERZY ANDRZEJEWSKI

Jerzy Andrzejewski is probably Poland's best-known modern novelist. His lifetime and professional career spanned the entire post-war communist period and virtually the whole Polish experience of the twentieth century: partition, independence, abbreviated democratic rule, military government, Nazi occupation, communism, opposition, Solidarność, Martial Law – only the collapse of communism and the start of the new democracy are missing. His life, his novel *Popiół i diament* (Ashes and Diamonds, 1948) and his trajectory as a Polish intellectual are important on a number of levels and essential to any attempt to understand the massive cultural, political, economic and intellectual changes that have taken place in eastern Europe since 1945. In 1993 the tenth anniversary of his death passed unnoticed outside Poland: in Poland what little comment there was proved guarded and cautious. Not everybody loved his writing, and his pre-war association with the right wing and his early support of communism set him apart. Many felt that he had not entirely redeemed himself with his later oppositionist activities. He had become even less acceptable with the anti-communist backlash after 1989. As with most writers from east central Europe, his professional career cannot be separated from his personal biography and from the political activities of the creative intelligentsia, and in order to understand something of the importance of his literary works it is necessary to see him not only as a powerful and original writer, but as an active and influential political figure in a very particular and difficult climate.

Andrzejewski was born in Warsaw on 19 August 1909 and died there on 19 April 1983. He had been a student at the Jan Zamoyski Gymnazjum, and later studied Polish philology at Warsaw University in the years 1927–30. He was also associated with small and frequently unpleasant right-wing Catholic-nationalist magazines. He made his literary début with a story called 'Kłamstwa' (Lying) in the right-wing anti-Semitic Warsaw daily *ABC*, for which he worked as a theatre and book critic. However, he was particularly associated with the right-wing, pro-Nazi, anti-Semitic weekly paper *Prosto z Mostu* (Straight Out), which was edited by Stanisław Piasecki, a member of the ONR-Falangist Party. In spite of this early connection with the Polish extreme right wing, Andrzejewski was no anti-Semite.[1]

Andrzejewski's literary career really began when *ABC* collected his short stories in a volume called *Drogi Nieuniknione* (Unavoidable Roads, 1936). Two years later his novel *Ład Serca* (Mode of the Heart, 1938), which had appeared as a magazine serial, was taken up and published to wide acclaim. The novel set an impressive moral conflict against a solemn and rather grand night-time backdrop. The central character of the novel was a priest and the 'action' was his late-night conversation with a murderer. Almost inevitably Andrzejewski was labelled a Conradian moralist, a conservative and a 'Catholic writer', which, as Miłosz has said, in Catholic Poland is no small thing. Short though very intense, Andrzejewski's period as a 'religious Catholic' established him as a writer of considerable talent. In 1939 Andrzejewski, among other awards, received the Polish Academy of Literature's Young Writers' Prize, and by public poll was also awarded the *Wiadomości Literackie* Readers' Prize. However, the war disturbed what was clearly a promising literary career. During the German occupation Andrzejewski became a member of the AK, ran a small underground magazine and was widely regarded as a moral authority in the unwritten patriotic code of relations with Germans and the conduct of the underground. Andrzejewski became an important part of the culture of conspiracy.

Andrzejewski threw himself into the reconstruction of post-war Poland. In the years 1946–7 he worked in Kraków and was elected president of the Kraków ZZLP (Trade Union of Polish Writers). Andrzejewski's first post-war book appeared under conditions that were absolutely different from anything that he and millions of other Poles could have predicted in 1938. *Noc* (Night, 1946), a series of short stories written during the war, was not particularly adventurous in terms of style or political content and told simply and effectively of the horrors of the occupation.[2] The book received the 1946 City of Kraków Literary Prize. In the years 1948–52 he lived in Szczecin before returning to Warsaw to become editor in chief of *Przegląd Kulturalny*. He became chairman of the Central Board of the ZLP in 1949, and in 1952 was awarded the state Banner of Labour Order as a reward for his 'social achievements'. In the years 1952–7 he also sat as a deputy in the Sejm and his circle of distinguished Party writer comrades included Ważyk, Wirpsza, Jastrun, Żuławski, Bocheński, Woroszylski and Hertz.

Popiół i diament (Ashes and Diamonds), which had originally appeared under the title *Zaraz po wojnie* (Right after the War) in serial form in *Odrodzenie* through 1947, was published in book form in 1948 and was at once hugely successful. It was awarded the *Odrodzenie* Prize in 1948. With the help of Andrzej Wajda's film (1957), which Andrzejewski co-directed, it became Andrzejewski's most famous work both in the west and in Poland. There can be little doubt that the appearance of *Ashes and Diamonds* was one of the major publishing events of the decade. It is the most widely reprinted of Andrzejewski's works and has become a classic of modern Polish literature. Along with Borowski's *Pożegnanie z Maria* (Farewell to Mary, 1948), Nałkowska's *Medaliony* (Medallions, 1946) and Miłosz's *Ocalenie* (Rescue, 1945) it stands out from most of the 'rubble literature' of the immediate post-war period, which was obsessed with simply and perhaps naively detailing the horrors of the Occupation. In the year 1948–9 was a crucial time in the life of the post-war regime, and Andrzejewski's novel is important both for what it reveals openly, for what it does not talk about at all and for the ambiguous place it occupies in the literary and political debate of those years.

Ashes and Diamonds takes place in a Polish town (probably Kraków) in the spring of 1945. It is set on the last day of the war and the action unfolds against the declaration that the German army is about to lay down its weapons in surrender. The novel shows a range of Polish characters in these final moments of war and the first moments of peace. It is a portrait of the very ambiguous and many-layered transition from war to peace, from the military society of pre-war Poland with its *szlachta* cultural and political values, to the communist values imposed at bayonet-point by the Red Army at the end of the war. It is a portrait of Poland making the very painful transition from the pre-war society of massive peasantry, small middle class and tiny but powerful nobility, to a new society of 'workers' and Party bureaucrats. The move from war to peace is not the end of violence, however; it is merely a shift from one kind of violence to another: hostilities between the incoming communists and those whose loyalties lay with 'old Poland' and the government in exile were taken up with a ferocious and intense savagery which both sides had learned and practised against the Nazis. For many it was a continuation in practice of the 'war against two enemies – Russia and Germany', already deeply embedded in the Polish political consciousness.

Ashes and Diamonds is a key text summing up many of the ambiguities, changes of attitude and the sacrifices necessary to accommodate the new regime. The subject of the book, the civil war that marked the transition to 'peace' in Poland, was still unfinished when the novel appeared. Andrzejewski probably focused on the issue of political assassination after the killing of General Karol Świerczewski, General 'Walter' of the French-Belgian volunteer contingent of the International Brigade in the Spanish Civil War. He had been a founder member of the Central Bureau of the Polish Communist Party in the USSR, a member of the Central Committee of the PPR and also of the National Land Council. In 1946 he became deputy minister of defence, served on the Sejm's Military Affairs Committee, was Inspector of the Army, commander of the Poznań military district and representative of the Polish military on the International Control Commission in Berlin. This central and very important member of the new authority was killed by 'Ukrainian nationalists' who attacked a convoy on an inspection tour of the eastern borders near the town of Baligród on 28 March 1947. He was given a state funeral on 1 April 1947. Roman Catholic funeral rites were observed by the chaplain-general of the Polish Army, a church choir sang *De profundis*, and *Salve regina* was intoned over the open grave.

In addressing a subject so closely bound up with the AK (Home Army, 1941–5) Andrzejewski was playing with fire. The AK was an umbrella term for a wide range of non-communist and anti-communist partisan groups who fought right through the war, some of whom continued to resist the new regime until 1947. With more than 300,000 members, the AK dwarfed the communist resistance movement, and as its membership owed allegiance to the Polish government in exile, rather than the incoming communist government, it was seen as a major threat to the new order. The AK were not the mindless Fascist wreckers described by Party propaganda. The fact was that in the period after the ambiguous dissolution of the AK up to the end of 1947, although an estimated 60,000 people continued armed struggle and violent opposition to communism, probably the only sizeable anti-communist organization was not the AK as such but its components, WiN (Freedom and Independence), Nie (No) and DSZ (Armed Forces Delegation). As a result of two amnesties in the period 1945–7 over 70,000 AK members left hiding and attempted to resume normal life: of these some 17,000 were arrested, tried and imprisoned. Many did not survive their brutal treatment at the hands of the authorities. Between 1945 and 1947 the assassination of PPR members, government officials and supporters averaged 200 per month, reaching a peak in May 1945 with 600 assassinations, and a second peak in September 1946 with 360 deaths. Although the AK had been officially dissolved by its own high command in January 1945, in June of that year sixteen AK leaders were charged with anti-Soviet activity and tried in Moscow – all had pleaded guilty. For most of the post-war period it was simply not allowed to portray or refer to the AK as anything more than Fascist bandits, wreckers and murderers. In spite of this propaganda war (perhaps even because of it), the spirit of the AK was to inform much of the dissident activity of the 1970s and 1980s: the AK anchor symbol PW (Poland Fights) was seen as graffiti throughout Martial Law.[3]

Ashes and Diamonds portrays a range of characters and their immediate social circle: Andrzej, son of Judge Kossecki, a member of an independent right-wing resistance group; Alek, the younger son, a member of a gang of juvenile thugs who pretend that they are part of a resistance movement; Maciek, an ex-student from Warsaw, in town to carry out the assassination of Szczuka for the AK. There are also the opportunists in the local government set-up, and in the local catering industry. There are representatives of the displaced and largely dispossessed nobility: Mme Staniewicz, the Puciatyckis and Teleżynski – all of whom found the war distasteful and who regard the incoming communists as upstart boors beneath contempt. More importantly there is the wretchedly pliable judge Kossecki, recently released from the Nazi concentration camp, who, although widely regarded as a lawyer without a stain on his character, was in fact, under the name Rybycki (*ryby*, fish), a concentration camp *kapo*, a trusty. The moral condemnation of these people resides, particularly towards the end of the novel, in the figure of judge Kossecki. His moral collapse is indicative of the wider failure and 'the bankruptcy of the petit bourgeoisie'; his plea that wartime has its own morality is set up to show that without the guiding light of communism, humanity is nothing more than a slave to circumstance. On the other side of the equation there is the self-righteous communist Podgórski. There is Szczuka, the Party official recently liberated from a concentration camp. And we also hear of Maria, a communist martyr who, in contrast to Kossecki, helped her fellow prisoners selflessly and died in Ravensbrück. We are told that Maria's devoted communist husband often thinks of her and cherishes her memory.

In setting up his gallery of characters Andrzejewski went to great lengths to show the deep divisions that had emerged in Polish society at the end of the war. Again and again the network of family and friends is riven by factionalism that had its roots deep in Polish history. *Ashes and Diamonds* was something of a departure from Andrzejewski's earlier books. Although it indicated misgivings about the communists and the situation at the end of the war, it was clearly not hostile to the new regime – its view of Polish class politics, its portraits of the resistance and the communists all made its attempted position quite clear. It condemned the old order and the continuing mainly right-wing elements of the underground movement and depicted the underground army as patriotic but tragically misguided. Andrzej, having bungled the assassination of Szczuka, goes to see 'the Colonel' – a cavalry officer who is very clearly a member of the pre-war military. After analysing what went wrong the colonel treats Andrzej to a disquisition on 'moral intelligence':

'We're living and fighting under very difficult and complex circumstances. But the war years, which were the testing years for everyone, have taught us that things have to be regarded in their elementary, basic set-up. There's no time for subtle discrimination, it must be simple and clear. Good is good, and evil evil. You agree? . . . So there's one thing we must get clear in the present situation. The Second World War is coming to an end. That's obvious. Another two or three days, perhaps a week – and it will be over. But we did not foresee an end like this. We thought that not only would Germany come out of the war defeated, but Russia too. Things have turned out rather differently. In today's set-up we Poles are divided into two categories: those who have betrayed the freedom of Poland and those who do not wish to do so. The first want to submit to Russia, we do not. They want communism, we do not. They want to destroy us, we must destroy them. A battle is going on between us, a battle that has only just started . . . What were you fighting for? Wasn't it for the freedom of Poland? But did you imagine a Poland ruled by blind agents carrying out orders from the Kremlin and

established by Russian bayonets? What about your colleagues, your contemporaries? How many of them died? What for? In the end how can people like
you and me – alive and still at liberty – how can we show our solidarity with our
friends if we draw back half way? . . . Now take Szczuka . . . Who's Szczuka? One
of the intelligentsia, a trained engineer, a communist, an excellent organiser into
the bargain. And he's a man who knows what he wants. Now he's working for the
Party in the provinces, but tomorrow if nothing changes, he'll hold a responsible
State job. He may be a Minister the day after tomorrow. Let's say he's an idealist.
He was put on trial several times before the war and was sent to gaol. He was two
years in a prison camp. He's the more dangerous. We're not worried by careerists.
When the time comes they'll leave the sinking ship like rats. It's a waste to risk
men like you – and bullets – on them. The cost is too high. But when it's a
question of ideas which bring us enslavement and death, then our reply can only
be death. The usual laws of battle. History will be the final judge as to who was
right. We have already decided . . . ' He inhaled his cigarette smoke and added
with emphasis . . . 'because we have already chosen.'[4]

Andrzej who has doubts about what he is doing, says that he wants to
be honest rather than intelligent about the armed struggle. The colonel
replies:

'Moral intelligence is precisely what I mean . . . Like you, I'm a soldier and carry
out orders of my superior officers. Blindly? No, I believe they're right, because as
a soldier I'm also a man and do not forgo the right to judge the world I live in. I
assure you, lieutenant, that a man who does not want to be a judge does not want
to be a man. And if one has the courage to judge, then loyalty towards oneself
applies too. It's a matter, if you'll forgive me using such a big word, of conscience.
That's all!'[5]

The colonel's position is almost certainly that of the many of the London-
backed AK, but equally certainly of the anti-communist WiN; the outline of
the noble, officer-caste style is easily apparent. In this passage Andrzejewski
makes a series of points, one of which is that after years of war, the ability to
decide clearly for oneself has become clouded, that it has become extremely
difficult to see the incoming regime, for a whole variety of reasons, as something with which it might be possible to co-operate. The moral position is the
important one, and that is simplified enormously by the Colonel. Yet
strangely the moral/political language used here is almost identical to that
used by Michnik in his essays on co-operation with the military government of
General Jaruzelski.[6] Thought is moral rather than political, and great stress is
laid on fidelity, honour, loyalty. Little serious political thought takes place in
laying out plans for an alternative future. It is a consistent feature of Polish
politics that the restoration of the previous incarnation of Poland takes
precedence over everything else.

Andrzejewski also shows how the moral damage to Poland's youth by the occupation fed into the chaos of the civil war. Andrzej's younger brother Alek is a member of an underground group – in fact they are little more than a gang meeting in a cave that was once their schoolboy hide-out. In an argument about finance their leader, Jurek, shoots and kills Janusz. Marcin remonstrates with Jurek: 'We were going to fight for Poland, for good and noble causes . . . Don't laugh, you said so yourself.'[7] They have just come through a war, which as it was visited upon Poland was very much concerned with notions of blood and race, but the effect of the war and the massive loss of human life has been to devalue. human life rather than elevate it. The good and noble causes of both sides slide into ugly, messy, personal disputes. This group, who plan to fight for 'freedom and justice', whose childish password is 'Freedom', remain just a gang playing at resistance. Beyond a childish brutality and spiteful variety of Fascism they have no sense of politics, no ideology that goes beyond the purely national. And that is part of Andrzejewski's point: because of the peculiarities of Polish history there is no socio-political agreement to resolve differences without recourse to violence:

'But what are we going to do now? With all this on our minds, with all this blood . . . '
  'Don't exaggerate. Why talk about it? Blood! Blood doesn't mean much.'
  'Jurek, please don't talk like that. You shouldn't!'
  'Of course blood matters, but not the blood of our enemies. We're going to shoot them down like dogs. That's our purpose and our justification. And the fact that he went first was only an accident . . . '[8]

Other members of the *inteligencja* do not come out of this situation too well either. The restaurateur Słomka, Mayor Świecki, Deputy Mayor and architect Weychert, the socialist chairman of the town council Kalicki, the editor of the local newspaper Pawlicki, are all morally flexible, that is they are corruptible. Drewnowski the mayor's secretary and Pieniążek the journalist show themselves to be little more than malleable, grafters, hangers-on who pander to the incoming communists with as much or as little conscience as they toady (*każdzić*) to the remaining members of the aristocracy. Indeed, Pieniążek hints very heavily that Pawlicki also collaborated with the Nazis. It is there in their names too, since rather in the manner of a morality play, some of the names have meanings indicating the characters of those concerned: Słomka – a straw; Świecki – worldly, mundane; Drewnowski – wooden, log; Pieniążek – small change. The values of the petit-bourgeois class – the 'rotten bourgeoisie' as Major Wrona (crow) of the security police calls them – may have collapsed in the war and in the camps, but Andrzejewski is saying that in spite of this, the values and style of this class, backed by the popular legitimacy of the

London government, still inform the political, social and moral patterns of the new Poland. Indeed we can see this in the way the official reception turns into a drunken debauch, a parade of snobbery, sentimentalism, furtive plotting, rampant opportunism and cynicism.

Nowhere are the potential and complexities contained within the moment of peace more in evidence than in the discussion between Major Wrona and Comrade Świecki:

'I know one thing. When we were in the forests, we imagined all this very differently. Some of our supporters are getting too tame and comfortable. If this goes on much longer, we shall lose the revolution. What's needed is to shake them up, like this.' He held up his clenched fists. 'Instead of doing away with the class war, we ought to intensify it, catch our enemy by the throat, because if we don't kill them in time, they'll put a knife in our backs.'

Świecki nodded with an understanding smile.

'That's all very well, major, but you're forgetting one thing. Politics isn't such a simple matter. At this stage we must first lessen various irritations.'

Wrona looked at him darkly.

'Whose? The kulaks? The landowners?'

'I'm speaking generally,' Świecki replied evasively. 'We must draw them to us, unite them with us.'

'But who?'

'What do you mean "Who?"' Świecki asked in surprise. 'The nation'.

Wrona's swarthy face darkened slightly.

'The nation? Comrade Świecki, do you really know the Polish nation, do you know what it's like and what it wants? Who do you want to unite? Those who think of nothing but pushing the workers and peasants back into poverty and degradation ? Or perhaps those who shoot from behind cover at our best men? Are they supposed to be the Polish nation?'

Świecki opened his hands. 'I understand your indignation, I myself was very upset about many incidents . . . '

'But you'd like to inscribe "Love one another, brother Poles" on the standard of the revolution?'

'The country's destroyed, the people are exhausted, we must think realistically.'

'No!' He brought his fist down on the table. 'That isn't the way, that's not the Bolshevik way. It's true our country is destroyed and the people are exhausted, but it looks to me as if you, Comrade Świecki, have no idea what great forces there are in this exhausted nation. These communist forces will grow and wake up in other people . . . ' His voice suddenly broke with almost boyish grief. 'It makes my heart ache to remember so many comrades who won't see this . . . '9

It may have been naive of Andrzejewski to suppose that Świecki's version of socialism would survive that of Wrona. Major Wrona has had a 'wholly admirable past in the underground movement', which is shorthand for belonging to the AL (People's Army, the communist resistance) rather than to the AK: his style of language, his use of the word *kulaks*, give him away as a creature made by the Party and its Moscow alliance.[10]

The novel was unusual in that it showed conflict between the forces supposed to be good and pure, and the 'Fascistic wreckers' of the AK. But, even though Andrzejewski had simplified the complexity and range of political opinion within the AK and had clearly skewed the political struggle between the AK and the communists to fit his own personal and still rather Catholic moral scheme, what he had also shown was that between the idealistic extremists of both left and right, there moved a host of confused, demoralized, exhausted Poles, many of whom saw no point in being other than opportunist. Further, the novel had as one of its main characters Maciek, a member of the AK.[11] Maciek Chełmicki (the name conjures up the word *hełm*, helmet) represents the moral confusion and political chaos that haunted Poland in those years. Presumably Maciek is a member of WiN, but one of the problems of the novel is that this is not clear, and no distinctions are made between the the various political strands that made up the AK. It looks as if Maciek stands for the whole of the AK, while the great range of AK opinion, and the fact that most members had already laid down their arms, goes unrepresented. At one point Maciek attempts to explain to his commander the difference between killing during the war and killing now: 'But what is it I'm supposed to sacrifice everything for? I knew in those days. But now? You tell me! What do I have to kill that man for? And others? And go on killing? What for?'[12] His attitude has changed, he has met a girl, he wants to leave the underground movement, settle down, have a normal life. In his stumbling, incoherent way he is trying to find a solution not only to his own problems but those of the whole country. In the end, however, he abdicates responsibility and decides to accept someone else's solution. His agreement to commit one last murder leads to his own death.

In Maciek we have someone who is trying to reject the old order (or parts of it) and who is trying to work out a new way forward. His efforts are thrown into sharp relief by the scene around him: in the hotel pompous politicians and leaders, *arriviste* local politicians and brutal local police meet in one room of the hotel. In the bar meanwhile the drunken, snobbish, plotting, hysterical old order dances a conga against a gross distortion of a Chopin Polonaise ('the one that goes Tam-ta-tam, ta-ra-tata-tata-tatam'). Of the eighteen Chopin Polonaises, Kotowicz calls specifically for the A-Flat 'Heroic' Polonaise, Op.53 (1842), but its highly charged, nationalistic overtones are parodied and distorted by the tired, bored musicians.[13] Meanwhile brutalized youngsters, liars and self-seekers returned from the camps attempt to work out some new *modus vivendi* for themselves in which their future is bright and their past is obscure. The old moral order has been turned inside out. The first day of 'Peace' marks the onset of an assault by communist Poles on traditional Polish cultural and hierarchical values, on Polish beliefs and myths about Poland and its place in the world. It takes great courage to carve a path through all this, to decide how the future will be, either as a communist politician or as a member of the anti-communist underground, or as an independent individual building or rebuilding a private life from the ruins. Maciek and his girlfriend Krystyna are ordinary Poles. If Maciek is a defeatist, then so is Krystyna.

Andrzejewski makes much of the heroic defeatism implicit in the references (quotation and allusion) to classical Romantic poetry and to the music of Chopin. He asks: is this like the defeats of the partition era? The novel is redolent of connections with Polish Romanticism in music and literature, indeed it takes its title from the poem 'Za kulisami' (Behind the Scenes) by Norwid (1821–83). Norwid's verses stand at the start of the book but are cut from the English translation:

> All around you, as from a charred splinter,
> Flaming rags let fall;
> Burning don't you know if you are free,
> Or if that which is yours may be lost?
> Will only ash remain, and chaos
> Blown by the storm? Or lying
> Beneath the ash will there be a starry diamond,
> Eternal victory's dawning.[14]

Indeed his use of the poem indicates very clearly that he wishes to consign evil to the ash and destruction of the past, and sees the possible moral victories of the socialist future as the diamonds hidden among the ash.

There are also passing references to the dramatist Juliusz Słowacki (1809–49). But perhaps the major reference to 'classical' Polish literature is in the scene where the banquet guests dance the conga to Chopin – that in itself is a direct reference to Polish classical literature. Wyspiański's play *Wesele* (The Wedding, 1901) is a still popular tale of the 'situation of the nation'. It shows an attempt by the Kraków *inteligencja* to bridge the cultural gap between gentry and the peasantry by a wedding between a peasant girl and a Kraków artist and is based on the carefully planned theatrical wedding which took place on 20 November 1900 when the poet Lucjan Rydel wed the peasant girl Jadwiga Mikołajczykowna. There is a scene in the play when at dawn the drunken wedding guests shamble grotesquely through a patriotic dance, out of the house and into the farmyard – a scene which Andrzejewski makes direct use of in his description of the hotel party on the evening before Maciek completes his assassination assignment.[15] These Romantic writers had their own independent and ironic grasp of the difficulties of Poland's situation. It is to them, rather than to images of the future, that Andrzejewski turns in trying to reconcile Poland to itself and its new rulers.

The Polish classics are a most peculiar and ultimately self-defeating set of references, since they point out very clearly that a Polish writer, a member of the *inteligencja*, could not easily imagine any Poland without those artistic and political traditions, that Polish tradition was deeply ingrained even among those who wished to accommodate the new regime. Andrzejewski, in his use of classical Romantic texts harks back to Poland's traditional anti-Russian feelings, and *szlachta* moral values. He reminds people of what they are giving up, implicitly contrasts the new order with the old, undercuts his own message of co-operation, affirms an ideal that is Polish not Russian, *szlachta* rather than proletarian or Party. At one point Kalicki and Szczuka discuss Poland's future under socialism:

'Do you honestly see no difference between the Soviet Union and Tsarist Russia?'
'Of course I do. It's a different system. I don't deny there are differences. But Russian imperialism and Russian aggression are the same. No, no!' he gesticulated, 'I know what you're going to say, but please spare me your propaganda. I know where I stand. The East will always be the East. That never changes. Anyhow, you'll see in a year or two. Poland won't exist any longer. Our country, our culture will all be lost, all of it . . . '
At this moment his voice broke painfully. He stopped.
Szczuka also said nothing for a time.
Kalicki shivered and sat up.
'I'm sorry for you, Jan,' he whispered at length. 'Life has beaten you.'
'Perhaps so,' he said in a controlled voice, 'but my life concerns me and me alone, whereas you're losing Poland.'[16]

Szczuka's last comment here is an ironic reference to the opening line of the Polish national anthem: 'Poland is not yet lost, as long as we are living . . .' Between them the resistance and the communists kill Szczuka and Maciek – the best and brightest, the most intelligent that either side has to offer. What they are left with are opportunists and drunks, rigid Stalinists, haughty and unyielding nobles, well-meaning but ignorant peasants, confused and tired workers; it is from these that the People's Poland will be built.

It must be said that the novel is badly flawed. Andrzejewski has doled out judgement, allocating right and wrong, according to the most superficial Marxist moral gloss. In true Romantic and Conradian fashion the communist heroes are solitary figures in a hostile environment, struggling with a lumpish, reactionary, un-responsive society which is caught up in trying to restore the past, and which lacks all vision of the future. The AK here bears the blame for death and destruction. Their sense of patriotism, their commitment to the cause, their courage and resilience all count for nothing because they have decided to resist the Party. The communists in the novel are not tortured by doubts in the way that Chełmicki is: only he experiences a longing for peace, a weariness of death and destruction, a desire to accept the situation as it is. But his doubts count for nothing because he has made a wrong choice. Only the AK fight on against the 'progressive' forces in order to carry out their misguided orders: it is the AK, not the Party, who are accused of suppressing their humanity and their compassion. The novel is also badly flawed in its depiction of Szczuka: we only know that he is a communist from what the author tells us about him, not from what Szczuka says or does. Drawing a communist character was a problem for Andrzejewski because for many to be a socialist was a failure of patriotism, a failure of Polishness: it was to be anti-Polish. In Poland nationalism often substituted for a more extended ideology of left and right, conservative and progressive. The idea of 'Poland' was invested during the partitions with all the power of ideology and all the mystery of a religious experience.

Although it is possible to show very broadly that *Ashes and Diamonds* went along with the notion that all art should now 'contribute to the ideological transformation and education of the workers in the spirit of socialism',[17] it managed to conform to a version of reality that was still close enough to the truth to disconcert those who believed in the Party line and who favoured total conversion to *socrealizm*. The novel offended the idea of *socrealizm* on a number of levels. Given the way the Stalinists behaved, the terms 'socialist' and 'realist' were mutually exclusive. The last thing the communists of eastern Europe wanted was a literature that showed the reality, that probed the actuality of the communist take-over or the construction of a new version of class politics. This was especially so in Poland where the Party lacked all legitimacy. The novel did not adhere to the tenets of *socrealizm* in depicting the communists as wholly attractive and blameless heroes in action. Wrona is presented as a line-toeing, insensitive, dangerous blockhead. Kalicki, son of a wealthy landowning family from Kiev, expelled from university for his socialist ideas, later an important member of the Polish co-operative movement, a member of the PPS (Polish Socialist Party), a deputy to the inter-war Sejm, is shown as full of scruples and doubts about the communist road to power. Szczuka too, it would seem, is a communist in name only: what he thinks about communism, what his hopes, plans and dreams for Poland might be are never revealed to the reader. The Party people drink, wench, have friends outside the Party, have ex-wives. They are not morally perfect, and because of this they are not Party literature banalities.

Also, it must be said that the portrait of the Party heroes as solitary figures was probably deeply questionable in Stalinist and *socrealizm* terms.[18] In this novel there are no positive and clearly identifiable socialist heroes, no absolutely good men, no converted proletarians, no justifiably routed bourgeoisie, no worker-heroes. Indeed, the working class and the agricultural labourers, the average, ordinary Poles, are almost entirely absent from the book, as it concentrates exclusively on the various aspects of the *inteligencja*.

Even Krystyna, the sole ordinary working girl who might be thought to occupy some special place in the pantheon of both Poles and communists, is no heroine of labour and no paragon of virtue. Her wants are bourgeois, and she falls in love with an AK assassin: if she believes in the socialist dawn then it does not show. The Party workers too seek their justification in weariness and in the idea of 'Poland' rather than in the socialist future. That is, their plans, where they are articulated at all, are more nationalist than socialist.

It is also clear that Andrzejewski had adapted his earlier moral schema to the requirements of the new situation, but he had not abandoned it entirely. Andrzejewski, who in his Catholicism, and in his later dissidence, always sought some form of total world vision, some all-encompassing sense of moral order, thought that he had found a resting-place within Marxism. It is a book shot through with internal Party strife, international and class conflict, and human opportunism. There is no harmonizing socialist principle at work. No dazzling radiance pours down from the summit of Soviet achievement to light the Polish path. There is no glimpse of the wonderful land that lies beyond immediate travail. There is no happy and definite conclusion in favour of socialism. There is no sense in this book that communism is the predetermined and inevitable end to class struggle, though Andrzejewski must have been aware that the failure to say that this was so left him open to charges of doubting the absolute necessity of communism. With hindsight it is possible to see that the book was aiming not to present socialism as a goal, but to explain why socialism might be considered at this particular point of Polish history.

The characters in *Ashes and Diamonds* do not so much renounce their past as make an accommodation with the present in the hope of picking up the old ways at some time in the future. There is no sense that any of the figures here are the cardboard-allegorical, personified abstractions favoured by Soviet *socrealizm* – though a few have suggestive names. These are not simple figures who appear as peasant, landlord, Party man, noble worker, loyal comrade-wife, young hero. The specifically socialist content of the book may be lacking, yet, perhaps in spite of itself, the book is rich in nationalist reverberations. Whether it will or no, the book harks back to lost dreams, shattered illusions, and shows the weariness of death and struggle that gripped Poland in those years. It is not an optimistic tragedy, it is a book filled with doubt, remorse and melancholy. It has very specific roots in the continuing social conflict and does not find any convincing resolution in socialism.

The success of *Ashes and Diamonds* was huge when compared to Andrzejewski's pre-war writings. It very quickly sold 100,000 copies, by 1966 had gone into fourteen editions and by 1989 had been reprinted in a total of twenty-five Polish editions. Long before this Andrzejewski rightly understood that under the new system his writings would reach a much wider audience than ever before. The patronage of the Party was now of vital importance, and after 1949 the minister of culture's calls to support the Party by writing a particular kind of literature could not be ignored with impunity. *Ashes and Diamonds* showed Andrzejewski veering, with some reservations, towards the new line of *socrealizm* and support for the Party. While *Ashes and Diamonds* did not conform to *socrealizm* it was nevertheless seen to be a book which would move other writers towards that style. In any case, the Polish authorities did not feel that they could impose such a style with any confidence just yet. *Ashes and Diamonds* had broken with convention by mentioning the AK and by writing, albeit rather cautiously, about the civil war. But this was something the Party was prepared to tolerate because it helped to show that the new regime was inevitable and offered Poland a new way forward. However guardedly, it supported the Party, and books which offered support to the post-war regime were few and far between. As if in reward for his acceptance of the Party Andrzejewski received the *Odrodzenie* Literary award in 1948 and the novel was awarded the state literary prize.

Miłosz had been a close associate of Andrzejewski during the war; he had narrowly escaped arrest with Andrzejewski in the first of the Nazi round-ups in Warsaw, had walked the rubble of Warsaw with him in 1945, and cooperated with him on a film at the end of the war. Miłosz wrote a little uncharitably of the success of *Ashes and Diamonds*:

A novel that favourably compared the ethic of the New Faith with the vanquished code [of the resistance and the exiled London government] was very important to the Party . . . One city donated to him a beautiful villa furnished at considerable expense. A useful writer in a people's democracy cannot complain of a lack of attention.[19]

Though he was later to revise his opinion, as far as Miłosz was concerned, Andrzejewski had merely exchanged the priest's cassock of the earlier novel for the leather jacket of the Party.

The poet Herbert spoke contemptuously of Andrzejewski as the oldest of the Stalinist 'old boys', and raged against the continued influence of the novel:

Ashes and Diamonds, reprinted again and again, poisoning the minds of the young. One hears that it was the 'Hegelian sting'. I am sorry, but Hegel was dead. He died a century earlier. It was Berman, Sokorski, Kroński who did the stinging. When I am speaking about a crime, it is the crime against the young generation, of those now in their twenties and thirties. They are still being raised on this kind of literature . . . Perhaps the times of terror were too much for the literary imagination. But what does it really mean? The spirit of history does not exist.

The system was built by people. One can list their names . . . The gang of agents badly needed the *inteligencja*, the elite – a kind of cultural *nomenklatura*. What did the governments have to offer? The divine status of a demiurge. Andrzejewski once told me that he was invited to visit by Berman. His host paced nervously in his office. Finally he stopped in front of his window and said, 'This country is on the edge of a civil war. Only a writer of your stature and talent could possibly . . .' Thus he suggested the subject of *Ashes and Diamonds*. They suddenly felt that 'the helm of history' rested also in their hands and that it was worth lying a bit to the confused nation upon which they looked with contempt . . . [20]

Milosz had defined the 'Hegelian sting' as the paralysis of the mind by the unavoidablity of dialectics and the proximity of the Red Army, but the young poet Zagajewski said that perhaps there was no real 'sting' at all, merely 'fear, fear of fear, the desire for a career, the need for safety, money, and an apartment in Warsaw, or just good old conformity'.[21] On the other hand, Kisielewski, who as an essayist for the Catholic *Tygodnik Powszechny* probably had every reason to despise Andrzejewski's espousal of the communist cause, offended the censors by praising Andrzejewski's even-handedness:

A good novel cannot portray only the bright side of life. It has to have elements of black and white, light and dark. This is why *Ashes and Diamonds*, a book which is in my view historically inaccurate, continues to be such a popular novel when so many others have faded into oblivion: because its author divided the light and distributed equal portions to both sides.[22]

For his part Andrzejewski was philosophical about the fate of his book and said:

You know the legend, handed down from generation to generation, that the work of a writer passes silently, and only later will there be a judgement whether to send it to Hell or to Heaven. Of course the majority go to hell. Hell in this case is to be forgotten. Only the chosen are taken to the Heaven of memory.[23]

However we now regard the book in terms of its politics, there can be no doubt at all that it is a landmark in Polish literature. It helped to establish some sort of accommodation between the reluctant population and the ambitious Party. The book sprang from the shock of the occupation and the shock of the liberation: it is about a people who stand at a crossroads in their collective life, but who are effectively denied a say in how they will move forward, or even in which direction they will go. It played out a longing to have done with conflict, to renew some kind of certainty and forge some kind of national unity to repair the ravages not only of the Nazi occupation, but the increasingly unpleasant rule of the colonels in the years before the war.

Although the novel is set in 1945 it is important to remember that it was written in 1947, that is before the full impact of Stalinization under First Secretary Bierut, before the attempted imposition of *socrealizm* by Berman, and that it therefore typifies only the immediate post-war dilemmas. Andrzejewski, for all his prescience, was not able to predict how Polish communism would develop. Although the book was criticized in the early 1950s for its attempt to transcend the differences between the various Polish political opinions and recent biographies, after the thaw of 1956 the idea that some sort of unity had to be achieved, that some sort of legitimacy accrued to the new regime, acquired new and rather ironic implications. The process by which Poland became a communist state had been presented as a unique possibility by which the whole Polish nation might become upwardly mobile. After 1956 increasing centralization, the suppression of opposition, the abandonment of collectivization, industrialization by police methods all meant that the achievement of *Ashes and Diamonds* was seen in quite a different light. Many felt that whatever value the book may have held when it first came out was put in jeopardy by the nature of the regime that it helped establish. Konwicki, for example, who was literary adviser to Wajda on the film of the book, came to see it as a very damaging piece of fantasy:

> The book that served as the basis for the film is the sort of political science fiction that we were writing at the time. It presented reality not as one saw it on the street but as created by an author well disposed to the newly arrived political doctrines and newly arrived regime... And so the novel depicted a Poland that was a bit fictitious, an ill-tempered society, politically turbulent, freed of its reactionaries, not shying away from feasting and revelry, precisely like the Roman Empire in the days before the final fall. But in reality that was a Poland of graves, of Auschwitz, deportation to Siberia, women and partisans slaughtered, a Poland of hunger and orphans, a Poland of torture and prisons, a Poland that had lost the war and lost hope.[24]

By 1983 the official line was:

> *Ashes and Diamonds* is devoted to the difficult problems of choice which faced many Poles on the eve of liberation. Andrzejewski's greatest merit lies in the acceptance of the new reality, while at the same time doing justice to those who had not solved their ideological problems and who were morally bound by oaths of loyalty to the decision of the Polish government in exile in London. Andrzejewski's sensitivity to moral problems places him at the head of the list of authors who summed up the failures of the Stalinist period and prepared the way for a literary thaw.[25]

During the early Stalinist years Andrzejewski was an apologist for the new regime. Perhaps in an effort to put his pre-war Catholic past away, sink himself entirely into the work of the new era and recover some impetus for his writing, perhaps to enhance his creative spark, Andrzejewski joined the Party in 1949. In 1950 he published a volume of speeches called *Aby pokój zwyciężył* (That Peace May Triumph). It was clear that Andrzejewski was committed to understanding and presenting the mechanisms by which people, but particularly artists and intellectuals, might change. To do this he identified two spheres that it was vital to understand: the Catholic Church and Marxism; and to understand Marxism, he claimed, it was essential to know Russia. In 1951 Andrzejewski, as a result of his work in support of the Party, was invited to the Soviet Union, after which he wrote a book called *O człowieku radzieckim* (On Soviet Man) in which he said it was necessary to choose liberty – either that offered by Truman or that given by socialism. Any 'middle road' would inevitably lead to imperialist servitude. He went on to claim that the only true freedom lay in the USSR. Andrzejewski became increasingly drawn into Party affairs, into the public support of the Party and open criticism of Vatican policy towards Poland, 'living in his beautiful villa, signing numerous political declarations, serving on committees and travelling throughout the country lecturing on literature in factory auditoriums, clubs and "houses of culture" '.[26]

In 1952 Andrzejewski published a long essay of *samokrytyka* (self-criticism) entitled *Partia i twórczość pisarza* (The Party and the Creativity of the Writer); this was followed by two volumes of essays called *Ludzie i zdarzenie* (People and Events). In these publications, which he referred to as *dialektyki, marxizm-leninizm-stalinizm*, he openly espoused and developed a Marxist world view. But he did so without great success. Years later Andrzejewski was to lament: 'I wrote books which even in the encyclopaedias are ignored. Just about all my books from that period . . . I wrote them very frankly, and *Partia i twórczość pisarza* even had a certain accent, you might even say it was prayerful.'[27] Looking back on these *dialektyki*, Miłosz thought his friend, in denouncing his failures through lack of Marxist faith, in admitting to faults in his personality in his early writing, was actually not damning those faults at all, but rather compounding them, glorying in a new-found humility which was in fact just a different version of the Catholic religiosity he had been so keen to display before the war:

> Other writers read his article with envy and fear. That he was first everywhere and in everything aroused their jealousy, but that he showed himself so clever – so like a Stakhanovite miner who first announces that he will set an unusually high norm – filled them with apprehension.[28]

However, while Andrzejewski was lauded by the Party, he was increasingly isolated from the Polish literati and became 'Alpha the Moralist', one of the devastatingly accurate portraits in Miłosz's *The Captive Mind* (1953). In conversation with Miłosz in 1991 I asked if he had changed his opinion of Andrzejewski: he replied that the more Andrzejewski had become involved with the Party the more his writing became 'flat and colourless', and that at this time Andrzejewski had been the protégé of the Stalinists, a 'respectable prostitute', though later, Miłosz agreed, Andrzejewski had gone to great lengths to redeem himself. Very quickly Andrzejewski's fame as a writer spread abroad. Within a very short time his work had been translated into French, German, English, Czech, Swedish, Bulgarian, Serbian, Hebrew, Persian and Japanese. However, Andrzejewski's efforts to follow the precepts of *socrealizm* were not successful. His next novel, *Wojna skuteczna* (Effective War, 1953) was a failure and seems to have prompted the beginnings of a crisis of conscience in which he began to react against the increasingly dogmatic Party line in both culture and politics. Although Andrzejewski was to comment that at every period of his life his 'temperament, intellect, intellectual predisposition and character' demanded the 'absolutely distinctive necessity of *fideizm* (fidelity)', 1953 was the year in which Andrzejewski began to lose his *fideizm* to the Party.[29] He was perturbed by the way in which the hugely enhanced state power was used in Poland. His collection of three allegorical novels, *The Slipper, Great Lament of a Paper Head* and *Golden Fox*, published together as *Złoty lis* (Golden Fox, 1954) showed a return to individualism and also a considerable disenchantment with the regime's aims and methods. *Great Lament of a Paper Head* was his first anti-Party piece, a satire on the twaddle dished up to desperate readers kept ignorant by the censor, an audience that was fickle and lacking in judgement. 'Golden Fox', written in the manner of Aesop, is the story of a boy who has a mysterious golden fox living in his wardrobe, but who by the end of the story has been forced through social and parental pressure, to say he no longer believes in the existence of the fox. The publication of *Złoty lis* was significant in that this was the period just prior to the political thaw of 1956, and it marked the beginning of Andrzejewski's public discontent with, and eventual open opposition to, the Party.[30]

Andrzejewski remained a member of the Party until 1957, and resigned when the planned magazine *Europa* was closed on Party instructions. Considering what Andrzejewski already knew about the Party this seems a small event to trigger such a decision, but perhaps it was the last straw: Andrzejewski was to say that it was as if *katarakti* (cataracts) had fallen from his eyes.[31] It is difficult to know what exactly prompted Andrzejewski's change of direction: some internal, personal decision, some argument with the censor, artistic discontent with the formulas of socialist realism, moral repugnance. Whatever it was, Andrzejewski's sensitive political antennae told him that a great wave of social and political unrest was building under the feet of the Party, and he, in his own way, was to make a significant contribution to that movement.

By 1956 most writers and intellectuals on the left did not see that the actuality of the PZPR came anywhere near to their idea of socialism, and the prospects for Polish literature were increasingly bleak. Most agreed that mass publication of the classics and the cheap large-scale publication of new works by living writers were progressive policies, as was the war on illiteracy and the opening up of the educational system to the entire population. However, they also realized that the literature of *partyjność* (Party-ness) would satisfy no one in the long run, would not interest an intelligent readership, would soon bore the new mass readership, and would satisfy the writers least of all. Andrzejewski's novel *Ciemnośći kryją ziemię* (Darkness Covers the Earth, 1957) appeared against a backdrop of gathering storm as writers realized the thaw of 1956 was to be a short-lived affair. Ostensibly the novel was about the Spanish Inquisition, but it was in fact a thinly disguised allegory about the nature of psychological and political pressure, about Stalinist repression of intellectual endeavour, and thus a very accurate gauge of the feelings of Poland's intellectuals. In the novel the young priest Fra Diego falls under the spell of the grand inquisitor Torquemada and is converted to the methods of the Inquisition. The novel ends with Torquemada recanting his beliefs and methods in a deathbed scene. Furious, betrayed, frustrated at being misled so abysmally, Fra Diego slaps the inquisitor's corpse across the face.[32]

By 1956 many Party writers like Andrzejewski felt the need to atone for their past gullibility and opportunism, and their implication in the crimes of the *czas błędów* (time of errors). It had become possible to debate the 'deformations' of socialism, the 'period of errors and mistakes', and it had become necessary to formulate a new programme for the ZLP which included the idea that the union should now defend the 'freedom of literary creation'. In practice, though, the Party could not accept individual initiative. Within a short time of his elevation to first secretary of the PZPR in 1956 Gomułka was at loggerheads with the writers. Gomułka saw intellectuals as a challenge to the power of the Party and began to fear that Andrzejewski and the *rewizjon<u>i</u>śći* (revisionists) were capable of forming the nucleus of a powerful opposition. Gomułka believed he needed greater control over the press and artists if he was to survive the 'threat' from Germany, the threat from Moscow and the threat of democratization from within Poland. He also felt he needed to narrow the base of his support and to make that support more definitely his own creation. For Gomułka 'leftism' and 'left-deviationism' included sectarianism, dogmatism and adventurism, and were, he claimed, characteristic of the immature actions of the exploited; opportunism and *rewizjonizm* (revisionism) on the other hand were examples of 'rightism' – that is, associated with those who exploit. For Gomułka 'leftism' was less of a threat than *rewizjonizm* such as Andrzejewski's.[33] Gomułka, almost immediately after his elevation to power, began to turn against his erstwhile supporters, Kott, Kołakowski, Woroszylski, Ważyk and Andrzejewski, and towards the end of 1957 began a purge in which over 200,000 people were expelled from the Party. Although the new magazines *Dialog* and *Współczes-ność* both appeared, a third magazine called *Europa*, edited by Ważyk, which was planning to publish new work by Andrzejewski, was suppressed at its first issue in mid-1957. In protest at this and the loss of *Po Prostu*, Jastrun, Hertz, Żuławski, Dygat, Kott, Ważyk and Andrzejewski all resigned from the Party in 1957. At the start of 1958 the journal *Nowa Kultura*, a leading outlet for the *rewizjoniści*, was forced to accept a new party line by Andrzej Werblan, causing the mass resignation of almost the entire editorial board.

Andrzejewski's books were highly praised by Polish critics, but his increasingly oppositionist stance did not endear him to the Party. It was said that he was flirting with treason to gain western currency in order to buy the Nobel prize for literature. Party newspapers slandered him mercilessly: he was said to be allied with Trotskyite revisionists, Zionists, anarchists, utopianists and West German Christian Democrats. He was accused of 'socio-political fickleness', of being a non-Marxist, non-Catholic. After 1962 it was increasingly difficult for him to get his work published in Poland, though it is thought that his international reputation protected him from any direct threat or punishment. In 1960 Andrzejewski's novel *Bramy raju* (Gates of Paradise) appeared. The subject was the medieval children's crusades from France into the Holy Land. The participants in the crusades weave together their stories and consciousness in an adolescent confessional. Stylistically the book flouted every tenet of *socrealizm*, and even normal typography – although it had commas, it lacked all other punctuation. Further, the novel, which was initially intended as a film script, posed questions about the nature of mass movements, revolutionary philosophy and the nature of paradise, seeing the urge to be 'part of the movement' as lying in the individual's reluctance to be or stand alone, an urge primarily located in sublimated sex urges. The novel may well have been influenced by *1984* and Orwell's ideas on the functioning of the inner Party and the use made of sex urges by the leadership. In *Bramy Raju* it is impossible to disentangle the adolescents' interest in flesh from their passion for the crusade.[34]

On 14 March 1964, thirty-four writers and intellectuals, including Andrzejewski, signed a 'Letter of the Thirty-Four' to the Polish government protesting at repressive cultural policies. They demanded the rights guaranteed them under the Polish constitution. At this stage they still hoped to reform the Party from within, so their protests were couched in reasonable, mainly Marxist and professional terms: they protested at limited allotments of paper for books and periodicals, restrictions in book publishing, reductions in the size of print runs and the size and number of titles published, at increasing censorship of the national culture, at the lack of open discussion and information as obstacles to progress:

> The limited allotment of paper for printing books and periodicals, as well as
> severe press censorship, is creating a situation that threatens the development of

national culture. The signatories below, while recognising the existence of public opinion, of the right to criticism, of free discussions and of honest information as indispensable elements of progress, and motivated by civic concern, call for a change in Polish cultural policies in the spirit of rights guaranteed by the Constitution of the Polish state and in harmony with the welfare of nations.[35]

The letter was delivered by Słonimski personally to the office of Cyrankiewicz, the prime minister. The response of the authorities was to arrest Lipski, who had collected the signatures, to ban the works of fourteen signatories, and drop all scheduled payments, performances and publication for the others involved. Fourteen signatories were invited to talk with Cyrankiewicz and warned from following up the letter with further action.

Kliszko (a close personal friend and supporter of Gomułka on the Central Committee where he controlled the Personnel Section) addressed a Conference of ZLP writers of the Western Territories and tried to get the membership to sign a petition of protest at the Letter of the Thirty-Four. He claimed that the letter was opportunistic, against the interests of Polish culture, that the authors had been swayed by the interventions of Radio Free Europe and by West German revanchists. Kliszko muttered angrily about the writers' failure to observe protocol in requesting the letter to be published abroad before the prime minister had seen it and before the government had a chance to consider it for publication in Poland. There were vigorous clashes between the internationally respected Maria Dąbrowska and Kliszko. Remarkably 600 writers signed the petition, 400 refused. The numbers signing probably indicates the fear of those living in the Western Territories in the days before any international treaty recognized Poland's western frontier, rather than any real appreciation of the issues in hand.[36]

The ZLP Warsaw branch meeting of June 1964 was dominated by the Letter of the Thirty-Four. It was rumoured the Central Committee were considering expelling those Party members of ZLP who had signed or supported the letter. Słonimski, accused by Kliszko of mismanaging the letter, spoke in his own defence at the Fourteenth ZLP Conference in Lublin in September–October 1964:

Who is really guilty here? One cannot hide one's head in the sand and pretend to see nothing. The whole affair of the 34 and the letter would not have existed had there been no reason to write this letter. And the reason was the fatal situation of Polish culture. The fruits of October have vanished, censorship has gagged the people, the most famous names have disappeared from the columns of the literary journals, the books published in limited editions do not satisfy the needs of the readers. For all this you are responsible and it will not help to look for scapegoats.[37]

Słonimski's speech received a standing ovation from the membership. Gomułka's reply was never made public – indeed it was unusual that he should have taken the trouble to attend the conference at all. This open, almost public row between the Party and ZLP, and the defeat of Kliszko's attack on Słonimski, marked the start of the Party's attempt to regain lost ground.

On 29 February 1968 Andrzejewski and 233 other writers attended an extraordinary general meeting of the Warsaw branch of ZLP to protest at the way the government had banned Mickiewicz's play *Dziady* (Forefathers' Eve, 1823) on 30 January 1968. The play occupies a far more focal position in Polish cultural and political life than any play in English literature – perhaps the nearest equivalent would be to imagine *The Bible, Paradise Lost* and *King Lear* all rolled into one. The play came out of the experience of armed struggle against partition and showed nineteenth-century Russian despotism and the violent struggle waged against the Poles. The play provoked enormous audience response, and lines like 'They only send us fools and drunks from Moscow' – seen by the authorities as too provocative or too accurate, or both – resulted in prolonged applause, multiple curtain calls and the audience singing the Polish national anthem. It is thought that complaints from members of the Soviet diplomatic corps in Kraków were responsible for intervention.[38]

The crudity of the banning provoked prolonged student protest in both Kraków and Warsaw, and proved to be a magnificent opportunity for ZLP to condemn the primitive and politically contradictory nature of the government's cultural policy. At their February meeting the ZLP Warsaw branch attacked government interference in cultural matters and warned that the failure of the government to listen to writers was steadily impoverishing Polish culture. Union chairman Putrament was doubtless under pressure and dismissed the writers' protest as an anti-government provocation and tried to persuade the writers to distance themselves from the protesters. He warned that Radio Free Europe was paying close attention to the banning. Andrzejewski confessed that he was vexed and angry at the political processes that were slowly sterilizing Polish literary culture. The government, he said, seemed determined to hold the thought and feeling of the Polish nation and its writers in contempt: every time the writers tried to initiate dialogue, social progress and reforms the authorities set out to damage and destroy the initiative. The authorities presented a wrong-headed and deliberately falsified version of Polish history and culture, Andrzejewski said, adding that criticism of the government and its policies did not grow out of some secret and alien plot to damage and destroy the nation, but out of protest at the government's contempt for the nation. Alluding to the work of Jan Kott, Kołakowski added:

I repeat, and we will repeat endlessly, the most banal truths, that cultural life requires freedom, that it requires freedom to reflect on culture, its values and possibilities. But even this reflection is not possible, for every discussion inevitably leads to fundamental problems fortified with prohibitions. For even particular evaluation of culture is systematically falsified . . . The administration of culture has now entered a spiral movement, whence there is no exit to be seen, but which would inevitably deepen the abyss between real cultural life and the administration, would waste energy the more and administer greater damage in all spheres of spiritual life. In a situation which has given rise to a great deal of inevitable antagonism, bitterness, disillusionment, of the feeling of importance and clumsiness in the management of culture, the stifling of the expression of these objections by administrative measures has only one result: it will spur their aggrandisement indefinitely. We have the classical, the most banal example of reflexive coupling – the measures preventing the disclosure of resistance, the real source of which nobody considers, create a situation where a still larger number of these means of repression is necessary and endlessly so. We have approached a shameful situation where the whole of dramaturgy, from Aeschylus through Shakespeare to Brecht and Ionesco, has become a collection of allusions to People's Poland.[39]

GUKPPiW (Main Office for the Control of Press Publication and Performance – the censor) banned a total of eighteen writers who attended the February meeting of the ZLP Warsaw branch. Several other writers were forced to resign influential editorships and some writers were put under police surveillance. A short while later Gomułka spoke out to condemn the Warsaw writers of the ZLP as a gang of front-men behind which *rewizjoniśći* and Zionist agents of imperialism operated to bring about Poland's destruction.

The *biurokracja*, led by General Moczar, sought to divert genuine political, economic and social grievances away from its own corruption and idiocy towards traditional scapegoats by setting off an anti-Semitic purge in an attempt to blame all Poland's troubles on the Jews and intellectuals. The venerable writer Paweł Jasienica, famous for his role in the Club of the Crooked circle in the 1950s and for his history of the Piast dynasty, dared to criticize the anti-Semitic campaign, and in return was attacked in a speech by Gomułka from the Palace of Culture on 19 March 1968. Jasienica was accused of taking part in the civil war of 1945–7 on the anti-communist side. It was said he had been arrested and had co-operated with the communist security services, informing against his comrades in order to save himself. It was also claimed that Jasienica had deserted from the Polish army and had been part of a gang that had committed a series of murders in Białystok in the years 1944–8. These slanders hastened Jasienica's death. By this stage there could be little doubt where Andrzejewski's loyalties lay, and at Jasienica's funeral in August 1970 he delivered a stinging criticism of the Party, the security services and the government as part of his graveside tribute:

He was accused of actions he did not perform, and of crimes he never committed. Publicly abused and insulted, he had no possibility of defending himself. The right to publish was taken away from him; old books were removed from bookstores, and his new ones were not allowed to appear. This is something that one would think would be inconceivable after all the experiences of totalitarian governments, but – sadly – it is true. An eminent Polish writer, a creator of permanent cultural values, enjoying the great trust and respect of thousands of readers, in the prime of his literary life, was in one day pushed to the margin of public life and condemned to civil death.[40]

In the summer of 1968 Andrzejewski compounded his 'errors' when he wrote to Edward Goldstücker, the Chairman of the Czechoslovak Writers' Union, to sympathize and apologize for Poland's part in the invasion of Czechoslovakia. He wrote:

I write to you so that you and all your colleagues should know that during the days of your creative search, so important for the future of the whole world, you have had in the Polish writers and intellectuals, friends full of hope, and when you were going through particularly difficult days for you and your people – we were with you, although deprived of free speech in our country. You must certainly know that the feeling of helplessness in the face of violence and force is the most painful of all human degradations, and that such a defeat becomes a particularly heavy burden when the best traditions of one's own country are insulted, freedom of speech annihilated and truth trodden down. I am quite aware that my voice of political and moral protest will not, and cannot, outweigh the shame that Poland has brought on herself in the progressive opinion of the whole world. But this protest, born of indignation, pain and shame is the only thing I can offer you and your friends and colleagues in the current circumstances.[41]

At once the Party newspapers began a tirade of criticism directed at Andrzejewski: *Życie Warszawy, Sztandar Młodych, Kultura, Trybuna Ludu, Słowo Powszechne, Walka Młodych, Żołnierz Wolności, Stolica*, and *Wrocławski Tygodnik Katolików* all accused him of anti-socialism, betrayal, cosmopolitanism, weakening the Warsaw Pact and mocking Polish traditions. During the next six months the police arrested large numbers of dissenting and critical intellectuals and students in Andrzejewski's circle of acquaintance. Mrożek, who had supported Andrzejewski, found that his plays were banned and not allowed on stage again until after December 1970. Mrożek left Poland to live in Italy.

For a while after March 1968 Polish writers were in such a state of ferment that many feared the Party might consider dissolving the ZLP. The union, and the Warsaw branch in particular, were proving to be not only centres of opposition such as Gomułka had always feared, but extremely resilient centres at that. The Party was nervous of outright demolition and instead decided to neutralize the ZLP from within. The 1969 Writers' Congress, held in

Bydgoszcz under the leadership of Jerzy Putrament, was shamelessly stage-managed – virtually all of the committees and positions of power were filled by Gomułka's men before the congress even began, and the statutes of the union were rewritten to give the executive greater scope to act without recourse to a mandate from the membership. By the end of the year the PZPR had established a very different kind of control over writers from that which existed in 1956. By the end of 1969 Gomułka's policies had effectively silenced the bulk of the writing community by censoring and distorting everything they wrote in protest, by cutting them off from their readership and from their public support and contact. Zbigniew Herbert said of the years 1956–68:

> In 1956 they [the writers] thought they brought about the thaw. Next there came a painful blow. Gomułka was not only primitive, he knew that the government was already firmly in the saddle. It had its own apparatus of repression, lots of prisons, a sufficiently corrupted judiciary. Who needed *Ashes and Diamonds*? Who needed literature? Suddenly the writers saw the social demand disappearing. They felt the emptiness, so they joined the opposition. They [the Party] loved us, they pampered us, and suddenly they dumped us. That's how it looked in general terms. 1956 destroyed the myth of the engineers of human souls – the myth of political usefulness of those who were ready to support the system with their poems, paintings and symphonies. The so called elite was sent away empty handed despite its good service because the new lord was an upstart and held intellectuals in contempt.[42]

The events of 1968 proved to be a turning-point in Andrzejewski's professional as well as political thinking. His book *Apelacja* (The Trial) was turned down by the censor. The refusal could hardly have come as a surprise since the novel charted a serious shift in the attitudes and perceptions of the public. It dealt with a man called Konieczny (the name means 'necessary, essential, indispensable') and his efforts to persuade the first secretary of the PZPR to remove the surveillance of some thirty thousand secret agents, working in co-operation with a great electronic brain. Konieczny's fears may have been pure paranoid fantasy, but his experience in the resistance, his suffering at the hands of the Gestapo and the Polish security service, and his rage at the exploitative nature of his work at the Prefabricated One-Family Home Factory were vivid and realistic foundations for his suspicions. Instead of bowing to the rejection of his novel, Andrzejewski sent it to the émigré publishing house Instytut Literacki in Paris.[43] He may have faced prosecution for slandering the state, but by the time the book was published in Paris officials of the Gierek regime took the line that his novel was about the final years of Gomułka, a period of 'mistakes and deviations', which they were anxious to disown. Gierek's officials were reluctant to appear punitive on behalf of a regime that they were trying to replace. It is significant that

Andrzejewski chose to turn to émigré publishing. As usual he was one of the first to sense new developments.

In 1970, amid mounting economic discontent, Gomułka fell and was replaced by Gierek, a leader who promised the workers riches if only they would 'help' him. The workers may have been fooled by Gierek, but others were not. In June 1971 Kołakowski published in *Kultura* (Paris) his 'Tezy o Nadziei i Beznadziejności' (Theses on Hope and Hopelessness) in which he defined the Polish political system as 'despotic socialism' and observed that the Polish system was not an example of the 'perfect or unadulterated socialism' in which Kołakowski still had some faith. For him socialism was only possible within a sovereign state, and Poland's subjection to the will and policy of the Soviet Union made this impossible. In Poland *sowietizacja* (sovietization) meant 'a situation where in public speech, nothing is or can be for real, all words have lost their original meaning'.[44] Under Gierek the government did not have any policy on the arts except to put writers and their works under political scrutiny by the censor.

Something of the underlying feel of artistic life can be seen in Andrzejewski's early experience of the Gierek regime. In 1970 he approached the state publishing houses with his latest project. This was his novel *Miazga* (Pulp), an 800-page monster of a book, a long extract of which had appeared in the magazine *Twórczość* in 1967. It had been written and rewritten over the long period 1963–70, and was described by one critic as 'the most important book written in Poland since the end of the war'.[45] Andrzejewski had detailed the slow cultural, linguistic and political decline of post-war Poland, but in doing so made no concessions at all to the censor. He had tried, he said, to write a book where 'black was black, white was white and where there was no double-think'. The book was delivered to the publisher in 1970, and, given that the Gierek regime was trying very hard to promote a new liberal image of itself over the grey memory of the Gomułka years, Andrzejewski had high hopes for his book's success. After lengthy negotiations he agreed to the in-house editors' suggestion that there should be some 600 alterations, plus cuts and deletions totalling over 100 pages. The book went to the printers in 1972 and the *pierwsza szczotka* (literally 'first brush' or galley proofs) were run off and – as normal – delivered to the censor for consideration. On Andrzejewski's birthday in August 1972, he was informed by the office of the censor that *Miazga* would not be published after all.[46]

In 1975 the Party began to amend the Polish constitution. They added three new areas; an article stating that citizens would be entitled to civil rights only if they fulfilled their obligations to the state; recognition that Poland's sovereignty was limited by its allegiance to the USSR; and recognition that the leading role of the Party was legally enshrined in the constitution. Very soon after the proposed constitutional changes became public Andrzejewski took on the task of co-ordinating signatures for what became known as the

'Letter of the 101'. In response a special GUKPPiW directive removed from the public domain all reference to those writers who signed. Their names were not to be mentioned in any publication or broadcast; any unavoidable mention of their name was to be referred upwards to a higher authority before publication. This was a manœuvre designed to rob individuals of the glory and the publicity of open blacklisting: Andrzejewski's name was first on the list.[47] By driving these people underground the censor did not stop them publishing and in fact only contributed to their growing intellectual disaffection. By 1976 there was a politically wide-ranging loose association of dissident writers and intellectuals, both in Poland and in enforced emigration, which included: the *rewizjoniśći* writers and artists of earlier days – Andrzejewski, Kołakowski, Lipinski; the historians who later worked in TKN – Geremek, Jedlicki, Kersten; the philosopher of science Amsterdamski; the writers Woroszylski, Bocheński, Kazimierz Brandys, Ficowski; the Catholics of the Znak group – Bartoszewski, Cywiński, Mazowiecki, Stanowski.

The Polish workers waited for the wealth promised by Gierek, but their patience snapped on 25 June 1976 when work ceased all over Poland in protest at proposed price rises on basic goods. At the Ursus tractor factory the workers blocked the rail line. At Radom, where workers were already angry at the aggressive and overbearing attitudes of a management which had increased shift quotas and refused to pay accident compensation, the workers marched to the city centre and besieged Party headquarters to loot the well-stocked canteen. Some say security service provocateurs ran amok, smashing shop windows and setting fire to buildings. By the end of the day four people were dead, seventy-five were in hospital and over a million dollars' worth of damage had been done. The price rises were withdrawn but 2,000 workers who had demonstrated were arrested: 150 were severely beaten by the police, thrown out of their dormitories, dismissed from their jobs and, at summary courts, were sent to jail with sentences of up to ten years. Most were charged with 'collective responsibility' for damage; some were charged with crimes that had taken place after their arrest. All were the victims of 'simplified legal procedures' introduced two days before the price rises had been announced.

For many intellectuals 1976 was the moment beyond which they could no longer give the Party the benefit of the doubt, the moment at which they realized the Party was not only incapable of reforming itself, but was barely in control of the state and the powers it claimed to lead. The realization was painful, especially for those with a conscience who owed their living to state appointments, people who were expected to uphold the regime. Professor Balbus, Party member and literary theorist of the Institute of Polish Philology at the Jagiellonian University, wrote:

> Not until when Gierek dealt so brutally with the protesting workers of Radom and Ursus did I realise I could no longer live like this. I began to worry I was

going crazy, that I'd become schizophrenic or insane if I didn't, once and for all, break from communism. I felt as though I was totally covered in shit and was searching for a way to shake it off . . . [48]

Andrzejewski wrote a 'Message to the Victimized Participants of the Workers' Protest' which was widely publicized in Britain, France, Germany, Italy and Japan, in which he comforted the workers, expressed his 'unceasing hope' for them, his solidarity with them, and called for an end to intimidation by the state and Party. The letter had a profound impact on the Polish workers concerned, many of whom had studied Andrzejewski's works when they were at secondary school. Further, the letter seems to have galvanized the bulk of the Polish *inteligencja* into recognizing that it could no longer remain silent in the face of such enormous and widespread official hypocrisy. In his essays Michnik had called for a new evolutionism, a new kind of positivism that would transform society by allowing it to organize itself by ignoring the state. He proposed to do this by a programme of working-class organization, linked with intellectuals to defend the working class, and by making the public independent of the state in a wide range of activities. Between them Andrzejewski and Michnik initiated a flood of samizdat material that far surpassed anything that Czechoslovakia or the Soviet Union produced.

Without doubt the most important step in the development of an independent literary life and society was the establishment of KOR (Workers' Defence Committee). Founded on 23 September 1976, with Andrzejewski as a founder member, KOR was a direct intellectual response to the police and judicial harassment of workers, and declared itself ready to fight authoritarianism. KOR sought to offer financial and legal support to those who were victimized by the authorities. Although its function was defined quite narrowly, its impact, coupled with the efforts of TKN (The Flying University, founded January 1978), was to go far beyond its stated aims. The organization had no common political purpose; indeed the diverse spread of its membership would have made this impossible. It is as well to stress the 'literary' input to KOR; in addition to Jerzy Andrzejewski, the other founder members were: Stanislaw Barańczak, Jacek Kuroń, Edward Lipiński, Jan Józef Lipski, Antoni Macierewicz, Andrzej Szczypiorski, Wacław Zawadzki, Bogdan Borusewicz, Anka Kowalska, Wojciech Onyszkiewicz and Adam Michnik. By 1979 the group had grown to thirty-four members of whom no less than thirteen had fought in the AK; most had spent time in prison for their oppositionist opinions; one of the founding members was a priest; several had spent time in Stalin's prisons. Many of the active members of KOR had been blacklisted for protest at changes to the Polish Constitution, and many were *rewizjoniści* who had been in close contact for several years and knew each other's backgrounds and political thought processes very well. Andrzejewski wrote a letter to inform the Sejm of KOR's existence:

> The victims of the current repressions cannot count on any help or defence from those institutions whose mission is to help and defend them, such as the trade unions, whose role has been pathetic. Social welfare agencies also refuse their help. Given this situation, this function must now be assumed by the society in the interest of which those who are now being persecuted were protesting against the price increases. Society has no other means of defence against lawlessness than solidarity and mutual aid.[49]

For many writers 1976 marked a watershed in their official state-subsidized publishing careers and it is possible to see a falling-off in the numbers of editions published from around this time: Andrzejewski's publishing career with the state was about to tail off: in the years 1945–55 he had nineteen editions in print; in 1956–65 he had twenty-three; in 1966–75 he had fourteen; by 1976–80 he had 7. In 1986 there was only one Andrzejewski novel still in print. As usual, Andrzejewski was one of the first to sense new developments and turn to underground and émigré publishing.[50] In 1977 Andrzejewski and several other writers launched the independent literary journal *Zapis*. The first issue contained an extract from an unpublished manuscript by Andrzejewski about the Russian novelist Pasternak. This independent literary journal proved a highly influential venture and, with the émigré publishing houses in Paris and London, was to give growing and wide-ranging dissident intellectual opposition a public voice.

Once Andrzejewski had established that it was possible to survive publication underground and abroad there was no turning back, and there could be no agreement to a refusal from state publishers. This became a general feeling among the writing community of the mid-and late 1970s. As well as making increasing use of the Paris Instytut Literacki, Andrzejewski worked with KOR. With British and Swedish émigré connections, KOR issued *The Black Book on Polish Censorship* (1977) and the *Documents on Lawlessness* (April 1978). These publications were based on documents smuggled out of Poland to Sweden the previous year by a defecting Kraków censor and were to have an enormous impact on the opposition's understanding of the censorship system. Poles had been aware that the 'grey areas' of their history were policed by the censor. But here, in detail, they could see for the first time exactly how far censorship controlled a whole range of cultural, political and social opinions. Andrzejewski wrote the introduction to the documents:

> We are dealing with one of the greatest revelations of the postwar period . . . The thesis that in our life lies and dis-information play the foremost role is confirmed again. Not only historical tradition, the ideological sphere and national culture

are falsified. Elementary facts are also suppressed or distorted, even those whose neglect is a crime against citizens – for instance the information that a popular floor tile commonly used by construction companies causes cancer and that chemicals employed in agriculture directly threaten human health. This suppression is performed apparently for the sake of social peace and order, to pacify society. But at the same time society has reason to feel anxious and keeping quiet or lying will not remove the causes of this anxiety. Documents of censorship also reveal another mystification. The censors have assumed the role of guardians and custodians of state secrets. According to periodical reports on the censor's activities the 'state secrets' rubric is very full, but there is no definite indicator as to what these secrets might be. In about 700 pages of reports one could perhaps find only six or seven interventions by the censor that were really linked to some state secret. All the documents clearly demonstrate that the censors continually justify their existence through the need to protect state secrets, and that they continue to create those secrets. It is now impossible to gain access to information on thousands of parasites afflicting cattle, on the hazards of certain kinds of labour in the chemical industry, the social and religious activities of the church, the names of writers and scientists – even the titles of their books and films – of historical events, of obituaries. It is not possible to investigate these things because they are state secrets . . . Convinced that the superior social interests require this decision we publish the following materials, revealing the precision of this anti-human machinery, this anti-citizen, anti-national device.[51]

By the end of 1977 Andrzejewski was a leading figure in a rapidly developing underground publishing movement, very active in the opposition and a 'father figure' to many young oppositionists.

The lecturers of TKN, the membership of KOR, ROPCiO (Movement Defending Human and Civil Rights, founded March 1975), the Free Trade Unions of the Coast, and the other growing independent social movements faced intermittent, brutal and sometimes fatal police actions. Most members of KOR and the larger underground publishing houses faced constant surveillance, unexplained arrest, forty-eight-hour detention and sudden release without charge. Yet it must be said that the response of the authorities was far from totalitarian. The spectacular growth of the Polish independent social movement and the underground publishing movement through the late 1970s, and the fact that they were tolerated by the security services, are hard to explain, especially since throughout the late 1970s there had been a persistent rumour that the budget of the Ministry of Internal Security was larger than that of the Ministries for Health, Education and Culture combined. The security services had the power and freedom of action to wipe out the entire independent social movement and to cover their tracks afterwards, but as T. G. Ash has written:

At a meeting in 1978 a Colonel of the security service was asked why the police did not destroy the underground publishers. 'We know all the addresses, we could destroy everything in one night,' he sighed, 'but the high-ups won't allow us to'. The 'high-ups', notably Gierek himself, seem to have thought that this flowering of intellectual opposition would not amount to a serious political threat, while tolerance might win them a broader measure of co-operation from the intelligentsia. Perhaps this reflected their low regard for ideas in general.[52]

The underground press was tolerated for several reasons. Strange as it may seem, no law was being broken by these activities unless lecturers or writers deliberately slandered the USSR or the People's Republic of Poland. The regime, where they thought about it at all, seem to have regarded the underground as something of a safety valve. They knew they could move against the underground if they wanted, but it actually provided them with a great deal of information they needed, particularly about the economy and society, information classified as secret which even they could not get through 'approved' channels. The authorities also knew that even if they managed to contain the underground they stood very little chance of ever destroying it completely.

Andrzejewski's role in KOR was highly public and there were various attempts to discredit him. In October 1976, for example, he was supposed to have circulated a letter to various institutions and organs of the state in support of legal recognition and equality for homosexuals. In Catholic and highly traditional Poland had he done any such thing it would have been sufficient to make him a social leper. However, thanks to the efforts of KOR, it soon emerged that his signature had been forged. A short while later, Roliński wrote a poisonous article in which it was said that Andrzejewski was using the foreign press to spread lies about Poland. The article characterized Andrzejewski as a political chameleon, claimed that his actions were damaging to the moral and social life of Poland, and warned him to keep away from the pseudo-intellectuals and politically bankrupt associates (utopianists, Trotskyites, social democrats, bourgeois anti-communists, Zionists, Christian democrats) that he rubbed shoulders with in KOR. The government also initiated legal proceedings against Andrzejewski and ordered him to report to a Warsaw court to hand over to a state bank some two million złoties collected for KOR. KOR refused to hand over the money and issued a public statement complaining that it was being harassed illegally. Andrzejewski did not go to court and as a result was fined 5,000 złoties – nearly double the monthly salary of a university teacher.[53]

That the wide-ranging opposition of the mid-1970s was a peculiarly loose coalition of the system's opponents drawn from very different social circles, and that it was largely non-ideological, was frequently reported by puzzled western observers. Andrzejewski, like most KOR, ROPCiO and TKN members, when asked by foreign journalists about the political ambitions and programme of the oppositionists, could do no more than shake his head and shrug his shoulders. In September 1981, as the independent trade union movement spearheaded by Solidarność moved towards bitter confrontation with the military authorities, Andrzejewski was interviewed by Trznadel. He said that it was very important to realize the difficulty of creating a socialist model that was different from that of the USSR, that the struggle to do so was in itself corrosive. In essence he said that it was vital to communicate that such a struggle was not a counter-revolution, nor was it a fight against socialism, or a fight against the USSR. He was reluctant to describe People's Poland as totalitarian, saying that totalitarianism was a system that claimed to be finished, completed, perfected, which Poland's communism had never been. He baulked at describing the communist culture of the post-war years as totalitarian, saying that it was necessary to see what happened in its international context: it was part of the times. On the subject of *Ashes and Diamonds* he was reluctant to speak. He claimed that he had not reread it since 1957 when Wajda was preparing his film script, admitted that he was simply too afraid to look at it again and that he could not remember it at all. 'This is not *kokieteria* (coquetry) . . . It was all a very long time ago.'[54]

What is fascinating about Andrzejewski's career is that as well as being a leading non-Catholic Pole, actively and crucially engaged with the political and cultural life of his society, he was to chart a path followed by almost all of his generation of the Polish *literati*; he was one of the first to give his support to the communists, and one of the first to withdraw it. Stefan Staszewski (b.1906), who had at various times been Party propaganda chief in Kraków, head of the Central Committee Press Section, deputy minister for agriculture, editor in chief of PAP and then editor of the *General Encyclopaedia*, when interviewed in 1982 by Teresa Toránska said of Andrzejewski's role in the establishment of communist control:

And what about members of the Polish *inteligencja* who helped the government – do we leave them out? What about someone like Andrzejewski – an example off the top of my head, but a typical one – who wrote *The Party and the Creativity of the Writer*, do we leave him out too? Here was, to put it bluntly, this intellectual, this humanist, this Catholic, and you mean to tell me he didn't know what he was doing? He came to us of his own free will; no one forced him, no one pressured him; and he joined the Party not because someone was urging him to, but because he accepted that Party's programmes and principles. And not only did he join it: he wanted to play an active role in it. He wanted to justify the Party's principles and persuade others that the Party was right. I don't know how you interpret his *Ashes and Diamonds* after all these years, but it's a novel whose function, if you'll forgive me, was among other things to bring the nation round to this regime and show that there was shooting on both sides and to show that Maciek was a victim of accident and misunderstanding. Whom does Andrzejewski justify, who does he think was right, historically right, in this novel? Maciek? No, Szczuka: a communist. No one asked Andrzejweski to do that; no one asked for the pamphlet *The Party and the Creativity of the Writer*. My question, then, is whether a writer, a moralist and a Catholic, a person raised in the Polish tradition of independence, who for the whole of the occupation was connected – not fighting, but connected – with the London independence camp, and who went over to the other side, burning his bridges behind him – whether or not such a person becomes answerable for the Party's mistakes. And let's not deceive ourselves by asking: did he know or didn't he? He knew. I could tell you, but I won't, that he knew more than I did, because he was in contact with persecuted circles whereas I wasn't. So he knew what was going on behind the security walls and I didn't . . . [55]

Those who did not follow the same twisting track as Andrzejewski were for the most part pre-war Fascists, nationalists or mere Party hacks. *Ashes and Diamonds* still occupies a profoundly ambiguous place in post-war Polish literature: not wholly against the old regime, not wholly for the new regime. Deeply opportunist, it is also an accurate and penetrating portrayal of the confusion and pain of those years.

Time, politics and literary fashion may eventually prove that Andrzejewski was too much of a pragmatist, too rooted in contemplation of the right course of action, the right moral response, to create literary works that would outlast his own lifetime by very much. However, anyone who wants to know how Poles thought and felt in the years 1936–83 about the differing directions of the political wind, the agonies of Poland's intellectual and cultural élite, and the response of the most sensitive of weather vanes, has to turn to the works of Andrzejewski. It has long been clear that Andrzejewski accepted the view that he was ever and always first to sense changing social opinion. However, it is also clear that he was hampered by his self-conscious concentration upon what was happening to the surface of political life rather than on how, beneath the surface, it affected the individual's existence, or how the individual's existence fed into changes in political life. In spite of this limitation, Andrzejewski's works have remained popular, even with General Jaruzelski, but especially with teachers and intellectuals now in late middle age, whose preference is for writers who grew up in independent Poland, who began writing before the war, who treat subjects related to the recent past, and who have not emigrated to the west.[56]

Andrzejewski died on 19 April 1983. One obituary said:

Andrzejewski went through his periods of born-again religion – Catholicism, Marxism, Existentialism – which he recanted with a frankness and scrupulousness uncommon among Polish writers, taking upon himself all the responsibility for false choices, delusions and privileges . . . he was a writer of universal horizons, but one who brought his gaze to bear on very specific and typically Polish situations, describing them with the anger, exasperation and indignation of a moralist obsessed with restoration of the moral order.[57]

It was an accurate assessment of his work and his achievement in politics and letters. By the time of his death Andrzejewski had covered a great deal of ground, both political and artistic.[58] His trajectory, from right to left, from Party apologist to dissident, from belief to scepticism, may be remarkable to western readers, but, as Miłosz has remarked, the twists and turns, the undoubted elements of opportunism that mark Andrzejewski's career, his 'metamorphoses and curious literary adventures' are not untypical of a writer of his generation from this part of the world.[59]

The situations described in *Ashes and Diamonds* are long gone, yet many Poles (even those too young to have experienced the period of the novel) testify to the novel's power and durability: indeed for many the novel is 'the truth' about the period, an accurate portrayal, almost a historical document. That *Ashes and Diamonds* alone among his works may survive is testimony not only to Andrzejewski's ability as a writer, nor even to his later efforts to redeem himself, but to the enduring and deep-rooted divisions and problems of political legitimacy that forty-five years of communism did nothing to resolve, diminish or render irrelevant. It is possible to see that even without Andrzejewski communist power would have been established in post-war Poland. It is also possible to see that without his principled resistance and opposition to communism after the thaw of 1956, life could have been very different, not only for those who read his books. Without Andrzejewski's moral stature and his public stand, the history of KOR and Solidarność would have been very different, and without them the challenge to the Party and to Soviet power would not have been so effective: Polish and Soviet communism might have endured much longer than it did. Whatever Poles may say about *Ashes and Diamonds* and his support for communism, it must also be said that Andrzejewski's withdrawal of support for the Party, his work in KOR and his criticism of the Party undermined the power and the certitude of the Party vision; that they were a major but unquantifiable contribution to the collapse of 1989 cannot be doubted.

4

JAN KOTT

In a real revolution the best characters do not come to the front. A violent revolution falls into the hands of narrow-minded fanatics and of tyrannical hypocrites at first. Afterwards comes the turn of all the pretentious intellectual failures of the time. Such are the chiefs and the leaders. You will notice that I have left out the mere rogues. The scrupulous and the just, the noble, humane, and devoted natures; the unselfish and the intelligent may begin a movement – but it passes away from them. They are not the leaders of the revolution. They are its victims: the victims of disgust, of disenchantment – often of remorse. Hopes grotesquely betrayed, ideals caricatured – that is the definition of revolutionary success. There have been in every revolution hearts broken by such successes . . . My meaning is that I do not want you to be a victim.

Joseph Conrad, *Under Western Eyes*

Jan Kott is Poland's best-known literary critic. He is internationally respect- ed, particularly for his inventive, sensitive and innovative Shakespearean criticism. His writing has had a profound influence on the work of theatre practitioners and literary critics the world over. Kott's literary criticism is in every sense Marxist, and much of his early career was given over to helping establish communism in Poland. During the war he was a member of the Moscow-backed resistance, and later helped edit the important socialist- realist magazine *Kuźnica* and even joined the Party.

Initially a favoured son of the regime, wooed and pampered by the Party, as the power structure of post-war Poland changed, Kott found himself relegated. Judged 'too weak for real political work' he was sent to teach in a provincial university. His faith in the Party, if not in communism, began to waver, and his criticisms of the Party were those of a once loyal, but struggling communist. He left the Party in 1964, but his idealistic and cultured vision of a communist future was finally shattered only by the attempted destruction of the Polish intellectual opposition in the anti-Semitic purge of 1968, when, through the persecution and expulsion of many of the surviving Jewish community the Polish Communist Party marginalized, gagged and forced into exile the bulk of the revisionist element within the Party. By doing so the Party ensured that the opposition movement would remain leaderless and atomized for nearly a decade. Kott's fascinating literary-political biography not only provides an interesting insight into the peculiarly Polish interface between literature and politics, but also a detailed and personal glimpse into the ambitions and failure of *rewizjonizm*.

Jan Kott was born in 1914 in Warsaw. He came from a literary family: on his mother's side of the family, his great-great-grandfather Hilary Nusbaum had published a history of the Jews and had translated the Pentateuch and Torah into Polish. Another relative on his mother's side, Józef Nusbaum Hilarowicz, an early Polish Darwinist, had converted to Catholicism when appointed to a Professorship at Lwów. Kott's father was a non-believer who knew only a few words of Yiddish, but he predicted that there would be little place for Jews in the newly independent Polish state. At his father's insistence Jan Kott was baptized into the Catholic Church at the Holy Cross in Warsaw in 1919. He attended Warsaw University, where he fell under the influence of the great essayist Jerzy Stempowski and the Marxist literary critic Stefan Żółkiewski. In 1934, already a member of the Association of Democratic Youth, but rapidly turning into a communist, Kott was arrested and imprisoned for two weeks after taking part in a 'red demo'. He took university courses in aesthetics, sociology and cultural anthropology, but graduated in law in 1936 and then did one year of military service. In 1938 he received a grant from the French Institute in Warsaw to study at the Sorbonne for a year. In Paris he met Tzara, Mme Apollinaire, Breton, Éluard, Jacques and Raissa Maritain. His doctoral thesis was supposed to be on Apollinaire as editor of de Sade, but instead he read international pornography in the basement of the Bibliothèque Nationale. He began his literary career with poetry and essays on French surrealism and Catholicism in Liebert and Rimbaud, and articles on Mauriac.

In 1939 Lance-Corporal Kott was called up for service in the army and took part in the defence of Warsaw. After his release from the German PoW camp (he claims he was certified dead of pneumonia) he crossed the German-Soviet frontier illegally and moved to Lwów, then under Soviet control. About a hundred Polish writers had taken refuge in the USSR. In the main these writers – Jerzy Borejsza, Władysław Broniewski, Mieczysław Jastrun, Jerzy Putrament, Julian Przyboś, Ewa Szemplińska, Wanda Wasilewska, Aleksander Wat, Adam Ważyk, Tadeusz Boy-Żeleński – were sympathetic to communism. In Lwów they organized themselves around the local chapter of the Polish Writers' Union, which already included such noted figures as Jan Brzoza, Leon Pasternak, Aleksander Dan, Ostap Otwin, Teodor Parnicki and Halina Górska, many of whom were very suspicious of the Soviets.

Unlike most of the left-inclined Polish writers in the USSR, Kott did not publish in the *Czerwony Sztandar* (Red Banner) or in *Nowy Widokręgi* (New Horizons) – the official Soviet-backed Polish journals, nor did he take part in public ceremonies. However, he did attend writers' meetings and was aware of the cost of belonging to the circle of Polish writers in the USSR accepted by the Party. Mieczysław Braun, a Jewish writer-refugee from Łódź, has left a description of these writers' meetings:

> I have never been in such a humiliating and absurd situation. Every day we have a meeting. I sit in the first row and they look at me, I hear propaganda, nonsense and lies. Whenever they mention Stalin my supervisor starts clapping and everyone present follows suit. I also clap, and I feel like a court jester. I do not want to translate Mayakowski, but I have no choice. I do not want to clap, but I am forced to. I do not want Lwów to be a Soviet city, but a hundred times a day I say the opposite. All my life I have been an honest person, and now I am playing the fool. I have become a scoundrel.[1]

Kott, with Borejsza, Jastrun, Przyboś and Hoffman, took part in a discussion where the poet Adam Ważyk was criticized for failure to include Soviet themes in his recent work (*Czerwony Sztandar*, 17 April 1941).

Kott may have had no taste for this kind of activity, but he nevertheless had close ties to the Polish communists. Once he was arrested for deportation to Siberia, but rescued from the train at the very last minute by Polish novelist and communist activist, Wanda Wasileska. For a while he worked at compiling a huge anthology of Polish translations of Ukrainian literature, and then resumed work for a doctorate, passing examinations in the history of literature, grammar and Marxism-Leninism with particular reference to the Bolshevik faction of the Communist Party as detailed in *A Short Course about the WKP(b)* – which was compulsory reading for Poles who wished to publish in the USSR. Soviet policy towards the Poles eventually meant that the Polish writers' union was absorbed into the Union of Ukrainian Soviet Writers. Kott applied to join the new Profspiłka, and in doing so acknowledged the Soviet right to annex the Ukraine, and went through the rigmarole of submitting his work for assessment by the committee before his membership was confirmed. In spite of his apparent co-operation with the Soviet authorities Kott was increasingly unhappy about literary life under the Soviets and did not display sufficient *dyspozycyność* (amenability) towards the regime. After the German invasion of the USSR, Kott and his wife Lidia returned to Warsaw, smuggled under a tarpaulin on the back of a truck.

In Warsaw Kott and Lidia managed to arrange forged papers but nevertheless they had to change address constantly. Kott's social circle in Warsaw included the distinguished young writers Jerzy Andrzejewski, Adolf Rudnicki and Czesław Miłosz. Kott was arrested by the Germans in a round-up, but after pretending to some medical knowledge, was briefly made a 'doctor' of the women's section in the transit department of Majdanek concentration camp. He was released without explanation, arrested again, mistaken for a murderer, but released, this time because he was mistaken by the Polish police for an influential AK (Armia Krajowa, London-backed resistance) colonel on false papers.

In spite of his left-wing sympathies Kott had never been a member of the Party. Indeed he was well informed about Stalin's destruction of the Polish Communist Party, the mass deportations and executions, and was firm in the belief that the liberation of Poland would come at the hands of the western Allies rather than from the USSR. Nevertheless, in 1942 Kott joined the newly created, intellectually enfeebled, Soviet-backed Polish Workers' Party (PPR) and the following year joined the AL (People's Army, Moscow-backed resistance), reading his oath from a cigarette paper in a friend's kitchen in Warsaw. Kott has not said much about the work of his underground unit but it is clear that it was involved in counter-intelligence work, in part directed against the London-backed AK. Kott's unit was directed by Marian Spychalski who was later to become minister of defence and chairman of the Council of State. During the occupation Kott met Comrade 'Tomasz', a member of the newly created National Council, who was in fact Bolesław Bierut, later to become Poland's first post-war communist leader. Kott recalled Comrade 'Tomasz' as a clean-shaven, nondescript, municipal functionary who spoke in a low monotone as if he were not speaking to Kott at all 'but rather repeating to himself phrases that he had learned by heart'.[2] Comrade 'Tomasz' persuaded Kott to write a long article on the planned post-war communist reorganization of Polish universities, and he was also given the task of writing brochures and tracts in the name of progressive Catholics. Kott also helped edit a clandestine journal. As Poles were denied access to any kind of higher education and forbidden to use the University Library, Kott's first book of literary criticism, *Mitologia i Realizm* (Mythology and Realism), was started behind a mound of German-language technical textbooks in the University Library. Some of his poems on the destruction of the Jewish ghetto (along with those of Miłosz, Jastrun and others) were published in the influential underground anthology, *Z otchłani* (From the Abyss).

As the war neared its end Polish society began to divide over the issues of what form post-war Poland should take, and over the issues of communism and relations with the USSR. Kott recalled literary gatherings at which the 'different milieux frequently intersected and merged'. At one such meeting Bieńkowski, Miłosz, Jastrun and Żółkiewski listened to Jerzy Andrzejewski read a story in which a hero betrays his friend to the Germans because he cannot stand the thought of dying alone. The story was one of the last written during the war:

> When Jerzy finished reading, a heated discussion ensued. More heated than was usual at such gatherings. Bieńkowski was the first to attack Andrzejewski, accusing him of justifying betrayal in a covert fashion. The group split into two camps. Miłosz defended Andrzejewski. Stefan, Jastrun and I attacked the story.

We talked of the judgement of history that would decide . . . In that passionate discussion which divided us so sharply, not once was the term Home Army used. And only later that night, when I could not sleep, did I realise that the discussion was all about the Home Army, about the defense or condemnation of loyalty in defeat. A few weeks later the uprising began.[3]

Kott, in reaction to Andrzejewski's story, felt very strongly that obedience to the process of history was more important than loyalty, honour and heroism.[4]

The Warsaw uprising caught the AL unprepared: Kott was cut off in the district of Ochota, sheltering with an AK runner. He worked on *Mitologia i Realizm* before being forcibly evacuated by the Germans. Eventually Kott made his way to Góra Kalwaria and, saying nothing about his membership of the AL or the fact that he was Jewish, joined an AK unit which carried out execution orders from the underground court. Instead of heading for Warsaw as ordered, the leader of the group attempted to cross the Wisła river and the unit was ambushed and scattered by the Germans. Doubtless he has not told everything. Although his underground career does not seem to have been a spectacular success, after official 'verification' Kott was awarded the Cross of Valour – presumably for his work with the AL rather than the AK.

At the end of the war Kott was recruited by Jerzy Borejsza to the growing Czytelnik organization in Łódź. He wrote two enormously successful pamphlets on Stakhanovite miners and the steadily improving coal production statistics for the Central Committee Department of Propaganda. The second of these pamphlets sold over 100,000 copies and was reprinted twice within a couple of weeks. As a result, the British Council invited 'coal expert' Kott to the north of England to look at coal-mines: he complained that he was underground almost the whole eight days of the visit.

Linked with the left and already well known as something of a Marxist essayist, Kott championed 'Grand Realism' in the influential Łódź journal *Kuźnica* (The Forge). This journal, 'the great tribune of the progressive intelligentsia', was meant to be hard-left, as a complement to the soft-left line of *Odrodzenie*. The title was meant to forge a link with the traditions of the Polish Enlightenment and the socialist Camp of Reform – a line which reflected the attitude of all those connected with the journal. The magazine took its name from a group of Polish writers grouped around Hugo Kołłątaj (1750–1812), a leading figure of the eighteenth-century Polish Enlightenment, and it was deemed the communist-Positivist flagship of the new situation, devoted to fighting against reactionary clericalism, misplaced *szlachta* idealism and outdated, outmoded Polish patriotism. Although it pushed the party line on *socrealizm*, it did not do so exclusively or dogmatically, but in a broad and questioning attempt to restore some of the best, humanist and socialist elements of nineteenth-century literature. *Kuźnica* grew out of circle of people with whom Kott was on familiar terms, namely the pre-war Circle of Polonists, a large and influential democratic-Catholic-leftist group at Warsaw University, one of the few student organizations to which Jews were admitted. It is significant that, with the exception of Stefan Żółkiewski, none of the editorial board of *Kuźnica* had been members of the Party before the war, though several had become members during the war. As Kott was to surmise, the destruction of the pre-war Polish Communist Party by the Comintern, and the attempt to brand all its members as Fascist Trotskyites, meant that virtually all surviving leftists wanted a clean start:

And perhaps that was the source of our enthusiasm and our arrogance in those first postwar years. It seemed to us that we had become Marxists of our own choice and of our own free will. In fact we had become 'Marxists' with the blessing of Borejsza and Jakub Berman.[5]

Kott became a close associate of Żółkiewski and was assistant editor at *Kuźnica*, and he, along with the writers Ważyk, Jastrun and Hertz, engaged in the battle for broad realism in literature. That is, they opposed the 'narrow realism of photographic verisimilitude and advocated broad realism such as Balzac or the English novelists and French Encyclopedists of the eighteenth century had practised'.[6] They admired Defoe, Fielding, Balzac and Proust, and they held Soviet *socrealizm* in low esteem, preferring Pasternak and Akhmatova. Intellectually the magazine was close to the style of the Hungarian Marxist György Lukács. The editors found that while they could write about the French Jacobins, Warsaw during the Kościuszko uprising of 1794, the Russian Decembrists of 1825, Polish revolutionary democrats (their aristocratic prejudices and utopian errors), the Polish 'reds' of 1830 and 1863, the Polish Communards, the Polish Proletariat Party, it was wiser to to let a fog descend on political life and events in Poland after 1905. They avoided publishing or discussing Dostoevsky and instead devoted a great deal of space to *inteligencja* self-criticism and the critical approach of the newer writers to the mental habits of the pre-war Polish writers and literary culture. The magazine gathered together and published writers like Żuławski, Brandys, Hertz, Ważyk and Jastrun. The liberal, anticlerical Kott stressed material considerations in human existence, distrusted intellectual constructions and was acutely aware of changes in political mood. Kott's wide-ranging and apparently unfettered writing in *Kuźnica* was mainly concerned with theatre reviews: Brecht, Dürrenmatt, Fredro, Wyspiański, Shakespeare, Mrożek, Witkiewicz, Chinese theatre, Beckett, the Edinburgh Festival, puppet theatre, Greek tragedy, Molière, Goldoni, Słowacki – even a very negative review of Kruczkowski's dull *socrealizm* play *The Visit* (1954).[7]

The Party attempted to swing this generosity of spirit and interest in resolving the issues suspended by the war around to its own ends by providing writers with a very comfortable existence in the new People's Republic and by focusing writers' attention on the meaning of the war and the coming of the new order rather than on the experience of war and the destruction of the old order. The Party, in regard to cultural policy, was engaged in a *łagodna rewolucja* (gentle revolution) and anxious to appear liberal. An example of this liberality was the publication of Kott's *Mitologia a Realizm* (1946) in which he outlined the 'Marxist-Leninist laws of history' as they applied to Polish literary, cultural and political values. This was an ambiguous subject which involved an attempt to show how the Marxist world-view and issues of human rights were compatible. This would certainly have brought Kott to the attention of the authorities if he had attempted it a few years later.

The end of the war may have brought Kott a literary appointment and some commissions, but it also saw the political differences between him and his wife surface. Within a week of the armistice Lidia Kott (daughter of Professor Hugo Steinhaus) had accused her husband of siding with the 'murderer' Stalin, and he, in response, had thrown her out. They did not manage a reconciliation until the late spring of 1946. The splits within Polish society were never simple, however, and often confound western assumptions of mindless communists versus selfless oppositionists. There was often more give-and-take than either side would easily admit to now. Even in conservative Kraków the Writer's Union was host to numerous meetings and discussions between opposing political factions within the writing community, all of which passed off without rancour or violence. Even in 1947, much to the annoyance of the poet Ważyk, it was still possible for Kott to have supper with Jerzy Turowicz, editor of the Catholic *Tygodnik Powszechny*, at the Kameralna restaurant in Warsaw. Indeed, Kott and the other editors at *Kuźnica* respected Turowicz and *Tygodnik Powszechny*, even though Kott criticized the journal for its Catholic obscurantism. The writers of *Kuźnica*, however, felt nothing but contempt for the ex-Falangist Catholic-communist Bolesław Piasecki and his Pax organization.[8]

In 1947 Kott, as well as writing for *Kuźnica*, completed his Ph.D. in French philology at the University of Łódż and took part in a fraternal delegation to Moscow. In spite of his support for the post-war regime, Kott was increasingly aware that the inner life of the Party was a dangerous business: whatever vision of a new world the rank and file may have had rapidly evaporated after the rigged referendum and election of 1946–7 and the increasing 'sovietization' of the Polish economy. The period 1945–9 was one in which almost all writers enjoyed large print runs, reprints, massively subsidized royalties, prizes, cheap accommodation and substantial gifts from their home towns. In return they were left pretty much to their own devices, to work out their own style, content, methods and relationship to the state and the reading public: the censor intervened only on clearly defined issues and on specifically forbidden topics of national security. However, after Gomułka's arrest and the show trial of Spychalski, Kott realized he was the only member of his AL cell still at liberty and that his connection with Spychalski's wartime counter-intelligence unit could well be a serious problem. By this time the writers at *Kuźnica* had become aware that they were likely to be at the forefront of any political clash and that the Party, which was beginning to push for a simpler version of Polish literature, would be much happier if Polish writers simply followed Soviet models of *socrealizm*:

> To a person, we all opted for realism. But what kind of realism? By that time we all knew quite well, although we would never admit it to ourselves even in the dead of night, that socialist realism and Zhdanovism meant death to all creativity. The problem was how to open the way to socialist realism – for after all, that was what we were doing – and yet at the same time somehow get free of it. In other words, how to put one's neck in a noose and convince others to do so – but prevent the noose from tightening. In *The Captive Mind* Miłosz, more effectively than anyone else either before or after, describes the games we played with the demon of double thinking.[9]

By the end of 1947 it was becoming clear that the Party was ambitious for totalitarian control. Kott, under increasing political pressure, found himself practising what Miłosz was to dub 'Ketman' or double-think, and he turned in his essays to Gorky's idea of 'critical realism', advocated by György Lukács. To his writings on Balzac, Stendhal, Tolstoy, Flaubert and Zola, Kott added Thomas Mann, Laclos, Breton and the surrealists, Defoe, Swift, Voltaire, the encyclopaedists and Diderot. He translated several of these writers for a classic publications series and called his list 'Grand Realism', as opposed to petty realism.[10] Kott was attacked at a closed Party meeting just before the Third Congress of Polish writers in Warsaw.

Woroszylski and the other impatient young communist writer-firebrands, the *pryszczaci* (pimplies) as Borowski had dubbed them, were rising to prominence. These younger writers were unhappy with *Kuźnica*, and at the Third Congress of the Writers' Union they 'heckled older writers, accusing them of flabby, bourgeois liberalism'.[11] Kott defended Maria Dąbrowska as a classic writer who, with her interest in the peasantry, the transformation of the gentry and the history of the co-operative movement, was necessary to the health of Polish literary culture: even if she was not on the 'side' of the Party, they had nevertheless awarded her several state prizes and many regarded her as the conscience of the secular left. In response Woroszylski attacked Kott, saying he had no time for bourgeois superstitions that allowed respect for class enemies. Woroszylski produced a copy of an ill-considered letter from Kott on the subject of Mayakovsky's verse and the audience applauded

Woroszylski's reading from the letter. Kott, shocked at the attack, collapsed and had to be taken home. Later he was to ponder the differences between the 'pimplies' and writers of his own generation:

> At *Kuźnica* we stood by the new order out of either conviction or a deep seated feeling of resignation not always recognised as such, but each of us brought along not only former tastes and predilections but also what proved more enduring – social habits and customs. We did not differ from the 'pimply ones' in political commitment . . . what distinguished us from the 'pimply ones' was our pre-war upbringing, while they had begun their conscious or barely conscious life during the war, the Occupation, the camps and deportations. Those of us who went to the forest had already finished university. We differed from them too in our abhorrence of denunciations and our absolute inability to repeat private conversations. We had a deeply ingrained respect for privacy, especially for the private life of friends. In those first post-war years a great wave of lying was bearing down, a mixture of peasant customs, petty-bourgeois hypocrisy, fulminations and castigations from on high.[12]

In 1949 Kott was summoned to Party headquarters. The secretary of the Central Committee and the chief of the Party propaganda section accused *Kuźnica* of 'rightist deviation'. Kott was told that he clearly had no backbone for political work and that henceforth he was to be professor of Romance languages at Wrocław University. Kott accepted the Party's 'objective judgement' of him. This 'conversation' marked the beginning of Kott's exile to the university system. To sweeten the pill he was awarded the state prize for literature and literary studies in 1951 and again in 1955 for his translation, editing and essays. In 1952 Kott was allowed to return to Warsaw when he was appointed professor extraordinary of Polish literature at Warsaw University, a post he retained until 1969. Kott's 'conversation' at Party headquarters also marked the beginning of his estrangement from the Party and the start of the dissolution of *Kuźnica*: within a short time the editor, Żółkiewski, was replaced by Central Committee member Paweł Hoffman, a neurotic hard-liner who ruthlessly scrutinized all copy for signs of 'right deviationism' or departures from *socrealizm*. A little while later the Writers' Congress in Szczecin was forced to adopt *socrealizm* as 'the sole artistic method of artistic creativity'.[13] In spite of the Party's drive for increasing power and control through the early 1950s, pressure for democratization grew, especially after the death of Stalin. On 6 March 1956 Kott, who was dissatisfied with the cultural policies of the Party and frustrated by the imposition of Stalinism on his vision of socialism, wrote in *Nowa Kultura* (New Culture) that writers were paralysed because they knew that the political establishment had no criteria of literary judgement and that the constant fear of writers was solely whether they had somehow inadvertently unmasked themselves as 'subjective enemies'.

On 24–5 March 1956 the Council of Culture and Art met for its nineteenth session. Party members and ex-Party members of the Writers' Union, people like Andrzejewski, Kott, Ważyk, Brandys, many of them winners of the state literary prize, led the debates. It was from among Party writers and ex-Party writers that the most vociferous and ferocious scourging of the Party came, and from their criticisms that Polish *rewizjonizm* (revisionism) developed. Kott, isolated after the changes at *Kuźnica* and increasingly alienated from mainstream Party opinion, opened the discussion with a talk entitled: 'Mitologia i Prawda' (Mythology and Truth: On Modernism and the Revolutionary Nature of Art, *Przegląd Kulturalny* 1–7 April 1956), in which he said that so far Marxist tools of analysis had been applied to the past, but not to the present. The perception of the leader in a mythical light, he said, was part and parcel of a mythical attitude towards the ideological struggle, and this was aided by the thesis of the intensification of the class struggle and the concept of 'enemies of the people'. Art, he said, served to legitimize the regime rather than the system; it degenerated into laudatory, exalting and decorative art.

Kott went on to say that in his view fatalism in the critique of the official ideology did indeed reflect some of the characteristics of Marxism, but that art was being used by the Party to legitimize itself rather than the philosophy the Party was supposed to serve. He said that over the last fifteen years Polish writers under Soviet power had been inclined to repeat that everything that was, was good, that everything that existed was right and proper. He stated that everyone was required to believe that things were as good as they could be, but that in doing this, art no longer told the truth, but furthered a totally fictitious version of reality. Art had been made to extract the truth of the human situation and experience. But in Poland reality had been 'justified' at the expense of the truth. Contemporary history was a great myth. Those who said that they liked Debussy or Stravinsky were condemned as public enemies; people had transferred from aesthetics to mythology, forgetting that aesthetics was a science. This strangulation of Polish culture had its roots in the USSR, in the first congress of the Soviet writers in 1934, when under Zhdanov literature had ceased to be the spirit and conscience of the revolution and had become the administration of the myth of *socrealizm*. Since then *socrealizm* had become the only model available to loyal communist writers, and thus literature could no longer speak of the crimes of the times; literature lived in falsehood and helped create a fictitious vision of reality. Soviet literature had canonized the myth of *socrealizm* and was now suffering for it culturally.[14]

In *Przegląd Kulturalny* (22–9 April 1956) Kott said: 'Only a writer's moral force and determination to oppose, his zeal and will to serve the truth, never to reconcile himself to mythology, would guarantee the future of Polish literature and culture.' He went on to argue that Soviet cultural life had already been thoroughly poisoned by official meddling during the Zhdanov years, and that as a result an atmosphere of lies and indifference prevailed in Poland; he refuted the idea that socialist art was permanently and by definition bound to improve, or that conversely bourgeois art was bound to decline; he also pronounced that *socrealizm* in Poland was a monumental blind alley, and that the strength of Polish literature probably lay in its ability to resist official policies in the arts. Now things were changing. and communist writers were learning to ask important questions concerning revolutionary dignity, the fate and future of the revolution. Writers were again the heart and soul of the revolution and the history of the nation. Writers, he said, did not wish to be separated from the people or from the Party, but they had a revolutionary duty as loyal party members to awaken conscience.

Kott's comments opened the way for serious debate within the Writers' Union at their annual conference in June 1956. Chairman Antoni Słonimski asked those Party members of the Writers' Union with 'dirty hands' to step down from positions of power within the union. Sandauer, Przyboś, Karst, Jastrun, Wirpsza and Żółkiewski all quibbled over Kott's use of Marxist terminology, but grudgingly agreed they had assisted the Party out of fear. Stalinists like Putrament (whom Kott once spotted on the back of a police wagon abusing demonstrators through a megaphone) defended the old Party line. But even they sensed that a new position was required. The minister of culture, Sokorski, who in 1949 had attempted to impose *socrealizm* as the official literary style of post-war Poland, now changed his position and revealed his distaste for attempts to direct literature or intervene in cultural and creative processes. He admitted that *socrealizm*, which he himself had introduced, at Berman's instruction, at the Fourth Writers' Union Congress in 1949, had been a mistake and that the basis for such literature did not yet exist in Poland. He criticized prevailing Party orthodoxy on *socrealizm*, saying that there could never be any such 'definite artistic school or style or recipe' for creative literature. While the idea of *socrealizm* was still valid it had been clumsily implemented and had stifled the individual 'free development' necessary to underpin objective truth. He also admitted that the Party's insistence on content over form had been misguided and promised that the system of Party directives to writers would now cease.

Commentators on 1956 have given prominence to the clashes on the streets of Poznań and the power of the Polish working class. Certainly Kott believed that after the 'feverish night' of 18–19 October, when Khrushchev himself had flown into Warsaw, when Soviet troops stationed in Poland were mobilized and the Polish military, making it clear that they would oppose any Soviet intervention in Polish affairs, had occupied key sites in Warsaw and armed the workers, the real master of Poland was demonstrably 'the revolutionary working class' (*Przegląd Kulturalny*, 25 October 1956). The protests in Poznań were a threat to the regime, but Soviet reaction had actually helped the Polish communists contain the threat by converting the crisis to one of national security. The Party also felt the demands of the writers and intellectuals had to be met in a different way from those of the workers. It was possible to disperse crowds with bullets, promises of more meat and threats of Soviet invasion, but none of these would greatly affect the intellectual threat to the Party's position. The main current of protest and even revolt may have been proletarian, but the main current of reform was intellectual and came from rebel party member writers: Ważyk, Hłasko, Brandys, Andrzejewski, Jastrun, Kołakowski, Kott, Iłłakowiczówna and Hertz. They had all gained valuable insight into the nature of the regime. Their opposition and ambition was now, quite by accident, associated and in harmony with demonstrating workers who were denied any means of communicating their political opinion and economic experience.

Władysław Gomułka, installed as Party first secretary during the crisis of 1956, was a product of the Party. At heart, while he was clearly a Polish patriot and had stood up to Moscow in the past, he was also a fairly orthodox Stalinist. Almost immediately after his elevation to power, Gomułka began to turn against his erstwhile supporters, the influential writers and editors Kott, Kołakowski, Lasota, Gottesman, Woroszylski, Ważyk and Andrzejewski. The mood of national unity on which Gomułka had ridden to power began to evaporate almost as soon as he had taken office. Towards the end of 1957 the ban on emigration was lifted for Jews. Anyone who could prove Jewish ancestry and expressed a desire to emigrate to Israel was allowed to leave. At about the same time Gomułka began a purge in which over 200,000 people were expelled from the Party and by 1959 some 40,000 people, mostly of Jewish origin and comprising the bulk of the surviving Jewish population, had left the country.[15]

Attacks on the highly readable student magazine *Po Prostu* (Plain Speaking) began to appear in print. Through 1954–5 *Po Prostu* had paved Gomułka's path and led the pursuit of reform by insisting that the Polish people had a right to expect, even demand, accountability from the Party. The journal supported the notion of workers' councils, agitated for new elections to the Sejm, supported the formation of independent clubs for intellectuals and the extension of cultural activities into the provinces. As an adjunct to revisionism the magazine was destined for trouble with the Party. In a short while the editor, Lasota, was dismissed; in June 1957 the magazine was forced to take a 'summer vacation'; on 7 September the current issue was seized while still on the printing presses; in October, exactly one year after Gomułka had come to power, the magazine, its editors labelled as *rewizjoniści* (revisionists), was banned. Ten Party members of the editorial board were expelled, six reprimanded by the Central Commission of the Party Control Board. Warsaw students demonstrated against these actions, but were met by riot police, and there followed four nights of violent confrontation in October 1957. The decision to close the magazine was criticized by the Writers' Union, but to no effect. Although the new magazines *Dialog* (Dialogue) and *Współczesność* (Contemporaneity) both appeared, a third magazine called *Europa*, edited by Ważyk, which was planning to publish new work by Jastrun, Żuławski, Hertz and Andrzejewski, was suppressed at its first issue in mid-1957. In protest at this and the loss of *Po Prostu*, Jastrun, Andrzejewski, Kott and several other writers resigned from the Party. But this was also to no avail: at the start of 1958 the journal *Nowa Kultura* was targeted, causing the mass resignation if its editorial team: Woroszylski, Konwicki, Mach, Marian Brandys, Kołakowski, Wirpsza, Piórski. In the months that followed Żółkiewski was dismissed from his post as minister of higher education, Władysław Bieńkowski lost his post as minister of education, the intellectual clubs that had grown up during 1956 were 'regulated' out of existence, and the journal *Przegląd Kulturalny* (Cultural Review) was closed down.

Doubtless Kott's health was affected by the the rigours of the war years and by the political climate of the time. In 1961, still in disgrace and outside the favour of the Party, he had to undergo surgery to remove the upper lobe of his right lung as a result of tuberculosis, but was refused permission to go to France for a rest cure until Leon Kasman, the supposedly 'inflexible' hard-line editor in chief of *Trybuna Ludu* (Tribune of the People) and member of the Party Central Committee, intervened on his behalf.

In 1963 the Party shamelessly manœuvred its own people into the leading positions within the Writers' Union. They ousted chairman Antoni Słonimski and elected the tame and compliant Iwaszkiewicz, supported by Kruczkowski and Putrament. (Within a year the union was to debate the 'collaborationist conduct' of these officers.) The Party renewed calls for *socrealizm*, responded to a letter of complaint from the writers by closing down the magazine *Nowa Kultura* and by setting up in its place the journal *Kultura* (Culture) – its name stolen from the independent Paris-based Polish literary magazine. At the XIII Party Plenum the attitude of Polish writers was debated. Gomułka dubbed them 'hostile elements' and accused them of *rewizjonizm*.

In March 1964 Kott, along with thirty-three other writers signed a letter protesting at government censorship and repressive government cultural policies in the allotment of paper for books and journal publishing, the restrictions in the size of print runs and the diminishing size and number of print runs and titles in print, the lack of open discussion. Kott claimed this was a 'mild and innocent' protest, but the Letter of the Thirty-Four was condemned by a petition of over 600 writers 'loyal' to the regime. Kott recalled the moment when he learned of the Party's reaction to the protest:

> I saw Sokorski in the hall of a theatre during intermission at the premier of a new Polish play. 'Those irresponsible idiots', Sokorski said right away, 'have drawn up a whole resolution directed against all of you who signed the protest. I've just

come back from the Building. (That was the Kafkaesque name used for the new Central Committee headquarters.) Your case has been put on the agenda. These fools have not cooled off yet and are still frothing at the mouth. None of you will be allowed to publish, and forget about trips abroad. But don't get too upset. The most important thing is to keep cool. They'll forget all about it in three months.' 'But Mr. Minister,' asked Lidia [Kott's wife], who was standing by my side and who wanted as usual to know everything, 'have you read the resolution?' 'Of course,' replied Sokorski, 'I wrote it myself.'[16]

A total of fourteen signatories of the letter, including Kott, were banned, fourteen others were given a personal warning by the prime minister. Kott could no longer get his writing accepted for publication in any magazine or journal. The clash between Kott and the Party illuminated the fundamental difficulty of reconciling literary and personal freedoms with doctrinaire Soviet-style Marxism. That said, the Polish Party were still not as inclined to brutality as their Soviet counterparts. They did not execute the writers or exile them to the *gulag*.

Since 1956, when he had reviewed politically powerful and influential productions of Shakespeare's *Hamlet*, Jarry's *Ubu Roi* and Mickiewicz's *Dziady*, Kott had been at work on a reinterpretation of Shakespeare, in which he linked the power struggles of Shakespeare's times with those of the twentieth century. This led to his most famous book *Szkice o Szekspirze* (1964) (Sketches on Shakespeare, English title *Shakespeare Our Contemporary*).[17] Kott had watched the events of 1953–6, the results of Stalin's death and the installation of Gomułka, very carefully. He saw Shakespeare's plays as very much in tune with their own era of cruelty, political murders, unscrupulous tyrants, the struggle for power, spying, duplicity and deceit – but the connection with Shakespeare enabled Kott to say things that many contemporary writers working in other literary media were unable to say. Heavily influenced by Malraux and also still under the sway of his wartime experience, Kott believed that a man who had not killed was a kind of virgin. Murder was a loss of innocence, very similar to the first biblical sex act, which provided knowledge of human fragility and a sense of contempt that was irreplaceable and irreversible.

Kott was clearly still working through the horrors and changes of the war and the new fears implanted by Stalinism – his contribution to a socialist Poland had been curtailed by his removal from *Kuźnica*, and by his later banning. In his work on Shakespeare he nevertheless presented a slightly veiled loyal-communist critique of power struggles in post-war Poland, and while it grew out of a specific experience of politics and history, it was to prove massively useful and illuminating to commentators from a very wide range of very different political backgrounds. In writing about Shakespeare in this way, Kott was clearly voicing his own growing cynicism about political life, the manipulation of public life and the human consequence of endless power struggle:

> *Romeo and Juliet* and *Troilus and Cressida* are, after all the same play. During the Nazi Occupation, years before *Shakespeare Our Contemporary*, I started to read Shakespeare through the experiences of the war. In times of terror, human dramas – even the most common and universal – somehow become final and are purified of anything accidental. They are sharply defined to a striking degree, and their clarity is sometimes appalling. In a hostile world the lover is taken away after their first night of love. Whoring or suicide are the only choices. There was still a third way out: planting mines on the tracks ahead of military transports. Of all Shakespearean heroines, Cressida was closest to my heart for a long time. [18]

For all this though, it was Kott's delineation of Lukács's Grand Mechanisms of History, and its immediate and vivid application to stage practice in Peter Hall's famous productions for the Royal Shakespeare Company, that found the book a popular readership in the west. In Shakespeare, Kott said, the history plays all begin with a struggle to consolidate the throne and end with the monarch's death and a new coronation. Every ruler drags a long chain of crimes, but has been unable to murder all those who might offer opposition. Those who gather against him hope for a new order, but their every step to power is marked by the same sequence of crimes: 'For Shakespeare power has names, eyes, mouth and hands. It is a relentless struggle of living people who sit together at one table.'[19] As Kott put it, having seen work by Peter Brook and also the continuous performance of six of Shakespeare's history plays at Stratford in Peter Hall's *Wars of the Roses*:

> The new bourgeoisie joined the ranks of the old aristocracy . . . The drama of the protagonists is the drama of history – sometimes even the tragedy of history. I showed the workings of the Grand Mechanism in Shakespeare's history plays. But that was ten years later, after Stalin's death . . . the scenery remained unchanged. The Usurper climbed the same stairs, and from the throne at the top of the stairs the Anointed, wearing the same crown, were toppled. The Grand Mechanism became visible on stage.[20]

For Kott, Shakespeare was more contemporary at some times than at others. In the late 1950s and early 1960s Kott judged Shakespeare to be very contemporary and it was primarily the notion that Shakespeare's experience mirrored and illuminated Stalinism that intrigued Kott. His fascination with the figure of King Richard III enabled many directors and actors to connect his character and schemes with those of Stalin: for a while there was a fashion, particularly evident in Yugoslav theatre and in western student theatre, of presenting the play as a 'contemporary event' with Richard wearing a moustache and dressed in a Stalin-style military jacket. Years later, thinking of Shakespeare's kings, Kott was to point to Stalin's funeral as a perfect example and vindication of the kind of connection he had been making:

> His [Stalin's] enormous coffin is borne on the shoulders of Malenkov, Molotov, Bulganin, Khrushchev, and Beria, all either in long coats or in military tunics, with huge fur caps on their heads. In the first week after Stalin's funeral, Beria was literally smothered by Malenkov (who threw himself at Beria during a Politburo meeting and strangled him with the help of some of the others) or, as a later official version reported, he was formally sentenced to death and executed only a month or more after that. All the rest of those mourners who carried Stalin's coffin to the Lenin mausoleum were shortly consigned to oblivion one after the other by Khrushchev. He himself was the last to go. But he was the first of Stalin's gravediggers.[21]

For Kott it was not surprising that given the prospect of the struggle to hold and maintain political power, Hamlet and Prospero should both, in different ways, seek revenge, attempt to right wrongs, sicken and then renounce their claims to power.

The British critic Alvarez wrote, the year after *Shakespeare Our Contemporary* was published:

> Polish art runs instinctively to allegory. It is all, whatever its appearance, written in what they call 'Aesopian language', in which each detail can always be translated into terms of something else – something relevant to the Polish situation. Hence when a scholar like Jan Kott writes about Shakespeare's Histories, in the west it is hailed as a revolution in Shakespearean criticism, while in Poland it is treated as political comment – as though there were an implied erratum: 'For "Tudor" read "Poland" throughout'.[22]

While the book cast a very searching light on Shakespeare's times and political culture, it told us just as much about the feverish, paranoid, plot-ridden, gossip-riddled life of the Warsaw intellectuals and their crumbling grey Stalinist world as it did about Shakespeare. The joy of an Aesopian reading of Shakespeare was that there was absolutely nothing the censor could do to guard against interpretation. This was clearly a very important discovery in the increasingly censored Poland of the 1950s and 1960s, but to read the book now is to enter a world of naked power, endless intrigue, overwhelming ambition, violence and deeply disturbing sexuality: it is a massively revealing book, deeply cynical and more than a little depressing for the relentlessness of its accurate observation of human nature and political activity – not only in communist societies. Miłosz wrote of it:

Historical experience enabled everybody to identify himself with Hamlet, who now, contrary to psychological interpretations, was just a brave young man forced to play the fool in order to deceive a dangerous master and his plainclothesmen. Thus, Shakespeare was integrated into the traditional Polish concept of the theatre as a public forum where problems of the community are debated by means of an artistic transposition. Since the existential frame of mind in Poland was nourished by the experience of people who felt the precariousness of the individual tossed around by the capricious forces of History, King Lear was played as Everyman, similar to the characters in 'absurd' plays. Kott formulated all this more cogently than any of his Polish colleagues, and to the scholarly objections raised by some Western professors he might oppose a valid argument: his Shakespeare has an immediacy that all Western directors, if not all Western professors, might well envy.[23]

In 1964 Adam Bromberg, director of the PWN publishing house, not only published *Shakespeare Our Contemporary*, but commissioned an English translation to be published by Methuen, paid for by the Polish Ministry of Arts and Culture in scarce hard currency. At the end of 1964, as a result of the publication of *Shakespeare Our Contemporary* in Polish, English, French and German, and the consequent award of the Herder literary prize in Vienna, Kott was invited to lecture at Yale. He had no trouble gaining permission from his university, but Kott was still in disgrace after his protest and the Central Committee refused to grant permission for him to go abroad. After a year Kott requested a personal interview with Zenon Kliszko, Gomułka's right-hand man and an acquaintance of Kott's from the period of the Occupation, and was finally granted permission to leave the country. In 1966 Kott left Poland as a visiting lecturer to Yale University. However, while Kott was away events in Poland moved to make his return difficult, even unlikely.

In February 1968, 234 writers attended an extraordinary general meeting of the Warsaw branch of the Writers' Union to protest at the way the government had banned a production of part III of Mickiewicz's play *Dziady* (Forefathers' Eve, 1823) on 30 January 1968. A production of this same play at the Warsaw Teatr Polski in 1955 had been a prime mover of political events and had helped shape public perceptions of the unfolding political crisis of 1955–6.[24]

The crudity of the banning provoked prolonged student protest in Kraków and Warsaw. At their February meeting the Warsaw branch of the Writers' Union attacked government interference in cultural matters, including direction of the content of literary works, as well as their distribution and reception in the press; arbitrary, damaging and woolly-minded censorship; the use of banning as a method of cultural policing; and warned that the failure of the government to listen to writers was steadily impoverishing Polish culture. Putrament, worried that Radio Free Europe was paying close attention to events, and doubtless under pressure to dismiss the writers' efforts as an anti-government provocation, tried to persuade the writers to distance themselves from the protesters. Gomułka spoke out to condemn writers (Kisielewski and Słonimski in particular) as a gang of front-men behind which *rewizjoniści* (revisionists) and Zionist agents of imperialism operated to undermine communism and bring about Poland's destruction. Moczar, the Minister now responsible for security, probably working on orders from Moscow, sought to divert genuine political, economic and social grievances away from government and party corruption towards traditional scapegoats by setting off an anti-Jewish purge.

Steadily, from 1956 onwards, the notion of *rewizjonizm* had come to stand as a kind of Party shorthand for Jewish influence. For Kott *rewizjonizm* meant 'breaking free from ossified thinking'.[26] There can be little doubt *rewizjonizm* had been a thorn in Gomułka's flesh for some time and by aiming at the Jewish and intellectual communities he was hitting the *rewizjonizm* movement and controlling the growing, disaffected, opposition within Party intellectual circles. The move against *rewizjonizm* was the start of an attempt to blame all Poland's troubles on the Jews, to purge the Party and *biurokracja* (bureaucracy) of independent-minded intellectuals and to divert attention from the real causes of economic and cultural unrest. Gomułka spoke of an Israeli fifth column operating in Poland, and made efforts to show that Israel and West Germany were involved in anti-Polish plots to relieve post-war Poland of its recently acquired western territories. Gomułka's supporters, particularly Moczar's ZBoWiD organization, Piasecki's Pax organization, the army newspaper *Żółnierz Wolności* (Soldier of Freedom), the Party newspaper *Trybuna Ludu* and Pax's *Słowo Powszechne* (Universal Word), all openly characterized *rewizjonizm* as a Zionist plot to overthrow Gomułka and bring down Poland.

In March 1968, against a background of growing crisis in Czechoslovakia, student protest at the banning of *Dziady* continued: riot police stormed Warsaw University and baton-charged a peaceful demonstration by 20,000 people in central Warsaw. In response to the banning of *Dziady* the censor banned eighteen writers of the Warsaw branch of the Writers' Union; two other members were forced to resign their influential editorships. Some writers were put under police surveillance. The writers Karst, Słucki and Wygodzki left for Israel. University professors Baczko, Brus, Morawski, Kołakowski, Bauman and Hirszowicz were accused of corrupting Polish youth, lost their jobs and left the country. Although Kołakowski was not Jewish, his wife was. Adam Bromberg, editor and director of PWN publishing house, was expelled from the Party, arrested, accused of leading an international criminal organization with the aim of overthrowing the Polish state and then, after a two-year 'investigation' was 'emigrated' to Sweden. Writers identified by the Polish press as resisting the anti-Jewish campaign were harassed: many went into hiding. The critic Kisielewski, after being attacked as an 'ignoramus' in *Życie Warszawy* (Warsaw Life), was twice physically assaulted and beaten:

two of his fingers were broken. Brandys's latest book received an insulting review questioning his 'Polishness'. Słonimski was hounded and insulted in the Party press. At the same time Nina Karsov, a 27-year-old philology student, was jailed for three years, found guilty of keeping a personal diary in which she recorded her feelings about the persecution of Polish intellectuals. By the end of 1969 some 20,000 Poles of Jewish origin had been granted, permission to leave the country.[27]

By attacking Jews the hard-liners within the Party effectively removed a slice of the independent intellectual opposition, silenced a large number of the old guard in the upper ranks of the Party, marginalized dissenting Party intellectuals and made Gomułka, whose wife was Jewish, acutely aware of how powerful his 'supporters' were. In effect Gomułka had been given notice, if he ever needed it, that liberalization was out of the question. Given the wide-ranging political, social, cultural and economic failure of Gomułka's regime, this outburst of repressive measures convinced many that primitive nationalism channelled through anti-Semitism was the only 'ideology' the Party could now muster. The anti-Semitic purge of 1968 broke the *rewizjonism* movement which had been so influential in Polish affairs since the early 1950s: effectively the opposition movement was not to surface again in any coherent and organized form until 1976. The fact that the Party could not make use of the goodwill and talent of its intellectuals, could not sustain the loyalty of writers, could not respond to the record of its policies presented by writers and artists, could not make positive use of comments from critics, and continually acted in bad faith, was an indication of the total lack of originality and intellectual dynamism within the Party, demonstrated the crippling effect of Moscow's dead hand, and was the measure of a Party still stifled by the Stalinists more than a decade after Stalin's death.

Kott and his wife Lidia realized that it would be very difficult for them to return to Poland. In spite of the virtual absence of Jews, anti-Semitism was still a powerful nationalist weapon, and in such a political climate their Jewishness, no matter how attenuated, would make them 'alien' and unwelcome, would be a constant source of worry and could prove their undoing. Kott was well aware that by choosing exile he was accepting the condition of a mute since he would in all probability be cutting himself off from his native soil, from his students, readers, friends, family, intellectual contact and most of all from his native language. He was clear that he was entering into a condition of alienness and of alienation, and that for him there could be no artistic cloak of Romantic artistic embellishment. Exile – or in Polish dissident parlance 'being emigrated' – was a hard fact to accept: there was very little chance that Kott would somehow 'translate himself', and there was likely to be little outlet in the USA for Kott's passion, wit, voracious intellectuality and wide-ranging interest in the world. Kott was also aware that he was condemning his own country for having fallen into 'the darkness of hatred', and there was an element of pride and steadfast perseverance in such a decision. In 1969 the Kotts requested political asylum in the USA. Their request was granted. Kott subsequently taught at Yale, Berkeley, the Catholic University of Louvain in Belgium, the Hebrew University of Jerusalem, lectured in Japan, was a Guggenheim Fellow 1972–3, lectured at the State University of New York at Stony Brook 1969–83, and taught at the Getty Centre in Santa Monica 1985–6. In 1984 he received the George Jean Nathan award for dramatic criticism. However, because of his membership of the communist PPR (Polish Workers Party) and the suspicion that he was still a 'hard-core communist', he was not granted a 'green card' by the US Immigration Service until 1978.

In 1979, after his residence in the USA was assured, Kott returned briefly to Poland. He found his works were no longer in print and all mention of his name and his writings had been removed by the censor from the public to the purely specialist academic domain. Kott found Poland completely altered, and the rising interest in right-wing, authoritarian, Polish nationalist figures from the past was deeply disturbing. He described a conversation with friends:

Three names were passionately stressed: Dmowski, Piłsudski, Daszyński. At first I simply could not understand what was happening. I rubbed my eyes. What did this bring to mind? In which émigration in London, in which anachronistic Warsaw did I find myself? Before the war . . . but which war? The second? No! Before the first! I had the impression that time had stood still. Even that History was running backwards. In the space of those thirteen years while I was away, absolutely different chapters of Polish history had returned. But this furious debate, in which names were brandished like evocative emblems, was about the choices and alternatives in 1979![28]

It was galling for *rewizjonist* Kott to witness, but the main achievement of Polish communism had been to turn Poles away from the figures and ideas of the left, even from those on the left who had consistently opposed Stalinism. The Party had created a hunger, not for a political alternative, but for a political opposite. For many, right-wing politics and solutions were the only alternative to communism.

In 'The Serpent's Sting' Kott considered his political past and his attitude towards communism and history:

If history is rational, reason can hasten it so that it becomes more rational sooner, or at least a bit more rational. If history is rational, whatever endows it with more reason, whatever accelerates it, is permitted and justified. From the top and in advance. At this point the Hegelian Sting takes effect. The *in blanco* justification of history has proven to be the most sinister. That was the pitfall we fell into when we were still twenty, during the first Moscow Trials and the Spanish Civil War. But solidarity with the *'No pasaran!'* of the International Brigades in Spain and silent acquiescence to the Moscow Trials were not the same choice. My political biography and that of my generation begins in those years. If I had to choose again, once more in the thirties, then I would once more choose *'No pasaran!'* and death to the fascists. For this was the choice against terror, and not for a history 'rational and necessary', the choice to be alive, not deaf, to the signs of human distress. The Moscow Trials began before the Spanish Civil War. The very same people who had chosen freedom from violence and oppression now covered their eyes and plugged their ears. The best went to Spain to join the International Brigades, and so gave their answer to the Moscow Trials. Others among us said that whatever is necessary is also rational. Years had to pass before painstakingly, bloodying our hands, we climbed out of this abyss. To avoid it, Nicola Chiaromonte's and George Orwell's clarity of vision and conscience would have been necessary. Intellectuals of my generation rarely possessed such lucidity in those years.[29]

For Hegel history was the unfolding of the potential of the human mind. History was the incarnation of the human mind in time. While it might have been possible to justify the past by understanding it, for Kott it was an infinitely more complex problem to justify the future. The Hegelian sting offered its Marxist adherents the prospect of being part of the Universal Mind, of turning history into *logos* and *ethos*, the prospect of belonging to history, of, quite literally, making history. The Hegelian vision saw humanity as a magnificent creation capable of great things, but saw individuals as 'dung, worthy only of contempt': adherents were 'trapped inside the charmed circle where only false oppositions hold':

> The serpent's sting overpowers the mind . . . Within the charmed circle, the mind moves in a fictitious universe unable to distinguish reality from illusion. The history of the schism of Communist intellectuals has yet to be written to the very end. Two of its chapters, two moments, deserve to be described in detail: joining the Communist movement and leaving it, enchantment and recovery. The moment of recovery is perhaps more important.[30]

By the mid-1980s Kott believed that Party censorship was the logical conclusion of the postmodernist belief that reality was a message that could be transformed at will.[31]

Like many writers of his generation who had been drawn to communism as a way of remaking Polish society and improving standards of living by shaping a new life through literature, Kott had been wooed by the authorities, ditched when they found him troublesome, banned when he became a nuisance, more or less forced into exile. The Party had made it increasingly difficult for him to work, marginalized him in a provincial university, and had made it impossible for him and his *rewizjonist* contemporaries to contribute to the creation of distinctive Polish socialism. Kott's experience was that literature could not *make* a new society to order, but if allowed, it could observe, comment, criticize and record: it could help shape consciousness. But this fact made literature both desirable and dangerous to the Party.

Kott's efforts, like most of his generation, had initially been to politicize the already highly sensitive Polish literati and literary traditions towards acceptance of communism. When he and his contemporaries realized the content of Soviet-style communism and the exceedingly narrow space allowed for their attempts to create a specifically Polish socialism with a human face, they redirected their efforts into criticism and away from the active construction of social models. Indeed, while Kott always acknowledged that it was impossible for literature to remain unaffected by politics, he was gradually to assume the position that literature was the opposite of politics, that while literature set out to improve the quality of human life through working on the imagination, under the decayed Stalinist regimes of eastern Europe, politics (if there was such a thing) was simply the exercise of power, in every way opposed to the liberating and critical faculties of literature. For Kott politics was entirely destructive both of imagination and of literature. Kott, who as a young man had been one of the most unashamedly political of *littérateurs*, was forced to conclude that in writing he was in retreat from politics.

Kott represents the 'compromised' older generation who helped impose communism in Poland. But his is a devastatingly sharp intellect turned against communism through the academically respectable examination of politics in Shakespeare. The politicality of Kott's writing cannot be denied, nor can the impact of Marxism on his thought. The outlines of his disagreements with the Party and his socialist-humanist principles show through all his writings. But his growing weariness with the grand mechanisms of theatre and politics, his impatience with naive writers and ambitious politicians and his perception that in Poland, while writers and politicians may have much to say on the subject of power, neither writers nor politicians necessarily have anything of importance to say on matters of ideology, are also clearly apparent. The twists and turns of his career and political experience, his ambivalence towards his Marxist past and the perhaps foolish hopes of his generation of young idealist communists, his anti-totalitarianism, his unease in exile, his distrust of public life, his suspicion of all those on the road to power, and his scaled-down notion of the role of literature in society, all have a direct bearing on the entire generation of Polish writers to which he belongs and reverberate through contemporary Polish literature and political life. Kott was like many intellectuals of his generation in that the Party could make nothing of his prodigious talent; indeed, the sharp focus of his intelligence was an embarrassment to the Party.

In December 1990 Kott, almost the last of the immediate post-war communist generation of writers, survived his fifth heart attack. He had spent more than ten years reviewing theatre productions, travelling the world to see plays and theatre festivals, a further ten years in Polish universities teaching theatre. He had made his reputation in the west with his writings about Shakespeare, but after leaving Poland his writing became increasingly contemplative, introspective, personal and philosophical. After his exile he wrote about sex and eroticism, heart attacks and illness, the twisting and twisted literary careers of other Polish writers, the difficulty of translation, death. In 1967 he wrote: 'I prefer to write about theatre. I take part in the great game, or at least I think I do.'[32] For him Polish theatre had been a vital political litmus paper, a kind of politics, a state-supported viper's nest of political protest, a cultural pressure point. However, his interest in theatre, he came to realize, was actually an interest in post-war Polish political culture and its mechanisms: the longer he was away from Poland, the more his interest in theatre waned. One of the closing remarks of his autobiography, *Still Alive*, was that theatre had long since ceased to be of any interest to him: he was now far more interested in his three-month-old granddaughter.

In many ways Jan Kott's career is a paradigm of the spiritual history of his generation. His life – somewhere between politics and literature, criticism and theatre, Poland and America, Shakespeare and communism – illustrates the despair of many involved in cultural politics. He has despaired at the way that literature, while attempting to record and interpret, is touched, influenced, manipulated and blocked by events which are not in themselves literary. It is, of course, possible to say that writers who get involved in politics are tarnished for ever and deserve all they get. But for writers of Kott's generation there was little choice. However, political life does not mean slavish adherence to the line of one particular party; indeed many writers, even those on the left, often refuse actually to join a party. And anyway, post-war Polish writers, especially those with a vision of a better future, were involved in the politics of literature whether they liked it or not, just by virtue of the fact that they wrote and lived in Poland.

Unlike many politically engaged writers in the USSR, Czechoslovakia, Nigeria or Iran, however, Kott got away from the 'meat grinder'. The Polish Communist Party was totalitarian only in its ambition: it did not kill and make a martyr of Kott. It preferred, as with Kołakowski, Brus, Baczko and the others, to marginalize them in some way and was happy simply to get them out of the country. In this, as in most things, provided it could hang on to power, the Party was never more than half-hearted. Kott's career trajectory, and those of the other *rewizjoniści,* indicates that while literature can (perhaps must) absorb and make use of political themes, political life cannot absorb writers except to their detriment, and does not know what to make of literature. The Party tried alternately to control writers and their work and then to ignore them.

The Party's achievement was to prevent Kott being of use in Poland, to deprive Polish readers and thinkers of his writing, to suppress, delay and spoil his contribution. Kott's depression, like that of many intellectuals in post-war Poland, is not that the Party hounded and harassed him, but that, while he had engaged with communist ideology, for its part the Party had tried to make a nothing of him: it could not absorb his commitment and had shamelessly squandered his energy and intellect. Kott, though he has not lived in Poland since 1966, is still shaped by his early socialism and his opposition to Stalinism. He is still a victim of the Party, prey to disgust, disenchantment and remorse. Like the other *rewizjoniści* his hopes for Polish socialism were grotesquely betrayed and his ideals caricatured by the victory of a half-hearted Stalinism over native Polish socialism.

5

STANISLAW LEM

The existing criteria of value have been falsified and distorted. The force brought to bear against consciousness must, sooner or later, develop into physical force. To take note of this and to give warning is the role of literature.

Stanisław Barańczak, passage cut from the Catholic journal *Więź*, in the Department of Censorship's internal journal *Bulletin on Themes of Materials Censored* (Second Quarter 1974)

Post-war writers of east central Europe have been fascinated by the way their societies have created and maintained themselves as closed information systems which control ideas. However, writers were rarely allowed to discuss the matter openly. Lem repeatedly presents human society as a complex mechanism for transmitting information and for furthering a common sense of identity through particular kinds of language, ideas, plots and characters. Lem's writings are the product of the specific political and social tensions that developed after the 'thaw' of 1956 and the collapse of Party efforts to promote *socrealizm*. In the former eastern bloc, science fiction could sometimes be seen as a form of dissidence, as an oblique way of considering important social and political themes, of side-stepping the censor in the never-ending battle to get unpoliced ideas out of the writer's head and into the heads of a reading public. This is directly related to the way the Party attempted to manipulate society and the cultural and political media via the office of the censor.

The jump from social and political problems to science fiction may seem huge, but virtually all of Lem's novels may be read as parables about what happens to society and to people when channels of communication are blocked, about the difficulty of making a revolutionary society or fundamentally changing human nature by social and political engineering on the slender basis of the knowledge of humanity that we have at our disposal. As such his novels are profoundly humanistic, a coded critique of the kind of societies that developed under Stalin and a plea for a socialism of gradual change and a human face. Before looking at Lem's work in detail it is best to set his novel *Solaris* (1961) in that specific literary-political context.

The Czech novelist Milan Kundera has described east central Europe as a laboratory where history made a strange experiment with humanity.[1] The defeat of Germany in 1918 brought forth a magnificent flowering of art and thought from among the 'smaller nations'. It was here that some of the most adventurous and far-reaching developments in modern fiction took place. Writers revealed what had been unleashed on the world in both personal and national terms by probing the collapse of the old empires and the rise of the new. They also anticipated many of the developments of the post-war world. East central European literature has a rich tradition of utopian and absurdist writing developed in reaction to censorship, the bureaucratic procedures and administration of the Austro-Hungarian, Prussian and Russian empires. Much east central European literature is marked by strong anti-authoritarian elements, grotesque appreciation of human contradictions, very perceptive reactions to power structures and a keen appreciation of the social, personal and familial structures that underlie government.

East central Europe up to the start of the Second World War was the haunt of artists and writers who, freed from a narrow concern for 'national survival', recorded the process of transition from agricultural folk cultures to modern industrial nation-states, and they recorded it in all its personal ambiguities. This was where Bartók, Kodály and Janáček transformed folk music into experimental work; where Freud explored dreams and the unconscious, and writers such as Musil, Broch and Roth, Kafka, Schulz, Witkiewicz, the brothers Capek, Karinthy, Nesvadba and Hašek explored not only the 'outer limits' but the inner limits of humanity and human identity. They all wrote of the effects of modern social structures and political systems on the inner life of the individual – the borderlands of perception, of consciousness and its links with citizenship. They pursued relentlessly those elements that go to make up personal, public and political decisions. East central Europe experienced the whole range of twentieth century possibilities within a very short time-span. The nations of east central Europe saw the growth and break-up of the old European empires, the development and impact of large-scale industry and the effects of increasingly centralized and often military governments upon their daily life. They experienced these developments first as distant provinces of the old empires, and then through the experience of building small, would-be democratic nations from the ruins of those empires. All experienced the totalitarian regimes first of Hitler and then of Stalin.

Without doubt Lem is a product of this intense history and literary tradition. Lem was born in the Polish-Ukrainian town of Lwów on 12 September 1921. Both his parents were doctors of very distant Jewish ancestry. His father had been a physician in the Austro-Hungarian army and had been captured by the Russians at the fall of the Przemyśl fortress in 1915. As an officer he was condemned to execution by firing squad, but was saved when a Jewish barber from Lemberg intervened on his behalf. Lem's father went on to become a successful (and therefore rather wealthy) laryngologist in Lwów. As an only child Lem did not lack for toys and had a French governess. As a child he found a German-language 'electro-technical experiment book' on his father's desk and with the help of a bilingual dictionary read it through and began devising his own experiments. He finished his schooling at the Karol Szajnochas Gymnazjum in 1939, and was rumoured to have an IQ of 180 – 'the most intelligent child in southern Poland'. By the age of eighteen he had read widely in chemistry and physics and had written a volume of poems. He started to study at the Lwów Institute of Medicine, but between 1939 and 1941 he was prevented from pursuing his studies by the Russian invasion of Poland and then, from 1941 to 1944 by the German invasion of Russia.[2]

Since under the Nazis Poles were forbidden any kind of further education Lem worked with false Polish papers as a garage mechanic. He scavenged ammunition from the local German Luftwaffe arms dump, and on one occasion transported a gun for the resistance under the noses of the occupation forces. Inevitably, in December 1942, his false papers were 'blown' and he was forced to leave his job with a German car-repair firm, hide the pilfered ammunition under the stairs in the garage and go into hiding while he obtained new papers. Hiding in the Lwów Botanical Garden he could hear the Nazis throwing grenades into the vaults of the Jewish Lyczaków cemetery as the last of the survivors from the Lwów ghetto were liquidated.

In 1944 Lwów was 'liberated' by the Red Army and Lem renewed his studies at the Lwów Institute of Medicine. However, in 1945 Lwów, along with the whole of eastern Poland, passed under Russian control. The following year Lem and millions of other Poles moved westwards to the new Polish People's Republic, leaving behind them their homes and most of their possessions. The Lem family lived in a single room in Kraków, and Lem senior, now aged seventy-one, was obliged to start work again. Tadeusz Konwicki recalls Lem at that time:

> Even with my lousy memory, I do remember Lem from 1945–46. In those days he wore a Jagiellonian University medical school cap and, if I'm not mistaken, knickers. Those slightly old fashioned trousers were engraved in my enfeebled memory cells because they were a certain sign of his provincialism. From those knickers I guessed that Lem came from the borderlands, probably Lwów.[3]

Lem resumed his studies in 1946, this time at Kraków's Jagiellonian University under the informal tutorship of the Kraków polymath Mieczysław Choynowski, director of the Scientific Institute. Lem read volumes, loaned by Choynowski, on cybernetics, cosmology, philosophy, biology. Eventually he finished his study of medicine in 1948, but he did so without taking his final diploma – the reason being that once qualified he would have been drafted for an extended period into the army medical corps. In 1947 he became a junior research assistant at the Kraków Naukoznawcze Conservatorium, where he made abstracts of scientific literature, many on the subject of cybernetics, for the journal *Życie Nauki*.

Lem's experiences of pre-war 'capitalist' Poland, of the Nazi and Soviet occupations and the post-war years in Poland made him profoundly aware that all human systems are profoundly fragile, and that under pressure human behaviour was impossible to predict. These were two observations to which he was to return again and again. Lem began writing in the late 1940s, short stories for a weekly crime magazine, as a way of supplementing his father's meagre earnings. His poems appeared in Katowice weekly newspapers and also in the Catholic journal *Tygodnik Powszechny*. His first published novel, *Człowiek z Marsa* (Man from Mars) appeared weekly in *Nowy Świat Przygód* in 1946; *Astronauci* (Astronauts) appeared in 1951; there followed a volume of short stories *Sesame*, and another novel *Oblok Magellana* (Cloud of Magellan, 1955). His early work was part of the very rigid Stalinist literary bureaucratic world, and these works conformed fairly closely to the conventional science fiction of the day in that they were largely optimistic, had faith in technological innovation and the powers of human ingenuity, and trusted in the idea of utopian worlds ruled by benign scientists and experts. His first 'serious' work, a trilogy entitled *Czas Nieutracony* (Time Not Lost, which includes the novel *Hospital of the Transfiguration*) though it was finished in 1948 (Lem's last student year), conformed more or less to the prevailing *socrealizm* mode, but apart from the first volume was clearly an artistic failure and was not published until 1956. This was virtually the end of Lem's flirtation with *socrealizm*.

Lem was expelled from the ZLP in 1951 for failing to produce enough to qualify him as a professional writer, yet by 1955 his novels and short stories had aroused sufficient interest for the city of Kraków to award him its Golden Order of Merit. Lem regards the period leading up to 1956 as one of mild brainwashing and has dubbed his early works as 'devoid of any value'. Certainly after 1956 although elements of detailed realism were incorporated in Lem's work, his novels and stories diverged ever more rapidly from *socrealizm*, and with the political relaxation of the 'thaw' Lem's work was accepted for publication far more frequently. While Lem was popular with science fiction enthusiasts, perhaps the first book to make a wider impression was *Eden*, published in 1959, a tale of exploration on a distant planet in which the outlines of his interest in human capacity for empathy with alien beings and ability to understand alien patterns of thought and social structure were already in evidence, as was his underlying concern with humans' capacity for understanding themselves. Increasingly, though, Lem was concerned with the discrepancy between the achievements of technology and human ability to put technology to good use. From the mid-1950s onwards Lem's novels portray power-hungry characters whose inner life is a mystery even to themselves, whose motives are cruel, greedy and destructive, and for whom hostility to whatever is alien is perfectly natural.

Between 1956 and 1968 Lem was enormously productive, and it is in these years that his publishing career peaked with four plays, ten volumes of short stories, five science fiction novels and an enormous book on cybernetic theory.[4] In 1973 Lem was awarded the Ministry of Art and Culture's literary prize (first degree). Lem is co-founder of the Polish Astronautical Society and a member of the Polish Cybernetics Association. He was elected an honorary member of the Science Fiction Writers of America, but his membership was revoked in 1975 after he was thought to have made rude remarks on western science fiction in a Frankfurt journal. By the late 1980s Lem had produced over thirty-eight volumes, totalling sales of over twenty-four million copies – six million in English. According to publicity material presented by André Deutsch, Lem's British publisher, his books have been translated into more than thirty languages, and approximately thirty new translations appear each year. His works proved to be particularly popular in what was the USSR, where two and a half million censored copies were in circulation. After the collapse of communism a further three million uncensored copies of his work were published. In post-1991 Germany he has sold over seven million copies. With his books reissued in a uniform Polish edition at the end of the 1980s, published in expensive transatlantic hardback and special editions, and in a two-volume paperback selection by Penguin, it is probably fair to say that Lem is one of the world's most successful science fiction writers.[5]

Lem's situation was the same as that of any other eastern-bloc science fiction writer. Because science fiction was seen to be a minority interest it had a very low priority within eastern-bloc publishing programmes; whenever the inevitable print and paper shortages showed themselves science fiction publication was one of the first casualties. This inevitably meant that serious Polish writers favoured work in other more stable and rewarding areas. At first the authorities said they could publish only a limited edition because he was unknown and because he was working in science fiction. Then, when his books sold out, received good reviews, came to the notice of foreign readers, the authorities worried that perhaps the public had read something into the work that they or the censor had missed. Reprints were not forthcoming until public interest had died down, or until the censor had checked that the work was perfectly safe, that there was, after all, nothing dangerous lurking between the lines.

It is often assumed that because Lem is now so well known in the former eastern bloc his work was somehow encouraged by state patronage and official favour. Lem, however, feels that his work was tolerated by the authorities rather than encouraged. Almost all of his books appeared first in editions of less than 20,000. *Summa technologiae*, for example, was first published in 1963 in an edition of 3,000 copies; even the highly successful *Bajki Robotów* (Robotic Fables, 1964) first appeared in an edition of 7,000 – small even by Polish standards. Lem has repeatedly complained that his books appeared in Poland in editions of only 25,000–35,000 copies. Only after 1978 did Lem achieve an edition of 100,000 on any of his books. The third edition of *Solaris* (Kraków, 1976) consisted of only 30,000 copies, but by the third joint 1986 edition of *Solaris* and *Niezwyciężony* (Invincible, 1964) the print run rose grudgingly to 100,000. Lem believes that state 'patronage' held him back. In its absence, he feels, he might have achieved greater recognition without having to wait more than twenty years for his international reputation to establish him in Poland. However, Lem admits that writing science fiction has made him a millionaire.[6]

Western readers encountering Lem for the first time sense the power of his writing, his literary and linguistic inventiveness, but find his playfulness, false naivety, grotesquery, his engagement with science fiction as a serious art form, and his willingness to use, undermine and break the conventions of western science fiction both daunting and unsettling – though in the terms of east European fiction these traits and manœuvres are perfectly acceptable. That western readers know little about him or the context of his work tells us more of the power of Anglo-American science fiction than it does about Lem. Science fiction from the eastern bloc is a rather difficult topic, not because it was subject to censorship – every variety of writing had to contend with that, and if anything science fiction was rather loosely policed – but because the writing itself, like western science fiction, tends to be poor. Also, since to western readers the literature lacks the hardware of conventional and dominant western science fiction models, it seems at first glance to be a very poor, imitative genre. The poverty, however, is rather a failing in the conventional expectations of the science fiction reader brought up on western hardware-orientated science fiction. It is necessary to appreciate that for all his talent Lem comes from quite a different tradition of writing: Lem's work lacks hardware and spectacular space opera techniques, but it is, if anything, over-rich in 'ideas', characters and human situations.

The planners, publishers and markets of both east and west are basically in agreement. In the west 'SF' is still a minority interest, regarded as a not altogether serious sub-species of literature akin to the detective story, romantic fiction and pornography, while in Russia, mainly as a result of the work of Lem and the Russian writers Boris and Arkady Strugatsky, it has only recently become fashionable to read *fantastyka*. In general both east and west regarded science fiction as a marginal and minority interest, a pulp industry. It was precisely this prejudice that gave Lem freedom to write almost anything he wanted. In Poland critics accused him of writing 'cosmic escapism', and of failing to engage with the communist regime. Lem's writings may be seen as pure fantasy, as 'escape literature', out into orbit, away from the problems of political ideology or even from daily life. But also, and more productively, his work can be seen as a series of deeply subversive, telling critiques of the prevailing political system and the mentalities it created. *Solaris* is a powerful parable about the difficulty of breaking into or out of closed information systems, whether that system be a language, a country or a political set-up. Lem anticipated the almost obsessive development of this theme in dissident writings of the 1970s and 1980s. Dissidents like Koła-kowski, Michnik, Bieńkowski, Kuroń, poets like Barańczak, and novelists like Brandys and Konwicki have all raised similar topics and have provoked the censor to take immediate action against them.

With *Solaris* (1961) Lem achieved considerable success. The book was translated into a number of languages but is probably best known as the basis for Andrei Tarkovski's film of the same name (1972). In *Solaris* Lem pursues the idea of society as a 'closed information system' through the image of Solaris, a huge, implacable yet apparently intelligent planet. The planet is covered by a mysterious sea which from time to time produces semi-solid 'mimoids' – forms of wondrous shape and size. There has been a long history of research into the planet – indeed the orbiting space station is equipped with a whole library of 'Solaristics' – yet after years of investigation and the accumulation of a vast amount of detailed data about the planet, Solaris remains an enigma:

> For a great many, particularly the young, the 'affair' gradually became a kind of touchstone for certain values: 'Basically', they said, 'there is greater matter at stake than the probing of Solaris civilisation. This is a game that turns on us alone, about the very borders of human cognition.[7]

Kelvin, a psychologist, is sent to investigate events on the space station. There he finds that, in response to human attempts to 'jolt' the planet into acknowledging humanity by bombarding it with massive doses of lethal X-rays, the planet has retaliated by digging into the subconscious of its human explorers to reproduce their most shameful fantasies and memories. For as long as they hover over Solaris they are doomed to relive their most severe failures of sympathy and humanity, doomed to live with their presumption and inability to recognize those aspects of their own life and mentality that are deeply and limitingly human. They are haunted by Phi-creatures, apparitions manufactured out of their deepest unconscious by the planet. Thus a giant negress, naked except for a grass skirt, persecuted the scientist Gibarian until he committed suicide; something childish and powerful lives in Dr Sartorius's room, and Dr Snow is tormented by a Phi-creature which he manages to keep hidden from view. At one and the same time these things are newly identified and as old as humanity. The scientist Snow explains to Kelvin:

> We moved out into the cosmos ready for anything. That means for loneliness, struggle, martyrdom and death. Modesty does not allow us to say so, but over a

period of time, we think we're rather excellent. Meanwhile this isn't it at all, and our readiness becomes a pose. We don't want to capture the cosmos, we want only to extend Earth to cosmic frontiers. One planet might be desert like the Sahara, another frozen like the poles, or tropical like the jungles of Brazil. We are humanitarian and noble, we don't want to enslave other races; we want only to pass on our values and in exchange to penetrate their heritage. We have become followers of the Knights of the Holy Contact. This is an expensive falsehood. We are searching for nothing other than people. It is not necessary to have other worlds. It is necessary only to own a mirror. We do not know what to do with other worlds. One world is enough, but still we are stifling. It has to be the 'right thing', an idealized picture; it must be a globe, a civilization higher than ours, but at the same time we hope again for a likeness that had developed like our own primitive past. At the same time on the other hand there is something unpleasant against which we defend ourselves, and we don't take with us from earth only the distilled virtue of humanity! We arrive here just like this, as we are in reality, and when we are shown that truth, that other part of us about which we would rather remain silent – we don't like it.[8]

Lem is mainly interested in the dilemma of investigator Kelvin. The planet very quickly digs into Kelvin's subconscious to find that he once had a girlfriend called Harey and that she, as a result of Kelvin's inattention and refusal to take her seriously, killed herself. Now the planet provides Kelvin with a new Harey, a woman who with her innocence and trust forces Kelvin to acknowledge the limits of his sympathy and his inabilities as a human being. Kelvin locks the new Harey in a space capsule and ejects her into space, but that night he wakes up to find her (or a new facsimile of her) beside him in bed again. She has no memory of the episode. The creation of Harey is linked with the planet's creation of huge, beautiful forms which crystallize into solid structures across the planet's surface, and which dissolve very slowly back into the sea. Sometimes these 'mimoids', which human research teams investigate and are large enough for planes to fly around inside, imitate huge human forms, but like the creation of Harey and the other Phi-creatures, their exact purpose can only be guessed at.

Lem does not tell us if the planet is self-aware, or hint what communication with the planet might be like. He is much more interested in looking at the basis of the human characters and their drive into space. In many of Lem's novels the human protagonists begin to understand their new and alien environment only after all attempts at communication in human terms have failed: at this point they often experience a difficult aesthetic encounter. Kelvin feels that the planet has played despicable tricks with his unconscious, but while he will never understand or be able to communicate with it, he still has to come to terms with that entity, and experienced it on its own terms rather than his. The only terms on which he can establish any contact with it are aesthetic. The beauty of the planet is a kind of truth, and truth resides in simply accepting that incomprehensible beauty. In the end the planet puts the humans in touch with a new perspective on their cosmic and personal failure, on their actual place in the universe.

Solaris forces the humans to face up to certain basic facts about themselves. What the planet has found in each of them is the core experience, the main-spring of their personality and presumption, their most shameful area of moral turpitude, the driving force that has led them to Solaris. The planet shows them that it is this which has driven them to conquer the stars, not a desire to meet or understand aliens. The planet, as far as we can know, has mastered its inner life, the humans have not. By its action it asks them to consider why it should respond and break its communication with itself when humanity is so lacking in self-knowledge and driven by piffling motives. The planet calls into question the human notion of 'I'. It asks them to consider that perhaps humans only mirror each other's preconceptions, run along in the tram tracks of human cognition, have not yet achieved the level of introspection and self-knowledge required to understand either the universe, the planet or even themselves. Humanity is pouring its own inner chaos out into the universe.

At the close of the novel Harey realizes that she is not human, that her presence is some kind of deception; if she is not fully human she has no place in Kelvin's life. The more human she becomes the less she accepts the mystery of her own existence. In secret Harey offers herself as a target for a new 'Matter Disintegrator' that Snow has developed. Kelvin wakes up one morning to find that Harey is not beside him. This time she does not come back. Kelvin recognizes that Harey's appearance on the space station had been a 'cruel miracle', but it was one that gave him a second chance and her presence was something that he had come to accept and appreciate. Now she is taken away a second time he despairs, alternating between a desire to renew attempts at communication with the planet and a desire to annihilate it. He dreams that somehow the planet is 'visiting' him in his sleep. He takes a flight out over the sea and experiences for the first time the power and mystery of the huge, intelligent entity, its massive boredom with him, the banality of his own personality and desires:

> Are we then to be a watch that measures the flow of time, now smashed, then repaired anew, whose mechanism the watchmaker sets in motion and which from its very first movement generates despair and love, knowing that it is the recapitulation of suffering, apparently profound, yet in sum, amounting only to a multiplicity of comic repetition. To repeat human existence, fine, but to repeat it like a drunk thrashing the same record, again and again throwing his newly minted coin into the depths of a capacious juke-box.[9]

All of Lem's protagonists are intellectually active, they want to solve the problems that beset them. Yet without exception they pay for their 'cognitive impulse', for their effort to recognize another way of processing, thinking, developing, being. They pay for the extension of their humanity with the painful recognition of their human limitations. In Kelvin's case, by repeating his earlier mistake of taking Harey's presence for granted, he pays with the loss of the thing he has come to love. Jarzębski, Lem's most perceptive critic, points to a passage in *Pamiętnik znalezony w wannie* (Memoirs Found in a Bathtub, 1971):

> What does it mean? Meaning. And so we enter the realm of semantics. One must tread carefully here! Consider: from earliest times man did little else but assign meanings – to the stones, the skulls, the sun, other people, and the meanings required that he create theories – life after death, totems, cults, all sorts of myths and legends, black bile and yellow bile, love of God and country, being and nothingness – and so it went, the meanings shaped and regulated human life, became its substance, its frame and foundation – but also a fatal limitation and a trap.[10]

Nature creates things; only humanity searches for and assigns meanings. To step outside that and accept the 'otherness' of another intelligence is perhaps to cease being entirely human.

Tarkovski's film version of the book displeased Lem. After seeing the shooting script he announced himself unpleasantly surprised at the long prologue set on earth, the undue importance given to Kelvin's mother – a figure who came to symbolize Motherland, ideas of home and Mother Earth, and which he felt had more to do with Russian folklore and Tarkovski's own preoccupations than with his novel. Lem managed to persuade Tarkovski to drop most of the alterations, but eventually realized that the novel was a stalking-horse for Tarkovski's own ideas and withdrew from the project. Although it is accounted one of the finest of all science fiction films, Lem has only seen fragments of *Solaris* on Polish TV:

> I was expecting a visualisation of the 'Drama of Cognizance', seen as a contrast between the images of 'home, sweet Earth' and the 'Cold Cosmos', a drama in which the characters affecting the men in the station originate from the ocean and symbolise the antagonism between the vast open spaces of the planet and the small enclosed Station. Unfortunately Tarkovski took sides and favoured 'home sweet Earth' against the 'Cold Cosmos'. For a drama of cognizance in which the people, the envoys from Earth, keep on struggling with the enigma that cannot be solved by the human mind, Tarkovski substituted a moral drama *par excellence*, which in no way relates to the problem of cognizance and its extremes. For Tarkovski, the most important facet was Kelvin's problem of 'guilt and punishment', just as in a Dostoyevsky book.[11]

Lem has said that the writer whose characters visit an alien intelligence is in a better position than a writer who has an alien intelligence visit Earth because the motives for an alien visit must be simple: to fight, steal, conquer, learn, play. If these motives are not sufficient, the only other strategy is to keep their motivation a secret. If humans stumble upon an alien intelligence, however, it is altogether a different matter: the alien is going nowhere, is living its life according to its own rules, and may therefore be utterly impenetrable. Thus in the encounter humanity may find only itself and its limitations. Lem was quite clear about the theory and direction that lay behind *Solaris*. When he began work on the novel he had a developing design in mind: 'I knew there was to be an ocean on the planet and that it would interfere with the lives of the people in the station, although I was not aware, at that point, what the ocean was truly "up to", or what the interference would in fact be.'[12] The process of construction gave him a great deal of trouble and the final chapter of *Solaris* was particularly difficult precisely because Lem was wrestling with his own self-knowledge and the limits of his own cognition:

> This process of writing, which is characterised by the signs of a creation by trial and error, has always been arrested by blocks and blind alleys that forced me to retreat; sometimes there has even been a 'burning out' of the raw materials – the manifold resources necessary for further growth – stored somewhere in my skull. I was not able to to finish *Solaris* for a full year, and could do it then only because I learned suddenly – from myself – how the last chapter had to be. (And then I could only wonder why I hadn't recognised it from the beginning.)[13]

Lem has said that the novel is 'a gnossological drama whose focal point is the tragedy of man's imperfect machinery for gaining knowledge'.[14]

Lem distinguishes between stories that have only a passing fashion (which interest us because they are parts of a world which is marvellous, but self-contained, with no bearing on the real world), putting most science fiction, in this category, and works like Franz Kafka's 'Metamorphosis' which, he says, is not a fantastic marvel of the imagination, but a deep-seated recognition of the deformations of the human 'socio-psychological situation':

> If the new phenomenon is of a qualitatively different scale – contact with 'aliens' in outer space, for example – it is all but certain that the repertoire of received, ready concepts will not be able to accommodate it without considerable friction. In all likelihood, a cultural, perceptual, and perhaps even a social-ethical revolution will be necessary. Thus instead of the assimilation of the new, we must imagine the re-ordering and even the destruction of fundamental concepts, the revaluation of truths that were previously indisputable, and so on.[15]

Lem blends the east central European tradition of humanist fantasy with his own psychological insights. There is also a subtle, wily, independent Marxism at work too, and he has no time for structuralist attempts to divorce his work from its cultural and political context. He insists on a very close relation and obligation to the social norms that helped create his work and has complained frequently about science fiction's lack of awareness of the problems of narrative and the relationship of the genre to the cultural and political problems of the real world. For Lem it is important that science fiction should depict a world that is not only morally neutral – where humans act out their own choices out of their own volition and motivation – but also a recognizable world at some point further along our space-time continuum:

> Only the outer shell of this world is formed by the strange phenomena; the inner core has a solid non-fantastic meaning. Thus a story can depict the world as it is, or interpret the world . . . or, in most cases, do both things at the same time. As in life we can solve real problems with the help of images of non-existent beings, so in literature can we signal the existence of real problems with the help of *prima facie* impossible occurrences or objects. Even when the happenings it describes are totally impossible, science fiction work may still point out meaningful, indeed rational problems.[16]

It is usual for writers to leave messages 'between the lines'. Indeed, recent Polish literature sometimes resembles a gigantic cryptic crossword to be read only by the initiate few. On a very crude level, the story could be said to portray a massively indifferent Party, its smugness at its own existence and its failure to respond to any outside overtures. It is tempting to look for some direct political correspondences in the novel, perhaps for veiled references to the events and atmosphere of Gomułka's Poland. It would, no doubt, be interesting if the planet 'stood' in some way for the Party, and the scientists 'stood' for the efforts of the Polish people to contact that entity; but it would be equally possible to reverse this, to claim that the planet 'stands' for the Polish people and that the rough and insensitive intruders who try to make the planet conform to their way of doing things, to prod it into a mode of contact and behaviour they can predict and understand, are the Party. But it is not possible to take either of these notions very far.

The novel is not a political allegory; we would be mistaken to look for a series of point-for-point correspondences with Polish political life. Lem was far too wary of the censor for that, even though the novel is informed by the experience of living in Gomułka's Poland. In the manner of all parables, the novel has much wider implications: it is very clearly about the human ability to think within and outside a given set-up, about the limitations of human comprehension of things which are not human, about humanity's refusal to believe that it may be of no interest to an alien intelligence. It is also about the obsessive 'I' of human culture, and since the role of the individual is one which the Party has sought to redefine, the subject has further repercussions in that it seeks to reveal some of the mechanisms by which our perceptions are shaped and informed, how we see and how we are allowed to see the world and the universe around us.

The novel is an open-ended parable, a speculative entertainment, a philosophical adventure: it airs the idea, in a highly entertaining and enigmatic fashion, of what happens when expected modes of behaviour and communication do not open up. It is important to realize that dissident objections to what the Party was doing were still in their early stages: major works by Michnik, Kuroń, Modzelewski, Geremek, Kołakowski, Bieńkowski, the oppositional literature of Herbert, Brandys, Konwicki, Andrzejewski and many others, and the events of 1968, all lay in the future. Also it is not necessarily a part of the science fiction writer's job to come to any conclusions on the subject – indeed, it could have been unwise for Lem to do so. In his own way Lem is as enigmatic as his planet. The philosophical objection to censorship, indeed Lem's objection to the idea of changing human nature, the effort to revolutionize human society on the basis of the slender knowledge currently available, are there for those that want them and who are open to receive them.

Censorship was the main and all-pervasive feature of the business of perception in the eastern bloc. It may be a characteristic of Stalinism, but it was not something which had much to do with Marx's ideas. A censored Polish press corrupted social life and meant that the government heard nothing but its own voice. In the post-war years censorship, rather than helping to smooth the path of progress towards socialism, actually suppressed legitimate grievances and set up a propaganda of success contradicted by everyday experience. This, as I hope to show in later chapters, in turn bred cynicism and antagonism towards the state and the authorities which the society had no way of satisfying, diverting or even easing. One of the effects of censorship, and one which literature continually struggles against, is that it makes the feelings and thought processes of human discovery and cognition increasingly difficult and irrational. Censorship blocks channels of information and feeling within society and individuals. It guards the difference between truth and propaganda: because it erodes the language and the processes of cognition it also effectively destroys the perception that there is a difference. Not only does a society not know what it thinks, but eventually it does not know what it feels; and before long that society does not know what it knows.

Not all Polish readers are prepared to seek comfort in science fiction, however, and it is important to note the social and political context in which *Solaris* was written, and the social and political developments by which its concerns became increasingly relevant. Through the 1960s and 1970s Poles turned increasingly to the art of 'reading between the lines' in a literature that became ever more oracular and Aesopian; they turned to sources of information and feeling that were not in any way 'approved' and which were uncontaminated by the hand of the censor. They listened regularly (and illegally) to Polish-language broadcasts from the west – Radio Free Europe, heard by seventeen million Poles per week; the Voice of America, heard by nine million Poles per week; and the BBC World Service and BBC Polish Service broadcasts, heard by nearly seven million Poles each week. They also came to depend increasingly on gossip. This meant that Poles became easy victims to malicious rumour-mongering and often tended to believe the most blatant nonsense simply because it came from some source other than their own official media.

Writers complained of the 'shell of falsification' that became increasingly effective in the 1970s. They regarded literature as an unofficial opposition that faced up to the moral bankruptcy of the regime and acted as an alternative ideal within society. The readership of semi-legal magazines was enormous – particularly after the demonstrations and unrest of 1976. It has been estimated that for each copy of an underground journal there were at least thirty readers and countless others who heard the contents over the 'bush telegraph'. While the underground press had virtually no contact with the authorities, their publications were read by those in power with a view to finding and suppressing publication. This was virtually the only transmission of ideas from the bottom to the top of Polish society. It was certainly not possible to voice criticism within the official trade unions, through elections to the Sejm or in newspapers: these 'organs of state' formed a one-way transmission belt for the orders and policies of the Party. The Party, like the mimoids of Solaris, created beautifully formed social organisms with no content, forms whose purpose and workings remained veiled and mysterious, shrouded in secrecy. Like the Party, the planet held out the promise of a miraculous reworking of creation, but delivered only 'cruel miracles'. The Party remained a self-contained, self-confirming entity locked in a dialogue with itself rather than with the society it led and shaped. Censorship shaped public consciousness and self-awareness as an incomplete and irrational, empty entity; it created a hunger for information, but did not foster introspection or provide any framework in which information could be assessed.[17] The inevitable consequences of these actions were pointed out to the regime by the semi-official DiP (Experience and Future) Group in 1978–9:

> The effects of politics and economic policies we experience literally every day, but we feel ourselves left out of the decision-making processes, not only as active subjects but even as mere observers. We are left out and hence cut off from responsibility. A Polish citizen experiences the meanderings of politics and planning more or less as he experiences changes in the weather: as important changes he must adapt to but whose causes – wholly external – are not worth exploring more deeply, since he has no way of influencing them . . . What is more,

this system has created something that is more dangerous than indifference and cynicism, something that surely was not intended: it has created a state of collective *informational* psychosis.[18]

Poles began to feel that in their own private lives they were no longer in control and that therefore they were no longer responsible for their actions. Somehow *oni* (they), the authorities, government, *nomenklatura* and Party were to blame for everything.[19] The result was mounting frustration, mutual hostility, a complete failure of social responsiveness and responsibility, undirected, unspecific antagonism towards the state and society.

Michnik, a political thinker with a rare sensitivity to literature, saw the growth of Polish right-wing opinion as a mark of confusion resulting directly from the work of the censor and the government's failure to establish or foster self-knowledge and responsibility within society:

I think that in Poland the conflict between the right and the left belongs to the past. It used to divide a society that was torn by struggles for bourgeois freedoms, universal voting rights, land reform, secularisation, the eight hour workday, welfare, universal schooling, or the democratisation of culture. A different distinction comes to the fore in the era of totalitarian dictatorships: one between the proponents of an open society and the proponents of a closed society. In the former, social order is based on self-government and collective agreements; in the latter, order is achieved through repression and discipline. In the vision of an open society, the state acts as the guardian of safety for citizens; in the vision of a closed society the state is a master and overseer who determines all modes of society's existence.[20]

At his grimmest Michnik claimed that every human move, feeling and reaction under censorship, even violent efforts to overthrow the regime, were nothing more than manifestations of 'slave mentality'.

As in Lem's novel, indifference provoked violence, but not necessarily further understanding on either side. Lem called into question the underlying human feelings that informed the processes of civil society. How can politicians remake society (or humanity dare contact aliens) when they know so little of how society works, and so little about the influence their own individual fears and ambitions have on the processes of power, or when there are no mechanisms of feedback on the effects of their re-structuring? They know themselves so little, yet are powerful enough to subvert and pervert political thinking and theory. Lem is interested in the mainsprings of human ambition and activity. He is concerned about the values and the true extent of the human knowledge and understanding that humanity is planning to export into space, and in the sense that the space race is also a revolution he worries about the presumption that humanity knows enough (morally and personally) to undertake any such engineering project when it has failed so spectacularly at home.

Władysław Bieńkowski has pointed out that censorship has made the business of integrating new knowledge about systems, social structures, the inner workings of human thought and its social and political manifestations almost impossible by creating barriers to resist all notions alien to a very narrow and highly selective interpretation of Marx. Bieńkowski believes that twentieth-century society has slowly abandoned force as a way of controlling its citizens and has concentrated on re-ordering social structures so that freedoms of all kinds are increasingly seen as some kind of commercial commodity – rights must be bought or earned by conforming to social norms. In east central Europe this has meant that the relationship between behaviour and consciousness, the very idea of internalization, of individual moral responsibility, have lost all meaning and instead have been replaced by learned behaviour patterns which have no personal rationale behind them. The Polish sociologist Julia Sowa has dubbed this phenomenon the 'dead field of public normative indifference'. It is a state of 'intellectual innocence' in which the citizen falls prey to chance impulse. While believing they are 'free' to decide for themselves on any issue, in fact they lack all self-knowledge and therefore lack all social and political judgement.[21] The result (as in Kelvin's case) is an increasingly chaotic social and inner life for the bulk of the population. In the same way that the failure of the planet Solaris to respond to the scientists provokes them to bombard it with massive doses of harmful X-rays, the monolithic indifference of the PZPR to public opinion and common sense provoked increasing hostility. Many writers and observers had warned that Polish society was heading for an explosion of discontent. Although the Party blamed Solidarność, the economic collapse of 1980 had been inevitable since the early 1970s. Had the government chosen to monitor the success of its own performance instead of using the office of the censor to suppress discontent, they would have picked up the first rumblings from deep within Polish society long before the earthquake of 1980 and the declaration of Martial Law in 1981.

Attempts to control the formation of opinion inevitably destroy the possibility of ever finding out what minds think or might think. Ultimately the bid for control destroys self-awareness and self-knowledge. In this way political power and social or self-knowledge are linked in opposition to each other. The office of the censor erected an insurmountable barrier between what Marxism might have offered the Poles and what the Party did in the name of Marxism. The great outburst of clandestine publication in Poland in the 1970s was a direct effort on the part of Polish intellectuals not to succumb to the Party's bid for total control, to maintain some level of self-knowledge and social understanding. Lem's particular choice of themes was to a very great extent a direct response to that bid to control minds and remake society.

Kazimierz Brandys has described the twentieth century in Poland as an era of 'self-diagnostic and self-critical culture', of 'thinking about thinking', a period of taking many senses and meanings each of which reveals some part of an overall truth. For him everything fulfils a cognitive function, and he characterizes the era as 'analysing itself while in the process of becoming', a process modified by introspection and self-analysis. For Brandys, as for Lem, it became essential to question the language in which the 'reality' of the closed, censored, communist world was presented. It became necessary to ponder anew the questions that tortured him as a schoolboy in order to restore some part of the faculty of cognition and introspection denied by censorship:

> What is man? Does God exist? Does death mean the end, and how ought one to live? These are actually adolescent's questions; if you ask them, the fear of being laughed at is well justified. Dare we ask them in a civilisation where research by specialists has replaced philosophy? Our world, which is interested in technology, in genetics, and in the structure of language, has grown humble in the face of the universal problems; it has set itself narrower, better defined goals. In such a world, to go deep within oneself and ponder the secrets of Being, without electronic microscopes, without laboratories or accelerators – that can only be the quirk of a thinker from the provinces seeking a proof of the existence of God. Yet sometimes there is nothing else to do. When choosing a way of life, only naive questions remain, because in such a world all questions with an ethical content appear to be naive.[22]

The critic and literary historian, Andrzej Zgorzelski, has argued that science fiction is a good location for the clash between reality and unreality simply because of its development as a genre – in science fiction the fictional world slowly disappears as the new world becomes apparent through the fantastic elements – and that it is these fantastic elements that dominate the setting. Thus, as the reader becomes more aware of the new world there is always a clash with 'objective reality' until new linguistic and cultural equivalents are established. Equivalents replace the signs and tokens of the old world that is no longer valid, but they cannot do so entirely or they would be incomprehensible, and they cannot of themselves produce the fantastic elements since they are bound by the parameters of 'the known'. As equivalents emerge, the apparent confrontation between the old world and the new disappears and attention can then focus on the meaning (if any) of the fantastic elements. In this way Lem presents the difficulty of ever breaking away from the basic dilemma outlined in *Solaris*.[23]

In the face of the implacable indifference of the cosmos Lem proposes a return to these considerations. In *Solaris* he questions the fundamentals of his own existence and the social order that both nurtures and stifles him. He writes out of a specific social and political context. What is it like to try to talk to an intelligent monolithic entity that consistently fails to respond? What are the effects of living under a regime/intelligence such as this? How can we know what we have created in a social revolution when we do not know ourselves sufficiently to understand what we are creating? Naive questions these may be. However, they undercut the 'ethics' of the one-party state, restore the status of self-knowledge and self-examination, they raise again the issue of humanity's right to make a social revolution and to explore the cosmos.

Solaris was published at a time when the east-west space race was just getting under way and when the burden of military spending was clearly more than the inefficient eastern-bloc economies could support. The novel appeared after the first of the post-war Polish upheavals, but before the increasingly serious demonstrations of discontent in 1968, 1970, 1976 and 1980–1. Lem could not be expected to predict exactly how the influence of the Party and the censor would operate on the formation of moral and political attitudes, but working in a genre of limited appeal and small circulation, and therefore largely ignored by the censor, he was able to pin-point one long-term effect of blocks and barriers to the free flow of information and feeling within that particular society. Lem was able to foresee and indicate a very precise formation of discontent, of political and moral failure within Polish society, and to predict an area of increasing concern taken up by dissidents and by the leaders and thinkers of Solidarność some twenty years later.

Though it is widely acknowledged that he is a science fiction writer with a taste for political commentary, Lem, perhaps wisely, has said little in public or in print that allowed any direct connection of his work to political life in Poland. He has had some harsh things to say about Poland's communist rulers in *Dialogi* (1957) and several of his stories have highly political implications – for example in *Eden*, *The Futurological Congress*, the short story 'In Hot Pursuit of Happiness', and several of the tales in *Star Diaries*. There can be no doubt about Lem's disenchantment with the regime, and the Party's unease at Lem can be seen in his publication history: his access to a reading public was certainly curtailed in spite if his increasing national and international reputation after the events of 1976. Lem did not take any high profile action to protest at Party actions, never courted censorship or confrontation and consequently was never banned. After Martial Law was declared Lem spent most of his time in Berlin and Austria. In 1982 he resigned from editing a science fiction series when a novel by Ursula Le Guin was banned by the military government because it was translated by Stanisław Barańczak, the dissident poet in exile.[24] This was one of the very rare occasions when Lem made an overt political act.

Lem has been able to produce 'serious' science fiction on his chosen themes precisely because he works in a medium that is considered to be an intellectual backwater of little or no serious thought, a trash medium where nothing lasts and whose readers are unlikely to be those who will fathom social messages, political commentary or moral significance. Although writers knew in detail how their work was related to political life and knew that it was impossible to avoid this connection, it was the writer who appeared to be non-political who was really the clever political writer – who knew exactly what to touch and what to avoid, what to appear to touch and appear to avoid. Anikó Sohár, writing of the ambiguous position of science fiction in socialist Hungary has said:

> One has to be aware that science fiction, being not part of the official cultural value system, was just tolerated, and because of this social-literary position, the readership consisted of not only the youth, the students and intellectuals with a technical-technological interest, that is the hypothesised usual readership of science fiction, but also of people opposing the officially established system, since it was a rather mild way to 'tease' the authorities, and meet otherwise unavailable views.[25]

These were also the writers whose work was most likely to survive on the commercial open market, who hoped to transcend their immediate context (time, politics and geography) to appeal to a wider and not necessarily Polish readership.[26]

Lem says now that he never believed in the communist Utopia, that although he knew he had to work within the system he would never be a part of it. The communists may not have trusted the in-built political messages of his science fiction, but one of President Gorbachev's first actions on assuming power was to recruit Lem to the Gorbachev Foundation and ask him to come up with a detailed prediction of problems for the year 2000: Lem spoke of viral epidemics, AIDS, overpopulation and global warming. However, with the collapse of Soviet communism, one of Boris Yeltsin's first actions on coming to power was to cut all funding for the Foundation with the result that Lem's report was never published. Lem says his task has always been to write prognoses: his warnings on the hazards of biotechnology and genetic engineering, penned more than thirty years ago, are only now being taken seriously by scientific journals. Lem worries about the gap between the legislative competence of governments and the speed of technical advance, warning about computer crime, artificial conception, genetic engineering, the limitations of human self-knowledge, the problems of language. He warns of overpopulation, over-whelming ecological damage, a coming war between the western world and Islam; he fulminates against 'this lunatic Derrida' and Francis Fukuyama's notion that the collapse of communism means the end of history, pointing to wars in Bosnia, the southern areas of the former Soviet Union, Rwanda and Algeria as proof. Lem's experience of capitalism since 1989 has not inspired him with confidence and he predicts it will collapse 'just like communism'.[27]

6

KAZIMIERZ BRANDYS

An older friend of mine, a man of outstanding intelligence and great novelistic talent, asked me a rather curious question: 'Did you notice that out there in the street everybody is acting abnormally? The salesman is pretending to sell, the bricklayer is building imaginary homes, newspapers don't have any news, the children's traffic warden is waving his lollipop like crazy, but there isn't really any traffic . . . ' This friend of mine remembered the pre-war years, but I later realized that even people who had never seen anything other than the People's Republic of Poland had the same kind of feeling.

Jan Błoński, *Tygodnik Solidarność* 21 (1981)

Kazimierz Brandys has been described by Timothy Garton Ash as 'the eastern prophet, the sage, the seer, righteous eyes ablaze, arms raised to high heaven as he denounces the whores of the rue de Babylon'. Adam Michnik has said that, in spite of Brandys's one-time membership of the Party, he is a politically radical writer intent on 'the destruction of the official canon of sovietised culture', who aimed to 'expose lies, lay bare hypocrisy, and mock the imprimatur of officialdom', and he has described *A Question of Reality* as one of the most precious achievements of post-war Polish literature. Certainly, and to an astonishing degree, Brandys's books proved inspirational. He popularized, confirmed and insisted on notions of truth, morality and human dignity, while the Party deemed 'reality' no more than a message to be rewritten at will. Since the mid-1950s Brandys, who as a Jew within Polish society never felt secure, has found that his ideas and observations were under attack from the 'unreality' of official political culture, of which anti-Semitism was a significant part.[1]

Brandys was born in Łódź on 27 October 1916, of a middle-class liberal-progressive Jewish family. His father was a professor, and later a school principal. Brandys attended the *gimnazjum* (high school), where he wore a black uniform with a high stiff collar, and studied mathematics and natural sciences. In 1932 his family moved to Warsaw, where he finished his secondary schooling. He then completed two years of military service as a cadet officer in the Signal Corps. He started to study law at Warsaw University in 1933, but dropped it after only two terms and took up philosophy. After a brief and unlikely membership of the right-wing

Piłsudskiite Society of the Lovers of Virtue and the Legion of Youth, in his third year Brandys joined the ZNMS (Union of Independent Socialist Youth). A leftist from his early youth, he quickly became the organizer of the university section of the ZNMS and entered the administration of the organization. While he was in the ZNMS he encountered the communists of the semi-legal Warsaw University 'Life' group, but found them stubborn, suspicious and dogmatic. While he was a student he was actively engaged in fighting anti-Semitism. He published an open letter protesting at anti-Semitism within the Warsaw University hierarchy and took part in a number of protests that ended in violent confrontation. On the day of his Roman law oral examination he was clubbed over the head by members of the Youth League. Looking back on his early political activities Brandys said his ambitions at this time had been for a democratic Poland, the liberation of the proletariat and social justice: in retrospect his ideas all seemed so 'good and noble'.[2]

In 1936 Brandys dropped out of university and enrolled at the National Institute of Theatre Arts to become a theatre director. He graduated in 1938 but was soon called up for military service. After the defeat of 1939 he managed to escape from a column of prisoners and lived in Warsaw throughout the war, though not in the ghetto. He lived under an assumed name, writing underground pamphlets and selling paintings. He was also, in the years 1940–5, a member of the AK (Home Army, the London-backed resistance). At first he trained high school students in the use of guns and grenades, then he operated a radio in the Warsaw suburb of Żolibórz, and in 1943 he taught the tactics of street warfare. It was at about this time that Brandys first heard rumours of assassinations and fighting between the AK and the AL (People's Army, the Moscow-backed resistance). After the Warsaw uprising, in which his father died, Brandys spent some time in a German PoW camp. At the end of the war he made his way to Kraków where he worked in the cloakroom of the actors' cafe and then as co-editor of the weekly magazine *Odrodzenie* (Rebirth).

Brandys was interrogated several times by the communist authorities about his membership of the AK, which they said made him 'objectively' a class enemy, and he was accused of anti-communist activities. Brandys denied that he was a class enemy or that he had ever undertaken anti-communist activities. Nevertheless, he felt that many of his wartime activities (particularly setting up his own phantom underground cell called Rondo) were frivolous. Eventually the security service dismissed him as something of a fool. Irritated and desperate to prove his independence, Brandys joined the Party in 1946. Looking back on this decision he wrote:

> For me socialism was not a confession of dogmatic faith: I went in because it was
> battling against a barbaric church that was hostile to me – fascism. Socialism's
> nineteenth century past had earned my respect, attracted me with its legends, the

lives of its heroes, its ethical tension. And also by its modest liturgy, its simple ways. A table, a chair, a speaker, a discussion. And so, though I professed no dogmas, I already had a gospel. It is without irony that I think of this today [1978]. I have no intention of reducing the significance of socialism in my life. And not only in my life. In history, culture. If I had to name the most important phenomena in our era, I would say the Roman Catholic Church, the Reformation, and socialism. I would further add that these constitute the historical trinity that delineates my idea of Christianity.[3]

Brandys had been born into a home that was progressively modern and Polish rather than conservative and Jewish. Like many other assimilated Polish Jews, he shared the difficulties of feeling that he was never an authentic part of Polish society. Between the wars, as a result of economic and political difficulties, anti-Semitism had been an increasingly unpleasant aspect of Polish political life. With the rise of Nazism in Germany, it could not be ignored. Even where Judaism was nothing but a very feeble family memory, there was still an enormous need for intellectual certainty, for human enlightenment, tolerance, a desire to identify with the progress of the proletariat, a need to belong to a community (literary or political), and to enjoy some form of solidarity and brotherhood. Many of these people felt the need to soothe their fears with action. These needs were felt by many Polish intellectuals at the end of the war, but for Polish intellectuals of Jewish origin these feelings were very complex indeed. For many the route out of uncertainty, into security and identity, was Zionism. As Hannah Arendt pointed out, it is no accident that Zionism was born in central and eastern Europe as a reaction to the steady rise of nationalist and ethnic intolerance from the mid-nineteenth century onwards.

However, Zionism represented a very wide range of political opinion – from extreme left to extreme right – and many Polish Jews did not feel comfortable in such company. Also, for secularized and assimilated Polish Jews this route was much more religious and much less Polish than they wished. For those who did not come from a Yiddish-speaking background, who felt themselves as belonging within the orbit of Polish affairs, for those who had built *inteligencja* social connections, who regarded themselves as assimilated, the possibility of learning to think and write in Hebrew, of emigrating to an uncertain future in Palestine, a land that was, if anything, even more hostile and unpredictable than Poland, was not a joyful prospect. It meant abandoning Polish literary nationalism, which was not a problem, but it also meant abandoning an established and well-defined literary culture, abandoning Polish as a literary language. It meant living in an environment and culture that were largely alien to them, learning a new language, beginning work in a language that had almost no modern literature, and which had as yet, no place for modern secular letters. For these people there was no question of 'redeeming' themselves by submitting to the 'judgement of Polish nationalism', especially if this involved turning into Jewish anti-Semites. For many, like Brandys, there was a striking, perhaps unavoidable, convergence between communism and a Jewish identity. Communism, with its language of international brotherhood and comradeship, its secular practicality, its faith in technological progress, its emphasis on the utopian ideals of liberating the proletariat of all races and nations, was both the alternative to emigration to Palestine and a universal answer to racism. As Stanisław Krajewski has written:

> If someone already had radical leanings, solidarity with the oppressed as an impulse led to Marxism or anarchism. Radicalism is a desire to break with the continuity of social institutions, and it is as a result of disbelief in their reformability. It requires distance from the existing social system. It was easy for Jews to develop this distance because they had occupied the social position of pariah for a long time. The age-old sense of expulsion, of not feeling comfortable, made it easier still. However, that sense was rather difficult to discern, particularly among those who chose communism, and thus anti-traditional assimilation.[4]

It was not unusual for Polish writers of the younger generation to join the Party towards the end of the war or in the immediate post-war years. Brandys was in excellent company: Mieczysław Jastrun, Julian Przyboś, Paweł Hertz, Adolf Rudnicki, Julian Stryjkowski, Jerzy Andrzejewski, Tadeusz Borowski, Jan Kott, Tadeusz Konwicki, Leszek Kołakowski all joined the party at about the same time. Many more simply agreed to co-operate in revolutionizing Polish literary culture. These people were a very small group within the Polish *inteligencja*, and a minute group within Polish society as a whole, but they regarded themselves as representatives of the future and hoped by the power of their example to persuade others to give their support to the new regime. It was possible for a writer to join the Party and believe this was the way forward. For many it appeared that refusal to join the Party meant they would be left 'outside history', marginalized.

Norman Davies has rightly referred to Polish-Jewish relations as one of the 'meanest' controversies ever to face a historian. However it must be said that there can be few such gross examples of 'reality' rewritten for political convenience as the manipulation of anti-Semitism in post-war Poland – a country now without a substantial Jewish population. From a total Jewish population of 3,350,000, only 369,000 (approx 11 per cent) survived the Nazi Holocaust. There was no possibility of return to the pre-war situation: countless Jewish communities including the enormous ghettos of Warsaw and Łódź had been completely destroyed by the Nazis, and few of the remaining communities could muster the *minyan*, the minimum number of males required for religious services. It was no longer possible to maintain a Jewish religious and community life in Poland. For Polish Jews the situation was stark:

emigrate and remain Jewish or go along with the new order and assimilate. Most of the survivors chose to emigrate to Palestine or the USA. For non-religious, mainly assimilated *inteligencja* Jews, who had not been active in the pre-war Jewish community, the new order beckoned with particular allure:

> It was party principle that, after taking power in Poland, the communists would put an end to anti-Semitism and all the sufferings of the Jews. Jewish workers and intellectuals would take part in the political and economic life of society and would enjoy equally the blessings of science and culture. Anti-Semitism and racism were considered nightmares that lay in the very nature of aggressive, capitalist society, racked by contradictions and ruled by the law of the jungle. Scientific Marxism, the basis of communism, proved – in a simple and ingenious manner accessible to all – that these contradictions would disappear when the means of production were socialised, and the divisions between exploiters and the exploited eliminated. Then there would be no struggle for existence, and persecution would disappear . . . Yes it was simple. Both for Jewish shoemakers and tailors, doctors and professors. Communism was the best way out for Jews, if not the only way. It was their best refuge. In the Party they were treated as equals, full-fledged members. They could develop themselves, dedicate themselves, display their talents.[5]

By 1945 the 40,000 remaining Jews in Poland were 'statistically insignificant' in a population of 24,000,000. They were to become even less statistically significant after the anti-Semitic purges and expulsions of 1959 and 1968. However, 'Jewish influence' and the notion of 'hidden Jews' was to haunt post-war Polish politics. It was important that the bulk of anti-communist Jews had either been killed in the Holocaust or had emigrated from the 'Jewish graveyard' of wartime Poland, leaving behind mainly Jews favourably disposed to the new regime. Many non-religious Polish Jews, some of whom had been socialists before the war, saw the 'building of socialism' in a positive light and embraced the new order, though not without reservation. But this very fact marked them out from the bulk of the Polish population. Most Poles could not, and never would, accept communism, since it struck at their national identity. Given the number of Jews in the post-war security services and the Party, many Poles began to see the rising spectre of the *Żydokomuna*, perceiving communism (and later the underground opposition of the 1970s and 1980s) as a Jewish plot to undermine and destroy Poland. Certainly the idea of Jewish influence proved to be very useful to the Party since it was a convenient peg on which to hang any purge of the opposition and was the one notion powerful enough to mobilize and unite large numbers of Poles.[6]

After the war Brandys lived in Kraków for a while, then moved back to Łódź where he became a member of the executive committee of the Writers' Union, and later an editor for the journal *Nowa Kultura* (New Culture). He became a fiction editor for *Kuźnica* (Forge), and helped draft the Party's policy statement on politically committed literature. Again, this was not unusual. Many of the writers who joined the Party just after the war worked for this magazine – indeed Ważyk and Kott also became editors at about this time. They attempted to forge a link between the Polish Enlightenment and the socialist 'Camp of Reform'. Although it advocated realism in literature Kuźnica was in favour of Balzac's realism rather than Soviet *socrealizm*. The magazine devoted a great deal of space to the *inteligencja*'s self-criticism and the critical approach of the newer writers to the mental habits of the pre-war Polish writers and literary culture. On the negative side the magazine reflected the Party line in failing to follow the very rich seam of experimental verse that had developed in Polish literature between the wars, and rejected most *awantgarda* (avant-garde) and foreign translations. Inevitably, there had been a vast flood of memoirs, recollections and analyses of the war years, and these had to some extent played into the hands of the Party and those in favour of *socrealizm* by emphasizing the role that the Party played in rebuilding Poland from the ruins. To a very great extent *socrealizm* seemed to offer a ready-made style and world-view to accommodate the events and the meaning of the war.

Writers like Borowski, Rudnicki, Brandys and Konwicki struggled to portray the events of the war and immediate post-war years in a shifting combination of story, reportage and personal memoir and within a few years had found the limits of the artistic form as well as the limits of the political content and social context. Brandys's first novel, *Drewniany koń* (Wooden Horse, 1946) is a detailed fictionalized portrait of the moral collapse of the Polish regime in the face of the Nazi occupation: it follows a well-meaning man of the *inteligencja* and shows his inability to deal with either Nazi occupation or the underground resistance movement. The novel was written in the years 1943–5 but was very much in the pre-war avant-garde style: in spite of this Brandys now saw himself as a man of the left and felt a need to show that any return to the politics and style of the pre-war military government, or that favoured by many of the exiled 'London Poles', would, for him, be a continuation of the latent fascism of the inter-war years.

Brandys's first important work was *Miasto niepokonane* (Invincible City, 1946) – a fictionalised and slightly satirical account of the Warsaw uprising – which was awarded the Warsaw City literary prize. Brandys returned to Warsaw in 1950 and was awarded the State Prize for Literature. His next work was *Między Wojnami* (Between the Wars, 1948–51), a four-volume account of vacillating and deluded Polish *inteligencja* life between the wars. In the final volume of the sequence *Człowiek nie umiera* (Man Doesn't Die, 1951), under the impact of *socrealizm*, Brandys vilified the opponents of 'communism'. In this novel only communists are aware of the threat of Fascism and Nazism and only communists and supporters of the regime are shown as decent examples of humanity: the 'positive' heroes of the Party, who see the threat of Nazism and link it with the history and development of capitalism, are little more than cardboard figures. This quartet established his concern for observation, psychology and political context, but also showed a certain readiness to explore the complexities of the human condition under the supposed certainties of a Marxist regime and a dim awareness of the limitations of *socrealizm*. In spite of the problems with the last volume, this series of novels established Brandys as one of the most powerful and original talents of his generation.

In 1953–4 Brandys wrote *Obywatele* (Citizens, 1954), a piece which was attacked by the critics for lacking proletarian heroes and 'positive themes', but which is regarded now as a fully-fledged, doctrinaire, *socrealizm* novel, bordering on manic parody of the form. Such a creation was possible only in a climate of what Miłosz calls 'collective psychosis', and betrayed a deepening unease at the required style. The book is often remembered for the hero, who undertakes tasks which push him to the limit of human endurance as part of a programme to achieve communist civic consciousness, and for the scene in which high school students zealously denounce the reactionary bourgeois views of their teachers to the authorities, and brand them class enemies. Although he was clearly attempting *socrealizm* at this time, it is sometimes claimed that Brandys was the least *socrealist* of the published writers of the Stalinist period. This may be wishful thinking, but certainly in the mid-1950s Brandys, along with many other creative intellectuals who had begun to feel that the actuality of the Party's policies fell short of their idea of socialism, began to change direction. The gradual increase in anti-Semitism in the closing years of Stalin's reign doubtless affected Jewish communists in Poland and, since it cut away the certainty that the Party would combat and eventually eradicate anti-Semitism, pushed them towards the growing *rewizjonist* trend within the Party. Brandys came to understand that under Party sponsorship the prospects for a Polish literature dominated by *socrealizm* were increasingly bleak. Mass publication of the classics and the cheap large-scale publication of new works by living writers were progressive policies, as was the war on illiteracy and the opening up of the educational system to the entire population. However, *socrealizm* and the literature of *partyjność* (Party-mindedness) satisfied no one in the long run: they did not interest an intelligent readership, soon bored the new mass readership and offered no joy to the writers. Brandys's stance as one of the Party faithful began to change into a desire to correct and affect the Party, to bring it back on course. In time this attitude melted into one of criticism, scornful cynicism and open opposition.

At the eleventh session of the Council of Culture and Art in February 1954, the minister of culture, Władysław Sokorski, revealed his distaste for attempts to direct literature or intervene in cultural and creative processes, and admitted that *socrealizm*, which he had introduced at the Fourth Writers' Union Congress in 1949, had been a mistake since the basis for such literature did not yet exist in Poland. Sokorski's comments opened up serious debate within the Writers' Union at their sixth annual conference in June of that year. Brandys, never an entirely uncritical Party member, was reported as saying that the Party had made ideological mistakes that had damaged the movement to establish a socialist literature; the Party had an immature and limited appreciation of ideology and, therefore, produced an immature and limited art. He claimed that since ideology and art grew out of a mature appreciation of human experience and cognition, the party and the writers had not so far been capable of producing anything other than a literature of poor self-knowledge since their appreciation of the world was grounded in an imperfectly understood ideology. The Party's mistakes had inevitably damaged progress towards a genuine socialist literature by producing and publishing a great many worthless books which, in reproducing the sterile propaganda of the Party and its definitions of literature, had avoided all discussion of vital problems and experiences. Brandys believed that for a genuinely socialist writer there could be no forbidden topic, no artistic formula, and that writers should be free to observe life, whether it matched a Marxist view or not.[7]

In 1955 Brandys was again awarded the state literature prize, but if this was intended as a bribe it was too little and too late. Brandys was never able to furnish a precise date for his departure from the Party orbit. While he was to say that a decisive factor in his disillusion with the Party was a series of conversations with people who had been in jail in the years 1954–6, he nevertheless remained a Party member for a while longer and somehow managed to justify this:

> I had my doubts from the beginning, but the stronger they were, the more I repressed them and the more vociferous were my denials of them. Every doubt damaged the logic and the ethics of the basic assumptions I had come to accept and burdened me with guilt. One was always on the lookout for signs of doubts in oneself and in others. In 1955 I was still trying to defend myself from myself against the facts. At bottom, I was only defending myself from myself. It may be that the most essential mechanism in the system known as communism is this curious twofold one: the counterfeiting and the denying of the self.[8]

Professor Stanisław Balbus was to recall a conversation between Brandys and Tadeusz Kwiatkowski in 1956, in which Brandys had rather naively said:

> Good God, look at what they've done with us! Who has? asked Kwiatkowski. THEY have. The communists, replied Brandys. I don't understand, said

Kwiatkowski, how you couldn't have known what was going on. Weren't you home? I didn't have a clue. Well then, you should have gone to the first tradeswoman on the market square, and she would have told you.[9]

Commentators on 1956 have given prominence to the violent clashes in Poznań. Although it is likely that the Party saw these as an immediate and dangerous threat to the regime, it is also clear that they felt the demands of the writers and intellectuals had to be met. It was possible to disperse crowds with bullets and promises of more meat, but neither of these would greatly affect the intellectual threat to the Party's position. The main current of revolt may have been proletarian, but the main current of reform was intellectual and came from writers: they had all gained valuable insight into the nature of the regime they had up to this point tolerated or, in some cases, actively supported it. The opposition and ambition of the writers was now, quite by accident, in harmony with demonstrating workers who had been denied any other means of communicating their political opinion and economic experience.

With the 'thaw' of 1956, Brandys's concern to follow the Party, or even argue with it shifted considerably. While it is safe to regard him as a supporter of the Party up to the mid-1950s, after 1956 he threw in his lot with the oppositionist *rewizjoniści* (revisionists). In books of this time it was not possible to blame the Party for any mistake or mishap: it was only possible to profess a mystic faith in the Party and say that whatever was wrong was the result of sabotage and manipulation by class enemies, US imperialists and anti-Polish elements. However, Brandys's famous short story 'Obrony Granady' (Defending Granada, 1956), broke substantially with the political and literary conventions of those days. It concerned the efforts of a theatre group to stage a play by Mayakovsky and the Party's successful efforts to get them to produce a worthless piece of *socrealizm* instead, with the result that the group becomes apathetic and breaks up. It was a tale in which idealistic young 'socialists' are defeated by Party dogmatism, soulless conformity and routine. The story more or less announced that Brandys, who had wavered somewhere between the orthodoxy of the Stalinists and the growing dissatisfaction of the revisionists, would henceforth be opposing the regime he had helped create. The story appeared in the journal *Twórczość* (Creativity), in January 1956. On 24–5 March 1956 the Council of Culture and Art met for its nineteenth session. Party members and ex-Party members of the Writers' Union, people like Andrzejewski, Kott and Ważyk, many of them winners of the state literary prize, led the debates, and it was from this group that the most vociferous, ferocious and thorough scourging of the Party came.

Brandys's *Matka Królów* (Sons and Comrades, 1957) was written during the months from March 1956 to March 1957, that is during the early part of the 'thaw'. The novel focuses on ways of understanding the 'new creed' which had not been dictated by the Party. Much to the embarrassment of the Party, by the power and experience of its characters and sheer narrative drive, the novel managed to penetrate the fog of falsity the Party was busy manufacturing. The story is that of a mother who loses her four sons (all devoted communists) not only to the blind and indiscriminately destructive forces of war and Nazism, but also to internal Party rivalries and purges. Brandys was determined to draw on his own experiences to explore the ethical conflicts that 'communism' provoked in Polish society and he was one of the first to observe the problem of what was happening to language under the influence of the Party. In the novel, Zenon observes the discrepancy between language and reality:

> 'What used to be has gone now, why don't they write about what *is*?' He cursed the trams and queues, the informers and careerists, the limousines the officials used. He hated life, himself and Roman [his brother], his own failed hopes and the voice of the announcer on the wireless, and when saying 'the people' or 'freedom' he contorted his mouth contemptuously.[10]

For many people, the thaw and the possibility of comment such as this meant that books became worth reading again. It has been estimated that in contrast to the period 1949–56 when a third of all books were unsold, in the years 1956–60 only 10 per cent of all books, and 5 per cent of fiction went unsold.[11] It was becoming clear that while many writers made use of *socrealizm*, the idea of a straightforward story and plot was still not very strong in post-war Polish literature. Novels like those of Brandys and Konwicki, in attempting to deal with censorship, the demands of the party and the enormous social and political changes in post-war Poland, were moving away from the simplicities of *socrealizm* towards a more contemplative style, with shifting and complex narrative methods. But the 'thaw' was short-lived: in the period 1957–9, in an effort to silence critics of the regime and remove the 'cosmopolitan intellectuals' who were the mainstay of *rewizjonizm* within the Party, some 200,000 Party members were purged by First Secretary Gomułka, and 20,000 Jews were persuaded to emigrate by the security services.

Gomułka's bid to rein in the *rewizjoniści* and to control the writers as a way of restoring the pre-thaw Party powers continued, but nevertheless, in 1963 Brandys was awarded the *Nowa Kultura* literary prize for his three-volume collection of letters, speculation and essays *Listy do Pani Z* (Letters to Mrs Z). In spite of his growing reputation Brandys was caught in an escalating conflict with the Party and it is clear that by this time he was trying to distance himself from it. In the years 1954–66 he resigned as chairman of the Warsaw committee of the National Unity Front, from membership of the Warsaw Party committee and from the Party Executive Committee in the Writers' Union. He refused his state publisher permission to reprint his novel

Obywatele. He refused all offers to participate in juries and state awards and turned down the opportunity to join the ideological committee of the Party Central Committee. He refused to join the Praesidium of the All Polish Peace Committee and refused to sign its appeal. He also refused to withdraw *Matka Królów* from publication in the west, even though the secretary of the Central Committee had made a direct request to him to do so. In the same period he was summoned to the Central Committee three times and charged with anti-Party activities. Doubtless his growing reputation abroad helped protect him: in 1964 he was awarded the Italian Alba prize.

After 1956 the Party had slowly recovered its grip on society, and by the early 1960s increasingly came to view writers (particularly Jewish writers) not as a loyal and imaginative opposition committed to the cause of Polish socialism, but as a hostile and negative 'enemy within', a fifth column in the pay of western capitalists and German revanchists. In 1966 no less than twenty-two Party writers (later joined by Brandys) sent a letter to the Central Committee arguing that it was 'excessive' and 'alarming' for a loyal oppositionist Marxist like Leszek Kołakowski to be expelled from the Party and harassed in his work. They stressed that the expulsion of Kołakowski would deepen the ideological rifts within the Party and would retard the hope of authentic socialist development in Poland. It was clear that it was no longer simply a case of the Party finding a young upstart lecturer to be a nuisance, but a matter of silencing dissent, especially within the Party. The Party responded to the 'Letter of the Twenty-Two' by attempting to intimidate the writers into withdrawing their signatures. It then set up a committee to interview and investigate the professional credentials of the protesting writers. When the writers refused to withdraw their signatures, sixteen were expelled from the Party. Brandys and Tadeusz Konwicki resigned from the Party in protest. From this date on writers of all kinds, who had come to believe that with the thaw they could say what was on their minds, realized that this was no longer so: they were expected to suppress their conscience – something which in Catholic Poland would have been difficult, and which the unique cultural position and political tradition of writers in Polish society made unlikely.

In 1968 Brandys wrote a letter to the minister of education to protest at the banning of Adam Mickiewicz's play *Dziady*, and as a result lost his teaching post at the PWST Theatre Academy, where he had worked since 1956. The banning marked the start of the Party's effort to silence intellectual criticism and political opposition within the Party by setting off an anti-Semitic campaign. Under the guidance of the interior minister, Mieczysław Moczar, and the ZBoWiD (Union of Fighters for Freedom and Democracy, a partisan organization), Poles of Jewish origin were 'revealed' and then purged from the Party, the film and entertainment industries, and the universities; several influential editors lost their posts. By the end of the year, in an increasingly hysterical anti-Semitic atmosphere, virtually the entire surviving Jewish element in Polish society – perhaps 20,000 people – had been given 'permission' to leave Poland. With this the Party had finally broken the back of *rewizjonizm* and silenced organized opposition for most of the next decade. It was to be the late 1970s before the scattered oppositionists would be in a position to draw together again. Brandys should have been intimidated by the campaign of 1968, but he and his wife resolved to stay on in Poland. In 1970–1 Brandys was allowed to lecture in Paris. Probably the authorities were glad to get him out of the country and almost certainly hoped he would not return. He returned. In 1972 Brandys published *Wariacje pocztowe* (Postal Variations), the history of a single Polish family over several generations told through a collection of letters. He was accused in the press of ridiculing Polish culture and history – a thinly disguised reminder of his Jewish origins.

In 1974 Brandys started the novel *Rondo*, which recalled his wartime folly in setting up a fake underground cell in order to win the affection of a Warsaw actress. The novel is set out as a letter designed to counter the publication of an academic book which purports to detail the activities of the underground cell. The author, a Professor Janota, claims that he was a member of the group. The narrator of *Rondo* explains that he spent several years in communist gaols, trying to persuade his interrogators that the cell was a fiction, but they were unconvinced and believed that an underground group about which absolutely nothing was known must have been incredibly efficient and was therefore still active and dangerous to the post-war regime. Only towards the end of the book is it revealed that the narrator Władek Sznej is also the academic historian Professor Janota, and that he is protesting at his own actions and earlier writings. The book attempted to show how a system of unreality could be created, and that once it was in existence could not be effectively challenged. It was a chilling warning that the 'reality of truth' was in fact self-contained and no longer had meaning or reference outside itself. Brandys, having embarked on the revelation of the 'unreality principle' at work within post-war Polish society found the subject too convoluted and painful. He could not finish the book, and dropped it to work on another project.[12]

By 1976, as a result of the workers' demonstrations in Radom and intellectual unrest at proposed constitutional changes, a politically wide-ranging, loose association of dissident writers and intellectuals, both in Poland and in enforced emigration, gathered around KOR (Committee for the Defence of Workers). Membership included numerous *rewizjoniści* writers and artists of earlier days, historians, philosophers, ex-Party writers and Catholics of the Znak group. All these people had distanced themselves from the Party. Brandys, who was part of this movement, had signed the 'Letter of the Thirteen' in July 1976 to protest at the treatment of demonstrating workers from the Ursus factory. In January 1977, Brandys and 172 other protesters petitioned the Sejm to investigate the violence and judicial victimization that followed the strikes in Radom and Ursus. Brandys and the other protesters were blacklisted by the authorities.[13]

In 1978 Jerzy Andrzejewski, Brandys and several other writers recognized that they could no longer look to official publishing houses as an outlet for their work. They took Adam Michnik's advice and set about re-creating an independent civil society. Bypassing the official media and the censor they launched the independent literary journal *Zapis* (Record or List). The first issue contained an extract from an unpublished manuscript by Andrzejewski about the Russian novelist Boris Pasternak. This independent literary journal was to prove a highly influential venture and, along with the émigré publishing houses in Paris and London, was to give the growing and wide-ranging dissident intellectual opposition a public voice. Before very long it had attracted to it the ex-Party poet Woroszylski as editor. Brandys also helped launch the KOR journal *Krytyka*, with an editorial board that included among others Barańczak, Jacek Kuroń, Michnik and the Hungarian dissident Miklós Haraszti. This journal paid particular attention to events and independent political and artistic thought in Hungary and Czechoslovakia. By the end of 1978 Brandys was a leading figure in a rapidly developing underground publishing movement. As a writer published by the underground NOWa, as co-editor of *Zapis*, and 'literary lecturer' for the Flying University, he felt he hazarded his life with these activities: he experienced a series of threatening letters and phone calls referring to his Jewish ancestry and foreign connections. Apart from this the authorities simply did not know what to do about the underground publishers or about KOR.

In 1978 Brandys courted possible legal action for slandering Poland when the Instytut Literacki in Paris produced *Nierzeczywistość*. This project had been started before *Rondo* and was closely related to its major themes. The book dealt with the 'reality' of political and literary questions in the People's Republic of Poland as matters of some urgency. With this publication it was clear that Brandys had finally abandoned the Polish state publishers. The book is a first-person introspective narrative in which the narrator tries very hard to come to terms with modern Poland and to accept the authoritarianism of the Polish 'socialists'. The book takes the form of a series of reflections on literature, history and Polish politics framed as replies to a questionnaire from a graduate American sociology student. In his answers Brandys drew together many of the strands of thought that had preoccupied him in his fiction, and displayed a multifaceted talent for thinking out loud on a variety of related subjects. He flayed Polish literature for its parochial obsession with Polishness and Polish history, for 'living in the national myth', lashed out at pre-war right-wingers who (with ease) became loyal left-wingers under the communists, and generally lampooned the culture of the communist regime as boorish peasant brutality garnished with a smattering of Marx; it is thought by some to be his best work. The book also spoke with disarming honesty about his conversion to communism and his Party membership:

> If I am not mistaken, I said yesterday that I had begun to believe in God in 1940; that is correct. But after the war, I began to believe in History. I mean by that a certain intellectual and moral condition having practically nothing in common with faith as a religious experience. It is a condition close to hypnosis, perhaps – almost magical. It is the making over of one's values to the bank of time. It is a kind of franchise granted not altogether deliberately, yet not under compulsion, and essentially disinterested . . . Yes the occupation had a metaphysics of its own; it was like passing from one realm of existence to another. I felt that my life could change utterly; I was expecting the ultimate, triumphant revelation. I would live the End and the Beginning.[14]

For Brandys submission to communism was not only a 'pact with necessity', but also 'the wisdom of the times', and the post-war social and political divisions between those who did and did not accept this wisdom were perfectly clear. Those who had been brought up in, or who had found for themselves, the traditions of the radical and secular *inteligencja*, enlightened rationalism, the peasant and proletarian political movements, made up the new order. Those who opposed the new order were the non-revolutionary bourgeoisie, traditional landowners, those who believed in national unity and those who felt the Catholic Church had a political role.

Through the early fifties, up to his resignation from the Party in 1966, Brandys, in line with Party rules, had largely kept silent about the injustices he had witnessed, and this bothered him. He had seen that the communists who interrogated him at the end of the war had very little capacity for argument. He recaptured the stultifying effect that reading Marx had on him, and described the resulting paralysis of his moral conscience in a way that disconcerted Party members and even upset fellow oppositionists:

> Why did I keep silent? Because I had come to the conclusion that History was right. Whatever I had thought and done until then was beginning to lose its importance in my mind, as if I were being wiped away by the gigantic, growing shadow of a colossus called the dialectic of change. A nervous curiosity made me read Marx and Lenin. I wanted to find in the original sources what this logic was that was undermining the foundations of my mind. Strange reading, supplying both the machinery and the key – a universal machine engaging all the gears at once – theories, arguments, and conclusions put together coherently: all you had to do was press a button and everything was explained – events, culture, religion, poverty, wealth, wars between nations, and relationships between men. But this universal explanation left one behind questionless. The result of accounting for everything was to preclude any possibility of evolution, and so the system of

thought is petrified through its own answers – its sort of suicide by certainty. In a world that is explained and with a self that is explained, man is reduced to silence in the midst of a truth that is explained . . . Of those who kept quiet, some now realise that their silence was not entirely due to fear of the terror which was raging. They had proof enough during the war that they were not cowards. But theirs was not a moral protest either. Sometimes, years later, they ask themselves why they weren't able to do more. If they kept silent, was it not in the face of a reality that paralysed the spirit? I think they, too, experienced an inner split, often without being fully conscious of it. In 1956 theatre directors and publishers were counting on the emergence of manuscripts full of revelations – plays, novels, poems written during the preceding years 'for the bottom drawer'. It turned out that the drawers were empty.[15]

He noted it was possible to say to oneself: 'I accept everything except the methods', without realizing that this gave assent to Party methods. He described his application for membership as a 'ridiculous gesture . . . an auto-nomous act in the midst of a collective catharsis'.[16] He summed up his years in the Party as comparable to a clinical case of depression, a 'period as in a mental illness that one hides'.[17]

Brandys was well aware that the younger generation blamed the former advocates of *socrealizm* and the writers and intellectuals of his generation for the imposition of 'socialism'. Trying to explain the 1950s, or his own biography, to one such student of literature, himself a product of 'Polish unreality', Brandys wrote:

I realised that it was futile. I would not be able to re-create those issues, to re-produce them as a whole or break them down into their component parts. They seemed enigmatic to me too. Each time I attempt to arrive at some formulation, my thinking snaps in two, stopped by that 'contradictory doubleness' I have written of elsewhere. For example, 'I didn't know what was happening because I was deceived' provokes the immediate reply, 'I was deceived because I didn't know what was really happening'. But at the same time neither of those two sentences says everything. They would both require numerous addenda, references to the war years, the pre-war years, to my own biography and that of other people, as well as to many ideas, like social reconstruction, revolution, socialism, and still other ideas from another tradition, like organic work, making up for lost time in a civilisation's development, reform, evolution. He wouldn't have understood any of it.[18]

Brandys was aware that reaction against the left could prove just as disastrous as the policies of the Party, and he was always mindful of the right-wing, religious, nationalist and anti-Semitic solutions lurking at the edges of the Polish political psyche:

In general those who have been disappointed by the outcome of revolutionary utopias run the risk of making a hundred-and-eighty degree turn; that is, of rejecting everything implied by revolution. But to reject revolution as too brutal a method of changing social life is not without consequences. I know intelligent and honourable people who moved away from Marxism, or from having an interest in Marxism, to opinions belonging to the traditional, conservative right. They were swept into it by one crisis, one shock after another; they tore off their old skin and ended up no longer able to understand the present-day world. The revolutionary movements in Asia and Latin America, as well as the tendencies on the new left in Western Europe, all of that is something inconceivable to them, suicidal. To them revolution heralds the slavery that is to come. They are beyond understanding that in certain situations revolution can get rid of obstacles to development and become one of the moral forces, while at other times it is up to the moral forces themselves to repair the damage caused by revolution. And there, too, lies another danger: that those who manage to escape one set of ready-made ideas can be engulfed by another set diametrically opposite.[19]

In spite of his criticisms of the Party, Brandys was absolutely certain that if Polish socialism had not been forced to remodel society in the image of the USSR, but had instead been allowed to 'draw upon the vital forces of the country', a socialist Polish regime based on human rights could have been created after the war. This was the dream of all those increasingly disillusioned intellectuals who stayed in the Party until 1956. It was not a dream that could be sustained in the years that followed 1956, though, when 'only the cynics still spoke of ideology' and 'illegality infected everything'.[20]

After his withdrawal from official publishing, Brandys lived on his royalties and income from foreign translations. For some observers, the fact that he was a Jew, that he had been a Party member, that he had 'abandoned' the Party and then Poland by publishing abroad, that he had 'gone over' to western patrons and 'sold out' to hard currency, made him a deeply untrustworthy figure, confirmed 'anti-cosmopolitan' feeling and brought into question the whole KOR underground movement.[21]

In December 1978 the Writers' Union sent Brandys a questionnaire which he completed:

1 *What form has your work with publishers taken in recent years?* For six years no publisher in the country has offered to sign a contract with me for a new book.
2 *With film?* For ten years all my proposals have been rejected (not by the film directors).
3 *With radio?* I have not received any offers for six years.
4 *With television?* No offers for seven years.

5 *What problems would you like to bring to the attention of the Executive Board of the Polish Writers' Union?* The censorship. The censorship's criminal actions with respect to persons and texts. The censorship, but not only as an agency. As an activity destructive of public property – the culture of the nation.[22]

These were the themes to which he was to return repeatedly, even obsessively, in his diaries. The appearance of Brandys's *Miesące* (Warsaw Diaries) was one of the opposition publishing high-spots of the closing years of the Gierek regime. The post-war years had given rise to a crisis in literature. By insisting on a realism that was not (could not, dare not be) realistic, it had forced writers to be far more literary, allusive and elusive, far more removed from the world of the senses and empiricism than they would have liked. The literary form that evolved was the hybrid genre, the 'lying diary'. The diary that was no such thing. It was a synthesis, part autobiography, part documentary, part confessional, part gossip column. It was nevertheless an authentic and highly successful literary fabrication. In response to the fabrications and manipulations of the Party the writers offered a fictional reality that only made sense in terms of the political situation.[23]

Brandys, who had for years shunned virtually all official literary gatherings and functions because of the predictability, was under no illusions about the kind of thing that Polish literature was becoming. For him, Polish literature lacked variety and a powerful range because it had not passed through the historical stages other European literatures had enjoyed. Polish literature had writing about the manor and the estate, but since Poland had not had a court it missed tightly plotted drama of court intrigue. Poland lacked a well-developed and numerous bourgeoisie and so lacked comedy of manners or literature showing the humbug and hypocrisy of middle-class ambition. Since it had only a tiny industrial working class, its literature largely failed to represent the ambiguities of working-class struggle and poverty. It lacked the genre of police and crime stories simply because the police represented alien authority. Poland lacked any colonies and so lacked adventure stories:

We had not passed through the school of historical plot development, which created the literature of the countries that possessed a court, a bourgeoisie, colonies, and police. The court was the school for intrigue, the bourgeoisie the school for careers, the colonies the school for adventure, and the police the school where crimes are reconstructed. Those are the fundamental elements of a story: intrigue, career, adventure, crime. Those countries produced Molière, Balzac, Defoe and Sir Arthur Conan Doyle. In Poland there was no court like at Versailles, a central focus for grand intrigues; the bourgeoisie developed late here and was weak; we had no colonies (Robinson Crusoe could not have come into being in a country without colonies); and we had no criminal police of the Scotland Yard variety. But we had the Miracle.[24]

Polish literature, Brandys said, remained 'constantly burdened by the legacy of the Romantic poets': they had bequeathed to literature 'the duty of creating a national miracle'.[25] As a result Polish literature was massively, obsessively, overwhelmingly and almost exclusively about the fate of the nation:

> Buried between the lines of every text printed are the names one is not allowed to mention, the facts about which one remains silent. The places and dates blotted from history create a dead zone where semi-poets gave interviews to semi-journalists and express their semi-truths to their semi-readers.[26]

Brandys had already identified what censorship and the resulting retreat from official media would do to Polish letters, but perhaps perversely he made no secret of his view that the clash between writers and state was an opportunity to renew the Polish writing élite. He saw the retreat from official publishing as the avoidance of officially sanctioned and directed mass culture, 'creativity that is bought and paid for'. He saw the exclusivity of underground literature as the ambiguous renewal of energy and the ancient vitality of Polish letters. The status of writer was offered by the authorities to anyone who satisfied conditions stipulated by the authorities, he said, but a writer was a person who 'did not accept offers'.[27]

Brandys was also well aware of the counter-arguments. If Polish literature had been built up despite the prevailing authorities of the previous hundred years, by smuggling in its messages through the chinks in the system, and had thrived on secrecy and martyrdom, then surely the police were doing it a great favour by driving it underground. Brandys saw the complexity and danger of this argument, and wondered if a cultural/political deformation was in the process of becoming a national norm. He asked: 'Are we deceiving the tyrant or is the tyrant deceiving us?' He countered by saying that by writing as he pleased in *Zapis* he was refusing to be driven underground, was coming out into the open, refusing to allow his work to be distorted, was trying to find personal literary forms:

> We are deviating from our years of being on the defensive, from the game we have been playing with our creative work. By employing tactics to deceive the tyrant, we were defending the last living values in our culture, we were ensuring their endurance, albeit in the form of allusions and sub-texts. In choosing open battle, we deprive ourselves of that possibility.[28]

Brandys also wrote off the western left's naivety in its understanding of 'socialism':

> There are the Western leftists. The left with its scruples about the world's first socialist country and its fear of providing grist to the right's mill. The left, the

right. In our part of the world self-respecting intellectuals realized long ago that this was an idiotic distinction. In Poland any sane person who does not wish to make a complete fool of himself keeps such ideas to himself. But they still have currency in the West. The left, belonging to the left, solidarity with the left, are articles of faith for them and are at the same time their alibi. The colossus should not be annoyed; in its barbarian skull slumbers the people's revolutionary soul. In the West, revolution is part of the catechism of the intellectual left.[29]

Brandys saw contemporary Soviet communism as watered down compared with the days of *The Captive Mind*, but all the more insidious and difficult to confront for being less violent. He saw the western left as merely a continuation of the Stalinist bureaucracies of east central Europe rather than as separate entities with different histories, experience and theories. For Brandys the west was obsessed with money, cars and sex, but for all its cries of freedom and democracy, it had lost its soul and did not know how to value its most treasured possessions. For Brandys the naive and foolish west was little more than a whore waiting for ravishment by the Soviets – 'No one', he wrote, 'is able to spread their legs more aesthetically, to lie down for the act with such *esprit* as the French intellectuals.'

In the face of these difficulties, and in spite of his own objections, Brandys felt obliged to fall back upon the unwritten code of the nineteenth century, a code of moral, nationalist behaviour based upon the *szlachta* values. For Brandys this was an ambiguous inheritance, since a substantial strand of Polish nationalist thought, and part of this code, had been anti-Semitism. Brandys was not anxious to offend and tried hard to emphasize the elements of the tradition that were tolerant and egalitarian. In his diary entry for January 1979 he wrote:

> There are moments when the unwritten values create the culture. Perhaps those are only the moments of tension and crisis, situations in which the boundaries of everyday endurance must be overstepped and the rules of the game broken. Then the majority of examples from the history of literature become useless and one must appeal to other ones. To the unwritten ones. To acts and attitudes that have not been anthologised but are part of the collective imagination, impregnating it with their gesture, scenes, faces.[30]

Though he felt that he had little choice but to accept the new regime in 1945, his naivety and feelings of guilt at his support for the Stalinists accounts for his desperate, even obsessive need to make sense of the world he saw around him, for the depth of his disappointment in the Party and his urgent need to re-establish himself and his credibility with friends:

> We talked about Poland, about ourselves and others, at night and during the day, drunk or sober. There was an obsessiveness in the talk that suggested an

addiction. None of us could do without it, and our need had a psychological source, like an interest in the occult. Returning home I would often say, 'Today was good, today we linked the chain.' The important thing was to establish an isolated, closed circuit. With the help of words we wanted to create a space of our own, a space in which we could be free. Our pronouncements on society, people, and books supplanted the injustice around us.[31]

Part of Brandys's literary pursuit had been to transcend the certainties of Polish Romantic literary traditions and its preoccupation with the tragic fate of Poland. However, Brandys was constantly frustrated in this. In assessing Poland's inward-looking literary patrimony and its intersection with political life, he complained that since the figure of the hero was automatically assumed to stand for Poland, it became impossible even in late twentieth-century Polish writing to present human passion in anything like its full complexity. For him the question of what Polish literature 'knew' hinged upon whether it was, or ever could be, universal and available to outsiders, or whether it would remain purely local. Brandys has attempted something unusual in Polish literature in that he tried to reveal the ways in which Polish national consciousness manifested itself – a kind of literary national pathology. Brandys had earlier dubbed this complex of literature, language, politics, resistance and deception *nierzeczywistość Polski* (Polish unreality).[32]

An important underlying factor in the life of Solidarność and a bone of contention in the months leading up to the declaration of Martial Law was the problem of what exactly the union wanted, where it was heading, how it framed its policies and made its alliances. These complex psychological, linguistic, economic and political features meshed in confusing and contradictory ways with 'Polish unreality'. Having lived in 'unreality' for so long it was difficult for the Party to acknowledge the reality of its situation, difficult for intellectuals to establish with any certainty that they understood the reality of Polish unreality, and for the workers to trust either the Party or the intellectuals to understand that the reality of the workers' lives was a poverty-stricken hell. Ironic speech and cynicism slowly but surely cut loose any link between reality and ideology. On one level it allowed the speaker to toe the Party line. At the same time it indicated to their peers that this was not what they really thought. This dual code meant that even though life became increasingly schizoid there was no large-scale disintegration of personality – the existence of professional life, the Church, the family, and the continued presence and awareness of pre-war cultural values and history, albeit altered, helped prevent any massively obvious social breakdown at least until the advent of Solidarność began the release of social and economic pressures. In the early 1970s Polish sociologists, linguists and writers began mapping the 'failure of the inner dynamic', the trend towards privatization – both in the economic sense and in the sense of social fragmentation, the internalization of intellectual, moral and political impulses. There was a very strong sense that things had been different before the war, that Poland had at one time been a 'normal country', that now 'real life' was elsewhere, that outside Poland things were normal. However, it was very difficult for people to express this feeling without allying themselves with the pre-war right-wing military regime, or with the West German revanchists, or, if they were Polish Jews, without appearing to be anti-Polish:

> The opposition between left and right reflects the ethical and religious dichotomies of good and evil, heaven and hell, truth and lie. Totalitarianism blurs the distinctions, and eliminates the struggle between good and evil, because the evil is good. Hell is Paradise. A lie effectively performs the function of the truth. Minus signs are replaced by plus signs and vice versa. We must leave it to the dialecticians of the West to decipher what is on the left in this hugely over-staged theatre of humanity. The Poles, the Czechs, the Lithuanians no longer think in Europe's political categories. They abhor the perfidious means by which they have been deprived of the humanist decalogue. They have experienced the horror of an ascendant technology of nihilism – a horror that the West cannot comprehend.[33]

In 1979 Brandys was asked by a friend if he did not regret the early *socrealizm* books he had produced and his early membership of the Party. Brandys replied:

> There's no reason to regret that things were different at some other time. It's more interesting like that. I don't regret my experience and I look back without horror and see myself 'in the shadow of my errors'. That's how I grew, how I learned – and continue to learn my portion of the truth. To grow and to learn. That's more interesting than finding the truth all at once.[34]

Brandys was acutely aware that Solidarność was the sole conduit for virtually every aspect and hue of protest within Poland – ranging from dissident communist opinion, through liberal socialist opinion right through to hard-line anti-Semitic and Falangist opinion. He was keenly aware that the union had allowed pre-war political groupings and opinions to re-emerge. He identified and was fearful of the stupid and ignorant, of the hatred and intolerance, the anti-intellectualism, chauvinism and fanatical xenophobia that suddenly emerged, and he was aware that the tensions of trying to shape, channel and contain these diverse strands of opinion could eventually blast Solidarność apart. He called the continued existence of the union a miracle. In September 1981, just before Brandys again left Poland to lecture abroad, he was accused in an anonymous pamphlet of belonging to a secret Zionist organization whose aim was the destruction of Poland. Brandys had no doubt this was a *prowokacja* (provocation) inspired by the security service. Brandys saw the best and the worst that was liberated within Polish society by the appearance of Solidarność, and he was to reflect on his early membership of the Party and on the connection with what later happened to Poland, squaring up to his burden of responsibility:

> Responsibility. I will be responsible for the worst that can happen, since it will have been caused by a political system that I at one time accepted. I have borne that knowledge within me for twenty-odd years. And it is of no great importance whether I might be able to elucidate psychologically what motivated me then or even whether I want to. What is important is that one cannot cast off the responsibility for those years and that one's later actions do not set one free from it. Only the simplistic interpretations and incorrect beliefs can be repudiated, but the error allows for no deletion. It casts its shadow back onto the past and one lives with that shadow. I foresee society becoming more acutely aware that the evil of those years is the source and beginning of the evils that now exist. And then that shadow will grow longer.[35]

Brandys admitted freely that Poland with Solidarność was a very complicated place. But, he said, when he attempted to think about the situation, to reflect on it rationally and make some judgement about how things were progressing, his thoughts collapsed into meaninglessness. However, he was sure that in time Polish literary culture and Polish liberal intellectual traditions would prevail to elucidate and give shape to events. The boorishness and ignorance of some Solidarność members (the anti-Semitic sentiments of Szczecin Solidarność leader Marian Jurczyk appalled Brandys) were matched by the dishonesty of the Party's own anti-Semitic front organizations, the Grunwald Patriotic Union and ZBoWiD. He railed against them and hoped:

> Culture has a higher wisdom than history: not only can it interpret facts, but it also posits a scale of values. Intolerance, stupidity and ignorance have inundated Polish society more than once before, but they have never created the nation's culture. Therein lies its greatness.[36]

Possession of Brandys's diaries during Martial Law was said by his British publishers to be sufficient to earn a ten-year prison sentence from the military regime of General Jaruzelski.

Critic Jan Błoński has located Brandys very firmly within the Polish-Jewish literary-political complex of the post-war years, pointing out that, like many others of his generation, Brandys joined the Party out of two contradictory impulses: out of a very clear sense of difference from mainstream Polish political opinion, and out of a very powerful need to belong. As Błoński said, Brandys hinted very early at his sense of otherness through the Jewishness of his character Samson (*Samson*, 1949). After this novel, the distance he felt from Polish society, the acute observation this distance and familiarity allowed him, and the strong need to belong were all clearly evident in virtually everything he wrote.[37] Brandys exchanged one minority for another even smaller, when he joined the Party. He joined another, even smaller, when he quit the Party and joined the dissident fraternity. As a dissident writer he deployed his edgy insecurity and his sense of marginality to analyse the literary and cultural impact of the Party on Polish society, which was something that was impossible from within the Party. In doing this he gave shape to the experience and confusion of marginality, described his need to identify with a group, a nation, a party, his frustration with the 'progress of history' and the 'reality' of Polish communism. His uneasy sense of himself as an outsider, his wry sense of disbelief, enabled him to pierce the fog of Polish 'communist' unreality. He did this as someone who was not entirely caught within the coils of either the Party or Polish culture. His notes from the margin illuminated the alienation, doubts and fears that the bulk of the Polish population were experiencing, but for quite different reasons.

At this point it is worth pausing to look briefly at one of the very few sources of information about Brandys available in English. W. Maciąg's pamphlet *Kazimierz Brandys* is part of a large series of similar publications on Polish writers published by the official Agencja Autorska, based in Warsaw. Although this pamphlet was written in 1983 and supplementary bibliographical material was added in 1988, it was not published until 1990. Presumably publication was delayed because Brandys, who was in France and refusing to return to Poland during the Martial Law period, was in disgrace. The pamphlet is an interesting judgement. Referring to how his experiences in the 1930s shaped Brandys's 'world outlook', Maciąg writes:

An artist, and a writer in particular, devoted to a creative pursuit, feels that he is caught up in a situation where he must make a choice of a world, hence also of a political outlook. That does not mean that he must choose immediately. The fact is, however, that he perceives the experience he goes through as a crucial question posed by society, that he views the world as a repertory of ideas among which he must choose and with which he must identify. Consequently personal independence is nothing more than an evasion that should be severely censured, that condemns the artist to banishment from our common history. That is not an iron rule. That period had its outsiders. But Brandys was particularly sensitive by nature to those pressures and the related questions. Many of his books dealt with what seemed as if his literary protagonists were motivated by a personal hostility towards nationalistic movements and ideologies, as if he were particularly incensed by the manifestations of anti-Semitism. Reports of Nazi brutalities in

Germany and closer to home the anti-Semitic riots he observed at the University of Warsaw, and on the other hand, the liberal progressive tradition in which he was brought up at home, conspired to push him toward the leftists.[38]

Clearly, as this pamphlet was produced in the final days of censorship it is impossible to know how much of this is the author's intent and how much is the result of interference. However, as it stands it is a judgement that smacks of 1950s *socrealizm* and a lurking anti-Semitism. The pamphlet simultaneously attempts to link Brandys to the discredited Party and to distance itself from the Party. It is ambivalent about the underground and émigré publishing movement – the hint, and it can never be more than a hint, is that these are financed by international Jewry. While it makes no secret of Brandys's departure from the Party in 1966 or his underground publications, it manages to make it appear as if Brandys left the Party because, however well-meaning, he was nevertheless a discontented and unstable outsider who was lucky that he had not been banished from 'our common history'. It is hinted that perhaps the underground and émigré press and the dissident KOR are all run by people of a similar disposition and character. The pamphlet skirts the issue of Brandys's Jewish identity, and in doing so makes it an issue of another sort. It is also clear that Brandys's 'particular sensitivity' to anti-Semitism is somehow unnatural, probably un-Polish, possibly even anti-Polish. Although the pamphlet never actually says that Brandys is Jewish, the key weasel-words, 'world outlook', 'our common history', 'outsider', 'liberal progressive tradition', are clear enough indications of what is taking place. The pamphlet avoids the Party's own nationalism and anti-Semitism, and gives no detail of Brandys's experience of anti-Semitism. It makes him sound like a fickle, over-sensitive, discontented outsider with a bizarre penchant for pre-war socialism; he is little more than a selfish bourgeois artist who dabbled with communism until that looked like failing, then dabbled with the opposition and underground publication, and finally went abroad to publish his diaries. In fact the pamphlet suggests that as a mere diarist Brandys is barely an artist at all.

It is hardly surprising that Brandys never felt welcomed or accepted by communism, or by Poland. He was in Poland but never quite of Poland; a socialist but never a Stalinist. In the eyes of those who insist on a 'true' Polish identity, his recognition of this, however reluctant, could only prove how Jewish he was and how un-Polish. Brandys's obsessive themes – the dissolution of personality, the nature of reality, his concern with the culture of 'we', the complexities of 'otherness', of the outsider who finds himself on the inside, the nature of citizenship, the masks of convention – can all be traced to this insecurity. Ironically, Brandys, in giving up his quest for a place in Polish 'communist' society, in deciding to write for his diary and to publish with the underground and émigré press, found a place within the Polish dissident community and through them was enabled to speak out on behalf of an increasingly repressed Polish society. Brandys, like many other Poles of Jewish origin, discovered that his quest for identity and a place within Polish society were not to be satisfied by communism, *rewizjonizm* or in opposition to communism. While his interest in left-wing politics may have followed a path that many Jewish intellectuals in Poland had trodden, his eventual decision to oppose communism paralleled, followed and informed anew a long tradition of Polish resistance. Dissident thinkers like Adam Michnik valued the honesty of Brandys's writing very highly, felt he illuminated their darkness, put a name to their fears, and made them feel less isolated and less marginal. Brandys's diaries and his essays on 'Polish unreality' stand as monuments of resistance to the deformations wrought by Polish 'communism' on Polish culture. In the final days of Gierek's regime, in the chaos and confusion of 1980–1 and in the long depressing months of Martial Law, that was no small achievement.

Brandys was abroad when Martial Law was declared in December 1981. Throughout military rule he lived first in Paris, then moved to New York. He continued to write his diaries and to observe and comment on what was happening inside Poland. Rather than return to Poland when Martial Law was suspended, Brandys took up a teaching post in the USA, denying the military regime a propaganda victory and undercutting their claim that Poland was returning to 'normal'. It is significant that Brandys declined to return to post-communist democratic Poland too. Doubtless age has something to do with it. By the time the communist regime collapsed in 1989 Brandys was 73. However, given the repeated anti-Semitic comments directed against the membership of KOR throughout the 1970s, the anti-Semitic remarks of Solidarność leader Marian Jurczyk in 1980–1 and the continued anti-Semitic activities of Pax, ZBoWiD and the Grunwald Patriotic Union during the Martial Law period, followed after 1989 by increasing social, political and economic turmoil, also the rise of the right-wing anti-Semitic nationalist party KPN (Confederation for an Independent Poland) and the Fascistic Party X, led by Stanisław Tymiński, not to mention Lech Wałęsa's anti-Semitic slurs against Adam Michnik and other leading opposition figures, it is probable that Brandys feared the worst. In this context his decision is not so strange.

There can be no doubt that Brandys's literary career and the experiences he set down in his diaries link up with and illuminate the intellectual development of a substantial section of the Polish *inteligencja*. However, Brandys's accidental exile has turned into a conscious voluntary emigration. Not the flight Polish nationalists may have wished for, not the emigration Zionists would have wished for, nor the unambiguous embrace of capitalism that Reaganites hoped for. Brandys, still an unrepentant *rewizjonist* who harks back to the socialist values of the pre-war years, has, without doubt assimilated and transcended Polish Romantic literary culture, bringing it face to face with some of its unpleasant components and internal contradictions. At the same time he has celebrated Polish literary culture's determination to fight free from the labyrinthine 'unreality' of the slowly decaying Stalinist system towards a more modern, less self-obsessed creativity. However, his bid for 'anti-traditional assimilation' into Polish politics, culture and national identity has not been such a success, and Brandys himself, it seems, has brought it to a conclusion by refusing to return to Poland.

7

RYSZARD KAPUŚCIŃSKI

Between western and eastern Europe – that is, at least Poland – there appears a certain distinct asymmetricality. In Poland the yearnings and ideas are European, but the civilisation is Asiatic: the means of production; the bureaucratic system; the appearance of the cities, towns and villages; the behaviour of the mob (when it is not a political, civic mob, but a throng hunting down a pair of shoes). This demonstrates how thin the crust of the élite's dream about Europe actually is, or, at least, how very Asiatic the rump attached to a European head.

Adam Zagajewski, *Solidarity, Solitude*, 1990.

The son of a village schoolmaster who had been driven from central Poland by poverty and unemployment to a post on the eastern Polish frontiers, Ryszard Kapuściński was born on 4 March 1932, in Pińsk, Polesia. It was a very underdeveloped area of eastern Poland, 'even poorer than Galicia – the Asia of Europe'. It was a town, Kapuściński was later to recall, of dirt roads, horse-drawn carts and wandering chickens; it had three motor cars, but lacked tarmac, concrete and telephones. Like most children in that part of Poland at that time, Kapuściński wore bark instead of shoes and ate flour and water pastries instead of meat and vegetables. The main language spoken in this area was Byelorussian (White Russian), along with Polish, Yiddish, Ukrainian, Russian, Lithuanian and German. The ethnic mix in Pińsk was 75 per cent Jewish, with substantial minorities of Muslim Tartars, Poles, Russians, Ukrainians and Armenians. It was a rich mix even by the standards of the old Polish Commonwealth. But it was a remarkably peaceful and harmonious community.

Pińsk was occupied by the Soviet Union in 1939. Kapuściński's education during this period was chaotic: he has spoken of a ruined classroom without roof or ceiling, of fifty boys to a class with only one Russian-language textbook, Stalin's *Voprosy Leninizma* (Studies of Leninism) which they took turns at reading aloud. The winter of 1939–40 was one of almost total famine in Pińsk, and Kapuściński's father, an officer in the Polish army and decorated with the Cross of Valour, noted that Poles who did not get a job with the Soviet administration or join the Party were liable for deportation to the Gulag. Kapuściński witnessed NKVD deportations of his teacher and almost half the students from his class. His father decided that they should move away as soon as possible and thus began a period in which the Kapuściński family 'wandered'. They eventually moved to a village near Warsaw.

Kapuściński's father was by then involved in the resistance and they hid with another underground family. After a year the authorities came looking for them and they were forced to move, this time to a small tenement block next to the Warsaw ghetto. As a child Kapuściński and his friends used to hide in the bushes to watch the Nazi firing squads at work, and would report back to his father on the numbers they had seen executed. After the war, with Warsaw totally destroyed by the Nazis and return to Soviet Pińsk unacceptable, the Kapuściński family wandered again. They eventually returned to Warsaw and took over a small fire-damaged building, which was all the shelter they could find in the ruins of the capital. Kapuściński's father became a stock clerk in a construction firm.[1]

Kapuściński's early years in Pińsk had a lasting effect on his vision of the world:

Because Pińsk, even though borrowing so much from Europe, was not part of Europe. It was not until I was seven years old that I saw my first train. I didn't have a telephone until I was thirty, and I am still learning how to use it. People are always having to stop me as I'm half way through the door on my way to deliver a message to someone who might live miles away because it simply doesn't occur to me to dial a number. I'm made uneasy by technology, I don't trust it, I'm uncomfortable around it. But I am not uncomfortable in the Third World. I have always rediscovered my home, rediscovered Pińsk in Africa, in Asia, in Latin America. In Ethiopia I am at home. Amid poverty I am at home. I know what the life means. The society of Polesia was, really, a feudal one, a tribal society: it prepared me for Africa. You know sometimes I am asked if I will leave Poland, if I will emigrate. And my reply, half joking, is always the same: there is no need to emigrate. I already have. I am an emigrant from Pińsk, from this other world.[2]

His first poems were published in the Pax-Catholic daily newspaper *Słowo Powszechne* (Universal Word), *Odrodzenie* (Rebirth) and *Twórczość* (Creativity) when he was still a high school student. In 1948 he joined ZMS (Union of Socialist Youth) and graduated from high school in 1950. It was his ambition to study philosophy: 'At that time there were no philosophy courses. Traditional philosophy had been dismissed as bourgeois, and, while there were lecturers in philosophy, the only philosophy they could teach was bourgeois philosophy, and the university was therefore prohibited from hiring them.'[3] He entered the history faculty at Warsaw University in the autumn of 1950. He graduated in 1955 having written a Master's dissertation entitled: *Rola inteligencji w królewstwie polskim na przełomie XIX i XX wieku* (The Role of the Intelligentsia in the Kingdom of Poland in the Late Nineteenth and early Twentieth Centuries) under the supervision of the historian Henryk Jabłoński, who later became chairman of the Council of State.

While still a student he began work for *Sztandar Młodych* (Youth Banner, joint journal of the Executive Committee of ZMS/ZMW, Union of Rural

Youth). In its time this was a militant investigative journal that maintained contacts with 'anonymous heroes' in industry and the bureaucracy. In 1953 (two years before Ważyk's famous 'Poem for Adults' on the same theme) Kapuściński wrote an uncompromising article about the new communist city of Nowa Huta and the Polish steel industry. In an article called 'This Too is the Truth of Nowa Huta' he showed that although the gigantic steelworks was a showpiece for the regime it was riddled with drunken supervisors, had poor management and appalling working conditions – facts which Kapuściński knew from friends who worked there and because he had worked in Nowa Huta during his student vacations. He concluded by saying that the people of Nowa Huta awaited justice for the skulduggery, insensitivity and hypocrisy that had been visited upon them, and waited for the Party and the government to explain themselves, knowing that there was no satisfactory explanation. Kapuściński was forced to go into hiding, protected by the workers at the plant. Eventually a special commission of inquiry was appointed and, after an investigation, the management of the steelworks was dismissed and the government set aside money for the construction of further municipal facilities. Kapuściński was rehabilitated and at the age of twenty-three was awarded a state prize, the Golden Cross of Merit, for investigative journalism.

Although he was invited to stay on at the university to teach he considered this rather boring and preferred instead to work as a journalist. In 1957–8 he began work on the weekly *Polityka*. His editor, Mieczysław Rakowski, sent him around Poland collecting material and writing articles about the consequences and the human truths that underlay Poland's economic and political changes of those years. This material eventually appeared as his first book, *Busz po Polsku* (Bush Polish-Style, 1962), which looked with a fresh and unsentimental eye at the people of the more remote (and not so remote) rural parts of Poland as if they were peculiar anthropological specimens from the African bush. In 1957 he first visited Uganda. In 1960, just as he was finishing work on his book about Poland, Kapuściński heard that conflict had broken out in the newly independent Congo and sought permission to go.

In 1964, having survived his hazardous journey to the Congo via Khartoum and Juba, he joined PAP (Polish Press Agency), the sole foreign correspondent Poland could afford. He asked to be sent to Czechoslovakia, but instead his editor sent him to India, Pakistan, Afghanistan, the Middle East, Japan, China, Latin America and again to Africa. He was Poland's first, and because there was very little hard currency available, often Poland's only foreign correspondent, working for what was by international standards a very small news agency. For nearly twenty years he was quite literally Poland's eyes and ears in the world; he went where most Poles could not go. His reporting earned him a considerable reputation and he is best known for his journalism covering social conditions, wars and revolutions in the Third World. By the time he returned to Poland in 1980 Kapuściński had covered wars in Honduras and El Salvador, a revolution in Zanzibar, a coup in Tanganyika, the South African invasion of Angola, a revolution in Burundi and civil war in Nigeria; he had met Che Guavara in Bolivia, Salvador Allende in Chile, Patrice Lumumba in the Congo, Idi Amin in Uganda, Ahmed Ben Bella in Algeria, and Aghostino Neto in Angola; he had observed the end of Haile Selassie's reign in Ethiopia and the collapse of the Shah's regime in Iran. In Uganda he suffered from cerebral malaria, in Dar es Salaam he suffered from pulmonary tuberculosis ('no pain but you feel bad, and you're coughing up blood') and he cured an attack of parasitic stomach worms by smoking forty cigarettes a day and refusing to eat. In total he had seen twenty-seven revolutions, coups and wars and had narrowly escaped death several times: in the Congo he was almost shot by a firing squad of Belgian paratroopers, he was frequently beaten up by one side or the other in the various civil wars and coups, and in Nigeria was doused with petrol but released just before he was due to be set alight. According to Kapuściński, he has been sentenced to death, 'actually facing the guns', four times.

From his experiences came a disturbing and fascinating series of books detailing the birth of the Third World: *Czarne gwiazdy* (Black Stars, 1963); *Gdyby cała Afryka* (If All Africa, 1969), a book that upset the Ethiopian government who refused to allow him back into the country for several years; *Dlaczego zginął Karl von Spreti* (Why Karl von Spreti Died, 1970) a challenging account of the kidnapping and death of the West German ambassador to Guatamala and the nature of dictatorship; *Jeszcze dzień życia* (Another Day of Life, 1976) about the liberation war and civil war in Angola; *Wojna futbolowa* (Soccer War, 1978) an account of political life and popular expectation in South America. However, his most striking successes have been with the books *Cesarz* (The Emperor: Downfall of an Autocrat, 1978) about the final days of Haile Selassie's regime in Ethiopia, and *Szachinszach* (Shah of Shahs, 1982) about the Iranian revolution and the overthrow of the Shah.[4]

Kapuściński is not only a very well-connected journalist, but an incredibly 'well-decorated' writer with numerous state awards and prizes for his literary works: the Golden Cross of Merit, 1953; the Bruno prize, 1959; the Ministry of Art and Culture prize, 1967; the Bolesław Prus prize, 1975; the *Miesięcznik Literatury* and the *Nowy Książki* prizes, 1975; the People's prize for literature (second category), 1976; the *Kultura* prize, 1978. By the mid-1970s he was part of a generation of well-known and respected journalists (Wojciech Giełżyński, Hanna Krall, Maciej Szumowski and Jerzy Lovell) who were about the same age, had largely come up through the Party youth movement, had developed a hard-hitting, wry, subtle and allusive style in response to censorship, and were increasingly worried by what they saw of Polish contemporary life, and increasingly disillusioned by the Party. Kapuściński in particular had become such a well-known figure in Poland that he attracted the attention of the film director Andrzej Wajda, who was interested in the idea of a Polish intellectual who no longer feels 'at home' in his own country and who is increasingly uneasy about the changes in Gierek's Poland. Kapuściński is believed to be the model for the journalist in Wajda's film *Bez znieczulenia* (literally 'Without Anaesthetic', English title: *Rough Treatment*, 1978).

Kapuściński's current renown hides the very difficult start his books had in Poland. Many Poles brought up on standard Polish national literary fare, on the classical 'matter of Poland', could not penetrate his stories of the Third World. They saw them simply as tales from another part of the world, exotica with little or no immediate relevance to Polish life:

> Most of my professional life has been spent outside Europe. As a foreign correspondent I witnessed the birth of the Third World and for me that completely changed the map of the world in terms of politics and culture. And I began to think that our literature was very parochial, very provincial. Its preoccupations were with Poles, with Poland, with our fate, with our tragedy, with everything Polish. It was all very inward looking. Our literary classics were written in the nineteenth century, often by writers living in exile, but even living abroad they wrote about Poland. They were unable to make contact with other cultures, other civilisations, other countries. Even our travel writers, when they went abroad, looked for other Poles: 'I came eventually to Guinea, or China or some such place, and I found there Pan Kowalski, and he is 100 years old now.' And there would be how he helped the writer and then the old man's story, how he was a sailor, how he went with British troops from somewhere to somewhere, how he found a wife, had children – his fate, simply, as a Pole . . . I realised there was a place in our literature that had been completely neglected, and so my aim was to write in Polish introducing something we didn't have until now. And this subject was the Third World – a world which has a lot in common with Poland: the role of our *inteligencja*, the structure of our society, our experience as a colony until the end of the partitions in 1918, the legacy of this experience. This was the connection I decided to explore. For a long time my early books went unread and I suffered a lot because of that: I grieved. My first book was published in 1962 when I was living and working in Africa. From time to time I came back and I could still see my books unsold in the bookshops – always a bad sign in Poland. My colleagues said: 'Look you should write more about here and in such a way'. But I refused. People asked me why I didn't write about Poland, but I always wrote about Poland! That's the one thing I always did, but of course, not in a text-book sense, or in an open way.[5]

Even though they were made available only in very small print runs, his books, once the Third World aspect had been penetrated by the readers, became remarkably popular in the late 1970s and 1980s, and usually sold out long before they reached the shops. There was a brisk trade in second-hand copies too, and Kapuściński used to buy all those he could find to give to friends. His books were released in a new uniform edition in Poland in 1988. Kapuściński's books also became international best-sellers: *Shah of Shahs* has been translated into twenty-six languages. *The Emperor* made it on to the Polish best-seller list in 1978, an unusual distinction for a book of 'personal reportage', and has been translated into thirty-two languages, including all the major European languages with the exceptions of Portuguese and Albanian.

The Emperor is a remarkable book. There is no plot or conventional story-line, and everything in the book takes place after the revolution that toppled the Emperor. On one level it is a piece of very superior political and historical reportage in which a Polish journalist, sometimes called 'Mister Kapoochitski', attempts to piece together the life of Haile Selassie's court and the events of the final days of the Emperor's régime. Kapuściński had first visited Ethiopia in 1963 and by the time of the revolution had extensive contacts there. His method of telling the story is deceptively simple: he allows people to speak, and the result is a collage of often unattributed voices. It is a kind of verbal post-mortem. He makes no pretence that this is legitimate 'straight' journalism built from 'attributable sources', and he has admitted many times that his practices would be unacceptable to the *New York Times* and most other serious newspapers. His method is to ask a few questions, collect papers, articles, letters and photographs, and reconstruct at a later date from memory; he takes few notes and does not often operate a tape recorder. The result may not exactly be journalism, but it is story-telling, political observation and human interest at a very high level of effectiveness.[6]

On another level, though, it is clear that *The Emperor* may also be read as a commentary on what was happening in Poland. Much had changed there while Kapuściński was writing about events in Africa and South America. Perhaps the most important single event was that in 1970 Edward Gierek became first secretary of the PZPR. Gierek had spent time in Belgium, working as a miner, and he knew something of the power of western capital. He used massive foreign trade credits and injections of borrowed hard currency to finance a number of huge industrial concerns: the Gdańsk North Port (construction by Skanska of Sweden, cranes and gantries installed by Finland), the Ursus Tractor Factory (Massey Ferguson), the Berliet Bus works (France), the Nowa Huta steelworks, Huta Katowice steelworks, the Włocławek PVC works (Lloyds Bank), the ethylene works at Płock. By the mid-1970s the Gdańsk shipyards alone employed 28,000 workers. Unfortunately the Party relied upon people of proven Party loyalty, rather than proven ability, to administer these funds. Many of these people were 'Gierek's Gang', cronies from his days as a Party official in Silesia.

The sudden influx of capital and personal wealth into an underdeveloped and mainly agricultural economy, an economy in which the leap into urban and industrial rhythms had still to be made by the bulk of the population, had huge and thoroughly unforeseen consequences. The economy was so centralized that it could not absorb huge amounts of money without 'leaking'. It had not the technical ability to put the money to good use. Not only was corruption a massive problem but much of the money was squandered on projects that could never come to fruition given the prevailing Polish economic and political conditions. Poland's international debt rose from $10 billion in 1976 to $29 billion by 1981, with 92 per cent of hard-currency earnings spent on servicing this debt rather than in creating new wealth. By 1980 there was a housing shortfall of 1,160,000 dwellings, and in the Gdańsk region alone there was a shortfall of 7,000 nursery school places and 11,000 kindergarten places. In the years 1978–80 real wages fell by 2.6 per cent; cancer, TB, hepatitis and alcoholism increased at an alarming rate. As economic pressure increased so the giant industrial enterprises abandoned safe working practices in an effort to improve production. The Gdańsk shipyards, Nowa Huta, Huta Katowice and the coal-mines of Silesia became particularly dangerous places.[7]

While the living standards of the bulk of the Polish population declined after the initial rush of foreign capital, Gierek's Gang, who were all in key political and economic positions, prospered. A phenomenon known as *sułtanizm* emerged in Poland: that is, the behaviour of powerful men, who with Party backing, lived pretty much as if they owned some primitive feudal sheikdom. In circumstances such as these the distinction between private and state budgets tended to get blurred. It was clear that in Poland and in Ethiopia the leader knew all about corruption, and he alone was responsible for the failures and the moral climate of his regime. Kapuściński's description of Gierek is important:

He was a typical Party apparatus man: not a very bright man, not very intelligent, very slow. Also – and this characteristic became more and more pronounced – he was very lazy. In the last days of his period as First Secretary of the Party he stayed at home, he didn't even go to the Central Committee to work any more. I knew Gierek's secretaries at the Central Committee. And I remember them complaining that they gave him daily reports of indescribable poverty and suffering, of drugs, prostitution, pollution, damage to health. Any normal man would have cut his own throat in despair after reading them. But Gierek either left them on the side of his desk unread, or he read and them and said nothing, simply retired to the sauna. At the time of the 1980 strikes Gierek was on holiday in the Trans-Caucasus, and he didn't want to return as he didn't consider the strikes important enough. But a delegation from the Central Committee flew out to him and General Jaruzelski forced him to return to Warsaw. Next day he made a speech on TV, and Gierek's press secretary told me that as Gierek emerged from the studio he handed him the text of the speech and said: 'Now everything will be

calm, you'll see.' He was completely out of touch with reality. But that was the
way he wanted to be. That was the way the Party wanted him to be. He didn't try
to be informed. He didn't want to be informed.[8]

That the leader was somehow misinformed or misled was perhaps the last
refuge of the political innocent. This was the myth that Kapuściński was
concerned to explode in *The Emperor*:

> The magical aspect is that the highest one is endowed, often unconsciously, with
> divine characteristics. The supreme one is wise and noble, unblemished and
> kindly. Only the dignitaries are bad; they cause all the misery. Moreover, if the
> one on the top knew what his people were up to he would immediately repair the
> damage and life would be better. Unfortunately these crafty villains pull the wool
> over their master's eyes, and that is why life is so hard, so low, so miserable. This
> is magical thinking because, in reality, in an autocratic system it is precisely the
> one on top who is the primary cause of what happens. He knows what is going on,
> and if he doesn't know, it's because he doesn't want to know. It was no accident
> that the majority of the people around the Emperor were mean and servile.
> Meanness and servility were the conditions of ennoblement, the criteria by which
> the monarch chose his favourites, rewarded them, bestowed privileges on them.
> Not one step was taken, not one word said, without his knowledge and consent.
> Everyone spoke with his voice, even if they said diverse things, because he himself
> said diverse things. The condition for remaining in the Emperor's circle was
> practising the cult of the Emperor, and whoever grew weak and lost eagerness in
> the practice of this cult lost his place, dropped out, disappeared. Haile Selassie
> lived among shadows of himself.[9]

The sudden influx of hard currency, 'real money', into Poland bore
startling resemblances to the arrival of economic and humanitarian aid in
Ethiopia: one of the first effects was that among the increasingly well educated
bureaucracy the 'cost of loyalty' suddenly escalated. In both places the influx
of unsupervised foreign capital had remarkably similar results: a period of
splendour and rapid growth, then corruption, structural waste, criticism,
frustration and revolt. As one of the courtiers says: 'Who destroyed our
empire? Reduced it to ruin? Neither those who had too much, nor those who
had nothing, but those who had a bit.'[10] When Kapuściński wrote about the
Ethiopian army officers finding dollars in between the pages of the Emperor's
copy of the *Bible*, and of the $100 million the Emperor held in a Swiss bank
account ('a few pennies to take care of my ailing son in a Swiss hospital'),[11]
Polish readers had their own strong suspicion that the very same would be the
case with the *nomenklatura*. Large numbers of Poles knew about individual
examples of embezzlement or corruption but doubted that they could effectively bring this to public attention in the Gierek-controlled media, and feared
lest they put themselves and their families at risk.

It took a while for the facts to be made public and confirmed. When they came, the revelations were as damaging and as massive as anything Kapuściński had revealed in Ethiopia, but conformed very closely to the outlines he had given. Local newspapers, after years of censorship, took great delight in exposing corruption and abuse. Between November 1980 and December 1981, *Echo Krakowa, Gazeta Krakowska, Życie Warszawy* and *Głos Wybrzeża* were packed with revelations. Gierek had a villa built at a cost of 27,200,000 złoties, but had submitted an inventory for only 4,100,000 złoties so that he could buy it back from the state legally at a ridiculously low price. Gierek also owned two other houses which had cost the state the best part of 21,000,000 złoties. Gierek earned about 336,000 złoties per year, so it is clear he could not have built these houses out of his own earnings. It has been alleged that he skimmed the money from housing budgets at a time when there was a fifteen-year waiting list for flats.[12]

Gierek had said 'enrich yourselves' in 1971, as part of his exhortation to make the industrialization programme effective. But only well-placed Party members and bureaucrats had been able to do so. In September 1980, just a few weeks after the dismissal of the Gierek government, the director of the Minex import-export concern was accused of stealing $700,000 worth of material benefits from foreign companies dealing with Poland over the previous seven years. And this was not an isolated occurrence. Under pressure from Solidarność, the Polish Politburo announced that it had set up a special commission to investigate charges of corruption against Maciej Szczepański, the powerful chairman of the State Committee for Radio and Television. In October 1980 it was announced by the Party Plenum after an all-night sitting that Szczepański had been found guilty of, among other things, misusing budget resources: as a specimen charge he was accused of embezzling 2,900,000 złoties at a time when there was no film for the cameras. Szczepański was dismissed from his post. Later, further charges were brought against him, and the court heard from the prosecution that although he earned only 284,400 złoties per year Szczepański had used his post on the Central Committee to buy seven private cars, a helicopter, two executive jets, a yacht, a farm, several villas including a sixteen-room mini-palace; that he ran a string of four black prostitutes, had two mulatto mistresses, an enormous collection of pornographic films, a villa in Kenya, and bank accounts in Switzerland and London. Gierek had been a frequent guest of Szczepański at a specially built private villa in the fashionable ski resort of Zakopane, so this corruption went right to the top. The extent to which the *nomenklatura* were implicated in the crimes of the Gierek Gang can be seen in the knock-on effects of his downfall. By May 1981 no fewer than thirteen ministers, forty deputy ministers, eighteen of the forty-nine regional governors, twenty-six deputy regional governors, twenty-six regional Party first secretaries, seventy-two regional Party secretaries, seven heads of central government departments, eight parliamentary deputies and fourteen directors of major industrial enterprises had been fired. Ex-first secretary Gierek, ex-prime minister Babiuch and ex-trade union chief Szydlak, along with three others, had been expelled from the Party. Two sacked ministers committed suicide rather than face expulsion and legal proceedings.[13]

In Ethiopia aid disappeared like water into the ground to a far greater extent than international loans evaporated in Poland. The gigantic and inefficient Polish factories and enterprises were to become monuments of proof that money had filtered through. But at the same time 'tribal' instincts had worked to divert huge amounts of money into private pockets. This mechanism was deeply embedded in the way the Party and its leadership operated, and it was an inevitable consequence of a society in which it was necessary to pilfer in order to make up for the deficiencies of the system. It had its correspondence in Ethiopia:

> The faction of 'personal people' was a peculiarity of our regime, created by the Emperor himself. His Supreme Majesty, a partisan of a strong state and centralised power, had to lead a cunning and skilful fight against the aristocratic faction, which wanted to rule in the provinces and have a weak, pliable Emperor. But he could not fight the aristocracy with his own hands, so he always promoted into his circle, as representatives of the people, bright young men from the lowest orders, chosen from the lowest ranks of the plebeians, picked often on little more than a hunch from the mobs that surrounded His Majesty whenever he went among the people. These 'personal people' of the Emperor, dragged straight from our desperate and miserable provinces into the salons of the highest courtiers – where they met the undisguised hatred of the long-established aristocrats – served the Emperor with an almost indescribable eagerness, indeed a passion, for they had quickly tasted the splendours of the palace, the evident charms of power, and they knew that they had arrived there, come within reach of the highest state dignities, only through the will of His Highness. It was to them that the Emperor would entrust the positions requiring greatest confidence: the Ministry of the Pen, the Emperor's political police, and the superintendency of the Palace were manned by such people. They were the ones who would uncover intrigues and battle the mean, haughty opposition . . . Not only did the Emperor decide on all promotions, but he also communicated with each one personally. He alone. He filled the posts at the summit of the hierarchy, and also its lower and middle levels. He appointed the postmasters, headmasters of schools, police constables, all the most ordinary office employees, estate managers, brewery directors, managers of hospitals and hotels – and let me say it again, he chose them personally.[14]

In Poland 'personal people' were called *nomenklatura*. Polish readers saw in the Emperor's patronage both the massive powers of the First Secretary of the PZPR and appointments made to key official positions, the *nomenklatura*.

These appointments were made more because of loyalty to the leadership or to the Party than as a result of superior talent or ability. This, coupled with the 'leading role of the Party', meant that a peculiarly powerful and primitive bond prevented effective change:

> Here let me mention that His Majesty did not oppose reform. He always sympathised with progress and improvement. But he could not stand it when someone undertook reform on his own, first because that created a threat of anarchy and free choice, and second because it might create the impression of there being other charitable ones in the Empire besides His Magnanimous Highness. So, if a clever and astute minister wanted to carry out even the smallest reform in his own backyard, he would have to direct the case in such a way and so present it to His Majesty that it would irrefutably, in the commonly accepted fashion, seem that the gracious, concerned innovator and advocate of the reform was His Imperial Highness himself, even if in reality the Emperor did not quite understand what the reform was all about. But not all Ministers have brains, do they? It sometimes happened that young people unacquainted with Palace tradition or those who, guided by their own ambition and also seeking popular esteem – as if the Emperor's esteem weren't the only one worth seeking! – tried independently to reform some little matter or other. As if they didn't know that by doing so they violated the principle of loyalty and buried not only themselves but also their reform, which without the Emperor's authorship didn't have a chance to see the light of day. I'll come right out and say it: the King of Kings preferred bad ministers. And the King of Kings preferred them because he liked to appear in a favourable light by contrast.[15]

Revelations of corruption and 'personal idiosyncrasy' in the highest places came as no surprise when they related to a feudal court. But Kapuściński was clearly pointing out (or better, making available) the idea that in any political system, even one laying claim to the determinism of Marxism, personality was an important factor. For a readership educated to believe in the all-knowing, all-seeing, ever-concerned Party, leading the people on the long march to a brighter future, the parallel with the overarching power of the medieval Emperor was clear enough. The conclusion to be drawn was that if these parallels held good, then the PZPR, the interlocked apparatus of Party and state, were no more than modern versions of the medieval court, Asiatic variations on an ancient theme, ancient methods of government (wearing ideological disguise) struggling to come to terms with industry and modern life.

The sudden arrival of hard currency and the growth of heavy industry in Poland meant that the emerging new 'technical' middle class began to acquire real political and economic power. But above the *technokracja* (technocracy) was a stratum of Party people and government officials who prospered in ways that the IMF and the West German credit banks had not imagined.

Although in newly independent ex-colonial Africa the processes by which international finance leaked into society, rather than supported the enterprises it was intended for, were slowly becoming evident, it had not been imagined that the situation would be repeated in a supposedly modern European state, particularly one where the overt expressions of state ideology indicated that this would be unacceptable. What no one had realized was that Poland in the 1970s bore startling resemblances to the emerging states and economies of the Third World. In fact, in giving money to Poland without attaching conditions to its use, to the proposed methods of repayment, to the internal financial and industrial structures that were supposed to administer the money, western banks and governments were repeating the mistakes they had made in giving money to Ethiopia in the late 1960s. Western bankers and financiers saw what they wanted to see in Poland: what appeared to be a highly disciplined and, above all, cheap labour force. They did not inquire much further.

Another fact they had not bargained for was what the new rich would do with their money. A rich man in a communist state would not reinvest personal wealth in business or industry, as in the west. In Poland personal wealth went into maintaining a life-style that echoed the courts and feudal lordships of the *szlachta* era: Gierek's top officials had small armies of loyal retainers: drivers, pilots, secretaries, courtesans, housekeepers, tame officials and *milicja*. And this was not so very different from the Third World: Selassie had a man to wipe the urine of his pet dog from the feet of visiting officials, and a man to assess the right-sized pillow to push under his feet on each of his royal thrones. Money, it seemed, had different qualities, depending on how and where it was spent:

> Do you know what money means in a poor country? Money in a poor country and money in a rich country are two different things . . . In a poor country, money is a wonderful, thick hedge, dazzling and always blooming, which separates you from everything else. Through that hedge you do not see creeping poverty, you do not smell the stench of misery, and you do not hear the voices of the human dregs. But at the same time you know that all of that exists, and you feel proud because of your hedge. You have money; that means you have wings. You are the bird of paradise that everyone admires . . . Money transforms your own country into an exotic land. Everything will start to astonish you – the way people live, the things they worry about, and you will say, 'No, that's impossible.' Because you will already belong to a different civilisation. And you must know this law of culture: two civilisations cannot really know and understand one another well. You will start going deaf and blind. You will be content in your civilisation surrounded by the hedge, but signals from the other civilisation will be as incomprehensible to you as if they had been sent by the inhabitants of Venus.[16]

The failure of repeated efforts to change the system, both in Poland and Ethiopia, had very similar effects on behaviour:

Everyone felt helpless before the seemingly magic force by which things autonomously appeared and disappeared, and nobody knew how to master or break that force. This feeling of helplessness, of always losing, always falling behind the stronger drove them deeper into negativism, into numbness, into dejection, into depression, into hiding like partridges. Even conversation deteriorated, losing its vigour and momentum. Conversations started but somehow never seemed to be completed. They always reached an invisible but perceptible point, beyond which silence fell. The silence said, Everything is already known and clear, but clear in an obscure way, known unfathomably, dominated by being beyond helping. Having confirmed this truth by a moment of silence, the conversation changed its direction and moved on to a different subject, a trivial, second-rate, secondhand subject.[17]

Clearly Kapuściński's comments on Ethiopia relate equally to Poland, to changes in the language and oppositional attitudes and strategies in the mid-1970s. It is very important to realize that this book was published less than two years after the 1976 protests in Radom. It was to overcome precisely this sense of isolation, dislocation and hopelessness, here ascribed to the Ethiopians, that KOR was formed.

Kapuściński had enormous difficulty in establishing the form of the book. It was very important to him that it was not just another piece of journalism. Even though the Warsaw *Kultura*, which had commissioned the work, was pressuring him for the first instalment, Kapuściński locked himself away in his flat and disconnected the telephone for two months while he wrestled with the material to find a form that satisfied him.[18] This context is important to understanding the *kind* of book Kapuściński was writing. As Jerzy Jarzębski has pointed out, one of the effects of Party control on public language was to compromise 'the document' as part of a continuing crisis of literature in which realistic novels and short stories, caught between *socrealizm* and attempts to render the shocking experience of twentieth-century Poland, succumbed to despair and to the schematism on offer from the Party. Realistic prose, as well as being hijacked by the Party, was unable to render the scale of war and the communist take-over within the terms of a conventional plot. *Socrealizm* forced prose into a enhanced 'realness' that was stylistically false to the experiences at hand, and made it distant from any but the most crass and simplistic psychology of depression. The literature of *socrealizm* offended with its baldness, its lack of hope, its dullness and its severe literary and intellectual limitation. The crisis of prose continued throughout the post-war period. It still continues. It has spawned a number of hybrid genres, among others the 'lying diaries' (that is, diaries that were no such thing) of Brandys, Konwicki, Herling-Grudziński and Gombrowicz, the pseudo-documentary prose of Hanna Krall and Kapuściński, the interviews with regime 'witnesses' by Trznadel and Torańska.[19]

Kapuściński has denied that his books are Polish political allegories, and has insisted that the political parallels between events in the Third World and in Polish politics should be the focus of attention.[20] *The Emperor* is not an allegory. It is about Ethiopia and about the downfall of the last Emperor. But the spirit that informs the work, the details that the author thinks worthy of note, the sense of circumstance and history, of cultural specifics, all have their roots in the typically Polish game of Hunt the Symbol, in the business of talking about Poland while ostensibly talking about something entirely different. For Kapuściński the Third World became a lens with which to focus upon world events. But he knew that a Polish readership would eventually find parallels and correspondences in his work, and it is clear from the text itself that what caught his eye as a writer was the similarity between Ethiopia under Selassie and Poland under Gierek. While it is possible for Kapuściński to point out correspondences in other people's books it would never have done for him to acknowledge too openly that this is what he was doing in his own work. After all, he had to submit his work to the censor along with everybody else, and it would serve no useful purpose if the censor were alerted that Kapuściński was actually trying to outsmart him with some smuggled message. Instead of complaining about the activities of the security service and the censor in Poland, Kapuściński wrote of the Shah's Iran:

'Oh, it's true', said the naive old man with a weak heart, trying to catch his breath, 'in such stifling weather it's difficult to breathe.' In a moment the Savak agent pounced and said: 'Now you'll get the chance to recover your strength'. And without a word further he placed the old man under arrest. The other people at the bus stop had heard everything with dread: right at the start the feeble old man had committed an unpardonable mistake in using the word 'stifling' to a stranger. Experience had taught them not to say out loud such words as stifling, darkness, burden, chasm, collapse, bog, rot, cage, grill, chain, gag, stick, boot, twaddle, screw, pocket, paw, insanity; also phrases of the kind – lie down, lay flat, straddle, on your head, waste away, weaken, go blind, go deaf, sink in; and even sayings such as – something here limps, something's not quite right here, something's not as it should be, something is rattling; because every one of them, these nouns, verbs, adjectives, pronouns, could all be allusions to the régime of the Shah, they were a semantic minefield in which one careless step could blast you to smithereens.[21]

The Shah was a subject on which the Polish Censor was very sensitive and for many years it had been difficult to discuss or even mention him. Iran was an important trading partner. The drive towards industrialization in the early 1970s depended on cheap Iranian oil, and in recognition of this Poland gave the Shah and his wife honorary degrees from the Jagiellonian University in 1978. Thus the relevant Censorship instruction reads:

All materials (including the most minor mention, photographs, etc) on the subject of the past or present of Iran, the Shah and his family, people connected to the Shah, or information forecasting the fate of the monarchy in Iran should be approved by the GUKPPiW leadership. In addition, matters related to the policy of Mossadek should not be discussed and Iran's role in the context of the politics of imperialist forces in the region of the Persian Gulf and the Indian Ocean should not be emphasised.[22]

Because Poland maintained no links with the military regimes of Chile, Paraguay, Guatamala and the Dominican Republic there was little restriction on reporting these countries. However, Poland's trade connections with Rhodesia, South Africa and Idi Amin's Uganda were protected by censorship. There were also regulations to hide Poland's connection with the increasingly unpleasant Iraqi Baath Party: the full extent of Poland's co-operation with these people did not become apparent until after 1989, when it was revealed that Poland was receiving one million tons of Iraqi crude oil per year as part payment for military hardware. The Party had also been planning to participate in a Korean-Brazilian consortium to build the new rail link between Baghdad and Basra. At the start of the Gulf War in 1991 Poland had 2,800 contracted 'specialists' working in Iraq, and 350 of Saddam Hussein's tanks were of Polish manufacture. The severance of trade at the start of the Gulf War cost Poland $300 million.[23]

Kapuściński's books are not allegories; they stand in their own right. However, Kapuściński was well aware of the long tradition of allegory and allusion in Polish literature. As A. Alvarez has written:

> The marriage of the arts and politics in Poland goes beyond any accident of the present political set-up or any Marxist theory of social awareness. It is a habit of mind which neither writers nor audience can shed, however politically indifferent, irresponsible, apathetic, or plain ignorant they feel themselves to be . . . in Poland it is impossible to write even about the birds and the bees without someone reading into it a political metaphor or allusion. Polish art runs instinctively to allegory. It is all, whatever its appearance, written in what they call 'Aesopian language', in which each detail can always be translated into terms of something else – something relevant to the immediate Polish situation.[24]

If anything, his works are sly Aesopian fables – that is, open to a political interpretation. Kapuściński has written:

> In Poland every text is read as allusive, every written situation – even the most distant in space and time – is immediately, without hesitation, applied to the situation in Poland. In this way, every text is a double text, and between the printed lines we search for sympathetic messages written in invisible ink, and the

hidden message we find is treated as the most valid, the only real one. The result stems not only from the difficulty of open speech, the language of truth. It is also because this country of ours has suffered every possible experience in the world, and is still exposed to dozens of different trials, so that now in the normal course of things every Pole sees in histories that are not ours, connections with his own life.[25]

This does not mean that Kapuściński has not had battles with the censor or with the Party, but simply that he is a far more wily opponent than many who, where they have opposed the Party, have done so headlong and publicly. He has preferred subtle manœuvre to open confrontation. Kapuściński has spoken of his battle to get *The Emperor* past the censor. He found that the censor blocked him in the cinema and the theatre:

> However, in the book version – and this is a good example of the bargaining process – *The Emperor* was published in a serialisation in *Kultura* [Warsaw]. It started very innocently and nobody noticed. First piece, second piece, third, fourth. Then the censor and the Central Committee began to complain that something had 'gone wrong' with this text. We decided that if anybody in censorship tried to make trouble for us we would report them to the Party Control Bureau, saying there is somebody who dares to compare this corrupt fascist dictatorship of Haile Salassie with the excellent leadership of Comrade Gierek. Who could say such a thing? Who could dare to see the text in this way? We were going to make a case against this censor and get him sacked from the Party. We said: 'Take away a piece of this text and next day you will be before the Party Control Bureau'. We silenced him, but we were careful just the same. Sometimes we took a long break, and then an isolated piece would appear. And so they allowed another extract and then another and another. Finally the whole thing was published. There was a rule that said when a piece has received the stamp of approval from the censor it need not be submitted a second time. So we took all these pieces to the publishing house and they said OK, no problem, everything has a stamp. When the book appeared, of course, there was an outcry: 'How did such a thing happen?' It's a good example of how we turned these handicaps to our own advantage. We used the distortion of language. These are tricks you can work when you know the system.[26]

Kapuściński was clear: the worlds of Gierek and Selassie were very close to one another. Poland under the communists, in spite of its European cultural heritage, was very much a part of the Third World. There was no doubt in his mind that Poland, along with vast tracts of the Soviet Union, had come to resemble the emerging Third World in the way the economy functioned (or failed to function) and in the mind-set of the people who lived there. In his blackest moments he attributed queues (the trademark of centralized, Soviet-style economies) to communism, but he also knew that socialism did not cause the basic problems from which the Third World suffers: years of colonialism, drought, corruption, tribalism, advancing desert, wars of independence, exploitation by the First World, military manipulation by capitalists and communists alike. He knew that Poland's economic problems stemmed from very deep-seated historical problems, its position between the developed west and the underdeveloped east, between democracy and autocracy. The queues were not what socialists had aimed for, but were a sure sign that Soviet-led communist attempts to solve these problems had not been successful.

Kapuściński sees history as a struggle between classes, and between competing systems, but he also sees it as a struggle between culture and the mob, between civilization and bestiality. His years as a professional observer of the Third World have made him a sharp-eyed and disconcertingly percept-ive critic of the new Poland emerging from the wreckage of the Soviet empire. Like many Poles he believed that the Soviet Union stood in a neo-colonial relationship to Poland. The main aim of the Soviets was not to destroy the Polish state but to weaken and deprive the Polish nation by governing it with an élite that had already 'sold out' to foreign powers. In his opinion, long contact with politics deforms and corrupts because of politics' greed to control human destiny and individual actions, and because of its expansive-ness into every sphere of human endeavour: progress, he once noted, is not a historical necessity, it is a possibility, and even an impossibility; he also said that the higher up the scale a crime was committed, the greater was the possibility that it would not be perceived as a crime, but as a necessary political manœuvre.[27]

For Kapuściński, in contrast to the material wealth of the First World, the mentality of Third World inhabitants could also be found in *homo sovieticus*:

> The communists failed in everything, but succeeded in one thing. They succeeded in creating Homo Sovieticus. A new type of man . . . Nobody trusts anybody. It's a question of cultural background. It's a question of organisation. It's not just a question of price, as everyone seems to think . . . They don't discuss how to produce a hundred or thousand refrigerators, but how to distribute ten of them. The mentality is distributive mentality, not productive mentality. The mentality is control mentality, not improvement and organisation mentality. You have thousands of different commissions who control each other, a huge bureaucracy that controls instead of producing.[28]

Homo sovieticus honoured the products of labour (consumer goods) and had statues and poems in praise of workers, yet the Soviet system divorced pro-duction and earnings, ruptured the connection between labour and wealth, sundered economic efficiency and consumption. In doing so it engendered enormous dissatisfactions, destroyed faith in the future, and turned Party ethics and communist economics into weapons against culture. Whereas people in the western capitalist states wonder how to produce more and to sell more, *homo sovieticus* gave huge amounts of time and energy to pondering the nature of the distribution of scarce resources. While westerners want to be rich, *homo sovieticus* does not want to be rich, only to ensure that his neighbour is no richer. Society is largely static because loyalty, not talent, is rewarded; bribery is normal simply as a respite from tension and worry: 'Things are arranged only for the members of the tribe . . . In this respect Russians are no different from the African tribes'.[29] Only in the Soviet attachment to the state is there any significant difference between them, but even in this the Soviet system was an anachronism, offering old and outdated solutions to new and rapidly multiplying problems.

Kapuściński's perception of what was happening to Polish society in the 1970s and 1980s was supported by sociological research, though very little of this revealing material was ever allowed past the censor. Walicki wrote:

An overwhelming majority of Poles do not identify with the institutions in which they work, do not think in terms of public good on the institutional level. Their loyalties and their feelings of belonging are two-sided. First they belong and are loyal to different primary face-to-face groups – from the family and groups of friends to informal cliques, mafias, and other personalised groups pursuing their interests in a half-legal way. From this lowest level of integration we have a sudden leap to the highest, most abstract and most sublimated, symbolic level: the level of national solidarity. Thus an average Pole does not belong to a large-scale institutionalised civil society; he belongs to different primary groups and, secondly, he belongs to his nation; not a nation as a system of political and economic institutions, but a nation as national tradition, national culture, the sphere of uniting symbols, of sublimated, lofty, patriotic feelings.[30]

It was clear from developments within the Polish language that the economic miracle had wrecked itself on this shoal, and that it had come dangerously close to making Poland an ungovernable entity. The language reflected the fact that the official economy no longer functioned and that the state survived because private enterprise and the black market bypassed state structures. In the years 1974–80 certain usages were particularly vivid in conjuring up the reality of Polish life: *załatwiać* (to arrange or to wangle); *kombinować* (to combine, but more specifically to improvise with materials at hand, for example in cooking, building, decorating); goods and materials, necessary papers, tickets, all could be obtained if one had the necessary *znajomości* (acquaintances, contacts) to fix things. Tea, coffee, meat and bread were not simply 'bought', it was necessary to *złapać* (grab, seize) them: such were the queues and the undignified scrum to get at scarce provisions that the shops no longer sold goods to customers, but in the language of the streets, *oni rzucali* (they threw) them to the *hołota* (rabble). As in the emerging African states it was often necessary to offer a *łapówka* (bribe) in order to get even small everyday things done. Anyone who did not conform to these norms, who did not offer a bribe, who believed in moral principles and who expected to get things done by observing the rules was idealistic, perhaps, but certainly a fool.

Kapuściński was aware very early that the power of the Party bosses was being abused, that Polish patience was exhausted, that without massive reform, which the Party was incapable of initiating or sustaining, something would snap. In August 1980, just after he returned to Poland, he was one of a very small group of journalists allowed inside the Gdańsk shipyards during the strike. He and thirty-five other journalists signed a declaration:

> We Polish journalists present at Gdańsk during the strike, declare that much of the news published so far, and especially the manner in which it has been commented upon, does not correspond with what is happening here. This state of things leads to disinformation. The cutting of telecommunications and the impossibility of publishing materials that would show the facts in their true light is profoundly distressing to us and totally prevents us from honestly fulfilling our professional duties. We consider that it cannot but favour the solution of the conflict and contribute toward social developments in the future to give the population the complete story of events.[31]

Kapuściński later spoke of his decision to sign this statement in spite of fears for his safety and worry about his job and family:

> For many journalists that signature was a huge decision. They wondered if there would be repression. I remember one colleague who signed and the next day came to me and said, 'Mr Ryszard, what do you think? I signed, but what will happen?' He was terribly upset. We all had the feeling that the decision was the right one, but risky . . . In the end, we were protesting against the whole propaganda line in connection with the Baltic coast . . . with what was going on there.[32]

As Kapuściński said

> The Gdańsk strike of 1980 was not just a strike. It was our fight for our own language, a question of how to defend our language, how to defend our dignity, how to defend ourselves against the riff-raff who were in power. I mean that each totalitarian power has the intention to destroy and to manipulate the language, and to distort the meaning of words simply because this is the most effective way to control the mind. Language has a most important role, although it is not 'officially announced'. The Stalinists, much more than in any other political system, put a lot of emphasis on the domination of the language. The destruction

of the language proceeds on different levels. Firstly, for example, by saying this is democracy when clearly there is no democracy. Secondly, the poetry of the language, using only particular formulations. I remember in the USSR when Aliluyeva defected to the west: she had been gone a long time, but they didn't admit it. Then one day a Party member came and he said – I was a witness to this – he said: 'I've just come from a meeting of the Propaganda section of the Central Committee, and we can now talk about Aliluyeva, it is allowed, but only using the word traitor: you have to say traitor Aliluyeva. This way, you can't say anything good about her. The third thing isn't very important – that most of the propaganda people are very uneducated people, with no cultural background. This primitiveness, this simplicity, this vulgarity was something very natural to them. They didn't have to practise or learn it. That is how they were. This combination of factors led to a terrible destruction and distortion of the Polish language. Probably the effects will be with us for a whole generation at least. For writers, of course, the fight for the language is a very important part of our obligation: it is a big problem and a challenge. The impoverishment of language is common all over the world, but here in Poland this tendency is especially pronounced because of the Stalinist legacy.[33]

The deformations of censorship and the corruption of language by the politicians were themes he was to return to again and again in his 'Warsaw Diaries'.

Kapuściński was a strong supporter of Solidarność and when Martial Law was declared he was dismissed from his job on *Kultura*. His *dowód osobisty* (identity card) was stamped to prevent him regaining his credentials or leaving the country. Throughout Martial Law he could not publish or work as a journalist and had to rely upon his wife's earnings as a doctor and on giving readings and talks where friends would pass the hat. His readership remained loyal:

Not so long ago I was asked to a town outside Warsaw to give a reading. It was scheduled to begin at five o'clock, and I arrived about half an hour early. But it was impossible to get in. The hall was packed. In fact, it was so packed that no one, with so many people squeezed up against the door-frame, was able to get out. By the time I succeeded in reaching the podium, I had been crushed and pressed and pulled by so many bodies that all my buttons had popped off. My shirt was torn, and I had lost my glasses. At around five-thirty, I began reading.[34]

He has, it seems, maintained a very special relationship with his readership: an example of the kind of moral and spiritual national leadership provided by a long tradition of Polish writers, so envied by the Party. In 1989, just before the collapse of the Berlin wall, Kapuściński's uncannily sensitive political antennae twitched and he took off for the Soviet Union where he began to travel and talk with ordinary citizens charting the collapse of the Soviet

Communist Party, to write of the moral and political chaos that was just becoming apparent under the surface of state control, and to warn of the massive tide of Soviet would-be migrants poised to flood westwards at the first opportunity. However, with the collapse of Polish communism, he took time off to recover physically from his gruelling travels in Soviet Central Asia, and to become involved with the Solidarność Citizens' Committees and help organize democratic elections to local government and to the Sejm.

There can be little doubt that *The Emperor* was a work of major importance in focusing attention on the nature of Polish economic development and the mechanisms at work within the minds of individual Poles. It revealed elements of the Third World within Polish society: for a nation that prided itself on being a modern European nation, the eastern bastion of Europe against an uncivilized Asia, a nation that took its cultural bearings from the west rather than the east, which looked to the west for its fashions and its political and economic ambitions, this was a bitter and frustrating observation. That these things were said by a man who was well connected in Polish government circles, a respected journalist, a decorated writer, and a man who had travelled throughout the Soviet Union and the rest of the eastern bloc and who had lived in the Third World for over twenty years, made the observation very difficult to dismiss or deny. Kapuściński's reflections fed into the growing stream of intellectual and economic discontent, increasingly focused on the disastrous leading role of the Party and its monopoly of power, that was building towards the revolt of 1980.

8

TADEUSZ KONWICKI

Millions of people in Poland no longer know what is and is not the truth, and what it means to be a 'sincere witness'. For decades, not only our language has been changed but our mental criteria – we are different now, though if you speak to us in the west you will think we are the same as you. We do a great many things without being forced to, instinctively, and that's the whole tragedy.

Stefan Kisielewski, 'School of Moronism', *Kultura* (Paris, July-August 1979)

Tadeusz Konwicki was born on 22 June 1926 in Nowa Wileńsk (Nowa Wilejka) near Wilno in Lithuania. His grandmother, and before her his great-grandfather, had leased a small grange from a neighbour at Bohiń. They had also owned a small estate at nearby Miłowidy, but this had been confiscated in the aftermath of the 1863 uprising. Konwicki's father, who was a metal-worker, died of tuberculosis aged fifty-three. Konwicki's mother stayed behind in Lithuania in 1945 and worked on a kolkhoz, where she died aged seventy-eight. Thus Konwicki, although he came from a working-class background, had a 'family memory' of a slightly grander past.

During the war Konwicki attended a *gimnazjum* (high school), run in secret by the underground because secondary education for Poles was forbidden by the Nazis. He graduated from high school in 1944, joined the London-backed AK resistance movement and fought in the area around Wilno. After the defeat of the local Nazi forces his unit remained in the Lithuanian countryside and forests, and from July 1944 fought the incoming Soviet troops and NKVD. Towards the end of 1945 most of the AK in the Wilno area were persuaded to give up their arms, only to be arrested and sent to the *gulag*: those who survived were not released until after Stalin's death. Konwicki was lucky. His commander suspected a trap and marched his troops away from the agreed surrender points. His unit disbanded deep in the Lithuanian countryside. Konwicki, cut adrift, made his way home on foot, pretending he had been helping relatives with the harvest. Upon reaching home he found that the region had been ceded to the USSR and that most of his friends and relatives had already departed westwards for the new Poland.

Konwicki succeeded in getting through to Warsaw and unlike many other AK members does not appear to have been arrested or imprisoned. He got a job in Gliwice for a while, working for the provisional government, and then, although he intended to study architecture, joined the department of Polish studies at the Jagiellonian University in Kraków. He became an editor and proof-reader on the magazine *Odrodzenie* (Renewal), which was initially based in Kraków, and as he already had what appeared to be steady employment he never bothered to graduate from university. It is from his period on *Odrodzenie* that Konwicki remembers Lem, and even from sight identified him as coming from the *kresy* (old Polish eastern borders).[1] The *kresy*, which figures very largely in Konwicki's personal mythology and in his fiction, had been territory of the old Polish Commonwealth which had united the Grand Duchy of Warsaw with the Kingdom of Lithuania; it was a conglomeration of national identities which over many centuries had, in spite of the many languages represented there, given rise to a remarkably unified and singular culture and set of ethical beliefs and shared customs. This border area is the same milieu that produced, among many others, Mickiewicz and Miłosz from Lithuania, Kapuściński in Byelorussia, and Słowacki, Conrad and Lem in Galicia. It is here in the borders that the pressure of Polish Romantic literature was felt with great clarity. Konwicki claimed: 'I visited those places in the closing decades of the nineteenth century. I experienced the time and breathed its air. The nineteenth century survived there in backwoods, in the deserted islands of central Europe, until World War Two.'[2]

Konwicki has repeatedly tried to convey the 'intricate, omnipotent and formidable pressure' of this area and the traditions behind its culture:

> Polish Romantic tradition has sunk its talons in us. We cannot escape it, or get detached from it. The mortal torture we suffer, the entire internal tension provoked by questions of what course of action to assume, and how to define ourselves in the face of developments in which we constantly get entangled: all this stems from our obedience to the Romantic code. At all times we act and behave in keeping with the bans and orders of the Polish Romantic tradition which was born at an extremely dramatic point in Poland's history, and so much differs from the quieter mainstreams of Western Romanticism.[3]

Konwicki's experience was typical of a whole generation – one brought up on Romantic virtues and traditions of patriotism, freedom and faith, the imperative of fight to the death with honour. After the war this generation was faced with the problem of obeying that imperative, remaining faithful to their oath in the face of a rapidly changing political and military situation, continuing their struggle for Poland's freedom by fighting the communists. For most of them the decision did not lie in their hands, but was made for them by historical events – hence the importance to so many of Konwicki's characters of a persistent sense of guilt and personal defeat that lingered for years, particularly evident in his *Sennik Współczesny* (Dreambook of Our Time, 1963). For many the lost land or place of their birth, and the time before the war, came to assume the value of deep-seated personal myth. Konwicki's approval of Romantic 'virtues' is not total, however. It is conditional. He mourns the passing of his world, and appreciates its values, but at the same time he points out frequent cases of maladjustment to contemporary life. He renders contemporary values in a grotesque way, with unstinting irony and not a little sneering, but he is not above flagellating himself when he feels he has deserved it.

In 1950 *Odrodzenie* was dissolved and Konwicki left Kraków and moved to Warsaw to work as an editor on the journal *Nowa Kultura*, where he stayed until 1957, when the board of the journal was sacked by Gomułka for 'too much revisionism'. For a while he was also on the editorial board of the Iskry publishing house. He made his début as a writer of short stories in both *Odrodzenie* and *Nowa Kultura*. His novel, *Rojsty* (Marshes), was written in Kraków in 1946, but had to wait ten years before it was published. His first published book, *Przy budowie* (By Building, 1950), was a collection of reportage. He wrote *Władzy* (Authorities, 1954), a socialist realist novel, and several short stories supporting the party line. For a while he was one of the 'pimplies', but like the others he became disillusioned as the grim life on the Polish streets steadfastly refused to conform to the dawn of the new era predicted and recounted in endless class-conscious and dutifully optimistic novels of the period.

Initially Konwicki was convinced that the Party was right to push Polish industrialization, and partly out of a misplaced sense of guilt he became a candidate for membership of the Party in 1946. Like many other Polish writers he saw social progress as linked to the rebuilding of Poland; like others he remembered pre-war Poland as a semi-feudal entity, an anachronism in modern capitalist Europe. He saw the Catholic Church as a force determined to keep Poland as it had been, backward, ignorant, provincial, and saw the Party as a way of liberating Poland from its feudal past while at the same time exalting and confirming the role of the intellectual within the new social structure. Through the early 1950s he insisted on giving the new regime a chance. As well as writing about the communist dawn that would put an end to backward, feudal Poland and usher in industrial wealth and prosperity, he also wrote against the AK, saying that they were wrong to resist the new order.

Konwicki was not alone in this. Andrzejewski and Brandys (who joined and left the Party in exactly the same years as Konwicki) wrote along similar lines; Miłosz too was a cultural envoy for the new regime in France and the United States; Borowski declared himself a follower of the new regime and worked actively for the communists for several years. Even several older writers (Tuwim, Broniewski, Nałkowska, Dąbrowska) some of whom had direct experience of the Soviet Union, were prepared to suspend their disbelief in the hope that a new, better Poland would emerge from the wreckage of the war. Konwicki has repeatedly said he is part of a generation that lost the war, whose dreams and aspirations were not fulfilled by fighting in the AK, nor by joining the Party. The war he had witnessed had first destroyed his material world and then steadily annihilated his moral world. His move towards the Party was an attempt to restore balance and direction, but he slowly came to see that he was aiding the destruction of the sense of morality and purpose he sought to restore.

He may have doubted the new regime from the very first, but the abortive anti-government protests in Poznań in 1956 brought on a severe crisis of conscience. It had become clear that the 'perfect democracy' Stalin had claimed for Soviet-style communism was itself a fiction: democratic socialism could not develop in the Soviet system, even after Stalin's death. Konwicki began to feel that he could not live with himself if he obeyed the party line or wrote socialist realist novels. He fell silent for nearly three years. When he started writing again it was not in agreement with any formula agreed by the Party. As he and many other writers abandoned 'approved social commissions' and began again to write out of their own feelings and compulsions, a gap opened up between their ambition and that of the Party. Although he later came to regret his writings of this period, and later still became an opponent of the regime, his colleagues in the AK never let him forget his past, and never quite forgave him:

> I am seriously worried. I could easily justify my whole biography. I could with dignity explain its most complicated events. There is, however, one thread in it that I am unable to justify, that cannot ever be justified, that will defile me forever, even if the present and the future generation should forget about it, and even if they would never notice that horrible scar similar to the stigma of a villain. I am thinking about a few or perhaps one tenth of my articles written in the years known sadly as 'the period of mistakes and misjudgements'. I am not ashamed of any of my books and I don't disown any of them. For better or for worse, they were documents, an authentic proof of the state of my consciousness and that of my contemporaries. They might be useful to historians – at least for some statistics. But my political journalism, the articles that I won't name for shame and irritation, these articles foisted on me by a particular hysteria of the environment and by my own hysteria, these articles are my bastards that I cannot dress up as tragic dandies or drown secretly at night in deep water.[4]

Konwicki, like his protagonists, suffers from a bad conscience, continually haunted by those who accuse him of selling out to the forces of reaction, and criticize him for his communism in the early days, yet are bored by his nagging sense of guilt and his long-standing public argument with his own past. He is tortured by a highly developed sense of guilt, a guilt that is Catholic, tribal, personal and deeply historical. Nevertheless he still musters sufficient irony and detachment to see that he is often seriously misunderstood by a readership that considers itself wise, cynical and too well versed in the art of reading between the lines:

> I did something rather provocative in *The Calendar and the Hourglass*. In a special little essay I presented myself as a veteran of the 'pimple-faced' movement, a staunch Stalinist from the fifties, someone who took part in the Party's most secret cells. The point was to provoke discussion, a certain state of mind, and a clinical analysis of what had been prettily referred to as the 'period of mistakes and distortions'. I expected that this would result in a cornucopia of similar confidences, confessions, intimate revelations, self-exposures, acts of contrition, or an unruly revolt. Meanwhile I met with a dead silence like that which ensues when an irresponsible guest makes some terrible gaffe at a respectable party. But it wasn't a total silence. Every once in a while someone would suddenly leap up with the euphoria of discovery and unmask me as a former Stalinist. Initially, I found this a cause for consternation and wondered why these discoverers were so late in coming out with their revelations, why only now they hastened to inform and warn their contemporaries. After long reflection, and after much surprise and astonishment, I realised that the source of their revelations was my heroic and swaggering confession in *The Calendar and the Hourglass*, which was supposed to benefit all of society, but which had only brought poor me shame and disgrace.[5]

Konwicki had never been involved in the work of the upper echelons of the Party, but as he once remarked to Brandys, the youngsters, Party and non-Party alike, would not let him rest: 'These kids are fascinated by moral pornography; they're excited by the idea of digging some smut out of us.'[6]

In fact, as a former member of the AK Konwicki had been forced to remain on the Party sidelines, 'not kosher, with a stain that could not be washed away'. Reaction to his pseudo-confession revealed some of the complex opposition to communism that was developing in Poland, a reaction that hunted for, and was fascinated by, political dirt, and which saw anti-Polish conspiracies in every turn of events:

> It is the young writers from the crannies of the opposition who have begun to show the greatest interest in that period. They even took me up, or perhaps I was high on their list of people connected with the crimes of the Stalinist era. I gave them my all, but I couldn't satisfy them. I searched my memory. I lashed my old body. I analysed my ego to its depths with utter cruelty. I referred them to the disclosures in *The Calendar and the Hourglass* and elsewhere. But it was never enough for them. They rejected my self-diagnoses, and my self-accusations as well. They demanded more.[7]

In 1963 Konwicki published *Sennik Współczesny* (A Dreambook for Our Time), and with that book seems to have begun a new publishing career in which he attempted to make a break with his own past and the mistaken allegiances of the immediate post-war period. The fact that the book was published at all is significant, but also exceptional. It deals with the experience of a man waking from a coma after a failed suicide attempt. It is set in a small provincial town where a strange religious sect is based, and the story is told through a mixture of details of life in the town and flashbacks to the conflict between the NKVD and the AK at the end of the war. Miłosz, who has described the scenes of the winter fighting in the Lithuanian countryside as 'hard to match in postwar literature', has also said that the novel, if it is not an indictment, is at least a complaint 'not directed against anybody in particular', raised in the name of 'all those in Poland who acted out of the best moral motives, only to get bogged down in a quagmire of all-pervading ambiguity where good and evil lose their clear distinctions'.[8]

As more writers revolted against the precepts of 'official culture' and refused lucrative 'social commissions', so it became less likely that any book as open and clear as *A Dreambook for Our Time* would ever be published again by a state publishing house. The books that followed (*Nothing or Nothing*, *Ascension* and *The Chronicle of Accidents of Love*) were all subject to censorship, and Konwicki's behaviour made it certain that he would clash with the Party. He signed the 'Letter of the Twenty-Two' protesting at the treatment of Kołakowski, who lost his job as professor of the history of philosophy at Warsaw University in March 1966 and was later expelled from Poland in the wake of the anti-Semitic purges of 1968. Konwicki, who says that from the moment he signed the letter he was a marked man, was promptly denounced by Gomułka as an enemy of order, an agent of the CIA and a capitalist stooge. He was summoned to a meeting of the Party at the Congress Hall in the Palace of Culture and told to explain himself. He was not expelled, but from that day no one in the Party spoke to him or rang him. Konwicki left the Party in 1966:

> I belonged to the Party for almost fifteen years. My friends dragged me into it, as if it were a beer house or a brothel. I had fallen into bad company, and they had convinced me, a good boy from outside Wilno, to join the Party; they got me addicted. I fell into bad company – comrades from the Party basic organisation – and my family, my relatives, and my mother were all worried sick that I'd gone to the dogs. I stuck in the Party's throat like a chestnut still in its greenish, spiky shell. Prickly, aggressive, outwardly unswallowable. But inwardly, in my unhusked centre, I was a super zealot, super engagé. Soft soap on the inside, sandpaper on the outside. Exactly the opposite of what should have been, according to the technical prescription for corrupting a person's morality and world view.[9]

His increasingly uneasy relationship with the Party and his disfavour with the cultural moguls is shown quite clearly in the fact that he has been awarded only two state literary prizes: People's prize (third category), 1950; *Nowa Kultura* prize, 1959. From 1975 his dissatisfaction with the attitudes and policies of the regime became more and more public and obvious. His clash with the authorities can also be seen in the record of his official state publications. After 1976, like Lem and Andrzejewski, he found the state publishing houses reluctant to accept new work or to reprint previously published works. He began to write as if the censor did not exist, ignored all taboos. In January 1977 he signed the 'Letter of the 172' demanding that the Sejm set up a special commission to investigate abuses of police powers in harassing strikers at Radom the previous year. Later that year he offered *Kompleks Polski* (The Polish Complex), for publication. It was a blend of time shifts and flashbacks designed to contrast an undignified and tawdry communist present with a heroic past. Predictably the censor tried to interfere and refused to license the whole book. Konwicki refused to kowtow and as a result was refused publication. Undaunted, he turned to the newly founded unofficial quarterly *Zapis*, published in London by *Index on Censorship*. *The Polish Complex* formed the third issue of *Zapis*, and although the initial market for the journal was mainly that of the émigré and exile community in Britain and the United States, many copies of the magazine found their way back into Poland illegally.[10]

Konwicki's novels have established him as one of Poland's leading literary figures. Miłosz, who collaborated closely with Konwicki in scripting and making the film *The Issa Valley*, has said that Konwicki's literary evolution, 'with even more zig-zags than Brandys', is 'indicative of general changes in the mood of the country'.[11] Konwicki, like Kołakowski, Brandys, Ważyk and Andrzejewski, came to see his early allegiance to the new order as a kind of worship of false gods. Increasingly he came to understand the links between the kind of literature available under communism and the kind of society that was being created. He related this to his feeling of what it was to be a 'provincial' in a literature that was itself an increasingly inward-looking and largely self-contained entity, in a literature that was historically provincial to world literature. One way or another communism seemed determined to keep literature as a provincial entity. That is, it would prevent national literature from relating to the world, from becoming a world literature, or it would keep national literature as purely provincial-based folk-entertainment and encouragement for collective workers. Communism, it seemed, was determined to cut off Polish literature from all that was modern, all that was radical, all that was newly perceived: the Party and the cultural moguls of the Ministry of Art and Culture were largely indifferent to literary convention, and cared not a jot for carefully developed theoretical works that opened up new areas of expectation or argument.

It was not only that Konwicki felt very keenly the trap of *socrealizm*. He also perceived clearly the trap into which the literature of any 'small' nation, but particularly Polish literature, with its national obsessions, might fall. In *The Calendar and the Hourglass* he explored the meaning of what it was to be a Polish writer. He recounted a trip to America and a meeting with Saul Bellow:

> Perhaps he thinks, with some surprise maybe, that on the threshold of Asia, in the desert steppes, this middle-aged writer is cobbling together novels to be read by nomads. Maybe these novels are pretentious and imitate in a harsh sounding language the contributions of Western litterateurs. Maybe this man is considered a classic, so well known that even the wayside goats stop to salute him. Maybe his life is safer and more bearable than that of authentic writers from a great metropolis . . . But there is also a pitiful epithet for me: 'One of the foremost', for in order to compensate for their smallness, small countries don't possess medium, average, good or very good writers; small countries have only great, most prominent and most illustrious artists. The most prominent artist of an unknown, exotic country is a most melancholy sight. The greatest artist from a provincial state – what could be sadder![12]

The life of Joseph Conrad might be thought to contradict Konwicki, but Conrad (no matter what his debt to Polish literature and political outlook) was writing in English. The experiences he recorded (the colonial world, seafaring, political intrigue, capitalism red in tooth and claw, spying, adventure) were not readily available as literary experiences within Polish culture. In order to gain these experiences, to find a way of writing about them and a readership, Conrad, like Ryszard Kapuściński after him, had to live and work outside Polish-language culture. The implication for Konwicki is that Polish writers are helpless provincials, just as their government too is helplessly provincial in the back garden of the superpowers. Even attempted totalitarianism makes writers provincial, both in personal behaviour and in literature. Konwicki had already noted that in communist countries literature was an 'incomplete torso', strong on social and political themes, but 'lacking in de Sades', pornography, and crime and science fiction. Every kind of 'deviation' in literature was thought to be either political or national sabotage.

Working as an artist under a 'totalitarian' regime created a whole series of problems for Konwicki, censorship and the necessity of ideological conformity being only the most obvious ones. Whenever conditions relaxed a little, the limits and boundaries of what the regime would tolerate could always be challenged, and perhaps even publicly satirized. The artist was invited to join the leadership of the intellectual wing of the government, and at the same time to join the leadership of the intellectual opposition. This too imposed conformism and limitations of its own. In times of stress the Ministry of Culture, GUKPPiW and the Party attempted to impose *socrealizm*. That is, they urged writers, painters and composers to create works which were directly accessible to the masses, to renounce the sins of bourgeois formalism, obscurantism, *angst*, and mental anguish in favour of the broad march of the successful proletariat. Yet in Poland, from the mid-1970s right through to the late 1980s the opposition, too, put pressure on artists to conform to a different ethos: they, too, began to demand simple, conservative, Catholic, Romantic art which harked back to the older literary forms studied at school, approved by the Church and the old *inteligencja*, themes and ideas which revived and fostered popular memory and patriotic emotions. Walicki has spelled out some of the complications:

> Under Stalinism it was the authorities who used and abused politico-moral pressure, while now it was the opposition who organised such pressure in the name of national unity, enforcing non-collaboration with the authorities and silencing dissidents within its ranks. 'Dual consciousness' was now the lot of many Party members still loyal to the Party but exposed nonetheless, to the 'moral terror' of its enemies. Gone and forgotten were the times when the Party was able to impose communist ideals on intellectuals and artists; now intellectuals and artists engaged in actively de-legitimising the system through both the political content of their works and ostentatious refusal to cooperate with official institutions . . . It is no exaggeration to say that in the 1980s (beginning, perhaps, in the late 1970s) a major part of the Polish intelligentsia underwent an extremely intensive process of anti-Communist self-indoctrination. Buying, reading and distributing all manner of anti-Communist, or potentially anti-Communist, literature – from classical analyses of Communist totalitarianism and first-rate historical monographs to disparate memoirs, novels and journalistic writings, including even vulgarly propagandist tracts – was seen as a primary duty of a conscious Polish patriot. As a result, the perception of the surrounding sociopolitical reality became profoundly ideologised and thereby heavily distorted. A weak and frightened regime, begging for a minimum of popular support and trying to woo intellectuals by an almost total ideological surrender, was perceived as a powerful, omnipotent and all-pervasive totalitarian system. Its timid and selective repressive actions were compared to the Stalinist terror, or to the brutal performance of the Gestapo. Its functionaries were presented as embodying an unshakeable belief in their historical mission – a position against which the opposition set its belief in absolute moral values. In fact this was a grotesque mythologization of the 'actually existing socialism' of the 1980s. But the mythological images held sway over people's minds, overshadowing the inconsistencies of reality.[13]

The conformity of opinion now required by the opposition worried others too. Barańczak said that continual confrontation with a powerful, relentless and cunning enemy produced a fortress mentality that was particularly damaging to cultural activity and that spontaneous creativity, in yielding to the obligation to defend certain values, unwittingly accepted the simplifications of collectivist restriction.[14] Taking up this theme, D. Pirie wrote of J. Krzysztoń's book *Madness* (Warsaw, 1986):

What distinguishes *Madness*, one of the most significant (as well as popular) works in Polish in the 1980s from the underground establishment's direct and highly erudite criticisms of the Party and its state apparatus, is that it elliptically attacks all the mechanisms (of the Party-State, Church and Opposition Nation) that are so destructive and from which there is no escape other than insanity.[15]

Zagajewski has described the way that 'Poland' became the all-pervading, ingenious justification for Polish resistants 'shackled by the immortal plural': for him the choice was between the uniformity of communism and the uniformity of society and 'the nation'. His solution was to withdraw from both into poetic solitude.[16] Zagajewski, Konwicki, Barańczak and others felt the conformity offered by Solidarność was no real solution, that their obligation was not to produce 'useful literature' (they could have done as much for the communists if that had been their aim) but simply to observe clearly and write well.[17]

It is clear that underground writers and intellectuals, who had enough of communism, curbed one authoritarian streak in Polish culture only to impose their own brand of 'moral terror' through their ostentatious refusal to co-operate with the regime of General Jaruzelski and their refusal to see any difference between his regime and that of the Stalinist terror. There is only one decisive factor that can explain such behaviour and that is the historical relationship of nationalism and national identity to the unique role of the Polish writer. Stanisław Starski has written:

> In the case of Poland . . . the loss of an independent Polish state, which did not survive the end of the eighteenth century and did not reappear on the map of Europe until 1918, has caused a profound intensification of the national frame of reference. The fact that Polish Romantic poets had to replace society's lawyers, teachers and politicians shifted the whole burden of socialization to national culture and away from practical activities of administration. The durability of this national pattern has been proven in the years since World War II. Sociological research carried on by Stanisław Novak since 1957 has confirmed a vague feeling on the part of Polish intellectuals that the majority of Poles view the state and 'state-leading groups' as historically coincidental . . . Devotion and loyalty go to the nation, the national community and tradition, which are felt to be definitely superior to the political organization of society. Thus what may appear as a purely demagogical slogan – 'We have signed the agreement, as a Pole does with a Pole' – which appeared after the Gdańsk, Szczecin, and Jastrzębie agreements had been signed, was actually an expression of loyalty to Poland on both sides of the class barricades. This loyalty to the national heritage which surpasses differences of class and politics is by no means an un-mixed blessing . . . [18]

It was into this background of mounting moral, political and artistic confusion that *Mała Apokalypsa* (A Minor Apocalypse) appeared in 1979.

A Minor Apocalypse is of interest not only because of its clear artistic merits, but because of the light it throws on the very specific political, literary and cultural atmosphere of the closing months of the Gierek era. It has been translated into at least thirteen languages including English, Swedish, Finnish, Norwegian, Dutch, French, German, Greek, Czech and Italian, and won the Italian Mondello prize for literature. It was a book that with its pessimistic and ironic attitude to official culture and its sharply derogatory portrait of life in the People's Republic of Poland, the state of things and the state of people's minds, could have expected no favour at all from state publishers. *A Minor Apocalypse* was not submitted to the censor but was published by *Zapis* in May 1979, over a year before Solidarność was formed and more than two and a half years before Martial Law was declared. The novel describes the feeling and atmosphere of that period with brilliant clarity and perception. It is here that some of the consequences of censorship in guarding the difference between reality and Party claims were shown.

The novel concerns a typical Konwicki-like narrator who is approached one day by Hubert and Rysio, representatives of the underground opposition, and instructed to set fire to himself that evening on the steps of Party headquarters in Warsaw on the day that the Soviet and Polish first secretaries are due to meet in Warsaw. The rest of the novel consists of the narrator's journey round Warsaw trying to find both matches and fuel, and his many and various encounters and conversations with people who know of the plan. It must be said that the novel cannot be read for its plot, which is almost non-existent, but rather for its attention to and presentation of significant and telling detail. It is a hideously accurate portrait of the cynical, confused, poverty-ridden, ailing, and opportunist Poland of Gierek's last year in office.

Konwicki is a tireless chronicler of the more absurd aspects of communism, and ambiguities abound right from the start. Hubert walks with a cane and has a blind eye as a result of having once been interrogated, not by the secret police but by the AK. During a campaign of persecution in the 1960s Hubert (the person now asking the narrator to immolate himself) had attempted to hang himself. The opposition is not very impressive and there is more than a hint that the act of self-immolation is to be undertaken by an opposition that has become desperate to be noticed, that has, in the face of a taciturn government's failure to respond to its petitions, 'gone to pot putting out all those semi-legal bulletins, periodicals, those appeals which are read by next to no one'. It is not even certain that the government bothers to keep an eye on this opposition: when Hubert and Rysio leave, the narrator notes that 'no one came running out from the half shadows' to follow them. Indeed, it seems that both the government and the opposition could benefit from the immolation.

Rysio's brother believes that the office of the censor has been one of the leading and dynamic elements for social change in Poland and he is about to give a lecture to the censorship's department of allusions:

Allusions in works of art, allusions in the mass media . . . I, my good man, am a devotee of allusions. I have created a theory of how allusions function in a socialist society . . . Allusions play a vital role. Not calling a thing by its name reveals what it is; allusions have suggestive power, they reach into the listener's subconscious. Therefore, an undisclosed truth becomes a public truth. The tension caused by the hunger for truth or, rather, I would say, by people's complex about the truth, those dangerous tensions are artificially eliminated by a skilfully employed allusion. For that reason, allusions should not be repressed; quite the contrary, they must be encouraged, people must be taught to make more intelligent, more meaningful allusions. After a certain amount of time, people will prefer an allusion to the truth itself. Because an allusion is, in its own way, a sort of art form. An allusion is truth clad in metaphor.[19]

The narrator muses on the thought that Poland has been 'overrun by the bourgeoisie, a Soviet bourgeoisie':

Things had looked better at one time. We were children of the nineteenth century. Our fathers had been members of Piłsudki's Legions or his secret army, and during World War II we had been in the Home Army or the Union of Fighting Youth. That means, how to say it now, that means, how to explain it after all these years, that means, the hell with it, that doesn't mean anything now, at the end of our splendid twentieth century, a century of tyranny and unbridled democracy, foolish holiness and brilliant villainy, art without punch and graphomania run rampant.[20]

To say that something means nothing runs counter to Marxist thinking, but to say that this legacy of Polish history and culture means nothing is to reduce something central to Polish life to an inevitable nothing. But the meaning of things, or rather the impossibility of ever approaching meaning in this kind of society, is a major theme of the book. Here it is possible to learn more from the censored obituary notices than from any official information almanac; cinemas advertise Soviet films, but in reality show Polish films behind locked doors; the meat industry celebrates fifty years of the People's Republic of Poland with a giant number 50 made from sausage, but in reality it is only forty years and the sausages are made from sawdust:

'It's wonderful and it's terrible that nobody knows what his own gestures, actions, and follies actually mean. We're worried about the death of our nation, but at the same time the entire galaxy is hurtling off into an abyss, nothingness. It's hailing again. What an autumn.'
'I'd say it was still summer.'[21]

In the late 1970s the censor was very sensitive to the subject of meat shortages and in state publishing houses the reference to sausage would almost certainly have been cut.[22] The confusion as to the date (they are not even sure what year it is), the season, and even the weather is a logical development from Poland's real censorship laws, interposed to prevent the accurate perception of reality. And Konwicki is not exaggerating. The censorship regulations in place in 1976 read:

> In censoring the calendar the following pattern should be strictly followed: The holidays from work are: New Year – 1 January; first & second days of Easter – variable; first day of Whitsuntide – variable; Labour Day – 1 May; Corpus Christi – variable; *odrodzenie Polski* (rebirth of Poland) – 22 July; All Saints – 1 November; Christmas – 25-6 December. The following days which are not holidays should also be indicated in the calendar: Victory Day – 9 May; October Revolution – 7 November; Others according to the judgement of publishers.[23]

In the streets there are crowds, enormous queues for basic commodities (matches are available only for hard currency) and long banners reading 'We have built Socialism' in both Polish and Russian. Also part of this are the crowds of Russian thugs that throng the streets and who are paid to attend official demonstrations chanting 'Polska, Polshe' in a language somewhere between Russian and Polish, intelligible to both, but neither Polish nor Russian:

> A bunch of guys, not young but dressed as newspaper boys, were fast approaching us from Aleja Jerozolimskie. It was a group of some sort of activists, probably from a youth organisation. They were scattering a special edition of *Trybuna Ludu* and calling out shamefacedly: 'Poland awarded honorary title of First Candidate for membership in the Union of Soviet Socialist Republics!', 'Extra! Poland a candidate for membership in Soviet Union!', 'Great Events in Polish history at the threshold of a new millennium. Extra!'[24]

The ironies and deformations within this society run very deep and those who perpetuate them are shameless. The minister of culture, who has spent his entire life 'making artists rot in jail and hounding poor art', has retired, only to find that he envies artists the attention they receive, and consequently he too has taken up painting. At an exhibition of his works the guests are men of distinction: 'generals from the security police, governors, high officials from the Censorship, vice ministers':

> They too had become part of the artistic elite. They too were writing their memoirs and sensationalistic novels, carving tree roots, composing hit tunes, and sculpting busts of their colleagues who had passed away. Any of their children who did not wish for a career in politics were placed in art schools. And so now

the regime had its own art. The regime is self-sufficient. It creates reality and mirrors it in art.[25]

The deformations extend deep into artistic creativity, even to respected members of the creative *inteligencja* opposition, making opportunist fellow travellers of even the best-intentioned artists. At one point the narrator is approached by a film-maker called Bułat (possibly a rather wicked portrait of Wajda) who confesses that 'lying has killed me', and describes his own intellectual cowardice:

> When I replay my films in memory, a sudden suffocating panic overwhelms me . . . Look I started with a film that slandered the Home Army, that is, the very milieu I came from, then I made a film glorifying the ill-fated Home Army. When the country was wasting away in a stupor, oppressed by the hopelessness of a situation that was half occupation, half freedom, I was making psychological films. I took a little of this and a little of that. I was trying to keep up with certain world trends. And then I made a film lampooning the intellectual elite and then I did one that smelled of anti-Semitism, though there really wasn't any in it. Do you see the iron logic in the path I've taken . . . ? My artistic biography is the curriculum vitae of a fellow traveller. I've always thought I was doing what could be done at a given moment. But look closer at the consistent thrust of my ideas and statements. I was carrying out the Party line in Technicolour. I rolled along with it from one error to the next.[26]

Bułat, like the poet Ryszard Schmidt, has accepted government subsidy all his working life, and yet at the same time has managed to court the applause of the public by presenting himself as a critic of the regime and dedicated oppositionist intellectual.

The ultimate logic of such a system of conspiracy and counter-conspiracy is that the resistance and underground opposition might well turn out to be unwitting police stooges, but that the police see themselves as the real connoisseurs of art and politics. Tadzio, the young man who follows the narrator around, is exactly the same age as the People's Republic of Poland; he is a police informer and writes satirical poetry and jokes against oppositionists and dissidents for the Police Department of Propaganda. However, he is also a great admirer of the narrator's writings and is always ready with an apt quote. A police chief who interviews the narrator in a secret vault somewhere underneath a restaurant cloakroom says that he would rather not enforce total silence or censorship:

> I even have an idea. You should write for one particular reader, that's always best. Me, for example. Reject censorship, raison d'état, all your fears, and write like a free man for other free men. You always were proud but never vain. The

size of the printing isn't the important thing for you. Better one intelligent reader with a literary head than tens of thousands of coelenterates with toilet paper between their ears. Your book won't die in my hands. Only in my hands will it have a chance of lasting, of living forever.[27]

The fact that this conversation took place in an underground chamber was ridiculed as exaggerated, paranoid nonsense by the novel's critics. Eight months after the novel appeared an underground tunnel connecting Party Headquarters and the basement of the Paradis Café on Nowy Świat was discovered during renovation work.[28]

This is a world where the 'reality' of communism is a subject for mourning, where indifference and opportunism, sanctioned by the Party, and the amorality that surrounds the Party, are finally victorious. But nevertheless there is a cynical, perverted underlying 'truth' that emerges about both the capitalist and the communist world. Comrade Kobiałka (the name means basket or pot), ex-first secretary and a neighbour of the narrator, and who is probably a portrait of Gomułka, says:

It's all being held together by a string, by the thread of domestic production, by a spiderweb of hope. We have demoralised capitalism. Utterly and absolutely. By our own horrible example. We have them so tied up in agreements, economic agreements, scientific, cultural, athletic, what have you, we've got them tied up as with barbed wire, and so we can fail to meet deadlines, cheat on quantity in deliveries, not pay what we owe on time, lie, drown them in vodka, so that after a while the total socialist chaos we have invented and sustained will bare its teeth even there, among them. And you should be aware, neighbour, that for a while now they have been letting people leave Poland and go abroad. And what have they been doing there? They've been breaking the pay phones, riding the subways without paying, slipping in ahead of the line everywhere, stealing silverware from restaurants, sneaking out on their hotel bills, getting people drunk, messing up public restrooms, and abusing the local women whenever they have the chance to. If we put all this together and draw our own conclusions, then, my dear neighbour, who will be surprised that the so-called free world is looking more and more like the Soviet world all the time. And here is the one last doctrine, it may be Lenin's, that hasn't been played out yet – if we don't overtake capitalism, then capitalism will wait for us.[29]

There is a thread of logic to this absurd extension and simultaneous demolition of Khrushchev's line on communist economic development, but it is a seriously damaged and wilfully perverse line of reasoning which suggests that the 'moral virus' of communism has even begun to affect capitalism. Also, clearly, this is a portrait of exactly the kind of people that communist social engineering had produced and the kind of internal logic and motivation it engendered among its citizens. Konwicki's fiction here chronicles the insidious spread of a 'moral virus' which is indifferent to morality or value systems of any kind, revels in its own subjectivity, is increasingly self-regarding, interested in nothing other than self-perpetuation and increase.

The narrator confesses his distaste for this 'indecent' world. He is used to secrecy, plots and the role of writers within specifically Polish conspiracy, but his idea of conspiracy is different from that of the Party writers, the bureaucracy, the police. He is a product of the old PPS and the AK, rather than the creature of the regime. He prefers that writing and political activity should be voluntary rather than the product of social and political blackmail; that writers should be disinterested rather than actively seek rewards; that writers and politicians should always be prepared to lose rather than desperate to win at any price. He acknowledges that it is almost impossible to transcend the conditioning of the time, the social mentality, the political system, the 'peculiarities of this phase of the historical process, the tightening or loosening of morality'. However, he feels that too many Polish intellectuals use the language of Marxism without pondering the moral and ideological problems that lurk within, and which decided the nation's fate for over forty years. For the narrator sin has become *the* form of virtue, moral imponderables have given place to amoral imponderables, amorality rules using the rules and language of morality: 'Evil has tapped into our ethical code and turned itself into good.'[30]

Towards the end of the book the narrator visits Hubert in the intensive care section of the hospital. Hubert, one of the writers who informed the narrator that he was to immolate himself, is now on a life-support machine. Sitting beside the dying writer he reviews Hubert's career, and in doing so reveals a picture of the moral and artistic nullity of culture at all levels that faced writers by the end of Gierek's period in office:

You didn't have much of a life, you had a tough life, and they say you were always changing your views. You stifled your own human impulses, or perhaps it was your philistine habits, and you condemned the bourgeois and the philistine in those you loved. Few people loved you, many hated you. You were loved carelessly but hated with full intensity. What sort of moral logic guided your actions, my pale, stiff, inhuman pang of conscience . . . ? When you started publishing in the émigré press and in the underground at home, the government's artistic salons chuckled and sneered that you were sucking up to the free West and trying to build a literary career on politics. When the students started copying your work on duplicating machines at night, when old cranks began knocking out copies on their typewriters, when your works, your desperate thoughts, and your hopeless hopes began to circulate through the country in editions of a few dozen copies, your colleagues, your faithful friends, keepers of Poland's flame, the vestal virgins of Poland's watchfires, they stepped up their ambiguous but profitable flirtation with our brainless regime. They rose to the top here in money and recognition, they took off abroad, availing themselves of the regime's support, diplomacy, money, the great machinery of the state. They winked significantly at people in the free world to say that they represented the moral strength of their oppressed country, that they both created and directed that moral force. But neither the one nor the other spared you any kicks, you poor beggar with your medieval upbringing . . . You're doing the right thing in dying, you old blackmailer. You'll slip away like a plumber who failed to fix the faucet. The world's evened out. There are no good or evil people. There is only a great unfathomable mob trampling itself underfoot. The life giving sources of the old morality have dried up and vanished in the sands of oblivion. There's no other source to draw from, no place to refresh oneself. There is no example, no inspiration. It is night. A night of indifference, apathy, chaos.[31]

A Minor Apocalypse gave vent to the bitter frustration of the opposition, but at the same time it showed that it was no longer possible to draw simple lines between the opposition and the government, between the writers and the Party, that the moral nullity of the Party had reached deep inside the psyche of Poles in all walks of life to create a despondency and apathy, an opportunism and amorality that were self-destructive and self-defeating and which had almost no resemblance to, or relationship with, any recognizable ideology. In this way the narrator's hesitant, hung-over shamble towards martyrdom on behalf of the nation is glorified and trivialized.

Perhaps the final irony of the book comes as the narrator kisses his girl-friend Hope (Nadzieżda in the Polish text) goodbye. The narrator, an ex-communist and anti-communist, a hopeful and faithful ex-Catholic and non-Catholic, discovers, like the author, that not only did people make the communist system what it is but that they also 'created God' in opposition. This God of mercy is also the ambiguous God of the people. One day, he assures us, God will take them 'the chosen race out of the promised land'.[32] The book closes as the narrator, finally armed with matches and petrol, moves towards the steps of Party headquarters. It is clear that what the Party has done is to rob human life of meaning and dignity, but this is apparent only when the annihilation of moral values is seen to have eliminated even the possibility of tragedy. It ends, not with an apostrophe to God but with an ironic and yet Romantic invocation to the People which inverts the Party's ideology and language:

> My legs are becoming heavy and my head is pulled down towards the earth from which I had arisen and to which I must, of my own free will, return. People, give me strength. People, give strength to everyone in this world who is, at this very moment, going, as I am, to make a burnt offering of himself. People, give me strength. People . . . [33]

It is clear that the book had a considerable impact, even in a limited underground edition, and in focusing attention on the absorption and normalization of the damage to moral and cultural values made a great contribution to the climate that created Solidarność. However, it must be said that some assumed the book was some kind of provocation set up by the security services to *osmalić* (smear) the underground. When Konwicki first approached NOWa with the manuscript they were very reluctant to take it, on the grounds that it did nothing to aid 'mobilization'. Konwicki's claim that honesty, even about the opposition, was necessary if literature was to deal in truth and wholeness was not something that was easily digested. Even émigrés opposed to the regime were unsettled by Konwicki's portrait of the demoralized communist Poland of the late 1970s. For Gustav Herling-Grudziński, Konwicki had become utterly and hysterically obsessed with himself and with his disgust at 'reality'.[34]

Konwicki said that contemporary experience was like a cake with 150 layers, and every layer was equally necessary.[35] He had made it clear that there was more than logic involved in the existence of the underground publishing and opposition movement; there was, even among Party members, a hunger, a desperate, deep-seated social, political and moral need for its existence.[36] Yet, for all the impact the book had at the time, and for all the accuracy of its perception that something in Poland was about to break, that something must break, on a massive, nation-wide scale, Konwicki later came to see that his attempt at satire had in fact been mocked by the course of events. Within a few months of the book's appearance the shipyard strikes in Gdańsk had produced Solidarność and the perfidy of the government was faced with widespread moral opposition and an insistence that the law must be upheld, even by the authorities. The country's economic position stood revealed as disastrous and what little social responsibility remained, even though enforced as far as possible by Solidarność, was soon under threat from a discontented and frustrated populace. Just over a year after the book appeared Martial Law was declared in an attempt, Jaruzelski said, to prevent the disintegration of the Polish nation.

In *Moonrise, Moonset*, which was written partly as a diary during the 'Solidarność year' and was to be the first wholly underground publication of a novel during military rule, Konwicki reconsidered the nature and accuracy of his satire in *A Minor Apocalypse* only to decide that Polish actuality continually beggared his imagination. He described how he found himself being interrogated by a policeman who was almost identical in mental attitudes to one he had had created in *A Minor Apocalypse*. This was either the ultimate vindication of his perceptions or the ultimate nightmare. Life in Poland after August 1980, Konwicki concluded, rapidly came to resemble the extreme vision of *A Minor Apocalypse*:

A kilo of chicken costs four hundred złoties. Turkey is two thousand a kilo. The prophecies I made in *A Minor Apocalypse* have long since come true. Reality is now outdistancing me at great speed. A rapist has been apprehended because of his sugar ration card, which his victim found after the rape. There are lines in front of newspaper kiosks which have no newspapers. A few thousand letters from the West were found in a garbage dump in Ursus. All the letters had been opened, by persons unknown. A ton of bacon is rotting in another garbage dump. The post office still has not delivered the packages which arrived from abroad last August. Local Party and state dignitaries pack their bags and flee to remote provinces. With the money a peasant gets from a litre of milk at a state purchase centre, he can buy three and a half litres of milk at the store next door . . . No one reads anything these days. If they do, they don't understand. If they read and understand, they forget it all immediately. That was said by Stanisław Lem in a television interview and it made me fall off my chair with delight.[37]

On the one hand the idea of creating an unofficial publishing industry seemed to solve many of the problems the opposition faced in dealing with a censorship that was not sanctioned by law, a government that had no mandate to rule and a Party that relied on the police to maintain its leading role. On the other hand the logic of such an opposition was that it inadvertently created another, alternative, parallel world that still failed to mesh with any open system for creating or exchanging views, information, and opinion. In its own way this was just as bad. At extremes it led oppositionists to mistrust everything the authorities said, and to believe everything that rumour chose to purvey. The underground opposition were moving steadily into territory where there were no real checks and balances on its thought or feeling. Polish life as a whole was becoming increasingly schizophrenic.

In Konwicki's vision it had become impossible to distinguish morally between the conspiratorial policemen encouraging writers to write in the old Polish nationalist tradition, and oppositionists, moving rapidly beyond the old Endecja positions by asking people to set fire to themselves for no good reason. Indeed it was no longer possible to divide the attitudes and opinions of the two groups satisfactorily on any level since there was no reliable way of saying who, in reality, was who. For that matter, in the chaos of Polish political life it was becoming increasingly difficult to maintain a grip on reality, to distinguish the *prowokacja* (provocation) from what was spontaneous, or to distinguish what was real from what was pure fantasy, gossip or censored nonsense. Konwicki's perceptions echoed the findings of sociologists too. By the end of the decade the Polish *inteligencja* were said to be 'much weakened psychologically, compared to the workers: their education and their social position, their awareness of social dissonance, their professional frustrations, their awareness of the meaning of social and political problems, and the unrelieved tedium of tension all served to increase anxiety and disquiet, and reduced their self-confidence'.[38]

Konwicki brought the clandestine and highly personal novel of opposition, and the idea of damaged conspiratorial thought, to their logical conclusion in

A Minor Apocalypse.[39] He showed a man for whom death for the cause of the nation is totally undermined, yet who still considers that act to be somehow morally imperative. It is a sacrifice for an uncertain cause, requested by people for whom he has little respect; it is an action called to protest at people who know his works and want him to continue writing, by people who have no particular interest in him or his work. There was no going back on that artistic, psychological or political revelation and logic. Polish literature had reached the end of the conspiratorial line. From this point on to stay underground, to continue the conspiracy, to refuse to rise into the gloom of Polish day, to refuse confrontation with the already deeply embedded social, political and moral deformations of Polish communist society, would have caused even further damage. The brief sixteen-month life-span of Solidarność was just such an attempt. The military coup of 13 December 1981 reversed all this. In the short term, while the shock of Martial Law lasted, it was successful in setting Polish literature back to its old conspiratorial habits.

However, in the long term there could be no return. For Konwicki, as for Lem, Barańczak, Herbert, Brandys and others it had become essential to question the language in which the 'reality' of the closed, censored, communist world was presented, to try to restore some part of the faculty of cognition and introspection denied by censorship. By 1980, such was the effect of censorship, the control of the media, and the damage wrought by Party language, that on the subjective level, and in the evidence gathered by numerous sociologists, it was clear that Polish society no longer knew what it thought, no longer knew what it really knew. Its perception of what was real and what was false had been seriously undercut; by and large Polish society was in the process of succumbing to the 'dead field of normative indifference'. It had begun to surrender to automatic patterns of thought and reaction. Even the underground opposition was beginning to succumb to the insidious effect of what Brandys had dubbed *nierzeczywistość Polski* (Polish unreality).[40] *A Minor Apocalypse*, published by the underground and émigré opposition only a few months before the great shipyard strike of 1980, sums up the feelings and tensions that marked the rise of Solidarność and the desperate cul-de-sac of both official and unofficial political and cultural life. The novel, with its view of the seedy underside of dissident and Party life, vividly delineated the confusions of both the authorities and the opposition, the deeply embedded economic chaos, the anarchy, the self-interest, the exhausting and exhausted moral, personal and cultural chaos that haunted Poland through the 1980s, and whose spectre still hovers.

9

ADAM MICHNIK

Adam Michnik has been called 'courageous and uncompromising', 'the real heir to Polish Social democracy', 'a formidable, courageous and prolific revolutionary spirit'. Timothy Garton Ash has praised his irony 'modulated by a fine sense of moral responsibility and a keen political intelligence'. Czesław Miłosz, who counts Michnik as a friend, has spoken of his talent as a 'combination of energy in motion, of moral purity and high intellectual qualities, a combination against the nature of public commitments'.[1]

Norman Davies, on the other hand, has described Michnik as holding 'eccentric left-wing or Marxist opinions'. Zdzisław Najder has accused Michnik of monopolizing virtue by claiming democracy, decency, morality, openness, tolerance and personal liberties for the left, while attempting to remove communism from the history of the left. Józef Mackiewicz has dismissed Michnik, along with Jacek Kuroń and Leszek Kołakowski as 'Soviets, only even more dangerous, because they appealed to democratic ideals'. Abbot Józef Tischner, for whom history took a wrong turn with the Enlightenment, has said that Michnik, while attempting to appropriate the moral high ground for social democracy, has compromised the Church by showing it at bottom to be chauvinistic, oppressive, reactionary, nationalist and obscurantist. And the poet Jacek Trznadel has claimed that Michnik is nothing more than an untrustworthy Trotskyite-revisionist communist, and has hinted very strongly that Michnik was, and always has been, a Party stooge within the democratic movement.[2]

Michnik's social democratic beliefs have never been hidden. His activism on behalf of Polish workers in opposing the Party was always open. If, in the 1970s, western policy-makers had paid close attention to Michnik's writings, instead of listening to First Secretary Edward Gierek's propaganda of success, they would have been better equipped to understand Polish politics through the 1980s and 1990s. His personal bravery is without question. Even his opponents note his generosity of spirit and his intellectual curiosity. If there is one Polish intellectual whose thought and argument affected all shades of opinion (the Party, the Church and the whole range of political opposition) it is Michnik. If there is a key personality in the history of the Polish democratic opposition it is not Lech Wałęsa, but Adam Michnik. And if there is a key moment in the history of that opposition it is not when Wałęsa climbed the Gdańsk shipyard wall to join the strike in August 1980, but in 1977, when Michnik's book *Kosciół, Lewica – Dialog* (The Church, The Left – Dialogue) laid out, for all to see, just how the left oppositionists, nationalists and Catholic Church could co-operate to create a life with dignity. It may be that western observers have overestimated Michnik's influence among Polish workers, but without Michnik, Solidarność could hardly have come into existence and could never have achieved anything like the social force it eventually mustered. Without his writings, his energy and his willingness to engage in dialogue with all comers, the democratic opposition, lacking focus, unity of purpose, political and legal strategies, would have remained fragmented and powerless. Michnik's writings and personality are central to the struggle against Polish communism, to the achievements of Poland's fragile democracy and to the slow regrowth of meaning for the discredited word 'socialism'.

Adam Michnik was born in Warsaw in 1946. He has described himself as 'son of Osjasz Schechter', the child of a 'Polish Jewish pre-war communist family'. Before the war Michnik's father had spent time in prison for political agitation. In the 1950s the precocious Michnik joined the 'Walterite' scout movement where his scoutmaster was Jacek Kuroń. The troop was named after the communist general Karol Świerczewski, who had fought in the Spanish Civil War and whose code name was 'Walter'. Politically the Walterites were diametrically opposed to the scout movement created by Baden-Powell and committed unequivocally to communism.

In 1961, Michnik (aged fifteen) became a founder member and 'leading spirit' of the Club of the Seekers of Contradictions, and that same year was introduced to the Warsaw *inteligencja* Club of the Crooked Circle, of which J. J. Lipski was president. Later that year Michnik gave a talk on school reform at the club. Almost immediately the club was informed that it was not the proper place for high school students, and Michnik was promptly expelled from school for 'illegal activities'. Michnik was expelled from his next high school too, but continued to attend the club until it was closed down by the authorities in February 1962. In 1963 Michnik, while walking in the park before his physics exam, was informed by Jacek Kuroń that he had been named by First Secretary Gomułka as a dangerous subversive.

In 1964 Michnik entered Warsaw University's department of history. He was part of a group of young nonconformist communist intellectuals, 'politically obstreperous young people', sometimes called the Revisionist Tots, but characterized by the regime as fearsome 'Commandos'.[3] This group began to redefine the political and intellectual tone of Warsaw student life. They had serious ideological criticisms to make of the Party and the ruling authorities. As the Party began to appreciate the ideological threat posed by the Commandos so they closed down the Commandos' avenues of expression: they dissolved the Walterites and expelled the troop leaders from the socialist scout movement. No longer able to attend meetings of the suppressed Club of the Crooked Circle, Michnik attended the Discussion Club of the ZMS (Union of Socialist Youth) until that too was dissolved by the authorities in 1964. In October 1966, Michnik and other Commandos held a meeting to demand the release of Jacek Kuroń and Karol Modzelewski who had been imprisoned for writing a critical left-oppositionist *Open Letter to the Basic Party Organisation of the PZPR and to the Members of the University Cell of the Union of Socialist Youth at Warsaw University*.[4] His support of Kuroń and Modzelewski was not Michnik's only crime. He also attended discussions where his teacher, Leszek Kołakowski, spoke very critically of the Party. Michnik was suspended from the university, reinstated, suspended again, expelled from ZMS, reinstated by the university, and then finally expelled. Michnik's expulsion sparked a petition of protest to the university rector, with over 1,200 signatures from staff and students. Michnik later said of his political understanding at this time:

> I began to criticise Polish reality as I became aware that official ideas clashed with everyday practice. I quickly came to realise that the revolution had been betrayed, socialism's ideas were being neglected, and that political and social democracy existed only on paper. But when I looked back to the inter-war period, it was only to contrast the magnificent personage of Wera Kostrzewa with the gloomy, cynical and dictatorial rulers of my own time.[5]

In spite of its physical disappearance the influence of the pre-war PPS (Polish Socialist Party) was a steady undercurrent in the left-humanist-liberal politics of the revisionists and of Michnik and was to surface again in the thinking of KOR. From this standpoint Michnik clearly resisted the 'present reality' with the image of a different kind of left-wing ideology. Thinking of the communist take-over he was to write:

> In line with official historiography we are accustomed to identifying the left of 1946 with support for the 'new reality' and for the new government installed by the Red Army. This is also how many people at the time viewed the matter, particularly among intellectual circles inside Poland. Not only did the ideologues of the PPR . . . always appeal to the 'ideals of the left', but so did those leaders of the 'official' PPS who were in favour of collaboration with the communists . . . The majority of the pre-war PPS leadership, however . . . came out in opposition to the 'new reality', as did several prominent intellectuals of the left, such as Maria Dąbrowska . . . There was now a real division within the traditional left. While the journal *Kuźnica* and its editor Żółkiewski emphasised the PPR's 'progressive' program of social reforms, moderate socialist leaders Maria Dąbrowska and Zygmunt Żuławski stressed the totalitarian and obscurantist methods of the reformers. This division within the left deserves to be kept in mind, for too many writers lightheartedly equate the ruling 'Progressive System'

with the political programmes of the entire left. As we shall see, not all left wing programmes entail acquiescence to lies and tyranny.[6]

This lament was to become a theme for much of Michnik's later writing.

Michnik took a leading part in the 30 January 1968 student demonstrations to protest at the banning of Mickiewicz's play *Dziady*. Michnik, after his arrest at the demonstration, spoke to a western journalist. A few days later he was rearrested on charges of having 'given false information' as part of a slanderous foreign propaganda campaign against Poland. On 4 March 1968 Michnik was expelled from the university by the minister for education, Henryk Jabłoński, acting on information not from any university inquiry but rather on information from the Party and the Police. Jabłoński had, however, exceeded his authority, and his action sparked further student unrest. On 8 March 1968, against a background of growing crisis in Czechoslovakia and continued student protest at the banning of *Dziady*, ZOMO riot police using tear gas stormed Warsaw University. On 9 March the police baton-charged a peaceful demonstration of 20,000 people in central Warsaw. At Warsaw University demonstrations and disturbances involving riot police continued for a month.

Gomułka's supporters, particularly General Mieczysław Moczar's violent anti-Semitic veteran's association ZBoWiD, Piasecki's 'Catholic' front organization Pax, the Pax newspaper *Słowo Powszechne*, the army newspaper *Żółnierz Wolności*, and the Party paper *Trybuna Ludu*, had been fighting a long, slow battle against the *rewizjonist* gains of 1956. They characterized *rewizjonizm* as a Zionist plot to overthrow Gomułka and bring down Poland and they launched a vicious campaign against Michnik, democratic socialist students and their literary and intellectual supporters. The Party set about 'restructuring' Warsaw University to bring it under closer Party control. In order to control dangerous intellectuals and revisionists Kuroń, Modzelewski, Karpiński, Michnik and the more active student organizers were arrested. *Trybuna Ludu* published a list of the 'golden youth' – student dissidents, children of top party officials and senior members of the *biurokracja*, many of whom were Jewish. Among those named were Szlajfer (the son of a senior Warsaw censor) and Modzelewski (son of the Polish foreign minister of 1945–7). Newspapers also revealed that Michnik was of Jewish extraction. The students, along with 1,600 others, were expelled from university. Professors Kołakowski, Bauman, Baczko, Hirszowicz, Brus and Pomian (all of whom were leading *rewizjonisci*) lost their university posts and decided to leave Poland.

The attack on the intellectual opposition was presented in the press as an effort to protect Polish patriotic values from Jewish radicals and alien influence. In the months that followed, six government ministers, eighty top Party members and over 500 top officials were sacked in Warsaw alone;

ninety-seven senior Party members and 1,404 other members, mainly Jews, were purged from the Party for 'offences against morality'; fourteen generals and over 200 other army officers lost their positions. Most were expelled because their 'concealed Zionist beliefs' had been revealed by the behaviour of their dissenting student offspring. The highly influential revisionist Władysław Bieńkowski (ex-minister of culture and also of education), Stefan Staszewski (senior editor at PAN), Roman Werfel (director of PAN) and Tadeusz Zabłudowski (ex-chief censor) – senior Party members with important literary connections and editorships – were sacked and expelled from the Party. Party members Paweł Hoffman and Adam Bromberg, both of whom had extensive connections among the *rewizjonisci*, lost their editorial jobs. Bromberg was 'emigrated' to Sweden.

Writers identified by the Polish press as resisting the anti-Jewish campaign or as being Jewish were harassed: many went into hiding. The critic Stefan Kisielewski, after being attacked as an 'ignoramus' in *Życie Warszawy*, was twice physically assaulted and beaten: two of his fingers were broken. Kazimierz Brandys's latest book received an insulting review questioning his 'Polishness'. Antoni Słonimski was hounded and insulted in the Party press. At the same time student Nina Karsov was arrested for keeping a diary recording the harassment of students, and expelled from Poland. The writer Adolf Rudnicki suffered physical assault and public vilification. The writers Roman Karst, Słucki and Stanisław Wygodzki were all blacklisted: they decided to emigrate to Israel; the historian Szymon Szechter was expelled and left for London. Sławomir Mrożek, who was in Paris at the time, and the literary critic Jan Kott who was in the USA, both refused to return to Poland.

Gomułka made it plain that if Poland's tiny surviving Jewish population wished to emigrate the authorities would not stand in their way. By the end of 1969 over 20,000 Jews – many of whom were unaware of their 'Jewish' identity until confronted by the authorities – had been forced out of Poland. Though Gomułka was to remain in office only until 1970, his demolition of the intellectual and political opposition in 1968 destroyed *rewizjonizm* as a political and cultural force and drove a wedge between intellectuals and workers that was to cripple organized resistance to the Party for almost a decade. Michnik, who was deeply shocked by the events of 1968, was expelled from the Party and sentenced, on charges of refusing to co-operate with investigations, to three years in prison. Although the Party wanted him drafted into the army, Michnik was rejected by the military because of his stutter. Jaruzelski, who had hatched the plan, was dumbfounded to find that someone who could organize student protest and address meetings could be rejected because of a stammer and protested that in the army oratory was not a requirement; it was only necessary to obey orders.[7]

On his release from prison in 1969 Michnik was barred from resuming his studies in Warsaw and worked at the Róża Luksemburg Enterprise (a lightbulb factory) until 1971. He commuted from Warsaw to Poznań as a special extension student in order to complete his MA. He graduated in 1975. In Poznań he met and became a close friend of Stanisław Barańczak. In December 1975 he initiated the protest 'Letter of the fifty-nine'. Also during this period Michnik acted as private secretary to the revered poet Antoni Słonimski (1895–1976). The choice of Słonimski was in many ways typical of Michnik. Słonimski was the son of a famous Jewish doctor. He had been educated as a painter in Warsaw and Paris, but made his début as a rebellious lyric poet in 1918 and became a founder member of the Skamander group. A prominent member of the pre-war liberal left, a poet of the Warsaw café and the liberal *inteligencja*, he was dedicated to the renewal of language and the perfection of traditional metrical forms. He was a Wellsian rationalist and pacifist who despaired of the attraction and power of Nazism in Germany and the rise of anti-Semitism and nationalist chauvinism in Poland. Słonimski had escaped to Paris after the defeat of September 1939 and then moved to England, where he edited the journal *New Poland*, returning to Poland only in 1951. In the People's Republic of Poland he became one of the most respected cultural journalists. In 1956–9, as Chairman of the ZLP, he showed himself an active spokesman for intellectuals opposed to Party controls and censorship. Michnik, who was Słonimski's personal assistant right through the early 1970s, regarded Słonimski as his mentor, a bastion of the liberal conscience, a peerless moral authority and a model for all oppositionists.

Unrest at proposed changes to the Polish Constitution grew throughout 1975. In June 1976 strikes and protests at Radom and Ursus were violently repressed by the authorities, and politically active workers were victimized. These events had a dramatic effect on the opposition movement. Although J. J. Lipski has credited Jacek Kuroń with giving form to the opposition movement, Barańczak remembers the moment the idea of an opposition organization was born:

It was in July 1976. We stood – Adam and a group of friends – in a corridor of a Warsaw court where the participants of the June strikes at Ursus were being tried. No one was admitted to the court room except close relatives of the defendants. Mostly the workers' wives. We did not know what was going on inside the court room, but after an hour or so we heard a sudden outburst of women's crying pierce the walls. And a while later those weeping, wailing, cursing women left the courtroom and made their way through the crowd – each of them stupefied by the fact that as a result of this sham of a trial she wouldn't see her husband for the next two, three, five years and that nothing, nothing could be done about it. I stood next to Adam at that moment. His eyes were dry but I knew him well enough to see that he had just hit upon one of those ideas of his.[8]

Following the events in Radom and Ursus, in July 1976 oppositionists began a series of private meetings in Laski, where Michnik was working on his book about the Church. Their intention was to found an organization that would effectively link worker and intellectual protest and opposition by providing professional legal advice for victimized workers. In September 1976 the founding committee of KOR (Committee Defending Workers) formally came into existence. Michnik was excluded from all practical work because he had an invitation, arranged by Jean-Paul Sartre, to visit France, and had been given his passport by the authorities. It was thought that once in the west, Michnik would be useful in publicizing the work of the Polish opposition movement and it was common sense that he should not come to the attention of the Polish security service before his departure. In November 1976 Michnik went to Paris, where he acted as KOR spokesman. On 27 April 1977 he was indicted (along with Lipski and Kuroń) for working with foreign organizations against the interests of the Polish People's Republic. It became clear that, personal slanders to one side, the authorities in attacking the leadership of KOR were preparing a move against the whole organization. Michnik formally became a member of KOR and then returned from France on 1 May 1977 to answer the allegations. He was arrested a few days after his return, imprisoned for two months as part of an ongoing three-month investigative process, then released.

Michnik's book, *The Church, the Left – Dialogue* (Paris, 1977), had been written in Poland but was published by the Instytut Literacki in Paris just after Michnik's release from prison. After March 1968 it had become clear to Michnik that critics could not look to the Party to reform itself, nor could they expect malcontents within the Party to win any power sufficient to bring about reform. The anti-Semitic purge of 1968 broke any hope that might have lingered for the revisionists; indeed it broke the revisionists. Now change would have to come from a different direction. In literature, said Michnik, who was a voracious reader, a great many creative writers became oppositionists after 1956; in 1968 intellectuals once more became dissidents. In 1976, after protests at proposed constitutional reforms and the repression of demonstrations in Radom and Ursus, many Marxists and critical intellectuals were again banned from state publishing houses and state-sponsored journals. For many intellectuals this meant a pragmatic shift in that the only avenue of publication left to them was the Catholic Church and its publishing houses and journals. For a while Michnik's book made it possible to bridge the rift that had existed between intellectuals and the Church since the sixteenth century, when the Church had suspected their freethinking Protestant sympathies and masonic connections.[9]

In order to judge the impact of Michnik's book it is essential to see the central role that the Catholic Church had mapped out for itself. Since the partition of Poland the Church had seen itself as central to Polish culture, spirituality and identity. Poland had been about 60 per cent Catholic before

1939. However during the war the Jewish population and virtually all the smaller Christian sects had been annihilated by the Nazis, and after the war the mainly Protestant German population had all been expelled to the west. While pre-war Poland had been the home of a wide range of religions and religious sects, post-war Poland was over 98 per cent Catholic. The Catholic Church in the People's Republic of Poland was not the hunted, harried, fugitive creature that many in the west suppose, but rather a major element in social, political and literary life. In the early years of communist rule the Church and the state had tussled and wrangled. Several hundred priests had been arrested and Cardinal Wyszyński had been put under house arrest. But gradually the Party and the Church had learned to tolerate each other. While the Church still refused to accept the Party's indifference to religion it refused to fade away. The Church learned that in return for underwriting the Party's social message the Church could appear to oppose communism when it was in fact merely protecting itself, preaching that industrial strife and political protest were undesirable and that peace on the streets was essential. The post-war Church may have confused the faithful, but it prospered nevertheless.[10]

Michnik knew the book would be read by people searching for practical answers to very difficult questions. He was also aware that he was looking at the history of the Catholic Church in a way that was a little too liberal, a little too critical and a little too independent for many Poles. For him disputes about the past were often arguments about culture and above all about identity. In Poland this meant questioning the role of the Catholic Church in defining Polishness:

> The episcopate has frequently emphasised the Catholic nature of our culture. It has often declared that there is an intrinsic connection between Catholicism and Polishness. This connection can be understood in two ways. It can mean that Catholicism is an integral part of Polish culture, or it can mean that only that which is Catholic is truly Polish.[11]

For the Church the temptation was to see Catholic culture as Polish culture. But for Michnik, Polish culture – Catholic, Protestant, Jewish, Muslim and non-believer – was one and indivisible. Michnik was convinced that a Polish culture in which the non-Catholic element was removed or ignored would be poorer, less attractive, even crippled. He refused to accept Kołakowski's description of the Church as a traditional, obscurantist, provincial, fanatical, dim-witted curse that had been strangling Poland for four hundred years. Michnik was clear that the power of the Church had helped it preserve its honour through the partitions and the Nazi occupation, but that this very strength also served to perpetuate a large number of negative features. He saw the Church as 'triumphant, shallow, anti-intellectual and extremely conservative', and complained of its philistine and obscurantist hangers-on.[12]

Michnik was aware that his plea for dialogue and co-operation was not something the opposition movement as a whole would necessarily agree with. Nor would his portrait of the Church flatter the hierarchy into co-operation. But it had became clear to Michnik that the repression of 1968 had effectively broken the power of the revisionist intellectuals within the Party. Since the Church consistently sought to avoid conflict and preached conciliation and accommodation rather than open opposition, this meant that in destroying the revisionists the Party had effectively silenced active opposition. Michnik saw that briefly in the late 1970s the interests of the Church, the oppositionists and the workers all coincided and could no longer be ignored. There can be little doubt that in emphasising the moral and social similarities between the *lewica laicka* (lay left) and the Church, Michnik placed the Church in an uncomfortable moral position, making it very difficult for it to ignore the fact that no matter how much the Church prospered under communism it had to oppose any system that placed restrictions on the liberty of the individual, as human liberty was a fundamental Christian virtue and central to Polish culture. Since Michnik did not seek to draft priests into the service of the revolution, the hierarchy probably felt that it could accommodate him and the *lewica laicka* in the short term and that his efforts would come to little in the long term. Either way a strategic alliance could be made without too much difficulty. Unfortunately a Polish Pope was elected, taking the matter on to an entirely different plane by opening up Church-state relations to international scrutiny. The Church found that the *lewica laicka* had occupied the moral high ground and dared the Church to join it: the Church had little choice but to co-operate with the godless Marxists of KOR.

Michnik spelled out exactly why oppositionist intellectuals should seek rapprochement with the Church and make better use of its institutional powers to protect freedom and dignity. Michnik regarded what had happened to Russian culture under Stalin as a total and unmitigated disaster and he was aware of the narrow margin by which the Polish defeat of the Bolshevik armies in 1920 had saved the Polish *inteligencja* from becoming 'fodder for polar bears'. He was also well aware of the social and political differences between Poland and the Soviet Union. In particular he was impressed by the independence and power of the Church and saw this as an important factor in the fight against *sowjetizacja* (sovietization). He took Polish intellectuals to task saying that since 1944 one of the major weaknesses of their opposition had been their failure to co-operate and make common cause with the Church. Michnik chose to ignore, or least overlook, that the Church had in the inter-war period been a major partner in power with the military regime and had supported the army when it fired on striking Polish workers. Michnik tried hard to distance the post-war Church from this association with power and chose instead to present it as threatened by the same political system that menaced dissident and oppositionist intellectuals. He pointed out that although in the inter-war period the Church had been a major ally of the military regime and an enemy to democracy, the post-war Church had, for some years, 'not been totally on the side of the authorities', a fact which seemed to have escaped the notice of the left-orientated intellectuals and ex-Party dissidents. For Michnik it was necessary only to read liberal Catholic journals and the pastoral letters of the episcopate to see that a huge shift had taken place in Polish Catholicism. However, although he repeatedly singled out the behaviour of Jerzy Turowicz, editor of the Catholic *Tygodnik Powszechny*, the journal *Więź* and the Catholic Znak deputies, Tadeusz Mazowiecki, Jerzy Zawieyski and Stanisław Stomma for praise, particularly over their protests in 1976, it was clear to Michnik that when 'communist obscurantism' struck a blow at the Christian virtues of the democratic socialist opposition in 1968, the episcopate had remained silent. Michnik did his best to interpret the Church's conduct in a favourable way for the *lewica laicka*, but his dissatisfaction with the behaviour of the Church showed through:

> The secular intellectuals issued no programmatic documents. Indeed, they did nothing whatsoever to make Catholic circles aware of their real position, which was anti-totalitarian rather than anti-religious. I suspect that the Church really did see the clash between the leftist intellectuals and the regime as part of some sharp, intra-Communist struggle for power. No doubt they saw the officially sponsored anti-Semitism in the same way, for anti-Semitism had long been used in intra-Party struggles. If we assume that this was their assessment of the situation, it is not surprising that the Church's response to 1968 was so moderate. Nor should we be surprised that the episcopate would not want to link the long-term interests of the Church to the confusing games of intra-Party struggles. Probably this explains the episcopate's refusal to speak in concrete political and ideological terms and its decision to restrict itself to a rather general statement on the students' elementary right to protest and the intellectuals' equally elementary right to scientific and cultural freedom. And yet even with all this in mind, I still tend to think that this restraint was a serious error on the part of the episcopate. Because, after all, apart from any internal factional struggles, there were real people suffering from racist demagoguery.[13]

Michnik's writing not only provided a treasure house of engaged thought and practical advice, but by insisting on his expression of a vote of no confidence in the ruling authorities he helped create cultural and political values and set a personal example. Moral values figure highly in Michnik's writing. He reasserts the fundamental ideals of Judaeo-Christian individualism by trying to 'live in truth' regardless of what is going on around him: he reverses the priorities of Stalinism, beginning not with the state and the Party, but with 'subjectivity', the resurrection of civil society, the individual, their duty, conscience and dignity. His strength (and his crime) were that he challenged the Church to put into practice the social virtues it preached and he refused the Church any unearned monopoly of moral high ground.

Michnik was determined not to let the official propaganda of the Church sever Polish Catholics from PPS traditions of left-wing trade unionism, protest and political organization. He made the point that after 1918, as the PPS recovered its unity and turned its attention from the struggle against the partitioning powers to the internal issues facing the infant Polish state, it had little choice but to move steadily rightward to encompass nationalist opinion. But for Michnik, Polish Catholicism and national feeling could still encompass left-wing ideas in a particularly Polish way:

> The Polish socialism of those years – after it broke with the anti-independence phraseology of the 'Proletarians' – was a peculiar synthesis of Marxist social doctrine, the ethos of Russian conspirators, and the romantic-insurrectionist tradition of Polish democracy of the nobleman's kind. The theory of class struggle was interwoven with stanzas out of Mickiewicz's poems. At demonstrations workers sang 'The Red Banner', while the red and white flags they pulled out from under their jackets sported images of Our Lady of Częstochowa . . . there existed socialist doctrine and the practices of socialists, but there was no Polish socialist thought which could bring theoretical assumptions to bear on everyday practice.[14]

In part this was a result of the deformations wrought by partition and the urgency of the issue of Polish independence. But as Michnik pointed out, one of the tragedies of the Polish left was that it had never managed to cut itself off from either the anti-national feeling of Róża Luksemburg's SDKPiL (Social Democracy of the Kingdom of Poland and Lithuania) or from the impact of Stalinism; nor had it ever presented its case and its social achievements as clearly and as coherently as the Church, the right wing and the nationalist camp led by Roman Dmowski had done.

Michnik was nevertheless clear about his definition of the secular-left traditions he had chosen to espouse:

> This left champions the ideas of freedom and tolerance, of individual sovereignty and the emancipation of labour, of a just distribution of income and the right of everyone to an equal start in life. It fights against national chauvinism, obscurantism, xenophobia, lawlessness and social injustice. The programme of this left is the programme of anti-totalitarian socialism.[15]

His insistence on the non-Catholic aspects of Polish culture, on the activities of the liberal Catholics of *Znak* and *Więź* and his insistence on the contribution of the left liberal *inteligencja* to the creation of social and moral values cannot have won him many friends in the Catholic hierarchy. His claim to political, spiritual and cultural kinship with Turowicz and Mazowiecki could well have simply undermined them rather than enhanced Michnik's bargaining power. Still less likely to endear him to the hierarchy was his defence of the independent spiritual qualities of Pax writer Anka Kowalska. Pax, in any shape of form, was not a subject on which the hierarchy was likely to change its mind. The defence of a member of Pax, while intended to show that Church values could be found in all sorts of unlikely places, could have been taken as simply insulting.

Michnik put the best possible face on the Catholic Church, but his book was not entirely without its darker side. Michnik made use of the ideas of Bohdan Cywiński's book *Rodowody Niepokornych* (Genealogies of the Indomitable, 1971) to outline his fears of possible Church conduct and the concept of the Julianic Church. Cywiński used the term Constantinian to denote a Church hierarchy such as that under the Roman Emperor Constantine, in which spiritual and temporal authorities co-operated to share power; the Julianic Church, drawing its name from the Roman Emperor Julian, was however a Church which had lost political power. Michnik and Cywiński both saw that it was possible for the Polish Catholic hierarchy to feel bitterness and resentment over the loss of their inter-war political powers, and frustration that they now held only powers of moral persuasion. They saw that current Church leaders could look back to the inter-war period and see there a model of correct social order. Though their alliance with the state had been interrupted by usurpers, the Church could content itself in the short term with moral authority in opposition while looking forward to a future resumption of its old powers and standing with a new and sympathetic state partner. Michnik quoted a lengthy passage from Cywiński:

Constantinism means participation in state power. Julianism is marked by bitterness and resentment over losing that power, and not by voluntary acquiescence to the loss. This is why the Julianic Church, with all its spiritual power, is never fully in solidarity with society, and never fully identifies with it. It does of course want society to identify itself with the Church, but this is not the same thing. Deprived of its political strength, it fights to preserve its spiritual leadership over the nation. It refuses to accept that there is any way other than the Church to bring about the spiritual or ideological integration of society, and it refuses to acknowledge the existence of any form of opposition other than that it itself promotes and controls. If the existence of another form of opposition becomes quite obvious – one that offers society some kind of ideological alternative, allowing it to come together apart from the Church – then the Julianic Church condemns this opposition, or at least tries to disavow and devalue it in the eyes of public opinion. Never will the Julianic Church be anxious to engage in any form of collaboration against the state with any independent centre of opposi- tionist thought. In its conflict with the secular rulers the Julianic Church prefers to act alone, without partners, towards whom it feels no sense of solidarity.[16]

As a result of this book the intellectuals and the Church (which still did not trust the left-orientated, ex-Party, atheist writers and intellectuals) shifted ground considerably, and the Catholic press by publishing many critical left-wing writers enjoyed a boost to its prestige and social standing. In particular *Tygodnik Powszechny*, edited by Jerzy Turowicz, and *Więź*, edited by Tadeusz Mazowiecki, published opposition intellectuals. However, J. J. Lipski has warned against reading Michnik's phrase 'secular left' as relating to a 'putative political group' rather than to a 'certain socio-cultural formation':

> This is as if one were to speak about a 'Catholic right', uniting the fascist Bolesław Piasecki, the liberal Stefan Kisielewski, the democratic neo-nationalist Aleksander Hall and several other similarly chosen people into a group and then claiming they were engaged in a common conspiracy.[17]

But equally, it was perhaps naive of the social democratic liberal-left in KOR to imagine that while for them under communism notions of left and right no longer made sense, this was the case for all Poles, or that this would always be the case. One of the problems Michnik and the *lewica laicka* faced was that the Party had hijacked the language of the left and turned it into nonsense. In September 1980 T. G. Ash wrote:

> If asked 'How do you recognise a leftist opposition intellectual in East Central Europe today?' the unkind answer might be: 'The leftist intellectual is the one who says that categories of left and right no longer have any significance in East Central Europe'. The right does not say that; and by now it is certainly possible to talk of a 'right' opposition. Indeed, for good or ill, the fashion in oppositional thinking . . . is now for liberal, libertarian, conservative, or revived pre-war nationalist/national-democratic/populist argument and/or rhetoric.[18]

In the successive political crises that marked post-war Polish life, the Catholic episcopate had consistently refused to do much more than defend itself and its position in Polish society: instead of backing protests it called for calm and order, insisting on sober hard work and care of the family and 'national values' rather than political action. There was no element of radical democratic ideology from the episcopate. The flock were sheep to be led. Wyszyński was, as far as possible, independent of Rome, and insisted that the Church in Poland had survived for a thousand years in spite of Poland's turbulent history. If it kept out of secular affairs and left politics to the Pope and the government, he was sure it would remain for at least another thousand years. It was no accident that Gierek supported the extension of Wyszyński's office when he reached seventy-five. In return for a promise that there would be no collectivisation of agriculture and for substantial institutional freedoms, the Church did not rock the political boat, did not openly side with dissidents and oppositionists, did not criticize the government, and several members of the Church hierarchy warned against godless Marxists and Jews.

There was a very strong tendency for what Michnik called *Paxizacja*, that is there was always a pressure for the Church to be integrated into the existing political structure simply by virtue of its insistence on the *status quo*. This current of thinking was a powerful influence on the leading conservative (and often nationalist) members of the episcopate and the central elements of the Church bureaucracy: Cardinal Glemp, Bishop Dąbrowski (secretary to the episcopate), Abbot Orszulik (episcopal spokesman), Bishop Modzelewski of Warsaw and Bishop Kaczmarek of Gdańsk. These men had all been handpicked by Wyszyński and remained true to his picture of the world and his view of the role the Church should play in Poland. Ranged against them in a loose (and not always reliable) alliance were the Catholic positivists: Pope John Paul II, Archbishop Macharski of Kraków, Abbot Józef Tischner, the liberal Catholic *inteligencja* of KIK, the Znak group and the writers and readers of *Tygodnik Powszechny*. Though they did not trust Michnik and the *lewica laicka*, these people were not afraid of the new populist trade union movement and were not quite so nervous of dealing with the secular left.

There can be little doubt that Michnik's book exerted a powerful influence throughout Polish society and enabled the non-violent alliance of intellectuals, workers and the Church. However, it placed the Church in a difficult position by showing what it had not been doing under communism and by saying out loud that even a liberal atheist like Michnik had expectations of the Church – expectations based in the teachings of the Church. The alliance between liberals and the Church could only be a temporary strategic alliance on all sides, but at the time it looked as if Poland had suddenly discovered something about itself, its spiritual life and its potential that was permanent. While the connection remained important from the mid-1970s until the collapse of communism in 1989 it was never without its uneasy moments. For Michnik it was always the case that 'all that is precious in Polish culture has arisen at the crossroads of its great historical paths: in the encounter between the Christian spirit and the free thinking spirit, in the mutually enriching conflict between these two opposed worlds'.[19] However, after 1976 a new independent underground publishing community developed in Poland and began to make extensive political and publishing connections in Paris, New York, London, Stockholm and West Berlin. Intellectually respected journals like *Zapis* and *Res Publica* began to appear, and independent publishing houses like NOWa developed extensive lists of banned books and writers, most of whom were still formally anchored in the ethos of a *lewica laicka*. As this new independent area of publishing and intellectual life grew, so the focus of Polish intellectual life again shifted away from the Church and the attitudes of the hierarchy towards the *lewica laicka* once again hardened.

For all its intentional naivety *The Church, the Left – Dialogue* is vital to twentieth-century Polish intellectual history since it marks a decisive change in mentality and a turn in the political climate. Michnik faced the Church with one basic question: 'Does the Church genuinely seek freedom for every human being, including believers in other religions as well as non-believers? Or does it only seek freedom for itself, its own faith, its own schools, its own press?[20] Though Michnik believed that the concept of a secular state was anti-totalitarian rather than anti-Catholic and that the conflict between the liberal intelligentsia and the Church was now a closed chapter in European history, this was clearly not what the Polish hierarchy thought. Michnik had put the Church in an awkward position. To his question the hierarchy could make no unequivocal answer. While Michnik and the liberal *lewica laicka* could tolerate the Church because they were not part of it or dependent on it, their values, though they coincided with those of the Church in general terms, did not acknowledge the temporal and spiritual power and authority of the Church. The Church could not tolerate the lay left since the left sought to be independent of the Church and as such focused on values and authorities outside Church control. Though in the short term the Church could accommodate a temporary alliance with Michnik and his kind, this was not the ultimate aim of the Church.

Without doubt the major achievement of Michnik's book was not that it embarrassed the Church, but that it demonstrated very simply and clearly that revisionists, ex-Party members, non-Party socialists and neo-Positivist liberal Catholics were all very close in their concerns. Michnik made the point that the most creative and active critics and the most wily and persistent oppositionists did not come from within the Catholic Church, where most western observers might have expected them, but from the secular left. While the Church had been busy protecting itself, the non-Catholic, often leftist, critics had begun to speak on behalf of the whole of Polish society, including the Church. The *lewica laicka* were often highly exposed ex-Party writers, but as Michnik repeatedly said, in the formation of independent public opinion, writers and their works played a decisive role.

Michnik claimed for the Polish liberal left specific works from a wide-ranging list of distinguished and internationally renowned contemporary writers. Among many others he included: Zofia Nałkowska, Maria Dąbrowska, Zbigniew Herbert, Czesław Miłosz, Antoni Słonimski, Adam Ważyk, Stanisław Ossowski, J. J. Szczepański, Kazimierz Brandys, Gustaw Herling-Grudziński, Tadeusz Borowski, Wiktor Woroszylski, Jacek Bocheński, Tadeusz Konwicki, Leszek Kołakowski, Oskar Lange, Edward Lipiński, Włodzimierz Brus, Krzysztof Pomian, Bronisław Baczko, Jan Strzelecki, Władysław Bieńkowski, Witold Kuła, Maria Hirszowicz, Stanisław Barańczak, Ryszard Krynicki, Adam Zagajewski, Bohdan Cywiński, Kazimierz Wierzyński, Juliusz Mieroszewski, Marek Hłasko, and Witold Gombrowicz. These were some of the best minds of their time. The inability of the Party to win the sympathy and retain the loyalty of intellectuals who were generally sympathetic to the cause of socialism, and who, as independent intellectuals, knew they stood to lose financially and socially in any capitalist 'open market', is a measure of the Party's failure. That the Party could not make use of their goodwill, could not make any effective use of their talent, could not absorb or respond to their record of life in the People's Republic of Poland is an indication of the total lack of originality and intellectual dynamism within a party crippled and made tame by the stifling hand of Stalin.

While Michnik was not prepared to praise Catholic writers simply because the Church had clashed with the communist state, he was prepared to praise Catholic writers (even those belonging to Pax) who had helped create 'a broad base for a culture independent of official norms and moulds', in particular the liberal Catholic Znak deputies Tadeusz Mazowiecki, Stanisław Stomma, Jerzy Zawieyski, the Catholic journals *Więź* and *Tygodnik Powszechny* and writers and editors Stefan Kisielewski, Jacek Woźniakowski, Anna Morawska, Hanna Malewska and Antoni Gołubiew, and the editors of the émigré journal *Kultura*. Michnik saw these people as his natural allies. For him, without a close reading of the works of these particular writers and editors (Catholic and *lewica laicka* alike) it was simply 'impossible to understand the moral and intellectual dilemmas of Polish oppositionist thought'. For what they held in common, rather than the differences that kept them apart, Michnik saw them all as New Evolutionists.[21]

Michnik pointed out that the first task of the various factions of the opposition movement was not to fight each other but to find common ground and link up with the Polish working class. Michnik felt that the only way to do this was outside the structures of the Party, which could be relied on only to destroy their efforts, but also outside the Church, which though its moral values were often inspiring, could not be trusted to follow through reforms from which it did not benefit or which it did not control. The opposition movement that grew up in the late 1970s comprised a wide range of opposition opinion but was led largely by the intellectuals of KOR (Workers' Defence Committee). They specialized in fronting legal cases for accused workers, and their membership included a large number of writers: J. J. Lipski, Jerzy Andrzejewski, Stanisław Barańczak, to name but a few.[22]

Michnik's achievement was that, while he distinguished between the pre-war and post-war Church and enlisted the more enlightened members of the *lewica laicka* and the hierarchy to a common cause, he also very boldly identified in literature a civil society and a repository of moral values, a focus of authority and political thought that lay outside the control of both the Church and the Party. At the same time he made the Church's ambition to regain its old powers, political, social and national, clear. Perhaps for the first time it became possible to see the post-war Church as an organization with a political ambition. The partnership of Church and state, though it was many times sorely strained, could admit a third member only with great difficulty – indeed the impact of Solidarność was a severe challenge to hegemony of the Church. While in 1980–1 the Church repeatedly underwrote the promises of the Party in the name of social accord and Christian charity, its persistent espousal of the role of honest broker between the Solidarność and the consistently dishonest authorities was hardly disinterested. The conduct of the hierarchy from the mid-1970s was filled with indications of intent, but the full extent of the hierarchy's Julianist ambition was not to be revealed until the collapse of communism in 1989.

In May 1977 KOR began publishing information about the intensification of the Party's action against dissident organizations and opinion, highlighting the fact that the death of student activist Stanisław Pyjas in Kraków on 7 May 1977 was linked to the undercover activities of the security services. Michnik, Kuroń and J. J. Lipski, the editors of *Biuletyn Informacyjny*, were all immediately indicted, accused of purveying false information with the intention of causing harm to the People's Republic of Poland. Michnik and Kuroń were arrested to prevent them attending demonstrations in Kraków, and a slanderous campaign against the defendants was started in the Press. The charges against the defendants were changed to collaboration with 'hostile centres' abroad, lest the issue of truth and the exact nature of the false information should be discussed in open court.[23]

Inevitably the defendants were all convicted, but almost immediately a campaign to get them released was started. Perhaps the most famous aspect of the campaign was the week-long fast at St Marcin's church on Piwna Street in Warsaw's Old Town. The eight people involved in the fast represented a wide range of opposition opinion including the wife and the sister of one of the imprisoned workers from Radom; Bohdan Cywiński, the editor in chief of the Kraków Catholic journal *Znak*; Jerzy Geresz, a Warsaw mathematics student; Father Aleksander Hauke-Ligowski, a Dominican priest from Poznań; Barbara Toruńczyk, the Warsaw sociologist; Henryk Wujec, a Warsaw based physicist and activist in KIK (Clubs of the Catholic Intelligentsia); Eugeniusz Kloc, a student of literature at Warsaw University; Ojzasz Szechter, Michnik's father, a former communist, an editor in a state publishing house; Joanna Szczęsna, a Warsaw journalist; Stanisław Barańczak, poet and university teacher from Poznań; Zenon Pałka, a Wrocław technician; Kazimierz Świton, a radio technician from Katowice. The spokesman for the group was Tadeusz Mazowiecki, editor in chief of the Catholic journal *Więź*. It was a mixed group of impeccable social credentials. Predictably the authorities attempted to exploit the fact that Szechter was Jewish. The fast focused attention both inside and outside Poland on the attempted repression. Michnik and the other

KOR activists in gaol as a result of the events in Radom and Ursus in June 1976 were amnestied in July 1977. The fast at St Marcin's was the first effective contact between the Church and the oppositionists.

At about this time KOR began publishing *KOR Communiqué* with Michnik as one of the editorial board. In August 1977 the independent publisher NOWa began production and was soon producing the journal *Zapis*, a serious literary journal of high quality edited by a wide-ranging but eminently respectable literary board. Michnik was chiefly responsible for recommending books for publication and for finding new materials; indeed it was through Michnik, with his substantial connections in intellectual circles, that many manuscripts came to NOWa. NOWa brought out Michnik's *Shadows of Forgotten Ancestors*. NOWa showed the way: within a very short time there were several other independent publishing houses including at least three that were closely allied to the Catholic Church.

In September 1977 KOR changed its name to KOR-KSS (Committee Defending Workers-Social Self-Defence Committee), acknowledging that it had broadened its sphere of action. As part of this change the organization began to publish a journal called *Głos* edited by Antoni Macierewicz. Michnik may have been the most articulate spokesman and the most lucid essayist that KOR-KSS had, but even within KOR-KSS his opinions and beliefs were strongly contested. Even before the first issue of *Głos* had appeared the editorial board were split over Macierewicz's rejection of an article by Michnik, who was in fact a member of the editorial board. Macierewicz saw Michnik's article as an attempt to reach an accommodation with the authorities and accused Kuroń and Michnik of attempting to exploit factions within the Party rather than to confront and defeat the Party as a whole. Macierewicz felt it was very important to get the first issue 'right' in terms of its stance. Michnik argued that the first issue was not so crucial that it could not present a range of possibilities – right or wrong. Neither side would back down or compromise. The writer Jerzy Andrzejewski sided with Macierewicz and the other editors, against Michnik. Within a short time Michnik, Kuroń and several others resigned from the editorial board. After the resignations *Głos* developed a suspicious and even hostile attitude towards the leftist KOR-KSS, and moved further to the right, towards a closer association with the Church and ROPCiO. Michnik, Kuroń and the others came to dominate the *Information Bulletin* and *KOR-KSS Communiqué* – which, as these were the official KOR-KSS journals, did not please *Głos,* who felt their independent social initiative, along with its journals, had been hijacked by the communists. Although there was no break between *Głos* and KOR-KSS, it was clear that a polarization within the democratic opposition movement was beginning.

The strategy and tactics of KOR-KSS's advice to the worker oppositionists and free trade unionists bore all the hallmarks of Michnik's gradualist thinking – indeed it is generally acknowledged that although KOR-KSS documents were the result of intense debate, they were largely authored by Michnik. Formal strike committees and workers' councils were to be avoided because they were easy targets for police action which left workers without leadership and because they were easily subverted by police agents. This was to be the same for journals and editorial committees too. As part of Michnik's attempt to 'live in dignity' everything had to be open to public scrutiny. Mimeographed issues of KOR-KSS's *Biuletyn Informacyjny*, in which police harassment of workers and breaches of the various Polish laws and international charters were monitored, were absolutely open. The journal even listed on the back page the names, addresses and phone numbers of the editorial committee: Adam Michnik, phone Warsaw 28-43-55.

Michnik's idea was that if workers could not produce their own unions and committees, they were to infiltrate existing structures (union branches and official self-management structures) and gradually render them representative. They were not to put demands on management, as these were to be deferred until they could be put publicly and supported by the irrefutable advice of professional economists, lawyers and engineers.

KOR-KSS also carefully exploited the discontent and cynicism in the middle ranks of the PZPR, and took care to stress the importance of a durable working relationship and compromise between KOR-KSS and the Party. The western press probably overstressed the importance the Polish workers attached to KOR-KSS. For most of them it was a distant noise and barely influenced them at all until the great upheavals of 1980. The workers were suspicious that so many of the membership were ex-Party and still clearly socialist in their outlook, and many listened to the rumour that KOR-KSS was a 'Zionist organization'. While influence on the bulk of the population was slight KOR-KSS had some influence on the Free Trade Unions of the Coast, at Ursus, the Silesian coal mines and the shipyards.

KOR-KSS was Michnik's 'new evolutionism' in action. Poles would cease to address the Party and address society itself. Civil society would steadily emancipate itself by organizing outside or alongside the state institutions, by simply ignoring or bypassing official structures, by gradually expanding the range of its activities and democratic and representative practices. It was a rolling, ongoing process of self organization. It was Michnik's hope that by rolling back the powers of the state while keeping the Party as a kind of umbrella Poles would be able to govern themselves and at the same time reassure the Soviets by presenting an economically, socially and politically stable Poland. On the surface, it would look as if nothing had changed, while underneath, the reality would be that the Party controlled nothing and was little more than a nominal leadership responsible only for state ritual. Michnik believed that 'New Evolutionism' was unfaithful to the church of Moscow, but faithful to the scripture of Marxism. As the collapse of communism and the Soviet Union was simply unimaginable at this stage,

Michnik thought his only chance of success lay in the long term, in harnessing popular discontent and in helping enlightened liberals to power within the PZPR and enacting a liberating and 'enlightened programme of socialist absolutism'.[24]

Michnik insisted that while revisionism had failed, it nevertheless had a positive and lasting effect on Polish intellectual and political life in that it had mobilized the *inteligencja* in an attempt to change the political orientation of the Party, and in that revisionist literature was of lasting importance in 'propagating persecuted ideas and defending truth and humanistic values'. The problem was that by the mid-1970s the few surviving revisionists still living in Poland were isolated from each other, from the working class, from all political life, from the Church, and as such were easily defeated by the Party. Michnik criticized the Catholics and the revisionists in that they both expected to reform the Party in some way and as such expected reform to be handed down to them from above, by some overarching authority. Building on Kołakowski's 'Hope and Hopelessness', Michnik and Kuroń developed a theory, not of confrontation or reforming alliance, but of gradual pragmatic evolution. As Kuroń was later to put it, 'Don't waste your energy burning down Party committees, just build your own.'

In the summer of 1978 the first issue of *Krytyka* appeared. This journal, whose title referred to an old social democratic PPS journal published in Kraków around the turn of the century, was closely connected to KOR-KSS, and Michnik was on the editorial board. In October 1978 Michnik was among a group of KOR-KSS activists who met Czech dissidents from Charter 77 in the Karkonosze mountains. Unfortunately at the third series of meetings the Czech dissidents were detained. KOR-KSS protested at the arrests and drew world attention to the brutality of the Czech police. After this Polish police attacks on 'independent lecturers' became increasingly frequent and it became clear that they had been targeted by the authorities.

On 16 October 1978, to the surprise of the whole world, the Vatican College of Cardinals broke with tradition and instead of electing an Italian, elevated Cardinal Karol Wojtyła of Kraków to Pope. For many on the Polish democratic left Cardinal Wyszyński, the Polish Primate, was an anti-communist conservative, rooted in the rural, traditional, paternalistic attitudes of the pre-war Polish Catholic Church who had found Vatican II's line on communism too soft. Michnik described Wyszyński as a man of monologue rather than dialogue: 'Modernity and the language of human rights left a foul scent for him.'[25] Michnik saw Wojtyła, who was now placed above Wyszyński in the hierarchy, as a very different personality: a man still rooted in the nationalist tradition, but who shunned nationalist rhetoric, a poet, philosopher, playwright, essayist, actor, who opposed communism in the name of human rights; a leader who understood the nature of tolerant, secular pluralistic society, and who maintained his reservations about it.

Michnik was also very clear that the election of the first Polish Pope, a man who, unlike his predecessors, knew the Polish situation intimately, would work a change in the Catholic hierarchy, and also in public thinking, that the Polish government would not be able to control.

The Party may not have been able to control public thought, but that did not prevent it from trying to squash independent organizations. In January 1979, during a meeting of TKN (Flying University), Jacek Kuroń's home was broken into by activist students from the Socialist Union of Polish Students and students from the Academy of Physical Education: several people, including Kuroń's wife and Michnik were hurt in an affray and Kuroń's father had to go to hospital with an aggravated heart condition. The Ministry of Justice (who were given a list of the names of the assailants) refused to investigate the incident adequately. In February Michnik and Barańczak were arrested at Kraków railway station while on their way to give a TKN lecture. The following day the security services burst in on a lecture by Michnik and used tear gas to clear the house. The next day Michnik and three associates were attacked and beaten in the street by a goon squad set up by the security service. On 3 April 1979, though his lectures on the Contemporary History of Poland had drawn a record attendance of 180 in the previous year and were scheduled for at least two more meetings, Michnik announced that in order not to provoke further attacks he was suspending his TKN lectures.[26]

In April 1979 Kuroń warned in *Biuletyn Informacyjny* of a possible explosion of popular anger against the regime, and pointed out that while the Soviets might invade Poland, the Polish authorities, if faced with the death of Party members at the hands of the mob, would not necessarily shrink from large-scale violence. Kuroń was arguing that KOR-KSS and the oppositionists should be prepared to make peace with whichever faction of the Party survived any upheaval. Such an attitude won him no friends in *Głos* and ROPCiO, and further polarized the wings of the democratic opposition movement. Indeed Kuroń's articles had hit on a constant theme, and for many a substantial weakness, in Michnik's writing: whether or not to talk to the corrupt authorities, and how to do so from a position of moral strength that would be recognizable to the Party. There was a constant tension in Michnik's writing between what is morally correct and what is politically necessary. The issue of whether or not to talk to the corrupt authorities was for Michnik a question of moral absolutism versus political pragmatism. For the right-wingers and nationalists of KPN Michnik had failed to get beyond this point, and had written little or nothing about economics and the economic strategies that should be put in place once the Party had been brought under control. Michnik on the other hand assumed that these issues were tied in some unspecified way to the notion of moral strength and that solutions would emerge of their own volition from the unpredictable soup of communist Poland.

The argument was a very Polish one. This was a question that generations of Poles had struggled with through the years of partition and occupation. In June 1979 the satirical feuilletonist Piotr Wierzbicki published his essay *A Treatise on Ticks* in *Zapis* and took up the subject again. He characterized those who co-operated with the authorities, on any level, as ticks. Michnik in his reply to Wierzbicki, published in the same issue of *Zapis*, never doubted that Polish ticks existed. However, he felt that comment as divisive as this was premature. He insisted it was too easy to condemn everyone who co-operated with the regime as ticks and he pointed out that many of those who conducted scientific and medical research, who preserved cultural and national values, had no choice but to co-operate with the authorities. He said these people should be attracted to KOR-KSS rather than repelled by criticism and ostracism, and he stated very clearly that KOR-KSS should regard all those who were not openly opposed to KOR-KSS as silently supporting it. He also warned of 'dissident conceit', of holier-than-thou-ism. For Michnik, Lipski and Kuroń there could be no question of KOR-KSS deserting its stance of resistance to totalitarian power. They argued that instead of accommodation, their policy had to be the creation of a broad sphere of co-operative public debate and civil liberty in opposition to the 'apparatus of coercion'.[27]

Relations between the nascent wings of the opposition movement soured further in September 1979. As KOR-KSS was transforming itself into a very active organization throughout Poland, it also began to debate the possibility of sending an observer to the Second Socialist International and to the Liberal International. Given that KOR-KSS was 'composed of persons of various ideological and political orientations', the social-democratic tendencies of the founding membership of KOR-KSS made it inevitable that *Głos* and ROPCiO would protest at any connection with international socialism.[28] As it turned out, the debate was futile and nothing came of the idea: neither of these organizations wanted contact with KOR-KSS, presumably because they saw it as politically ambiguous and at worst anti-socialist in intent.

Although a political activist, Michnik was also a theorist and strategist, and it was precisely his ability to think and to organize that the Party feared. In February 1980, at the Eighth Plenum of the PZPR the 'moderate' Politburo member, Tadeusz Grabski, named Michnik as one of the ringleaders of KOR-KSS and said that a judicial investigation had been launched into KOR-KSS activities. On 28 August 1980, just as the government was beginning to get serious about the negotiations in the Gdańsk shipyards, the public prosecutor in Warsaw issued warrants for the arrest of Michnik and several other members of KOR-KSS on the grounds of 'criminal intent'. Michnik had recently become an adviser to Solidarność. He was arrested, then released after protests from Wałęsa, then rearrested every forty-eight hours. On 1 September all the prisoners were released. Later in September 1980 Michnik attempted to make clear to the strikers and negotiators of Solidarność what was at issue:

What does all this show? It is clear that every attempt to rule against the wishes of society has led to disaster; it is also clear that every attempt to overthrow communist rule in Poland is seen as an attack on the interests of the USSR. Nevertheless pluralism in all spheres of social life is possible: removal of preventive censorship is possible, rational economic reform and more just social policies are possible, a competitive press and television speaking the truth are possible, freedom of scientific research, the autonomy of universities are possible, social control and organized defence of consumers' interests are possible, independent courts and a police that does not beat people up are possible . . . But we have to wrest and extort these things from the government because no nation has ever been given its rights as a gift. Yet while wresting and extorting we should take care not to destroy what makes the Polish state; not a sovereign independent state perhaps, but still a state without which our lot would have been much worse.[29]

Although he consistently advocated compromise with the authorities, he made it clear that he did not trust those in power to keep to agreements. Michnik was one of the first to realize that Solidarność could not sit back and simply defend itself. It had to push the government for ever greater reforms and changes, permanently to alter the environment in which Solidarność existed so that defence was not necessary. But Michnik was also aware that he was opening a can of worms, not only by threatening the interests of the USSR, but by releasing long-suppressed ambitions within Polish society. Within the opposition movement, long before the Solidarność Congress of September 1981 it was clear that the left and right were emerging from the democratic opposition movement. Michnik and his *lewica laicka* were increasingly ranged in opposition to the supporters of KPN, nationalist fundamentalists and fans of Stefan Kurowski. Michnik had enough contact with the Polish right-wingers of KPN (particularly Leszek Moczulski) to know that Polish reformers were riding several tigers.

On 9 February 1981 a Polish Press Agency communiqué announced that Michnik, in addition to being charged with violations of the criminal code, was also to be investigated under the charges levelled against KOR-KSS three years previously. Throughout March 1981 the Party-backed Grunwald Patriotic Union, under the guidance of Moczar, warned of the treachery of the Polish Zionists, claimed that Jews had made a major contribution to the abuses of power in the 1950s, and revealed (not for the first time) that Michnik's real name was Szechter (or Schechter) and that he had been adopted. Radio Moscow mentioned Michnik by name and warned that KOR-KSS was run by Zionists and their friends. On 6 March 1981, while formal charges were made against four KOR-KSS members held in gaol, the security services tried to arrest Michnik in Wrocław on charges of 'slandering the state'. Michnik, however, refused to co-operate and the local Solidarność provided him with a Workers' Guard. Later that month there was a rally in

Warsaw to commemorate the anniversary of the March 1968 student demonstrations. General Moczar, who was now restored to the Politburo, launched another attempt to bring charges of sedition against Michnik. In response the miners of Wałbrzych threatened to strike and Michnik announced that he was ignoring a summons to present himself at the public prosecutor's office.

The Party were not the only ones unhappy about Michnik's activities. In January 1981 the Revd Alojzy Orszulik, director of the episcopate press office, commented to foreign journalists that it was particularly necessary for KOR-KSS to behave reasonably in the present situation: the implication was that they were, in some vague and unspecified way, behaving badly. A Vatican spokesman promptly disowned Orszulik's comments and on 5 January 1981 Primate Cardinal Wyszyński accepted a delegation from KOR-KSS which included Michnik, thus signalling the end of any uncertainty the Church might have had about the role KOR-KSS had in advising Solidarność.

In May 1981 Michnik was in Otwock where the police had detained and severely beaten two people. This was the latest in a long string of violent incidents involving the Otwock police, and now locals wanted revenge. Solidarność activists alerted Mazowsze Solidarność who immediately sent Jan Walc and Zbigniew Romaszewski. They managed to restrain the mob, which had surrounded the local police station and wanted to lynch a police corporal and to burn down the police station with a prosecutor and the local police captain inside. Walc and Romaszewski had debated such a possibility within KOR-KSS and had no intention of allowing violence. They talked to the crowd until they were hoarse, then entered the police station, where the police had already put out two attempted fires. ZOMO riot police waited nearby but it was clear that any move on their part would mean death to those inside the police station. As the little wooden police station was again doused in petrol Michnik and Zbigniew Bujak arrived. Michnik climbed up on to a car and, quoting a recent description of him in *Trybuna Ludu*, shouted: 'My name is Adam Michnik: I am an anti-socialist element.' He persuaded the crowd to release the policemen by recounting how the police had beaten him, and pleaded with the crowd not to use violence, but to release the policemen unharmed. The crowd asked for guarantees that those who were guilty would be punished, but Michnik said that there could be no guarantees and that only through solidarity would they bring the police under social control. Early in the morning the crowd dispersed. The captain of police saluted Michnik, thanked him and offered his hand. Michnik shook his hand. Next day the petrol-soaked police station burnt down and the Party press accused KOR-KSS and Solidarność of inciting the riot.[30]

Throughout the summer of 1981 the Polish economy continued its rapid disintegration. Ration cards could not be honoured and there were hunger marches. Some commentators, though Solidarność had suspended strikes and had no control over the economy, maintained that the union had gone too far. Others complained that it had not gone far enough or fast enough. Certainly by the time of the first Solidarność Congress in the sports hall at Oliwa in September 1981, there were those within the union who were very frustrated by the inability of the Party to deal honestly, by the reticence of the Church in not siding openly with the democratic movement, and with the union for not confronting the Party head-on. Wałęsa became involved in discussions about about how the union might enter power politics and the spectre of Solidarność actually seizing power was floated, particularly by the membership of the right-wing nationalist KPN (Confederation for an Independent Poland).[31]

Michnik's first requirement for success (harnessing popular discontent) had long ago been met. But it had begun to look as if Moscow would prevent any liberal intellectual reformers from coming to power within the Party. Indeed, it began to look as if such a creature no longer existed within the ranks of the Party. Even the criticisms of Mieczysław Rakowski were, in the end, negated by his adherence to the Party line. It may be that Michnik's New Evolutionism had gone as far as it could within that particular political climate. But in any case, though the authorities had lost every argument and behaved disgracefully at every opportunity, they could neither sort out the mess they had created nor could they abdicate power. The military coup and declaration of Martial Law on 13 December 1981 put an end to the Party's brainlock and to the whole experiment in New Evolutionism. Depressing and frustrating though it was, the leadership of General Jaruzelski was to be the culmination of the Party's ability to spoil and its inability to create.

When the military government published its first list of internees in December 1981 it was clear that there was a straight fifty-fifty split between KOR-KSS and Solidarity – which, given the difference in the sizes of the two organizations, was remarkable. Michnik had already spent more than three years in prison at various times. Although he was again interned in December 1981, he was only formally arrested on 3 September 1982. He was imprisoned first in an internment camp at Białołęka, then transferred to the isolation wing of Mokotów prison, then to Barczewo prison. It was announced that he was to stand trial with Jacek Kuroń, Henry Wujec and Jan Lityński and J. J. Lipski – all members of KOR-KSS – accused of 'preparing the violent overthrow of Poland's socio-political system'.

Imprisonment gave Michnik the chance to write, and he embarked on a series of essays and open letters that once again displayed his characteristic generosity of spirit and political determination. In a 1982 analysis of Piłsudski's legacy he lamented the destruction of the social-democratic tradition within the Polish left: 'The achievements of Polish socialism were marked with the specific stamp of the Polish, chivalrous, freedom-oriented tradition which consistently reappeared in the ideology of the workers' revolution. This atmosphere remained in the PPS as long as the party existed.'[32] Michnik concluded that the moral strength of the PPS may well have been its naivety in the face of the power of Endecja nationalism, the Church and the ruling military regime. This naivety appealed to Michnik's own Ghandi-esque character. However, he had to admit that for post-war socialists, little of use was left of PPS traditions:

> Indeed, in Poland the word *socialism* is both discredited and ambiguous. From this point of view it should be abandoned. Nonetheless, the Polish workers' movement and its party, the PPS, which upheld the ideals of the rights of working people and of national independence, the principle of 'Poland's freedom and the freedom of man in Poland', used the word for decades. It is true that the PPS's socialism was the child of another era, the product of different social and intellectual circumstances.[33]

Michnik clung stubbornly to his use of the word 'socialism'.

The Party (which Michnik now referred to as a trade union for rulers) was unsure about how to proceed with show trials. In November 1983 General Kiszczak, minister for internal affairs, who claimed to have been attempting to seduce Michnik's partner while Michnik was in prison, offered him the chance to emigrate – Christmas on the Côte d'Azur. Michnik refused and penned a withering attack on the honour, morality and mentality of Kiszczak:

> (1) To admit one's disregard for the law so openly one would have to be a fool. (2) To offer a man who has been held in prison for two years the Côte d'Azur, in exchange for his moral suicide, one would have to be a swine. (3) To believe that I could accept such a proposal is to imagine that everyone is a police collaborator.[34]

Michnik was released with the suspension of Martial Law, then arrested again in 1984. He did not waste away in jail. In spite of the strict regime of isolation Michnik used his time to produce a long series of passionate, tightly argued, wide-ranging essays on politics, literature, morality and Poland's situation, most of which were smuggled out for clandestine publication. His essay on Thomas Mann and his reaction to Nazism clearly presented events of the past through the prism of the present. Michnik summed up Mann's attitude, describing him as a kind of Don Quixote, struggling endlessly to make the world a better place, revolted by Nazism, but desperate to stay out of politics. Michnik was able to produce from Mann's experience not only 'a few ideas worth noting' but also counsel for his own hours of despair:

> First: Do not worry about the future – this is the only possible life strategy in today's times. Second: Immerse yourself in innocent and internally equanimous work – this is the only thing that can help us deal with this nightmare. Create one's work calmly and persistently amid upheavals, coups and threats. Third: Be

one's own signpost when there are no other signposts. Fourth: Know how to wait and endure; know how to create decent works in sad, wicked, barrenly resistant times. Fifth: Maintain the bravery and the patience that Schopenhauer so beautifully associated with courage. Sixth: Call baseness, base.[35]

Michnik was amnestied in 1986. In total he had spent over six years in prison.

Michnik played an important part in the round-table talks leading to the 'almost democratic' elections of 1989. These talks were something of a shock for General Jaruzelski who had assumed, as Security reports told him, that Michnik was just a hooligan. Almost at first contact Jaruzelski discovered that he had much more in common with Michnik than with Party hard-liners. Michnik for his part seems to have realized that, compared with the illiberal 'new radicals' of KPN, the hard-liners of Solidarność who had resisted all dealings with the Party, demanding that the round-table talks be boycotted, and the increasingly sultanic Wałęsa, Jaruzelski was someone to whom he could actually talk. But this was no dewy-eyed romance. Michnik has consistently supported amnesty for former communists, but is dismissive of their claims that they were frustrated reformers and that someone else was responsible for the mess the Party created. Michnik has often remarked that all communists were reformers, that there was no other kind of communist. The party taught that it must always reform itself, but in fact was incapable because it had no machinery for reform. The reformer might have been subjectively right, but the party, in all its inertia, was always objectively right and that was an overpowering factor in maintaining the *status quo*. No matter what individual members may have thought or wanted, the Party was deeply conservative and reactionary: 'If they were all reformers, where did communism come from?' Michnik insists that unlike the actions of the democratic opposition, any Party talk of socialism with a human face was by definition a nonsense, an argument for what he called 'totalitarianism with the teeth knocked out'.[36]

Release from gaol and the advent of even a limited form of democracy meant a whole new range of problems for Michnik. By the summer of 1989 'socialism' had virtually disappeared from the language of the democratic opposition.[37] Unless they were covered by the umbrella of Solidarność sponsorship Michnik's aims could not be stressed simply because the vocabulary was tarred as a creeping apology for communism – a fact which was to play into the hands of Wałęsa after the elections, when he split Solidarity and turned against his erstwhile advisers. It was increasingly clear that social democracy was not a saleable commodity simply because the Party had appropriated the terms 'socialism', 'socialist' and 'social democracy'. In May 1989 Michnik launched and became editor in chief of Solidarność's *Gazeta Wyborcza*, which, though still subject to censorship was still eastern

Europe's first independent opposition newspaper. At the same time, in June 1989 Michnik was elected as a deputy to the Sejm.

That Solidarność had survived so long without being crippled by its own internal political divisions is nothing short of miraculous. Rivalry between on the one hand the members of ROPCiO, the increasingly nationalist *Głos* group, the Catholics and KPN, and on the other the social-democratic groupings, had become increasingly bitter. With Solidarność's electoral success at the June 1989 elections to the Sejm and Senate, the gap between Wałęsa and Michnik began to open up. On the very eve of the election Cardinal Glemp issued a clear warning that Wałęsa should distance himself from his former advisers when he snubbed the *lewica laicka* by receiving in audience the Christian Democrats standing against Michnik and Kuroń, the official Solidarity candidates. Michnik and Kuroń were elected anyway, but Wałęsa blamed Michnik for the fact that the Communist Party had been split into two rather than three parts by the election. Michnik, for his part, was mystified and unaware of any plans Wałęsa might have had for the Communist Party.[38]

It was well known that Michnik favoured a slow transition to a market economy and disliked the Balcerowicz reforms as too abrupt. At the start of 1990, knowing full well that Polish workers were complaining precisely because the economic reforms put in place by Leszek Balcerowicz were having a devastating effect, Wałęsa began to proclaim that 'egg-head intellectuals' like Michnik were blocking reforms and that Mazowiecki's government was moving too slowly. Michnik's *Gazeta Wyborcza* published a series of unflattering and downright critical articles about Wałęsa, including comments on his manners and on his churlish refusal to travel to Warsaw to meet Czechoslovak President Václav Havel. Hurt by the behaviour of the intellectuals, in March 1990 the increasingly Piłsudski-like Wałęsa appointed the recently returned exile, literary historian and broadcaster, Zdzisław Najder, as head of the Solidarność Citizens' Committees, directly responsible to Wałęsa. Virtually all of Wałęsa's intellectual advisers expressed consternation at this decision.

Almost immediately, and probably on Najder's advice, Wałęsa launched a bitter and wounding attack on Michnik and Solidarność's liberal wing, on leftist intellectuals like Andrzej Wajda and on the government and leadership of liberal-Catholic Prime Minister Tadeusz Mazowiecki. Wałęsa announced that he was declaring *wojna* (war) on Mazowiecki's government and made *akceleracja* (acceleration) the new buzz-word. It became clear that Wałęsa, in spite of protestations to the contrary, intended to run for president, and that, if elected, was prepared to consider the possibility of calling in the army to control the democratic government. In May 1990 Wałęsa stated clearly that if he were president he would not hesitate to rule by decree.

In preparation for his presidential campaign, on 1 June 1990 Wałęsa, again probably acting on the advice of Najder, tried to sack Michnik from his post as editor in chief of *Gazeta Wyborcza*. Michnik replied in a dignified manner that the newspaper was not Wałęsa's personal property and that as he had been appointed by an election of the Citizens' Committees rather than by Wałęsa, it was they, not Wałęsa who would dismiss him. Wałęsa insisted that the Solidarność logo be removed from the journal's front page. Wałęsa was well aware that coming on top of the forty-fourth anniversary of the Kielce pogrom (Najder wrote him a speech for the occasion) the move against Michnik could be seen as anti-Semitic. On 5 June, Wałęsa, Bishop Głogowski, the secretary of state, Nowina Konopka, and several Solidarność officials, took a plane to Warsaw to meet Agostino Casaroli, the Vatican Secretary of State. On the plane the Solidarność press spokesman Kurski noted that Wałęsa, opening his mail with a large kitchen knife, said, to the consternation of all:

> I believed in my friends – Jews – and they made a fool out of me . . . I was warned many times not to get involved with Jews, that I should not get into their circle and take their advice. I always answered that these were my friends, colleagues. So what happens? They worked me over! Now I won't let them manipulate me.[39]

A short time later Wałęsa was in trouble with Yad Vashem and the Israeli Knesset for anti-Semitic remarks, and was widely reported in the western press for complaining that he could not understand why Jews in the Polish government and Sejm were trying to hide their true identity. His comments at a press conference on 13 September 1990, the day before he received a letter from the Israeli minister of religion clearing him of anti-Semitism, show that Wałęsa was playing with something he claimed he did not understand. Saying that he was only responding to anti-Semitic questions put to him, often anonymously, by the public he declared:

> I have nothing in common with Jews, I am not a Jew, there are no Jews in my family, but I am not anti-Semitic . . . My approach to this matter is as follows. Why should a man be ashamed of his background? We know that you cannot be held liable for your origin or punished for it and so forth, but that is something else altogether. But in my opinion you should not be ashamed – why should you? If I were Jewish I would admit it proudly. But I am not – I don't have anything to explain.[40]

This is the language of innuendo. It insinuates that Poles have nothing to explain while the Jews do, that it is impossible for Jews to become assimilated, that there may be very good reasons for Jews in Poland to remain silent about their identity, that a Jew cannot be a 'real' Polish citizen. While denying that anti-Semitism was a problem Wałęsa reinforced the notion that Jewish identity was a divergence from the true Polish norm and therefore a legitimate concern for Poles. He reinforced a hierarchy in which 'true Poles' and shameful Jews both had a place. As Michnik put it: 'By mouthing nonsense about egg-heads and separating people into Jews and non-Jews he made a bow towards those nursing anti-intellectual, populist and anti-Semitic phobias.'[41]

Writing in July 1990, Michnik was clearly engaged with the emerging mechanisms of post-communist Poland. He was aware that many Poles held 'aliens and foreigners (Russians, Germans, Jews, cosmopolitans, Freemasons) accountable for bringing communism to Poland'. However he was equally clear that while the debate about communism formed much of the surface pattern of political life, political conflict in Poland was no longer about this issue and he was keen to show anti-Semitism as part of a wider pattern of political thought:

The greatest threat to democracy today is no longer communism, either as a political movement or as an ideology. The threat grows instead from a combination of chauvinism, xenophobia, populism and authoritarianism, all of them connected with the sense of frustration typical of great social upheavals . . . The most important conflict in Polish culture today is being fought between those who see the future of Poland as part of Europe and those characterized by the Polish sociologist Jerzy Szacki as 'natiocentric' – although the first do not by any means reject national values and traditions and the latter are not necessarily chauvinist. In any case, these two approaches today divide the Polish *inteligencja*; they cut across all political lines and can be found among adherents of the *ancien régime* as well as within Solidarność and the Catholic Church . . . What we have learned during the past year (the most unusual in the forty years of my life) is that there is no determinism in history, that our history depends far more on ourselves, on our will and our decisions, than any of us thought. If we want to stand up to the danger, we have to know where it comes from, and we have to call it by its name. And if there are reasons for assuming that this danger is deeply rooted in certain social attitudes that can only promise new injustice and new oppression, then it is our duty as inheritors of European culture to fight against those attitudes – in the name of all those values of Judeo-Christian culture that were defended for centuries at the cost of great sacrifice. Just as France showed two faces during the Dreyfus trial, two faces are now being shown in Eastern and Central Europe. Even then, however, the forces of good and evil were not neatly divided along the lines that separated leftist republicans from rightist national conservatives. It is never that simple. For that reason we must always be prepared to understand and acknowledge the values of our opponents, even those we are fighting against. Only then are we truly Europeans.[42]

Wałęsa's presidential election campaign of December 1990 put further distance between Michnik and himself. Although he later made strenuous efforts to correct the impression that he was anti-Semitic, Wałęsa made use of anti-Semitism to gain support from KPN, the less sensitive members of the

Catholic hierarchy and from the right wing of Solidarność. Wałęsa claimed publicly that unlike some of his opponents he was a 'true Pole, a Slav and a Catholic', 'a full-blooded Pole with documents going back to his great-grandfathers to prove it', 'a pure Pole, born here'. He consistently failed to condemn those who attacked his opponent, Tadeusz Mazowiecki, allowing them to accuse Mazowiecki of being a crypto-communist subject to Jewish influence (a reference to Michnik) and to claim that Mazowiecki was descended from converted Jews. Dazed, offended and humiliated, Mazowiecki was driven to ask his parish priest to testify publicly that he was a real Pole and a good Catholic. At the very start of his campaign Wałęsa made a speech in which he argued that 'persons of Jewish origin should not conceal this by changing their names' because when they 'hid' under a Polish name they created suspicion about Jews in government. Wałęsa said:

> Chauvinistic and anti-Semitic views and manifestations . . . appear because the present set-up lacks clarity. There is confusion . . . as to whose interests the administration represents. The personal configurations and the question of responsibility are unclear . . . The functioning mechanism of the state structure must be made transparent, cliques smashed, and competence – not mafia arrangements – be relied on. Then this suspiciousness will disappear.[43]

There could be little doubt that this was aimed directly at the intellectuals of the left and at Michnik, Kuroń and Mazowiecki in particular. For Michnik at least, insofar as it was a tactic designed to smear the opposition by the use of anti-Semitism, it was reminiscent of 1968. Wałęsa's presidential campaign succeeded. He defeated Mazowiecki.

By 1991 there was a growing rift between Gdańsk and Warsaw, between the populist workers' movement and its links to the nationalists and the Church, and the *lewica laicka* intellectuals. Wałęsa nailed his colours to the mast by aligning himself with the conservative Catholic right-of-centre Porozumienie Centrum (Centre Agreement). Michnik saw this party and its leader as representing an important strand of Polish political experience and characterized them as xenophobic nationalist mythologizers. Michnik and the other opponents of Wałęsa moved towards Mazowiecki's Unia Demokratyczna as part of the broad left ROAD (Civic Movement-Democratic Action), an alliance which reached out to the revived but struggling PPS under J. J. Lipski, and which stressed its connection to western European traditions of secular thought, tolerance and modernity.

In the spring of 1991 the Church took advantage of the communist collapse to advance its own influence in precisely the way the Michnik had warned of in his discussion of the Julianic Church. Under Prime Minister Mazowiecki the first post-communist government had been forced to agree to the reintroduction of Catholic education classes into state schools and, without parliamentary or public debate, to curtail abortion rights. Cardinal Glemp now began to agitate for the abolition of divorce for Catholics and non-Catholics alike. He also campaigned that the constitutional provisions guaranteeing the separation of Church and state should be abolished as part of a move to protect 'Polish majorities' from non-Polish minorities, particularly: Jews, gypsies, homosexuals, communists and foreigners. The vice-minister for health said only perverts caught AIDS and the teachings of the Church did not allow him to sanction the use of condoms.

The general election of October 1991 failed to produce a clear governing party and left another splintered and less than effective Sejm. Although the UD (Democratic Union – led by Mazowiecki) won 14 per cent of seats and was the largest party in the Sejm, President Wałęsa refused to offer the party even one ministerial post in the coalition government. Michnik, isolated, worried aloud that the Church had not accepted that it was possible for atheist humanists and religious believers to live side by side and share the same set of ideals. The Church did not accept that it should occupy a limited place within modern Polish society, and saw in *lewica laicka* and liberal indifference to religion only hostile competition for political power and for the souls of good, decent God-fearing Poles. Michnik was made aware that the Church, having outlasted communism, was gearing itself up to combat liberalism, and he warned that once again simplistic solutions were on offer from President Wałęsa:

> It would be very dangerous if the philosophy of revenge became the basis for a pro-presidential government, and the main plank of its programme becomes ambiguous phrases about the Polish nation being a Catholic country and the policies of producing worthless money. Then Poland may well face chaos.[44]

In 1993 President Wałęsa, having hamstrung the Sejm and the government by refusing to accept the UD into the coalition, complained of the ineffect-iveness of both the Sejm and the government and created the BBWR (Non-Party Block Supporting Reform). This was a conscious echo of Piłsudski's inter-war military regime and his advisory body, also known as BBWR (Non-Party Block Co-operating with the Government) For Michnik it was another indicator of Wałęsa's ambitions and dictatorial potential. Michnik's portrait of the president in *Gazeta Wyborcza*, linked to the populist need for a 'vision of a sovereign and ethnically pure nation state' and the resulting ethnic hatred seen throughout the former eastern bloc, was far from flattering:

> I don't think Wałęsa has any of the traits of a bloodthirsty tyrant. On the contrary, Wałęsa loves applause, he needs approval, he wants to be loved. The style of power which he dreams of is a paternalistic dictatorship sanctioned by democracy. The problem is the extent of the president's dictatorial powers, which can be obtained by democratic and legal means . . . Wałęsa plays a key role on the

Polish political scene. He does not represent any ideals – having no programme is the very essence of his character: he is constantly changing his advisers, his language and his ideas. He constantly demands more and more power for himself. He has no patience with democratic procedures, he cannot tolerate strong independent personalities, and he does not recognise partner-style relationships in his personal dealings. He is a politician with great instinct; he has mastered the art of destabilisation, and he is excellent at taking advantage of his opponent's weaknesses. Once he was a myth. Before the presidential elections, he promised mountains of gold and now the electors are showing him the bill. Once he had great charisma – today he is an impenetrable authority available only to his aides at the Belvedere Palace. People still believe in his instinct and intuition, but he is no longer credible to anyone as a democratic leader. Situations like these have often cleared the way for authoritarian solutions . . . Democratic order can win, if more people can decipher the present situation: that the success of populist forces offering electors empty money and empty words, together with anti-presidential rhetoric, clears the path for the supporters of presidential dictatorship sanctioned by democracy. Or even unsanctioned.[45]

While Michnik is generally forgiving of his erstwhile opponents and even of his gaolers, he is less well disposed to those allies in Solidarność who turned against him. It is not the fact that Wałęsa came to oppose Michnik politically, nor Wałęsa's continuing closeness to the episcopate that causes Michnik discomfort. It is the manner of Wałęsa's opposition, the undemocratic nature of Wałęsa's ambition and his willingness to use (but not admit to) racist opinions that Michnik finds primitive and deeply offensive. Wałęsa, after all, had been a close friend in difficult times and was godfather to Michnik's child.

Michnik saw Wałęsa's defeat in the presidential elections of 1996 as no great cause for satisfaction. He feared that Wałęsa had already substantially damaged the emerging Polish democracy by sanctioning 'obscurantist trends' and by floating the possibility of dictatorial solutions. Having survived a boorish and unimaginative Polish communism, since 1989 Michnik's ambition for a western-style liberal Polish democracy has been in constant danger from an upsurge of clericalism, anti-intellectualism and national chauvinism. As early as 1985 Michnik observed that the sudden politicization of thousands of people who had previously been passive and unfamiliar with political life or political thought of any kind, the transformation of society from 'a sack of potatoes', had created a whole series of problems, not the least of which was that the original idea of Solidarność was increasingly set against 'the populist-totalitarian tendency, whose screaming drowned out every proposed strategic initiative'. Polish public life, Michnik observed, was producing a new kind of *Endecja* totalitarianism: 'a combination of populism and nationalism richly decorated with religious symbols'.[46]

Forsaking his earlier generosity towards the Church, Michnik has spoken repeatedly of the danger of *Iranizacja* (Iranization) in Poland, through the combination of retrograde nationalism and the political ambition of the militantly conservative mullahs of the Catholic Church. He has warned of what he calls a *czarnokracja* (literally a blackocracy, referring to the black vestments of the Catholic priesthood). He has repeatedly emphasized the ease with which popular opinion has been manipulated by nationalists and clerical leaders, the fact that the Polish electorate has demonstrated massive indifference to democratic political processes, and the great difficulty Poland has had in electing a government with a clear mandate. Michnik, clinging doggedly to his belief in liberal values and social-democratic ideals, has been forced to begin a slow, thoughtful re-examination of his earlier communitarianism. The presidency of Lech Wałęsa was a low point for him. While he insists that his political credo still consists of the Ten Commandments and the Sermon on the Mount, it is also clear that for *lewica laicka* liberals like Michnik democratic politics became personal and unpredictable under President Wałęsa. Wałęsa's populist totalitarianism meshed with the Church's Julianic ambitions: his anti-intellectual, anti-communist, anti-Semitic gamble put lives at risk: not for the first time in their history the Polish *inteligencja* realised how vulnerable they were to a very different definition of national identity and political action. For Michnik and the rest of the tiny, fragmented and politically powerless *lewica laicka* the problems in post-communist Poland, as in communist Poland, are to find an identity which is socially acceptable, a commonly accepted political language, a political space in which to operate and allies with whom to work.

10

WRITERS, LANGUAGE AND PARTY

I suppose I became a bit cynical. I even had on my desk a text written by a girl from my old sociology department. She worked hard on it, and then I worked hard, but in the end the whole thing was thrown out. It was an article on the language of official party documents. A really super piece of work . . .

K-62, 'I Censor', *Tygodnik Solidarność*, 8 May 1981.

In order to appreciate the important and increasingly difficult role of writers within Polish society after 1945 it is essential to look at changes in the Polish language – that is, at the medium of both writers and politicians.

In 1945 Poland lost to the Soviet Union territory roughly equivalent in size to that of the United Kingdom. In exchange Poland gained from Germany an area equivalent in size to England. In effect Jagiellonian Poland was abandoned, and after a gap of some 600 years, the territory of medieval Piast Poland was resumed. As a result, over 1,500,000 Poles from the east were moved to the new western Poland – now designated Recovered Territory to signify Poland's 'historical claim' to the area. It was forbidden to say that these people had been expelled: there was a whole government department devoted to 'repatriation'. Some 1,500,000 Poles returned from abroad after the war and they too settled mainly in the new western lands. A further 7,000,000 Poles from central Poland moved west and north to take up the opportunities now on offer in places like Gdańsk and Wrocław. The result of these massive population shifts was that for the most part regional accents were weakened – the only exception was the gradual acceptance of various words and structures from Mazowian-Warsaw dialect into standard speech. The German minority had by this time been expelled; Poland had lost most of its Lithuanian, Ukrainian and Byelorussian subjects; the Jewish population had been exterminated during the war.

These developments were reinforced by the post-war government's mass literacy campaigns. The Ministry of Education claimed to have reduced illiteracy from 5,945,900 (1931) to 1,144,600 (1950) and then to 644,000 (1960). It is generally said that illiteracy in Poland was 'wiped out' in the 1950s, and that by 1960 only the aged were resistant to tuition. This too helped further standardize Polish.[1]

The kind of change that took place in the language after 1945 was wide-ranging, but most obvious in the area of vocabulary. By the end of the nineteenth century the corpus of the Polish language held more than 60,000 words, of which some 15,000 were of old Slavonic or old Polish origin. Shortly after the end of the Second World War it was estimated that more than 30,000 new words had been added, so that by the 1980s the Polish language contained perhaps 100,000–120,000 words. The average Pole, it is thought, uses a vocabulary of about 7,000–8,000 words in daily speech, while a well-educated Pole may use perhaps 10,000. Foreign words (particularly from English, American-English and Russian) entered the language in large numbers. English words, some passing via Russian, became accepted: *adapter, tranzystor, trend, nylon, dżinsy, dżin, relaks, parking*. The introduction of Osram lightbulbs caused great joy (from the verb *srać*, vulg. imperfective): *O, sram*, Oh! I'm shitting. Particularly evident were words connected with politics and sociology of the *izm* variety – *egoizm, leninizm, marksizm-leninizm, komunizm, trockizm, gaullizm, maoizm, reakcjonizm, liberalizm, reformizm*. There were probably only about twenty-six 'ism' words in Polish at the end of the nineteenth century, but when Doroszewski's great etymological dictionary appeared (1958–69) there were over 1,000.[2]

There was a great increase in nouns ending in *owiec*: *szybowiec* (glider), *stoczniowiec* (shipyard worker). This was also the case in political language, where words such as *lewicowiec* (leftist), and *prawicowiec* (rightist), made an appearance. There was also, as a direct response to the need to develop a fuller range of political vocabulary, a growth in the suffix *szczyzna* meaning something like 'ishness': *gomułkowszczyzna*; a growth in the use of derivative words ending in the suffix *ista* or *ysta*: *centrysta*; a growth in the use of the prefix *anty* – *antyfaszystowski, antyimperialistyczny*. Also there was a growth in the use of prefixes like *pro*: *proreformistyczny, kontr*: *kontrrewolucja*, and *neo*: *neofaszyzm*.

Among the words that became 'popular' with the advent of communism are a very great number of words and phrases taken from military language: *oręż* (weapon), *wojna psychologiczna* (psychological war), *wojna z alkoholem* (war on alcohol), *walka* (fight), *ranga* (rank), *arsenał* (arsenal), *front robót* (work front), *kampania* (campaign), *kampania cukrownicza* (sugar campaign), *ofensywa* (offensive), *ofensywa gospodarcza* (economic offensive), *strategia* (strategy), *strategia polityczna* (political strategy), *mobilizacja* (mobilisation), *manewr* (manœuvre), *manewr gospodarczy* (economic manœuvre), *natarcie* (advance). These were characteristic of speech-making and political journalism in the immediate post-war years and most survived into the 1980s.

For a while Party members (particularly those who had spent their early years or the war years in the Soviet Union) tried to import and adapt Russian formal terms for Polish use, employing the various forms of the plural pronoun *was, wami* and *wy* (you), and the plural conjugation *cie*. However, this was considered by most Poles to be an unnatural affectation, since in Polish, *wy* is only used for emphasis. Unlike the other Slav languages Polish did not use the plural for formal address to an individual, but used instead the words *Pan* or *Pani*. These words were technically anathema to the Party since they mean literally, 'Lord' and 'Lady', though in common speech they have come to mean no more than 'sir' and 'madam'. As K. S. Karol wrote of his experience in the Soviet Union:

> I am called *polski pan*, even though I have explained a thousand times that in Poland, anybody is a *pan*, that it doesn't constitute a title, but a term equivalent to 'Mr' or 'Monsieur'. My colleagues . . . don't want to believe me. They are victims of a stupid propaganda campaign against the *panska Polcha* (the Poland of the *pans*) which has persuaded them that in Poland it is only the rich and the oppressors who are called *pan*.[3]

Polish Party members addressed each other after the Soviet fashion, using the word *towarzysz* (comrade). These innovations were confined to the Party and almost certainly after the early attempts to make them general were not used outside Party meetings and offices. While their use marked out Party members, they hardly had any impact on the usage of the majority of Poles. The word *rewolucja* (revolution) did not at this time enter Polish political vocabulary from Russian. It was already a part of the Polish language – a borrowing from Latin *revolution* or from modern French. Russian usage of the word was a nineteenth-century borrowing from Polish.[4]

Under the impact of Soviet-styled military and increasing bureaucratization there was a great proliferation of abbreviations and contractions – PRL, PAN, MO, PKO, PKP, *Cepelia*, *Pewex*. Abbreviation became something of a mania, thus: *1 sek KC PZPR*, instead of *Pierwszy Sekretarz Komitetu Centralnego Polskiej Zjednoczone Partii Robotniczej* (first secretary of the Central Committee of the Polish United Workers' Party). The precise use of initials became a reliable guide to the Party's attitude to certain states and organizations. The full and unabbreviated name of a state or organization was deemed to be a gesture of solidarity; initials were often deemed pejorative. West Germany for example was often referred to as the NRF, but when it handed over money it became Niemiecka Republika Federalna (German Federal Republic). East Germany, though it was often referred to as the NRD, was nearly always *Niemiecka Republika Demokratyczna* (German Democratic Republic) whenever public ritual demanded reaffirmation of friendly links. The censor made sure that *Związek Socjalistycznych Republik Radzieckich* (Union of Soviet Socialist Republics), though often referred to simply as the *Związek Radziecki* (Soviet Union), was rarely reduced to ZSRR.[5]

It is now generally agreed that 1956 was a kind of watershed in Poland's relationship to communism – the failure of the Party to reform itself meant that while the public were living in a 'post-communist' society, the state existed as if communism were in some way 'actual'. Neither side had the language or the cognitive faculty to understand the other, nor did room for manœuvre exist within the Warsaw Pact. The struggle of the dissidents and of the whole of Polish civil society was to re-establish a language in which the state and society might talk to each other, and the Party's refusal to allow such a language to develop, meant that there was no dialogue, that Poland was doomed to a series of increasingly serious and desperate repetitions, the upheavals of 1956, 1968, 1970, 1976, 1980–1 – and that the political options available upon the collapse of the Party would be significantly altered.

The first signs of the deep-seated damage done to Polish by the post-war regime emerged in the thaw of 1956. While the *inteligencja* – particularly the writers – had a very exhilarating time of it, the reaction of the bulk of the population to the thaw was silence. Professor Jadwiga Staniszkis has said that most people found themselves prey to a very complex reaction to change – rejoicing did not come easily: many, after the impact of Nazi occupation followed by eleven years of communism, had severely hampered cognitive capacities and were unable to analyse their own feelings:

> In spite of the invitation to 'public discussion', most people remained silent because of an instinctive and deeply imprinted fear of using words and epithets so long forbidden. This shame combined with the self-hatred of a people who, having been raised in a totalitarian regime, were trained to think in terms of power as the small animals in a jungle.[6]

By the late 1960s it was clear that the *rewizjoniści* of 1956 had not been able to formulate a new or different ideology or proposals. They had argued that they, rather than the Party, represented the correct application and interpretation of Marx's ideas. However, they were forced to operate on ground of the Party's choosing and had to use the language of the Party. They were forced to use words in limited context rather than in the elaborated code of an ideology of their own making since the Party had already grabbed the content of the language of communism. They were after all merely revising what had gone before.

In the 1970s, as Gierek took over and his style permeated the country, there was a conscious increase in the Party use of the words *Polska* (Poland) and *naród* (nation) as Gierek tried to equate the continuance of the PZPR in power with the well-being and economic progress of the country and the nation.[7] Under Gierek those who had mastered the elaborated linguistic code of the Party found it easy to imitate the required style of expression, preserving the impression of calm and authority, neutrality and command, of utilizing genuine knowledge. Under Gierek the Party developed a style of speech that was 'devoid of inner dynamic'. The distancing effects of this style limited speech to statements that were on the surface true, even if delivered in a style that was highly ironic, but which were in fact deeply misleading. A whole range of phrases suddenly acquired and required inverted commas whenever they were used in order to indicate that these things were 'so called': *wolny świat* (free world); *prawa człowieka* (civil or human rights); *swobody demokratyczne* (democratic freedoms); *czerwone niebezpieczeństwo* (red menace); *kultura Zachodu* (western culture); *wolność duchowa* (freedom of spirit); *niezawisłość myślenia* (independent thought); *democracja zachodnia* (western democracy); *żelazna kurtyna* (iron curtain).

Inevitably the populace became increasingly cynical. Middle-class speech 'abounded with quotations, parenthetical insertions, and turns of phrase that clearly indicated the speaker's distance from his own statements'. The impact of Party language resulted in the 1970s in the growth of an ironic style among the middle classes and the growing *technokracja*. This also meant that very soon the Party, the *biurokracja*, the *nomenklatura* and the professions were populated by people who cynically manipulated speech – they said what the regime wanted to hear, while they reserved their own 'private stance':

> On the surface, this appears to be a very good mechanism of adaptation. The misleading statement addressed to the establishment was sufficiently 'recognisable' to enable the speaker to function and even be promoted in the official hierarchy. On the other hand, the 'distance-indicating' part of the sentence, recognisable by the speaker's own group (which as a rule was critical of 'officialdom') allowed him to save face and preserve a feeling of identification with the group. Thus, for the middle class there was no question of the disintegration of personality that was often the case with the workers, whose limited semantic ability prevented them from resorting to mechanisms of self-defence based on language decomposition. It was difficult for workers to construct phrases with an internal structure that would indicate their distance from their own statements. On the other hand the misleading official language was more tangible to them, because of their respectful attitude to the spoken word. As we have seen, during the strikes of summer 1980, this attitude resulted in a global rejection of everything that was said by the government sources and the creation of Solidarność's own sources of information.[8]

For the middle class this dual code of public front and private reservation meant that even though life became increasingly schizoid there was no large-scale disintegration of personality – the existence of professional life, the Church, the family, and the continued presence and awareness of pre-war cultural values and history, albeit altered, helped prevent any obvious social breakdown. The phrase 'so to speak' became particularly popular as a result of this style. On one level it allowed speakers to toe the Party line. At the same time it indicated to their peers that this was not what they really thought. The novelist Kazimierz Brandys for example found:

For several years I was not able to do without the phrase 'in a certain sense'. I would use it at the beginning of one sentence out of three. When I realised what I was doing, I came to the conclusion that this linguistic habit reflected my awareness of the ambiguity of things.[9]

This was not the case with the workers. The development of ironic speech and cynical stances hindered and made more difficult the articulation of both working-class and *inteligencja* interests, and slowly but surely cut loose any linguistic link between reality and ideology, between reality and language. As early as the 1960s Polish sociologists had begun mapping the trend towards privatization – both in the economic sense and in the sense of social fragmentation, the internalization of intellectual, moral and political impulses – among both the Polish working class and the *inteligencja*.[10]

Under Gierek the language and ambition of the streets and the language in which the new gigantic economic projects were presented (the new language of ideology) were briefly in harmony. Gierek's call to 'enrich yourselves' was taken simply and literally. Yet whatever social mobilization had taken place after 1970 had reached its limit by 1975–6. As the economy became more out of balance, as professional life became less rewarding, as political and public life diverged again from the language used to describe it, so everyday life became internalized and intensely private. The regime was happy to promote the values of family life and consumerism as its sources of legitimacy and its ideology. This did not conflict with the teachings of the Church, which still found its direction in family life, in personal responsibility and morality, and in the work ethic of Positivism. At the same time, while Polish society was driven in upon itself, the Party denied efforts to create an independent civil society.

The 1970s saw words and phrases increasingly located solely in terms of daily context rather than in references outside immediate context to ideological content and a system of belief. In 1973 it was still possible to sing the jaunty popular ballad 'Well, let's go, farmers, we're building the new Poland', but by 1980 this same lyric had become a jeering, cynical period piece in which singer and audience mocked their own earlier beliefs and hopes in Gierek. During the late 1970s the increasingly ironic, detached and restricted code of the *inteligencja* and *technokracja* came to resemble a variation of the working-class 'restricted' code. That is, as the symbolic content of all statements was felt to be steadily 'impoverished', there was a conscious avoidance of words which had been exploited and used excessively by the Party and by official propaganda. Public speech on matters of political and economic policy became increasingly a matter of ritual.

In its own relentless way *Nowa-mowa* (Newspeak) created a new pseudo-reality. The language of Party speeches and articles illustrated all the dangers and simplifications that Orwell warned of, and many more that he had not imagined. The verb as an indicator of time and causation came under pressure. Active and passive voice were a problem area; instead of the active voice, the Party much preferred the passive: 'It was decided . . .', 'A new factory was built . . .', 'A new policy direction was decided . . .', 'A project was undertaken . . .' There was little room for doubt about the outcome of government strategies – things were no longer 'said to lead', but instead simply 'led to' predestined and agreed ends. The people responsible for particular actions or policies were rarely named and the actions were never reported as if the outcome was in doubt. A statement such as 'Mistakes were made' left the reader frustrated and ignorant: what mistakes, when, made by whom, affecting us in what way? Conditionals too began to disappear from Party language: 'If we continue on our present course we should be successful' slowly but surely metamorphosed into the simple assertion: 'We will succeed' or 'We are succeeding.' It was not only that the iron will of the Party and the inevitable 'progress' of history were represented in such a style, but that the Party actually managed to leap over and ignore all unpleasant failures in the here and now.[11]

Words which had once had one simple and clear meaning slowly acquired new and rather different meanings. The word *nastrój* (atmosphere), instead of carrying the more traditional pleasant connotations, under Party influence came to mean an atmosphere of unpleasantness, something antisocial, something out of tune and tending towards social disharmony. More particularly it came to mean criticism of the Party and anti-Russian feeling. There was a growing use of double meanings in words like *rewizjonizm* – meanings that could not be precisely pinned down. The word *obcy* (foreigner, stranger, alien) had a tradition of steady and friendly interest in 'the outside world' behind it. It had been possible to refer, without necessarily being hostile, to *obcy klasowa* (foreigner class), *obcy ideologycznie* (foreigner ideology), but between 1956 and 1968 the word narrowed down considerably in its application and came to mean an ideological group or class within Polish society who were not a part of the nation, but whose existence was a cause of concern: shorthand for 'Jewish'.

The use of *eufemizm* and hyperbole also helped the ritualization of political language. The word *historyczny* (historic) for example became greatly overused so that everything was historic: *historyczna wizyta* (historic visit), *historyczny plenum* (historic plenum). Simple judgements of worth came under pressure as the Party adopted a steady stream of superlatives: everything became the most serious, the most important, the most urgent, the most superb, the wisest, the biggest, the best, the heaviest, the greatest. There was greater use of circumlocution and 'enigmatic paraphrase' in referring to events the Party would have preferred to ignore: *wydarzenia marcowe* (the March events, 1968), *wydarzenia w radomie* (events in Radom, 1976), *wydarzenia w Ursusie* (events in Ursus, 1976). In talking of the death of Stanislaw Pyjas for example it was common to hear: *To, co się stało w Krakowie* (This, which happened in Kraków), or: *To, co się zdązylo w Krakowie* (This event in Kraków). At the same time the Party began to reserve to itself use of the word *kierowniczy* (guiding) and through its vocabulary and its poster campaigns began to turn the leading role of the Party into a political and economic fetish that even the total economic collapse of 1980–1 did little to shift.

The Party's use of language slowly destroyed the ability to assess the worth of evidence. It increasingly passed off pragmatic changes of policy as slight alterations of plan, and in doing so increasingly ritualized political processes even within the Party. Since language and reality were increasingly divergent, political and economic decisions were also increasingly arbitrary. The magical elements of language and power were abused in the over-use of slogans, which became either an unquestioned part of life or caused a negative reaction: few people could remain indifferent or withstand the daily repetition. Party language promoted uniformity of opinion, Byzantine ritualism and an *ewaluacjonizm sugerujący* (insinuating evaluationism) that was incapable of realistic evaluation.

Language was a valuable technique of domination and manipulation, the principal way of making that domination if not acceptable, then at least unavoidable. The various modes of speech and semantic codes developed by the Party served as substitutes for ideology. Instead of a developing ideo-logical consciousness allowing analysis of the situation and corrective measures, consciousness became segmented, society and the opposition re-mained fragmented. The prevailing social and economic forms presented themselves as the norm and since attack on them entailed the construction of a counter-ideology, the language for which had already been destroyed by the Party, opposition remained for the most part individual and hazardous. Words and linguistic codes became means of identity rather than dynamic means of communication. The work of KOR, TKN and the underground publishing houses of the 1970s and 1980s, on the other hand, was to undercut propaganda, to restore meaning to words, to show again that words might have a meaning outside their immediate context, and could refer to an abstract idea that did not change.

In spite of its apparent homogeneity Polish society was fragmented. Throughout the 1970s it was exceedingly difficult even for a well-educated person to gain any perspective on the links between the various social and economic subsystems. Poles in all walks of life had very little sense of society outside themselves and their immediate circle – this often resulted in a feeling that 'I am a typical Pole, I am Poland.' There was a feeling that one's own position was clear and universal, that any attempt to clarify it, tie it up in 'language', must be designed to sink it. One had only to do the right things to be victorious; those who saw the world in a different way, who worried that an agreement might need to be watertight, and have definite aims and objectives, were seen as somehow dubious, possibly 'political' and certainly 'against' morals. Since they lacked any way to overcome this feeling there was a growing tendency throughout the 1970s to believe in simple moral solutions to all problems.

There was almost no ideological debate after 1956 mainly because the Party itself was ideologically bankrupt and intent only on preserving the *status quo*, but also because the Catholic Church was non-metaphysical and its visible achievements were primarily moral and social. That is, as long as its institutional survival was not threatened the Church remained non-combative towards the PZPR. The Church continually advised against efforts to change the system, and while it reluctantly sheltered those atheist dissidents who ran to it, it also warned against both oppositionists and the Party, holding on to a very deeply embedded suspicion that all intellectuals were communists in disguise. Both the Party and the Church based their considerations on their own earthly and institutional survival. The Church continually said that calm and order were the prime requisites for life in Poland. The Church was prepared to offer succour, but it was not prepared to confront the Party openly or develop publicly a wide-ranging critique of Party practices. Because of this the populace lacked any substantial intellectual perspective on its plight and (with the exception of the mirage of western consumer society) lacked a coherent vision of an alternative society. In the absence of any way of communicating feeling from the bottom of society to the top, the workers themselves increasingly turned to the Church and to the creative intellectuals outside the Party to mediate their case and articulate their demands and their problems, force the Party to take them seriously, prevent confrontation between striking workers and violent repression by the armed forces, give content to the 'consultation' between workers and Party – increasingly regarded as nothing more than mere ritual. Only after 1976, with the birth of KOR and the link-up between underground intellectual oppositionists and unofficial Free Trade Unions of the Coast activists did this situation begin to change.

Also, it must be said, the illegal opposition was deeply non-ideological. Thus it was possible through the 1970s for all sorts of tensions and tendencies to coexist in Poland simply because there was no common ground in language for conflict or varying ambition to find expression. The peculiar non-ideological climate of the Polish opposition has several sources, but is mainly located in the old Polish social hierarchy, and is reinforced by the impossibility of thinking ideologically from within the communist system. A wide-ranging non-ideological opposition formed only in the mid-1970s, a peculiar very loose coalition of the system's opponents from different social milieux. Later the relative absence of ideology was also evident in Solidarność right through the 1980s. Jadwiga Staniszkis, who worked as an adviser to Solidarność in the shipyards in 1981, noted that more than 55 per cent of shipyard workers could not label their political attitudes as characteristic of right or left, and most of the 36 per cent who supported opposition groups (KOR, KPN) could not give any ideological reason for their behaviour other than the argument that 'the opposition tells the truth'.

That the opposition were non-ideological was frequently reported by puzzled western observers. Jerzy Andrzejewski, when asked about the political ambitions and programme of the KOR oppositionists, would merely shrug his shoulders. Only very slowly did it become apparent that such was the degree of diversity of ambition and platform within the opposition, that this movement – including Solidarność – could be no more than a conduit for voices of all kinds from within Polish society. In themselves KOR, ROPCiO and Solidarność were not political parties. They were agents which fostered the possibility of political parties and democratic opinion.

The Party devalued the language of ideology and art with its poster and slogan campaigns. There, where language was reduced to its functional minimum, we can see some of the processes at work. Along with the posters advertising the latest PZPR Congress, the hundredth anniversary of Lenin's birth, the nintieth anniversary of the founding of the Proletariat Party, the thirtieth anniversary of the Polish Workers' Party, the 'idea' of the 1917 Revolution, the year 1917, or Peace and Co-operation in Europe and Poland, there were others whose message was more destructive but less obvious. When the Party put out posters like the one that read: 'For us there is no business more dear than that of the Polish People', or the poster saying: 'That Poland should grow in strength and the people live in prosperity – the Sixth Party Congress' – it was to ask for a comparison with life on the streets of Poland and provoked a cynical response. In 1975 it was the International Year of Women and there was a huge poster campaign to glorify and pay tribute to the role of women in Polish society. In spite of the posters telling them otherwise, Polish women knew that there was no adequate contraception available to them, that they could expect on average four abortions in their lifetime, that no adequate provision had been made by the centralized planning system for tampons, make-up, tights and stockings, hair bands, hair-grips and children's shoes; the average Polish woman spent three hours every day waiting in queues. There were no women on the Party Central Committee, no women in the government, few women in Parliament, and as far as anybody could tell there were very few women among the *nomenklatura*.

The Party's use of language rested largely on an attempt to destroy any alternative vision of the future and also to rewrite the Polish anti-Soviet, anti-communist, anti-Russian past by damaging the sense of time and sense of history. One example of the way the Party tried to undermine perceptions of history by killing the perception of time lies in the favoured phrase *dalsze umocnienie* (further strengthening), usually employed to describe ties between Poland and other communist countries, or to describe the position of the Party and its 'leading role' in Poland.[12] The phrase is remarkable in that it manages to reconcile two quite opposite ideas: things are just the same as they were, only now they are more so. The phrase also implies that the process is inevitable, while denying the possibility of failure – it offers only faster progress, greater strength, even greater success. The 'destruction of time' is a theme to which Kapuściński often refers: 'The main objective of authoritarian systems: to arrest time, because time brings about change.' For Kapuściński it was clear that with phrases like this the Party hoped to 'sneak up' on the Polish public.[13]

An example of favoured vocabulary extending the destruction of time, is the poster slogan *Naród z Partią* (Nation with Party, a parody of the phrase *Polska z Bogiem*, Poland with God), the model for a host of similar slogans: *Młodzież z Partią* (Youth with the Party), *Górnicy z Partią* (Miners with the Party). Polish makes no use of articles and does occasionally form sentences without obvious verbs – yet even so, the phrase still contains an ellipsis, a verb, particularly the word *jest* (is). The phrase is not exactly 'The Party is with the Nation.' Without some form of time marker to indicate when this event took place the slogan became a peculiar cross between an exhortation, a prediction, a prophecy and a description – but that was the peculiar strength of this kind of language usage. Contrast, for example, the possible grammatically correct phrases which the Party did not adopt: *Młodzież będzie z Partią* (Youth will be with the Party), or *Młodzież była z Partią* (Youth was with the Party), or even *Młodzież była, jest i będzie z partią* (Youth was, is and will be with the Party). The meaning of these phrases is much clearer, though probably the message is no more acceptable.[14]

The aspect of language isolated in these Party posters is called 'disjunctive grammar'. Normally one word operates on or affects another; semantic relations between a combination of words decide the meaning of any phrase or sentence. However, in poster and advertising language the world over, and particularly in that of *Nowa-mowa*, words are atomized – they do not operate on combinations of propositions, but rather each word is itself a proposition. Disjunctive language communicates at a sub-logical level by reinforcing associative meaning as opposed to cognitive meaning, cognition or analysis. That is, judgements of truth or falsehood can only be applied with great difficulty when this language is used; it is impossible to challenge an utterance because it is impossible to frame an adequate question, since the relationship between the component parts of the statement is unclear. The 'message', however, is always abnormally simple, much of the 'meaning' being inferred from the circumstances of the utterance rather than the overt transmission of information, and includes situational factors to such a degree that particular meanings are dispensed with almost entirely. In fully discursive grammar, minor and non-finite clauses are dependent; in fully disjunctive grammar they are independent:

> It means, in effect, that in disjunctive language a sentence need not contain a finite predicator, and this in turn means that a single nominal group or single adverbial group may be grammatically independent. Either of these groups may in turn consist of a single word. In other words there is no limit to the simplicity of a grammatical unit. But to the extent that the higher units of grammar are left unexploited, they can be disregarded in description.[15]

The poster that simply read *Przewodzi Partia* (Party Leads) was another example of undistributed meaning – just what did the poster advertise? Was it a recommendation, a comment on actual fact, an exhortation, a prediction? Some posters and hoardings read *z Partią* (With the Party). Who is, was, or will be with the Party? Other posters read simply *Partia* (Party). Ultimately Party slogans like *PRL zawsze z partią* (People's Republic of Poland always with the Party) and *Niech żyje PZPR kierownicza rola budującego się socjalizmu* (Long live the PZPR leading role of inspiring socialism) made use of disjunctive grammar to reinforce the simple association of ideas. They had the function of a declaration, an observation, an obligation: in time they neutralized meaning, and in meaning they neutralized time by grammatically and politically blending past, present and future. It was not so much that these slogans had no meaning, but that their meaning was almost impossible to pin down. The lasting impression of a series of such statements – these models formed the basis of the Party's poster campaigns through the 1970s 1980s – served not to place any section of society in a meaningful relationship to the Party, but simply emphasized the dominant position of the Party. This in turn increased frustration and cynicism among those forced to read these huge roadside hoardings every day of their lives.

The blatant contradiction between posters declaring the International Year of Women, and the actual condition of women's lives was particularly galling. Women achieved suffrage in Poland in 1919 and were guaranteed equal rights under the 1952 Constitution. By 1989 women made up 50 per cent of the population, 55.5 per cent of all students and 46 per cent of the work-force, and of these 60 per cent worked in shops, clerical positions or service industries. Although 70 per cent of the cost of modern contraception was paid for out of national insurance, contraceptives were generally unavailable in the shops and only 26 per cent of women in 'spousal unions' used contraception of any kind. By 1989 abortions were estimated at 70–100 per 100 live births, so more than 60 per cent of Polish women had experienced at least one abortion. As many as 60 per cent of Poland's 500,000 single-parent families lived below the official poverty line.[16]

Censorship, propaganda and Party language functioned to ensure not that anyone believed what they were told, but solely to disarm doubt, to hamper the articulation of doubt, to prevent the formulation of a vocabulary of protest and to suppress the language of opposition. That is, to atomize society. Nowhere was this clearer than in Tomasz Rumiński's 1973 poster, *Polska 73 74 75*. The poster is enormous – in some versions the size of a roadside hoarding, in others the length and height of a whole building – and it is very difficult to give an adequate impression. Basically it consists of a huge title running along the whole right hand of the poster from top to bottom: *POLSKA 73 74 75* (Poland 1973, 74, 75). Under that, in much smaller lettering, is the sentence: *Polska Ojczyzna Ludzi Świadomych Kwalifikowanych Ambitnych* (Poland fatherland of people purposeful competent aspiring). Under the number 73 of the title sequence the following appear as a list running down to the bottom of the poster: *Rzetelnie Realizując Program Partii Przyspieszyliśmy Rozwój Kraju Polepszyliśmy Warunki Naszego życia* (Honestly realizing the programme of the Party we have speeded the development of the country improved our conditions of living). To the right of this appears a message in bold capitals: *WZROST EFEKTYWNOŚCI GOSPODAROWANIA, RZETELNA I WYDAJNA PRACA – DROGĄ DO PEŁNEJ REALIZACJI UCHWAŁY VI ZJAZDU PZPR* (Augmenting effective management, solid and honest work – the road to full realization of the resolutions of the VI Congress of the PZPR).[17] The effect of this huge poster was to fragment words and phrases until no consistent message was left, only an isolated series of emotive buzz-words, one-word slogans and exhortations. It was like a political acrostic which inadvertently but accurately revealed the Party's own linguistic and ideological style.

The Party's abuse of the Polish language called forth its own response from the public. During the 1970s the art of the political joke – verbal resistance – assumed awesome proportions:

'Daddy, is it really possible to build socialism in one country?' 'Yes of course it is son, but then, you have to live somewhere else.'

Definition of alcoholism: a transitional stage between capitalism and communism.

The difference between the communist system and the capitalist system is that under capitalism you have rigid discipline in production and chaos in consumption, whereas under communism you get discipline in consumption and chaos in production.

The four crucial periods in the history of Soviet agriculture are . . . winter, spring, summer and autumn.

The difference between capitalism and communism is that under capitalism man exploits man, but under communism it is the other way round.[18]

Another example of the way that humour challenged Party language was in the Polish response to the imported East German car, the Trabant. For the East Germans it was the *Trabi*, but because of its glass-fibre body and under-powered engine the Poles claimed it was only 'something like a car'; they dubbed it the Martin Luther after his comment 'Here I stand, I can do no more.'

Although Polish literature does not make much use of the pun, wits had enormous fun with the word *zjazd* – the word chosen by the Party to describe the annual Party Congress. As well as meaning congress the word also meant a downward slope. The use of the pun is a sign that words contain within them enormous pressures, pressures that can only be resolved through a joke. But both the pun and the joke are personal and private forms of revolt. They are not large-scale and they are not public. This was not the case in July 1981, however, when hunger marchers' banners parodied Party slogans: 'With ration books to socialism'; 'The hungry will eat the authorities'; 'Hungry of all lands unite'; 'Citizens we are marching towards communism – you are requested not to eat on the way'; 'A spectre is haunting Poland – the spectre of hunger.'[19] In political jokes and on the marchers' banners it was the language and the litany of Party language, the expected Party phrase or slogan, the Party catechism that was subverted and contradicted.

There was a very strong sense that things had been different before the war, that Poland had at one time been a 'normal country', that now real life was elsewhere, that outside Poland things were normal. However, it was very difficult for people to express this feeling without allying themselves with the pre-war right-wing military regime, or with the West German revanchists, or without appearing to be anti-Polish in some way. Nevertheless it was a feeling that showed itself in small ways. For example, the joke: 'Grandad why do you, an atheist, still go to Church?' 'Well, where else can I get pre-war quality these days?' The decline in quality at all levels was manifest. In the 1970s it was quite normal for professional people to add 'pw' to the letters after their name, meaning *przed wojna* (pre-war).

A large number of Polish revisionists have assured us and demonstrated that under Soviet patronage the PZPR hijacked the language of socialism and so deprived any left opposition of a way of voicing its dissent from what was done in the name of communism. The rulers of Poland did not for the most part believe in the ideals of socialism, or in Marxist theory, indeed for most of them there is little evidence that they were even vaguely aware of Marxist methodology. Their propaganda resembled Marxism only in its phraseology. The post-war Polish regime followed the Soviet example, blurring and ignoring the distinction between state ownership and social ownership.

By linking the existence of the Polish state to the existence of the PZPR and its guarantor, the Soviet Union, and by constant recourse to the threat of West German revanchism, the Party made opposition of any kind a form of disloyalty. All opposition was characterized as deeply anti-socialist, and that included anti-social and anti-national. Indeed the Party made a substantial effort to shift national perception towards understanding 'anti-socialist' to be the same thing as 'Fascist', and see all opposition as an anti-patriotic alliance with foreign Fascists.[20]

Abbreviated and truncated versions of powerful revolutionary slogans were displayed in hopeless, shameless pastiche. The meaning of fundamental terms was transformed beyond recognition: 'socialism' came to mean the existing social order, or the power of the PZPR; 'fraternal socialism' meant the military power of the USSR to bend its geographical periphery to its will; 'counter-revolution' meant any activity that sought to undermine either the PZPR or its guarantor, the USSR; 'democratization' an attempt to undermine communism; 'socialization' meant state ownership; 'internationalism' meant subordination to the interests of the Soviet Union; 'anti-socialist force' meant any form of political opposition; 'anarchists' meant opportunists belonging to some current of the European socialist tradition outside Soviet control; 'cosmopolitan' meant Jewish influence; 'reasons of state' indicated a clash with the interests of the USSR. Even the word 'ideology' came to assume a different meaning. To the increasingly embattled and outnumbered membership of the PZPR 'ideology' meant the function of stabilizing the *status quo* and existing social relations by influencing individual opportunities, social groups and classes through their ability to frame grievances and get those grievances heard and acted upon. On the subject of Party slogans: although the military *coup* was planned as early as March 1981, it was only when Solidarność, during the September 1981 Congress in Oliwa, put into effect the slogan 'Workers of the world unite' by contacting the workers of the Ukraine and Lithuania and urging them to form their own independent trade unions that the Polish military decided to move towards declaring Martial Law.

The particular Party use of these words and slogans was part of a general phenomenon of what Stanisław Starski has called 'conceptual embezzlement' – a process that reached deep into the possibilities of vernacular speech and writing, an Orwellian process, which fundamentally limited people's conceptual framework and rendered inexpressible a wide range of protest and oppositional ideas.[21] In consequence, those ideas vanished deep into the collective subconscious. In times of social and economic crisis those ideas struggled to emerge, often transmuted into ugly, simplistic, moralistic solutions.

As far as the Polish authorities were concerned the Polish public could believe what it wanted just so long as its beliefs remained inchoate, unspecified, local. In general the machinery of the Polish state was content to spoil public opinion rather than actively to shape it. That is, Poland remained a stable place just so long as people remained uninformed and disunited. As soon as people began to inform themselves, to find a language with which to question the official version of life, then the place became unstable and the ruling class came under threat. In 1967, Jacek Kuroń and Karol Modzelewski, lecturers at Warsaw University, showed how the absence of a left opposition and a language of opposition affected Polish political and moral life:

> The bureaucratic system provokes natural antagonism and hate among the masses; it identifies itself with socialism but ruthlessly suppresses all opposition from the left, thus creating conditions favourable for spreading rightist ideologies among the masses. People look for ideological symbols to express their protest against the existing dictatorship and in the absence of opposition from the left expressing their real interests, they find the old symbols of the traditional right. In this manner, the bureaucratic dictatorship aids the traditional right and even enters into agreements based on collaboration with them as with Pax and agreements with the Church hierarchy.[22]

For daring to say this (and their analysis was in itself a perfect example of what a left opposition might do) the authors were sent to prison.

Linguistic dispossession has far-reaching and often totally unforeseen consequences. As Eva Hoffman put it, 'Linguistic dispossession is sufficient motive for violence, for it is close to the dispossession of one's self.' Later she expanded on one aspect of this a little further:

> Does it still matter, in these triangulations, that my version of reality was formed in eastern Europe? It is well known that the system over there, by specialising in the deceit, has bred in its citizens an avid hunger for what they still quaintly call the truth. Of course, the truth is easier to identify when it's simply the opposite of a lie. So much eastern European thinking moves along the axis of bipolar ideas, still untouched by the peculiar edginess and fluidity created by a more decentred world.[23]

In the absence of a left opposition Poles looked to the right, to the western leaders and to the Catholic Church, for help and guidance. The result was not just naive confusion, but often tragic misalliance and bitter despair. The bulk of the *inteligencja* suffered from the Party's conceptual embezzlement of the language of socialism and found that by the early 1980s they no longer 'knew' anything about politics; their ideas of right and left were hopelessly confused and deeply cynical. Writers of all kinds protested at this state of affairs and also charted its depths and course. Effectively this class, under the impact of Gierek's regime, had ceased to function in any ideological sense and functioned rather, on the one hand, as a moral agent of the Church on whom all moral authority had now devolved, or alternatively as an opportunistic victim of the Party. Members of the Party came to believe, particularly after the failure of Martial Law, that the Central Committee had lied to them. The Central Committee in its turn claimed that it had been misled by its leaders in the government; they in their turn, like Gierek, claimed that oppositionists and opportunists within the upper ranks of the Party and among the government ministers had misinformed the leadership. Government ministers, however, claimed that their leader had been deaf to all warning.[24] The sad and insidious fact was that Nowa-mowa made it possible to know, and at the same time not know, a great variety of things.

The distortions of an absent left opposition were made even worse by the activity of the censor. Andrzej Szczypiorski, who was later to become an active Solidarność supporter, one of the first to be arrested during Martial Law, wrote:

> If the Polish press says that the West is suffering from continual recession, then there is no doubt in people's minds that the Western economy must be thriving; when Polish television recites unemployment figures for the USA (or for West Germany or Great Britain) this must mean that unemployment there is inconceivable. No one will even hear of abuses or terrorism in some countries of the so-called free world. Foreigners thus sometimes find Poland to be a country of bizarre reactionaries who refuse to believe the crimes of the Chilean junta, are sceptical about the problem of terrorism in Italy, reject as untrue reports of racial segregation in South Africa, approve of the *Berufsverbot* in West Germany, and so on. A mind fed on garbage becomes poisoned.[25]

However Szczypiorski was writing in 1979. By the mid-1980s his list had begun to look very bland. In 1986 it was possible to hear Poles in conversation argue that there must be no *détente*, that the west should support the South African regime as a bastion of anti-communism, that the African National Congress was just a communist front; Poles expressed dismay at the US defeat and withdrawal from south-east Asia, supported the idea of direct US intervention in Nicaragua, supported Ronald Reagan's Star Wars plan since one of its objectives was to bankrupt the Soviet Union, and argued that it was essential for the naive and foolish west European governments to keep US cruise missiles on their soil simply because Soviet talk of peace was just a manœuvre to disarm the west. Intellectual distortions were such that Poles were, understandably, far more interested in the increasingly reactionary sentiments of Leszek Kołakowski than in the possible development of independent socialist thought, theory and practice in the emerging African states, in Latin America, in Italy, China, Yugoslavia or Nicaragua.

It is perhaps as well to point out that the word 'socialist' by this time signified not a philosophy or world-view, but rather loyalty to the current ruling authorities. When B. Rogowski came to address the Łódź Party in November 1980 he openly admitted that the Party had fallen victim to its own inability to accept independent organizations, its own choice of an incompetent leadership, and its manipulation of information, and went on to say that if the Party were to attempt 'renewal' it would have to rename itself and tie the new party very firmly to a thoroughly revamped notion of socialism: 'Socialist – that is, with the goal of constructing a society based on social ownership of the principal means of production, and on the principle of redistributing goods in accordance with the quality and quantity of the work performed . . .'[26] But even this perception by a Party member was long past the time when anything effective could be done to reverse the processes at work. When, in 1982, Michnik circulated his essay 'Conversation in the Citadel', Janusz Onyszkiewicz replied: 'Socialism is a thoroughly discredited term. Is it good that you use it in your conclusion?'[27]

Given that it was very difficult to be well informed through the official Polish media, it was impossible to form any sensible perspective on the world. Working on the principle that help from the western left was unacceptable, many Poles reasoned that their enemy's enemy must be their friend. An example of the pressure on language and the confusion of the time, as well as a the narrowing down of options – an essential tactical part of opposition to the Party – can be seen in the following:

> I want to struggle in a free and democratic society, by using political means, against conceptions of society such as those proclaimed, for instance, by the Confederation for an Independent Poland. However, in order to make this possible, today I plan to co-operate even with the KPN in a common struggle against a totalitarian, alien occupation regime.[28]

It is clear that in this context the growing influence of the right-wing anti-Semitic KPN and its sympathizers within Solidarność during the period just before the declaration of Martial Law becomes thoroughly understandable, even if it is still unedifying. There was a great deal of confusion about who possible allies in the west might be – many Poles were heartened at the support they received from Margaret Thatcher and Ronald Reagan since these leaders were anti-communist: that they were also anti-trade union either did not register or was felt to be inapplicable in the case of Solidarność. This confusion even led to suspicion of left-wing supporters in the west. Ryszard Kapuściński, who was in the shipyards throughout the 1980 strike, remembers two Spanish Trotskyites who visited the yards with a request to be allowed to 'join the revolution'. The MKS Praesidium (Inter-Factory Strike Committee) thanked them for their concern and said: 'We are not making a revolution here. We are arranging our affairs. Sorry, but please leave the shipyards at once and do not try to come back.'[29]

The paranoia and schizophrenia induced by this system could only be relieved by certain courses of action: withdraw from all public life; attempt to change the system by steadfast opposition both within and without the law; create an alternative underground society; exploit and take advantage of the system through self-interest and cynical manipulation, even to the extent of joining the Party. Jadwiga Staniszkis lamented that the birth of Solidarność had not relieved the stress of this situation, but rather provided a single avenue of expression for a whole range of discontent. In doing so Solidarność constricted expression, simplifying the kind of political opinion it was possible to hold. Solidarność became the channel for all public opinion – a burden it could not easily bear or contain:

> It may sound like heresy, but Polish political life and especially the flow of ideas after August 1980 and the creation of Solidarność has been impoverished as a result of the impact of the populist and solidarist perspective pressed upon society by Solidarność. This view contrasts with the segmented, often morally ambiguous but nevertheless less uniform and less aggregated course of society in the 1970s. The earlier atomization of PZPR led to the pluralization of positions and ideas. They varied from totalitarian utopians from the Sigma Club at Warsaw University, with their abstract, dialectical imagination, to the primitive demonstrations of a need to dominate, that were often fed by personal frustrations and rationalised in terms of 'class dictatorship', of the Club Warsaw 80. Varied reactions to the ritualisation of ideology were observed from the Karl Marx Club, which gathered a few dozen tired party intellectuals (and semi-intellectuals) to the much more primitive and populist Katowice Forum.[30]

It was inevitable that the confusion of Polish society should be channelled into the only available outlet over which the government had no control. Solidarność was a forum which, whether it knew it or not, struggled to create an environment where politics and opinions of the left and right could once again assume some context and significance, where left and right, and politics itself, could become meaningful concepts again. Over the years the government monopoly of information produced a public that in its alienation, cynicism and indifference, clearly suffered a 'collective information psychosis'. Censorship guarded the distinction between the real situation and the Party's public pronouncements. But that was only one of its functions. Even those who were of an independent cast of mind, widely read, well connected socially, widely travelled and incurably inquisitive – principally the writers – could not entirely shake off the ramifications of the false consciousness engendered by censorship and the destruction of political and moral language.

In the late 1970s Edward Gierek's regime set up the DiP discussion group as a forum in which to analyse what was happening within Polish social and public life. The group met once and had its Party sponsorship withdrawn, but eventually produced two reports, neither of which was published in Poland. They too located the failure of Polish public life in ideology and language, and did not hesitate to spell out the consequences of what they saw:

> The system has created something that is more dangerous than indifference and cynicism, something that surely was not intended: it has created a state of collective informational psychosis. One week a couple of fires break out in a capital city of one and a half million people: well then, some mysterious arsonist must be on the prowl! Perhaps it is a sign of a power struggle! Posters are put up – as they are every year – announcing a call-up for military service: well then, it must be a general mobilisation; they are sending our boys to Vietnam! Or what about the explosion in the General Savings Bank at the Rotunda? Obviously a time bomb, dynamite, sabotage, a provocation . . . People who for decades have not been informed or who are misinformed, about the critical issues facing our country, people who see only the results of actions taken by the leadership (and to see them it is enough today just to walk into a shop), but who know neither the motives nor the reasons for those actions have a reflex reaction to every piece of news: 'they can't fool us! . . .' No, this is not even understandable scepticism. It is naive credulity in reverse. People who trust no-one and believe nothing will tomorrow accept the most improbable rumours and trust the first clever demagogue who comes along. A society that has no trustworthy political figure can easily become, in times of crisis and panic, an unpredictable society, a 'blind force'.[31]

Ordinary shipyard workers may not have been able or willing to frame their protest in a way the Party recognized as legitimate, but by 1980 they had nevertheless developed a very sharp suspicion of communist vocabulary. The language of communism was now inadequate to the task of clearing up the mess the PZPR had created simply because the Party lacked the language to recognize in depth the reality of its situation. Ryszard Kapuściński for example wrote of the 1981 strike:

> On the coast they played out a battle about language, our Polish language, about its purity and clarity, about the reinstatement of unmistakable sense, about the purification of our speech from ready-made phrases and nonsense, about freeing it from a worrying plague – the plague of insinuation. 'It's like everything is wrapped in cotton wool', said one of the shipyard workers. 'Our language is hardened, but it isn't tempered.' I remember the first meeting of the MKS with a government delegation. The MKS said: 'We request that our grievances are heard'. The government spokesman said: 'As you like, then I'll reply generally.' The MKS: 'No.

We want you to reply in detail. Point for point.' They naturally mistrust the general reply, the generality of language. They protest at everything that promotes falsity, gaps, moulding like putty, mere soap suds, cheating. They are against sentences that begin 'Well as you know . . . ' (really we don't know!), 'Well as you understand . . . ' (really we don't understand!). One of the shipyard delegates: 'Better the bitter truth than sweet lies. Sweeties are for kids, we are grown ups.'[32]

Many Polish workers took the view that what they wanted was good for Poland, even that they were Poland, that the authorities had simply made a mistake, that no one could treat them in this way because they represented the real Poland. This was a simplistic moral and nationalist view encouraged by both Church and state. Again and again workers assumed that somehow the guiding idea of duty to the nation would keep everyone on the rails. The authorities exploited specific features of the workers' restricted linguistic code to suit their own purposes. They asserted that the regime required no justification or legitimation to issue orders, make laws and order the economy as it saw fit. This coincided with traditional Polish social structures in that the working class respected those who had a good command of the language and who demonstrated they occupied superior social status through their use of the literary code.

However, there was still tension between the workers and the intellectuals. Public language had become a form of ritual, but one which has lost its flexibility and which has ceased to be an instrument to communicate feeling or information. Spread through a whole nation the effect was to propagate a change from the mass paranoia of the 1950s to massive and widespread social and political schizophrenia in the 1970s, a move away from a language-embodied ideology towards the absolutes of Catholic morality, towards the transparency of ritual gesture, and towards faith in symbols rather than words. Inevitably this also led to anti-intellectual feeling among workers: they no longer trusted anybody who retained linguistic competence. Worker-leaders were quick to fix on Catholic symbols to communicate with the led, but a consequence of this was a continuing gap between workers and their intellectual advisers: 'The indecisiveness of the intellectuals, their second thoughts, their tendency to operate on a level of pure analytical models were often met with suspicion.'[33]

The Party's achievement in the 1970s was to present current reality as if there was no alternative, no other form of social or political life. It was a cumulative definition of reality that could only work as long as Polish society remained atomised. It was effective because, while the liberal and reformist ethos was not allowed any open forum, the gentry ethos was still very powerful in keeping traditional social groups – notably the workers and the *inteligencja* –

apart. As a result of this, notions such as democracy, worker management and self-government dropped out of ordinary speech and, if they had ever figured even marginally on the political agenda, now disappeared altogether. Control of the vocabulary in which needs could perhaps be perceived, identified and formulated also created a structure of alternatives, and was therefore another way – aside from creating a polarized social structure – of containing possible actions, of consolidating the political *status quo*. For the most part the regime managed to keep conflicting interests below the level of articulation.

Many aspects of pre-war Polish society contributed to these developments and influenced Polish workers. There was still considerable stress on social stratification. Workers tended to see society in terms of their own immediate problems. They did not see their problems in abstract, ideological or institutional terms. The one-dimensionality of their vision was further enhanced by the influence of the Church and backed up by Polish national feeling. There was still considerable faith in the existence of simple criteria of correctness, criteria that could not be reached by discussion and compromise or by mutual agreement, but which, though they existed outside the political and economic sphere,were nevertheless still believed to be important to all Poles.

Deputy Premier Jagielski's concluding speech to the striking shipyard workers of Gdańsk of August 1980 is a perfect example of how *Nowa-mowa* could take advantage of this situation and set of beliefs, and at the same time illustrates how difficult it was even for top-ranking members of the government to avoid this linguistic style and talk plainly and, above all, honestly:

Esteemed audience, I regard it as my duty to add a few words. Our joint work has ended as the Chairman said. It really was not easy. The talks were difficult and demanded great effort. But they were concerned with vital issues. They concerned problems of employees, both those present here and those who are not, of their families, their wives and children, friends and colleagues at work. We tried throughout to understand the aims that prompted you. Sharp words were addressed to us. We used some ourselves. We tried to show the practical limits of what we could undertake and actually implement. I reiterate and confirm what has been said: we talked as Poles should talk to one another: as Poles with Poles. (applause, acclamation) I strongly confirm one final thing: we should take from this hall the same spirit that accompanied us throughout the negotiations. There are no winners or losers: no victory and no vanquished. What matters most is that we have reached agreement. We came to an understanding. The major guarantee of implementing our Agreement will be work and its results. Only effective work can produce the goods which we then share out. The whole country is watching us. Let us set an example of selfless, reliable work. We will manage it together, as stated. I am profoundly convinced that this will be the best proof of our patriotic, Polish, civic intentions. It will prove that we want, to the best of our abilities, to serve the cause of all working people, of our nation, of our socialist Fatherland: the Polish People's Republic. (applause, noise, renewed applause)[34]

Jagielski clearly draws on Party, liturgical and national sentiments in a shameless mishmash of ready-made phrases to dispel lingering uncertainty about the validity of any agreement made by the Party – but the same liturgical and nationalist sentiments can be seen in the closing speeches of Lech Wałęsa too. And he earns applause, in spite of the fact that throughout the negotiations the yards had been surrounded by troops, the city of Gdańsk had been isolated and the phones cut off, in spite of the fact that the workers had been reviled in the media as 'hooligans' and 'wreckers', and that during negotiations the Party had tried to whittle away the more generalized social and political protests and tried to limit the workers' demands to simple pay increases. A month after the agreement was signed the authorities were saying that as it did not formally acknowledge the 'leading role' of the Party, and had in any case been exacted under duress, the agreement had no validity in law.

The Bydgoszcz crisis of March 1981 arose when – against a background in which the Party again attempted to restore its own meaning to the words 'partnership', 'trust', 'consultation' and 'socialist renewal' – the police severely beat several Solidarność members attending a local council meeting. The union threatened a general strike unless those responsible were brought to trial. A Party investigation affirmed that the victims had not beaten themselves, but would not take matters further. Wałęsa personally took over negotiations with the government, leaving his advisers outside meetings with Deputy Premier Rakowski. Eventually he announced that the threatened general strike was suspended, but gave no satisfactory reasons. The police responsible for the beatings were never caught. After this Wałęsa was referred to as 'King Wałęsa', his authority came under pressure and union support began to wane. The historic agreement between the government and Solidarność, eventually legalized on 31 March 1981 after the Bydgoszcz crisis, had been negotiated mostly by the experts of both sides, was in the typical *inteligencja* style – full of allusions, mutual winks and unbinding signals – and for the working-class membership was a terrible shock. They could see very plainly that nothing they had fought for had been unequivocally agreed. The obscure language made it impossible to deduce from the text what was won and what was lost. A hierarchy built on semantic skills had reappeared and in the deal which appeared to have been struck between the intellectuals of both sides, proved as stable and as disadvantageous to the workers as their previous situation had been. Nearly all expressive functions in the movement were executed by its middle-class members, and workers felt their own creative powers had been expropriated. They no longer perceived Solidarność as the vehicle of upward mobility; faith in their peaceful revolution and in their 'advisers' disappeared. The combination of the climb-down over the Bydgoszcz beatings, the appearance of the agreement, the failure of the advisers and Lech Wałęsa's increasingly autocratic behaviour meant huge disillusionment among the union membership. The initial stage of

Solidarność's development ended with a visible demobilization of its rank-and-file members over the spring and summer of 1981.[35]

It was not until the Party had reneged on almost every promise made to Solidarność that the workers finally tried a new tack. They began to suspect that the *inteligencja*, the Party and the KOR advisers to Solidarność were, perhaps unwittingly, playing games with each other. The conflict about intellectuals and Jews functioning as advisers and experts within Solidarność can be seen as confused conflict, at one remove, over the rediscovery of argument and abstract thinking on precisely the issue of how the union was to control its leaders, how to relate to intellectuals, and how to assess advice. These were reactions to the intellectually undigested remnants of Poland's pre-war self, coupled with the barely understood response to a whole range of pressures that could not easily be explained. Many workers saw all intellectuals as the Party in disguise, and many saw both opposition intellectuals and the Party as Jews: intellectual class interests were not those of the workers. They mistrusted complication, sought simple solutions, feared betrayal from every direction. This too drove union members further to the right, into sympathy with the KPN.

Language is the most impure, the most easily contaminated, the easiest-exhausted of all the materials available to an artist – witness the difficulties post-war German writers experienced in trying to overcome the damage done to their language by the Nazis.[36] The Nazis were in power in Germany for twelve years; in Poland the communists were in power for forty-five years. Language is a local and personal as well as national experience. It is a social experience, but it is experienced not merely as something shared but as something corrupted. It carries with it historical baggage, it is weighted with an accumulation of definitions, usages and historical events. For all writers, the unacknowledged legislators of the world, the creation of a new work is a struggle to make readers see words in a new context, to make people see what is happening to words and to the meanings they, and the society which made them, contain. Language is a means of dealing with two opposed areas of meanings and the relationships words have to the world. Writers have their own meaning for a given word and they use words in their own way. On occasion, however, writers also struggle with the other accumulated public meanings for a word, meanings that develop the writer's ideas and language, but which at the same time clutter, compromise, and adulterate the meaning the writer is trying to assign. As Stanisław Barańczak has said:

> Collectivist uniformity finds its remedy in poetry's individual point of view and natural subjectivity (the principle of a first person speaker). The tyranny of empty

generalities is countered by poetry's disposition to concrete vision (the principle of poetic image and metaphor). Falsifications of language and worn-out slogans are met by linguistic explorations which bring the word's potential meanings to the attention of a reader (the principle of decomposition of set phrases). Finally, schematic monotony is countered by one of the oldest principles of poetry, namely, by a dynamic equilibrium of regularity and irregularity, of stable and changing elements (the principle of poetic rhythm).[37]

Barańczak has testified to the continuing debilitating effects of the Party's influence on his sense of political language and his decision-making processes:

> Someone who comes from Central Europe, who in his own country declared himself in favour of democracy and freedom, someone who has actively opposed the repressive machinery of government – well, that newcomer to America may begin to have problems with his choice of 'ideals'. I don't mean 'ideology', but he will have difficulties in translating one mentality into another. There is a semantic problem. For example, if someone in America declares himself a 'liberal' it means he's on the left; in Poland it would be ridiculous to associate these two notions.[38]

It was not so much that the Party had invented a whole new language in which it became impossible to think certain thoughts, as suggested by Orwell's Newspeak, but rather that *Nowa-mowa* was a language where concepts of moral, economic and political significance had been emptied of agreed, normative, social meaning and refilled at will by the Party. Polish writers have been forced again and again since contact with Soviet communism to examine the nature of words and the content of language. Aleksander Wat, who had experimented with words and meanings to a remarkable degree in his early Futurist poetry, discovered after being locked up for several months with a mad etymologist in the Moscow Lubyanka jail during the Second World War that the idea of the 'liberated word', the the word as an 'object with which you can do as you please', was an avant-garde recipe for 'nihilism: linguistic materialism'. Wat was brought face to face with the same set of problems and realizations that were to face all Polish writers outside the Party and all those who felt themselves to be in any degree part of the opposition movement. Wat began to feel

> the biological connections of words on a higher level, not a mineral, biological, or even archetypal level but in the connection to history, to the incredibly alive tissues of human destiny, the destinies of generations, the destinies of nations. And the responsibility for every word, to use every word properly. And then, intuitively – for I realised all this only later on – I had an intuitive sense both of the responsibility and of that which is perhaps the only thing that distinguishes a

poet from the others who speak the language: the poet's task, or mission, or instinct to rediscover not the meaning of each word but only the weight of each word.[39]

Within the Party and throughout public life the spontaneous creation of new language, of innovation in thought and speech, died. That which had been spontaneous became mechanical, frozen, habitual: stale, over-used metaphors, stock similes, ageing, inappropriate and anti-grammatical slogans became the order of the day. Political speeches and articles grew longer while their content became more ambiguous. Instead of individual style there was only an increasingly anonymous and conformist rhetoric, jargon and gesture. Where once there had been precise daily usage, now there were jargon, bluster and lies. Foreign words and borrowings – particularly those from American-English, and from western consumer goods – were swallowed whole, as if they could give some vitamin of vitality, some taste of another way of life. It became essential to keep the labels on all foreign jars and pots of food even after the contents had long since been used up. By the 1980s, as Jan Prokop said in an article entitled 'Poland Disappeared or the Glacier of Shit', the Polish language stood in great danger of being 'officialized into nothingness by a million local party secretaries'.[40]

Censorship attempted to erode Poland's stormy past and to elide the difficult but important areas of conflict with communism and the Soviet Union. Leszek Kołakowski, who was to conclude his efforts to reform communism with the equation: Democratic Socialism = Fried Snowballs, believed that it was impossible for the Party to rebuild society or make a fresh start without ditching the entire corpus of the historically compromised Polish language. A consistent destruction of the past would require forgetting a language that carried cultural traditions, imposed certain structures of thought and thus limited the possibility of creating a New Man. Polish contained words and grammatical forms which should not be known by a New Man. Perfect Revolution would require techniques for throwing people back to the pre-linguistic stage. Indeed, there could be no hope of real success without 'genocide, slavery and bestiality'. For Kołakowski the idea of liberation for, from or by the Party was in itself a dangerous nonsense. Though there is a great deal of truth in what he said, such reductionism was rare. Kołakowski had nevertheless located an important limitation on what the Party could hope to achieve: 'The perfect revolution presupposes a perfect cultural desert.'[41]

Officially one of the primary aims of accelerating educational reform in Poland had been to overcome semantic and linguistic differences based in class. The idea of overcoming the Sarmatian hierarchy of semantic codes had been a part of socialism's promise to those who made up the new proletariat. However, the system developed in Poland, though it made great use of the idea of the unity of the Party and the workers, still prevented workers' grievances from being publicly articulated or even formulated, and it did this by robbing the workers of the language of socialist protest. Thus, in periods of economic uncertainty the workers found themselves made inarticulate, demobilized, blocked by the organizational hierarchy of the party, and without *inteligencja* assistance. Official solutions to worker protest were often based on a semantic code which the workers either could not crack or which they took at face value; the workers could not make themselves understood, and were continually abused by the government. Understandably Polish workers came to believe that the way they spoke was shameful and inappropriate to registering grievances about their way of life in anything other than purely financial terms. The Party did nothing to help the workers overcome their traditionally 'restricted' linguistic code; indeed the Party regarded worker protest as strictly ritual, a hangover from a previous era, unthinkable in modern communist society. That they could think this was an indication of the damage the Party had done to its own cognitive faculties: language no longer served to get at thought, to pass thought from one head into another. It only served to blur thought, to pass off habit as ideology, to pass off power as leadership. Instead of allowing people to express feeling with energy and direction, the language relaxed any sense of reality and urgency, dispersed all feeling of responsibility, purpose and direction. There was a feeling prevalent in the late 1970s that real life lay outside Poland, that somehow the life Poles led was surreal, a bad joke, an imitation. Kazimierz Brandys dubbed it *Polski nierzeczywistość* – Polish unreality.

Literature shows us what is happening to words. Words show us what is happening to thought. Stanisław Lem, Ryszard Kapuściński, Tadeusz Konwicki and a host of other writers all reveal in their different ways, that the manipulation of information distorts public opinion in unpredictable ways simply because it engenders a false consciousness, and this in turn promotes mistrust, social and political misunderstanding and the generation of irrational beliefs and attitudes. The effect is to block the formation of social and political micro-structures, to disrupt a whole range of social contacts and to turn society from a dynamic developing body into an inert, manipulable, unpredictable mass. By 1981, as Jacek Kuroń was later to recall, society – students and workers – *Pytali, pytali, pytali* (they questioned, questioned questioned) Solidarność and the dissident speakers who toured the countryside. But, as Kuroń was quick to realize, they had no common language. The dissidents did not hear answers in the questions, and the students and workers heard only more questions in dissident answers: 'For the last thirty or forty years all we had in common with which to talk about politics was the language of the bureaucratic picture of reality.'[42]

11

SOCIALIST 'UNREALITY' TO CAPITALIST 'REALITY'

The language of politicians is made up of stock phrases: we don't believe them, even when they extol first aid for the drowning. We do not believe in words. Words are reproducible. Modern day hell is paved with words. Words supply information: but values, essence, spirit, one expects to obtain those from art. Today the biographies of artists are like the lives of the saints, their works are like relics, they are priceless.

Kazimierz Brandys, *A Question of Reality*

In Poland industrialization plus the proximity of the Red Army did not mean communism. It meant, after an initial honeymoon period in which the Party offered writers remarkably favourable conditions in return for a nominal adherence to the tenets of *socrealizm*, the continuation and adaptation 'in opposition' of older formations – even within the Party itself. It meant an almost irresolvable clash between culture and system; it meant that Polish culture was suspended, frozen, warped by considerations that were not its own. Polish society, even after the massive upheavals of the war and the attempted restructuring by the communists, never quite managed to break with the past or do more than improvise from day to day.

The Party was led by men who needed to woo writers but who mistrusted intellectuals. The cultural needs of the new leadership were more than modest and grew from a desire to stem the tide of reformism and preserve their own authority, rather than from a need for inner refreshment or quest for self-knowledge. As a result the Party failed to inject any element of dynamism into post-war cultural life. The aims of many Polish writers were only slightly at variance with the ambition of the less dogmatic members of the Party, but the fact that writers and their ideas maintained independence from the Party did not fall easily within the comprehension of the Party as a whole and meant that clashes were inevitable. The often contradictory conservative and progressive social elements in the make-up of individual writers persisted, but the profession as a whole remained unaccommodated to the Party. Indeed to a very great extent the changes the Party attempted to make in human understanding, its glaring failures in social and economic conditioning and its enormous programme of self-perpetuation, rather than genuine social change and improvement, were all grist to the writers' mill.

The role of the writer in Poland, fundamentally different from that of writers in western Europe, was never one of simple opposition to communism.

In a monopoly situation the pressure was on post-war writers to forsake traditional paths and conform to the political and aesthetic principles deemed useful and even necessary by the Party and bureaucracy. The aim of the Party (in theory at least) was to transform the writer into a socialized producer, a 'useful' member of society. The Party's definition of 'usefulness' was 'usefulness to the Party', rather than to Polish society. In return for co-operation (or at least silence on key issues) they offered writers social standing, prestige, material rewards, prizes, substantial subsidy, almost guaranteed publication. In short, in a profession that elsewhere was regarded as risky and very insecure, the Party offered an assured publishing career, even to many of those who opposed it. The Party operated not to exterminate opposition, but simply to spoil it.

The stubborn struggle of writers, their insistence on loyalty to their conception of Polish society, characterized relations between the writer and the state and is part of a much larger struggle over the nature of political authority that has its roots deep in Polish history and social structure. By definition the Polish *inteligencja* helped create society's consciousness of itself, and it is precisely in the area of social consciousness, self-awareness, reflection and analysis that the Party operated with particularly destructive skill (hampering creativity, information-gathering, information dissemination, opinion formation and rational analysis by undermining language and controlling access to public expression) leaving a terrible and bewildering legacy for the post-communist governments.

In 1981 Solidarność seemed to be the solution to Poland's problems, but it became clear, over the sixteen months of its existence, that all Solidarność could do was reveal the depth of the complex problems deeply rooted in the psyche of the nation, and act as a conduit for a wide range of often contradictory moral and spiritual protest at prevailing economic conditions and political behaviour. Solidarność was not and could never be a party. It had neither a mandate nor the remotest chance of being allowed to form a government. The union, for all its special and remarkable qualities, was deeply mired in the very problems it sought to relieve, deeply rooted in the actuality of communist Poland and in the social and intellectual structures created by the Party. Although the bulk of the population were either Solidarność members or supporters, most were only 'paper members' and after the first few weeks activists were outnumbered by the vast majority of 'grey masses' who simply awaited the outcome of the struggle. While many believed the 'unity' of the workers, farmers, intellectuals, students and dissatisfied Party members would allow them to launch an effective programme of *odnowa* (renewal), the entrenched bureaucracy and the reactionary elements in the Party combined to create a situation of incredible confusion and ensure that renewal could not proceed without major social conflict.

This complex nexus of psychological, linguistic, economic and political features meshed in confusing and contradictory ways with what the novelist Kazimierz Brandys dubbed 'Polish unreality'. Having lived in 'unreality' for so long it was difficult for the Party to acknowledge the reality of its situation, difficult for intellectuals to establish with any certainty that they understood the reality of Polish unreality, and for the workers to trust either the Party or the intellectuals to grasp that the reality of the workers' lives was a poverty-stricken hell. In spite of the initial enthusiasm for the union, it soon emerged that unity of opinion was an illusion: unanimity of belief was often supposed by union members, but in fact the membership were united only in their opposition to the Party. The political ambitions contained within Solidarność were diverse, often difficult to extract in any coherent form. The Solidarność leadership had increasing difficulties in reining in members who were impatient for some kind of 'action'. As 1981 staggered from crisis to crisis, the populace, many of whom now felt ready for desperate remedies, began to react against Solidarność, and many came to see the union exactly as the government described them – as wreckers and hooligans. Solidarność became increasingly influenced by the right-wing, nationalist KPN (Confederation for an Independent Poland) and developed a growing minority intent on anti-intellectualism, anti-Semitism and anti-socialism.

As 1981 unfolded, writers and intellectuals in KOR (Committee for the Defence of Workers) and the advisers to Solidarność gradually realized that rather than 'forging links with the masses' since 1976, they had been talking to only a handful of active oppositionist workers, who, while they were happy to accept assistance from the intellectuals, did not necessarily have any interest in the social-democratic ambitions of most of the KOR membership. Opposition intellectuals were shocked to realize that they were often considered to be irrelevant to the solution of workers' problems and that they were regarded with considerable suspicion. Many union members saw Michnik, Kuroń, Geremek and KOR as covert communists bent on leading the workers deeper into some other form of bondage – an attitude encouraged by Cardinals Wyszyński and Glemp. Many felt that the intellectuals were intent only on humanizing the immoral and godless communist system. But when it came to the question of whether the workers wanted to retain some form of socialism or to abolish the system entirely and install a market system there could only be a pained silence. The workers, who did not trust the communists, trusted the intellectuals only on practical matters, and even then often felt confused and betrayed by them, had no experience of the free market, but could see it glittering and beckoning on the horizon. Although their needs were consistently greater, Solidarność was prepared at first to settle for independent trade unions: later they began to realize that there could be no such thing as an independent trade union operating within the existing political set-up. And in any case, whatever the workers of Solidarność may have wanted, the overwhelming power of the Soviet military (whose fleet was visible manœuvering in the Gulf of Gdańsk throughout the first Solidarność Congress in Oliwa) marked the limits of possibility.

In the absence of any way of communicating feeling from the bottom of society to the top, the workers increasingly turned to the Church to mediate their case, articulate their demands and problems, force the Party to take them seriously, prevent confrontation between striking workers and violent repression by the armed forces, and give content to the 'consultation' between workers and Party which was increasingly regarded as mere ritual. However, the Catholic Church was resolutely 'neutral'. Its achievements were primarily moral and social, and as long as its institutional survival was not threatened the Church remained non-combative towards the Party. Contrary to popular opinion the Church in Poland was not a semi-underground organization. It was very successful and expanded enormously under the communists. While it reluctantly sheltered atheist dissidents like Adam Michnik, the hierarchy also warned against both oppositionists and the Party, holding to a deeply embedded suspicion that all intellectuals operating outside specifically Catholic enterprises were communists in disguise. The Church was prepared to offer succour, but not prepared to confront the Party or publicly develop a critique of Party practice. Beyond moral condemnation and a sense that somehow the Party and its values were 'not Polish', the populace lacked any substantial intellectual perspective on its plight and, with the exception of the mirage of western consumer society, lacked a coherent vision of an alternative society.[1]

In spite of KOR the influence of intellectuals was socially and politically very limited, but the opposition intellectuals were in any case deeply non-ideological. The wide-ranging opposition of the mid-1970s was a peculiarly loose coalition of the system's opponents, often from very different social circles. That the opposition were non-ideological was frequently reported by puzzled western observers. Later the relative absence of ideology was also evident in Solidarność. All sorts of tensions and tendencies coexisted within it. Such was the degree of diversity of ambition and platform within the opposition that Solidarność could be no more than a conduit for voices of all kinds from within Polish society. These were not in themselves political parties, they were agents fostering the possibility of political parties. Piotr Ikonowicz, commenting from the perspective of his own efforts to found a new independent PPS (Polish Socialist Party) in the winter of 1988, wrote:

> In the 1960s and 1970s the structure of oppositional thinking still remained in the dialectical range of class conflict . . . The common feature of [their] models was, apart from a simplified bi-polar vision of social conflict, its ideological

anachronism. This consisted of a consistent use of one, and only one – Marxist – method to explain social phenomena and conflicts. It was not by coincidence that such people were called revisionists. They were trying to revise a doctrine they were unable to discard. It was not only too deeply rooted, but above all it was tempting for its grace and formal consistency . . . This was nevertheless the source of impotence of the opposition and the durability of the system. The ideology of the opposition remained one of the variations of the state ideology. It was therefore just as distant from the vivid, complex and changing social reality. With growing consciousness of that situation such groups as KOR tried to avoid ideological phraseology, proclaiming only slogans of a generally democratic nature and refraining from deeper analysis of social structure and ramifications.[2]

The peculiar non-ideological climate of the Polish opposition had several sources, but was mainly located in the failure of the revisionists in the late 1950s to bring about any breakthrough in making a humanist Marxism possible in Poland, reinforced by the political strait-jacket of decayed, barely functioning, Polish Stalinism.

Throughout 1981 the impact of 'freedom' on the economically and politically repressed populace, combined with the economic and social consequences of widespread shortages of even basic foodstuffs, resulted in increasing chaos in both public and private life.[3] The economic situation was such that neither the government nor Solidarność could hope to rectify things without massive co-operation from the populace, and this the public was not prepared to give. The workers had been squeezed, the budgets shaved, the statistics massaged for so long that the economy and people were bankrupt financially, physically and emotionally. In July 1981 the Party, embracing reform before it was seen to have lost control, proposed sixty-six articles designed to streamline the economy, recognized that the effect of thirty-five years of central planning and manipulation had resulted in economic and social stagnation, that for young people in particular life had become alienated and burdensome, and that what passed for 'political thought' within the Party was merely dreary and routine conformism.[4]

The idea of reform was welcomed, but the Party's ideas were much beside the mark of public opinion and did little to stabilize the economy. Their proposals did not include the demolition of the *nomenklatura*, did not do away with the leading role of the Party, did not address the problem of censorship, did not effectively rein in the power of the *milicja* or the UB, did not democratize election procedures, did not address the problem of Poland's relationship to the USSR and did not discuss Poland's role in the Warsaw pact. For the writers and intellectuals, who had borne the brunt of organizing and articulating opposition since the mid-1950s, there were no guarantees of intellectual freedom, and no mention of reducing the Party's hold on university appointments, the mass media or publishing industry. By late 1981 the membership of Solidarność had made the same discovery that the revisionists had made before them – namely that as long as the Party was backed by the USSR, as long as the bureaucracy and *nomenklatura* had a vested interest in keeping things as they were (no matter how bad that was), no amount of idealistic talk about *odnowa* would help revitalize Poland.

On 13 December 1981 writers attending the annual ZLP (Union of Polish Writers) congress at the Palace of Culture arrived to find the hall locked and a handwritten note from the Mayor pinned to the door saying that in view of Martial Law he had taken it upon himself to cancel the remainder of the congress. Martial Law was greeted by an exhausted populace with a mixture of anger and a sense of relief.[5] The *coup* temporarily crushed Solidarność and ended a major attempt to restore the idea of an independent civil society; the Party was suspended along with Solidarność. Writers and publishing were particularly hard hit by Martial Law. As well as the harassment of the underground, 'official' publications and 'officially recognized organizations' suffered in the clamp-down.

Among the other organizations banned by the military between 1981 and 1983 were: the Students' Union, the Union of Stage Artists, the Union of Visual Artists, and the Club of the Catholic Intellectuals. The Association of Film Makers only survived after its chairman, Andrzej Wajda, agreed to resign. The suppression of SDP (Journalists' Union) was one of the most fierce. By the end of March 1982 it is likely that over 1,200 of Poland's 10,000 professional journalists had been dismissed or forced to resign – thirty journalists resigned from *Polityka*, twenty from *Słowo Powszechne*, thirteen from *Kurier Polski*. Among TV journalists 513 were dismissed and forty suspended. Ryszard Kapuściński, who had been a firm supporter of Solidarność throughout the shipyard strikes, was prevented from working and had his passport confiscated.

Given the massive resources available to the military authorities, one can only wonder that they made such a poor job of suppressing dissenting writers. The Polish authorities were consistently inconsistent and reliably unreliable in their half-hearted totalitarianism, but there can be very little doubt about the feasibility of repression. Polish PEN was presented with an idiotic list of political charges which, with grave and admirable dignity, they ignored; nevertheless they found themselves proscribed. In the interest of consolidation the Kuźnica club, a venerable relic of the old days of *socrealizm*, was disbanded by the military on 30 January 1983, when it was claimed that it had become a private club for the Kraków Party *inteligencja*. Predictably ex-KOR-KSS activists Lipski, Modzelewski, Michnik and Kuroń were arrested. Polish writers, many of whom had long since forsaken the state publishing houses, were also among the first to be arrested – Andrzej

Szczypiorski, Marek Nowakowski, Wiktor Woroszylski, Anka Kowalska, Janusz Anderman, Władysław Bartoszewski and Tomasz Jastrun, to name but a few. Janusz Krupski, the editor of *Spotkania*, was only arrested after nine months in hiding. ZLP, seen by the military as one of the main foci of unrest, was vilified in the surviving press. Over the next few months ZOMO riot police broke up demonstrations and smashed printing presses. ZLP was instructed that it was no longer possible to run a writers' cafeteria as this constituted an illegal assembly under Martial Law regulations. The novelist Kazimierz Brandys was to recall in his diaries that there was a big debate in the papers and on TV as to what to do with ZLP – some wished to reform it, others to abolish it entirely. A small minority of members supported the military, but as soon as they were known, the public boycotted the purchase of their books.[6]

Under Martial Law all 'normal' ZLP union activity was impossible and Chairman J. J. Szczepański and his executive committee spent most of their time trying to trace and contact arrested writers, send parcels of food and medicine, and petition the authorities for their early release. In December 1982 all writers were released from prison under an amnesty, but ZLP was instructed to purge itself of anti-socialist elements. The newspapers began a campaign to discredit ZLP, its officers, and Szczepański in particular – the police even went so far as to forge a letter from him to the Council of State in February 1983. In the autumn of 1983 the military decided that the union was unable or unwilling to co-operate and should be suspended. A short while later ZLP was dissolved. The Committee of ZLP wrote a seventeen-page letter to the Ministry of Internal Affairs to protest: they criticized ministry officials for attempting to force the union into expelling and blacklisting opposition writers, and for attempting to stage-manage the union's congress. ZLP, they pointed out, had been founded some sixty-three years ago, was probably the single most influential cultural organization in Poland and had its roots deep within Polish culture, and its dissolution 'would lead to huge and irreparable damage, not only to the literary community, but to the whole of Polish society and culture'. The abolition of the union did irreparable damage to relations between the creative *inteligencja* and the authorities.[7]

In March 1984 government spokesman Jerzy Urban announced that in future those writers associated with the 'second circuit' would no longer be eligible for consideration by the state publishing houses, nor would they be eligible for membership of the new writers' union. On 3 March *Życie Literackie* published comment from Kazimierz Molk and the Military Committee for Literary Guidance and Active Culture in which twenty-eight writers, the worst offenders against the authorities, were named and effectively banned. Among these were: Miłosz, Kornhauser, Bocheński, Konwicki, Woroszylski, Żuławski. Shortly afterwards a new ZLP was created by the government. This took over the offices and finances of the old union, and even kept the old name. It was clear that any writer who remained outside the new union would not have access to the café, the library, the grants and pensions, the subsidized publishing incentives, the insurance scheme, the holiday homes, the medical care, and vacation opportunities abroad. In spite of this only unknown Party writers joined. Virtually all those who had any reputation refused.[8] Waldemar Łysiak never had a very high opinion of the ZLP, but by 1989 his view that the union consisted not of 'full writers', but only of incompetents, 'half-writers, quarter-writers and still worse', those 'whom the gods had allowed on to Parnassus without credentials, photographs and stamps', was more than justified.[9]

Martial Law was a time of moral crisis. Writers were faced with choices: continue with their work, co-operate with the military authorities, refuse 'collaboration', go underground, or just fall silent. They were aware that the Polish reading public looked to them not to fall silent in times of crisis, and expected them to offer guidance. The decision often depended on how the writers viewed Martial Law. If they saw it as occupation by the military, forced suspension of civil liberties, crushing of free expression and refusal to reform, then publication with the state was out of the question. For many Martial Law was not only a national, political and cultural shock, but a deep personal wound. Daily life, which had already become chaotic, now became completely unreal, and many felt that the values of their world had been shattered. They searched for historical antecedents and found them in Kościuszko's 1794 uprising, the 1830–1 Russo-Polish war, the great uprising of 1863, and the Russian-German invasions of 1939. They took their bearings from these events, and many still speak of this period as *wojna* (war).

If, on the other hand, writers saw Martial Law as a simple annexation, or even as a temporary set-back, then withdrawal from writing was an unsatisfactory short-term non-solution. Some saw truth in Jaruzelski's claim that he would push through the reforms initiated by Solidarność, and agreed that some effort had to be made to restore calm and order to a dangerously unbalanced society. They felt that in the long run history would absolve Jaruzelski from some of the blame and judged that co-operation with the new regime would be a kind of Positivism within a political set-up that offered no other possibility: they rationalized co-operation with the military as essential, healthy 'organic' work on behalf of the nation. One of the first journals to treat literary developments under Martial Law seriously was *Res Publica*, a paper which had been published 'privately' for some time, and had become such a respected journal that the authorities offered funds if it would accept a minimal level of censorship. The editors did not see co-operation with the military as a rational way of treating the situation, and characterized acceptance of the offered bribe as certain social suicide. They refused the offer.[10]

Zbigniew Bujak was one among many who had begun to talk of the differences between an underground society and an underground state – he had had enough of living underground. Kuroń wanted to conspire to seize power and proposed a general strike and programme of mass resistance. But Michnik, who had anticipated many of the struggles that would develop in the 1980s in a discussion with Kuroń and Lipski in the pages of *Biuletyn Informacyjny* in 1979, said that a non-violent struggle was taking place between an organized civilian society and the repressive apparatus of power. The aim of the opposition, he said, was not to take power, but simply to limit it; the real problem was how to limit it in the open, rather than through an underground system that was itself limited and subject to deformation. Michnik knew that to 'live as if they were free' was not the same thing as 'living in freedom'. *Samoorganizacje* (self-organization) was no substitute for democratic government and an open market for information. The parallel civil society, with all its distortions and reflections of 'Polish reality' (itself distorted by the Party) was the only one that offered them satisfaction, self-respect, dignity and an inner life:

> The publication of uncensored books and periodicals is the most frequently cited product of the opposition's tactic of creating independent institutions. The uncensored press is not just free from censorship, but it has virtually no contacts with the official system. I write 'virtually' because it often happens that these publications are read by people who are concerned with the system. And there is another point of contact: the police take every opportunity they can to confiscate copies of these publications. This is how the independent press can and should function under today's conditions.[11]

However badly shocked the Poles were by Martial Law, it did not destroy the will to restore civil society. Indeed the *coup* forced the public back on itself and, far from suppressing the need for a civil restoration, it extended that feeling into the thinking of even loyal Party members.

General Jaruzelski's legacy will doubtless prove complex and ambiguous. A communist from his youth, but of gentry descent, Jaruzelski seems to have finally seen through the charade of Polish communism only in 1987–8, but he had been wavering for some time. In declaring Martial Law he spoke, not of the Polish state, but of the survival of the Polish nation, promising that he would carry through the reforms initiated by Solidarność. Even without the Party, which he had suspended, he was as good as his word; but eventually he came to realize that while the communist system may have been very useful in the post-war reconstruction of Poland, the Party had 'exhausted its locomotive power' and was incapable of leading Poland's energy into 'constructive channels or towards genuine democracy'.[12] Jaruzelski slowly realized that without some form of social legitimacy (such as was accorded by democratic dialogue) he could not push through his reform of the economy, and could not make the Party anything less than odious to the majority of Poles. Jaruzelski was far more aware of Polish literary culture than any of his predecessors, which was not difficult. He was certainly more aware of Polish literature than Wałęsa.

At school Jaruzelski is said to have excelled in Polish literature. One of his classmates was the poet Gajcy, and his speeches were peppered with references to Polish literary classics (particularly Andrzejewski, Wyspiański, Prus and Mickiewicz) in a way that was most unlike other post-war leaders. Furthermore, he was not afraid of making connections between literature and politics, even when this went against the grain of received opinion:

> What I have to say may sound harsh, but the truth may not be trimmed. Polish shortcomings are not a product of socialism. They have a combination of causes stemming from the complicated, centuries-long vicissitudes of our nation. Have those ascribing all the evil in Poland to the socialist authorities never looked into the great sages of our political journalism? From Modrzewski and Skarga, Staszic and Lelewel to Prus and Pruszyński – almost every generation faces the bitter question: Why is our understanding of the interest of the state so weak, our ethics of public life so low, our attitude towards work so frequently improper? Why is there so much envy and pig-headedness? Why does slander spread so easily and gossip find so ready an audience? The quality of human relationships also has an impact on the shape of civic attitudes. Last year, I asked in Parliament how it could happen that in Poland democracy turns so easily into anarchy, while the authorities so easily succumb to deformation. This subject has yet to be accorded sufficiently thorough reflection, reaching back to its roots. I think our movement should take up this issue, discuss it and bring it home to all sections of society.[13]

Jaruzelski chose his writers with care, however. He was careful not to quote anyone still living. Andrzej Frycz Modrzewski (1503–72), a priest and utopian intellectual had believed the state should be the guardian of Christian ethics and that the duties as well as the rights of citizens should be defined and enshrined in law. Piotr Skarga (1536–1612), a Jesuit preacher active mainly in Lithuania had attacked the gentry for their belief that Poland stood because no one ruled and had sought to make the state responsible for creating and keeping just laws in return for civic responsibilities from the populace. Stanisław Staszic (1755–1826), was a priest who had supported the emancipation struggles of the peasantry and saw the state as a combination of the middle class, burghers and the enlightened landowners in the struggle against the retrograde and conservative elements among the gentry and foreign powers. Joachim Lelewel (1786–1861), a historian who took part in the 1831 uprising, is best remembered for his negative opinions on the stifling impact of the Catholic Church and the nobility on native Slav structures. Bolesław Prus (1845–1912), a novelist wounded during the insurrection of 1863, was a progressive intellectual who had little time for the rich and who spent his free time in endlessly educating himself (he believed in the co-operative system and said that Polish society had made a serious error in modelling itself on *szlachta* values). Finally, Ksawery Pruszyński (1907–50), a member of the gentry, writer and journalist, a republican reporter during the Spanish Civil War, Polish ambassador to Holland 1948–50, had held right and left in equal contempt.

However sensitive he was to literature, Jaruzelski did not necessarily respect or admire living writers, especially when they opposed his policies and the Party. He dissolved ZLP and a whole range of other cultural organizations, and severely restricted those few that survived; the military even extended the censorship system to post-publication, in order to enable them to seize books already passed by the civilian censors. Jaruzelski's sensitivity to literature did not prevent several hundred deaths in the imposition of Martial Law, or the torture and death of Father Popiełuszko. Hundreds of independent intellectuals, writers and Solidarność advisers were imprisoned or forced into exile, thousands of ordinary Poles were punished for carrying, reading or possessing 'forbidden literature'.

Polish society resisted Martial Law, but it could hardly do so through open confrontation. In 1983 the underground opposition announced the KKN (Committee for Independent Culture), founded to promote the work of oppositionist writers and artists through tours, prizes, performances and exhibitions; a little later the SKN (Social Committee for Learning) came into existence to promote independent social and scientific research in history, sociology and politics. In addition the KOS (Committee for Social Resistance, founded 1981) published its own journal *KOS* (Blackbird); KOS and ZON (Committee for Independent Education) published *Tu i Teraz* (Here and Now), a journal devoted to literature, history, economics and philosophy. By this time some of the underground publishing houses, like NOWa, had become very big indeed, and were destined to play a vital role in underground culture during Martial Law and the years that followed. In 1981–2 alone over forty books and 500 periodicals appeared from unofficial publishing houses. It was here that the works of Gombrowicz, Żeromski, Zbigniew Brzeziński, Kuroń, Günter Grass, T. G. Masaryk, Orwell, Joseph Brodsky, Osip Mandelstam, Bartoszewski and many others found a Polish readership. Krąg, the largest of the underground presses, managed to publish more than fifty-two books and journals in 1982, including Joseph Conrad, Mikhail Bulgakov, Bohumil Hrabal, Konwicki, Nadiezhda Mandelstam, Michnik, Miłosz and Artur Schnitzler. NOWa even exhibited its work at the Frankfurt International Book Fair. The success of these publications may be judged from the fact that without hesitation, virtually all the best and most respected writers in Poland contributed to them under their own names. By 1985 underground publishing was such an extensive business that an Independent Publications Fund was set up by Solidarność to assist the work of the larger houses. In October 1986 a Social Council for Independent Publishing was set up to oversee the quality of product, offer advice and settle disputes. Polish underground publishing had become a formidable cultural and political phenomenon.

From 1983 onwards Jaruzelski's government steadily liberalized the print and publishing industry.[14] With the demise of the censor, the reform of the economy and the end of police harassment many writers began to worry that by staying with underground publishers they were actually contributing to the further deformation of Polish culture. Jaruzelski, true to his word, had reined in the censor and the *milicja*, and created a more or less free market for comment and public opinion. His reforms undermined the moral purity of the writers' stance. Not only writers, but actors, film directors, theatre directors, editors, historians, journalists, artistic sponsors of all kinds, having spent a couple of years in the unsubsidized underground, or working in the west, had felt the chill blast of the free market and decided that if socialism was to have a human face after all, then they might as well make a living from it. This return to the state was not accomplished without bitterness, but in a situation where it was possible to say and publish virtually anything, there was no point in maintaining a high moral profile and a poor bank balance. Tadeusz Konwicki, whose book *A Minor Apocalypse* (1979) had anticipated the social collapse and confusion of the 1980s, was persuaded to resume contact with state publishing. His conversion was frank, disarming, cynical and self-critical:

> Now I return again to my yoke. Of my own accord, I submit to the loving embrace of the noble office [GUKPPiW, the censor], which resides in Warsaw on Mysia Street. Here I am already safe. Here my pen is followed by the watchful eye of my known protector, my intellectual father, my spiritual guide. How heavenly and safe I feel. At last.[15]

The collapse of the Party came at the very moment of social surrender – a fact which has implications for the whole of Polish society: Party membership was growing again, many writers had abandoned the underground presses and their boycott of the state, and were once again showing their manuscripts to state publishers.

In order to set Martial Law and the events of 1989 in context it is important to realize the extent of Poland's long-term compromise with communism. It was not that Poles simply refused to co-operate with the Party right from the first. In spite of its constant clashes with the system, Polish society had a growing Party membership throughout the post-war period. Most Poles saw the benefits of the system (even if they could not experience them as their own) in the post-war reconstruction, in the growth of towns, in the growth of the *czerwona burżuazja* and the professions, in the staggering upward mobility that shifted huge numbers off the land and into towns and factories, in the falling illiteracy rates, in the modest affluence that frequently threatened to show itself. Each successive political upheaval occurred at the same time as a rise in Party membership: in fact, as far as it is possible to tell from the figures available, membership rose throughout the post-war period until at its high point in July 1980 Party membership stood at 3,150,000. This, coupled with the 2,000,000 *nomenklatura* (Party-approved appointments system), meant that nearly one in ten of the population were members of the Party or owed their jobs to direct Party patronage. This probably indicates not satisfaction with the Party, but rather that people felt increasingly demoralized to the point where they had no option but to join the Party in order to preserve their standard of living, further their career, protect their family. The Party created opportunists with a minimal commitment to ideals.

In Poland communism was an uneven opponent for literature, and after the mid-1950s the least of literature's enemies was Marxist ideology. With the death of Stalin *socrealizm* was slowly abandoned in favour of censorship. Writers had found ways round their problems, new ways of publishing, new kinds of writing, a language of hints and guesses, a literature of enormous national responsibility which in many ways harked back to the partitions. On the surface this new literature promised that it was highly political, wily and inventive in its opposition to communism. Moreover, it was a literature that was tolerated and even subsidized by the communists, and was clearly desired by the reading public, *nomenklatura*, Party and *inteligencja*. Nobody, it seems, not even the UB (security service), wished to suppress the literature of opposition in its entirety, nor to replace it with the literature of *partyjność* (literally party-ness, political consciousness). However, under the surface appearance there was a void: writers were united in what they opposed, but divided and uncertain about what they would replace it with, and they had no forum in which to establish these things.

Communists and intellectuals alike had discovered that under the post-war leadership they were to be patronized but unhoused. Polish communism took over the intellectual framework of Soviet Marxism but refused to foster further thought on matters of politics, society, art or economics. The intellectual structures suggested by Marx as the shape of things to come stood as the absolute limit of legitimate thought. Inside that framework intellectual endeavour was supposed to cease, all questions answered. Polish communism did not challenge, never faced up to the fact that illegitimate intellectual activity was far more vital to the health of the society than were the legitimate activities of the Party and the *nomenklatura*. Throughout the post-war period the knowledge and technical expertise of the new *technokracja* were central to the development of the modern industrial society proposed by the Party. Yet the aims of the Party (centralized control and planning) were contradicted by social and economic needs and the requirements of the professional *inteligencja* the Party had created. And without that technical *inteligencja* the Party's project could not succeed. As Andrzej Walicki pointed out, the *nomenklatura* appeared to operate as a new social class, but enjoyed corporate rather than ideological thinking: that is, they preferred to preserve their continued existence and privilege rather than further the aims of communism:

> In post-Stalinist Poland members of the *nomenklatura* were, as a rule, thoroughly de-ideologised, belonging to different 'special interest groups', closely connected with the 'second economy' and comprising also non-Party members. The inevitable pluralism of these groups contradicted the totalitarian ideal of a fully controlled, centrally planned economy.[16]

It was among these people that the writers found their readers. Indeed, to a great extent the Party, *nomenklatura* and opposition overlapped socially and politically. Without an undecided and sometimes sympathetic bureaucracy the writers would have had a very different time of it. Writers, unlike other sectional interests or pressure groups within Polish society, sought to express much more than their own limited professional and social interests. While the Party asked writers to chart the course (positively) of social change in Poland, the writers were more interested in witnessing the change of genuine revolutionaries into reactionary bureaucrats, in spelling out the implications of this change for Polish society, in showing the human consequences of delaying the development of independent Polish political thought.

Although under Bierut the party attempted to foist *socrealizm* on to the writers, under Gomułka the party sought to silence them through censorship, and under Gierek sought to buy them or ignore them, and developed the vague notion that somehow culture (folk-dancing) was a good thing, but possibly irrelevant, and that too much culture (writing, debate, literature) was probably dangerous. Beyond this the Party never managed to formulate or articulate any serious cultural policy. They never worked out a relationship to the traditional role of Poland's writers. The highly centralized political establishment was never in a position to discover the real state of cultural life simply because there was no mechanism for discerning what the Polish public wanted to read, hear or see – and even if there had been, it is unlikely the Party would have obliged, since high on the public's list would have been a whole series of topics which were all too embarrassing to be aired. Instead the Party's cultural apparatus concentrated on bulk publication, cheap editions of foreign classics, 'safe' literature, undemanding poetry. What Polish writers achieved in this period echoed the achievement of the Party, a magnificent rambling improvisation that was no more than a 'holding action'. The cultural experience of Polish communism was a long detour down a blind alley – the same blind alley that Polish culture had been consigned to by the partitions. Within this the conflict between writers and Party, if it can be described as such, was no more than extended wrangling about the real seat of social, political and moral, historically vested, authority.

Polish communism could not challenge this state of affairs because Polish communism was neither Polish nor communist. Whether it knew it or not, Polish communism was never more than a compromise, a holding action within a given, and for the time being unalterable, political situation. Polish communism was slow to acknowledge that class politics had not yet developed by the time they 'took over' in 1945. Class struggle, the separation of Church and state, the development of local capital, the growth of an urban industrial working class and an urban commercial middle class, the growth of trade unions – none of these things had happened in Poland in the way that they had happened in western Europe. Class struggle had been irrelevant in Polish history and communism had preceded the emergence of right and left. Poland's development from the Enlightenment to the present has often been buried in a struggle to exist. Poland is an 'undeveloped culture', closer in many ways to the emerging countries of the Third World than its neighbours to the west: even by 1980 much of the nineteenth century had yet to happen to Poland.

In Poland the survival of the nation had been the only political considera-tion. Poles divided not into left and right, but into those who were against the government, who favoured the patriotic poetic insurrectionary conspiratorial mode, and those who were for the government in a limited and reluctant fashion, who favoured the Positivist collaborationist 'organic work' mode. The emerging post-war *inteligencja* were very different from the pre-war *inteligencja*. They were integrated into the state in a way that the pre-war *inteligencja* had never been. The links between the economy and the government were much closer, yet at the same time, while the professional ethos developed within the *inteligencja*, many saw politics and opposition as a waste of time. What mattered was a well-paid job, a secure home, professional status. If communism and Party membership were the modern equivalent of 'organic work' for many, protest through petty theft, chiselling, absenteeism, alcoholism, conspiracy and a general refusal to give consent to actuality (a range of attitudes symbolized by the graffiti symbol of the tortoise) were the real life of many more. For a few, conspiracy and resistance became a way of life.

Even a casual glance into the essays of Adam Michnik, Stanisław Barańczak or Adam Zagajewski reveals Polish culture as possessing a highly developed moralistic and emotional streak, a culture that placed greater emphasis on loyalty to the nation than on any ideology of class or division of left and right. Many writers (Miłosz, Brandys and Zagajewski in particular) lamented that their options lay either in solidarity with the traditionalist masses, or in solitude. These were options that an earlier generation of writers (Bruno Schulz, Stanisław Witkiewicz and Witold Gombrowicz) would have recognized. At the same time the old gentry vices of egoism, and haughty, cultured independence, became national virtues, just as they had during the nineteenth century partitions: the Polish *inteligencja* saw itself as the major force for preserving national tradition, identity and the idea of independent political life. Working within the inherited and refined tradition of the gentry ethos supplemented by the moral authority of the Catholic Church, they recorded the human effects of the 'Asiatic mode of production' on the Polish people, the effects of crude and inefficient industrialization, the moral and spiritual effects of the one-party-state. They charted the continuing failure of political thought in Poland.[17]

Poland was never a fully communist state, and Poles were never so serious about the idea of communism as when free-marketeers began the demolition of communist structures after 1989. Nor, after 1956, did Poland have a totalitarian regime on the Soviet model. Each successive post-war government consistently failed to turn its authoritianism into totalitarianism, failed to push through the collectivization of farm lands, failed to suppress dissent, tolerated underground publishing, punished but did not eradicate or liquidate opposition, failed to promote social ownership, failed to move towards a moneyless or marketless economy, and failed to reduce the need for private enterprise. Indeed by accepting the 'second' economy (and creating the dollars-only PEWEX stores to make use of it) they recognized their system was inadequate and provided themselves with legal access to black-market goods and finance. By the 1980s all pretence to communism had gone and the regime sought minimal assent for its existence rather than active collaboration. For many members of the Party, Polish communism was a necessary evil, something to be tolerated, taken advantage of, used; it was a realistic acknowledgement that circumstances could not easily be altered, that nothing inside Poland could be solved until events outside Poland (in the USSR) were more favourable. The Party promoted reluctant acceptance of its continuance not on ideological grounds but solely on geopolitical realities, namely the proximity of the Soviet Union and the threat from Germany. At the moment Jaruzelski is seen as a pariah, and his regime is characterized in the blackest terms by most Poles. In spite of this, it may be that at some future date his *coup* and the 'social and political restructuring' of Martial Law will be seen as a clumsy attempt to dissolve irreconcilable elements in Polish social and political life.

Since 1976 Polish writers have proved to be the (sometimes distant) ally of the proletariat against a wavering and opportunist bureaucracy, and against the monopoly power of the Party. By making available a portrait of the authorities the writers wrote a limit to the insensitive and decaying values favoured by the heirs of Stalin. At the same time they showed that while the

Party took Moscow's opinion into account at virtually every stage of its supposedly internal processes, moral life in Poland was untenable simply because Poles were denied responsibility for themselves. At least until the mid-1970s, in spite of the blandishments offered by the state cultural apparatus, writers refused to equate socialism as a moral vision with the bureaucratic reality of communism. Most writers refused to believe that the continued institutional survival of the bureaucracy, Party and *nomenklatura* was synonymous with the survival of the nation. The writers articulated non-Party, national and nationalist, Catholic, middle-class ambitions, opinions and values, through which garb the old *szlachta* ethos peeps out. The creative *inteligencja* faced the spoiling powers of an authoritarian society with enormous bravery and resilience: against the threat of violence they pitted knowledge gleaned at great personal risk, and intellect fostered in obscurity. They interpreted and elucidated the difficulties and social problems the Party and the *czerwona burżuazja* were creating but which they could not contain. Polish intellectuals – even those inside the Party – needed the independent writers because they could find out about these things nowhere else.

It is clear that most underground writers and intellectuals, who had had enough of what they understood to be communism, curbed one authoritarian streak in Polish culture only to impose their own brand of 'moral terror' through their ostentatious refusal to co-operate with Jaruzelski and their refusal to see any difference between his regime and that of the Stalinist terror. There is only one decisive factor which can explain such behaviour, and that is the historical relationship of nationalism and national identity to the unique role of the Polish writer. As Stanisław Starski has written:

> In the case of Poland . . . the loss of an independent Polish state, which did not survive the end of the eighteenth century and did not reappear on the map of Europe until 1918, has caused a profound intensification of the national frame of reference. The fact that Polish Romantic poets had to replace society's lawyers, teachers and politicians shifted the whole burden of socialization to national culture and away from practical activities of administration. The durability of this national pattern has been proven in the years since World War II. Sociological research carried on by Stefan Novak since 1957 has confirmed a vague feeling on the part of Polish intellectuals that the majority of Poles view the state and 'state-leading groups' as historically coincidental . . . Devotion and loyalty go to the nation, the national community and tradition, which are felt to be definitely superior to the political organization of society. Thus what may appear as a purely demagogical slogan – 'We have signed the agreement, as a Pole does with a Pole' – which appeared after the Gdańsk, Szczecin and Jastrzębie agreements had been signed, was actually an expression of loyalty to Poland on both sides of the class barricades. This loyalty to the national heritage which surpasses differences of class and politics is by no means an unmixed blessing . . . [18]

The years 1988–90 saw remarkable and entirely unpredicted change in east central Europe. In 1988 President Gorbachev let it be known that the Soviet Union was no longer prepared to prop up the regimes on its periphery. Almost at once the discredited, inefficient and hopelessly antiquated communist regimes of east central Europe became untenable. Freed from the cloak of Moscow at last, Polish communist thought stood naked. One of the first organizations to scent the change was Polish PEN. They had been suspended by the Martial Law authorities in December 1981, and their democratically elected management body had been replaced by a military commissar. Their protests and a visit from the President of International PEN had been to no avail. Polish PEN refused to accept military interference and instead declared itself dormant. The military responded by initiating legal charges claiming PEN were agents of the west. PEN refused to answer the charges and simply waited for better times. Juliusz Żuławski, Polish PEN President, explained:

> It was complicated. I believe that many Polish communists were afraid of Russia and some acted in a double way: they wanted it to be seen that they were very good communists, but at the same time they were also Poles, and they also tried to preserve what they could of the Polish identity. Many Polish communists acted this way – double thinking, double acting. Of course they mouthed communist propaganda, but behind that they tried not to spoil everything. In Poland this was especially the case, much more so than in other communist countries. In 1987, the government started trying to speak about how it might be possible to do something with PEN. They explained about how it might be possible to resurrect PEN if we would agree to do this without any elections, with people on the board suggested by the government. The minister of culture, Mr Krawczuk, made this proposal. I told him that according to our constitution there was only one way to reopen PEN and that was to call a free election of the board (and that in itself was a compromise, because we already had a board from 1981). But he was very nervous. A free election, he said, is very dangerous. He tried to make a secret deal with me. He said: 'You will be president for life, we guarantee it, if we can put our people on the board'. I refused any such malversation [*sic*] and told him that normal elections were the only way, in accordance with the International PEN charter and regulations. Then they sent me two different Party members (members of PEN, writers who were on the government side) to try to persuade me to make a deal, somehow, with the government and set up PEN without elections. I laughed and refused. I refused any and all preconditions. Several times I tried to get my point of view on this whole subject printed in the newspapers, but always the censors withheld it. Then suddenly I was allowed to write something in *Tygodnik Powszechny*, an open letter addressed to the president of the Council of State and to the speaker of the Sejm, and this was followed by a letter signed by most Polish PEN members (about 150) in support. And after that we were all invited to the Belvedere Palace to discuss things . . . suddenly, in 1988, the government agreed to ask me to call a general assembly of PEN and agreed to free elections. They accepted PEN's own normal running, and agreed to restore PEN,

without any preconditions. It is important to realize that PEN was restored a long time (several months) before Solidarność. We were the very first organization to resume normal working. Our first meeting was held on 19 September 1988.[18]

ZLP was also affected by a change in the political climate. Suspended and then disbanded by the Martial Law authorities, who saw it as a focus of intellectual discontent and opposition, it had been replaced by another ZLP, set up by the Party, using the same name, offices and finances. The bulk of the writing fraternity simply failed to join, indeed they refused to have anything to do with it. In June 1989 the SPP (Association of Polish Writers), was founded as a free and democratic alternative to the 'official' ZLP, with the ex-ZLP president J. J. Szczepański as its elected chairman. The new organization did not seek to replace the state-run ZLP, merely to bypass it and if possible ignore it entirely. Membership was a matter of choice, no rewards were offered, and it was open to writers living abroad.

In the spring of 1989 the Party offered underground Solidarność round-table talks. These were followed by free elections in which the Party suffered a humiliating defeat, handed over power quite meekly to anyone who would take it, but could not call upon any organization other than Solidarność to assume the mantle of leadership. Solidarność was itself in difficulties: it had no ideology beyond national feeling and no agreed policies. There was no clear social agreement to follow Solidarność's lead and the union was weaker in 1989 than it had been at any time since its birth. Its membership was declining while membership of the official trade unions was rising; its efforts to call a general strike had ended in disaster raising only patchy support; at the same time it had no control over the latest wave of independent strikes which were quite separate from the Solidarność initiative, and Lech Wałęsa's personal public standing was at its lowest ever in May 1988. In many ways Poland was as unprepared for its liberation in 1989 as it had been in 1918, and the same temptation loomed to surrender power to an authoritarian father figure.

Timothy Garton Ash has assured us that there was nothing new in the 'velvet revolution' of 1989 – that this was a quiet, simple return to the old eighteenth-century central European concept of civil society, of democratic and egalitarian relations assuming prominence over the post-war exploitative social relations and violent suppression of discontent.[19] But this is wishful thinking. Poland was and remains unstable and unpredictable: it is a nation superbly strong in patriotism, but with little or no sense of itself as a society. In the words of the adage, Poles still find it easier to die for Poland than to work for it. As the poet Cyprian Norwid (1821–83) warned at the time of the partitions, the virtues that sustained Poland through its darkest days could yet prove to be supremely antisocial in more liberal times. Dissident intellectuals like Michnik, Geremek, Kuroń and others have made it clear that their model of civil society is not that of the free market, nor of a bourgeois democracy;

they do not have in mind the simple transfer of western models. Poland has its own history of noble democracy, which some characterize as anarchic, to draw upon. The emphasis of Michnik, Geremek, Kuroń and others is upon the enabling aspects of government, upon the strength of autonomous, self-governing, self-organized, local civic groupings; they seek to abandon state power and hope for the oppressive spoiling powers of the state to wither away. But they are faced with a conservative working class that rightly sees marketization as a threat, does not trust any political leadership, and which, if it could have its cake and eat it, would like to see individual profit alongside a socialist system under any other name.

The sudden transition to a free-market economy and a convertible currency, while the enormously expensive state-owned industries still limped along producing little that was saleable, caused a massive rise in unemployment, drug abuse, prostitution, gun ownership, car theft, house breaking, violent crime, divorce and suicide. As well as knee-jerk anti-communism there was also a growth in anti-Semitism and anti-intellectualism. The power of the Catholic Church also grew as it bid for a place enshrined in the new constitution, campaigned for religious worship in schools and for new anti-abortion laws. What was revealed by the collapse of communism was a frightening susceptibility to demagoguery, an enormous sympathy for simplistic solutions. Poland stood as a complex blend of the industrial and the irrational; modern Enlightenment and modern ambition mixed with rural prejudice; eighteenth-century Enlightenment mixed with frightening ignorance. Where these contradictions were too great to contain in the transition to an open society, the almost intact structures and forms of past political thought surfaced, and though often inappropriate they rose to impose some kind of order, vision and perspective on the swirling maelstrom of political life, where over 600 political parties, few with a membership of even 2,000, vied with each other. Much that is 'new' in the Republic of Poland (the People's Republic disappeared early in 1990, when the crown was restored to the Polish eagle) is in fact recycled pre-war history, a history that has been held in abeyance. When Wałęsa was inaugurated as president in December 1990 he received his insignia not from Jaruzelski, the outgoing president who was not even invited to the ceremony, but from Kaczorowski, the London-based president of the émigré pre-war regime. Adam Michnik was alone in protesting at this. All this spoke, not of the end of history, but of a resumption of the history interrupted by the Nazi invasion of 1939, and perhaps even a return to the history interrupted by the partitions.

After the 1989 elections the floors of both Sejm and Senate (now graced with internationally renowned figures like Andrzej Wajda and Andrzej Szczypiorski) looked more like professional gatherings of writers, historians and film-makers than legislative assemblies. However, for many writers the end of communism was the end of a career. There was a feeling that writers, in opposing communism without forming an alternative that protected their privilege, had killed the goose that laid the golden egg. Writers in Poland now faced a vastly different world from anything within their previous experience. If Polish writers had finally won the right to ignore politics, they were just about to learn that politicians had finally earned the right to ignore writers: indeed it seems that writers had earned the right to become politicians.

The political threat posed by writers was never as great as the Party imagined. Writers stood to lose too much by the destruction of the system of state subsidy. Polish writers wanted to alter the relationship between central authority and civil liberty, not necessarily to dismantle entirely the system that afforded them such privilege. Most realized that their privilege as artists could not be maintained in an open society. They could not reconcile their work with the communist set-up, but many, understanding that Poland would eventually have to go through a period of class politics such as it had never before experienced, realized that socialism need not always be of the Soviet variety. Many would have preferred greater freedoms within socialism to the total freedom of the free market. Many saw they could not guarantee civil freedom under socialism as long as the Soviet Union was still in existence and still powerful. Writers sought change without seeking power. They gained power because they sought change, but the change they wanted was to make human conscience a political and artistic force. That may be why in 1990–1 they lost power almost at once to the rising populist element in the fragmenting ranks of Solidarność. Intellectuals may have been on the road to class power, but the workers were on that same road, and they were moving faster, travelling harder, pushing for power in ways that the intellectuals were not. The writers had not sought to capture state power, and were unprepared for total political power to drop into their laps. Indeed, after forty-five years of struggle, having just reached an accommodation with the Polish government which now allowed them to say and write almost anything and still receive a state subsidy, the collapse of communism was a grave and shocking blow which denied the opposition the moral victory it wanted and needed.

The Party had been obsessed with the problem of its authority. By the time the Party was prepared to listen to independent intellectuals and was free of the stifling Soviet control, Polish society as a whole was no longer prepared to accept the leadership of writers, no longer saw anything even remotely useful in what it understood to be socialism, placed its trust in the free market and the western right and began, under the leadership of Lech Wałęsa (who has a bust of Piłsudski on his desk and whose proudest boast is that he has never read a book in his life) to see writers as covert communists and Jews who had done very nicely out of the old regime. At first Solidarność needed intellectuals and writers to advise it. Once they had established a toehold on power, Solidarność began to attack writers and intellectuals. In 1990 Wałęsa launched a *wojna* (war) against the first democratic Polish government, saying that its ministers were crypto-communists: he tried to get Jacek Kuroń, the minister of labour, dismissed from his post; clashed with Tadeusz Mazowiecki, the prime minister (a devout Catholic intellectual, who it was said was also of distant Jewish descent); stripped the union's newspaper *Gazeta Wyborcza* of its Solidarność logo and tried to oust Adam Michnik (who is of Jewish descent) from his editorial post. Wałęsa's election to president made 'Polishness' a criterion for high office. He split Solidarność into a number of tiny feuding factions in which writers and intellectuals were mistrusted by the bulk of the population, and tried to set the provincial workers against the Warsaw intellectuals.

The transition from 'communist unreality' to 'capitalist reality' has been incredibly painful for all Poles. As Ryszard Kapuściński said:

Polish society is very complex and contradictory: it has been fighting a long time for its independence. And unlike our Czech neighbours, who found a way to wait for better times, our struggle has largely been a frontal assault. Now people here are very emotional. They are used to fighting, but they are exhausted. They have lost their enemy and as a result they are mistaken and confused. Society has no visible guidance. The old system is finished, but it has not quite disappeared, and whatever will replace it has not yet emerged. People don't know how to act, where to go, what to do. They are happy that there has been a change in the power system, that they don't have communists above them any longer, but on the other hand they don't know what they are any more. You don't find a lot of happiness here, only a lot of uncertainty and that is very tiring. We've come out of communism, but not as a clean society; there is a lot of riff-raff here, and as in any big change the scum always rises to the surface. Some people are using democracy. For them it is only a pretence. These are developments which make us fearful simply because there is no institution which can control them. At this moment there is almost no Polish state. The police are afraid to act, Customs and Tax cannot collect revenues, the Party doesn't exist, the government is weak. There are government structures, of course, but these don't extend into society. If a hundred men decided to go on the street and start shooting tomorrow there is no one who could stop them. There is a power vacuum. And the riff-raff are using this moment. We have a rise of terrible mental backwardness, a *ciemnota* – a darkness of the mind, primitive hate, anti-Semitism, anti-all races, something which is anti-everybody. The trouble is historical. Everything has a historical explanation – but that of course is no justification. This was always a very backward country with a very backward peasantry. The *inteligencja* was always very small, and most of them perished in Katyn and Oświęcim, emigrated or died in the Stalinist prisons. This nation now has a very, very tiny, limited *inteligencja*. There is no real middle class here; there is no stable element here; there is no tradition of bourgeois culture here. Ninety per cent of the inhabitants of our towns are not town-dwellers of more than one generation – they are a mixture from all over the old Poland, they don't even come from the same parts of Poland, and their fathers and grandfathers were illiterate peasants. This is very different from the society of Budapest or Prague. We are much closer to the society of the USSR. The problem is that there are no socially accepted, cultural, European, civilized institutions or organizations on a mass scale in this country. There are individuals and small groups, but they are unable to influence the mentality of the whole nation and the level of their civilization. This country is in a very dangerous situation because if we cannot raise the level of our civilization, our culture, very quickly we will be in trouble. We will be left aside for the next hundred years. Some people are aware of this, but the nation as a whole is not.[20]

What will happen to Polish writers now that the power of Party patronage and subsidy has crumbled away, now that Poland is in the process of becoming a 'free'-market economy with a democratic electoral system? Nobody can say for sure. Wałęsa gave an interview to *Playboy* in which he showed a deep misunderstanding of what writing could be like in a 'free' Poland. When the current troubles of Martial Law were over, Wałęsa promised, he would write a book: 'I'll talk the way I'm talking. I'll say to someone, "Listen, write this." And out of it should come a book. Not a boring one. It has to be interesting. It has to overturn the old theories. And at the same time describe them, restore them in order to overturn them.' Wałęsa was under the impression that he would 'write books and earn lots of money'.[21] That was in 1982. By 1991 the breakneck pace of economic reforms sponsored by Wałęsa, reforms which he said were proceeding too slowly, were being sabotaged by crypto-communists, reforms which had all but destroyed the readership, alienated intellectuals, demolished the state publishing industry and replaced it with uncontrolled, independent, piratical, low-brow and pornographic publishing, making it unlikely that anyone would earn a living from serious writing in 'free and democratic' Poland for a long time to come.

The privatization of the giant RSW publishing combine was a matter of urgent concern to the first post-communist government of 1990: the enabling laws took precedence over the seizure of Party property, the election of a national president and the redrafting of the Polish constitution. Between March and November 1990 the Liquidation Commission, set up by special Act of the Sejm, estimated that RSW had been running with an annual government subsidy of 260 billion złoties. The commission sold off fifty-five of its newspapers and proposed the sale of RSW's entire distribution network, nine printing houses and those parts of CAF (Central Photographic Agency) that were most closely involved in working with RSW. A further 107 RSW newspapers and journals were sold at auction: *Sztandar Młodych, Dziennik Bałtycki, Dziennik Łodzki, Express Wieczorny* and *Życie Warszawy*, this last for 40 billion złoties to a Polish bidder backed by a Sardinian consortium. Many complained that these operations had been sold too cheaply to foreign buyers – for example *Dziennik Bałtycki* was sold for 12 billion złoties. but in the previous year had shown a profit of 4 billion złoties.

This, however, was only one of six newspapers bought by the right-wing French publisher Robert Hersant. Bids by the British press magnate Robert Maxwell were turned down (Polish revenge for publishing a sycophantic English-language volume of interviews and speeches by General Jaruzelski during Martial Law, in which Maxwell referred to military rule as safe-guarding Poland from Solidarność and the threat to socialism). Another seventy newspapers were offered free or as worker buy-outs to journalists, to be run as smaller co-operative concerns. The Liquidation Commission also broke up the ownership of the RSW specialist publishing houses, namely: Interpress (the Party's outlet for foreign-language publications about Poland); KAW, (National Publishing Agency) specializing in social and political science books, albums, tour guides and serious books for young adults; KAR, (National Workers Agency), publishing economics and political literature; KiW (Books and Knowledge), a co-operative publishing books on sociology and political science; MAW (Youth Publishing Agency), social and political literature, *belles-lettres* for young adults; WW (Contemporary Publishing), popular science, children's books, books for young adults, serious science texts for young adults, social and political science texts.

By the end of 1991 the privatized Ruch kiosks were still the main distrib-utors of newspapers and journals, and were still massively inefficient: they owed billions of złoties to publishers from counter sales, and even the most popular newspapers expected to recover only 10–20 per cent of their costs through circulation via Ruch. As a result of these sales and changes approximately 1,000 of Poland's 10,000 journalists lost their jobs, and most independent writers found that they were no longer offered contracts or commissions for the future. Former RSW employees were unable to find work: such was the political and economic climate. The liquidation of RSW in 1990–1 marked the effective end of the communist political monopoly in Poland.[22]

The advent of the free market hit writers very hard. The collapse of ZLP and the withdrawal of state subsidy meant that the writers' retreat at Obory, the writers' café and restaurant, the whole way of life the writers had known under communism (prizes, readings, the Club of International Press and Books, even the possibility of publication itself) were about to disappear. The collapse of the state publishing industry had not been foreseen, and when it came the effects were swift. Within a few weeks of the departure of the Party Poland's publishing industry was in ruins. Leszek Balcerowicz's economic reforms devastated the Polish readership by introducing inflation at an average of 25 per cent per month: in some parts of the economy inflation reached 1,000 per cent per month. While incomes remained pegged, subsidy was withdrawn from a whole range of Polish industry, and 'real' costs were passed on to the consumer. Inevitably book sales plummeted. PIW, which had regularly sold 30,000 volumes per year from its Contemporary Thought series, failed to sell even 5,000 by the end of 1990. PIW cancelled its plans to publish contemporary Polish poetry, translations of foreign classics and a series of contemporary Polish literature. A crippling 12 per cent interest rate on bank loans meant that by the end of 1990 even independent publishers found themselves in difficulties. Publishers now found it difficult to get their books into the shops. The new independent distributors would only take books they felt they could sell at once and preferably at a huge profit. Publishers and authors found that their profit margins were wiped out by the speed of inflation before they could even collect their receipts. By the autumn of 1991 there were 880 registered publishing houses in Poland, 600 of them private. In the period 1989–92 an average of 200 new publishing houses appeared each year, and an average of 200 publishing houses per year went bankrupt. These enterprises operated without effective copyright laws, without paying taxes or keeping accounts, without price control and without any legal restraint on publishing pornography, politically extreme or racist opinion.

Further, writers were afforded little guarantee for past work. The state bureau for the protection of intellectual property had acted as a clearing house to avoid duplication but had not arranged effective legal protection of writers' work, assuming that state monopoly would make this unnecessary. Writers, editors, publishers and readers were astonished at the speed and extent of the collapse. Within a few weeks a host of small publishers appeared: writers began to see pirated editions of their books appear on the stalls and could do nothing about it. Between 1989 and 1992, among many others, *Mała Encyklopedia*, Herman Wouk's *The Caine Mutiny*, Erich Remarque's *Arc de Triomphe*, EFL text books by Alexander, the EFL series *Kernel Lessons*, Alastair Maclean's novels *Circus, Puppet on a Chain* and *Floodgate*, Leopold Tyrmand's books *Życie towarzyskie i uczuciowe* (Life, Social and Emotional) and *Rok 1954* (The Year 1954), Milan Kundera's *La Valse aux Adieux*, Margaret Mitchell's *Gone with the Wind* and six books in the *Namiętności* (Passions) series from ALFA were all the subjects of legal complaints regarding piracy. In some cases small independent publishers had produced one book and then disappeared so that no legal action against them could proceed; in other cases print employees were bribed to produce more copies than had been agreed, and then to 'slip' them to a pirate. In some cases tiny 'club editions' were made, numbering less than 500 copies. Some of the smaller publishers tried to brazen the matter out in court claiming that they had received verbal permission to print; others said that their edition was too small to cause any real damage to the sales of the authorized versions.[23]

Many of the new publishers specialize in cheap and often inaccurate translations of foreign best-sellers, cheap crime novels, horror novels and lurid pornography sometimes in editions of 100,000–200,000 copies. It is possible to buy *Światowy program żydowskiej masonerii* (The World Program of the Jewish Masons), the Polish edition of *The Protocols of the Elders of*

Zion. A Polish-language edition of the still banned *Mein Kampf* (Scripta Manent, Krosno) proved to be incredibly popular, even when the Ministry of Justice and the attorney-general took steps to prosecute the publisher for 'publicly supporting Fascism and fomenting nationalist agitation'. The Polish ISBN service, rather than the state copyright protection agency, turned out to be the only organization that kept track of publishers, and they estimate that by November 1991 they were dealing with over 900 Polish publishing concerns (not all of which were registered) plus an untold numbers of 'pirates'. Although copyright protection in Polish law followed the principles of the Berne Convention, in practice, because of loopholes in the domestic law and the tardiness of the courts, publishers were not required to request an ISBN number, did not report insolvency, did not supply full publication details to either the tax office or the ISBN office and did not send copies of their publications to the National Library. Even after an act of piracy was reported to the courts and legal proceedings were initiated it often took more than sixty days before any action was taken to uphold the law and move to find the pirate – by which time the pirate had made his 'killing' and had moved on. The Society of Polish Book Publishers was lobbying for changes to the law to protect the publisher's rights, as well as those of the authors, by extending copyright from twenty-five to fifty years and by punishing infringements with a maximum prison sentence of two years or fines up to one million złoties.[24]

After 1989 writers and publishers could no longer rely on sales of books to libraries, since there was no longer any subsidy available and there was no reliable guidance from the Party, Składnica (Repository, the central book distribution service) or from the publishers as to what librarians should purchase. Beyond the rather limited work of the *Krakowski Ośrodek Badań Prasoznawczych* (Kraków Centre for Press Studies) there was no guide to the new commercial publishing industry. Librarians lacked professional advice and even lacked their own professional newspaper to review new publications.

In conditions where it was possible to say anything and publish what the market wanted at the highest price it could bear, the writers' product ceased to hold value. The sudden marketization of the Polish publishing industry meant an abrupt end to *ambitna literatura* (serious literature) and the arrival of *literatura wagonowa* (literally, wagon literature: pulp fiction). It was not only that by coming out into the light of day the writers now had to face the open market and compete with the pornography and dross of a 'free society'; they had in fact lost almost overnight the role, built up over 200 years, as the moral conscience, speakers for a downtrodden, occupied and conspiratorial national culture. It is hardly surprising that many writers now see no future (or at least no substantial income) in literature, and have gone into politics – the only job that a career dealing in words has fitted them for.

For the first time writers were thrown on to the free market at a time when Polish society was experiencing an indescribably chaotic range of transitions.

Polish writers faced 'freedoms' new to their national culture; they were without the ready-made audience provided by underground publication or the 'muse of censorship'. Perhaps for the first time since the partitions there was no restraint upon what they could say. For writers brought up within an intense, inward-looking, conspiratorial, moralistic, anti-authority tradition, the lush indifference of the free market was a terrifying prospect. By the end of 1991 very few writers had written anything since the round-table talks of 1989. Some had ceased writing because they did not know what to write any more, some because they were 'giving their energy to the formation of democracy', some because they were now politicians, others because they had lost their bearings and could no longer make sense of what they saw or heard. Many had stopped writing because their publishers collapsed.

The state budget could no longer afford to offer subsidy. The economy was too weak to produce private patrons, the public too poor to afford works of literature. For nearly forty years Polish communists and secret policemen had failed to suppress the writers: the free market managed it rather more efficiently within a matter of weeks. In May 1991 I attempted to arrange a meeting with the state Czytelnik publishing house to discuss the change to democratic government and the free market and their effect on Polish writers and the publishing industry. It was very difficult to get anyone at this or any other publishing house to talk; finally over the telephone a man said wearily: 'We are dying. These are our last days. Can't you leave us in peace?'

Czesław Miłosz was sure that Polish communism, with all its talk about the redistribution of wealth as a primary social task, was fundamentally interested only in the issue of the source of authority. Speaking of the future of Polish literature he explained:

> On the one hand you have this pseudo-Polish pseudo-communist pseudo-culture, working its peculiar deformation of the consciousness for forty-five years through pseudo-literature. On the other hand you have the literature of the underground, which even though it tries to be 'free', follows every twist and turn of official culture – if only to combat it. The two march in lockstep, they are inseparable, and yet both are deeply unnatural. And now we are faced with the prospect of creating something from this mess. And the problem is that even when you put the official and unofficial cultures, and the people who made them, together you still do not have Polish literature. You have only the peculiar literature and culture, the mind-set, of the People's Republic of Poland. What we have to realize is the full implication – for our literature, culture, moral and spiritual life, as well as our politics – of the fact that our communism, for all its connection with Moscow, was a Polish affair, that its collapse was peculiarly Polish. And that the failure of our underground opposition to effect a clear victory was also fully and intimately a Polish failure.[25]

Miłosz also put the new dilemma of Polish writers clearly:

Does the victory of the multi-party system in the countries of central and eastern Europe mean the end of their estrangement from the west? Will they, by introducing the classical division of powers – a legislature, executive and judiciary – recognize the supremacy of all western values? Will the years of suffering under totalitarian rule be obliterated, erased and the people start from scratch? Should the thinkers, poets and artists join their western colleagues in the somewhat marginal role assigned to them in societies busy with selling and buying?[26]

Miłosz had no doubt that the downfall of communism in Poland had been brought about because writers and artists had insisted on the idea of personal vision and personal responsibility. True, the writers led intellectual protest, showed exactly how and why the Stalinist system could not work. Yet Miłosz is simplifying. The writers and oppositionists did not win: victory of a kind was handed to them. In the end the Party's surrender denied them the moral, social and political justification for their struggle. Was the collapse of the intellectuals a part of the collapse of communism? Are Polish intellectuals a spent force? Do they have any vestigial power in a Poland dominated by disgruntled and confused industrial workers in crumbling and polluted cities?

Zagajewski is clear about the nature of the failure:

In my part of Europe, intellectuals played a very important part in bringing down totalitarianism by educating the political élite in liberal and anti-communist ideas, but they didn't reach the whole people. It's quite sad that now, when they should be acting even more vigorously to educate the nation, they seem to have capitulated in front of new-born capitalism and the phenomenon of mass culture, the vulgarity of mass culture.[27]

Perhaps Zagajewski is right. But it is also possible that the Party preserved the power and influence of writers far beyond its normal lifetime by courting them and then by attempting to suppress them. In the same way that Poles flocked to support their Church whenever it was under threat, they supported their dissident and oppositionist writers whenever they were seen to be in difficulties: under Polish communism both writers and Church prospered, in spite of their opposition, in the most unexpected ways. But Poland can be a very confusing place. It is possible that in a 'free' market the power of both writers and the Church will evaporate.

That literature in east central Europe had been political life by other means was demonstrated clearly after the collapse of communism in 1989, when, right across the former Soviet bloc, large numbers of writers abandoned their profession for party politics and positions in the new national leadership. In the Ukraine writers ceased all creative work to give their time and energy to the process of reform and the creation of a democratic opposition. In Hungary, where Geörgy Konrád had done so much to publicize anti-politics (a 'third way' between communism and capitalism), the playwright and short-story writer Arpád Göncz became president; the poet Sándor Csoóri, an outspoken defender of 'national values', became a key adviser to the first post-communist government; dramatist and short-story writer István Csurka became a founder member of the first post-communist governing party. Csurka and Miklós Haraszti were among many who entered party politics either as highly visible government ministers, MPs or spokesmen for the newly created parties. Konrád became president of International PEN (the first time a writer from 'eastern Europe' had ever held the post), and then as a member of the Free Democratic Party helped form a coalition government with the (reformed communist) Socialist Party. In Bulgaria the new government heard that several countries had requested that the poet Blaga Dimitrova should be their new Bulgarian ambassador – in fact she became vice-president. One of the first acts of the liberalizing Bulgarian government was to set up an investigation into the assassination by poisoned umbrella of the writer Georgy Markov, who had been living in exile in London. In Romania the poet Mircea Dinescu, who was under house arrest as the December revolution started, hitched a ride on the first liberated tank and rode to the Bucharest TV studios; after a short and dramatic appearance on national TV he became chairman of the new democratic Romanian Writers' Union. In Czechoslovakia politics lurched to the right and most writers found themselves elbowed into the shadows by professional politicians, advisers and entrepreneurs. However, the admired and respected playwright Václav Havel, only recently released from prison, took a leading part in the Civic Forum and was soon elected Czechoslovak president; Ivan Klíma, who in 1989 organized the revival of the Czech PEN Club, threw himself into what he called 'democratic agit-prop'; the novelist Jirí Grusa became Czech ambassador to Bonn.

In Poland, where writers had played an important role since the time of the partitions, the movement came slightly later, but was nevertheless highly visible. As Polish PEN and the new writers' union began to organize themselves for the new conditions, so the writers rethought their careers. Tadeusz Mazowiecki became prime minister, then later leader of the Democratic Union Party. Stanisław Stomma, Andrzej Wajda, Andrzej Szczypiorski and Karol Modzelewski all became Solidarność senators; Modzelewski went on to become leader of the Social Democratic Labour party and honorary chair of the Union of Labour. J. J. Lipski became head of new PPS. The socio-logist Andrzej Siciński became minister of arts and culture. Ryszard Kapuściński threw himself into the new Solidarność Citizens' Committees. The poet Ewa Lipska was appointed cultural envoy to the key Polish Cultural Institute in Vienna and Tomasz Jastrun was appointed cultural attaché to Sweden. Zdzisław Najder, his death sentence for collaboration with the CIA quashed, returned from exile as an adviser to Wałęsa, acting as Wałęsa's minder for the Solidarność Citizen's Committees, then later as adviser to

Prime Minister Olszewski. J. J. Szczepański became president of the new STP (Writers' Union). Adam Michnik, after a spell as a senator, became editor of *Gazeta Wyborcza*. Jacek Kuroń became a Sejm deputy, then minister of labour and then vice-chairman of the Democratic Union Party. Antoni Macierewicz became president of the Christian National Union and then minister for internal affairs. The journalist Aleksander Małachowski became a Sejm deputy for the left-orientated Solidarność Labour Party then chairman of the Solidarność Review Committee. Jan Polkowski renounced poetry and the life of contemplation for direct political action, becoming owner-editor of the right-wing nationalist Kraków daily newspaper *Czas*. Jerzy Turowicz, after serving as a member of the opposition delegation to the round-table talks of 1989, became an active member of the Citizen's Committee under Wałęsa. Andrzej Wielowiejski became a member of the Citizen's Committees, then leader of the Democratic Union party and a senator. Piotr Wierzbicki, a close associate of Lech Wałęsa, supported his bid for the presidency in *Tygodnik Solidarność* before parting company with Wałęsa to publish in the nationalist, anti-Semitic *Gazeta Polska*.

Clearly a very special epoch in the history of literature has come to an end. We have reached the end of the road as far as the idea of writers as engineers of human souls is concerned. The experiment in shaping human consciousness was for the most part a hugely expensive waste of time and paper, and produced results that were far from those intended. For all that it has been through, Polish literature has little apart from the fact of its survival and a substantial and ambiguous contribution to the literature of anti-totalitarianism to offer the free market of world literature. As Miłosz wrote:

> It's bewildering to think that in selling ourselves to the communists, in return we obtained no great masterpiece. In Polish contemporary literature, even in the latest publications after the fall of communism, there is no book or books which could turn the moral collapse into something of artistic value. Not even one Doctor Faustus . . . The real drama of Polish literature is not only based on the fact that so many writers acceded to communism, but also – and maybe most importantly – not one of them was able to truthfully, courageously and with talent describe his mistake.[28]

This lack of moral certainty and lack of political reliability reverberates deep within the emerging social structure of the new Poland and is manifest in, among many other things, a deep mistrust of the morality of the older generation of writers by younger writers and readers, and a deep suspicion of the older writers' involvement in contemporary political and cultural life. As the young critic Piotr Rypson put it:

Even when the older generation of writers protested, they did so in comfort. This was the group who had agreed to allow Stalinism. Even when they disagreed with the Party, the Ministry of Culture protected them. You have to remember that the peasants in the Party and in the government were in awe of writers. They still wanted the writers on their side. And this generation of writers who formed the 'Stalinist laureate' – they are the main barrier to our culture. After 1968 many new and young writers simply felt blocked by these people. They had to find other avenues for their work. It was as if they refused the patronage of these people. Débuts in official magazines became increasingly rare. Many, of course, found themselves 'emigrated' in 1968, 1970, 1976, 1981. Others simply went underground – which was, after all, only partly underground. But a large number of writers simply did not publish at all – they refused the whole thing, they wrote for themselves and for a small circle of family and friends. After 1970 and its promises began to fade away, this development, of living privately, of having a small circle of close friends, of not even going to certain places or certain events, of not coming into contact with certain parts of society in case you became somehow contaminated, this became a real socio-political phenomenon, a cultural phenomenon. It was this way for poetry, for music and for the visual arts. Now, in the 1990s you look around at our literary culture and you say: Where are the younger writers? Whole generations are missing. Our writers are all due for their pensions it seems. There are very few under sixty years of age. With the exception of the *nowa fala* (New Wave) of 1968, Barańczak, Kornhauser and Zagajewski (and two of these lived abroad after Martial Law), the younger generation of writers hardly exists at all. That is the work of the Stalinist generation. They blocked the younger writers in ways they did not know – with their approval, with their protest, with their taste and with their guilt. This older generation has terrible difficulties in admitting its mistakes or its part in what is happening now – this terrible, wonderful confusion. They write their memoirs, give interviews, but they don't tell the truth. They can't admit that they found their situation very comfortable. They were the hierarchy who sat in judgement.[29]

Few writers emerged from the wreckage of Polish communism with their reputation intact – Zbigniew Herbert, Stanisław Lem, the writers around *Tygodnik Powszechny*, exiles and émigrés, a few others. Those who had continued to publish 'overground' after 1976 were deemed 'compromised'; those who had signed letters of protest in the 1970s but continued to enjoy the benefits of state publication, official favour and a comfortable life-style were also suspect. For many, particularly those in Solidarność who had been imprisoned, writers who were published officially after 1981 were traitors and collaborators. In Stanisław Lem's view, Polish literature did not, perhaps could not, take the chance to become universal under communism, and stood no chance of doing so under capitalism. When asked about the future of Polish literature after the collapse of communism he said:

It's incredibly difficult to write under present conditions. Until recently it was possible to employ Marxism as a point of reference but now, not only is it a closed formation, but one which is entirely decaying. After all, despite everything else, Marxism supplied Polish literature with a chance to be universal. At the moment I can see no problem which in being Polish would at the same time reach beyond the limits of our local interests to the rest of the world. By way of consolation we could say that in countries with a strong market economy literature does not blossom either.[30]

In Hungary, György Konrád, who had been watching events in Poland very carefully, described post-communist writers as the 'new noble poor' and put the issue bluntly:

Books have become more expensive, whilst readers are poorer. Trash overflows and there is less time and money for literature, so many writers have joined the ranks of the unemployed. Gone is the sense of security that a book a year will support us, that we can keep on writing up to our dotage. The place of literature in life has shrunk.[31]

The fate of the younger poets of the New Wave generation of 1968 does not bode well for any continuity of talent from the communist era into the democratic era. They have almost all fallen silent or retreated into right-wing politics.

A disturbing aspect of the 'normalization' process of 1991–2 was the obliteration of communist homage to writers of the left in the naming of streets. For example on 15 March 1992 the Kraków street *ulica* Ignacego Fika was renamed *ulica* Józefa Mackiewicza. Ignacy Fik (1904–42) had been a graduate of Kraków and Lwów universities and an important member of the Union of Independent Socialist Academic Youth. He had been imprisoned for several months in 1925, but had gone on to become a respected critic, poet and political writer. During the occupation he was the organizer of the underground publications *R-Rewolucja* and *Polska Ludowa*, and was Kraków city organizer for the PPR (Polish Workers' Party). On 21 October 1942 he was arrested by the Gestapo and taken to Montelupich. After torture he was shot on 26 November 1942. He betrayed no one. His wife, arrested two days later, died of typhus in Oswięcim in June 1943, but his daughter survived to become a well-known theatre critic. Józef Mackiewicz (1902–85), was a Lithuanian Pole from Wilno, and quite a different case. Adam Michnik described him as 'a controversial author and not exactly my favourite'. While a staunch supporter of the idea of a multiracial commonwealth, he was also a bristling opponent of communism. His most successful works are those written in the west after the war, in which he portrayed the vicious struggles between the London- and Moscow-backed resistance groups. After the war Mackiewicz resided and published abroad. He had been sentenced to death by a Polish underground court for collaborating with the Nazis out of hatred for communism: that is, in 1943, while working as a journalist in Wilno, he visited the site of the Katyń massacre, which was then under German control. He voiced the opinion in the German-controlled Polish-language press, and again in a later book, that the Soviets were responsible for the massacre. This, along with some outspoken observations on the 1920 Russo-Polish war and his insistence that, while the Nazi occupation had made heroes of the Poles, the Soviet occupation had broken Poland's moral backbone, was sufficient to make him an un-person in the People's Republic of Poland. At least one observer thought this particular change of street names to be a 'charlatan manipulation of history', deeply revealing of 'hypocritical shame in attempts to efface the heroic deeds of people whose only fault was that they were communist, to negate any achievements of communist rule, to overlook the works of great artists just because they were left-wing':

> Zealous hypocrisy has become the most popular attitude towards a communist past. It's easy to pretend that real Poles had nothing in common with communism, that it was fate, nobody's fault and nobody's doing. That it was only the Kremlin and its agents dropped into the country from parachutes who shaped the country's image for nearly half a century. That nobody ever marched in a May Day parade under a red banner, raised his hand in consent during party meetings, cast his vote during elections, got an apartment and a coupon for a car after prostrating himself in the party cabinet. That all were born anti-communist and from their very first day knew that communism was hideous and was pushing Poland into an abyss. Only they didn't show it.[32]

In Poland, for most of recent history, literature was the continuation of politics by other means. While politics was impossible, literature was an imperative: as soon as politics became possible, literature became an expensive irrelevance, a cultural extra. In part, it is a matter of what has happened to the word 'communist'. From the late nineteenth century up to the 1930s the word 'communist' became popular with the poor subjects of largely dictatorial regimes of eastern Europe simply because their rulers used it as a term of abuse against ordinary men and women who asked for economic reforms and democratic rights, protested against bureaucratic abuse, and resisted the authorities in the execution of wanton and casual brutality.

Forty-five years after the communists took power that same mechanism made the word 'capitalism' popular. Capitalism was the price Polish society paid for democracy, and no one was to understand this better than writers, particularly those of the older generation whose hopes for socialism had been complex and, it seems, doomed to frustration. The underground republic of letters and the concept of writing as a standard-setting intellectual activity are very probably things of the past. In the future the high moral stance taken by critics of the government will be tempered by the market, and literature itself will be influenced by commercial considerations. Stefan Kisielewski, the aging satirical scourge of Polish life and letters throughout the post-war period, echoing dozens of writers across the old eastern bloc, lamented that no republic of letters emerged from the ruins of communism or from the underground opposition and wrote: 'We are "normalizing" here. The age of the prophets – Sienkiewicz, Prus, Wyspiański – is over. The age of the "engineers of human souls", as communist prophets were called, is also over. From now on only common books, be they interesting or not, will be published.'[33] In Poland the age of the prophets has gone. In its stead has come the age of profits.

NOTES

Notes to Preface

[1] A. Michnik, *Letters from Prison* (Berkeley, 1987), 135–48; J. J. Lipski, *KOR* (Berkeley, 1985), 360–2.

[2] A. Michnik, *The Church and the Left* (Chicago, 1993), xii, 208; Michnik, *Letters from Prison*, 18, 140.

Notes to Chapter 1: Cultural Pathology: The Roots of Literary Opposition

[1] P. Hertz, 'Rozważanie na marginesie lektury', *Twórczość* (July 1959), 90–5.

[2] A. Alvarez, *Under Pressure* (Harmondsworth, 1965), 20.

[3] *Dziady* (Forefathers' Eve) has a complex history. Parts II & IV were published in Wilno as two short plays in 1823. Part III, complete in itself but labelled 'act one' of a much longer piece, appeared in 1832. A fragment of part I was discovered and published posthumously. Why Mickiewicz should have numbered the parts of the play in this way is unknown. H. B. Segal (ed.), *Polish Romantic Drama* (Cornell, 1977).

[4] N. Davies, *The Heart of Europe* (Oxford, 1980), 177–8; M. Gardner, *Poland: A Study in National Idealism* (London, 1915); G. Gömöri, *Polish and Hungarian Poetry 1945–56* (Oxford, 1966); D. Lane and G. Kolankiewicz (eds.), *Social Groups in Polish Society* (Columbia, 1973); P. Anderson, *Lineages of the Absolutist State* (London, 1984), 282; A. R. Myers, *Parliaments and Estates in Europe to 1789* (New York, 1975); O. Halecki, *The Limits and Divisions of European History* (London, 1950).

[5] A. Mickiewicz, *Pan Tadeusz* (Paris, 1834; London 1966).

[6] H. Sienkiewicz, *Tales from Sienkiewicz* (London, 1946), 208; B. Prus, *The Doll* (Warsaw 1890: London, 1996); B. Prus, *Pharaoh* (Warsaw, 1895–6; London, 1991).

[7] Tadeusz Bobrowski, *Pamiętniki I* (Lwów, 1900), 362; *Z Bożej Łaski i Woli Narodu: Konstytucja 3 Maja* (Warsaw, 1991).

[8] J. Conrad, *Heart of Darkness* (London, 1969), 92. This conflict, and the theme of work as a solution to political problems, has survived as an undercurrent into recent Polish literature and can be seen in the poetry of Pope John Paul II, particularly the poem cycle 'Profile Cyrenejczyka'. K. Wojtyła, *Poezje i dramaty* (Kraków, 1979), 49–57.

[9] K. Brandys, *A Question of Reality* (London, 1981), 17–18.

[10] The revival of interest in Sarmatianism in Poland in the mid-1970s coincided with increased interest in Daco-Roman origin myths in Romania, Thracian origin

myths in Bulgaria and the Great Moravian Empire in Czechoslovakia. These phenomena are clearly part of a process whereby national feelings, submerged under Stalinism, emerged again as an outlet for frustrated political and economic aspirations. F. Glatz, 'Hungarians in the Carpathian Basin', *Hungarian Book Review* 2/3 (1989), 9–10.

11 T. Konwicki, *Moonrise, Moonset* (London, 1987), 81; A. Wat, *My Century*, 273; N. Davies, 'Poland's Dreams of Past Glory', *History Today* (November, 1982), 23–30; N.Davies, *God's Playground: A History of Poland*, I (Oxford, 1981).

12 O. A. Narkiewicz, *The Green Flag: Polish Populist Politics 1867–1970* (London, 1976).

13 A. Polonsky, *Politics in Independent Poland 1921–1939* (Oxford, 1972), 28; N. Davies, *God's Playground*, *II*, 417–18; J. Topolski, *An Outline History of Poland* (Warsaw, 1986), 231.

14 Maria Dąbrowska born in Russów near Kalisz, studied natural sciences, sociology and economics in Warsaw, Switzerland, Belgium, France and England. She also studied the peasant and co-operative movements in Finland and returned to Poland to marry a noted social worker. She worked in the Polish co-operative movement for ten years and then began to write fiction. She made her début with a collection of startlingly realistic stories in 1925. Her major work is *Noce i dnie* (Nights and Day), published in the years 1932–4, a four-volume epic of life in Kalisz from the 1860s up to 1914, portraying the transformation of the gentry into the urban intelligentsia. Frequently nominated for the Nobel prize, she is considered the foremost realist in Polish fiction, a link between contemporary literature and the nineteenth-century Positivists. She was the conscience of the intellectual lay left after 1956, and the recipient of many awards from the post-war regime.

15 W. Doroszewski, *Słownik języka polskiego* (Warsaw, 1958–69); W. Here and W. Sadowski, 'The incompatibility of system and culture and the Polish crisis', in S. Gomułka and A. Polonsky (eds.), *Polish Paradoxes* (London, 1990), 119–38.

16 G. Konrád and I. Szelényi, *Intellectuals on the Road to Class Power* (London, 1979), 125.

17 B. Schulz, 'An Essay for S. I. Witkiewicz', in Jan Kott (ed.), *Four Decades of Polish Essays* (Evanston, 1990), 109; B. Schulz, *The Fictions of Bruno Schulz* (London, 1988); J. Ficowski (ed.), *The Letters and Drawings of Bruno Schulz* (New York, 1990); J. Ficowski (ed.), *The Drawings of Bruno Schulz* (Evanston, Ill. 1990).

18 W. Gombrowicz, *A Kind of Testament* (London, 1973), 53–4; also: D. De Roux (ed.), *Rozmowy z Gombrowiczem* (Paris, 1969), 89–91.

19 W. Gombrowicz, *Ferdydurke* (Warsaw, 1938; Harmondsworth, 1986); *Possessed: A Gothic Novel* (Warsaw, 1973; London 1980); *Operetta* (Paris, 1967; London 1971); *Princess Ivona* (Warsaw, 1937; London, 1969); *The Marriage* (Paris 1953: London 1970); *Diaries* (Paris, 1957–69; Evanston, 1993); *Trans-Atlantyk* (Paris 1970; New Haven, 1994); *Pornografia* (Paris, 1960; London 1966); J. Kott, *The Theatre of Essence* (Evanston, 1984) 83–96.

20 S. I. Witkiewicz, *Insatiability* (Warsaw 1932: London, 1985); The Madman and the Nun and Other Plays (Washington, 1968); D. Gerould (ed.), *The Witkiewicz Reader* (London, 1993); B. Schultz, 'An Essay for S. I. Witkiewicz', in Jan Kott

(ed.), *Four Decades of Polish Essays* (Evanston, 1990), 109; J. Kott, *The Theatre of Essence* (Evanston, 1984) 61–82; C. Miłosz, *Emperor of the Earth: Modes of Eccentric Vision* (Berkeley, 1981), 32–49.

21 N. Bethell, 'Soviet Agent Reveals Terrible Truth of Polish Massacres', *Observer* (6 October 1991), 1–23; C. Moorhead, 'Out of the Darkness', *Independent Magazine* (26 January 1991); L.Fitzgibbon, *Katyń Massacre* (London, 1976); *Documents on Polish-Soviet Relations 1939–45* (London, 1967); S. Kot, *Conversations with the Kremlin and Despatches from Russia* (London, 1963).

22 A. Wat, *My Century: The Odyssey of a Polish Intellectual* (London, 1977; New York, 1990).

23 K. S. Karol, *Solik* (London, 1986); B. Porajska, *From the Steppes to the Savannah* (London, 1990); W. Sagajłło, *The Man in the Middle: A Story of the Polish Resistance 1940–45* (London, 1984); Z. Zajdlerova, *The Dark Side of the Moon* (London, 1989); G. Herling, *A World Apart* (Oxford, 1987).

24 On Soviet treatment of Polish writers see: K. Sword (ed.), *The Soviet Takeover of the Polish Eastern Provinces: 1939–41* (London, 1991).

25 C. Miłosz, *The Captive Mind* (London, 1953).

26 On Nazi attempts to destroy Polish culture: S. Korboński, *The Polish Underground State: 1939–45* (New York, 1978); J. Garliński, *Poland in the Second World War* (London, 1985).

27 M. Bernhardt and H. Szlajfer (eds.), *From the Polish Underground: Selections from Krytyka 1978–93* (Pennsylvania, 1995).

28 M. Pinior, 'Solidarity at the Crossroads', *International Socialism* 41 (Winter 1988).

29 J. R. Fiszman, *Revolution and Tradition in People's Poland* (Princeton, 1972), 289–90; A. Michnik, *The Church and the Left* (Chicago, 1993), 159–63.

30 J. Kowalski, *Zarys historii polskiego ruchu robotniczego w latach 1918–39* (Warsaw, 1959); L. Kołakowski, *Main Currents of Marxism* (London, 1987); T. Deutscher, 'In Memoriam: Proletariat Party, 1882–1886', *New Left Review* 143 (January-February, 1984), 109–19; I. Deutscher, 'The Tragedy of the Polish Communist Party', in M. Eve and D. Musson (eds.), *The Socialist Register 1982* (London, 1982), 124–63; G. D. Jackson, *Comintern and Peasant in East Europe 1919–30* (New York, 1966); E. H. Carr, *The Twilight of the Comintern 1930–35* (London, 1986); M. K. Dziewanowski, 'The Communist Party of Poland', in S. Fischer-Galati (ed.), *The Communist Parties of Eastern Europe* (New York, 1979), 245–80; M. K. Dziewanowski, *The Communist Party of Poland* (Cambridge, Mass., 1959); N. Davies, *White Eagle Red Star: The Polish-Soviet War 1919–20* (London, 1983); N. Davies, *God's Playground: A History of Poland* (Oxford, 1991); O. A. Narkiewicz, *The Green Flag: Polish Populist Politics 1867–1970* (London, 1976); A. Polonsky, *Politics in Independent Poland 1921–39* (Oxford, 1972).

31 R. Luxemburg, *The National Question: Selected Writings* (New York, 1976); H. Arendt, *Men in Dark Times* (Harmondsworth, 1968); P. Frölich, *Rosa Luxemburg: Her Life and Work* (New York, 1972); E. Ettinger, *Rosa Luxemburg: A Life* (Boston, 1986). N. Geras, *The Legacy of Rosa Luxemburg* (London, 1985).

32 Davies, *White Eagle, Red Star.*

[33] M. Hirszowicz, 'The Polish Intelligentsia', in S. Gomułka and A. Polonsky (eds.), *Polish Paradoxes* (London, 1990), 156; *PPR: Rezolucje, odezwy, instruktcje i okólniki komitetu centralnego – 1946–47* (Warsaw, 1961), 212; J. Wiatr, 'The Hegemonic Party System in Poland', in J. Wiatr (ed.), *Studies in Polish Political System* (Wrocław, 1967), 115; J. Szczepański, 'Osobowość ludzka w procesie powstania społeczeństwa socjalistycznego', *Kultura i Społeczeństwo* VIII/4 (1964), 3–25; G. D. Jackson, *Comintern and Peasant in East Europe: 1919–30* (New York), 1966; J. Topolski, *An Outline History of Poland* (Warsaw, 1986), 260–76; A. Polonsky and B. Drukier, *The Beginnings of Communist Rule in Poland* (London, 1980), 97; J. Coutouvidis and J. Reynolds, *Poland: 1939–47* (Leicester, 1986), 181, 236 and 284; K. Kersten, *The Establishment of Communist Rule in Poland, 1943–48* (Berkeley, 1992), 466; B. Bierut, 'Sprawozdanie KC na II zjazd PZPR', *Trybuna Ludu* (12 March 1954); M. K. Dziewanowski, *The Communist Party of Poland* (New York, 1959); G. Sanford, *Military Rule in Poland: 1981–83* (London, 1986), 189; N. Bethell, *Gomułka: His Poland and His Communism* (Harmondsworth, 1972), 93.

[34] L. Kołakowski, 'The Intelligentsia', in A. Brumberg (ed.), *Poland: Genesis of a Revolution* (New York, 1983), 54; W. Wesołowski, 'Changes in Class Structure in Poland', tables 12 and 13, in J. Wiatr (ed.), *Studies in Polish Political System* (Warsaw, 1967), 65 and 78–79; A. Polonsky, *Politics in Independent Poland 1921–1939* (Oxford, 1972), 28; J. Topolski, *An Outline History of Poland* (1986), 274–5.

[35] M. Hirszowicz, *The Bureaucratic Leviathan* (Oxford, 1980), 193.

[36] L. Kołakowski, *Marxism and Beyond* (London, 1969), 178–9.

[37] L. Kołakowski, *Modernity on Endless Trial* (Chicago, 1990), 207–8. Kołakowski's assumptions are challenged in E. P. Thompson, *The Poverty of Theory and Other Essays* (London, 1980).

[38] A. Piekarski, *Freedom of Conscience and Religion in Poland* (Warsaw, 1979), 44–54.

[39] *Ibid.*, 59.

[40] B. Szajkowski, *Next to God ... Poland* (London, 1983), 19.

[41] A. Piekarski, *Freedom of Conscience and Religion in Poland*; Szajkowski, *Next to God ... Poland*; Anon., *Kościół katolicki w polsce 1945–78* (Warsaw, 1979).

[42] C. Cviic, 'The Church', in A. Brumberg (ed.), *Poland: Genesis of a Revolution* (New York, 1983), 307; Piekarski, *Freedom of Conscience and Religion in Poland*, 149–50.

[43] B. Cywiński, *Rodowody niepokornych* (Warsaw, 1971), 262–4.

[44] C. Miłosz, *History of Polish Literature* (Berkeley, 1983), 504.

[45] *Ibid.*, 508.

[46] A. Michnik, *The Church and the Left* (Chicago, 1993), 157.

[47] J. Schatz, *Generation: The Rise and Fall of the Jewish Communists in Poland* (Berkeley, 1992).

[48] E. Czarnecka and A. Fiut, *Conversations with Czesław Miłosz* (New York, 1987), 159.

[49] J. Błoński, 'Is there a Jewish School of Polish Literature?', in A. Polonsky (ed.), *Studies from Polin*, 471–86; L. Q. Mincer, 'A Voice From The Diaspora', *ibid.*,

487–501; J. Schatz, *Generation: The Rise and Fall of the Jewish Communists of Poland* (Berkeley, 1990); M. Fuks (ed.), *Polish Jewry* (Warsaw 1982); H. Mendel, *Memoirs of a Jewish Revolutionary* (London, 1989); A. Kainer, 'Jews and Communism', in Bernhard and Szlajfer, *From The Polish Underground*, 353–438.

50 W. Czapliński and T. Ładogórski, *Atlas Historyczny Polski* (Warsaw, 1974), 25 and table 41; M. Hirszowicz, *The Bureaucratic Leviathan* (Oxford, 1980), 176.

51 J. J. Lipski, *KOR: Workers' Defense Committee in Poland 1976–81*, 137–8.

52 *Ibid.*, 338.

53 I. Deutscher, 'The Ex-communist's Conscience' (1957), in C. Wright Mills (ed.), *The Marxists* (Harmondsworth, 1973), 341–51.

54 A. Michnik, *Letters from Prison* (Berkeley, 1987), 137.

55 L. Kołakowski, *Modernity on Endless Trial* (Chicago, 1990), 207–8; also L. Kołakowski, *Marxism and Beyond* (London, 1969), 178–9; E. P. Thompson, *The Poverty of Theory* (London, 1980), 92–192.

56 Michnik, 'A New Evolutionism' (1976), in *Letters from Prison*, 135–48; Lipski, *KOR*, 360–2.

57 Michnik, *The Church and the Left*, xii, 208; Michnik, *Letters from Prison*, 18 and 140.

58 W. Woods, *Poland: Phoenix in the East* (Harmondsworth, 1972), 134–5.

59 J. Staniszkis, 'Evolution of Forms of Working Class Protest: Sociological Reflections on the Gdańsk-Szczecin Case', *Soviet Studies* (April 1981).

60 Z. Herbert, *Report from the Besieged City* (New York, 1985), 69.

61 A. Międzyrzecki, in D. Weissbort (ed.), *The Poetry of Survival* (London, 1991), 194.

Notes to Chapter 2: The Writing Profession

1 A. Szczypiorski, *The Polish Ordeal* (London, 1982), 55.

2 J. Peterkiewicz and B. Singer (eds.), *Five Centuries of Polish Poetry* Oxford, 1970), 106.

3 Interview with J. Żuławski (Warsaw, 29 May 1990).

4 *Rządowy raport o stanie gospodarki* (Warsaw, July 1981), 126; M. Duskov, 'I don't have the Soul of an Anarchist', *Euromaske* 1 (Autumn 1990), 23–4. Izabella Cywińska, minister for arts and culture, said that after the withdrawal of most state subsidy in 1990, the Polish arts budget still stood at 1. 55% of the national budget. British arts subsidy, which lags far behind all other west European states, in 1995 stood at less than a quarter of 1% of the national budget. 'Letter on Arts Funding to MPs', WGGB (November 1993); 'Arts Council Grants', *WGGB News Letter* 11/1 (Spring 1995), 19.

5 'Apparatus Power', *Labour Focus on Eastern Europe* 4/4–6 (Winter 1981), 55–6; J. L. Curry, *The Black Book of Polish Censorship* (New York, 1984); G. Schöpflin (ed.), *Censorship and Political Communication in Eastern Europe* (London, 1983).

6 Z. Krzystek, 'Kim Jesteśmy?', *Prasa Polska* (August 1977), 30.

7 *Ruch wydawniczy w liczbach XXXIII: 1987* (Warsaw, 1989), tables 30 and 36.

8 *Ibid.*, table 47.

[9] 'Listy', *Polityka* 2/723/xv (9 January 1971); 'The Dissemination of Culture', VI, 1–1, *Facts About Poland* (Warsaw, 1980); *Rocznik Statistyczny: 1966*, XXVI (Warsaw, 1966), 34.

[10] S. Lec, *Unkempt Thoughts* (Warsaw, 1957).

[11] R. F. Staar, *Poland: 1944–62* (New Orleans, 1962), 172; A. Siciński, *Literaci polscy: przemiany zawodu na tle przemian kultury współczesnej* (Wrocław-Warsaw, 1971), 90, tables 37 and 40.

[12] A. Michałów and W. Pacławski (eds.), *Literary Galicia* (Kraków, 1991), 28.

[13] T. Torańska, *Oni: Stalin's Polish Puppets* (London, 1987), 268–9; K. Kersten, *The Establishment of Communist Rule in Poland: 1943–48* (Berkeley, 1992), 416–17; J. Topolski, *An Outline History of Poland* (Warsaw, 1986), 277.

[14] J. J. Szczepański, *Kadencja* (Kraków, Znak, 1989), 5–7.

[15] K. Brandys, *A Warsaw Diary* (London, 1983), 72–3.

[16] T. Konwicki, *Moonrise, Moonset* (London, 1988), 167.

[17] O. Budrewicz, *Incredible Warsaw* (Warsaw, 1972), 147.

[18] T. Torańska, *Oni: Stalin's Polish Puppets*, 269–70.

[19] M. Wesołowski and A. Sarapata, 'Hierarchie zawodów i stanowisk', *Studia Sociolgiczne* 2/2 (1961), 104; A Sarapata, 'Przemiany w hierarchii zawodów', *Studia Sociologiczne* 1 (1964).

[20] L. Kurowski, 'Reforma podatkowa 1949r', *Państwo i Prawo* 12 (1949), 377–8.

[21] A. Siciński, *Literaci polscy*, tables 48–53; F. Fejtö, *A History of the People's Democracies* (Harmondsworth, 1974), 550; W. Woods, *Poland: Phoenix in the East* (Harmondsworth, 1972), 156.

[22] Tables 44 and 45, *Ruch wydawniczy w liczbach XXXIII: 1987* (1989); Topolski, *An Outline History of Polish Culture*, 279; 'Dissemination of Culture' VI, 1–1.

[23] 'Literature' VI. 7–1, *Facts About Poland* (1980).

[24] Interview with Artur Międzyrzecki (Warsaw, 1 June 1990). See also: J. Szczepański, 'Materiały do charakterystki ludzi świata naukowego w XIX i początkach XX w. ', *Odmiany czasu teraźniejszego* (Warsaw, 1971), 50–1; N. Davies, *God's Playground*, II (Oxford, 1980), 196 and 406; M. Hirszowicz, 'The Polish Intelligentsia', in S. Gomułka and A. Polonsky (eds.), *Polish Paradoxes* (London, 1990), 156; M. Hirszowicz, *The Bureaucratic Leviathan* (London, 1980), 193; J. Szczepański, 'The Polish Intelligentsia: Past and Present', *World Politics* 14/3 (April 1962), 419; J. Szczepański, 'Osobowość ludzka z processie powstania społeczeństwa socjalistycznego', *Kultura i Społeczeństwo* 8/4 (1964), 3–25; J. J. Szczepański, 'Sociological Research on the Polish Intelligentsia', *Polish Sociological Bulletin* 1–2 (1961); A. Gella, 'The Life and Death of the Old Polish Intelligentsia', *Slavic Review* 30/1 (March 1971), 17; J. Chałasiński, *Kultura i naród* (Warsaw, 1968); J. Chałasiński, *Przeszłość i przysłość inteligencji polskiej* (Warsaw, 1958); J. Żarnowski, *O inteligencji polskiej lat międzywojennych* (Warsaw, 1965).

[25] *Statystyka szkolnictwa: 1964–65*, 4 (Warsaw, 1966); *Rocznik statystyczny szkolnictwa: 1944–67* (Warsaw, 1967), 434–5; *Rocznik statystyczny 1970* (Warsaw, 1970), 40.

[26] Siciński, *Literaci polscy*; G. Gömöri, 'The Cultural Intelligentsia: The Writers', in D. Lane and G. Kolankiewicz (eds.), *Social Groups in Polish Society* (New York,

1973), 159; W. Wesołowski, 'Changes in the Class Structure in Poland', in J. Wiatr (ed.), *Studies in Polish Political System* (Wrocław, 1967), 79–80.

27 Siciński, *Literaci polscy*.

28 J. Wiatr, *Studies in Polish Political System* (Warsaw, 1967), 110–11.

29 Z. Herbert, 'Interview', *Partisan Review* LIV/4 (1987), 574

30 'Zbigniew Herbert, A Conversation with M. Oramus', in D. Wiessbort (ed.), *The Poetry of Survival* (London, 1991), 328.

31 Interview with J. Żuławski (Warsaw, 29 May 1990).

32 T. Borowski, *Wybór opowiadań* (Warsaw, 1959); T. Borowski, *This Way for Gas Ladies and Gentlemen Please* (Harmondsworth, 1976).

33 T. Torańska, *Oni: Stalin's Polish Puppets* (London, 1987), 141.

34 L. Kołakowski, 'Światopogląd i krytyka', *Nowa Kultura* (16 January 1955).

35 J. Błoński, 'Za pięć dwunastu I–III', *Życie Literacki* (17 April, 24 April and 1 May 1955). Błoński's assertions about the impact of Party policies were later confirmed in Siciński, *Literaci polscy*; E. Fischer, *The Necessity of Art* (Harmondsworth, 1978), 107–15; D. A. Pirie, 'Engineering the People's Dreams', in A. Czerniawski (ed.), *The Mature Laurel* (Bridgend, 1991), 135–59; J. J. Szczepański, *Kadencja* (Kraków, 1989), 5–7.

36 J. Lewiński, 'Nowa Huta Soul's Project', in A. Michajłów and W. Pacławski (eds.), *Literary Galicia*, 59–64; 'Metallurgy' VIII. 3–1, *Facts About Poland* (1980); L. Ludwikowski, *A Guide to Kraków and Environs* (Warsaw, 1979); J. Adamczewski, *Kraków od A do Z* (Kraków, 1986).

37 A. Ważyk, *Poemat dla dorosłych i inne wiersze* (Warsaw, 1956), 5; 'Poem for Adults', in A. Gillon and L. Krzyzanowski (eds.), *Introduction to Modern Polish Literature* (London, 1968), 460–3.

38 K–62, 'I, The Censor', in A. Brumberg (ed.), *Poland: Genesis of a Revolution* (New York, 1938), 260.

Notes to Chapter 3: Jerzy Andrzejewski

1 J. Andrzejewski, 'Zagadnienie polskiego antysemetizmu', *Odrodzenie* (14 and 27 June 1946).

2 'The Trial', from this collection: A. Gillon and L. Krzyzanowski, *Introduction to Modern Polish Literature* (1968).

3 J. Coutouvidis and J. Reynolds, *Poland 1939–47* (Leicester, 1986), 216 and 241; see also K. Kersten, *The Establishment of Communist Rule in Poland: 1943–48* (Berkeley, 1991), 222–3; A. Polonsky and B. Drukier, *The Beginnings of Communist Rule in Poland: 1943–45* (London, 1980); J. Garliński, *Poland in the Second World War* (London, 1985).

4 J. Andrzejewski, *Ashes and Diamonds* (Harmondsworth, 1980), 49–51. A new edition lists corrections and supplies missing passages: J. Andrzejewski, *Ashes and Diamonds* (Evanston, 1991). Reference to Puciatycki's nasal tone: in post-war Polish the two nasal vowels are dying out, but those who identify with pre-war *szlachta* cultural and political values and insist on speaking 'proper Polish', as opposed to *po ludsku* (people's Polish), often emphasize nasal vowels and are thus

sneeringly referred to as 'ą-ę'. M. Zagórska-Brooks, *Nasal Vowels in Contemporary Standard Polish* (The Hague, 1968).

[5] *Ashes and Diamonds* (Harmondsworth, 1962, 1980), 51.

[6] A. Michnik, *Letters from Prison* (Berkeley, 1986).

[7] *Ashes and Diamonds*, 73.

[8] *Ibid.*, 73.

[9] *Ibid.*, 117.

[10] J. Andrzejewski, *Popiół i diament* (Warsaw, 1963), 178–9.

[11] Andrzej Wajda chose Maciek as the protagonist for his film. *Popiół i diament* was released on 3 October 1958 and was very successful, winning numerous awards: FIPRESCI Award, Venice, 1959; CFFMA Award, Vancouver 1960; Otto Selznick Silver Laurel, West Berlin, 1962; the Crystal Star of the French Motion Picture Academy, Paris, 1962; Prague Annual Film Critics' Award, 1965. Andrzejewski did not like the film and complained it did not represent the spirit of the book since it portrayed only selected *wątki* (threads) of the plot. Andrzejewski doubted that any film could adequately portray the full complexity of the novel. J. Trznadel, *Hańba domowa* (Paris, 1988), 82; A. Wajda, *Ashes and Diamonds, Kanał, Generation* (New York, 1972); Andrzej Wajda, *Three Films* (London, 1984).

[12] *Ashes and Diamonds*, 213.

[13] *Ibid.*, 171; *Popiół i diament*, 277.

[14] Prologue to *Tyrtej, Tragedia fantastycna*, in Cyprian Norwid, *Pisma Wszystkie*, J. W. Gomulicki (ed.), (Warsaw, 1971). In the film Wajda has a white horse running around in the background just after this poem is quoted, an allusion to General Anders, commander of the Polish army in the Middle East. In 1946 Anders boasted he would return to Poland on a white horse, signifying he would restore the pre-war alliance of Church, military, bourgeoisie and landed gentry interests. Anders never returned. He died in London in 1972.

[15] S. Wyspiański, *Dzieła zebrane*, L. Płoszewski (ed.) (Kraków, 1958–60).

[16] *Ashes and Diamonds*, 148–9.

[17] Anon., 'Socialist Realism', *Universities and Left Review* 7 (Autumn 1959) 57–67; Teresa Torańska, *Oni: Stalin's Polish Puppets* (London, 1987); D. Pirie, 'Engineering People's Dreams', in A. Czerniawski (ed.), *The Mature Laurel* (Bridgend: 1991), 133–60.

[18] M. Kierczyńska, 'Młodzież podziemia w powieści Andrzejewskiego', *Kuźnica* 23 (1947).

[19] C. Miłosz, *The Captive Mind* (Harmondsworth, 1980), 105.

[20] Z. Herbert, 'Interview with Jacek Trznadel', *Partisan Review* LIV/4 (1987), 564–65.

[21] A. Zagajewski, 'From the Little Larousse', in J. Kott (ed.), *Four Decades of Polish Essays* (Evanston 1990), 371; S. Mrożek, 'Popiół? diament?', *Kultura* 1 (Paris, 1983), 22–41.

[22] Comments cut from *Tygodnik Powszechny* 50, in *Report on Materials Censored*, GUKPPiW (1–5 December 1974).

[23] Trznadel, *Hańba domowa*, 85.

[24] T. Konwicki, *Moonrise, Moonset* (1988), 57.

[25] B. Klimaszewski (ed.), *An Outline History of Polish Culture* (Warsaw, 1983), 314.

[26] Miłosz, *The Captive Mind*, 107 and 109.

[27] Trznadel, *Hańba domowa*, 77.

[28] *The Captive Mind*, 109.

[29] J. Trznadel, *Hańba Domowa*, 75–76.

[30] J. Andrzejewski, 'The Slipper' (1953), 'Great Lament of a Paper Head' (1953), 'Golden Fox' (1954) collected as: *Złoty lis* (Golden Fox) (Warsaw, 1954); 'Golden Fox', in M. Kuncewicz (ed.), *The Modern Polish Mind* (1963), 208–28; 'The Great Lament of a Paper Head' *Polish Perspectives* XXVI/3 (1983), 40–8.

[31] Trznadel, *Hańba Domowa*, 78.

[32] J. Andrzejewski, *Ciemności kryją ziemię* (Warsaw, 1957).

[33] W. Gomułka, *O aktualnych problemach ideologicznej pracy partii* (Warsaw, 1963), 53; M. Waller, *The Language of Communism* (London, 1972), 64–5; D. S. Mason, *Public Opinion and Political Change in Poland: 1980–82* (Cambridge: 1985), 14.

[34] J. Andrzejewski, *Bramy raju* (Warsaw, 1967).

[35] P. Raina, *Political Opposition in Poland: 1954–77* (London, 1978), 80–1.

[36] J. Karpiński, *Count-Down*, 151; W. Woods, *Poland: Phoenix in the East* (Harmondsworth, 1972), 169.

[37] Raina, *Political Opposition in Poland*, 164–5.

[38] Mickiewicz's *Dziady* occupies a special place in Polish Romantic poetry, but many claim its length, style and allusiveness make it unacceptable to modern audiences. Parts of the play have been translated into English, but the full work is not available: B. Taborski, *Polish Plays in English Translations* (New York, 1968). Part III can be found in: H. B. Segal (ed.), *Polish Romantic Drama* (New York, 1977).

[39] Raina, *Political Opposition in Poland*, 121–2. The allusion is to Jan Kott's *Shakespeare our Contemporary* (London, 1967).

[40] J. Karpiński, *Count-Down* (New York, 1982), 151.

[41] Raina, *Political Opposition in Poland*, 164–5.

[42] Z. Herbert, 'Interview with Jacek Trznadel', *Partisan Review* LIV/4 (1987), 570–1; J. Rupnik, *The Other Europe* (London, 1989), 217.

[43] J. Andrzejewski, *Apelacja* (Paris, 1968).

[44] L. Kołakowski, 'Tezy o nadziei i beznadziejności', *Kultura* 6/285 (June 1971), 3–21.

[45] R. Hammer, 'Poland', *Index on Censorship* 4/1 (1975), 30.

[46] The book was eventually published by NOWa: J. Andrzejewski, *Miazga* (London and Warsaw, 1980).

[47] J. L. Curry, *The Black Book on Polish Censorship* (New York, 1984), 385–6.

[48] S. Balbus, 'The Great Silence of the Black Hole', in A. Michałów and W. Pacławski, *Literary Galicia* (Kraków, 1991), 48–9.

[49] J. J. Lipski, *KOR* (Berkeley, 1985), 467–8: *Amnesty International Report 1977* (London, 1977), 259–63.

[50] Table 48, 'Tytuły i nakłady dzieł niektórych pisarzy polskich', *Ruch Wydawniczy w Liczbach XXXIII:1987* (Warsaw, 1989).

[51] J. J. Lipski, *KOR*, 138; Introduction to *Czarna księga cenzury PRL* (Uppsala-London, 1977–78); Curry, *The Black Book on Polish Censorship*.

[52] T. G. Ash, *The Polish Revolution* (London, 1983), 19.

[53] A. Chmielewska, 'The Campaign', *Zapis* 4 (1977), in A. Brumberg (ed.), *Poland: Genesis of a Revolution* (New York, 1983), 227–36; Lipski, *KOR*, 138.

[54] Trznadel, *Hańba domowa*, 83.

[55] Torańska, *Oni: Stalin's Polish Puppets*, 130–1.

[56] J. R. Fiszman, *Revolution and Tradition in People's Poland* (Princeton: 1972), 223.

[57] Anon., 'Jerzy Andrzejewski: Obituary', *Polish Perspectives* XXVI/3 (1983), 38–9. The same journal also published a short extract from 'The Great Lament of a Paper Head', carefully dated 'September 1953' to show that this was nothing new. Before that only 'Running Low', an extract from *Już prawie nic*, had appeared in the journal in September 1980.

[58] Andrzejewski's involvement in the underground publishing industry and in KOR were clearly a grave embarrassment to the Party. His career after the flirtation with socialism is hardly mentioned in official biographical material such as J. Krzyzanowski (ed.), *Literatura polska: przewodnik encyklopedyczny* (Warsaw, 1984); W. Sadowski's *Andrzejewski* (Warsaw, 1975) devotes most of its space to his early life and an extended discussion of *Ashes and Diamonds*.

[59] C. Miłosz, *The History of Modern Polish Literature* (Berkeley, 1983), 493.

Notes to Chapter 4: Jan Kott

[1] Quoted in: Y. Litvak, 'The plight of refugees from the German occupied territories', in K. Sword (ed.), *The Soviet Takeover of the Polish Eastern Provinces 1939–41* (London 1991), 66. Braun could not tolerate the steady degradation of personality and belief in the USSR and returned illegally to the German zone, where he died.

[2] J. Kott, *Still Alive* (New Haven, 1994), 98.

[3] *Ibid.*, 98.

[4] *Ibid.*, 164. 'Przed Sądem' appeared as 'The Trial', in A. Gillon and L. Krzyzanowski (eds.), *Introduction to Modern Polish Literature* (London 1964), 224–35.

[5] *Ibid.*, 234.

[6] C. Miłosz, *History of Polish Literature* (Berkeley, 1981), 455.

[7] J. Kott, *Theatre Notebook 1947–67* (London, 1968), 89.

[8] Kott, *Still Alive*, 186.

[9] *Ibid.*, 181.

[10] *Ibid.*, 189–90.

[11] Miłosz, *History of Polish Literature*, 457.

[12] Kott, *Still Alive*, 194.

[13] *Ibid.*, 193.

[14] J. Błoński, 'Za pięć dwunastu, I–III', *Życie Literackie* 17 April, 24 April, 1 May 1955; A. Siciński, *Literaci Polscy* (Warsaw, 1971).

[15] Eva Hoffman, *Lost in Translation* (London, 1991).

[16] Kott, *Still Alive* 180–1.

[17] Kott's other books include: *Four Decades of Polish Essays* (Evanston 1990); *The*

Bottom Translation (Evanston, 1987); *The Theatre of Essence* (Evanston, 1984); *Memory of the Body* (Evanston, 1992); *The Eating of the Gods* (New York, 1974); see also: C. Wieniawska (ed.), *Polish Writing Today* (Harmondsworth, 1967).

18   Kott, *Still Alive*, 165.

19   J. Kott, *Shakespeare Our Contemporary* (London, 1964), 7. Writing of the east European contribution to the 1996 Edinburgh Festival, Neal Ascherson listed a Russian *Othello* about Stalin, a Polish *Hamlet* about General Jaruzelski, a Georgian *Richard III* referring to Eduard Shevardnadze, Zwiad Gamsakhurdia and Tengis Kitovane, an Estonian *Romeo and Juliet*, and a Georgian *Coriolanus* clearly portraying the political world of Tblisi, testifying to Kott's continuing influence: 'In that part of the world, the bible for directors and dramaturges seems still to be *Shakespeare Our Contemporary*, first published nearly 40 years ago . . .' N. Ascherson, 'The dead leave their wisdom behind', *Independent on Sunday* (1 September 1996), 18.

20   Kott, *Still Alive*, 188,

21   *Ibid.*, 201.

22   A. Alvarez, *Under Pressure* (Harmondsworth, 1965), 22.

23   Miłosz, *History of Polish Literature*, 517.

24   Kott had in fact reviewed the 1955 production of *Dziady*. J. Kott, 'Why don't you want to write about it, Gentlemen?', *Theatre Notebook 1947–67*, 52–56.

25   P. Raina, *Political Opposition in Poland: 1954–77* (London, 1978) 120–2.

26   Kott, *Still Alive*, 205.

27   J. Bauman, *A Dream of Belonging* (London, 1988).

28   *Zapis* 13 (1980), 36.

29   Kott, *The Theatre of Essence*, 203.

30   *Ibid.*, 204–5.

31   S. Barańczak, *Breathing under Water* (Harvard, 1990), 68.

32   Kott, *Theatre Notebook 1947–67*, 3.

Notes to Chapter 5: Stanisław Lem

1 Milan Kundera, 'A Kidnapped West or Culture Bows Out', *Granta* 11 (1984), 93–123.

2 Biographical details can be found in: J. Krzyzanowski (ed.), *Literatura polska: przewodnik encyklopedyczny* (Warsaw, 1984); A. Wójcik; 'Ambassador polskiej literatury', in A. Wójcik and M. Englander (eds.), *Budowniczowie gwiazd,* I (Warsaw, 1980), 36–92; P. Nichols (ed.), *The Encyclopedia of Science Fiction* (London, 1981), 350–2; R. E. Ziegfeld, *Stanislaw Lem* (New York, 1985).

3 T. Konwicki, *Moonrise, Moonset* (London, 1988), 129.

4 Lem's publishing history, in terms of the number of editions in print reflects economic and political trends very accurately: 1944–5, 10; 1956–65, 26; 1966–75, 45; 1976–80, 14; 1981–5, 16; 1986, 3; 1987, 2. Table 48, *Ruch wydawniczy w liczbach XXXIII: 1987* (Warsaw, 1989).

5 The main works and collections available in English: *Solaris*, (Kraków, 1961; Newton Abbot, 1973), *The Star Diaries* (Warsaw, 1957; London, 1978), *The*

Investigation (Warsaw, 1959; New York, 1976), *Eden* (Warsaw, 1959; London, 1989), *Return from the Stars* (Warsaw, 1961; London, 1981), *The Invincible* (Warsaw, 1964; Harmondsworth: 1976), *The Cyberiad* (Kraków, 1965; London, 1975), *His Master's Voice* (Warsaw, 1968; London, 1983), *Tales of Pirx the Pilot* (Kraków, 1968; London 1980), *Memoirs Found in a Bathtub* (Kraków, 1971; New York, 1973), *A Perfect Vacuum* (Warsaw, 1971; London, 1979), *Imaginary Magnitude* (Warsaw, 1973; London, 1985), *The Chain of Chance* (Kraków, 1976; New York: 1978), *Hospital of the Transfiguration* (Kraków, 1957; London, 1989), *The Futurological Congress* (Kraków, 1971; New York, 1975), *Memoirs of a Space Traveller* (Kraków, 1957; New York, 1982), *Mortal Engines* (New York, 1982), *More Tales of Pirx the Pilot* (London, 1983), *Microworlds* (London, 1985), *One Human Minute* (Warsaw, 1986: London, 1986), *Fiasco* (Warsaw, 1986; London, 1987); *Peace on Earth* (Warsaw 1987: London, 1995). Several shorter pieces have also appeared in English: 'In Hot Pursuit of Happiness', in F. Rottensteiner (ed.), *View From Another Shore* (New York, 1978); Introduction to W. Bartoszewski, *The Warsaw Ghetto: A Christian's Testimony* (London, 1989), vii–x; 'To My Readers', *Poland* 225 (May 1973), 6–9; 'Culture and Futurology', *Polish Perspectives* XVI/1 (1973), 30–8. In addition Lem has given a number of revealing interviews: 'Stanisław Lem', in A. Michałów and W. Pacłowski (eds.), *Literary Galicia* (Kraków, 1991), 110–11; 'Stanisław Lem: Profile', BBC2 TV (13 November 1991); A. Szostkiewicz, 'Where Fact and Science Fiction Meet', *The Warsaw Voice* 2/168 (12 January 1992), 12–13; P. Swirski, *A Stanislaw Lem Reader* (Evanston, 1997).

[6] In order to put Lem's complaint in perspective it is essential to realize that in the west the average edition of a new book is of about 2,000 copies. In 1978 Poland published 54,000,000 books, including 12,000,000 'modern classics' in translation and 11,849 new fiction titles by contemporary Polish writers in editions of about 10,000 copies, approximately 11,849,000 volumes of new fiction. 'Literature', *Facts about Poland* VI 1/1 and 7/1 (Warsaw, 1980); S. Lem, 'Lem in a Nutshell', in P. Swirski, *A Stanislaw Lem Reader* (1997), 115.

[7] S. Lem, *Solaris* (Kraków, 1976), 26. My translation. The English-language edition of *Solaris* is a translation of a French translation from Polish. The English 'version' has: 'It was essentially a test of ourselves, of the limitations of human knowledge': *Solaris* (1973), 23. In spite of his fame Lem was initially served very badly by his translators and publishers in Britain and America. Theodore Sturgeon has complained about the treatment given to writers from the Soviet Union and east central Europe, saying that in passing through two or more languages the hazards of translation are more than doubled and that this is a process in which 'even a laundry list could hardly be expected to survive': T. Sturgeon, Introduction, to A. and B. Strugatsky, *Roadside Picnic and Tale of a Troika* (New York, 1978), viii.

[8] S. Lem, *Solaris* (Kraków, 1976), 76–7.

[9] *Ibid.* 208–9.

[10] J. Jarzębski, 'Stanisław Lem, Rationalist and Visionary', *Science Fiction Studies* 4/2 (July 1977), 119; S. Lem, *Memoirs Found in a Bathtub* (New York, 1973), 148.

[11] 'Stanisław Lem Answers Questions', *Foundation* 15 (January, 1979), 46.

12 *Ibid.*, 42.
13 S. Lem, *Microworlds* (1985), 22.
14 *Ibid.*, 196.
15 *Ibid.*, 35–7.
16 *Ibid.*, 37.
17 J. L. Curry, *The Black Book of Polish Censorship* (New York, 1984).
18 M. Vale (ed.), *Poland: The State of the Republic* (London, 1981), 25. Lem is thought to have contributed to the forum and, under various pseudonyms, to have written a great deal of material critical of the regime for émigré journals.
19 T. Torańska, *Oni: Stalin's Polish Puppets* (London, 1987).
20 A. Michnik, *Letters From Prison* (Berkeley, 1985), 91.
21 W. Bieńkowski, *Motory i hamulce socjalizmu* (Paris, 1969), 82; W. Bieńkowski, *Theory and Reality* (London, 1981), 72–3; J. Sowa, 'Teoria grup odniesnia', *Studia Socjologiczne* 4 (1966).
22 K. Brandys, *A Question of Reality* (London, 1981), 158.
23 A. Zgorzelski, *Fantastyka: Utopia: Science Fiction* (Warsaw, 1980), 40–102.
24 J. J. Szczepański, *Kadencja* (Kraków, 1989), 30; R. Sukenick, 'Poland', *Granta* 9 (1983), 245.
25 A. Sohár, 'Cultural Importation of Genres: The Case of SF and Fantasy in Hungary', *Translation in Hungary* III/4 (1997), 126.
26 G. Konrád, 'A New Europe', interview with E. P. Thompson, in B. Bourne, U. Eichler and D. Herman (eds.), *Writers and Politics* (London, 1987), 44.
27 S. Lem, 'Reflections on Literature, Philosophy, and Science', in P. Swirski, *A Stanislaw Lem Reader*, 62; R. Boyes, 'Mystic Lem', *Times Magazine* (11 May 1996), 23–4.

Notes to Chapter 6: Kazimierz Brandys

1 T. G. Ash, *The Uses of Adversity* (London, 1989); 153; A. Michnik, *The Church and the Left* (Chicago, 1993), 161 and 208; A. Michnik, *Letters From Prison* (Berkeley, 1985), 137 and 178–9. For basic biographical information on Brandys: J. Krzyzanowski, *Literatura Polska: przewodnik encyklopedyczny,* I (Warsaw, 1984).
2 K. Brandys, *Warsaw Diary: 1978–81* (London, 1982), 109. The diaries first appeared in an underground edition in Warsaw in 1980, but were later published in Paris: *Miesące 1978–79* (Paris, 1981), *Miesące 1980–81* (Paris, 1982), *Miesące 1982–84* (Paris, 1984), *Miesące 1985–87* (Paris, 1987). A further diary selection in English was made: K. Brandys, *Paris, New York: 1982–84* (New York, 1984). For a personal account of Jewish communist activity under the Piłsudski regime see: H. Mendel, *Memoirs of a Jewish Revolutionary* (London, 1989).
3 *Ibid.*, 11.
4 S. Krajewski, 'Jews and Communism', in M. Bernhardt and H. Szlajfer (eds.), *From the Polish Underground: Selections from Krytyka 1978–93* (Pennsylvania, 1995), 368.
5 H. Grynberg, *The Victory* (Paris, 1969; Evanston, 1993), 69–70. Other novels

attempting to deal with the issue of Polish-Jewish relations are: C. Miłosz, *The Seizure of Power* (London, 1995); A. Szczypiorski, *The Beautiful Mrs Seidenman* (Paris, 1986; London, 1990); A. Szczypiorski, *A Mass for the Town of Arras* (Warsaw, 1988; London, 1993). A personal account of the 1959 anti-Semitic campaign can be found in: E. Hoffman, *Lost in Translation: Life in a New Language* (London, 1991); and of the 1968 anti-Semitic campaign in: J. Bauman, *A Dream of Belonging: My Years in Postwar Poland* (London, 1988). Perhaps the most accessible account of Polish-Jewish relations is: E. Hoffman, *Shtetl: The History of a Small Town and Extinguished World* (London, 1998).

[6] N. Davies, *God's Playground: A History of Poland*, II, (Oxford, 1981), 240–65. J. Schatz, *Generation: The Rise and Fall of the Jewish Communists in Poland* (Berkeley, 1990).

[7] *Nowa Kultura* (13 June 1954), 5–7.

[8] Brandys, *Warsaw Diary: 1978–81*, 93–4.

[9] S. Balbus, 'The Great Silence of the Black Hole: Literature in the Face of Communism', in A. Michajłów and W. Pacławski (eds.), *Literary Galicia: From Post-War to Post-Modern* (Kraków, 1991), 41.

[10] K. Brandys, *Sons and Comrades* (*Matka Królów* (Warsaw, 1957; New York, 1961), 82. Brandys's works available in English include: 'Memories from the Present Time', in C. Wieniawska (ed.), *Polish Writing Today* (Harmondsworth, 1970); 'How to be Loved' (1960), in A. Gillon and L. Krzyzanowski (eds.), *Introduction to Modern Polish Literature* (London, 1964); *Letters to Mrs Z*, (Evanston, III. 1987).

[11] H. Stehle, *The Independent Satellite* (London, 1965), 198.

[12] K. Brandys, *Rondo* (New York, 1989); S. Barańczak, *Breathing under Water and Other Essays* (Cambridge, Mass., 1990).

[13] 'Letter of the Thirteen Polish Intellectuals' (7 July 1976), in P. Raina, *Political Opposition in Poland* (London, 1978), 249–51.

[14] K. Brandys, *A Question of Reality* (London, 1978), 61–2. The manuscript of this book had been rejected by the official Polish publishing houses in 1975 and was first published in Polish by the Paris Instytut Literacki in 1978.

[15] *Ibid.*, 70–4.

[16] *Ibid.*, 87.

[17] *Ibid.*, 76.

[18] *Ibid.*, 17–18.

[19] *Ibid.*, 158–9.

[20] *Ibid.*, 153.

[21] This attitude underlies comment on Polish-Jewish writers during the 1970s and 1980s in A. Sandauer, *O sytuacji pisarza polskiego pochodzenia żydowskiego w XX wieku* (Warsaw, 1982).

[22] Brandys, *Warsaw Diary: 1978–81*, 31.

[23] J. Jarzębski, 'The Document: Polarities of its Employment', in S. Eile and U. Philips (eds.), *New Perspectives in Twentieth Century Polish Literature* (London, 1992), 87–104.

[24] Brandys, *Warsaw Diary: 1978–81*, 26.

[25] *Ibid.*, 25–6.

[26] *Ibid.*, 42.

[27] *Ibid.*, 25–6.

[28] *Ibid.*, 42.

[29] *Ibid.*, 166.

[30] *Ibid.*, 43.

[31] Brandys, *Paris, New York: 1982–84*, 140.

[32] Brandys, *A Question of Reality* (1978).

[33] *Paris, New York: 1982–84*, 32–3.

[34] *Warsaw Diary: 1978–81*, 123.

[35] *Ibid.*, 226.

[36] *Ibid.*, 253.

[37] J. Błoński, 'Is There a Jewish School of Polish Literature?', in A. Polonsky (ed.), *Studies from Polin: From Shtetl to Socialism* (London, 1993), 471–86.

[38] W. Maciąg, *Kazimierz Brandys* (Warsaw, 1990), 8–9.

Notes to Chapter 7: Ryszard Kapuściński

[1] Biographical details can be found in: J. Krzyzanowski (ed.), *Literatura polska: przewodnik encyklopedyczny* (Warsaw, 1984); A. Pawluczuk, *Kapuściński* (Warsaw, 1980).

[2] W. Buford, 'Interview', *Granta* 21 (1987), 84–92.

[3] *Ibid.*, 85–6.

[4] Kapuściński's publications in English: *The Emperor: The Downfall of an Autocrat* (Warsaw, 1978; New York, 1983), *Shah of Shahs* (Warsaw, 1983; London, 1985), *Another Day of Life* (Warsaw, 1976; London, 1987), *The Soccer War* (Warsaw, 1976; Cambridge, 1990), *Imperium* (Warsaw, 1993; London, 1994); 'Christmas Eve in Uganda', *Granta* 26 (1989), 9–19; 'The Snow in Ghana', *Granta* 28 (1989), 47–56; 'Fever Pitch', *Independent on Sunday* (28 October 1990), 8–15; 'Bolivia, 1970', *Granta* 33 (1990), 159–66; 'Stiff', *Granta* 21 (1987), 115–25; 'Outline for a book', *Granta* 21 (1987), 99–115; 'Warsaw Diary I', *Granta* 15 (1985), 213–26; 'Warsaw Diary II', *Granta* 16 (1985), 195–204; 'A Tour of Angola', *Granta* 20 (1986), 187–200; 'Africa's New Order', *Independent on Sunday* (1 September 1991), 2–5; 'A Period of Transition', *Independent on Sunday* (27 October 1991), 10–12; 'Nagorno Karabakh', *The Guardian* (20 March 1992), 25–7; 'Power to the Peoples', *The Guardian* (14 August 1992), 19; 'Startled in the Dark', *Granta* 48 (1994), 203–16.

[5] C. Tighe, 'Interview', in N. Jenkins (ed.), *The Works* (Swansea: 1991), 97–108.

[6] 'Ryszard Kapuściński', *Third Ear*, BBC Radio 3 (29 January 1991).

[7] C. Tighe, *Gdańsk* (London, 1990), 241–6.

[8] C. Tighe, 'Interview', 1991.

[9] R. Kapuściński, *The Emperor* (New York, 1983), 153–4.

[10] *Ibid.*, 158 and 160.

[11] *Ibid.*, 113.

[12] A. Brumberg, *Poland: Genesis of a Revolution* (New York, 1983), 50; D. Singer, *The Road to Gdańsk* (New York, 1982), 235–6.

[13] J. Taylor, *Five Months With Solidarity* (Nottingham, 1981), 85.

[14] R. Kapuściński, *The Emperor*, 30–1.

[15] *Ibid.*, 33.

[16] *Ibid.*, 44–6.

[17] *Ibid.*, 82–3.

[18] 'Writers in Conversation: Ryszard Kapuściński', ICA Video, n. d.

[19] J. Jarzębski, 'The Document', in S. Eile and U. Philips (eds.), *New Perspectives in Twentieth Century Polish Literature* (London, 1993). Jarzębski's point is reinforced by publishing statistics. In 1986 Poland published a total of 1,084 titles (47,295,000 copies) of *literatura piękna* (belles-lettres), of which forty-two titles (1,080,200 copies) were memoirs and letters. In 1987 there were 1,217 titles (55,545,500), of which seventy-four titles (6,463,800 copies) were letters and memoirs, only thirty-one of which (1,292,200 copies) were by contemporary authors. *Ruch wydawniczy w liczbach XXXIII: 1987* (Warsaw, 1989), table 28.

[20] R. Kapuściński, *Szachinszach* (Warsaw, 1988), 199.

[21] Buford, 'Interview', 92–3.

[22] GUKPPiW instruction to Branch Offices, section III, Relations with Foreign Countries, numbers 10 (n) and 12, revised 22 April 1975, cancelled 12 January 1976, in G. Schöpflin, *Censorship and Political Communications in Eastern Europe* (London, 1983), 37.

[23] Marcin Święcki (minister for foreign economic relations), 'Gulf Crisis Affects Poland', *Warsaw Voice* (7 October 1990), 13.

[24] A. Alvarez, *Under Pressure* (Harmondsworth, 1965), 21–2.

[25] R. Kapuściński, 'Z Warszawy 1982', *Lapidarium* (Warsaw, 1990), 39.

[26] C. Tighe, 'Interview', 103.

[27] Kapuściński, 'Z Warszawy 1983', 5.

[28] S. Schiff, 'Interview', *Vanity Fair* 54/3 (March 1991), 193.

[29] R. Marszalek, 'Interview', *The Insider* (21 March 1991), 10.

[30] A. Walicki, 'The Three Traditions in Polish Patriotism', in S. Gomułka and A. Polonsky (eds.), *Polish Paradoxes* (London, 1990), 33; J. Koralewicz, I. Bialecki and M. Watson (eds.), *Crisis and Transition* (Oxford, 1987).

[31] M. C. Albright, *Poland: The Role of the Press* (New York, 1983), 41.

[32] *Ibid.*, 41.

[33] C. Tighe, 'Interview', 102.

[34] W. Buford, 'Interview', 93.

Notes to Chapter 8: Tadeusz Konwicki

[1] Biographical details can be found in: J. Krzyzanowski (ed.), *Literatura polska: przewodnik encyklopedyczny* (Warsaw, 1984); J. Wegner, *Konwicki* (Warsaw, 1973).

[2] R. Piętrzak, 'Polish Syndrome', *Poland* 1/357 (1989), 24.

[3] *Ibid.*, 24.

[4] J. Rostropowicz-Clark, 'Introduction', in T. Konwicki, *The Polish Complex* (Harmondsworth, 1984), xv; Anon., 'Tadeusz Konwicki', *Index on Censorship* 11/6 (December 1982), 10; L. Kołakowski, 'Introduction', Tadeusz Konwicki, *A*

Dreambook for Our Time (Harmondsworth, 1976). Even Party members realized that *socrealizm* was not a style that suited all writers and Konwicki had been warned that his novel *Władzy* was not a success for this reason. Stefan Staszewski, director of the Central Committee press and publishing section, recalled: 'Sometimes writers displayed a quite irrational stubbornness. I remember my conflict with Konwicki when he wrote his book *Władzy*. I was against publishing it because I thought the book was bad and written in a large degree under the influence of Borejsza, so Grzegorz Lasota went off to complain about me to Berman, on his own behalf and Konwicki's. Berman had *Władzy* published and to this day Konwicki is still ashamed of having written the book' (T. Torańska, *Oni: Stalin's Polish Puppets* (London, 1987), 142).

5 T. Konwicki, *Moonrise, Moonset* (London, 1981), 28–9.
6 K. Brandys, *Warsaw Diary: 1978–81* (London, 1984), 61.
7 Konwicki, *Moonrise, Moonset*, 29.
8 C. Miłosz, *The History of Polish Literature* (Berkeley, 1983), 500.
9 Konwicki, *Moonrise, Moonset*, 228–9.
10 Konwicki's publishing history: 1944–5, twelve editions; 1956–65, ten; 1966–75, eleven; 1976–80, five; 1981–5, five; 1986, one; 1987, one. Table 48, *Ruch wydawniczy w liczbach XXXIII: 1987* (Warsaw, 1989).
11 Miłosz, *The History of Polish Literature*, 535.
12 Rostropowicz-Clark in: Konwicki, *The Polish Complex*, x. Also Brandys, *A Warsaw Diary: 1978–81*, 26.
13 A. Walicki, 'From Stalinism to Post-communist Pluralism', *New Left Review* 185 (January/February 1991), 96–8.
14 S. Barańczak, *Breathing Under Water* (Cambridge, Mass. 1990), 76.
15 D. Pirie, 'Private States of Mind', *Edinburgh Review* 81 (1988), 65–74.
16 A. Zagajewski, *Solidarity, Solitude* (New York, 1990), 138.
17 N. Ascherson, 'Tungsten amid the Turmoil', *Independent on Sunday* (13 January 1991), 18.
18 S. Starski, *Class Struggle in Classless Poland* (Boston, 1982), 227–8.
19 T. Konwicki, *A Minor Apocalypse* (London, 1983), 35.
20 *Ibid.*, 14–15.
21 *Ibid.*, 68.
22 S. Barańczak, 'My Ten Uncensorable Years: Or How Liver Sausage lost its Political Implications', *Index on Censorship* 10/6 (1981), 38–40.
23 G. Schöpflin (ed.), *Censorship and Political Communications in Eastern Europe* (London, 1983), 63–4.
24 *A Minor Apocalypse*, 105–6.
25 *Ibid.*, 82.
26 *Ibid.*, 92.
27 *Ibid.*, 119. An earlier version of this theme can be found in Mrożek's play *Policja* (Warsaw, 1958), where the last dissident has gone over to the government side; if the police are to survive they must provide dissidents from their own ranks. The last dissident, now working for the police, though he sees the error of his previous activities, volunteers to act again as a dissident, this time as a gesture of loyalty to his new comrades and masters.

[28] S. Nowicki, *Pół wieku czyśćca* (Warsaw, 1990), 209.

[29] *A Minor Apocalypse*, 124.

[30] *Ibid.*, 169.

[31] *Ibid.*, 187–8.

[32] *Ibid.*, 231.

[33] *Ibid.*, 232.

[34] G. Herling-Grudziński, *Dziennik pisany nocą 1973–9* (Paris, 1980), 339.

[35] S. Nowicki, *Pół wieku czyśćca*, 299–300.

[36] A. Michnik, *Letters from Prison* (Berkeley, 1985), 55.

[37] Konwicki, *Moonrise Moonset*, 128.

[38] J. Koralewicz (ed.), *Społeczeństwo polskie przed krzysem w świetle badań sociologicznych z lat 1977–79* (Warsaw, 1987), 80–110.

[39] His early *socrealist* works have not been translated, but several of his more recent works have appeared in English: *A Minor Apocalypse* (*Zapis* 10, NOWa, Warsaw, 1979; London, 1983); *A Dreambook For Our Time* (Warsaw, 1963; Harmondsworth, 1976); *The Anthropos Spectre-Beast* (Warsaw, 1969; Oxford, 1977); *The Polish Complex* (London, 1978; New York, 1982); *Moonrise, Moonset* (London, 1982; *Bohin Manor* (London, 1992). Konwicki has also enjoyed a distinguished career in films, working with directors such as Kawelerowicz and Morgenstern. He scripted the films: *Winter Twilight* (1957), *Mother Joan of the Angels* (1961), *Pharaoh* (1964) and *Jovita* (1967); he directed: *The Last Day of Summer* (1958), *Halloween* (1961), *Salto* (1965), *How Far and Yet How Near* (1972) and *Ława* (1989).

[40] K. Brandys, *A Warsaw Diary: 1978–81*. Also K. Brandys, *A Question of Reality* (London, 1981); J. Koralewicz, I. Bialecki and M. Watson (eds.), *Crisis and Transition* (Oxford, 1987); S. Nowak, 'A Polish Self Portrait', *Polish Perspectives* 2 (Warsaw, 1981).

Notes to Chapter 9: Adam Michnik

[1] A. Szczypiorski, *The Polish Ordeal* (London, 1982), 104; M. Glenny, *The Rebirth of History* (Harmondsworth, 1993), 69; *The Struggles for Poland* (London, 1987), 186; T. G. Ash, *The Uses of Adversity*, (London, 1989), 164; T. G. Ash, *The Polish Revolution* (London, 1983), 341; C. Miłosz, Foreword, in A. Michnik, *Letters From Prison* (Berkeley, 1987), xiv.

[2] N. Davies, *God's Playground*, II (Oxford, 1981), 630; Z. Najder, 'Dialog z Michnikiem', *Ile jest dróg* (Paris, 1982); for Mackiewicz see M. Bernhard and H. Szlajfer (eds.), *From the Polish Underground* (Pennsylvania, 1995), 193–206. J. Tischner, *Marxism and Christianity* (Washington, 1987); J. Trznadel, 'Interview', *Puls* (May/June 1992).

[3] J. J. Lipski, *KOR* (Berkeley, 1985), 12.

[4] J. Kuroń and K. Modzelewski, *An Open Letter to the Party* (London, n. d.).

[5] A. Michnik, *Letters from Prison* (Berkeley, 1987), 203.

[6] A. Michnik, *The Church and the Left* (Chicago, 1993), 31–2. This is an updated English version of *Kościół, Lewica – Dialogue* (Paris, 1977).

7 T. Rosenberg, *The Haunted Land* (London, 1995), 154.

8 S. Barańczak, *Breathing Under Water* (Harvard, 1990), 46.

9 C. Miłosz, *History of Polish Literature*, 538. Also: L. Kołakowski, 'Christian Poland and Human Rights', *Index on Censorship* (November/December 1979), 27–32; L. Kołakowski, *Modernity on Endless Trial* (Chicago, 1990).

10 A. Piekarski, *Freedom of Conscience and Religion in Poland* (Warsaw, 1979); B. Szajkowski, *Next to God . . . Poland* (London, 1983); Davies, *God's Playground*, II; *Kościół katolicki w Polsce 1945–78* (Warsaw, 1979); *Ruch Wydawniczy w Liczbach XXXIII: 1987* (Warsaw, 1989).

11 Michnik, *The Church and the Left*, 152.

12 *Ibid.*, 153–4 and 181.

13 *Ibid.*, 101–2.

14 A. Michnik, *Letters from Prison*, 292.

15 *Ibid.*, 33.

16 B. Cywiński, *Rodowody Niepokornych*, (Warsaw, 1971); Michnik, *The Church and The Left*, 132–3.

17 Lipski, *KOR*, 76.

18 T. G. Ash, *Uses of Adversity* (London, 1989), 237.

19 Michnik, *The Church and the Left*, 246.

20 *Ibid.*, 133.

21 Michnik, *The Church and the Left*, xii and 208; Michnik, *Letters from Prison*, 18 and 140.

22 Michnik, *Letters from Prison*, 135–48; Lipski, *KOR*, 360–2.

23 Lipski, *KOR*, 154–55.

24 Michnik, *Letters from Prison*; P. Raina, *Political Opposition in Poland 1954–77* (London, 1978); Z. A. Pełczyński, 'Solidarity and the Rebirth of Civil Society 1976–81', in J. Keane (ed.), *Civil Society and the State* (London, 1988).

25 Michnik, *The Church and the Left*, xiv.

26 C. Pszenicki, 'The Flying University', *Index on Censorship* (November/December 1979), 19–22.

27 P. Wierzbicki, 'A Treatise on Ticks', *Biuletyn Informacyjny* 3/29 (April 1979), and A. Michnik, 'Ticks and Angels', *Biuletyn Informacyjny* 7/33 (May 1979), in: A. Brumberg (ed.), *Poland: Genesis of a Revolution* (New York, 1983), 199–218. Also: M. Król, 'The Polish Syndrome of Incompleteness', in S. Gomułka and A. Polonsky, (eds.) *Polish Paradoxes* (London, 1990), 68–9.

28 Lipski, *KOR*, 360–62.

29 Michnik, 'Czas nadziei' *Biuletyn Informacyjny* 6/40 (September 1980), 4.

30 J. Walc, 'Otwock, 7 Maja',*Tygodnik Solidarność* 7 (15 May 1981).

31 Michnik, *Letters from Prison*, 321.

32 *Ibid.*, 333.

33 *Ibid.*, 67. Also: E. Hoffman, *Exit into History* (London, 1993), 50.

34 A. Michnik, 'Don Quixote and Invective' (1986), in J. Kott (ed.), *Four Decades of Polish Essays* (Evanston, 1990), 392–3.

35 T. Rosenberg, *The Haunted Land* (London, 1995).

36 Ash, *The Uses of Adversity*, 237.

37 T. G. Ash, *We the People* (London, 1990), 30.

[38] J. Kurski, *Lech Wałęsa* (Colorado, 1993), 30.

[39] *Ibid.*, 42.

[40] *Ibid.*, 42–4.

[41] *Ibid.*, 44.

[42] A. Michnik, 'Two Faces of Europe', in *Writing on the East* (New York, 1990), 1–5.

[43] A. Polonsky, 'Loving and Hating the Dead', *Financial Times* (3 May 1991), ix; N. Ascherson, 'A Breath of Foul Air', *Independent on Sunday* (11 November 1990), 3–5; Kurski, *Lech Wałęsa*, 43–4.

[44] A. Michnik, 'A Bad Day for Reform', *Guardian* (1 November 1991), 29.

[45] A. Michnik, 'The Worship of Wałęsa', *Guardian* (25 June 1993), 15.

[46] Michnik, *Letters from Prison*, 90 and 158.

Notes to Chapter 10: Writers, Language and Party

[1] *Rocznik Statistyczny: 1966, XXVI* (Warsaw, 1966) 34.

[2] B. Klimaszewski (ed.), *An Outline History of Polish Culture* (Warsaw, 1984), 306–8; W. Doroszewski (ed.), *Słownik Języka Polskiego* (Warsaw, 1958–69); O. Budrewicz, *Poland for Beginners* (Warsaw, 1974), 171–2.

[3] K. S. Karol, *Solik* (London, 1986), 125.

[4] Doroszewski, *Słownik Języka Polskiego*.

[5] J. Bralczyk, *O Języka Polskiej Propagandy Politycznej Lat Siedemdziesiątych* (Uppsala, 1987), 100–3.

[6] J. Staniszkis, *Poland's Self-Limiting Revolution* (Princeton, 1984), 304.

[7] J. Karpiński, *Count-Down* (New York, 1982), 175.

[8] Staniszkis, *Poland's Self-Limiting Revolution*, 128–9.

[9] K. Brandys, *A Question of Reality* (London, 1981), 31; Staniszkis, *Poland's Self-Limiting Revolution*, 128–9.

[10] A. Malewski, 'Attitudes of the Warsaw Employers', *Polish Sociological Bulletin* 2 (1971); W. Adamski, 'Postawy społeczno-zawodowe mlodzieży', *Studia Socio-logiczne* 2 (1974); A. Sarapata, 'Z badań nad hierarchią prestiżu zajęć w polsce', *Studia Sociologiczne* 1 (1975); A. Sarapata and W. Wesołowski, 'Evaluation of Occupations by Warsaw Inhabitants', *American Journal of Sociology* 66 (1961); S. Nowak, 'Social Structure in Social Consciousness', *Polish Sociological Bulletin* 2 (1964).

[11] S. Amsterdamski, A. Jawłowska and T. Kowalik, *Język propagandy* (Warsaw, 1979), 12–20; P. Wierzbicki, *Struktura Kłamstwa* (Warsaw, 1987); M. Głowiński, *Nowamowa Po Polsku* (Warsaw, 1990).

[12] This example donated by Jerzy Jarzębski.

[13] R. Kapuściński, 'Z Warszawy 1982', *Lapidarium* (Warsaw, 1990), 48; also J. Bralczyk, *O Języku Polskiej Propagandy Politycznej*, 107 and 191.

[14] *Nie ma dla nas sprawy droższej niż Polska Ludowa*, H. Hilscher, Archiwum WAG, n.d.; *Aby Polska rosła w siłę a ludzie żyli dostatniej – VI zjazd PZPR*, M. Chwedczuk, W. Lącki and M. Modzelewski, Archiwum WAG, n.d.; *Z Partią*, I. Rybicka, n. d., archiwum WAG; *Partia*, W. Zakrewski, n.d., archiwum WAG;

Przewodzi Partia, K. Śliwka (1973), in A. Przedworski (ed.), *Polski Plakat Polityczny XXX-Lecie PRL* (Warsaw, 1974); K. Zmijewska-Borowicz (ed.), *1948–73: 25 Lat PZPR Plakat* (Warsaw, 1973).

15 G. Leech, *English in Advertising* (London, 1966), 93.

16 S. Drakulic, 'In Their Own Words', *Ms* (July/August 1990), 36–47; J. Tilbury and P. Hockenos, 'Catholicism Reigns in Poland's Halls of Power', *In These Times* (10–16 April 1991), 9.

17 T. Rumiński, *Polska 73, 74, 75* (Warsaw, 1973); in A. Przedworski (ed.), *Polski Plakat Polityczny XXX-Lecie PRL* (Warsaw, 1974).

18 See also G. Benton and G. Loomes, *The Big Red Joke Book* (London, 1976).

19 D. Singer, *The Road to Gdańsk: Poland and the USSR* (New York, 1982), 240.

20 J. J. Lipski, *KOR* (Berkeley, 1985), 450.

21 S. Starski, *Class Struggle in Classless Poland* (Boston, 1982), 183.

22 J. Kuroń and K. Modzelewski, *An Open Letter to the Party* (London, n. d.), 71.

23 E. Hoffman, *Lost in Translation* (London, 1991), 124 and 211.

24 J. Rolicki, *Przerwana Dekada* (Warsaw, 1990).

25 A. Szczypiorski, 'Poland – the Fiction and the Reality', *Index on Censorship* 8/6 (November/December 1979), 4–5.

26 B. Rogowski, 'What is to be Done?', *Labour Focus on Eastern Europe* 4/4–6 (Winter-Spring 1981), 54.

27 A. Michnik, *Letters from Prison* (Berkeley, 1985), 333.

28 D. Warszawski, 'An Open Letter From Solidarność to the Left', *In These Times* (3–9 November 1982), 17.

29 R. Kapuściński, 'Z Gdańska 1980', *Lapidarium* (Warsaw, 1990), 32–3.

30 Staniszkis, *Poland's Self-Limiting Revolution*, 145; A. Walicki, 'Poland's Flawed Socialism', *New Left Review* 185 (January-February 1991), 92–121; T. Konwicki, *Mała Apokalypsa* (Warsaw, 1989).

31 M. Vale (ed.), *Poland: The State of the Republic* (London, 1981), 25.

32 Kapuściński, in *Lapidarium* (1990), 31–2.

33 Staniszkis, *Poland's Self-Limiting Revolution*, 124–5.

34 A. Kemp-Welch, *The Birth of Solidarity* (London, 1983), 141–2. The scene can be witnessed in Andrzej Wajda's newsreel *Robotnicy '80* (1981).

35 Staniszkis, *Poland's Self Limiting Revolution*, 19–20.

36 G. Grass, *Dog Years*, (1965); V. Klemperer, *LTI*, (East Berlin, 1946); G. Steiner, 'A Note on Günter Grass' (1964) in: G. Steiner, *Language and Silence* (Harmondsworth, 1969), 152–9; M. Townson, *Mother Tongue and Fatherland*, (Manchester, 1992).

37 S. Barańczak, 'Poems and Tanks', *Tri-Quarterly* 57 (Spring/Summer 1983), 57.

38 S. Barańczak, 'Translating the Self', *Gazeta International* 13 (31 May 1990), 7.

39 A. Wat, *My Century* (Berkeley, 1988), 220.

40 J. Prokop, 'Polska znijączona albo lodowiec z gówna', *Zapis* 6 (1978), 139–43.

41 L. Kołakowski, *Modernity on Endless Trial* (Chicago, 1990), 224.

42 J. Kuroń, 'Zaczęły się schody', *Polityka* 47/XXXV (23 November 1991), 8–11.

Notes to Chapter 11: Socialist 'Unreality' to Capitalist 'Reality'

[1] *Kościół katolicki w Polsce 1945–78* (Warsaw, 1979); B. Szjakowski, *Next to God – Poland* (London, 1983); A. Michnik, *Kościół, lewica, dialog* (Paris, 1977); A. Piekarski, *Freedom of Conscience and Religion in Poland* (Warsaw, 1979).

[2] P. Ikonowicz, 'The Courage of Ideological Thinking', *International Socialism* 41 (Winter 1988), 70.

[3] C. Tighe, 'A State of Mind', *Planet* 64 (1987).

[4] *Fakty i Komentarze* 14 (Warsaw, 17 April 1981), 5–10; *Kierunki reformy gospodarczej* (Warsaw, July 1981); J. Staniszkis, *Poland's Self-Limiting Revolution* (New York, 1982), 19.

[5] J. Kopeć, *Dossier Generała* (Warsaw, 1991); W. Jaruzelski, 'The General's Story: Why I Declared Martial Law', *Warsaw Voice* (15 December 1991), 7–10; W. Jaruzelski, *Stan Wojenny. Dlaczego* (Warsaw, 1992); W. Jaruzelski, 'I've Told Everything I Know', *Warsaw Voice* (24 May 1992), 12–13.

[6] K. Brandys, *Paris, New York 1982–84* (New York, 1984); T. G. Ash, *The Polish Revolution* (London, 1983), 175.

[7] J. J. Szczepański, *Kadencja* (Kraków, 1991).

[8] 'Literature', *Facts about Poland* VI/7–1 (Warsaw, 1980); 'Index Index: Poland', *Index on Censorship* 12/6 (1983), 46; R. Stefanowski (ed.), *Poland under Martial Law*, Radio Free Europe (March 1984), 161–75 and 187–200; C. Pszenicki, 'Freedom of Expression in Jaruzelski's Poland', *Index on Censorship* 12/6 (March 1983), 19–24.

[9] W. Łysiak, *Lepszy* (Warsaw, 1990), 29.

[10] M. Orski, 'Nowa proza stanu wojennego', *Res Publica* (July 1989), 58–65; J. J. Szczepański, 'Każdy ma swój podręczny Panteon: Z Janem Józefem Szczepańskim rozmawia Krystyna Czerni', *Res Publica* (January 1989), 89–97; T. Sobolewski, 'Dąbrowska sama w sobie', *Res Publica* (November 1988), 114–18. Of the literature of Martial Law, and its obsessions with moral justice and Polish unreality, see in particular the writing of Janusz Anderman and Marek Nowakowski.

[11] A. Michnik, *Letters from Prison*, 151–2.

[12] H. Pick, 'Lapsed Communist Ushers Poland into Democracy', *The Guardian* (1 May 1990), 9; T. Rosenberg, *The Haunted Land* (London, 1995); R. Kuklinski, 'The Suppression of Solidarity', in R. Kostrzewa (ed.), *Between East and West* (New York, 1990), 72–98.

[13] *Jaruzelski: Selected Speeches* (London, 1985), 64–5.

[14] C. Tighe, '*The Tin Drum* in Poland', *Journal of European Studies* XIX (1989), 3–20.

[15] T. Konwicki, 'Nowy Świat i okolice', *Czytelnik* (Warsaw, 1986), 6.

[16] A. Walicki, 'From Stalinism to Post-Communist Pluralism', *New Left Review* 185 (January/February 1991), 103.

[17] M. Hirszowicz, 'The Polish Intelligentsia in a Crisis-Ridden Society', in S. Gomułka and A. Polonsky (eds.), *Polish Paradoxes* (London, 1990), 139–40. M. Hirszowicz, *The Bureaucratic Leviathan* (Oxford, 1980), 171–99.

[18] Interview with Juliusz Żuławski, 29 May 1990.

[19] T. G. Ash, *We the People* (Cambridge, 1990).

[20] C. Tighe, 'Interview with Ryszard Kapuściński', in N. Jenkins (ed.), *The Works*, 106.

21 L. Wałęsa, 'A Candid Conversation with the Charismatic Leader of Poland's Solidarity', *Playboy* (February 1982), 61–162.

22 'Forms of Ownership', *Facts about Poland* VII. 2–1 (Warsaw, 1980); E. Gajewska, 'Press Market: Workers of RSW Disband!', *Warsaw Voice* (11 November 1990), 4; C. Bobiński, 'Catching up with Information', *Financial Times Survey: Poland* (3 May 1991), xv; K. T. Toeplitz, 'Ludzie zbędnie', *Polityka* 16 (21 April 1990), 16.

23 D. Ślepwrońska, 'Red Devils and Bogeys, *Warsaw Voice* (31 May 1992), 10–11; P. B. Kaufman, 'Remaindering Marx', *Nation* (20 May 1991), 660–4; A. Dubrawska, 'Book Publishing in Poland', *Warsaw Voice* (12 May 1991), 9.

24 R. Gott, 'A Headache After the Party', *Guardian* (26 February 1991), 21; A. Waldoch, 'Freedom to Print?', *Warsaw Voice* (17 November 1991), 9; L. Zukowski, 'Crime and Publishing', *Warsaw Voice* (24 November 1991), 9; A. Nagorski, 'Read All About it', *Newsweek* (10 June 1991), 10–15; *Nowe Książki* 49/50 (May-June 1990).

25 C. Miłosz, Interview, 26 May 1990; C. Miłosz, *The Witness of Poetry* (Cambridge, Mass., 1983), 105.

26 Miłosz, 'The State of Europe', *Granta* 30 (Harmondsworth, 1990), 164.

27 K. Jackson, 'Beliefs for the Millennium', *Leonardo* 1, (3 April 1992), 34.

28 C. Miłosz, 'The State of Europe', 164.

29 Interview, 5 June 1991.

30 A. Michajłów and W. Pacłowski (eds.), *Literary Galicia*, 110–11.

31 G. Konrád, 'Something Has Gone', *PEN International* XLI/2 (1991), 79–81.

32 S. Majman, 'Departure of King Lear', *Warsaw Voice* (15 March 1992), 8; J. Adamczewski, *Kraków od A do Z*, (Kraków, 1986), 42; C. Miłosz, *The History of Polish Literature*, 524–25 and 536; A. Michnik, *Letters from Prison* (Berkeley, 1987), 44; J. Mackiewicz, *The Katyn Wood Murders* (London, 1951); J. Surdykowski, 'According to Mackiewicz', in M. Bernhard and H. Szlajfer (eds.), *From the Polish Underground* (Pennsylvania, 1995) 193–206.

33 S. Kisielewski, 'On Books and Money', *Warsaw Voice* (10 March 1991), 7.

BIOGRAPHIES

ANDERMAN, Janusz, b.1949. Studied Slavonic literature at Jagiellonian University, worked as a journalist on *Student*, became increasingly involved in underground politics, co-editor for the uncensored periodical PULS in 1978. State publishers accepted *Deaf Telephone Games* (1977), and *Playing for Time* (1979). He has also produced screenplays and translations. In 1980 responsible for liaising between the ZLP Committee and Solidarność. After Martial Law was declared he helped organize the Committee for Aid to Internees until he was arrested and imprisoned for six months at the Białołęka Camp. State publishers refused his anti-Martial Law collections *Poland Under a Black Light* (London, 1985; Warsaw, 1983) and *The Edge of the World* (London, 1988; Paris, 1988), but these were published abroad or underground. He is generally considered one of the most important of the writers of the Martial Law period.

BACZKO, Bronisław. Former Party member and leading revisionist, dismissed from university history teaching post after March 1968, after which he became a Professor of History at the University of Geneva. A supporter of TKN, author of *Utopian Lights: The Evolution of the Idea of Social Progress* (New York, 1989).

BARAŃCZAK, Stanisław, b.1946. Born in Poznań. A member of PZPR for several years, lived in Poznań and recognized as one of the most talented of the younger generation of Polish poets and teachers. Active in the student movement of 1968, lectured at Poznań University from 1969. By 1976 he had translated Dylan Thomas into Polish, had made significant translations from Russian and German, published three volumes of verse and was the winner of the A.Bursa literary prize, the All Poland Festival of Poetry prize in Łódź, and the Koscielski Foundation prize. His poetry is distrustful of linguistic clichés and official jargon and is often said to have paved the way for the New Wave of post-1968 poetry. Recognized as one of the most talented of the younger generation of Polish poets and teachers. In 1976 he became a founder member of KOR and later became editor of several journals including *Zapis* and *Krytyka*. He fell from grace with the authorities, suffered police harassment, was dismissed from his post in 1977 and was arrested on charges of attempting to bribe an official. Poetry published by NOWa. Lecturer for TKN, for which he was arrested in February 1978. Offered post of Professor of Slavonic Studies at Harvard University, but because of support for KOR was refused a passport by the Polish authorities; able to take up the post only after 1981.

Now edits the *Polish Review* and frequently contributes to *Salmagundi* and *Partisan Review*.

BARTOSZEWSKI, Władysław, b.1922. Born in Warsaw, studied at Warsaw University, was imprisoned in Oświęcim and released in 1941. Member of the AK and Żegota, a wartime organization to aid Jews, founder member of the Polish Jewish Aid Council, awarded a medal for his work by the Israeli government. Catholic historian and journalist specializing in the Holocaust, Polish resistance movement and Polish-Jewish relations, gained his Ph.D. in Cambridge; professor of history at the Catholic University of Lublin; author of eighteen books and over 400 articles. Arrested on trumped up charges in 1946, released 1954; a leading member of the Catholic Znak group and TKN lecturer, general secretary of Polish PEN; protested at the 1976 constitution changes and was dismissed from his post in 1977. Imprisoned during Martial Law for his work with Solidarność.

BAUMAN, Zygmunt. Former Party member, leading revisionist, writer and professor of sociology; lost his post at Warsaw University after March 1968 and left Poland soon afterwards; later a supporter of TKN from his home in Leeds.

BERMAN, Jakub, 1901–84. Born of a modestly successful Jewish middle-class family, he graduated in law from Warsaw University, taught the history of social systems and gained a Ph.D. on the structure of Polish cities. Joined the communist youth movement in 1924, joined the KPP in 1928 and was appointed to the section of the communist youth movement dealing with *inteligencja*, where he became director of editors. In 1939 he took refuge in the USSR, where he edited the Byelorussian communist paper, *Standard of Freedom*, worked for Radio Kosciuszko and lectured and directed the Polish section of the Comintern. In December 1943 he was appointed to the Central Bureau of the PPR and was made responsible for communications in Poland. In 1944 he became a member of the Central Committee and was clearly a member of Bierut's inner circle. He was later under-secretary of state for foreign affairs and under-secretary of state on the Council of Ministers. He helped found Cominform, was one of the architects of the PPS-PPR 'unification congress' that founded the PZPR, edited the new party's programme declaration documents, was one of the main movers in the decision to collectivize agriculture and in the condemnation of the Jugoslav Party. A member of the Politburo, Central Committee and the Central Committee Organization Bureau, a member of the Praesidium, deputy premier, Member of Parliament: responsible, among many other things, for ideology, education, culture, security, propaganda and foreign affairs. Under Berman's guidance it became Party policy to foster and publish *socrealizm* in a Polish variant. It is understating the case to say that in Berman contradictory functions overlapped. Jan Kott, commenting on the power Berman and Borejsza exerted in the arts and in security, said: 'This osmotic and reciprocal infiltration of culture and security on all levels, starting with the district committees and going up to the Central Committee and the Politburo, was one of the most diabolical tricks devised by Stalinism, of which even Orwell had only vague forebodings, failing to grasp the full implications' (*Still Alive*, 175–6). Fell from grace and lost all his posts with Bierut's death in 1956: judged responsible for the Stalinist period of 'errors and distortions' and expelled from the Party in 1957. Became a senior editor for Książka i Wiedza until his retirement in 1969.

BIAŁOSZEWSKI, Miron, 1922–83. Born in Warsaw, graduated 1942 from an underground high school, began the study of Polish literature at an underground university. As a result of the Warsaw uprising he was deported to Germany. He spent the rest of the war working as a bricklayer's apprentice near Oppeln. He returned to Warsaw in 1945, but failed to complete his studies, working instead at a number of odd jobs, as a letter sorter in a post office and as a reporter. He also wrote verse for children. He published a few poems, but was unable to conform to *socrealizm*, suffered the humiliation of consistent rejection for his idiosyncratic and often unpoetic, jarring verses. Like Herbert he decided to write for his desk drawer. Białoszewski, living in destitution in a shabby Warsaw apartment, was something of a hermit, and refused to take any part in public life. This did not change very much even after 1955 when a handful of his poems appeared in *Życie Literackie*. He helped start a small theatre in a friend's apartment and began to stage his plays. After 1956 he published several volumes of poetry, but remained a virtual recluse. He surprised his readership in 1970 by publishing his *Memoir of the Warsaw Uprising*. His last book, *Oho* (1985) was a grim realistic portrayal of martial law. In general his writing was wide-ranging, lyrical, minutely observed, linguistically detailed, hilarious, unorthodox and highly individual.

BIEŃKOWSKI, Władysław, 1906–91. From a middle-class background, had a university education. Professional journalist. A member of communist youth movement, member of central editorial office of KPP. A distinguished member of the AL. Joined PPR in 1942 and became a member of KRN, departmental director and a member of the Central Committee 1945–8, where he was part of the secretariat. In spite of his close association with Gomułka, an exceedingly liberal personality. He was a key revisionist and played an important part in normalizing relations between the Church and state in 1956. Director of the National Library 1949–56, minister of culture 1956–9, minister of education 1956–60. Dismissed from his post by Gomułka in 1960 after he lent his support to the growing democratic opposition movement and popularized his criticisms of the Party in *The Motors and Brakes of Socialism* – first published in Paris. He broke with Party discipline by not restricting his criticisms of the Party to the Party membership and by publishing abroad his comments on the failings of the regime; for this he was expelled from the

PZPR in 1968; an influential revisionist and Flying University lecturer, his later works were published by NOWa. In 1977 he, with Kijówski and Kisielewski, audited the books of KOR in order to defend it against government propaganda.

BIERUT, Bolesław, 1893–1956. Educated by the Party in the USSR. Before the war a professional Comintern agent of the NKVD in Bulgaria, Czechoslovakia and Austria; spent seven years in gaol, in prison at the time of the destruction of the KPP. President of KRN, joined the Central Committee in 1948, 1947–52 Polish president, general secretary of PPR Central Committee 1948, chairman of PZPR Central Committee 1948–54, prime minister 1952–4, first secretary of PZPR 1954–56. Died in Moscow during the Twentieth Congress, some say from shock at hearing the full extent of Stalin's crimes.

BŁOŃSKI, Jan, b.1930. Literary critic and translator, currently professor of Polish Literary History at the Jagiellonian University in Kraków. In the early 1950s he had the nerve to point out that literary débuts were declining in number, that the poetry that was published was dull and poor, and that the amount of verse being published was also declining. Accused in 1955 of a nihilistic attitude towards the achievements of socialist Poland, he identified the failures of Polish literary culture in the slavish imitation in pseudo-revolutionary verse of Broniewski. His comments paved the way for the publication of Drozdowski, Białoszewski, Herbert, Harasymowicz in 1956.

BOREJSZA, Jerzy (Jerzy Goldberg), (1905–52). Professional journalist. Active in left-wing organizations in France and Spain 1922–7, joined KPP in 1929, spent the war in the USSR. When the Soviets entered Lwów they appointed him director of the Ossolineum publishing house and editor in chief of *Wolna Polska* – the organ of the Union of Polish Patriots. He attempted to keep Ossolineum in Polish hands and to create through it a repository of Polish labour history, which, coupled with his lack of enthusiasm for the Soviet Ukrainization policies, made him less than a malleable tool of the Soviets. His efforts came to nothing, however, and in March 1940 the Soviets removed him and turned Ossolineum into the Ukrainian Academy of Sciences. Borejsza continued to head a large team of Polish writers and academics producing Polish-language school textbooks. In 1944 he was appointed head of the Czytelnik publishing house and made responsible for non-Party publications. He was to become a key figure in the post-war cultural/political set-up and is generally regarded as the man the Party entrusted with the task of restructuring Polish intellectual life. In particular he was responsible for reorganizing the Polish press and the publishing industry after 1945, and in 1948 he was general secretary of the International Congress of Intellectuals in Wrocław, when dozens of foreign intellectuals were invited to Poland. He later edited *Rzeczpospolita*. If we are to judge from the range and variety of material in *Kuźnica*, it is possible that if Borejsza had not fallen from power after a motoring accident his 'liberal' cultural empire could have tempered the Polish communist regime and might well, as Kott suggests, have tempted the bulk of the émigré and exile writing community to return to Poland. Borejsza was brother to Jacek Różański, head of the Internal Security Department, who, when he was removed from his security post after the Światło spying scandal in the mid-1950s, was appointed head of the PIW publishing house. Borejsza worked directly under Jakub Berman.

BROMBERG, Adam, b.1912. Editor and director of PWN publishing house 1953–68. Expelled from the Party in 1968, arrested and accused of leading an international criminal conspiracy to subvert the Polish state. After two years of 'investigation' he was 'emigrated' to Sweden where he runs a publishing house.

BRONIEWSKA, Julia, 1904–81. From a middle-class background. The first wife of poet Władysław Broniewski. Spent the war in the USSR working for the Union of Polish Patriots. Afterwards appointed secretary of ZLP to watch over the political activities of the membership.

BRONIEWSKI, Władysław, 1897–1962. Although presented as a proletarian poet by the Party he was in fact born of an *inteligencja* family in Płock. He fought with the rank of captain in Piłsudski's legions in 1915 under the name Orlik, and again in the Russo-Polish war of 1919–20, when he was decorated for bravery. He made his literary début in 1925. A socialist slowly turned communist, he developed a highly political view of literature as a weapon in the class struggle. He was skilful at blending Polish Romantic elements into his patriotic poems and was critical of inter-war Poland. In 1939 he wrote the famous patriotic poem 'Fix Bayonets'. Arrested with Aleksander Wat in Lwów and imprisoned by the NKVD in 1940, he was accused of having written anti-Stalin poetry. He was released to join Anders's army in 1941 and journeyed though Persia, Iraq and Palestine. In spite of appalling treatment by the Soviets he remained a communist. He returned to Poland in 1945 and, although he had written anti-Stalinist poetry in prison, became the PZPR's favourite poet. A slavish *socrealist* and propagandist, his poetry was an outstanding example of the tedious revolutionary pseudo-poetic style favoured by the Party. Traditional Romantic verse shot through with *socrealizm*, verse veering between sentimental lyricism and revolutionary rhetoric, much of his output was tedious, pedantic and downright damaging to truth – poetic or otherwise. In 1950, when even those who had embraced *socrealizm* were becoming dissatisfied and sensed that Stalin might not live for ever, Broniewski, whose ideological fervour had been waning, wrote his hymn of praise 'A Word about Stalin' and was proclaimed a 'national poet'. In spite of this he does not seem to have ever been a member of the Party. Although he is judged to be the most significant Marxist poet of the inter-war period (in itself a dubious distinction), it is widely acknowledged that his best poetry followed the death of his daughter – poetry written in spite of himself and far better than his revolutionary self could ever achieve. After 1956 his revolutionary poetry was increasingly out of place: his anti-Stalinist poetry was published in Paris after his death.

BRUS, Włodzimierz, b.1921. Professor at Warsaw University, former Party member and leading revisionist, a distinguished economist with an international reputation, supporter of market socialism, dismissed from university post after March 1968 for supporting student protests, left Poland in 1972 and became a tutor at Wolfson College Oxford. A founder signatory of KOR and supporter of TKN. In March 1998 he was offered an apology and his Polish citizenship was restored by President Kwasniewski.

BRYLL, Ernest, b.1935. Allusive, and highly intellectual poet with an interest in Greek, medieval and Renaissance history. His refusal to write about emotions is often seen as a response to the aridity of public life and bureaucratic rhetoric after 1945. He became a very popular poet in the 1960s, but Miłosz suspended judgement when he first compiled his *Post-war Polish Poetry*, and by the 1983 edition he had decided that Bryll was an obscure, wilful poet who, Miłosz hinted, shunned his moral responsibilities. He was a supporter of the communist establishment and only became a critic after the imposition of Martial Law. In 1986 he had a volume of poems published in Paris.

CYWIŃSKI, Bohdan, b.1939. A Kraków Catholic historian and literary critic associated with Znak, editor in chief of *Znak*. Author of *The History of the Catholic Church in Independent Poland*. A founder member of KOR and a TKN lecturer. He had a profound influence on KOR circles in that he showed the importance of both the secular and Catholic nationalist traditions for modern Polish intellectuals and illustrated his idea of the harmony of ethical consciousness that could exist between Polish Catholic and secular social aspirations in his book *Genealogies of the Indomitable* (1974).

DOBRACZYŃSKI, Jan, b.1910. Born in Warsaw, he began his publishing career in 1934 and has published more than thirty books, mainly novels. His main interest was in the moral problems of Catholicism in the modern world. He was a soldier in the September 1939 campaign, later was a member of the AK and took part in the Warsaw uprising of 1944. He was arrested by the Nazis and sent to Belsen. Lucjan Blit (the biographer of Bolesław Piasecki) calls him a pre-war Fascist. An early member of Pax and a stalwart hack, primarily associated with the Pax journal *Dziś i Jutro*; in 1953 he was one of the Pax editorial board that took over *Tygodnik Powszechny*. In 1977, writing in *Kierunki*, he argued that the Catholic Church should beware of offering support to dissidents since the bulk were Jews and Trotskyites acting on behalf of the west – and that these people were to blame for Poland's post-war misfortunes.

EDELMAN, Marek. Doctor of medicine specializing in heart problems. Last living leader of the Warsaw ghetto uprising. Lived in Łódź where he became a Solidarność activist, then a member of the Citizens' Committees and later a member of the Democratic Union Party.

FICOWSKI, Jerzy, b.1924. Served in the Polish army at the start of the Second World War. Made his début in 1948, and has since published literary criticism, poetry and numerous articles, essays, books. He was frequently banned during the Stalinist era and afterwards. An ethnographer and expert on Spanish poetry, gypsy and Jewish culture in Poland, tireless biographer of Bruno Schulz. His poetry, which only appeared abroad or in underground editions, is a bare, stubborn exercise in remembering. *A Reading of the Ashes* (1981), thought to be his most effective writing, concerns his wife, who was smuggled out of the Warsaw ghetto shortly after she was born. Member of KOR from 1977, editor of *Zapis* in the late 1970s.

GAŁCZYŃSKI, Konstanty Ildefons, 1905–53. Born of a lower middle-class family in Warsaw, he and his family moved to Russia during the First World War. They returned after 1918 and Gałczyński entered Warsaw university to study classics and English, but did not complete his studies. His sympathies with the anti-Semitic right wing were well known. Like Andrzejewski, a frequent contributor to the right-wing anti-Semitic journal *Prosto z Mostu*. Captured by the Germans in the invasion of 1939, and liberated from a POW camp by the Americans at the end of the war. After spending time in Paris, Brussels and Rome in 1946 he returned to Poland amid loud and official (in spite of his past) acclaim. He was no avant-gardist, but regarded politics as a handy prop in a private life that resembled a circus; was often censured for his failure to write verse *socrealizm*, swung from left to right, was happy to satirize capitalists and communists alike. He adopted the pose of the man in the street faced with irreconcilable demands of a highly politicized existence: he faked co-operation, wrote popular lyrics and nonsense rhymes and played the part of jester. He was perhaps the most peculiar of the apologists for the Party, and only briefly found favour with his 'Poem on a Traitor', about Miłosz's defection to the west. Miłosz has described him as a 'buffoon . . . a weak man, a drunkard, a vagabond . . . trying to survive and to bring people something of beauty.' (*The History of Polish Literature*, 411). Significantly his work does not figure in either version of Miłosz's famous anthology of post-war Polish poetry. In the early 1950s, fearful of the Stalinists who had labelled him a 'petit bourgeois in socialist clothing' he stopped writing poetry and switched to translation. After 1956 his work found a popular audience.

GIEDROYĆ, Jerzy, b.1906. Fought as an officer in the Carpathian Brigade at Tobruk and in Italy. Started the Instytut Literacki in Rome, but soon moved to Paris. His ambitions were literary, but his motivation was primarily political. The journal *Kultura*, published by Instytut Literacki, was a focus for émigré and exiled Polish writers and also for dissident writers in Poland. He clashed with the the Union of Polish Writers in Exile and refused to follow their instruction not to deal with writers published by communist state publishing houses in Poland. The journal avoided Catholic pietism, the rigid political attitudes of many émigrés and the rabid anti-communism of many right-wing Poles in exile, publishing a wide cross section of writers and opinions. The journal, though it was never produced in vast numbers, probably reached the height of its influence in the late 1960s, and was important right through the 1970s.

GROCHOWIAK, Stanisław, 1934–76. Born in Leszno, western Poland. Poet, playwright, novelist and editor. Made his début in 1956. Reacting against the puritanism of the 1949–56 years he made a cult of ugliness, which he called 'turpism', even in dealing with love. He mocked the difference between the language and the reality of communism with a frank satirical intent, but from a clear metaphysical anguish and need for a new moral order. In 1962 he won the Ministry of Arts and Culture literary prize.

GRYNBERG, Henryk, b.1936. Born in Warsaw, emigrated to the US in 1967. Author of numerous books including *Jewish War, Life Ideological, Life Personal* and *Khadish*. Winner of the Alfred Jurzykowski award. His best-known work is probably *Victory* (Paris 1969) about the fate of Holocaust survivors in post-war Poland.

HARASYMOWICZ, Jerzy, b.1933. Born in Puławy, central Poland, son of a Ukrainian major in the Polish legions. A professional forester. Lives in Kraków, took part in the early ZLP discussions about *socrealizm*, but tired of it. Writes poetry about remote highlands, villages and forests; he refuses to assign a socially useful meaning to his poetry and is indifferent to literary and political argument, but founded the Muszyna literary group. First volume of poetry published in 1956, followed by seven more volumes by 1965. Indifferent to religion, though very aware that his ancestors were of the Orthodox Church, he feels that anyone who is not a Catholic inpost-communist Poland is very much a second-class citizen.

HERBERT, Zbigniew, 1924–98. Born in Lwów. Graduated from an underground high school. He took part in AK activities and studied Polish literature at an underground university. After the Soviet annexation of Lwów he moved to Kraków and graduated in economics in 1947. He later graduated in law at Toruń University and then in philosophy at Warsaw University. He resigned from ZLP in 1947 and worked for a while at the editorial offices of the Catholic *Tygodnik Powszechny*. Herbert was doubtless penalized for his association with the journal and took up a series of underpaid jobs – in a bank, a peat co-operative and a small industrial enterprise – that kept him out of the public eye, away from the literary scene and relatively safe, until after Stalin's death and the start of the thaw. Although he had begun publishing poems in *Tygodnik Powszechny* this ceased in 1953 when the magazine was taken over by Pax as a result of its refusal to publish a sycophantic obituary to Stalin. In 1954 Herbert published a handful of poems; in 1955 a few more poems appeared in *Życie Literackie*, and in 1956 his first volume *String of Light* appeared to great critical acclaim. This was swiftly followed by *Hermes, Dog and Star* (1957) and *Study of the Object* (1961). His poems were a reaction against the gloom and physical hardship of life under communism, against the corruption of public and private life, the dismal effect of official ideology on individual moral responsibilities. His poems were not widely read in Poland, however, and he was far better known abroad as a result of the Penguin translation of his work which appeared in 1968. Herbert began working as an editor and critic for *Tworczość* (1955–76). However, sensing that the thaw would not last, he began a series of long study tours abroad. He was abroad in 1958, and in the years 1965–71. In 1962 he published *Barbarian in the Garden*, a collection of art/history essays on west European culture, highlighting the wider context of Polish history and quietly insisting on a European rather than eastern connection and ambition for Poland. In 1973 he left Poland for Berlin. The publication of *Mr Cogito* (1974) was one of the literary high spots of the mid-1970s: in these poems Mr Cogito is tantalized by an endlessly elusive moral and spiritual dimension to human life. In 1976 Herbert signed a letter of protest at the Party's planned constitutional amendments. On his return to Poland in the spring of 1981 he joined the board of the underground journal *Zapis*, and expressed himself a supporter of Solidarność. His poems about Martial Law, *Report from a Besieged City* (1983–84), were first published underground in Poland (but all copies were confiscated) and later in Paris. The politicality of Herbert's poems cannot be denied, but in general he has maintained a low and non-confrontational profile in his opposition. Among several other prizes, he has been awarded the Polish Institute of Sciences and Arts in America prize, and the Austrian Nicholas Lenau prize in 1965.

HERLING, Gustaw (Herling-Grudziński), b.1919. Born in Kielce, fourth child of a flour- and saw-mill owner. He began to study Polish literature at Warsaw University and was in his second year when the Nazis invaded. He took part in the September 1939 campaign. In 1940, after setting up one of the first underground resistance cells, he was arrested crossing the Soviet border and sentenced to five years in an NKVD labour camp on the White Sea. He was released in 1942, joined Anders's Polish Army, formed in the USSR. He moved with them to the Middle East and served in the Second Polish Corps in Italy where he fought at Monte Cassino and was decorated with the Virtuti Militari. After the war he resumed writing, married the daughter of the philosopher Benedetto Croce, and lived in Rome, London, Munich and Naples. After 1948 he became co-founder of, and regular contributor to, *Kultura*. His writing was promptly banned in Poland. In the following years *Kultura* was to publish many of his essays and short stories and his *Daybooks Written at Night*. His most widely read work is his account of the Soviet prisons, *Another World* (London, 1953). A founder member of the Paris-based Instytut Literacki and founder contributor to *Kultura*, he is regarded as a prominent liberal essayist and writer of fiction.

HERTZ, Paweł, b.1918. Made his début in the late 1930s; a poet, novelist, essayist and editor. An early champion of 'broad realism' in literature, a member of the *Kuźnica* group and a supporter of the Party until the thaw of 1956.

HIRSZOWICZ, Maria. Held a post in sociology at Łódź. As associate professor of sociology at Warsaw University, sacked in March 1968. She is currently reader in sociology at Reading University.

HŁASKO, Marek, 1934–69. The James Dean of Polish literature, and a 'lost-generation' youth-cult rebel-hero of Michnik's youth. He started publishing in the socialist-realist style in 1954 and became editor of *Po Prostu*. His collection of stories, *First Step in the Clouds* (1956) won him the state Polish Publishers' Literary prize. This book and *Eighth Day of the Week* (1956) established his reputation as an 'angry young man'. In 1958 he received a visa to visit the west for two months. While he was away, *Next Stop – Paradise* and *Cemetery*, the only books in which he displays any concern for ideology or *socrealizm*, were refused publication in Poland. Hłasko gave both books to the émigré magazine *Kultura* (Paris), opening himself to legal charges of slandering the state. His short story 'The Graveyard' was due to appear in *Trybuna Ludu* but the paper panicked at its own boldness and dropped the idea; a film based on *The Eighth Day of the Week* was banned. The authorities refused to extend his visa, but Hłasko decided to stay abroad anyway; he travelled in Italy, Switzerland and West Germany. In 1959, though he was not Jewish, he emigrated to Israel where he worked as a truck driver and pimp. In 1966 he moved to the USA, where he worked illegally and wrote very little. In 1969 he moved to West Germany where he took an overdose of sleeping tablets and died. George Steiner said of him: 'The intriguing thing . . . is not the fact that he found "socialist" Poland stifling and sought freedom in the west, but that he found the "free world" almost equally intolerable.'

HOFFMAN, Paweł, 1903–78. Dealt with propaganda and the press in a wide range of official positions: in 1948 editor in chief of *Kuźnica*, and then editor of *Odrodzenie, Nowa Kultura*. Dismissed from all his literary posts in 1968.

HOŁUJ, Tadeusz, 1916–85. Born in Kraków, a graduate in law from the Jagiellonian University. Made his début in 1935 and published two volumes of verse before the war. Imprisoned in Oświęcim 1942–5. His novel about this experience, *End of Our World* won him the Ministry of Arts and Culture literary prize and the City of Kraków prize in 1962. Well known as a communist, but of a rather unorthodox kind. He believed that under a Marxist regime all artists had a very important role within the national tradition of creating and fostering social awareness and consciousness, in evaluating reality. In 1976 he was Kraków deputy to the Sejm. In May 1981, writing in the local Party newspaper *Gazeta Krakowska*, he bravely stood up to the Grunwald Patriotic Unions's anti-Semitic campaign, saying that such activities were not compatible with the party's ideology.

HORODYŃSKI, Dominik. A member of the pre-war nobility and an early member of Pax, primarily associated with the journal *Dziś i Jutro*. In 1956 he left Pax as a 'secessionist' and joined ODiSS before taking up a diplomatic post as Poland's ambassador to Rome. In 1974 he became editor in chief of the reformed and liberalized *Kultura* (Warsaw). In 1977 he characterized a Warsaw hunger strike in which several distinguished and respected public figures took part as 'political exhibitionism'. Lipski lists him as one of those who slandered KOR in *Trybuna Ludu* in 1976–7.

IŁŁAKOWICZÓWNA, Kazimiera, 1892–1983. Born in Wilno, later lived in Vitebsk and Warsaw, then studied literature at St Petersburg, Kraków and Oxford. At the start of the First World War she was in Russia and worked first as a nurse then as an editor in one of the St Petersburg publishing houses. She went to Warsaw at the end of the war and became a civil servant in the Ministry of Foreign Affairs. She published her first volume of poems in Kraków in 1912. In the years 1926–35 she was personal assistant to Marshal Piłsudski. At the outbreak of the Second World War she escaped to Romania and took asylum. She taught foreign languages and translated German and Hungarian poetry into Polish. She returned to Poland in 1947 and settled in Poznań. She published at least ten volumes of poetry, essays and memoirs.

IWASZKIEWICZ, Jarosław, 1894–1980. Born near Kalnik in the Ukraine, son of a white-collar worker but descended from a landowning gentry family. Cousin and biographer of Karol Szymanowski. He studied at Elizavetagorod, graduated in law at Kiev University in 1918, began to study music at the Kiev Conservatory, but he and his family moved to the newly independent Poland and settled in Warsaw in 1918. He made his début as a poet, writing in the manner of the Russian Symbolists in 1919. Co-founder and most controversial member of the inter-war post-Romantic and modernist Skamander group of poets, who in general considered life to be a primeval force, larger, more irrational and wiser than any intellect could ever grasp; though prolific, he was criticized by the younger generation for his complete lack of interest in social and political affairs. His works are tinged with homosexual eroticism and demonism. Considered an exotic easterner by many, he was often said to be the Polish Thomas Mann, but more often described at the Polish Oscar Wilde because of his poetic sense and personal style. He was a pre-war diplomat for Poland in Copenhagen, Brussels, Paris and in Persia. While he remained a pessimist, he confounded critics with his sheer output, his determined amorality and Dionysian qualities. He remained in Poland throughout the war and took part in the literary and cultural resistance to the Nazis, and his home was a meeting place for the resistance movement. After the war he became president of ZLP for several years and from 1956 was editor of *Twórczość*. Novelist, poet, playwright, music critic, editor, biographer of J. S. Bach and Chopin, he received numerous state awards for his prolific literary output, the most successful part of which will probably prove to be his short stories.

JASIENICA, Paweł, 1909–70. Arrested during the war for his membership of the AK, sentenced to death but later released. A Catholic essayist and author of extremely popular histories of the Piast and Jagiellonian dynasties. He played an important role in the opposition movement of 1956 as chairman of the influential independent Club of the Crooked Circle. He criticized the anti-Semitic campaign of 1968, and in return was attacked in the press and by Gomułka himself before being slanderously accused of murder. After his death his works were republished by NOWa.

JASTRUN, Mieczysław (Mieczysław Agatstein), 1903–83. Born in Koralówka, near Tarnopol, of Jewish origin. Completed a doctorate in Polish literature at Kraków University, worked as a teacher 1929–38. Published his first volume of poems in 1929, followed by four more volumes before the war intervened. He tried to keep out of literary arguments, but was opposed to the inter-war Skamander group of poets. He risked his life to stay in Warsaw throughout the war, teaching in schools for the underground Polish administration and writing for the resistance press. Although a collection of his verse appeared after the war, and his biography of Mickiewicz appeared in 1949, he was reluctant to publish in the early years of the People's Republic and suffered horribly at the moral collapse (particularly among his fellow writers) during the Stalinist repression. His poem 'Man' is eloquent testimony to his feelings. He was divided over his 'metaphysical needs' for isolation, and his need for a commitment to a morally stable political world. He devoted himself to translations for several years, and only began to publish his poetry again with the thaw of 1955–6. Much of his writing from this period is existentialist, an attempt to accept both good and evil, intelligence and stupidity – his best contemplative poetry stems from the period after 1956. He also wrote a great deal about Mediterranean culture and history. Something of a recluse, he was deeply interested in metaphysics and moral themes in his later years, managed to keep out of post-war literary and political squabbles and published with *Tygodnik Powszechny*. He left behind him a huge body of work which includes poetry, essays, fiction and translations from Russian, German and French.

JASTRUN, Tomasz, b.1950. Son of Mieczysław Jastrun. Made his début in 1978 and published several collections of poetry underground during the Martial Law period and before the collapse of communism. In the late 1970s he worked with the underground publishing house NOWa and in August 1980 joined striking shipyard workers in Gdańsk. He edited the Mazowsze region Solidarność *Biuletyn Kulturalny* and in 1981 was an editor for the Solidarność press agency. With Martial Law he went underground, but was finally arrested and interned in November 1982. His poetry appeared in the underground *Tygodnik Solidarność* in 1982, and in two samizdat editions. An outspoken critic of the Martial Law regime and the regime that followed it, in the late 1980s he edited *Res Publica* and in 1990 was appointed cultural attaché to Sweden.

KARPIŃSKI, Jakub. A leader of the student demonstrations in 1968, imprisoned 1968–71. Later a lecturer in sociology at Warsaw University and

LSE. Associated with the journal *Głos*, with NOWa, KOR and the Instytut Literacki in Paris, he helped smuggle *Kultura* into Poland over the Tatra mountains. He often used the pen-name Marek Tarniewski.

KARPOWICZ, Tymoteusz, b.1921. Born in the tiny hamlet of Zielona, near Wilno. Studied Polish philology at Wrocław university, where he also received his doctorate and took up a lecturing post. Made his début in 1948, but remained little known or published before 1958, when his second volume of verse was published. Four more volumes of verse were to follow between 1958 and 1972. A journalist and editor of the weekly Wrocław magazine *Odra*, he was also president of the Wrocław branch of ZLP for several years. In 1958 he was awarded the Wrocław city literature prize. He somehow managed to lead a rich inner life while outwardly conforming to the social and political pressures of the Party. Mainly known as a nature poet with four collections in the years 1957–62 and four more by 1972, he is also known as an essayist and literary critic. Among Polish post-war poets his roots are clearly drawn from the modernist tradition, but his use of language borders on the edge of unacceptability in that he often reads like a badly translated foreign author. He ceased publishing in 1972, left Poland in 1973 and since 1978 has been teaching Polish literature at Illinois University.

KARSOW, Nina. Adopted daughter of wartime resistance workers, she had by the age of three narrowly escaped going to the gas chamber, while her mother was imprisoned in Mokotów jail. Originally of Jewish family, she was arrested in 1966 for political offences – namely collecting material on political trials and on official anti-Semitism. In prison she married Professor Szymon Szechter as part of a complex plot to obtain her release. Expelled from Poland in 1968, settled in London where she translated Szechter's stories and started her own publishing house.

KARST, Roman. Young revisionist who reported for Radio Free Europe's Polish-language broadsheet *Na Antenie* in the late 1960s, and left Poland for Israel after being blacklisted as a result of the party's investigation into protest at the banning of *Dziady* in 1968.

KASMAN, Leon, 1905–84. Member of Communist Youth Movement, joined KPP in 1922, and spent a total of ten years in gaol. Spent the first three years of the war in the USSR where he worked for the Comintern. Parachuted into Poland to help organize the PPR in 1943. After the war he worked on Party propaganda, was editor in chief of *Trybuna Ludu* and editor of *Trybuna Wolności* 1951–4 and 1957–67. Member of the Central Committee 1948–68. Dismissed from his post during the anti-Semitic campaign of 1968.

KIJOWSKI, Andrzej, 1928–85. Born in Kraków, died in Warsaw. He studied humanities at Kraków University and began his career as a critic in 1950. In 1955 he became an editor on *Twórczość*, and in 1958 moved on to the staff of *Przegląd Kulturalny*. He was particularly outspoken and popular in the early 1960s, and is best known as a critic working mainly in the Catholic

Tygodnik Powszechny. He also wrote short stories, novels, essays and the film scenarios *The Wedding* and *The Orchestra Conductor* for Andrzej Wajda. In the 1980s some of his prose was published by NOWa, and he was one of the Citizens' Commission appointed to audit KOR's finances. In August 1980 he was one of the commission of experts appointed by Szczecin Solidarność.

KISIELEWSKI, Stefan, 1911–91. Born Warsaw. Writing under the pen-name 'Kisiel', a multi-talented liberal who nevertheless supported the Catholic Church insofar as it defended individual freedoms against communism. An intellectual star in the Polish artistic firmament since the 1930s. One of the few writers of his generation not associated with *Kuźnica*, he maintained his independent opinions throughout the whole of his career, and for doing so earned the respect of the entire literary and cultural community and the endless attention of the censor. Censorship regulations stated that as a matter of course all his work had to be seen and approved. In the years 1957–65 he served as a Znak deputy to the Sejm and in the 1960s was a co-editor for *Tygodnik Powszechny*, which also published much of his work. In February 1968 at a ZLP meeting he labelled the regime a dictatorship of dim-wits and was later beaten up by unknown assailants. He remained close to the liberal Catholic milieu of the Znak group and of Turowicz. He wrote the original preface to Michnik's *Church, Left, Dialogue*. A member of the ZLP Committee in 1980. He frequently published his articles in *Kultura* (Paris) under the pseudonym Tomasz Staliński. His connections with the dissident community were never disguised or hidden, yet his stature as a satirist was so great that although the Party kept a close watch on his work, he was able to write very much what he wanted and to fend off serious interference until Martial Law was declared. He was one of the Citizens' Commission appointed to audit KOR-KSS finances.

KOŁAKOWSKI, Leszek, b.1927. Born in Radom. An influential philosopher. Probably the most outspoken of the Marxist oppositionists and revisionists. Studied philosophy at Łódź University. Taught the history of philosophy at Łódź University. In 1954 became a lecturer in the history of philosophy at Warsaw University. In 1959 he became a professor. In the years 1952–4 he taught at the Central Committee's Institute for Training Scientific Workers. In the years 1955–7 he edited the communist intellectual journal *Po Prostu*, which was censured in 1956 for its deviationism and then in 1957 suspended altogether. He became editor of *Studia Filozoficzne*, and after he resigned in 1959 remained on the editorial board. His essay 'The Priest and the Jester', which appeared in *Twórczość* in October 1959, occasioned considerable debate within Party circles. He was expelled from the PZPR in 1966, and lost his post in 1968 after being accused of inciting student riots. In 1969 took up a post at All Souls College, Oxford; for many he remains a potent symbol of opposition. Although best known for his three-volume *Main Currents of Marxism* (Paris, 1976–8), he has also written extensively on religion and the spiritual aspects of modern politics and culture. He is also the author of at least three collections of short stories and several plays. In March 1998 he was offered an apology and his Polish citizenship was restored by President Kwasniewski.

KORNHAUSER, Julian, b.1946. Born in Gliwice, he had made his début in 1972, but is generally considered a leading figure in the 'New Wave' 1968 generation. Co-founder of the journal *Teraz*. A distinguished poet, translator, novelist and essayist, with over a dozen books to his name, taught Slavonic studies at the Jagiellonian University in Kraków and is an expert on the history of Yugoslav literature. His essays *The Unrepresented World* (1974, with Adam Zagajewski), caused considerable controversy as they advocated a return to reality via plain speaking in politics *and* literature, and attempted to bypass 'tribal tyranny' by writing about the things that were not 'normally present in Polish literature'. This was what they meant by the phrase the 'unrepresented world'. With the shock of Martial Law Kornhauser almost stopped writing, and he is an example of the sudden paralysis that afflicted many Polish poets right through the 1980s. In the mid-1980s he appeared to make a come-back and published in *Zeszyty Literacki*, *Pogląd* and *Tygodnik Literacki*, but apart from his volume *Another Order*, which was almost ignored by the critics, he has published little. Kornhauser, when asked at the 1995 Cheltenham Literature Festival how his poetry had been affected by the changes of 1989 remarked: 'After 1989 it was all different, everything changed. Suddenly words and ideas were far more slippery. It was not possible to describe anything as it all changed so fast. Now my poetry is only silence: that is the only possible way that I can respond. It is the only way I can draw attention to, and comment on, the hole, the gap, the nothingness that now exists at the centre of Polish society and in my head.'

KOSSAK, Zofia (Kossak-Szczuka, Kossak-Szatkowska), 1890–1954. Spent her youth on an estate leased by her father in Skowrodki in Wołhynia. Best known as a traditional Catholic novelist of historical themes. Her first novel *Blaze* (1922), about political life in the closing years of the First World War, has been described by Neal Ascherson as 'one of the most viciously anti-Semitic books I have ever read' (*Games with Shadows*, 232), and this may be why she is not even mentioned in Miłosz's *History of Polish Literature*. However there is another aspect to her life. During the occupation she was hunted by the Nazis for the anti-Nazi views she had expressed before the war, and lived in Warsaw illegally. With the help of Witold Bieńkowski (later a member of the Pax *Dziś i Jutro* group) and the Catholic historian Władysław Bartoszewski she co-founded Żegota, organizing aid to Polish Jews. In 1942 she published an underground pamphlet entitled *Protest* asking all Poles, even those who disliked Jews, to take a morally unambiguous stance in regard to the crime of genocide. She was arrested and sent to Oświęcim for a while. After her release in 1941, she made her way to England and returned to

Poland only in 1957. She often shows her protagonists as victorious in defeat, and links her study of religious problems with political and psychological insight, and with the narrative of Polish political history. Her best-known novel is probably *Blessed Are the Meek*, a life of St Francis.

KOWALSKA, Anka, b.1932. Born in Sosnowiec in Upper Silesia. Studied literature at the Catholic University of Lublin. Poet and editor at Pax, where she stood out from the bulk of the membership, operating as a link between Pax dissidents and KOR. Although she resigned from Pax in March 1968 she retained her job as an editor with Pax. Editor of KOR's illegal *Communiqué* and *Information Bulletin*. Winner of the Pax Pietrzak literary prize. Arrested by military authorities in 1981, her descriptions of life in the prison camps are vivid and committed political poetry of a high order.

KOZIOŁ Urszula, b.1931. Born in Biłgoraj in south-eastern Poland (or in 1935 in Rakówka in central Poland), she studied humanities (or Polish literature) at Wrocław University and graduated in 1953. She was refused access to postgraduate work on political grounds and sent to teach in provincial secondary schools. After 1953 she was allowed to resume her studies in Wrocław. Her poems appeared in a variety of journals, but her first volume of poems appeared in 1957, her second in 1963. In the 1960s she returned to teaching and in 1971 she was appointed co-editor and poetry editor of *Odra*. Since then she has written a novel, plays for the student theatre and radio, and a collection of essays. She lives in Wrocław.

KRALL, Hanna. Of Jewish family, she is one of Poland's most distinguished journalists. She worked for many years on the weekly *Polityka* but resigned with the imposition of Martial Law and began to publish underground and abroad. In 1986 she was awarded the Solidarność cultural prize for her autobiography *The Subtenant* (1983). She has published three collections of articles. Her book *Shielding the Flame* (Warsaw, 1977), a series of interviews with the Warsaw Jewish ghetto survivor Marek Edelman, appeared in twenty-two editions and helped raise the issue of anti-Semitism for Solidarność. A great deal of her writing centres on Polish-Jewish relations and the legacy of the Holocaust.

KRUCZKOWSKI, Leon, 1900–62. Born and lived in Kraków, studied science at Kraków University. Fought in the September 1939 campaign and spent five years in a prisoner-of-war camp in Germany. A dedicated Marxist who held several important positions after the war. He took over the chair of ZLP at the start of the campaign to impose *socrealizm* and he continued until the thaw of 1956. In spite of the fact that he was rather unpopular with other writers, they almost all grudgingly admit that he could tell a good tale and did not strain history too much in telling stories from a Marxist perspective. He employed documentary methods for added authenticity and opened up post-war Polish literature to Marxist influence and a revaluation of its traditional 'virtues' – even in *socrealist* mode he was interested in individuals.

KRYNICKI, Ryszard, b.1943. Born in Sankt Valentin in Austria. Studied Polish literature at Poznań University. Poet and translator of German, Austrian and English literature. A (possibly the) leading figure of the 'New Wave' 1968 generation, dedicated to exposing the evils and ills of communist Poland, advocating moral and social commitment as a reaction against *socrealizm* and the *hermetizm* of the previous generation of poets. His first volume of poetry was published in 1969, and his second appeared in 1975 but he was blacklisted immediately afterwards for his protests at the proposed changes to the Polish constitution. His next three books were published in Paris, and much to the annoyance of the authorities were reprinted by the clandestine press in Kraków. He is fascinated by language and the unmasking of the language in which the party presented itself on various levels: he called his work 'linguistic poetry'. Miłosz has dismissed his poetry as 'the result of an unflinching adherence to principles', but other critics have been more impressed and it is said that his sparse meditations border on prayer. He has recently turned away from extreme lyrical gnomism to develop a more aphoristic and concise form of poetry to encapsulate his metaphysical and moral concerns. An editor of *Zapis* in the late 1970s, he won the Koscielski award in 1975 and the Polish PEN award.

KUNCEWICZ, Maria, b.1899. Born in Samara, Russia, educated at Kraków and Nancy Universities, and at the Warsaw Conservatory. She made her début in 1926 and is mainly known as a novelist, translator and anthologist. In 1937 she was awarded the City of Warsaw literary prize; in 1938 she was awarded the PAL Golden Laurel prize. She spent the years 1940–5 in England, where she founded the International PEN Centre for Writers in Exile. She made her home in the USA, where she became president of PEN USA and visiting professor of Polish literature at Chicago University.

KUROŃ, Jacek, b.1933. A charismatic figure, a historian, teacher, and prominent democratic activist. Originally a communist pedagogue, he was expelled from the Party in 1953 and again in 1956. He lectured at Warsaw University in the early 1960s, was arrested in November 1964 and sentenced to three years in gaol in 1965, accused of attempting to overthrow the regime by writing (with Karol Modzelewski) *Open Letter to the Party*, a Marxist analysis in which they accused Gomułka of having abandoned the ideals which had brought him to power. Prominent during the student disturbances of 1968, he was arrested again. Frequently detained by the authorities in the 1970s, he abandoned his Trotskyite stance and became an advocate of anti-politics, urging the reconstruction of civil society. He was a founder member of KOR in 1976 and also of the TKN, adviser to Solidarność 1980–1. Identified by the KGB as part of the 'Zionist conspiracy' plotted by Solidarność, he was arrested during Martial Law, accused of plotting to overthrow the government by force, and spent two and a half years in gaol. In total he has spent nine and a half years in gaol. A leading negotiator for Solidarność at the round-table talks in 1989. In the years 1989–90 he was minister of labour in Mazowiecki's post-communist government; in 1990 he became a Sejm deputy for, and vice-chairman of, the Democratic Union Party which was part of the Union of Freedom caucus. He became minister of labour again 1992–3.

LEC, Stanisław Jerzy (de Tusch-Letz), 1909–64. Lec ran the gamut of twentieth-century experience. Born in Lwów of a rich Viennese-Galician Jewish family with an aristocratic title, educated in Lwów and Vienna, died Warsaw. Studied Polish literature and law at Lwów University where he became a poet of extreme leftist opinions, made his début in 1929 in the radical left periodicals. Wrote for the Warsaw Cabaret Theatre in 1933. Imprisoned by the Nazis in 1941, he escaped from a concentration camp in 1943 to join the AL in Warsaw where he edited underground publications, achieved the rank of major and was decorated for bravery. In 1945–50 became a member of the Polish Political Mission to Vienna. Broke with the Stalinist regime in 1950 and emigrated to Israel, but returned to Poland after only two years and settled in Warsaw. He began to write his famous aphorisms in 1956. His aphorisms and satires appeared in a wide range of journals. With jibes as delicious as 'Illiterates must dictate', his first collected *Unkempt Thoughts* (1957) appeared only after the thaw was well under way. His aphorisms border on poetry and cannot be divorced from the public mood of 1956–66, but were also extremely popular under Gierek.

LECHOŃ, Jan (Leszek Serafinowicz), 1899–1956. Born into a poor white-collar family, studied literature at Warsaw University. A co-founder of the Skamander group, he made his début as a poet in 1920. His themes were a search for form and the life of the nation. A poet turned diplomat, he was cultural attaché in Paris from 1930 to 1940. After the defeat of France he fled to Brazil with Julian Tuwim and later moved to New York where he edited the journal *Polish Weekly* and directed the Polish-language programmes on culture for Radio Free Europe. Although he began to write early in his life he was intensely self-critical. He sought to maintain the standards of the precocious genius of his early years and thus produced only a modest output. After going to the France he made use of the mask of his role as a diplomat to disguise the failure of his talent and his interest: indeed his early success seems to have paralysed his talent. In the USA he seems to have published very infrequently, and even then his patriotic laments were out of place in the USA. Some of his later work, the most personal and the most desperate, regained and even surpassed the intensity of his early work, but he suffered severe bouts of depression and committed suicide by jumping from a New York skyscraper.

LIPSKA, Ewa, b.1945 in Kraków. From 1963 she studied art history and painting at Kraków Academy of Fine Arts. Although she began writing at the age of fourteen, she did not belong to any poetic group and published very little, until her first collection of poetry appeared in 1967. She believed that

communism had deprived Poles of 'true biography', that her generation had
no heroic struggles, no arms to take up. This changed after March 1968. Close
to the *nowa fala* poets of the 1968 generation in her concern with the power of
public language. In 1970 she became editor at the Wydawnictwo Literackie
publishing house. In 1973 she received the Kościelski Fund award (Geneva)
for her poetry. In 1975–6 she lectured at Iowa University and in 1979 received
the Robert Graves PEN Club award. In 1981 she was one of the founders of
the Kraków journal *Pismo* and continues to edit it. Her 1985 collection
Storeroom of Darkness was published underground by the Warsaw Independent Poets' and Artists' publishing house. In 1990 she became Polish
cultural attaché to Vienna.

LIPSKI, Jan Józef, 1926–91. Literary critic and historian. A member of
PPS between the wars, a soldier in the AK at the age of sixteen, wounded and
decorated with the Cross of Valour for his part in the Warsaw uprising;
profoundly influenced by Miłosz's poem 'Moral Tract' (1948). After the war
studied Polish literature at Warsaw University. In the years 1956–62 he was
chairman of the Club of the Crooked Circle (KKK), and in 1957 worked as an
editor for *Po Prostu* and *Nowa Kultura*. After the suppression of *Nowa
Kultura* in 1957, he was refused a passport. In 1961 he joined the staff of PAN
Institute of Literary Research (IBL), where he consistently campaigned
against censorship. In 1964 he was chief sponsor and signatory of the 'Letter
of the thirty-four', and was banned from publication on numerous occasions.
He left the Party in 1966. Although he remained a socialist, after 1968 he
maintained close links with the Catholic Church and in 1976 was a founder of
KOR. Helped found *Zapis*, the first of the important underground journals.
In 1980 he was one of the leaders on the executive committee of the
Solidarność Mazowsze chapter. In 1981 he organized a strike at the Ursus
factory in protest at Martial Law, for which he was arrested and dismissed
from his post at the Literary Institute. Released by the authorities because of
ill health (at the time of his initial arrest he had just undergone heart surgery),
he was soon rearrested. Throughout the 1980s he worked to unite the non-
communist left under the banner of the PPS. In 1989 – believing that the new
Poland would need a democratic left – he made contact with the London
remnants of the pre-war PPS and attempted to unite it with the fragmented
and bickering groups of the reborn PPS in Poland. Became chairman of the
revived PPS, elected to the Senate on the Solidarność ticket, representing the
town of Radom. Regarded by all as a moral authority, he is best known
outside Poland for his history of KOR.

MACHEJEK, Władysław b.1920. Born near Miechów. Spent virtually his
whole working life in Kraków. First secretary of the Basal Party Organization
within ZLP. A pre-war communist and notorious post-war communist hack.
He served each and every post-war leadership with slavish zeal, praising the
new leaders and criticizing those who were deposed. He firmly believed that

literature was a means to fight for a great idea and was a great help to the Party. He was editor in chief of *Życie Literackie* from 1951 – a haven for the obscurantist and reactionary elements of Polish literary life, and occasionally, when he sensed the wind blowing from another direction, even dissenting political opinion – from Kraków. His *magnum opus* is *Waiting for the Last Word* (1976) a four-volume novel about the life of ordinary Party members, which blamed intellectuals, homosexuals, liberals and Jews for all Poland's post-war problems. The censor judged it such an outrageous representation of the Party that he intervened to prevent favourable reviews appearing, and stopped the novel being serialized (except in *Życie Literackie*) or reprinted. Irena Grudzińska-Gross, writing in *ANEKS* in 1977, had no hesitation in labelling him a Fascist. Lipski lists him as one of those who slandered KOR in 1976. In 1980–1 he praised Solidarność, but turned against it after Martial Law was declared.

MACIEREWICZ, Antoni, b.1948. Historian, expert on Maya Indians. Anti-Vietnam campaigner in the 1960s and early 1970s, protested against Polish constitutional changes in 1976. Co-founder of KOR in 1976. In the late 1970s he moved steadily away from a revisionist position towards Catholic nationalist and populist ideas. In 1980 became an adviser to Solidarność and member of the Mazowsze chapter of Solidarność. In 1990 became president of the Christian National Union; in 1992 minister of internal affairs.

MAJ, Bronisław, b.1953. Born in Łódź. Studied Polish literature at the Jagiellonian University and co-edited the influential magazine *Student* which was suspended during Martial Law. Worked as a scriptwriter and actor with the KTO theatre 1977–81. Published his first book of poems in 1980 and has since published four more volumes. After 1981 his poetry was published abroad or underground. His latest volume was published by Puls in 1986 in London. In 1983, during Martial Law, he became editor in chief of *NaGłos*, a unique and very popular oral literary journal published in Kraków which managed to circumvent the military authorities and censorship. Compared to Krynicki and Barańczak the political and satirical aspects of his work are much more muted, but his insistent line that poets 'always talk about freedom', his belief that Stalinist poets had lied to preserve the truth, that surviving communism as a clean human being meant trying to reconcile the irreconcilable, along with his preoccupation with the language of communism, all made him very popular with Solidarność: he was awarded the Solidarność literary prize in 1984 and Miłosz dubbed him 'a Polish poet' in the line of Mickiewicz. His reputation rests on three volumes of verse published in 1980, 1981 and 1986. Since Martial Law, Maj has written very little and has devoted himself to editing *NaGłos*, which since 1989 appears in printed form, but which, as Maj says, is 'completely non-political'.

MALEWSKA, Hanna, 1911–83. Born in Grodzisk, near Warsaw, daughter of a doctor. Studied at KUL, and graduated in history in 1933. Published her first novel in 1937, but her writing career was interrupted by the war. She worked as a teacher, was active in the resistance and took part in the Warsaw uprising in 1944. A Catholic conservative rightist, after the war she lived in Kraków where she edited *Tygodnik Powszechny* and directed and wrote for *Znak*. She published a biography of C.K.Norwid; her novels on historical themes were set in ancient Greece, the Holy Roman Empire, ancient Rome, medieval France and eighteenth-century Poland. She lived in Kraków.

MAZOWIECKI, Tadeusz, b.1927. Lawyer, essayist and Catholic activist. He was chairman of the state-run Student Publishing House 1947–8, but was dismissed for 'clericalism'. Although an early member of Pax he was never a Party member. His association with Pax was concluded in 1955–6 – some say he was expelled in 1955, others say he left in 1956. In 1958 he founded and was for many years editor of the respected Catholic journal *Więź*. This journal was in favour of pluralism and advocated that the Church should be far more open to contemporary life and thought. For Pax, which had accepted Stalinism, the journal was an example of socialist humanism, and as such far too close to the Church. For the Church it was seen as the acceptable face of communism, a kind of Trojan Horse. From 1961 Mazowiecki was a Sejm deputy for the Catholic Znak group, but in March 1968 he blotted his reputation with the Party by signing a letter of protest to the government, and by speaking out in the Sejm to support the rights of student and intellectual demonstrators, and to ask the Party to restrain the brutality of the riot police. His period in the Sejm came to an abrupt halt in 1968. As an editor and essayist he was active throughout the 1970s in KIK, TKN and the democratic opposition to communism. In the 1970s he often published work by writers that the state and Church publishers refused to accept. In December 1970, after the massacre of shipyard workers in Gdynia he attempted without success to get a Sejm investigatory commission set up. In August 1980 he went to the Gdańsk shipyards during the strike to take a letter of support entitled 'The Appeal of the Sixty-Four Intellectuals' to the infant Solidarność. He was invited to stay and to select and lead a team of expert advisers. He became a member of the Solidarność Inter-Factory Strike Committee and an adviser to Lech Wałęsa. In 1981 he became co-founder and editor in chief of *Tygodnik Solidarność* and was interned during Martial Law. Afterwards he was a member of the Citizens' Committee and took part in the round-table discussions of 1989 and went on to become the first post-communist prime minister in the coalition government of 1989. In the presidential elections of 1991 he ran against Wałęsa and lost. Wałęsa's vague smear that Mazowiecki was tainted by his early communism referred to his membership of Pax and was fuelled by the Catholic hierarchy's suspicion of liberal Catholic journal *Więź* rather than anything of substance. Michnik had long been an admirer of Mazowiecki's generosity and patience as well as his democratic liberal Catholic spirit; he has expressed profound admiration of *Więź* and for the patience and far-sightedness of Mazowiecki as both a writer and editor. Currently Mazowiecki leads and is Sejm deputy for the Democratic Union Party, part of the Union for Democratic Freedom, which with 14 per cent of the vote was the largest party in the 1992 Sejm.

MICEWSKI, Andrzej. Catholic biographer. Popularized the views of Endecja with his biography of Roman Dmowski. Barańczak accused his biography of Cardinal Wyszyński of sycophancy.

MIĘDZYRZECKI, Artur, b.1922. Born in Warsaw, served with the Polish division of the British army as a junior artillery officer in Italy during the Second World War; afterwards studied literature and history in France and Italy. Married to the poet Julia Hartwig. Made his début as a poet in 1943 while serving in Jerusalem. After the war he studied journalism in Paris and returned to Poland in 1950. His first volume published in Poland appeared in 1951, but he did not become well known until the late 1960s. He is best known as a poet of 'despairing civic passions' and as translator of Racine, Molière, Rimbaud, Apollinaire, René Char and Yves Bonnefoy. He has also translated Osip Mandelstam, Emily Dickinson, e.e. cummings and William Carlos Williams. In 1965 he was elected vice-president of the Executive Board of the Writers' Union as part of a compromise between the union and the Party. He lost this post in the upheavals of 1968. In 1976 he was banned for his protests at the constitutional changes. He was a respected member of ZLP, frequently called upon to chair meetings, and was vice-president of Polish PEN when it was dissolved by the military in 1983. He was involved in a large number of underground publishing ventures throughout the 1980s, and published collections of verse in 1983 and 1987. In 1971 he won the Polish PEN Club prize, in 1977 the French Prix Annuel de Traduction, and in 1981 the Polish Society of Authors' ZAIKS literary award. Since 1989 he has resumed his post as vice-president of Polish PEN. Author of ten volumes of verse, four books of criticism and five collections of fiction, his constant theme is the struggle of culture with despotic politicians.

MIŁOSZ, Czesław, b.1911. Born in Sztejnie, Lithuania. A pupil at the local grammar school and then in 1929 went to study law at Wilno King Stefan Batory University and co-founded the Żagary group of poets. Started to publish in 1930 as part of the Second Vanguard movement (in reaction to Skamander and its opponents in the First Vanguard) and was branded a catastrophist. Published his first book of poems in 1933, graduated 1934, lived in Paris for a year before returning to Poland to work in the Wilno office of Radio Polski. His second book of verse appeared in 1936, but he lost his job because of his alleged leftist sympathies. He moved to Warsaw and found another job with Radio Polski. He escaped from Warsaw to Wilno at the start of the war and returned to Warsaw clandestinely a few months later. He edited an anti-Nazi anthology of poetry. His wartime poems *Rescue* (1945) as well as revealing some of the moral dilemmas faced by Poles during the occupation, outlined Miłosz's sense of guilt at having survived: this was to be his only collection of verse published in Poland until 1980. In 1948 he published his verse 'Treatise on Morals' criticizing rule by terror. For several years he served in the Polish diplomatic corps, working as second secretary to the Polish embassy in the USA and then as cultural attaché in Paris. After his passport was withdrawn by the Polish authorities in 1950, he obtained an exit permit and requested political asylum in France in 1951. He lived as a freelance writer in Paris for most of the next decade, but had little literary success. His works were banned for many years in Poland and he was mainly published by the Instytut Literacki in Paris. In 1960–1 he moved to California. He is now professor of Slavonic literature at Berkeley. Awarded the Neustadt International prize for literature in 1978, and the Nobel prize for literature in 1980. Although his work had been published by underground presses it was only with the Nobel prize that the official publishing houses in Poland were allowed to produce his work.

MINC, Julia, b.1910. Born into a lower middle-class family of Warsaw traders, she had a high school education. Her father had been a member of the SDKPiL; she joined the communist youth movement and then graduated to the KPP. She spent two years in prison. She and her husband Hilary Minc lived in France for a while, then in 1939 they moved to the USSR. Summoned to Moscow, she worked on Radio Kosciuszko, while her husband joined Berling's army. They returned to Poland in 1944 where she became editor in chief of PAP, a position she occupied until 1954 when for ideological reasons she was dropped. Worked in the State Commission on Employment until 1956 when her post was dissolved and she retired.

MOCZAR, Mieczysław, 1913–86. Came from a rural background, had only an elementary education and no profession or trade. Joined the KPP in 1937, spent the war in Poland as an AL partisan commander. In the years 1945–8 he worked as deputy chief of security services in Łódź. He was deputy minister of internal affairs 1957–64, minister for internal affairs 1964–8, member of the Council of State, 1969–76, Central Committee Secretary, 1948–81, member of the Politburo, 1968–71 and 1980–1 and chairman of the Supreme Chamber of Control. He had close connections with the Soviet security service. His power and the appeal of his simple policies of nationalism, anti-Semitism and plain race hate should not be underestimated in the challenge they represented to both Gomułka and Gierek. Doubtless in 1967–8 it was Moczar who was seeking to oust Gomułka, appealing for popular support through an anti-Semitic purge led by his organization ZBoWiD. There was a very real chance that in 1970, when Gomułka's policies came unstuck over the Szczecin shipyard strikes, Moczar would become first secretary of the Party. Moscow and most of the Party, however, backed Edward Gierek. Once installed, Gierek purged Moczar from the Politburo and reined in ZBoWiD.

MOCZULSKI, Leszek, b.1930/8. A Catholic historian of Polish-German relations in the Second World War, journalist, politician and Catholic lyric poet. Began work in 1960 with the journal *Stolica*, which was associated in 1968 with hard-liner Moczar's anti-Semitic policies: he wrote attacking students and intellectuals. His early historical writings were praised by the Polish Ministry of Defence, but he fell from favour in 1972 with the publication of *Polish War*, in which he presented a rather unglamorous portrait of the Soviet military. In spite of this he has since published seven books. He made his début as as a lyric poet in 1971. His poems are close to the spirit of the generation of 1968. In 1977 he was a founder member of the oppositionist ROPCiO, a movement that was consistently more nationalist, overtly Catholic and conservative than KOR. ROPCiO split up in 1979 and Moczulski founded and led the right-wing, nationalist, anti-Semitic party KPN. For this he was imprisoned for most of the 1980s. The problem of whether or not KOR and Solidarność should campaign for the release of Moczulski was much discussed in 1980–1. Eventually it was decided that no matter how odious KPN policies were, Poland should have no political prisoners and Moczulski should be freed. Today he is a leading KPN Sejm deputy.

MODZELEWSKI, Karol, b.1937. Historian and prominent opposition activist. Son of Zygmunt Modzelewski, Poland's first post-war ambassador to the USSR and later minister for foreign affairs. Expelled from the PZPR in 1964, arrested in 1965 for his part in writing *Open Letter to the Party* with Jacek Kuroń. Arrested again in 1968 for his part in the 'March events', released in 1971. In 1980 he was co-organizer of independent trade unions in Wrocław and is widely credited with coining the name of Solidarność. In 1980 he became leader of Wrocław Solidarność, and then press officer for Solidarność, serving on the union's National Commission until April 1981. He was elected delegate to the National Board at the Oliwa Conference in September 1981. During Martial Law he was arrested in December 1981, sentenced without trial to three years in gaol and held until 1983. Elected to the Senate as a Solidarność deputy in 1989–91, he was a critic of admired but untried free-market shock-therapy idea, and went on to become leader of the Social Democratic Labour party and honorary chair of the Union of Labour.

MROŻEK, Sławomir, b.1930. Born near Kraków, son of a postal clerk. Started to study a wide variety of subjects at university – architecture, fine arts, oriental languages – but never finished any of them. Began his career in 1950 as a cartoonist and satirical pamphleteer with the magazines *Szpilki* and *Przekrój*. He took part in the cabaret movement of the late 1950s, joined the Party after Stalin's death, and after 1956 revealed himself as a master of the satirical short story in a collection entitled *Elephant*. In 1958 his first stage play *Police* appeared to great acclaim, and this was followed by several experimental pieces in the manner of the theatre of the absurd. His play *Tango*

(1965) is a masterpiece recounting the power struggles within three generations of a single family. He travelled in Italy in 1963. Following his protest at the Warsaw Pact invasion of Czechoslovakia in 1968 his work was banned for several years. Mrożek stayed in Paris. He currently lives in Mexico.

MYŚLIWSKI, Wiesław, b.1932. Born in Dwikozy near Sandomierz. Graduated from KUL in Polish literature in 1956, and appointed assistant editor at Ludowa Spółdzielnia Wydawnicza. In 1958 he was promoted to director of contemporary literature publishing. In 1975 helped found the literary and cultural journal *Regiony*. Best known for his novels *Naked Court* (1967) and *Palace* (1970), which display his complete lack of a sentimental vision of peasant life, his lack of interest in the Warsaw *inteligencja* and his devotion to the life and culture of the Polish provinces.

NAJDER, Zdzisław. Literary historian, expert on Joseph Conrad, onetime research scholar at St Antony's College, Oxford. An activist in the cause of Polish independence, also on behalf of PPN (Polish Independence Compact) since its foundation in 1979, he helped publish numerous anonymous reports on important political issues. Outside the country during Martial Law, he worked as director of the Polish section of Radio Free Europe, where he was reputed to be a man of intrigues and factions. He was sentenced to death in his absence by the Polish authorities for alleged collaboration with the US security services. At the round-table talks in 1989 Tadeusz Mazowiecki intervened with General Kiszczak to get Najder's death sentence rescinded. Najder returned to Poland in 1989 and was appointed by Wałęsa to steer the Citizens' Committees. Adviser to Wałęsa (briefly) and then to Prime Minister Olszewski. In 1992 the satirical journal *Nie* (No) published a signed document dated 1958, showing that Najder had agreed to co-operate with the Polish security service. As a result, Jerzy Urban (editor in chief of the journal and former media spokesman for General Jaruzelski's regime) was found guilty of publishing classified state secret, was given a one year suspended prison sentence, fined $4,000 and banned from managing a magazine or working as a journalist for a year.

NAŁKOWSKA, Zofia, 1885–54. Born in Warsaw, daughter of a famous geographer, she showed an early interest in politics and the arts. Her first novel, published in 1906, was the product of a Positivist outlook and a strong understanding of sociology and psychology. She was an early adherent to modernism, but shifted to a more social and traditional style in the inter-war years, moving to a frankly experimental style at the start of the war. Active supporter of the post-war regime. She wrote fifteen novels and two volumes of short stories, but the most translated of her works, published in 1947, is *Medallions*, an account of her work and harrowing experiences with the International Commission to Investigate Nazi War Crimes.

NOWAK-JEZIORAŃSKI, Jan. Legendary soldier of the AK. Emissary for the AK during the Second World War, made five secret journeys from

London to Warsaw via Stockholm; his experiences were recounted in his *Courier from Warsaw* (Warsaw 1981; London, 1983). The printer and publisher Mirosław Chojecki of NOWa was put on trial for publishing it without permission in Poland, but it was awarded the PULS prize. After the war remained abroad and worked as founder member and director of the Polish section of Radio Free Europe, 1952–76. Currently he lives in the USA, and is a member of the Polish American Congress and an adviser to the US National Security Council.

NOWAKOWSKI, Marek, b.1935, Warsaw. A graduate in law from Warsaw University. Published his first story in 1957. Fascinated by the tough margins of society, a satirical commentator and sharp observer of Warsaw low life, both official and unofficial. Produced seventeen volumes, of which four were clandestine. In 1969, under the pseudonym Seweryn Kwarc he began publishing in *Kultura* (Paris), chronicling the profound disintegration of Polish society, morality and culture under communism. He protested at the constitutional changes of 1976, signed the letter of the 101, edited *Zapis*. Interned during Martial Law. *The Canary and other Tales of Martial Law* was smuggled out of prison and published underground by Solidarność in 1982. After this he began to publish in *Kultura* under his own name.

ORŁOŚ, Kazimierz, b.1935. Opposed to Gierek's policies, in 1980 a member of the ZLP Committee, author of several novels and short stories that present a grimly detailed portrait of the decay of morality and the destruction of family life and social order in the Gierek years. Convinced that the Party could never be reformed by conscientious and honourable Party members.

PIASECKI, Bolesław, 1915–79. From a middle-class background. Leader and founder of the extreme right-wing ONR-Falange party in the inter-war years. Fought in the campaign of September 1939. Arrested by the NKVD in 1945, but did a deal in return for his life, released to form and direct the tame pro-regime 'Catholic' Pax organization; editor of *Słowo Powszechny* and *Kierunki*, and author of several books, including *Important Problems, Forces of Development* and *Polish Patriotism*, all published by Pax. Opposed Gomułka in 1956, slowly lost control of Pax, but remained a member of the State Council from 1971 until his death.

POBÓG-MALINOWSKI, Władysław. Émigré pro-Sanacja historian, author of a three volume *History of Poland 1864–1945* (London, 1956–61). He claimed that the Soviets had betrayed Polish communists to the Nazis, but also that key Polish figures had collaborated with the Nazis.

POLKOWSKI, Jan, b.1953. Brought up in Nowa Huta and lives in Kraków, studied Polish literature at the Jagiellonian University. One of the most gifted poets to emerge in the 1980s, his work, which appeared in *Zapis*, is tough, staccato, street-wise and tempered. Edited the clandestine journal *kos* 1977–9. An activist in the Kraków Student Solidarność Committee and in the Kraków Students' Press, he was co-founder and editor of the independent journal *ABC*. He also worked for Małapolska region Solidarność. He made his début in the underground press in 1980. Arrested and interned on the first night of Martial Law. Three of his volumes of verse were published underground and a fourth volume was published by Puls in London. When he was released he edited the underground journal *Arka*. Later he edited and owned the right-wing nationalist Kraków daily newspaper *Czas*. His most recent collection of poems was published by the Catholic Znak organization in 1990. Incapable of being one of Kołakowski's jesters, he announced in 1991 that he had given up writing and poetic reflection in favour of direct involvement in political affairs.

POMIAN, Krzysztof, b.1934. Assistant professor of philosophy at Warsaw University, historian of philosophy and leading revisionist, author of *The Warsaw Uprising* (London, 1945); expelled from the Party in 1968 after lecturing (with Kołakowski) on the fate of culture under the post-war regime and criticizing the Party; one of his 'crimes' was that he had published abroad; left Poland to live in Paris; a supporter of TKN.

PROKOP, Jan, b.1931. Poet, translator, fiction writer, essayist and literary historian; member of the PAN Institute for Literary Research (IBL); in 1953 he was one of the Pax editorial team that took over *Tygodnik Powszechny*; author of three slim volumes of verse in 1971, 1978 and 1989; lecturer at the Jagiellonian University and at the University of Turin in Italy; most of his work in the 1980s appeared underground or abroad.

PRZYBOŚ, Julian, 1901–70. Born into a peasant family in southern Poland, but studied Polish literature at the Jagiellonian University and graduated in 1923. A great enthusiast for the 'modern'. He was a provincial secondary school literature teacher for most of the inter-war period. A member of the pre-war Kraków avant-garde, a follower of Tadeusz Peiper's theories, condemned the Skamander poets for letting a demon work through their poetry without let or hindrance and set up a series of poetic prescriptions for how poetry ought to be. Disillusioned by Piłsudski's failure to improve rural Poland and bring the peasantry into the twentieth century, he saw communism as a breakthrough for Poland and became steadily more committed and political. He spent the early part of the war in Lwów, but returned to his village in 1941, where he wrote resistance poetry for the clandestine journals and worked as an agricultural labourer. In 1945 he became the first post-war chair of ZZLP. He later joined the party to help organize literary life in post-war Poland. He was a diplomat for People's Poland in Switzerland 1947–51, and later became an editor and a head librarian. He seems to have realized on his return to Poland that Soviet-style communism was not going to create the democratic cultural and political life he had imagined. He felt that *socrealizm* was a return to outdated forms rather than an adequate response to the new. He withdrew to live in the countryside and offered distant sympathy to the revisionist opposition in the 1950s.

PUTRAMENT, Jerzy, 1910–86. From a middle-class background, university education. A writer, revolutionary Marxist and anticlerical leftist even before the war. During the Soviet occupation of Wilno he supplied Ivan Klimov of the Byeorussian Communist Party Central Committee with a list of Byelorussian nationalists and political activists and with suggestions for possible measures to be used against them (K. Sword (ed.), *The Soviet Takeover of the Polish Eastern Provinces 1939–41* (London, 1991), 264). He was a member of the press corps for the Union of Polish Patriots, contributed to *Czerwony Sztandar*, supported the sovietization of the Ukraine and the idea that Polish writers should be absorbed into the Union of Soviet Ukrainian Writers. He declared Stalin to be 'the greatest man of our times' (*Czerwony Sztandar*, 6 September 1940) and returned from the USSR as an officer in Berling's Polish Army. In the years 1945–50 he was Polish ambassador to France. He was an active member of ZLP and editor of several journals, a member of the Central Committee and a staunch advocate of *socrealizm*. He is generally seen as Berman's main assistant in attempting to neutralize the ZLP as a political force. Few outside the Party have anything good to say about Putrament: most writers regard him as untalented. Czesław Miłosz has described him as a 'less than first-rate' writer, and made him the model for Gamma in *The Captive Mind*. For J. J. Szczepański, Putrament fell from favour in 1950, after handing some of Szczepański's stories to the security service. For Tadeusz Konwicki Putrament was 'simply a Chekist'.

RAKOWSKI, Mieczysław, b.1926. From a middle-class background, university-trained journalist. Joined the PZPR in 1957. Long-time editor of *Polityka*; vice-prime minister 1981–5. The ninth and last communist prime minister 1988–9, the last first secretary of the PZPR.

ROLIŃSKI, Bohdan. One of the most unpleasant characters on the Polish literary scene. Lipski lists him as one of those involved in the slander campaign against KOR and against Andrzejewski in particular. His article, 'It had to be a Diamond' (a reference to Andrzejewski's novel), *Życie Warszawy* (8 January 1977), accused Andrzejewski of socio-political fickleness, and characterized KOR's guiding principles as a mix of utopianism, Trotskyism, Social Democracy, Zionism, Christian Democratism and NEP (Lenin's New Economic Policy, introduced in 1921); he also accused KOR of being in the pay of western – primarily West German – intelligence services. Roliński's book *Interrupted Decade* (1991) was a series of interviews in which the ex-first secretary, Edward Gierek, claimed he was kept in ignorance by the bureaucracy and therefore knew nothing of Poland's economic difficulties in the late 1970s.

RÓŻEWICZ, Tadeusz, b.1921. Born in Radomsko, central Poland. Began publishing poetry in 1939. In the war he worked in a factory and taught Polish in an underground high school for the AK. He joined the AK in 1943. After the war he read art history at Kraków University, then moved to Gliwice in 1949 and finally to Wrocław in 1968. Made his début in 1947. Much of his poetry stems from the traumatic events of the war and his horror at the collapse of human values. His landscapes and characters are bleak, desperate, nihilistic and deeply humanitarian, and Różewicz's search is for a way out, for another way of feeling. Prodigious output – marred by his unsuccessful attempt to find comfort in ideology and his efforts to conform to *socrealizm* – brought him numerous state literary prizes including the state literary prize for poetry in 1955 and 1966, and the City of Kraków literary prize in 1959, and the most prestigious national award, the state literary prize first class in 1966. His poetic style is central to understanding post-war literary aesthetics: he always claimed that he wrote for horror-stricken survivors and those condemned to remember butchery. In 1971 young Polish poets voted him the most important living Polish poet. His poetry belongs to the anti-poetic style which often sees art of any kind as an offence to suffering, and his surrealist plays arouse strong critical feelings among both Catholics and communists, for both of whom his attack on sentiment, dream and wonder is unacceptable. For Różewicz humans are alone in a universe that lacks metaphysical justification – the only reality is that which they create in contact with other human beings, and that contact is usually mistaken, failed and generally bloody. He has been successful in failing to find solace in ideology of any kind; his writings undercut the supposed virtues of revolt. Różewicz has accepted Miłosz's description of him as a poet of chaos with a nostalgia for order. He has also written numerous avant-garde theatre works.

RUDNICKI, Adolf, 1912–91. Born in Zabno, made a name for himself chronicling life in the Warsaw ghetto, and Jewish life in the provinces. Made his début as a novelist in 1931, chronicled his military service in 1937, described Polish life in the artistic colonies 1938, and then produced five volumes of short stories. Although he was Jewish he survived the war by living on false papers. He attempted in later life to describe the fascinating and volatile interaction between Polish and Jewish cultures. A member of the *Kuźnica* group.

RYPSON, Piotr, b.1956. Instrumental in introducing punk music into Poland and was involved with the alternative music circuit. Author of *Picture Words*, a history of visual poetry (1989).

SŁONIMSKI, Antoni, 1895–1976. Born in Warsaw, son of a famous Jewish doctor. Educated as a painter in Warsaw and Paris but made his début as a rebellious lyric poet in 1918 and became a founder member and leader of the inter-war Skamander group, dedicated to the renewal of poetic language and the perfection of traditional metrical forms. A poet of the Warsaw café and the liberal *inteligencja*, a Wellsian rationalist and pacifist who despaired of the attraction and power of Nazism in Germany and the rise of anti-Semitism and nationalist chauvinism among the Polish right. Noted as a prominent and outspoken member of the pre-war liberal left, he wrote regularly in Warsaw literary magazines. He escaped to Paris after the defeat of September 1939 and then moved on to England, where, he edited the journal *Nowa Polska*. He returned to Poland only in 1951. Although part of a group of writers and intellectuals who were unhappy at the prevailing political orthodoxy and increasingly unhappy with Stalinism, he became one of the most respected cultural journalists. He came to prominence during the October crisis of 1956, when as chairman of the ZLP (1956–9) he showed himself an active and courageous spokesman for intellectuals opposed to Party controls and censorship. Adam Michnik, who was his personal assistant in the early 1970s, regards him as a prestigious moral authority for all Polish dissidents and as his mentor. Published several plays and more than a dozen volumes of poetry, very little of which has been translated into English.

SOKORSKI, Włodzimierz, b.1908. Became a member of PPS in 1926, imprisoned for political activities, 1931–5. Spent the war in the USSR where he became deputy head of the Polish Union of Patriots, a political officer in the First Division of Berling's army. In 1947–8 deputy minister for education; 1948–52 deputy minster for arts and culture; 1952–6 minister for arts and culture; 1956–72 head of the Radio and Television Committee. 1948–75, a deputy member of the Central Committee. He thought of himself as a writer and had written what Kott called a 'quasi revolutionary, quasi pornographic novel'. Of his career as minister for the arts Kott wrote:

> It was only after a number of years that I saw how efficiently and effortlessly that grinding machine had been crushing all opposition – from the very start, during the first five year plan. Everybody got ground to a pulp: not only those who were turning the handle but also those who merely touched it or happened to get too close. Only one person somehow survived unscathed, and that was Sokorski . . . After almost half a century, the only one to survive the meat grinder was Włodzio Sokorski. And there is nothing strange about that. Only the eternally smiling clown survives everything. Like the clown Pandarus in Shakespeare's *Troilus and Cressida*. (*Still Alive*, 180–1).

In 1980 he became president of ZBoWiD.

STAFF, Leopold, 1878–1957. Born in Lwów, he studied law, philosophy and Romance languages at Lwów University. Made his début as a poet in 1901. He moved to Warsaw at the end of the First World War. For a Polish writer Staff led a remarkably uneventful life. In spite of the fact that most of his manuscripts were destroyed in the Second World War, he managed to publish sixteen books of poetry – a seventeenth volume appeared posthumously. He also wrote plays and essays, and made translations from several languages. He was awarded honorary doctorates from Warsaw and Kraków Universities and received the PEN Club prize for his translations. A benign old man of Polish letters, Staff's publishing career spans three very different eras of Polish history: he nevertheless achieved critical acclaim and the respect of fellow poets, particularly Różewicz.

STANISZKIS, Jadwiga. Associate professor of sociology at Warsaw University, author of *Poland's Self Limiting Revolution* (Princeton, 1986).

STASZEWSKI, Stefan, b.1906. Born in Warsaw. Joined the communist youth movement at fourteen, studied at the Comintern school in Moscow. Worked for communist youth movement as first secretary in the western Ukraine. After arrest he returned to Moscow in 1934 to lecture for the Comintern. In 1936 he was expelled from the Party, arrested and sentenced to eight years in a labour camp in Kolyma. (His elder brother was killed by the NKVD in the 1937 purge.) Released in 1945 he was appointed propaganda secretary in Katowice, then head of the Central Committee press section, a post he retained until 1954. In 1954–5 deputy minister for agriculture; 1955–7 first secretary of the Warsaw Party Committee. Editor in chief of PAP until 1958, then senior editor at PAN publishing house. Expelled from the Party in 1968 and retired. A supporter of Solidarność.

STEMPOWSKI, Jerzy, 1893/4–1969. Born in Kraków, died in Berne. Born into a gentry family, he studied humanities at Kraków, Munich and Zurich Universities. Emigrated to Switzerland in 1939. Under the name of Paweł Hostowiec became a regular contributor of essays to *Kultura* (Paris). As an émigré he took an interest in a wide range of modern culture, and built on his classical schooling to produce a large number of philosophical essays on European history and society. He disliked mechanization and the increasing power of groups over individuals, frequently citing the superiority of Greek culture to contemporary life.

STOMMA, Stanisław, b.1908 or 1910. Born in Wilno. Holds a doctorate in law from Kraków University, where he also taught. Legal expert and Catholic publicist, co-editor of *Znak* and contributor to *Tygodnik Powszechny*. A Znak deputy to the Sejm, 1957–76; editor and journalist for *Tygodnik Powszechny*. In 1976 Stomma realized that he was involved in an impossible undertaking; he alone of the Znak deputies walked out of the Sejm rather than cast his vote in favour of the constitutional reforms. Adam Michnik has likened him at this moment to Tadeusz Rejtan, the eighteenth-century Sejm deputy who tore his clothes and threw himself on the floor in front of the other deputies in an attempt to prevent them ratifying the partition of Poland. By the following session of the Sejm, Stomma was no longer acceptable as a deputy, and Znak was replaced by another group of deputies who operated under the name of Znak. In 1981 Stomma, by then emeritus professor of law at the Jagiellonian University in Kraków, served on a number of advisory councils to Cardinal Glemp and Lech Wałęsa, and headed the Catholic Church's 'crisis team' set up by Cardinal Glemp to gather information about Martial Law, contact the military authorities, find out who had been arrested and negotiate for their release. Continued to write for *Tygodnik Powszechny*, *Res Publica* and *Znak*. Led the Catholic Church-supported, conservative, right-oriented, Dziekania (Deaconery) group from the mid-1980s up to 1989 when it was dissolved.

Elected to the Senate on the Solidarność ticket in 1989 to represent the town of Płock. Now retired.

STRZELECKI, Jan, 1919–88. Sociologist, socialist activist, underground youth organizer during the war. Joined PZPR and advocated 'socialist humanism'; in the mid-1950s he began to rethink the party's traditional hostility towards the Church. In spite of his belief that change could come from within the party itself he remained a figure of moral authority among intellectuals. In 1980 he became an adviser to Solidarność.

SZCZEPAŃSKI, Jan Józef, b.1919 or 1920. (Not to be confused with the sociologist, Professor J. Szczepański, b.1913.) Born in Warsaw, son of the former Polish consul-general to Chicago. Lives in Kraków. A keen alpine climber in his youth. Fought in the Polish army during the September 1939 campaign and then in the AK throughout the occupation. After the war studied Sanskrit and Hindi at Warsaw and Wrocław Universities. He has stated that for him, in the immediate post-war years the division into left and right was a falsity and entirely artificial in view of the humanistic, intellectual and moral decisions that need to be made. He claimed that most Polish intellectuals made the same decision, knowing that the communist function-aries were mystificators, primitive and arbitrary in their use of power, and that Polish intellectuals in giving their support in this way had not given sufficient thought to how things were to be realized or what it really meant to be on the left under Stalin. Although he had begun publishing before the war he considers that he made his début in 1953 as a writer of film criticism in *Tygodnik Powszechny*. In the 1950s he wrote a series of novels and short stories that detailed the ethical and psychological aspects of wartime savagery. His first collection of stories was called *Boots* (1956) and displayed great awareness of moral problems, and a close, almost *socrealist* attention to observed documentary detail. The collection was to have appeared in *Twórczość* but Kazimierz Wilka lost his nerve, so the stories were published by Turowicz in *Tygodnik Powszechny*, with the result that the magazine received over 300 letters protesting at the anti-patriotic nature of the stories. In 1959 he received the Ernest Hemingway award. In the 1970s he produced a series of essays on Conrad, Father Maksymilian Kolbe and Charles Manson. In 1971 he criticized, in the pages of *Polityka*, the emerging phenomenon of 'sultanism'. In the late 1970s he was a TKN lecturer. He served on the editorial board of *Tygodnik Powszechny* before it was given to Pax, and again when it was taken away from Pax. He had a long and fruitful collaboration with Turowicz and *Tygodnik Powszechny*, a magazine which he described as 'po prostu liberalny' (simply liberal), but never quite reconciled himself to appearing in a Catholic journal. He felt that the Catholic Church very explicitly chose to engage the Party only on issues where it could muster the greatest popular support, and that it used that popular support to defend important strategic positions. It did not engage in debate over issues where it could not present itself as under threat and could not muster popular support. In 1980–1 he was a Solidarnośc supporter and a non-Party deputy to the Sejm where he criticized the media for their failure to alert the country about the looming economic crisis. A non-Marxist, non-communist, non-Catholic of scrupulous integrity he was not afraid to point out that the interests of the Catholic Church did not necessarily coincide with those of the Polish nation, and his 'collaboration' with the authorities made him a target for Catholics, independent intellectuals (like Lipski) and party hacks alike. He served as chair of ZLP in 1980–3 and proved to be the most distinguished, popular and effective of all the ZLP chairs. His battles to keep ZLP in existence after Martial Law was declared are chronicled in his *Cadence* (1990). He was one of the few Sejm deputies who refused to ratify the formal ban on Solidarność in 1982. In 1983 the regime attempted to blacken his reputation by forging a letter to the Council of State with his signature on it. He described the Martial Law years as a 'golden age' for the Catholic Church, in which it grew intellectually and found for itself tasks which it had previously been unable to identify clearly. In June 1989 he was elected chairman of the newly formed STP (Association of Polish writers). Trznadel described him as a writer who dreamed of dictators without boots.

SZCZYPIORSKI, Andrzej, b.1920 (or 1924) in Warsaw, where he still lives. He was a member of the resistance movement and took part in the 1944 Warsaw uprising, when he was captured and sent to a concentration camp. A novelist, journalist, author of more than eighteen books and of a great many essays published by the underground press, mainly dealing with issues of ideological conflict and moral authority within the post-war generation. He was at first sympathetic to communism but later changed his mind. He also writes fantasy and detective stories under the pseudonym Maurice S. Andrews. In the late 1970s he was treasurer of Polish PEN. A member of the ZLP executive and leading Solidarność activist, he was arrested by the military in 1981 and kept in gaol for a year. He helped found the Solidarność Congress of Polish Culture. His novel *A Mass for the City of Arras* (1971, 1993) is about the persecution of Jews and heretics as examples of mass psychosis crushing rights and liberties and destroying individuals. In *The Polish Ordeal* (1982) he attempted to explain his experience of the last fifty years and set it in the context of Poland's political problems. His novel *The Beautiful Mrs Seidenman* (1986, 1989) won international acclaim and was widely translated; partly as a result of this he was awarded the Austrian state prize for literature in 1988, and also the PEN Club prize. In June 1989 he was elected to the Senate to represent Solidarność. Like Aleksander Wat, Szczypiorski has commented that in his opinion many writers turned to the 'new faith' of communism in reaction against the continuing influence of the inter-war Polish military regime's mind-set, the rise of Nazism, the continuing threat of West Germany to Poland, and Polish anti-Semitism. Both *The*

Shadow Catcher (1976, 1997) and *Self Portrait with Woman* (1994, 1995) have been translated into English.

SZECHTER, Szymon, b.1920. Professor, academic historian, political scientist and satirist, author of an unpublished book on the genesis of the peasants' strike and the Peasants' Party (SL) in the years 1936–7; his first book of short stories was confiscated by the censor in 1965, and had increasing problems with the authorities until in 1964, along with Nina Karsow, he was arrested for collecting information about official anti-Semitism and political trials. Released in 1966 he divorced his wife Lida and married Nina Karsow as part of a complex plot to obtain her release. They were both expelled from Poland in 1968. After that he lived in London, working closely with Nina Karsow, who translated many of his stories into English. He and Nina Karsow had their marriage annulled in Britain in 1970 so that Szechter could re-marry Lida. Author of *A Stolen Biography* (1972) and, with Nina Karsow, *In the Name of Tomorrow* (1971).

SZYMBORSKA, Wisława, b.1923. Born in Prowenta-Bnin in western Poland, she and her family moved to Kraków in 1931. She attended an underground high school and then studied Polish literature and sociology at the Jagiellonian University, 1945–8. She abandoned her studies as the university lost its independence after the communist take-over. Made her début as a poet in 1945 but publication of her first volume of poems in 1948 was delayed for political reasons, and her first volume only emerged in 1952. *That's Why We Live* and her second volume *Questions Put to Oneself* in 1954 were both highly political. She joined the Party after Stalin's death, and in the years 1953–81 she worked under Machejek, editor of the Kraków literary weekly *Życie Literackie*, as a poetry editor, book reviewer and columnist. In 1954 she received the Kraków City literary prize, in 1955 the state literary prize, and in 1963 the Ministry for Art and Culture prize. She was a 'believer' in communism, but later said she fulfilled her 'rhymed duties' for the Party in the naive conviction that she was doing right. Her reputation is not founded on any poetry of *partyność*: she was an outspoken supporter of Solidarność and an associate of Lech Wałęsa in the 1980s. She has published eight volumes of poetry and much of her output has appeared in *Twórczość*, *Odra* and *Puls* (London). She has also published essays and translations of French poetry. Her 1986 collection *People on the Bridge* was widely acclaimed one of the most important collections of post-war Polish verse. She still lives and works in Kraków and is widely regarded as the outstanding female Polish poet in the post-war period. Her constant theme is support for the individual's right to doubt in utopias. Awarded the Nobel prize for literature 1996.

TOEPLITZ, Krzysztof Teodor (used the pseudonym KAT). Published regularly in the official journals. In the mid-1950s he was noted as an enthusiastic feuilletonist of reform, so much so that *Nowa Kultura* ceased to accept his work for a while in 1956. In the mid-1970s a book of his collected writings was published, but the censors decided not to allow publication of any reviews. In spite of this he went on to hold a government post in the Martial Law period. In the era of *glasnost* he warned against taking reform too fast or opening up the reform process to democratic pressures.

TRZNADEL, Jacek, b.1930, in Olkusz. Poet, essayist and translator. In his youth an ardent member of the communist youth movement, later a member of the Party who for many years kept a portrait of Stalin on his wall. Later became a critic of the regime and noted right-winger. Like Michnik, he signed the letter of the fifty-nine intellectuals in 1975. In the years 1978–83 he was professor of Polish literature and director of the Polish section in the department of Slavonic studies at the Sorbonne in Paris. A leading member of the Independent Historical Committee for research in the Katyń Massacre. He is also the author of five books of poems, four books of essays, and translations of de Sade, Sartre, Lévi-Strauss and other French literature. His best-known work is *Domestic Shame* (Paris, 1986), a series of critical and revealing interviews with ex-Stalinist writers, which was awarded the Independent Solidarity Cultural Committee prize in 1986. In May/June 1992 he was interviewed by the magazine *Puls* and claimed that Adam Michnik was still nothing more than an untrustworthy Trotskyite-revisionist communist, hinting very strongly that Michnik was and always had been a communist plant within the opposition movement.

TUROWICZ, Jerzy, b.1912. Born and lives in Kraków. Member of the Catholic Odrodzenie and Pax Romana movements between the wars. Graduated in history and philosophy from Kraków University. Journalist and then editor in chief of the Catholic *Głos Narodu* 1945–53. Co-founder and editor in chief of *Tygodnik Powszechny* 1945–53 and 1956 to the present; he designed the journal to formulate Catholic opinion to the extent permitted by censorship and the Catholic hierarchy. He did not see it as subject to the political guidance of KIK, despite its ties, nor did he see it as a simple pulpit for the Church. A democratic Catholic sympathetic to the idea of Christian socialism, and he consistently demanded democratic moral values in cultural and political life was sometimes referred to as the 'Dean' of the opposition movement; he was a figure of huge moral authority for the secular left oppositionists. He signed the 'letter of the thirty-four' in 1964, published the essays and articles of purged and persecuted liberals and Jews in 1968, and published pro-Solidarność writers during Martial Law. Member of the opposition delegation to the round-table talks of 1989. A member of the Citizens' Committee under Wałęsa, he is also the author of *Christians in the Contemporary World* (1963) and is a close associate of Pope John Paul II.

TUWIM, Julian, 1894–1953. Born of middle class Jewish parents in Łódź, he was educated at a Russian *gymnasium* and later moved to Warsaw University where he graduated in law and philosophy. A leader of the Skamander group of Futurist poets, he was popular between the wars and contributed light verse and songs to the Warsaw cabaret circuit; as well as pursuing his antiquarian interests he was a distinguished translator of Russian poetry. He spent the war years in the USA and returned to Poland in 1946 to become an enthusiastic supporter of the Stalinist regime. He was radical and conservative by turns, and his enthusiasm for the regime was probably an emotional reaction to the exciting potential of post-war reconstruction, rather than a serious ideological position.

WALICKI, Andrzej. Professor at the PAN Institute of Philosophy in Warsaw until 1981. Now professor of history, specializing in Russian and Polish intellectual history, at Notre Dame University, Indiana.

WAŃKOWICZ, Melchior, 1892–1975. Author of numerous picturesque gentry tales and of a three-volume history of the Battle of Monte Cassino. Signed the Letter of the Thirty-Four in 1964 and was tried for slandering the state.

WAT, Aleksander, 1900–67. Born Chwat, of Warsaw Jewish *inteligencja* family. Studied philosophy and psychology at Warsaw University. Poet, editor, translator, literary critic. A founder of the Polish Futurist movement in the years before the Second World War, he published a book of precocious Futurist experimental verse in 1919, which caused quite a stir. In the years 1921–5 he edited *New Art* and *Almanac of New Art*. In 1927 he published the story collection *Lucifer Unemployed*. He was editor in chief of the Party magazine *Miesęcznik Literacki* in the years 1929–32, but this was closed down by the Polish authorities and he spent some time in prison. In the years 1932–9 he was literary director of a publishing house. He became a Marxist, and, though never a member of the Party, was an important 'fellow traveller' on the intellectual left. His conversion to Marxism coincided with a literary silence. In 1939 he escaped to the Russian zone of occupied Poland and in 1940 was arrested by the NKVD as a Trotskyite and Zionist agent of the Vatican. He was imprisoned in the Lubyanka and then deported to Kazakhstan in Soviet Asia where he converted to Catholicism. After his release as part of the 1941–2 amnesty for Poles, he went to Alma-Ata to search for his wife and child. He found them on a kolkhoz, but shortly afterwards, as they would not accept Soviet citizenship, they were all exiled to Ili. They were released and returned to Poland in April 1946, but in the years 1949–56 Wat was labelled a 'hostile element' and was refused publication. After earning his living as a translator for a while, he was publicly castigated by his fellow writers for failing to support the regime's policies, and suffered a stroke which left him in considerable pain for the rest of his life. After 1956 he was able to resume his publishing career and his poetry appeared to great acclaim among the younger generation. The Party apologized lavishly, showered him with awards, appointed him editor in chief of the PIW publishing house and allowed him to travel abroad. In 1959 he left Poland to live in Italy and France. In 1963 he visited California where he recorded *My Century* (London,

1977) with Miłosz. His health was poor, though, and his planned volume of philosophical investigation into the phenomenon of Soviet communism never materialized. Several of his most important works and many of his notes and essays were only published after his death. He died in Paris. As Miłosz put it, Wat's life-Odyssey charts the political pressures that writers worked under at this time, and the twists and turns they were obliged to make (C. Miłosz, *The Captive Mind*, x).

WERFEL, Roman, b.1906 in Lwów of bourgeois family. Joined communist youth movement at the age of fifteen, joined KPP in 1923. Spent two years in gaol. Was sent to work for communist youth movement in the western Ukraine. Expelled from the KPP in 1936. Spent the war in the USSR, first in Lwów, then in central Asia. Edited *Czerwony Sztandar* and the Polish-language *Nowy Widokręg*, where he worked with Putrament, Broniewska and Jędrzychowski. After the war he worked for the Party in Lublin, as director of Książka i Wiedza, and senior editor of *Nowe Drogi*, *Głos Ludu*, and *Trybuna Ludu*. Sacked in 1956, in 1959 he was appointed propaganda director of the Wrocław Party Provincial Committee; in 1963 became director of the PAN Institute for the History of Polish-Soviet Relations. In 1968 he was expelled from the Party and retired. He was rehabilitated by the Party in 1983.

WIELOWIEJSKI, Andrzej. An active member of KIK, member of the Citizens' Committees under Wałęsa, later a leader of the Democratic Union party and a senator.

WIERBŁOWSKI, Stefan, 1897–1973. From a middle-class background, trained at university as a chemist. In 1925 joined the KPP, spent seven years in gaol. Spent the war in the USSR. Became a member of the Central Committee in 1945 and then worked in propaganda; secretary of *Sztandar Wolności*, editor of *Nowe Drogi*.

WIERZBICKI, Piotr, b.1935. Born in Warsaw, graduated in Polish studies at Warsaw University in 1957, the year in which he made his début in the fortnightly *Współczesność*. For ten years he wrote in *Literatura*, and from 1977 published his satires, pamphlets and prose sketches in *Tygodnik Powszechny*. After *The Enthusiast in School* (1976) his work appeared underground or abroad. An uncompromising black humorist, he wrote for a wide range of the underground publications throughout the 1970s and for the Solidarność press throughout the 1980s. Best known for his 'Treatise on Ticks' (to which Michnik penned a reply), his merciless satire on the Polish intellectuals' ability to compromise with the authorities. He was arrested and interned during Martial Law. His book *Structure of Lies* (London, 1987), an analysis of Party language, won the Solidarność Culture prize for 1986, and the Independent Journalists' prize for the best book of 1986. In the years 1989–91 he was a close associate of Lech Wałęsa and wrote to support his bid for the presidency in *Tygodnik Solidarność*. Later he and Wałęsa parted company. He now publishes in the nationalist, anti-Semitic *Gazeta Polska*.

WIERZYŃSKI, Kazimierz, 1894–1969. Born in Drohobycz, son of a railway station-master. Studied in Kraków and Vienna, before being drafted into the Austrian military during the First World War. Spent three years as a Russian prisoner, escaped, took part in the 1920 Polish-Soviet war as a correspondent, settled in Warsaw. A founder member of the Skamander group, he made his début as a poet in 1919. Thought by some to be a naive enthusiast of things modern, by others to be a classicist of the Romantic school. He went into exile just after the outbreak of the Second World War, making his way to France, Portugal and Brazil before settling in the USA in 1941, thus becoming one of the few members of the pre-war Polish Academy of Literature to survive; his profound frustration, strong sense that he was an anachronism and his unhappiness with his conventional verse strategies led to a crisis of creativity in the years 1930–49. His *Life of Chopin* (1949) was a bestseller in the USA. After living in New York for a while he moved on to New England, Italy and the UK. A staunch opponent of communism, he felt Poland's fate was tragic and never returned.

WIRPSZA, Witold, 1918–85. Poet, playwright, fiction writer, essayist, translator of German literature. Party member and early poet of *socrealizm*, he published several collections in the years 1949–56, but only emerged as an interesting and original poet in the 1960s. Then his verse provoked a heated debate because of its interest in the aesthetics, semiotics and politics of poetry. Increasingly active in the opposition from the mid-1950s, when he published anti-Stalinist poems in *Przegląd Kulturalny* in March 1955. After publishing in German a controversial book, *Pole wer bist Du?* (Pole, who are you?), on German-Polish relations, he was attacked and abused by the official media and felt forced into exile. From 1969 he lived in West Berlin and his work appeared only in underground or émigré editions.

WOJTYŁA, Karol, b.1920, in Wadowice near Kraków, son of a captain in the Polish army. In 1938 started to read Polish philology at the Jagiellonian University but his studies were interrupted by the outbreak of war. He worked for a while in a stone quarry, then in a water purification plant, and kept up his studies with the underground university as well as taking part in underground theatrical productions. With the death of his father in 1941 Wojtyła enrolled as a theology student in the underground seminary. He completed his studies and entered the priesthood in November 1946. For the next two years he was sent to study at the Pontifical University in Rome, after which he was awarded a doctorate. On his return to Poland in 1948 he was sent as priest to a small village. He was eventually appointed parish priest in Kraków, and in 1951 resumed studies at KUL, where he lectured and held a professorship. In 1958 he was appointed auxiliary bishop of Kraków and five years later became Archbishop. In October 1978 he was elected Pope. By 1978 he had published five books, forty-four philosophical essays and twenty-seven essays and other articles, plays and poetry numbering some 400 items. Many were issued under the pen-names Andrzej Jawień and Stanisław Gruda. Much of his work was published by KUL and Pallotinum, and appeared in *Rocznik Filozoficzne* and *Znak*, but the bulk of his articles and poetry seems to have appeared in *Tygodnik Powszechny*. It is proving difficult to integrate the various aspects of his personality. As a writer the young Wojtyła was an innovative radical humanist, frustrated by the Church; as a member of the Church hierarchy he was popular, outgoing, diplomatic and sternly unyielding towards communism; as Pope he has been reactionary and conservative.

WOROSZYLSKI, Wiktor, b.1927. Born in Grodno, son of a doctor. An enthusiastic supporter of communism in the 1940s and 1950s, a distinguished translator of Russian literature, essayist, fiction writer, biographer and poet. When eastern Poland became part of the USSR in 1945, his family moved to Łódź. That same year Woroszylski graduated from high school, joined the Party as a young communist, published his first poem, and began work as a journalist. Later he studied medicine at Łódź University and then humanities at Warsaw University. His first volume of poetry appeared in 1949. He attended the Moscow Gorky Institute of Literature, 1952–6 and gained a master's degree in philosophy, followed by a Polish state literary prize for his poetry. While he was a student in Moscow he travelled extensively in the Ukraine, Byelorussia, Caucasus, Baltic states, central Asia and Siberia. He started his literary career as a convinced *socrealist* and ardent communist, but while he was in Moscow he became aware that his poetic talent was not developing and that this was connected with the way the Party had dictated how poetry should be written. On his return to Poland wrote mainly for *Nowa Kultura* and *Po Prostu*, where he published several articles critical of the Party over the previous decade and supporting the idea of reform. He also published several anti-Stalinist poems in *Po Prostu*. He had become increasingly disgusted by the ideological barrenness of the Party. *Nowa Kultura* sent him to Budapest and Poznań in 1956. His support for the *rewizjoniści* was confirmed by direct personal observation; what he witnessed in 1956 finally broke his faith in Soviet communism and cured him of any further interest in working with the USSR. Some of his comments to the VII ZLP Congress of November-December 1956, when he urged the writers to support the Hungarian cause by condemning Soviet intervention, were reported in *Nowa Kultura*, 9 December 1956. In 1958 he published a volume of verse; in 1966 he published his *Life of Mayakovsky*; he also published several novels for children, translations of Russian poetry and editions of Saltikov-Shchedrin and Yesenin. The last of his poems to be published by a state publishing house appeared in 1974, when he was supposedly non-political. Though he never renounced his socialist beliefs, in the late 1970s he became a leading dissident figure. As well as taking part in numerous protests, demonstrations and rallies, he was a co-founder and editor of the opposition journal *Zapis*. Although associated with no party or political faction, he was still seeking 'socialism with a human face' at a time when it was unfashionable to do so. Though it was clear that he was revolted by the ideological sterility and rigidity of Stalinist communism, his poems were still unrepentently socialist in outlook. He was interned for one year during Martial Law after helping to organize a strike at the Ursus tractor factory.

WOŹNIAKOWSKI, Jacek, b.1920. A Catholic writer, art historian and essayist who viewed communism and capitalism with equal contempt. Professor at KUL, affiliated with *Tygodnik Powszechny*, director of the Znak publishing house. He took a very dim view of the Church's desire to squash polemic and all criticism of the hierarchy in the name of unity against the Party, saying that the desire to silence criticism of the hierarchy after 1989 was part of the Church's effort to reassert its pre-war position, an unacceptable bid to impose conformism, even a kind of communism.

WYGODZKI, Stanisław b.1907. Member of KPP, later of PZPR. His book *Remanded in Custody* was suppressed in 1957. He was banned after the *Dziady* protests and emigrated to Israel in 1968.

WYKA, Kazimierz, 1910–75. Born in Krzeszowice. Influential critic and professor at Kraków University. Strongly aware of the experience of the 'independent' inter-war generation. Often credited with 'liberating' the younger generation of critics from the bardism of *socrealizm* and schematism of the 1950s and 1960s. A supporter of compromise: defender of individual status as opposed to totalitarian claims: he also saw the social and moral value of limiting individualistic narcissism and aestheticism.

ZABŁOCKI, Janusz, b.1926. By 1950 a member of Pax. In 1956 Zabłocki led the defection of the 'Fronde' group, which consisted of most of the Pax youth movement. In 1958 founded, with Tadeusz Mazowiecki, the journal *Więz*. After this more or less abandoned writing to become a Znak Sejm deputy. In 1969 he set up an organization called ODiSS (Centre for Documentation and Social Studies) designed to find middle ground between Pax and Znak: this Pax-like organization published several journals, research on Polish Catholicism, Zabłocki's *On the Polish Crossroads* and Andrzej Micewski's biography *Roman Dmowski*. In December 1981 Zabłocki protested in the Sejm at the imposition of Martial Law but soon fell into line with the government.

ZABŁUDOWSKI, Tadeusz, 1907–84. Spent the war in the USSR where he was editor for the Union of Polish Patriots. 1944–8, chief censor; dismissed in 1948 when it was discovered that he had once translated the works of Leon Trotsky. Until 1968 he worked in publishing and the press, but was dismissed from his job and expelled from the Party in the anti-Semitic campaign of 1968.

ZAGAJEWSKI, Adam, b.1945. Born in Lwów, but forced to move to Gliwice in October 1946. Studied philosophy and psychology at Kraków University, where he also edited the magazine *Student* and the dissident journal *Zapis*. Described by Miłosz as 'a disillusioned young socialist', he is generally considered typical of the generation of 1968, the *nowa fala* (new wave). In 1968 he founded the Kraków literary group *Teraz* (Now). Made his début in 1972 with the collection *Komunikat*, and was immediately recognized as leading representative of the generation of 1968, and has since published six collections of verse, three novels and five collections of essays. Like his contemporaries he perceives the Polish language to be damaged by the Party: he is concerned to restore simple truths to language, is obsessed with the philosophical aspects of language and with restoring civic responsibility to society through poetry. In 1974 he received the Koscielski award for the volume of essays *The Unrepresented World* (with Julian Kornhauser), a book which was significant in locating his generation's response to the language of Polish communism. He was banned several times from 1976 onwards, after protest at proposed changes to the constitution. In 1979 he received a scholarship to travel to West Berlin. A strong supporter of Solidarność he has lived in Paris since 1981, teaching at the University of Houston every spring, and editing a Polish-language journal. Two volumes of his poetry, *Tremor* and *Canvas*, and two volumes of essays, *Solidarity, Solitude* and *Two Cities* have been translated into English.

ZAWADZKI, Wacław, 1900–78. He had been a member of the PPS but had been expelled in 1948 when it was merged to form the PZPR. Worked as the director of the PPS Wiedza publishing house, and joined the PZPR after October 1956 in the hope that the Party could and would reform itself, and became deputy editor in chief of PIW, the State Publishing Institute. In 1967 he resigned from the Party in protest at the expulsion of Kołakowski. He is the editor of many memoirs, an expert in the field of publishing, a bibliophile, member of ZLP and Polish PEN. A member of KSS-KOR from October 1976.

ZAWIEYSKI, Jerzy, 1902–69. Born in a small village near Łódź. Studied philosophy and art history at Warsaw, Wilno and Paris Universities. A professional actor, he made his début as a novelist in 1932 and went on to write plays, diaries and novels. He travelled extensively in Africa and Europe. A noted figure of the Catholic liberal left, close in outlook to the Catholic intellectuals trained at KUL. One of a small but strong group of Catholic writers to take part in the 1949 Writers' Congress in Szczecin, at which Sokorski introduced *socrealizm* and the ideological offensive to writers. Zawieyski and other Catholics were prepared to go along with the reconstruction of Poland and to co-operate with the communists, but they objected to *partyność* as a legitimate literary aim. His group was isolated at the Congress; many found it difficult to publish outside the Catholic *Tygodnik Powszechny* and *Znak* in the years that followed. He was unable to publish at all until 1956. One of the first Znak deputies to the Sejm in 1957; in recognition of his integrity he was elected president of Clubs of the Catholic Intelligentsia (KIK), and vice-president of ZLP. He also became a member of the Council of State, 1957–68. Author of twenty-five plays, four novels, two collections of short stories, several volumes of essays and articles. While labelled a Catholic writer for his use of biblical themes and Symbolism, he always objected that there was no such thing, that religious subjects were limiting and that he wrote on moral and psychological themes from a purely human perspective. In 1968 he was the only Znak deputy to protest at the anti-Semitic and anti-intellectual course of events, was removed from his post on the State Council and died in obscure circumstances. Miłosz said: 'His spiritual adventures . . . are moving in their evocation of the authentic torment of a modern Catholic.'

ŻÓŁKIEWSKI, Stefan, b.1911. Studied humanities and later taught at Warsaw University, where he appears to have joined the KPP in 1936. During the war he stayed in Poland and edited underground communist newspapers in Warsaw. A *socrealist* essayist and critic associated with *Kuźnica*, which he edited in the years 1945–9, during which time he was also professor of Polish literature at Warsaw University, head of the Party's Department of Culture and in 1948 founded the PAN Institute for Literary Research (IBL). In the years 1955–9 he was minister for education and from 1957 was the first editor of *Polityka*. He edited several cultural journals in the 1960s and was a full member of the praesidium of the Polish Academy of Science. Until 1962 director of *Nowa Kultura*.

ŻUŁAWSKI, Juliusz, 1911–99. A distinguished poet, essayist, novelist and the translator of Byron and Walt Whitman. He was President of Polish PEN from his election in 1978 until he handed over to Jacek Bocheński. His handling of the government on Polish PEN's behalf brought him enormous respect from the literary community. His best-known works are *Past Tense Imperfect*, *Time Regained* and his memoirs *From Home*. In 1971 he was awarded the American PEN Kister prize, and the New York Jurzykowski Foundation award.

INDEX OF PRINCIPAL NAMES
AND PUBLICATIONS

ABC 100, 101
Ajdukiewicz, Kazimierz 55
Akhmatova, Anna 139
Aliluyeva, Nadezhda 222
Allende, Salvador 206
Almanac of New Art 19
Alvarez, Arthur 149, 217
Amin, General Idi 206, 217
Amsterdamski, Stefan 55, 126
Anderman, Janusz 311, 362
Anders, General Władysław19
Andrzejewski, Jerzy 32, 55, 59, 67, 74, 95,
   100–33, 137–8, 143, 145, 146, 170, 180,
   185, 189, 226, 230, 259, 261, 287, 314
   The Appeal (Apelacja) 124
   The Gates of Paradise (Bramy Raju) 119
   Darkness Covers the Earth (Ciemnośći kryją
    ziemię) 118
   'Message to the Victimized Participants of
    the Workers' Protest' 127
   Miazga 125
   O człowieku radzieckim 116
   Partia i twórczość pisarza 116, 131, 132
   Ashes and Diamonds (Popiół i diament) 100,
    101–16, 124, 131, 132, 133, 136
   Golden Fox (Zloty lis) 117
Arendt, Hannah 179
Ash, Timothy Garton 129, 177, 244, 256, 323
Aulaytner, Wacław 54

Babiuch, Edward 212
Baczko, Bronisław 55, 59, 151, 156, 247, 258,
   362
Baczyński, Krzysztof Kamil 20
Baden-Powell, Lord 245
Balbus, Professor Stanisław 126, 184
Balcerowicz, Leszek 271, 328
Balzac, Honoré de 139, 141, 182, 193
Barańczak, Stanisław 32, 51, 59, 127, 158, 164,
   175, 189, 232, 233, 243, 249, 258, 259,
   260, 264, 301–2, 319, 335, 362–3
Barlicki, Norbert 23

Bartoszewski, Władysław 56, 126, 311, 315,
   363
Bauman, Zygmunt 50, 51, 151, 247, 363
Bella, Ahmed Ben 206
Bellow, Saul 231
Berent, Wacław 7
Beria, Lavrenti 149
Berman, Jakob 77, 78, 80, 83, 84, 99, 113, 114,
   139, 144, 363–4
Białoszewski, Miron 364
Bieńkowski, Władysław 55, 59, 137, 146, 164,
   170, 173, 248, 258, 364–5
Bierut, Bolesław 39, 65, 67, 78, 99, 115, 137,
   318, 365
Biuletyn Informacyjny 260, 262, 264, 313
Black Book on Polish Censorship, The 128
Błoński, Jan 50, 96, 177, 198–9, 365
Bobrowski, Kazimierz 8
Bobrowski, Stefan 8
Bobrowski, Tadeusz 7, 8
Bocheński, Jacek 55, 59, 101, 126, 258, 311
Borejsza, Jerzy 78, 135, 136, 138, 139, 365–6
Borowski, Tadeusz 59, 67, 92, 93–4, 102, 141,
   180, 182, 226, 258
Borusewicz, Bogdan 127
Brandstaetter, Roman 48, 49
Brandys, Kazimierz 9–10, 32, 50, 55, 59, 67,
   74, 83, 94, 126, 139, 143, 145, 152, 164,
   170, 174, 177–202, 215, 226, 228, 230,
   243, 248, 258, 282, 304, 305, 307, 319
   Sons and Comrades (Matka Królów) 185–6,
    187
   Warsaw Diaries (Miesące) 193
   A Question of Reality (Nierzeczywistość)
    177, 189
   'Obrony Granady' 185
   Rondo 187, 189
   Samson 199
Brandys, Marian 146
Braun, Mieczysław 136
Brecht, Bertholdt 122, 139
Broch, Hermann 159

Brodsky, Joseph 315
Bromberg, Adam 150, 151, 248, 366
Broniewska, Julia 366
Broniewski, Władysław 67, 91, 135, 226,
    366–7
Brook, Peter 148
Brus, Włodzimierz 55, 59, 151, 156, 247, 258,
    367
Bryll, Ernest 367
Brzeziński, Zbigniew 44, 315
Brzozowski, Stanisław 23, 58
Bujak, Zbigniew 267, 312
Bulgakov, Mikhail 315
Bulganin, Nikolai 40, 149
Bunsch, Karol 48
Byron, Lord 92

Capek, Karel and Josef 159
Casaroli, Agostino 272
Chłopska Droga 70
Chesterton, G. K. 72
Choynowski, Mieczysław 160
Churchill, Sir Winston 91
Cioran, E. M. 91
Conrad, Joseph 7, 8, 9, 134, 225, 231, 315
Csoóri, Sándor 333
Csurka, István 333
Cywiński, Bohdan 43, 45–6, 56, 59, 61, 126,
    255, 258, 260, 367
Czas 334
Czechowicz, Józef 20, 79
Czerwony Sztandar 135

Dąbrowska, Maria 14, 24, 50, 55, 59, 120, 141,
    226, 246, 258
Dąbrowski, Bishop 257
Dan, Aleksander 135
Davidson, Basil 54
Davies, Norman 5, 14, 180, 244
Debussy, Claude 143
Defoe, Daniel 139, 141, 193
Derrida, Jacques 176
Deutscher, Isaac 31, 54
Dialog 71, 72, 119, 146
Dimitrova, Blaga 333
Dinescu, Mircea 333
Dmowski, Roman 22, 153, 254
Dobraczyński, Jan 48, 72, 94, 367
Documents on Lawlessness 128
Dostoevsky, Fyodor Mikhael 139, 167

Doyle, Sir Arthur Conan 193
Dürrenmatt, Friedrich 139
Dygat, Stanisław 119
Dziennik Bałtycki 327
Dziennik Łodzki 327
Dziennik Polski 72
Dzierżyński, Feliks ('Bloody Feliks') 26, 29

Echo Krakowa 72, 211
Edelman, Marek 367
Endecja 32
Europa 117, 119, 146
Express Wieczorny 327

Ficowski, Jerzy 56, 126, 368
Fielding, Henry 139
Fik, Ignacy 336
Forum 71
Frankfurter Allgemeine 84
Frederick the Great, Emperor 4
Fredro, Aleksander 139
Freud, Sigmund 159
Fukuyama, Francis 176

Gajcy, Tadeusz 20, 314
Gałczyński, Konstanty Ildefons 15, 67, 95,
    368
Gazeta Krakowska 211
Gazeta Polska 334
Gazeta Wyborcza 270, 271, 272, 275, 326, 334
Geremek, Bronisław 42, 55, 61, 126, 170, 307,
    323, 324
Geresz, Jerzy 260
Giedroyc´, Jerzy 51, 368–9
Giełżyński, Wojciech 206
Gierek, Edward 44, 124–5, 130, 201, 208, 209,
    211, 214, 216, 218, 234, 239, 244, 256,
    281, 283, 294, 297, 318
Giertych, Jędrzej 52
Glemp, Cardinal 45, 257, 307
Głogowski, Bishop 272
Górska, Halina 135
Głos 261, 264, 265, 271
Głos Pracy 71
Głos Wybrzeża 211
Goetl, Ferdinand 79
Goldstücker, Edward 123
Gołubiew, Antoni 48, 49, 55, 59, 259
Gombrowicz, Witold 3, 16–17, 18, 51, 59, 64,
    215, 258, 315, 320

Gömöri, George 89
Gomułka, Władysław 30, 32, 75, 118, 120, 121, 122, 123, 124, 141, 145, 146, 147, 150, 151, 152, 169, 186, 229, 247, 248, 318
Göncz, Arpád 333
Gorbachev, Mikhail 19, 176, 322
Gorki, Maxim 141
Grabski, Tadeusz 265
Grabski, Władysław 48
Gramsci, Antonio 54
Grass, Günter 315
Greene, Graham 72
Grochowiak, Stanisław 369
Grusa, Jirí 333
Grynberg, Henryk 369
Guevara, Ernesto Che 206

Hall, Aleksander 256
Hall, Peter 148
Harasymowicz, Jerzy 369
Haraszti, Miklós 189, 333
Hašek, Jaroslav 159
Hauke-Ligowski, Father Aleksander 260
Havel, President Václav 271, 333
Herbert, Zbigniew 61, 59, 68, 91, 95, 113, 124, 170, 243, 258, 335, 369–70
Herling-Grudziński, Gustav 51, 59, 215, 241, 258, 370
Hersant, Robert 328
Hertz, Paweł 4, 49, 67, 95, 96, 101, 119, 139, 145, 146, 180, 370–1
Hilarowicz, Józef Nusbaum 135
Hill, Christopher 54
Hirszowicz, Maria 35, 55, 59, 151, 247, 258, 371
Hitler, Adolf 49, 67, 159, 330
Hłasko, Marek 51, 59, 145, 258, 371
Hlond, Cardinal 43
Hobsbawm, Eric 54
Hoffman, Eva 51, 293
Hoffman, Paweł 99, 136, 142, 248, 371
Hołuj, Tadeusz 371
Horodyński, Dominik 371–2
Hrabal, Bohumil 315
Hussein, Saddam 217

Ideologia i Polityka 70
Ikonowicz, Piotr 25, 308
Iłłakowiczówna, Kazimiera 48, 145, 372
Information Bulletin 261

Irzykowski, Karol 20
Iwaszkiewicz, Jarosław 13, 67, 79, 83, 89, 146, 372

Jabłonski, Henryk 204, 247
Jagiełło, Władysław 11
Jagielski, Mieczysław 299–300
Jarry, Alfred 147
Jaruzelski, General 105, 111–12, 132, 198, 209, 233, 248, 268, 270, 312, 313–16, 320, 321, 324, 328
Jarzębski, Jerzy 167, 215
Jasieński, Bruno 31
Jasienica, Pawel 122, 372–3
Jastrun, Mieczysław 49, 67, 68, 95, 96, 101, 119, 135, 136, 137, 139, 144, 145, 146, 180, 373
Jastrun, Tomasz 311, 333, 373
Jedlicki, Jerzy 55, 126
Jeleński, Konstanty 51
John XXIII, Pope 41
John Paul II, Pope 40, 44, 54, 257, 263, 399–400
Jurczyk, Marian 198, 201

Kaczmarek, Bishop 43, 257
Kaden-Bandrowski, Juliusz 15, 20
Kafka, Franz 16, 159, 168
Kamiena 71
Kapuściński, Ryszard 32, 203–23, 225, 231, 295, 297, 304, 310, 326, 333
    Emperor, The (Cesarz) 206, 208–10, 216, 218, 223
    Another Day of Life (Jeszcze dzień życia) 206
    Shah of Shahs (Szachinszach) 206, 208
    'This Too is the Truth of Nowa Huta' 205
    'Warsaw Diaries' 222
    The Football Wars (Wojna futbolowa) 205
Karinthy, Frigyes 159
Karol, K. S. 280
Karpiński, Jakub 247, 373–4
Karpowicz, Tymoteusz 374
Karsow, Nina 152, 248, 374
Karst, Roman 144, 151, 248, 374
Kasman, Leon 146, 374
Kelles-Krauz 23
Kersten, Krystyna 55, 126
Khrushchev, Nikita 94, 99, 144, 149, 238
Kierunki 71
Kijowski, Andrzej 374–5

Kisielewski, Stefan 43, 49, 59, 114, 151, 224, 248, 256, 259, 338, 375
Klíma, Ivan 333
Kliszko, Zenon 120, 121, 150
Kloc, Eugeniusz 260
Kobieta i Życie 72
Kochanowski, Jan 50
Koestler, Arthur 54
Kołakowski, Leszek 32, 34, 35–6, 51, 54, 55, 59, 67, 96, 118, 125, 126, 145, 146, 151, 156, 164, 170, 180, 187, 229, 230, 244, 247, 246, 258, 263, 294, 303, 375–6
Kołłątaj, Hugo 138
Konopka, Nowina 272
Konrád, Geörgy 332, 333, 336
Konwicki, Tadeusz 11, 32, 59, 67, 83, 95, 115, 146, 160, 164, 170, 180, 182, 186, 187, 215, 224–43, 258, 304, 311, 315
  Dreambook for Our Time, A (Sennik Współczesny) 225, 228–9 229
  Polish Complex (Kompleks Polski) 230
  A Minor Apocalypse (Mala Apokalypsa) 233–43, 316
  Moonrise, Moonset 241
  KOR Communiqué 261
  KOR-KSS Communiqué 261
Kornhauser, Julian 311, 335, 376
Korżeniowski, Apollo 7–8
Korżeniowski, Hilary 8
Korżeniowski, Józef Teodor Konrad Nałęcz *see* Conrad, Joseph
Korżeniowski, Robert 8
Korżeniowski, Teodor 8
Kościuszko, Tadeusz 312
Kossak, Zofia 48, 72, 376–7
Kostrzewa, Wera (Maria Koszutska) 23, 31, 246
Kotarbiński, Tadeusz 55
Kott, Jan 50, 51, 54, 67, 74, 94, 95, 118, 119, 121, 134–57, 180, 182, 185, 248
  'Serpent's Sting, The' 153
  Shakespeare Our Contemporary (Szkice o Szekspirze) 147, 148, 149–50
  Still Alive 156
Kott, Lidia 136, 140, 147, 152
Kowalska, Anka 127, 255, 311, 377
Kozioł, Urszula 377
Krajewski, Stanisław 180
Krall, Hanna 206, 215, 377
Krasiński, Zygmunt 5, 6, 50

Kruczkowski, Leon 67, 80, 95, 139, 146, 377
Krynicki, Ryszard 59, 258, 378
Krytyka 24, 189, 263
Krzystoń, Jerzy 48, 232–2
Kula, Witold 55, 59, 258
Kultura 17, 51, 52, 71, 72, 123, 125, 146, 215, 218, 222, 259
Kuncewicz, Maria 378
Kundera, Milan 158
Kuroń, Jacek 24, 32, 42, 61, 63, 127, 164, 170, 189, 244, 245, 246, 247, 249, 260, 261, 263, 264, 265, 268, 271, 274, 293, 304, 307, 310, 313, 315, 323, 324, 326, 334, 378–9
Kurowski, Stefan 266
Kuźnica 24, 71, 77, 84, 98, 134, 138, 139, 141, 142, 147, 182, 246
Kwiatkowski, Tadeusz 184–5

Lange, Oskar 55, 59, 258
Lasota, Grzegorz 95, 145
Le Guin, Ursula 175
Lec, Stanisław Jerzy 75, 379
Lechoń, Jan 7, 51, 379
Lehr-Spławiński, Tadeusz 94
Lelewel, Joachim 314
Lem, Stanisław 74, 91, 158–76, 225, 230, 242, 243, 304, 335
  Eden 161, 175
  Futurological Congress, The (Kongres Futurologiczny) 175
  'In Hot Pursuit of Happiness' 175
  Memoirs Found in a Bathtub (Pamiętnik znalezony w wannie) 167
  *Robotic Fables (Bajki Robotów)*162
  The Investigation (Śledztwo) 81
  Solaris 58, 81, 163, 164–8, 170, 174–5
  The Invincible (Niezwyciężony) 81, 163
Lenin V. I. 26, 27, 28, 29, 97, 190, 238, 287
Leo XIII, Pope 38
Leśmian, Bolesław 49
Limanowski, Bolesław 21
Lipiński, Edward 55, 59, 126, 127, 258
Lipska, Ewa 333, 379–80
Lipski, Jan Józef 25, 52, 59, 120, 127, 245, 249, 256, 259, 260, 265, 268, 274, 310, 313, 333, 380
Literatura 71, 72
Literatura na Świecie 71, 72, 74
Lityński, Jan 268

Lovell, Jerzy 206
Lukács, György 139, 141, 148
Luksemburg, Róża 22, 23, 26, 27, 29, 31
Lumumba, Patrice 206
Łysiak, Waldemar 312

Macharski, Archbishop 257
Machejek, Władysław 380–1
Maciąg, Włodzimierz 199
Macierewicz, Antoni 127, 261, 334, 381
Mackiewicz, Józef 51, 244, 336–7
Magazyn Kulturalny 71, 72
Maj, Bronisław 381
Małachowski, Aleksander 334
Malewska, Hanna 48, 49, 59, 259, 381–2
Malinowski, Bronisław 17
Mandelstam, Nadiezhda 315
Mandelstam, Osip 315
Mann, Thomas 141, 269
Manteuffel, Tadeusz 55
Marchlewski, Julian 26
Maritain, Raissa 135
Markov, Georgy 333
Marx, Karl 190, 281, 317
Masaryk, T. G. 315
Maxwell, Robert 328
Mayakovsky 136, 141–2, 185
Mazowiecki 255, 258
Mazowiecki, Tadeusz 43, 53, 54, 56, 59, 61,
    126, 253, 256, 259, 260, 271, 274, 326,
    333, 382–3
Mendelson, Stanisław 21
Micewski, Andrzej 54, 383
Michnik, Adam 24, 32, 42, 49, 50, 55, 55,
    56–8, 59, 61, 63, 64, 105, 127, 164, 170,
    172, 177, 189, 201, 244–77, 259, 307,
    308, 310, 313, 315, 319, 323, 324, 334,
    336
    *Church, The Left – Dialogue, The (Kosciól,
    Lewica – Dialog)* 42, 244, 250, 258
    'Conversation in the Citadel' 295
    'New Evolutionism, The' 57
Mickiewicz, Adam 5, 6, 37, 50, 121,140, 151,
    187, 225, 247, 314
Międzyrzecki, Artur 88, 383
Mieroszewski, Juliusz 59, 258
Miesęcznik Literacki 19, 71
Mikołajczykowna, Jadwiga 109
Miller, Jan Nepomucen 24
Miłosz, Czesław 20, 44, 48, 50, 51, 61, 59, 67,
    92, 94, 101, 102, 113, 114, 116–17, 133,
    136, 137, 141, 149, 183, 195, 225, 226, 229,
    230, 244, 315, 319, 331–2, 334, 311, 383–4
Minc, Julia 384
Moczar, General Mieczysław 122, 151, 187,
    247, 267, 268, 384
. Moczulski, Leszek 43, 268, 385
Modrzewski, Andrzej Frycz 314
Modzelewski, Karol, Bishop of Warsaw 42,
    170, 246, 247, 257, 293, 333, 385
Molk, Kazimierz 311
Morawska, Anna 59, 94, 151, 259
Morożek, Sławomir 248
Mrożek, Sławomir 123, 139, 385–6
Musil, Robert 159
Muskie, Senator 44
Mycielski, Andrzej 94
Myśliwski, Wiesław 386

Najder, Zdzisław 4, 244, 271, 333, 386
Nałkowska, Zofia 58, 59, 102, 226, 258, 386
Nałkowski, Wacław 27
Narutowicz, Gabriel 12, 79
Nesvadba 159
Neto, Aghostino 206
New Art 19
New Poland 249
New York Times 84, 208
Norwid, Cyprian 6, 50, 109, 323
Novak, Stanisław 233
Novak, Stefan 321
Nowa Kultura 71, 81, 84, 96, 97, 119, 142, 146,
    182, 226
Nowa Wieś 82–3
Nowak-Jeziorański, Jan 386–7
Nowakowski, Marek 311, 387
Nowakowski, Tadeusz 51
Nowe Drogi 70
Nowe Książki 71
Nowe Widnokręgi 98
Nowy Świat Przygód 161
Nowy Widokręgi 135
Nowy Wyraz 71
Nusbaum, Hilary 135

Ochab, Edward 99
Odra 71
Odrodzenie 71, 84, 101, 138, 178, 204, 225,
    226
Onyszkiewicz, Janusz 295

Onyszkiewicz, Wojciech 127
Orłos, Kazimierz 387
Orszulik, Revd Alojzy 257, 267
Orwell, George 54, 119, 154, 283, 302, 315
Orzeszkowa, Eliza 6
Ossowska, Maria 24, 55
Ossowski, Stanisław 24, 55, 59, 258
Otwin, Ostap 135

Pałka, Zenon 260
Pamiętnik : Literacki 71
Panorama 71, 72
Parnicki, Teodor 48, 52, 135
Pasternak, Boris 128, 139, 189
Pasternak, Leon 79, 135
Paul VI, Pope 41
Perspektywy 71, 72
Piasecki, Bolesław 77, 140,151, 247, 256, 387
Piasecki, Stanisław 100
Piechowski, Jerzy 48
Pieterkiewicz, Jerzy 51
Piłsudski, Józef 11, 12, 21, 22, 28, 29–30, 32,
    38, 53, 79, 153, 268, 325
Piotrowski, Andrzej 48
Pirie, D. 232
Pismo 71
Pius XI, Pope 38, 41
Pius XII, Pope 41
Po Prostu 96, 119, 145, 146
Pobóg-Malinowski, Władysław 387
Poezja 71, 72
Poglądy 71, 72
Polityka 71, 72, 205
Polkowski, Jan 334, 387–8
Polska 71, 72
Pomian, Krzysztof 55, 59, 247, 258, 388
Popiełuszko 315
Pravda 84
Prokop, Jan 94, 303, 388
Prosto z Mostu 100
Prus, Bolesław 7, 22, 314, 338
Pruszyński, Ksawery 67, 314, 315
Przedświt 21
Przegląd Kulturalny 71, 96, 101, 146
Przekrój 72
Przyboś, Julian 55, 67, 77, 79, 95, 135, 136,
    144, 180, 388
Przyjaciółka 72, 82
Putrament, Jerzy 67, 83, 91, 92, 95, 121, 124,
    135, 144, 146, 150, 389

Pyjas, Stanisław 44, 260, 284

Rakowski, Mieczysław 205, 268, 300, 389
Reagan, Ronald 294, 295
Res Publica 257, 312
Reymont, Władysław 6, 83
Rocznik Literacki 71
Rogowski, B. 295
Roliński, Bohdan 130, 389
Romaszewski, Zbigniew 267
Różewicz, Tadeusz 389–90
Ruch Literacki 71
Rudnicki, Adolf 49, 67, 136, 180, 182, 248, 390
Rydel, Lucjan 109
Rypson, Piotr 334, 390

Sade, Marquis de 135
Sandauer, Artur 49, 96, 144
Sartre, Jean-Paul 250
Schechter, Osjasz 245
Schiller, Leon 55
Schnitzler, Artur 315
Schopenhauer, Arthur 270
Schulz, Bruno 16, 18, 159, 320
Selassie, Haile 206, 208, 214, 216, 218
Sempołowska, Stefania 27
Shakespeare, William 122, 139, 147–9, 155
Siciński, Andrzej 87, 89, 91, 333
Sienkiewicz, Henryk 6, 50, 338
Skarga, Piotr 314
Słonimski, Antoni 15, 49, 55, 59, 67, 94, 120,
    121, 144, 146, 151, 152, 248, 249, 258,
    390–1
Słowacki, Juliusz 5, 6, 109, 139, 225
Słowo Powszechne 71, 123, 151, 204, 247
Sokorski, Włodzimierz 80, 81, 95, 113, 144,
    146–7, 183–4, 391
Sowa, Julia 173
Spotkania 311
Spychalski, Marian 137, 141
Staff, Leopold 391
Stalin, Josef 16, 26, 30, 31, 39, 49, 59, 75, 79,
    81, 91, 94, 95, 98, 99, 127, 136, 137, 140,
    142, 148, 149, 159, 183, 203, 224, 227,
    317, 320
Staniszkis, Jadwiga 281, 287, 296, 392
Stanowski, Adam 56, 126
Starski, Stanisław 233, 292, 321
Starzyńska, Maria 48
Staszewski, Stefan 95, 131, 248, 392

Staszic, Stanisław 314
Steinhaus, Professor Hugo 140
Stempówski, Jerzy 51, 135, 392
Stolica 123
Stomma, Stanisław 48, 49, 53, 54, 59, 253, 259, 333, 392–3
Stroiński, Stanisław 20
Strug, Andrzej 27
Strugatsky, Arkady 163
Strugatsky, Boris 163
Strykowski, Julian 49, 67, 180
Strzelecki, Jan 258, 393
Świerczewski, General Karol 39, 102, 245
Świton, Kazimierz 260
Szacki, Jerzy 273
Szajkowski, Bogdan 39
Szczęsna, Joanna 260
Szczepański, Jan Józef 59, 89, 258, 311, 323, 334, 393–4
Szczepański, Maciej 211
Szczypiorski, Andrzej 67, 127, 294, 310–11, 324, 333, 394–5
Szechter, Ozjasz 260
Szechter, Szymon 248, 395
Szelburg-Zarembina, Ewa 48
Szemplińska, Ewa 135
Sztandar Młodych 123, 204, 327
Sztande, Ryszard 30
Szumowski, Maciej 206
Szydłowski, Roman 96
Szymborska, Wisława 395
Szymanowski, Karol 13

Tarkovski, Andrei 164, 167
Thatcher, Margaret 295
Thompson, E. P. 54
Tischner, Abbot Józef 244, 257
Toeplitz, Krzystoz Teodor 395–6
Tolstoy, Count Leo 141
Torańska, Teresa 131, 215
Toruńczyk, Barbara 260
Truman, President 91, 116
Trybuna Ludu 70, 71, 72, 123, 146, 151, 247, 267
Trybuna Robotnicza 72
Trzebiński, Andrzej 20
Trznadel, Jacek 131, 215, 244, 396
Tu i Teraz 315
Turowicz, Jerzy 48, 49, 59, 94, 256, 140, 253, 255, 334, 396

Tuwim, Julian 15, 49, 51, 67, 92, 95, 226, 396–7
Twórczość 71, 72, 81, 82, 84, 96, 98, 125, 185, 204
Tydzień 71, 72
Tygodnik Powszechny 39, 41, 47, 53, 55, 56, 77, 94, 95, 114, 140, 161, 253, 256, 257, 259, 322, 335
Tymiński, Stanisław 201

Umiński, Zdzisław 48
Urban, Jerzy 311

Wajda, Andrzej 101, 115, 131, 207, 271, 310, 324, 333
Walc, Jan 267
Wałecki (Horwicz) 31
Wałęsa, Lech 10, 12, 33, 61, 63, 201, 244, 265, 268, 270, 271–6, 277, 300, 314, 323–7, 333, 334
Walicki, Andrzej 220, 232, 318, 397
Walka Młodych 123
Wandurski, Witold 30
Wańkowicz, Melchior 397
Warsawski (Adolf Warski) 31
Waryński, Ludwik 21
Wasilewska, Wanda 135, 136
Wat, Aleksander 3, 15, 19, 51, 67, 135, 199, 302, 397–8
Ważyk, Adam 55, 59, 67, 91, 94, 96–9, 101, 118, 119, 135, 136, 139, 140, 143, 145, 182, 185, 205, 230, 258
Werblan, Andrzej 119
Werfel, Roman 248, 398
Wielowiejski, Andrzej 334, 398
Wierbłowski, Stefan 398
Wierzbicki, Piotr 265, 334, 398
Wierzyński, Kazimierz 51, 59, 258, 399
Więź 41, 47, 53, 56, 61, 253, 254, 256, 259, 260
Williams, Gwyn Alf 54
Williams, Raymond 54
Wirpsza, Witold 51, 101, 144, 146, 399
Witkiewicz, Stanisław Ignacy 17–18, 139, 159, 320
Władysław, Broniewski 15
Wojtyła, Karol *see* John Paul II, Pope
Woods, William 60, 85
Woroszylski, Wiktor 55, 59, 101, 118, 126, 141, 145, 146, 189, 258, 311, 400–1
Woźniakowski, Jacek 49, 59, 259, 401

Wrocławski 123
Współczesność 83, 119, 146
Wujec, Henry 260, 268
Wygodzki, Stanisław 151, 248, 401
Wyka, Kazimierz 55, 401
Wyspiański, Stanisław 58, 109, 139, 314, 338
Wyszyński, Cardinal 39, 41–2, 43, 44, 60, 251, 256, 257, 263, 267, 307

Yeltsin, Boris 176

Zabłocki, Janusz 54, 401
Zabłudowski, Tadeusz 248, 401
Zagadniena i Materiały 70
Zagajewski, Adam 59, 114, 203, 233, 258, 319, 332, 335, 401–2
Zapis 56, 128, 189, 194, 230, 234, 257, 265
Żarski, Tadeusz 30

Zawadzki, Wacław 127, 402
Zawieyski, Jerzy 48, 49, 55, 59, 253, 259, 402–3
Żcie Literackie 311
Żeleński, Tadeusz 'Boy' 20, 135
Żeromski, Stefan 6, 27, 58, 315
Zgorzelski, Andrzej 174
Znak 39, 41, 47, 53, 56, 61, 254, 260
Żółkiewski, Stefan 67, 135, 137, 139, 144, 146, 246, 403
Żołnierz Wolności 123, 151, 247
Żuławski, Juliusz 68, 92, 101, 119, 139, 146, 311, 322, 403
Żuławski, Zygmunt 24, 246
Życie Literackie 71, 72, 96
Życie Nauki 161
Życie Parti 70
Życie Warszawy 72, 123, 151, 211, 248, 327